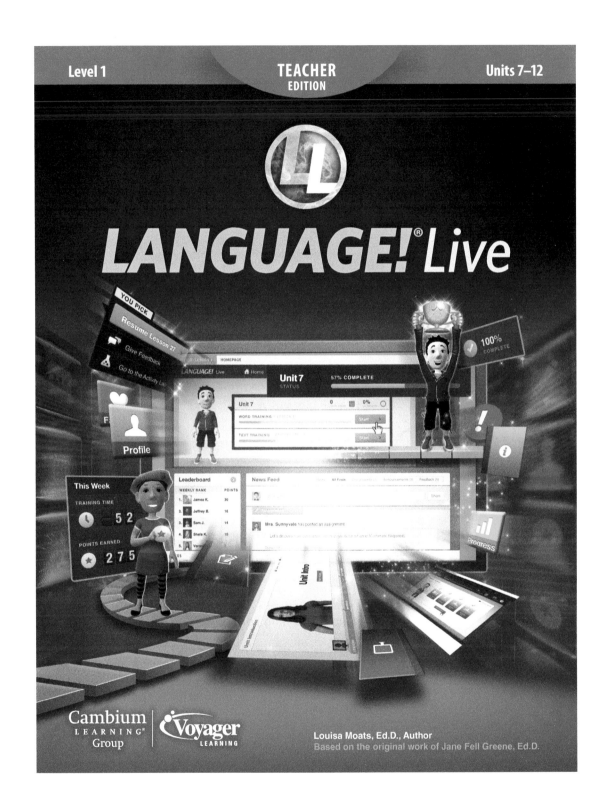

Level 1

TEACHER EDITION

Units 7–12

LANGUAGE!® Live

Cambium LEARNING® Group

Voyager LEARNING

Louisa Moats, Ed.D., Author

Based on the original work of Jane Fell Greene, Ed.D.

2 3 4 5 6 FRD 18 17 16 15 14

978-1-62489-930-0
1-62489-930-7
322974

Printed in the United States of America

Published and Distributed by

17855 Dallas Parkway, Suite 400 • Dallas, TX 75287 • 800 547-6747
www.voyagerlearning.com

Table of Contents

Table of Contents

Unit 11 "Twisters"

Primary Text: Twisters
Genre: informational
Content Focus: tornadoes

Instructional Texts:
Earthquakes
Genre: informational
Frightening Powers of Nature
Genre: informational
Compare Internet and Print
Genre: informational
Contrast Internet and Print
Genre: informational

Unit 12 "The Gorgon's Head"

Primary Text: The Gorgon's Head
Genre: literary
Content Focus: mythology

Secondary Text:
Mythological Women
Genre: informational

Decodable Text:
A Trip to Crete
Genre: literary

Instructional Texts:
Heroes from Mythology
Genre: informational
Myths from Ancient Cultures
Genre: informational

About the Author

Dr. Louisa Moats has been a teacher, psychologist, researcher, graduate school faculty member, and author of many influential scientific journal articles, books, and policy papers on the topics of reading, spelling, language, and teacher preparation. She began her professional career as a neuropsychology technician and teacher of students with learning disabilities. She earned her master's degree at Peabody College of Vanderbilt and her doctorate in Reading and Human Development from the Harvard Graduate School of Education.

Dr. Moats spent four years as site director of the NICHD Early Interventions Project in Washington, D.C. This longitudinal, large-scale project was conducted through the University of Texas, Houston under the direction of Barbara Foorman. It investigated the causes and remedies for reading failure in high-poverty urban schools. Dr. Moats spent the previous 15 years in private practice as a licensed psychologist in Vermont, specializing in evaluation and consultation with individuals of all ages who experienced learning problems in reading and language.

In addition to *LETRS*, Dr. Moats' books include *Speech to Print: Language Essentials for Teachers* (Brookes Publishing); *Spelling: Development, Disability, and Instruction* (York Press); *Straight Talk About Reading* (with Susan Hall, Contemporary Books), and *Basic Facts About Dyslexia* (with Karen Dakin, International Dyslexia Association). She is well known for authoring the American Federation of Teachers' "Teaching Reading IS Rocket Science."

Dr. Moats has authored numerous books on language, spelling, reading, and dyslexia. She is Vice President of the International Dyslexia Association.

Based on the original work of Jane Fell Greene, Ed.D.

Jane Fell Greene has been at the forefront of the nation's literacy movement for many years. Prior to creating *LANGUAGE!®, The Comprehensive Literacy Curriculum*—used to teach reading, writing, vocabulary, grammar, spelling and language to at-risk and ESL students since 1995 and now in its 4th edition, Dr. Greene earned credentials in and taught English, speech, and ESL at both middle and high school levels for twenty years. Subsequently, she taught undergraduate and graduate courses in reading, reading disabilities, ESL, and clinical diagnosis for another ten years.

A tireless advocate for students who experience delays in literacy acquisition, Dr. Greene has been a frequent presenter at national and international conferences. She oversaw the *National Council of LANGUAGE! Trainers* until 2010. She has served on the Board of Directors of the International Dyslexia Association and is a Fellow of the Orton Gillingham Academy of Practitioners and Educators.

Program Contributors

Contributing Developers

Debra D. Coultas, M.A.
National Literacy Consultant and Trainer

Sheryl Ferlito, Ed.S.
Co-author of Sortegories
Secondary Special Education Literacy Teacher

Anne Whitney, Ed.D., CCC-SLP
Clinical Professor
University of Colorado
Speech, Language, Hearing Department

Program Validation

Arlington Independent School District
Arlington, Texas
Nichols Middle School

Central Unified School District
Fresno, California
El Capitan Middle School
Glacier Point Middle School
Rio Vista Middle School

Kent Independent School District
Kent, Washington
Cedar Heights Middle School
Northwood Middle School

Orange County Unified School District
Orange County, California
El Rancho Middle School
Portola Middle School

Walla Walla School District
Walla Walla, Washington
Garrison Middle School

Program Overview

Welcome to *LANGUAGE! Live*. This exciting new program blends personalized, online learning with teacher directed instruction to empower struggling learners to close the learning gap between themselves and their peers. The carefully crafted learning progression in *LANGUAGE! Live* improves students' basic decoding, spelling, grammar, comprehension, vocabulary, and writing skills. The flexible and easy-to-implement program allows students in grades 4–12 to move at their own pace online to improve their reading while being exposed to complex text and rigorous vocabulary in the teacher-directed instruction. This combination ensures student success and growth.

Why *LANGUAGE! Live*?

- An early emphasis on speech and language to build literacy skills
- Adaptive technology that leverages social media to promote learning
- All-inclusive system to support a broad range of academic levels that simplify intervention and teacher training
- User-friendly, flexible implementation model
- Embedded assessment system to track and measure progress, and differentiate instruction

Instructional Design

Word Training—Online

Lesson 1	Lesson 2
Skill Review *Review of previous skills* **Tutorials and Check for Understanding** *Introduction of new skills* **Cumulative Practice** *Decoding, Encoding and Fluency Practice* **Sight Words**	**Skill Review** *Review of previous skills* **Tutorials and Check for Understanding** *Introduction of new skills* **Cumulative Practice** *Decoding, Encoding and Fluency Practice* **Sight Words**

Text Training—Print

Lesson 1	Lesson 2
Reading • Purpose for reading • Preview text • View content video • Read passage • Check comprehension **Vocabulary** • Preteach words from text • Rate word knowledge	**Vocabulary** • Multiple-meaning words • Graphic organizers **Grammar** • Skill introduction or practice **Reading/Writing** • Skill introduction or practice
Lesson 6	**Lesson 7**
Vocabulary • Use context to define words • Vocabulary concept introduction or practice **Reading** • Comprehension strategy **Writing** • Sentence expansion and enhancement	**Reading** • Read passage • Close reading • Guided highlighting

Lesson 3	Lesson 4	Gateway – Lessons 5–10
Skill Review *Review of previous skills* **Tutorials and Check for Understanding** *Introduction of new skills* **Cumulative Practice** *Decoding, Encoding and Fluency Practice* **Sight Words**	**Skill Review** *Review of previous skills* **Tutorials and Check for Understanding** *Introduction of new skills* **Cumulative Practice** *Decoding, Encoding and Fluency Practice* **Sight Words**	*Practice, Adapt and Assess* **Goal: Say Sounds** **Goal: Read Words** **Goal: Spell Words** **Goal: Sentence Reading/ Passage Reading**

Lesson 3	Lesson 4	Lesson 5
Reading • Word fluency practice • Read passage • Critical understanding **Vocabulary** • Review passage vocabulary • Vocabulary concept introduction or practice	**Reading** • Read phrases • Read passage • Critical understanding **Grammar** • Skill introduction or practice	**Vocabulary** • Use context to define words **Reading** • Read passage • Ask and answer questions • Guided reading with text analysis **Writing** • Respond to text questions
Lesson 8	**Lesson 9**	**Lesson 10**
Writing • Writing in response to reading • Writing process » Plan and prepare » Two-column note-taking » Review and revise » Use Writer's Checklist	**Reading** • Word fluency • Passage fluency **Vocabulary** • Building depth of knowledge • Graphic organizer: Four-Square **Grammar** • Skill introduction or practice	**Vocabulary** • Review of vocabulary • Demonstrate vocabulary knowledge through Cloze procedure **Reading** • Confirm understanding of concept or topic • Author point of view **Review Game or Activity** **Content Mastery** • Grammar • Vocabulary • Reading

Literature and Informational Text

Unit 1

Primary Text
- Batty About Bats (Informational)

Unit 2

Primary Text
- Africa Digs (Informational)

Instructional Texts
- Boston's Big Dig (Informational)
- Benefits of Exercise (Informational)
- Two Giant Animals (Informational)

Unit 3

Primary Text
- Gemini: The Twins (Informational)

Decodable Text
- The Big Dogs and the Rams (Literary)

Instructional Text
- Earthly Twins (Informational)

Unit 4

Primary Text
- Jazz: The Recipe (Informational)

Decodable Text
- Stuck in the Mud (Literary)

Instructional Text
- What a Wonderful World of Jazz (Informational)

Unit 5

Primary Text
- Coming Clean About Toxic Pollution (Informational—Persuasive)

Decodable Text
- Quite a Bike Ride (Literary)

Instructional Text
- Rachel Carson (Informational)

Unit 6

Primary Text
- Censorship (Informational)

Secondary Text
- Dear Congressman Whipple (Literary—Letter)

Instructional Texts
- Web Wins (Informational)
- A Day in the Life (Informational)

Unit 7

Primary Text
- Whale Song (Informational)

Secondary Text
- Dolphin Talk (Literary—Poem)

Instructional Texts
- Whale Watching (Informational)
- Two Types of Whales (Informational)

Unit 8

Primary Text
- How Bugs Bug Us (Informational)

Secondary Text
- Bugs in Medicine (Informational)

Decodable Text
- Plans for the Big Bash (Literary)

Instructional Texts
- Bugs Live (Informational)
- Chinch Bugs (Informational)
- Spider Webs (Informational)
- Point of View excerpts (Literary)
- Jill and Rosa (Literary)

Unit 9

Primary Text
- The Time Machine (Literary—Narrative)

Instructional Texts
- Cars of the Future (Informational)
- Butterfly's Bet (Literary—Folktale)
- My New Respect for Spiders (Literary—Narrative)

Unit 10

Primary Text
- Hurricane! (Informational)

Decodable Text
- The Storm (Literary)

Instructional Texts
- Tsunami (Informational)
- Cloud Seeding (Informational)
- This is Jack Olsen, the voice of KOKA Radio. Yesterday: Sunday, April 14, 1935 (Literary—Radio Narrative)

Unit 11

Primary Text
- Twisters (Informational)

Instructional Texts
- Earthquakes (Informational)
- Frightening Powers of Nature (Informational)
- Compare Internet and Print (Informational)
- Contrast Internet and Print (Informational)

Unit 12

Primary Text
- The Gorgon's Head (Literary—Mythology)

Secondary Text
- Mythological Women (Informational)

Decodable Text
- A Trip to Crete (Literary)

Instructional Texts
- Heroes from Mythology (Informational)
- Myths from Ancient Cultures (Informational)

Assessments

Effective Measurement Tools

LANGUAGE! Live Level 1 is designed for struggling students who read significantly below grade level. To provide the highest quality of assessment information for placing and monitoring student progress, Cambium's assessment system includes the tools that have proved to be reliable and effective measures of reading.

LANGUAGE! Live Benchmark Assessments

Benchmark 1	Benchmark 2	Benchmark 3
LRS	LRS	LRS
TOSCRF	TOSCRF	TOSCRF
TWS-4		TWS-4

LANGUAGE! Live Benchmark Assessments consist of three norm-referenced assessments that measure students' literacy skills two to three times per calendar year. These assessments are taken online to provide immediate results. The three measures include:

LANGUAGE! Live Reading Scale (LRS)

The LRS assesses reading comprehension and yields a Lexile (L) score powered by the Lexile Framework® for Reading. This series of assessments monitors each student's reading level and matches text that presents the right degree of challenge to the reader. This assessment consists of 49 questions. Students will need 30 to 45 minutes to complete the LRS.

Test of Silent Contextual Reading Fluency (TOSCRF)

The Test of Silent Contextual Reading Fluency (TOSCRF) is a measure of silent contextual reading fluency. It measures the speed with which students can recognize the individual words in a series of printed passages that become progressively more difficult in their content, vocabulary, and grammar. This three-minute, norm-referenced test measures a wide variety of essential interrelated silent reading skills.

The Test of Written Spelling, 4th edition (TWS-4)

The Test of Written Spelling, 4th edition (TWS-4) is a norm-referenced test of spelling administered twice per year. It can be used to document the overall improvement in spelling as a result of intervention instruction. The test is administered using a dictated word format. The TWS-4 has consistently high reliability and a demonstrated high degree of validity.

Assessments

Ongoing Progress Monitoring

There are several means for progress monitoring within *LANGUAGE! Live* online and in print. The two online progress monitoring assessments in Word Training are Gateways and Text Quizzes. In the Text Training component, additional opportunities are available to monitor fluency and comprehension through Fluency Practice, Content Mastery Tests, and Writing.

Gateways

Gateways occur at the end of every Unit, and they assess students' level of mastery of critical elements taught within the Unit. They are composed of adaptive practice and reteach based on students' level of proficiency. The time to complete Gateways varies by student since the program adapts based on each student's level of proficiency.

Each Gateway is structured by individual goals; three in each Unit. Earlier Units include Say Sounds, Read Words, and Spell Words. After students have moved into later Units, the Say Sounds goal is replaced with Read Sentences, then Read Passages. These carefully scaffolded Gateway goals demonstrate a student's ability to read and spell words and build to fluency passages.

Gateway Goals by Unit

	Say Sounds	Read Words	Spelling	Read Sentences	Read Passages
Unit 1	•	•	•		
Unit 2	•	•	•		
Unit 3		•	•	•	
Unit 4		•	•	•	
Unit 5		•	•	•	
Unit 6		•	•		•
Unit 7		•	•		•
Unit 8		•	•		•
Unit 9		•	•		•
Unit 10		•	•		•
Unit 11		•	•		•
Unit 12		•	•		•

Text Quizzes

Text Quizzes are also implemented at the end of every Unit. Each Text Quiz comprises 15 test items, focusing on basic comprehension and vocabulary from the Text Training component. These criterion-referenced assessments measure comprehension and vocabulary that have been taught in the current Unit. The online program alerts students when it is time to complete a Text Quiz at the discretion of the teacher.

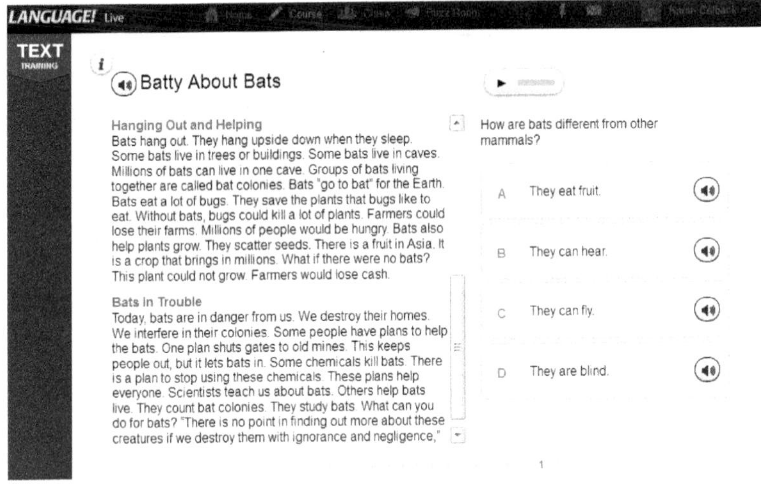

Fluency Practice

Fluency activities linked to skills taught are in place throughout Text Training and Word Training. Students are able to practice and improve fluency through word, phrase, and passage reading activities. Students are provided opportunities online and in print to monitor their own fluency growth and rate of improvement.

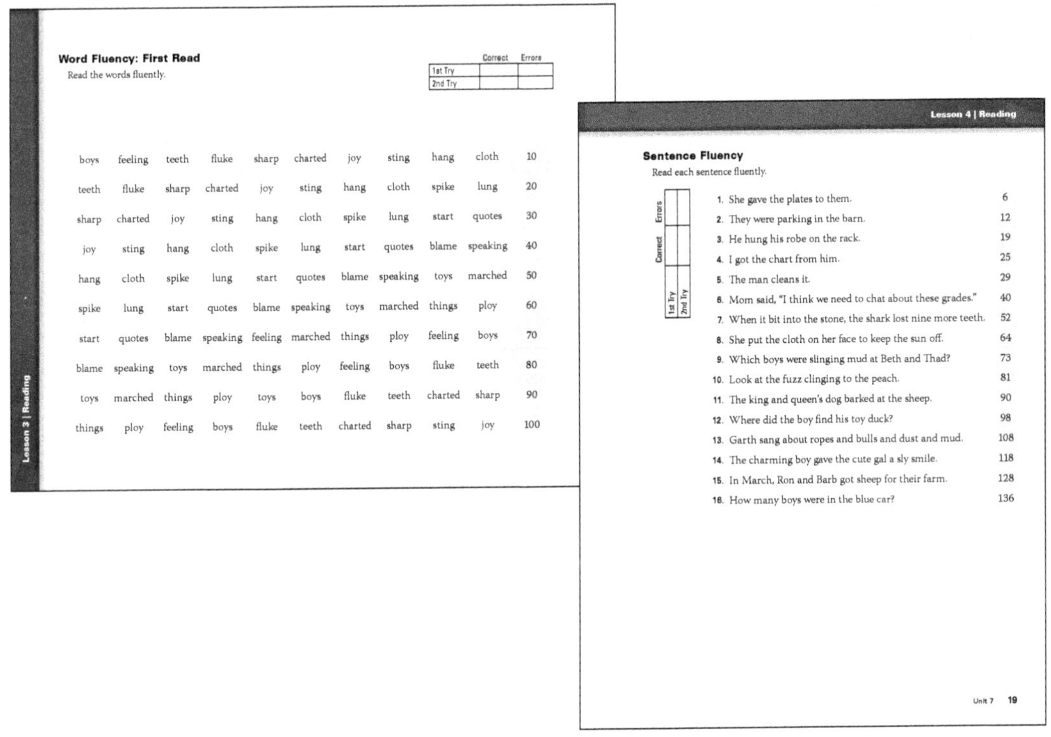

Word Fluency: First Read

Read the words fluently.

	Correct	Errors
1st Try		
2nd Try		

boys	feeling	teeth	fluke	sharp	charted	joy	sting	hang	cloth	10
teeth	fluke	sharp	charted	joy	sting	hang	cloth	spike	lung	20
sharp	charted	joy	sting	hang	cloth	spike	lung	start	quotes	30
joy	sting	hang	cloth	spike	lung	start	quotes	blame	speaking	40
hang	cloth	spike	lung	start	quotes	blame	speaking	toys	marched	50
spike	lung	start	quotes	blame	speaking	toys	marched	things	ploy	60
start	quotes	blame	speaking	feeling	marched	things	ploy	feeling	boys	70
blame	speaking	toys	marched	things	ploy	feeling	boys	fluke	teeth	80
toys	marched	things	ploy	toys	boys	fluke	teeth	charted	sharp	90
things	ploy	feeling	boys	fluke	teeth	charted	sharp	sting	joy	100

Lesson 3 | Reading

Lesson 4 | Reading

Sentence Fluency

Read each sentence fluently.

	Correct	Errors
1st Try		
2nd Try		

1. She gave the plates to them. 6
2. They were parking in the barn. 12
3. He hung his robe on the rack. 19
4. I got the chart from him. 25
5. The man cleans it. 29
6. Mom said, "I think we need to chat about these grades." 40
7. When it bit into the stone, the shark lost nine more teeth. 52
8. She put the cloth on her face to keep the sun off. 64
9. Which boys were slinging mud at Beth and Thad? 73
10. Look at the fuzz clinging to the peach. 81
11. The king and queen's dog barked at the sheep. 90
12. Where did the boy find his toy duck? 98
13. Garth sang about ropes and bulls and dust and mud. 108
14. The charming boy gave the cute gal a sly smile. 118
15. In March, Ron and Barb got sheep for their farm. 128
16. How many boys were in the blue car? 136

Unit 7 19

Assessments

Content Mastery

Content Mastery assessments are short, end-of-unit assessments on objectives not assessed in online measures. These include grammar, comprehension, and vocabulary.

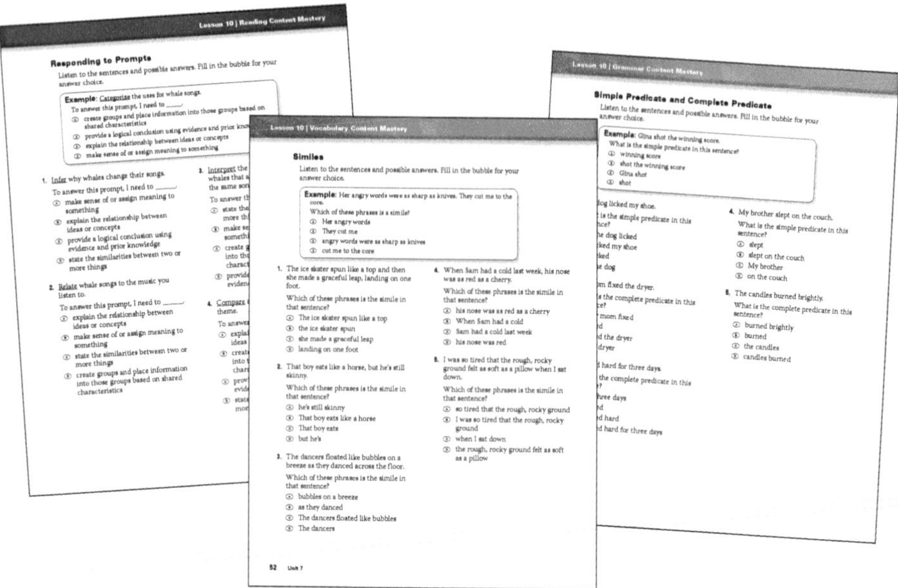

Lesson 10 | Vocabulary Content Mastery

Similes

Listen to the sentences and possible answers. Fill in the bubble for your answer choice.

Example: Her angry words were as sharp as knives. They cut me to the core.
Which of these phrases is a simile?
Ⓐ Her angry words
Ⓑ They cut me
Ⓒ angry words were as sharp as knives
Ⓓ cut me to the core

1. The ice skater spun like a top and then she made a graceful leap, landing on one foot.
Which of these phrases is the simile in that sentence?
Ⓐ The ice skater spun like a top
Ⓑ the ice skater spun
Ⓒ she made a graceful leap
Ⓓ landing on one foot

2. That boy eats like a horse, but he's still skinny.
Which of these phrases is the simile in that sentence?
Ⓐ he's still skinny
Ⓑ That boy eats like a horse
Ⓒ That boy eats
Ⓓ but he's

3. The dancers floated like bubbles on a breeze as they danced across the floor.
Which of these phrases is the simile in that sentence?
Ⓐ bubbles on a breeze
Ⓑ as they danced
Ⓒ The dancers floated like bubbles
Ⓓ The dancers

4. When Sam had a cold last week, his nose was as red as a cherry.
Which of these phrases is the simile in that sentence?
Ⓐ his nose was as red as a cherry
Ⓑ When Sam had a cold
Ⓒ Sam had a cold last week
Ⓓ his nose was red

5. I was so tired that the rough, rocky ground felt as soft as a pillow when I sat down.
Which of these phrases is the simile in that sentence?
Ⓐ so tired that the rough, rocky ground
Ⓑ I was so tired that the rough, rocky ground
Ⓒ when I sat down
Ⓓ the rough, rocky ground felt as soft as a pillow

52 Unit 7

Writing Samples

Text Training also includes writing in response to reading and writing samples to include in students' portfolios.

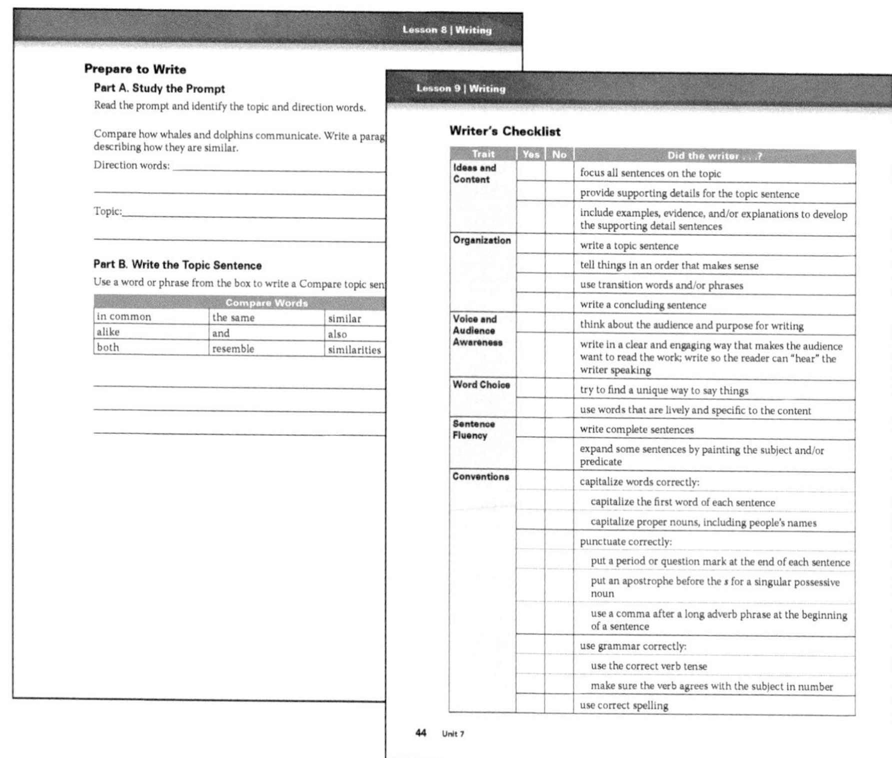

Lesson 8 | Writing

Prepare to Write

Part A. Study the Prompt

Read the prompt and identify the topic and direction words.

Compare how whales and dolphins communicate. Write a parag
describing how they are similar.

Direction words: ______

Topic: ______

Part B. Write the Topic Sentence

Use a word or phrase from the box to write a Compare topic sen

Compare Words		
in common	the same	similar
alike	and	also
both	resemble	similarities

Lesson 9 | Writing

Writer's Checklist

Trait	Yes	No	Did the writer . . . ?
Ideas and Content			focus all sentences on the topic
			provide supporting details for the topic sentence
			include examples, evidence, and/or explanations to develop the supporting detail sentences
Organization			write a topic sentence
			tell things in an order that makes sense
			use transition words and/or phrases
			write a concluding sentence
Voice and Audience Awareness			think about the audience and purpose for writing
			write in a clear and engaging way that makes the audience want to read the work; write so the reader can "hear" the writer speaking
Word Choice			try to find a unique way to say things
			use words that are lively and specific to the content
Sentence Fluency			write complete sentences
			expand some sentences by painting the subject and/or predicate
Conventions			capitalize words correctly:
			capitalize the first word of each sentence
			capitalize proper nouns, including people's names
			punctuate correctly:
			put a period or question mark at the end of each sentence
			put an apostrophe before the *s* for a singular possessive noun
			use a comma after a long adverb phrase at the beginning of a sentence
			use grammar correctly:
			use the correct verb tense
			make sure the verb agrees with the subject in number
			use correct spelling

44 Unit 7

Instructional Routines

Fluency Procedure

Thoughtfully pair students.

Consistent pairing is important to save time. One technique is to informally rank order your students by ability (most to least fluent). It doesn't make sense to pair the top and bottom readers because the bottom reader may not be able to keep up with the top student. If you have 10 students, think about pairing your highest reader with a mid-range reader. You might pair 10-5, 9-4, 8-3, 7-2, and 6-1. Take personalities into account—avoid pairing two easily distracted students. If you have an odd number or absentees, you take on the partner role.

Set up the ideal physical setting.

To save time, think about how you will organize your students as they read and record. They will need to know how they will sit and where you want them located in the room. Think about suitable locations for students who might be distracted by noise or movement.

Here are some seating ideas:

- Have pairs sit across from each other at a table.
- Have students move chairs or desks to sit side-by-side or sit facing opposite directions shoulder-to-shoulder or knee-to-knee.
- Have students sit on the floor facing each other. Provide clipboards for ease of marking.

Establish the routine and procedure.

- Fluency drills start with a choral read of the first row (at least). Read loudly enough and at a pace at which students can match their voice to yours.
- For the second row, continue to choral read. Create a rhythm (snap your fingers, tap your foot, tap your pencil) as you and students read aloud. As you proceed through the row, fade the level of your voice.
- On the third row, students (only) chorally read the words. Snap or tap a rhythm.
- If students are doing well with the words, they are ready to move into the partner reading activity. **Note:** If the students need additional support, use an echo read technique. Say the word, then have the students immediately repeat the word.
- Explain the specific steps for the partners. There are two roles for students: the reader and the recorder.

Instructional Routines

- Readers and recorders move left to right tracking each word with a pencil eraser. (It is important for readers and recorders to touch every word, at least initially, to keep students on target.)
- Demonstrate how recorders should mark errors in a way that the word is still legible.
- Demonstrate how a recorder places a mark (star or bracket) on the last word read when one minute is up. Indicate how it should be double marked if they are able to get through the words and begin again.
- Demonstrate how readers should count and record scores.

Preteach Vocabulary

Key passage vocabulary should be mastered by end of unit. Students will benefit from multiple exposures to each word—orally, in reading, and in writing. Thus, students are not expected to achieve mastery of the words during Lesson 1. This procedure was designed to take five to ten minutes only and is an introduction to the words.

Research has proven that vocabulary is best learned when students represent their knowledge of words in linguistic and/or nonlinguistic ways. Thus, drawing a picture and writing a definition will help students remember the words. However, these processes are secondary to the conversation about the words. If your students are visual learners and would greatly benefit from copying the definitions, please have them do so outside of instruction time. The definitions can be found in the margins of the passages.

Text Reading

Guiding Students Toward Independent Reading

While the lessons are written for a teacher read aloud, it is important that students read as much and as often as they can. Assign readings that meet student needs, based on observations or data.

Options for reading text:

- Teacher read aloud
- Teacher-led or student-led choral read
- Independent read of small sections with frequent comprehension checks
- Paired read or independent read

Unit Plans and Lessons

Unit 7 Unit Plan

Primary Text:
"Whale Song"

Text type: informational

Secondary Text:
"Dolphin Talk"

Text type: poetry

Lesson 1	Lesson 2
Reading • Determine the topic of the text. • Determine the author's purpose. • Discuss the topic of the text. • Preview the passage. **Vocabulary** • Determine the meaning of key passage vocabulary. **Reading** • Demonstrate an understanding of the text by asking and answering questions and referring to key details in the text.	**Vocabulary** • Determine the meaning of the multiple-meaning word *mean.* • Demonstrate their understanding by using *mean* in written sentences. **Grammar** • Demonstrate an understanding of the function of object pronouns in sentences. • Write sentences using object pronouns in place of a direct object and in place of the object of a preposition. **Writing** • Demonstrate an understanding of the function of commas and quotation marks in dialogue. • Use commas and quotation marks correctly in written dialogue.

Lesson 6	Lesson 7
Writing • Know spelling-sound correspondences for words with the digraph /ng/ with /ă/ and /ŭ/. • Know spelling-sound correspondences for words with the *oy* vowel team. **Vocabulary** • Use context to determine the meaning of words in text. • Demonstrate an understanding of compound words. • Brainstorm and write compound words. **Writing** • Demonstrate an understanding of the conventions of English by editing their writing for punctuation, capitalization, spelling, and word order. **Reading** • Discuss characteristics of poetry. • Describe how words and phrases supply rhythm and meaning in a poem. • Read to identify rhyme and figurative language in a poem. • Reread a poem for key information. • Take notes of key information in a poem.	**Reading** • Read with purpose and understanding. • Answer questions to demonstrate comprehension of text. • Determine the main ideas of the text. • Explain explicit details from text.

Lesson 3	Lesson 4	Lesson 5
Reading • Read to develop fluency. **Vocabulary** • Review passage vocabulary. • Demonstrate an understanding of simple similes. • Write simple similes. • Identify similes in popular music. **Grammar** • Identify singular and plural subject pronouns. • Identify singular and plural object pronouns. • Demonstrate an understanding of subject and object pronouns in sentences. **Reading** • Ask and answer questions to demonstrate an understanding of a text. • Use inference, interpretation, comparisons, and categorization to analyze a text.	**Reading** • Read phrases to develop fluency. **Grammar** • Listen to oral sentences and accurately write them. • Demonstrate an understanding of the function of pronouns in sentences. • Demonstrate an understanding of the function of subject pronouns and object pronouns in sentences. **Reading** • Read sentence phrases with fluency to support comprehension. • Preview a text. • Respond to specific questions to demonstrate an understanding of a text using interpretation, inference, comparison, and categorization to answer questions.	**Vocabulary** • Review and clarify the meaning of key passage vocabulary. **Reading** • Write questions or prompts about the passage to deepen comprehension. • Respond to questions or prompts orally. **Writing** • Write responses to prompts to categorize, infer, compare, and interpret information from the passage. • Support written answers with evidence from text. **Reading** • Interpret information presented orally. • Identify structural elements of a poem, including rhythm and rhyme.

Lesson 8	Lesson 9	Lesson 10
Writing • Gather relevant information from notes about the passage. • Orally review key ideas from the passage. • Write a clear introductory topic sentence for a comparison piece. • Write a concluding sentence for a comparison piece. • Write a comparison paragraph.	**Reading** • Read words to develop fluency. **Vocabulary** • Demonstrate an understanding of a word by relating it to its antonyms, synonyms, and related words. • Write similes. **Writing** • Revise and edit their paragraphs according to ideas and content and organization. **Grammar** • Demonstrate an understanding of the function of action verbs and linking verbs in sentences by diagramming sentences. • Demonstrate an understanding of the function of simple subjects and complete subjects in sentences. • Demonstrate an understanding of the function of simple predicates and complete predicates in sentences. **Writing** • Create sentences using a word as a different part of speech in each sentence. • Ensure pronoun-antecedent agreement in sentences.	**Vocabulary** • Clarify the meaning of key passage vocabulary. • Demonstrate an understanding of passage vocabulary by using the words in sentences. **Reading** • Discuss and answer questions to demonstrate an understanding of the passages' main ideas and key details. **Vocabulary** • Review key passage vocabulary from Units 4–7 by matching words to their definitions.

Unit 7

Lesson 1

Lesson Opener

Before the lesson, choose one of the following activities to write on the board or post on the *LANGUAGE! Live* Class Wall online.

- *Write two statements: one factual and one opinion. Ask your partner to determine which is which.*
- *Use the word* censorship *in a sentence. Write another sentence using a subject pronoun to replace* censorship.
- *Use at least one adjective to write an opinion statement about* LANGUAGE! Live.

Reading

Objectives

- Determine the topic of the text.
- Determine the author's purpose.
- Discuss the topic of the text.
- Preview the passage.

Unit Introduction

Direct students to page 1 in their Student Books.

Discuss the content focus of the unit.

Content Focus

whales

What is this passage about? (whales) What do you think you will read in this passage? (Answers will vary based on prior knowledge of whales.)

Type of Text

informational

Informational text is also called nonfiction. Nonfiction is not fiction. *Non-* is a prefix or word part that means "not." Fiction is made up. Is nonfiction made up or real? (real) So, what do you think will be in this passage? Facts or fiction? (facts) This passage will give us information, or facts. What will the information be about? (whales)

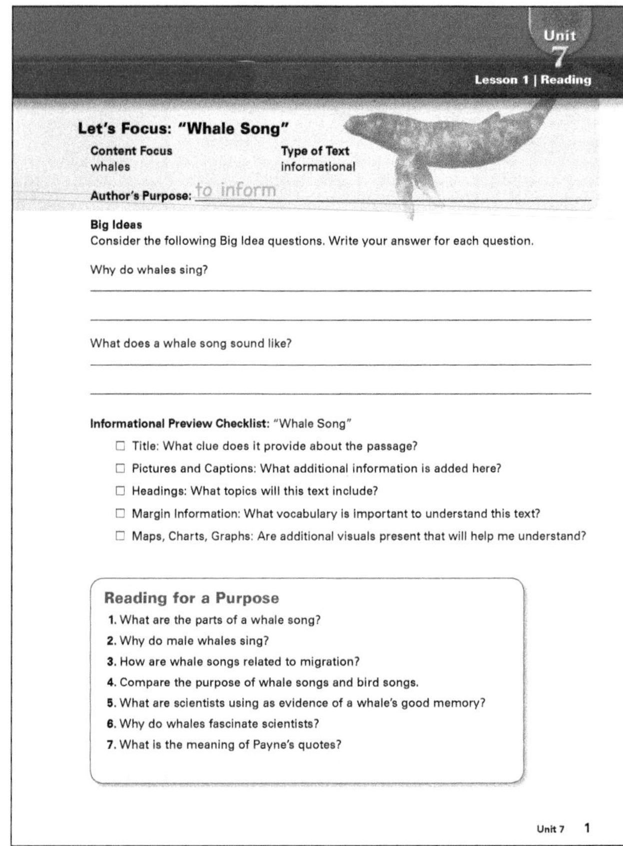
Unit 7
Lesson 1 | Reading

Let's Focus: "Whale Song"

Content Focus whales

Type of Text informational

Author's Purpose: to inform

Big Ideas
Consider the following Big Idea questions. Write your answer for each question.

Why do whales sing?

What does a whale song sound like?

Informational Preview Checklist: "Whale Song"

- ☐ Title: What clue does it provide about the passage?
- ☐ Pictures and Captions: What additional information is added here?
- ☐ Headings: What topics will this text include?
- ☐ Margin Information: What vocabulary is important to understand this text?
- ☐ Maps, Charts, Graphs: Are additional visuals present that will help me understand?

Reading for a Purpose

1. What are the parts of a whale song?
2. Why do male whales sing?
3. How are whale songs related to migration?
4. Compare the purpose of whale songs and bird songs.
5. What are scientists using as evidence of a whale's good memory?
6. Why do whales fascinate scientists?
7. What is the meaning of Payne's quotes?

Unit 7 1

Author's Purpose

The author's purpose is the reason that the author wrote the text. Authors write for different purposes. Turn to your partner and tell him or her why authors write texts. (to entertain, to persuade, and to inform or teach) **Have students share reasons.** Knowing an author's purpose can help a reader understand a text better. "Whale Song" was written to inform others about whales. Was "Whale Song" written to inform or entertain? (inform) **Have students write *to inform* on the line next to "Author's Purpose."**

Background Information

Prepare a clip of whale sounds and play as you discuss background information.

Whale Song. What does that mean? First, let's look at the word *whale*. What do you know about whales? (Answers will vary.) Whales swim in the world's oceans, like fish, but they are mammals. This means they are warm-blooded and breathe air like us. They are related to dolphins and porpoises. Are whales large animals? (yes) What else do you know about whales? **Have volunteers share information.**

Whale Facts

- They breathe through a blowhole into lungs.
- Whales, dolphins, and manatees are the only mammals that live their entire lives in the ocean.
- Like other mammals, whales have hair and feed and care for their young.
- Like bats, whales use echolocation to hunt their prey.
- Some classify killer whales as the largest member of the dolphin family.
- Humpback whales are acrobatic, have two blowholes, and travel in groups with their young nearby. They are the noisiest and most creative with their sounds.
- Adult whales have very few predators. Humans are the primary hunters of whales.
- Some whales are in danger of going extinct.

Next, let's consider the words *whale song*. In this title, *whale* is an adjective that describes *song*. What kind of song? (whale song) Have you ever considered the sounds that whales make? **If possible, play an audio clip of whale sounds.** Why are these sounds called songs? **Have volunteers share predictions about why whale sounds are called songs.** In the passage, we will learn more about how and why whales sing.

Play the Unit 7 Text Training video found in the Teacher Resources online.

Before we read the passage about whale songs, we will watch a short video to help build background knowledge. I want you to combine what you just learned with what you are about to watch on this video. Listen for two things that you did not know about whales. You will share this new information with a partner after the video. **Play the Unit 7 Text Training video. Have partners discuss what they learned from the video.**

Direct students to page 1 in their Student Books. Read the following Big Idea questions aloud:

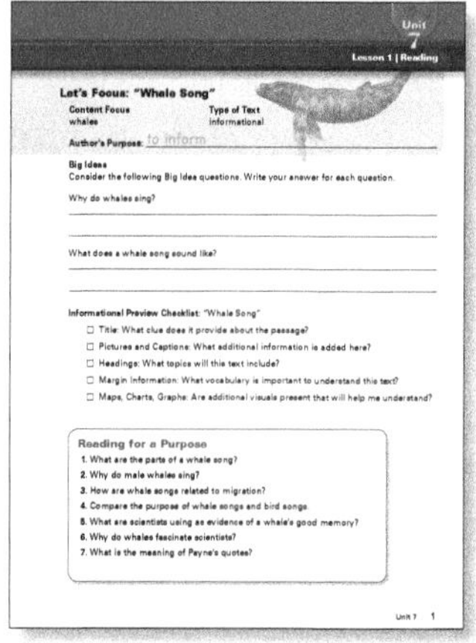

Unit 7

Lesson 1 | Reading

Let's Focus: "Whale Song"

Content Focus
whales

Type of Text
informational

Author's Purpose: to inform

Big Ideas
Consider the following Big Idea questions. Write your answer for each question.

Why do whales sing?

What does a whale song sound like?

Informational Preview Checklist: "Whale Song"

- ☐ Title: What clue does it provide about the passage?
- ☐ Pictures and Captions: What additional information is added here?
- ☐ Headings: What topics will this text include?
- ☐ Margin Information: What vocabulary is important to understand this text?
- ☐ Maps, Charts, Graphs: Are additional visuals present that will help me understand?

Reading for a Purpose

1. What are the parts of a whale song?
2. Why do male whales sing?
3. How are whale songs related to migration?
4. Compare the purpose of whale songs and bird songs.
5. What are scientists using as evidence of a whale's good memory?
6. Why do whales fascinate scientists?
7. What is the meaning of Payne's quotes?

Unit 7 1

Big Ideas

Why do whales sing?

What does a whale song sound like?

As a class, consider the two Big Idea questions. After discussing each question, have students write an answer in their Student Books. We'll come back to these questions after we finish learning about whales. You will have much more to add to your answers. You can edit your answers as you gain information.

Preview

Good readers preview the features of a nonfiction text independently and automatically. To develop this reading habit, you will preview today's text on your own, and then discuss what you noticed with a partner.

Direct students to page 3 in their Student Books to preview the text. Remind them of the Informational Preview Checklist in their Student Books on page 1. Give them permission to refer to the checklist during the preview if they need a reminder of text features.

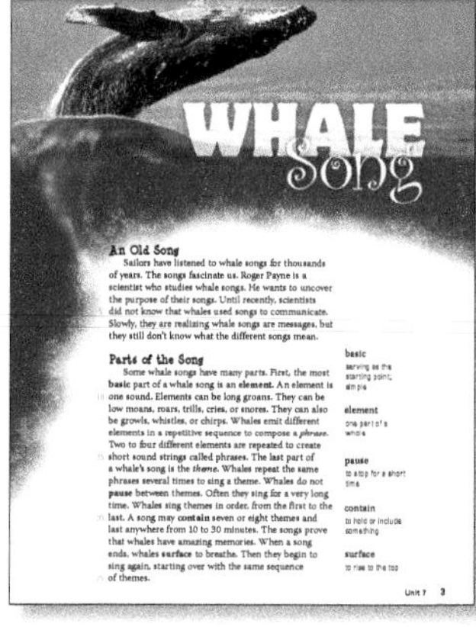

Lesson 1 | Reading

WHALE Song

An Old Song

Sailors have listened to whale songs for thousands of years. The songs fascinate us. Roger Payne is a scientist who studies whale songs. He wants to uncover the purpose of their songs. Until recently, scientists did not know that whales used songs to communicate. Slowly, they are realizing whale songs are messages, but they still don't know what the different songs mean.

Parts of the Song

Some whale songs have many parts. First, the most **basic** part of a whale song is an **element**. An element is one sound. Elements can be long groans. They can be low moans, roars, trills, cries, or snores. They can also be growls, whistles, or chirps. Whales emit different elements in a repetitive sequence to compose a *phrase*. Two to four different elements are repeated to create short sound strings called phrases. The last part of a whale's song is the *theme*. Whales repeat the same phrases several times to sing a theme. Whales do not **pause** between themes. Often they sing for a very long time. Whales sing themes in order, from the first to the last. A song may **contain** seven or eight themes and last anywhere from 10 to 30 minutes. The songs prove that whales have amazing memories. When a song ends, whales **surface** to breathe. Then they begin to sing again, starting over with the same sequence of themes.

basic serving as the starting point; simple

element one part of a whole

pause to stop for a short time

contain to hold or include something

surface to rise to the top

Unit 7 3

Note: Create a small teacher-led group for students who displayed dependence or confusion with the previewing process during the previous unit. New students and truant students should also join this group until they reach independence.

Preview the text using text features. Afterward, you will debrief with your partner, using the checklist as a reminder to be sure that you didn't skip an important text feature.

Have individuals preview the text. After sufficient time, have partners use the checklist to evaluate each other's previewing skills. Gauge individual success as you circulate around the room. Determine which students need extra practice with the skills and provide them with alternative practice sources.

Vocabulary

Objective

- Determine the meaning of key passage vocabulary.

Rate Your Knowledge

Direct students to page 2 in their Student Books.

You will rate your word knowledge. The purpose of this activity is to measure how familiar you are with this unit's key vocabulary words.

Vocabulary Rating Scale poster

Review the Vocabulary Rating Scale with students.

Vocabulary Rating Scale

0—I have never heard the word before.

1—I have heard the word, but I'm not sure how to use it.

2—I am familiar with the word, but I'm not sure if I know the correct meaning.

3—I know the meaning of the word and can use it correctly in a sentence.

Lesson 1 | Vocabulary

Key Passage Vocabulary: "Whale Song"

Rate your knowledge of the words. Define the words. Draw a picture to help you remember the definition.

Vocabulary	Knowledge Rating	Definition	Picture
basic	0 1 2 3	serving as the starting point; simple	
element	0 1 2 3	one part of a whole	
pause	0 1 2 3	to stop for a short time	
contain	0 1 2 3	to hold or include something	
surface	0 1 2 3	to rise to the top	
migrate	0 1 2 3	to move between habitats or places	
guideline	0 1 2 3	a rule or piece of advice about how to behave	
coordinate	0 1 2 3	to organize or arrange	

2 Unit 7

Read the list of words. Have students repeat each word. Provide time for students to rate their knowledge of each word.

Have partners discuss the words they rated as 3s and tell each other the meanings.

Preteach Vocabulary

You've rated your knowledge and talked about what you think the words mean. Now, let's discuss the words.

Preteach Procedure

This activity is intended to take only a short amount of time, so make it an oral exercise if your students aren't capable of writing quickly.

- Introduce each word as indicated on the word card.
- Read the definition and example sentences.
- Ask questions to clarify and deepen understanding.
- If time permits, allow students to share.

* Do not provide instruction time to write definitions or draw pictures, but explain that students should complete both as time permits during the unit.

Note: Research has proven that vocabulary is best learned when students represent their knowledge of words in linguistic and/or nonlinguistic ways. Thus, drawing a picture will help students remember the words. This strategy is especially effective for English language learners.

basic

Let's read the first word together. *Basic.*

Definition: *Basic* means "serving as the starting point, or simple." Something that is the starting point or simple is what? (basic)

Example 1: Babies make only *basic* cooing and babbling sounds before they say more complex words.

Example 2: A *basic* guideline for behavior at our school is that all students must treat others with respect.

Example 3: A *basic* outfit consists of pants, a shirt, and shoes, but many people like to add extra colorful items, such as hats and scarves.

Question 1: Are addition and subtraction *basic* skills needed before doing higher-level math? Yes or no? (yes)

Question 2: What are the two *basic* parts of a sentence? (subject, predicate)

Pair Share: Turn to your partner and tell how you think the word *basic* will be used in the passage "Whale Song."

element

Let's read the next word together. *Element.*

Definition: An *element* means "one part of a whole." One part of a whole is what? (an element)

Example 1: Addition and subtraction are *elements* of arithmetic.

Example 2: No matter what the language, consonants and vowels are sound *elements.*

Example 3: The *elements* in smog are smoke and fog.

Question 1: Are passing and dribbling *elements* of basketball? Yes or no? (yes)

Question 2: Is oxygen an *element* of air? Yes or no? (yes)

Pair Share: Turn to your partner and name the *elements* of chocolate chip cookies.

pause

Let's read the next word together. *Pause.*

Definition: *Pause* means "to stop for a short time." To stop for a short time is to what? (pause)

Example 1: When I need to leave the room, I *pause* the movie I am watching.

Example 2: On Veteran's Day, we *paused* for a moment to honor those who have fought for our country.

Example 3: When I was studying for the test, I *paused* because my eyes were getting tired.

Question 1: When we read, do we *pause* at commas? Yes or no? (yes)

Question 2: Should you *pause* before you cross a street? Yes or no? (yes)

Pair Share: Turn to your partner and define *pause.*

contain

Let's read the next word together. *Contain.*

Definition: *Contain* means "to hold or include something." To hold or include something is to what? (contain it)

Example 1: The FCC censors songs that *contain* coarse language.

Example 2: I lost my wallet, which *contained* my driver's license, cash, and a debit card.

Example 3: The science book *contains* a chapter on pollution.

Question 1: Does a refrigerator *contain* things? Yes or no? (yes)

Question 2: In what is sand *contained*? (possible answer: a sandbox)

Pair Share: Turn to your partner and categorize what your locker *contains* into "needed for class" and "needed outside of class."

surface

Let's read the next word together. *Surface.*

Definition: *Surface* means "to rise to the top." To rise to the top means what? (surface)

Example 1: A bottle-nosed dolphin can hold its breath underwater for seven minutes before it needs to *surface* to breathe.

Example 2: Moles spend most of their time in underground tunnels but *surface* occasionally to find water.

Example 3: The submarine had been underwater for two weeks and needed to *surface* for supplies.

Question 1: If I *surface,* do I rise above something or sink below something? (rise above something)

Question 2: If you are swimming, do you *surface* to breathe? Yes or no? (yes)

Pair Share: With your partner, name two animals that need to *surface* to breathe and two that do not.

migrate

Let's read the next word together. *Migrate.*

Definition: *Migrate* means "to move between habitats or places." To move between habitats or places is to what? (migrate)

Example 1: Some hummingbirds *migrate* 500 miles across the Gulf of Mexico.

Example 2: My grandparents live in Michigan but *migrate* to Arizona during the winter.

Example 3: Some farm workers *migrate* from one area to another, following the crops that are ready to pick.

Question 1: Does *migration* involve movement? Yes or no? (yes)

Question 2: Do all animals *migrate*? Yes or no? (no)

Pair Share: Tell your partner four things that *migrate.*

guideline

Let's read the next word together. *Guideline.*

Definition: *Guideline* means "a rule or piece of advice about how to behave." A rule or piece of advice about how to behave is a what? (guideline)

Example 1: Teachers usually give *guidelines* on how to behave during group work.

Example 2: The *guidelines* for the concert said that we could not use any recording devices.

Example 3: Our school has a student handbook that lists the *guidelines* for behavior.

Question 1: Which is stronger, a *guideline* or a law? (law)

Question 2: Are there *guidelines* for computer use in your school? Yes or no? (yes)

Pair Share: Turn to your partner and state two *guidelines* for this class.

coordinate

Let's read the last word together. *Coordinate.*

Definition: *Coordinate* means "to organize or arrange." To organize or arrange is to what? (coordinate)

Example 1: To get students to school on time, bus drivers *coordinate* the order in which they pick them up.

Example 2: We do not have enough computers for everyone in school, so the teachers *coordinate* who uses them on which days.

Example 3: We are having a party on Saturday and will need to *coordinate* who will bring food, napkins, plates, and silverware.

Question 1: If you are going to a party with your friends, do you need to *coordinate* a time to leave? Yes or no? (yes)

Question 2: Does someone *coordinate* the assemblies at your school? Yes or no? (yes)

Pair Share: Tell your partner about a time you *coordinated* something.

Reading

Objective

- Demonstrate an understanding of the text by asking and answering questions and referring to key details in the text.

"Whale Song"

Direct students to page 3 in their Student Books.

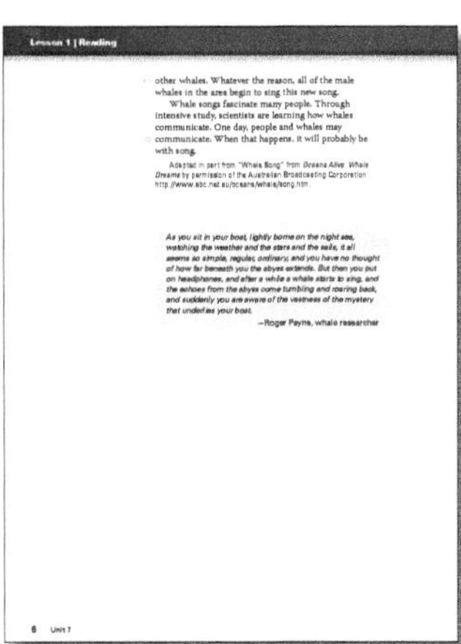

Words to Know

In addition to the vocabulary words, here are some words students might have trouble with:

remain to continue; to stay

similar like; almost the same as other things

compete to try to win or get something that others are trying to get

attract to make (cause) people or animals to want to be near

behavior the way that people or things act

alter to change in some way

dominant most powerful

You and your partner have already previewed the text. Let's discuss some key points before we read.

- Text features can provide readers information about a text before they begin reading. Often, text features can help readers identify the topic, which is the subject of the passage. What is the topic of this passage? (whales)
- Notice the picture behind the title "Whale Song." Use the pictures to predict what the text will be about. What do you see? (Answers will vary.) **Guide the discussion toward the size and actions of the whale. Ask probing questions such as these:** What body of water is this? (ocean) How can you tell? (vast water with large waves) Is this fresh water or salt water? (salt water)
- Look at the picture on page 5. What do you see? (swimming humpback whales)
- Remember that captions provide clues about the text. Put your pencil eraser on the caption while I read it aloud. Ready? "Humpback whales in the singing position." Turn to your partner and tell how the caption relates to the picture.
- Nonfiction text often has headings that divide the text into meaningful sections.

Scan the headings. What do you learn from reading the headings? (Whale songs have parts. Whale songs have a purpose.)

- What other text features do you notice? (two quotes) Who is Roger Payne? (whale researcher)

Read both quotes aloud.

> Some of my happiest hours have been spent at night lying back in the cockpit of a sailboat, alone on watch, steering with one foot and watching the mast sweeping across vast fields of stars, while the songs of the humpback whales poured up out of the sea, to fill my head, my heart, and finally my soul as well.
>
> —Roger Payne, whale researcher
>
> As you sit in your boat, lightly borne on the night sea, watching the weather and the stars and the sails, it all seems so simple, regular, ordinary, and you have no thought of how far beneath you the abyss extends. But then you put on headphones, and after a while a whale starts to sing, and the echoes from the abyss come tumbling and roaring back, and suddenly you are aware of the vastness of the mystery that underlies your boat.
>
> —Roger Payne, whale researcher

Have students discuss their interpretation. We will revisit Payne's quotes during the first read.

Direct students to page 1 in their Student Books. Have them follow along as you read the prompts aloud.

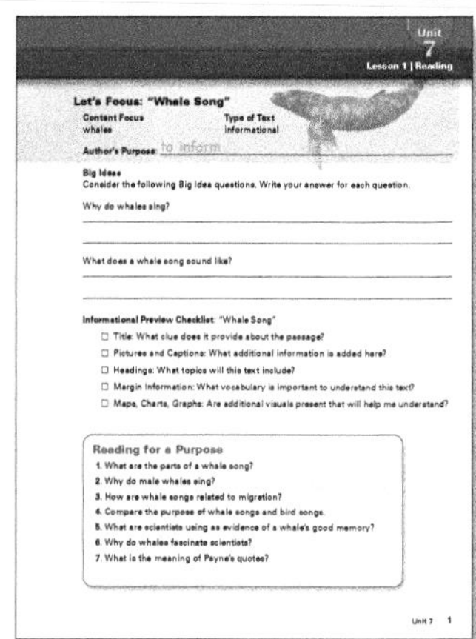

Reading for a Purpose

1. What are the parts of a whale song?
2. Why do male whales sing?
3. How are whale songs related to migration?
4. Compare the purpose of whale songs and bird songs.
5. What are scientists using as evidence of a whale's good memory?
6. Why do whales fascinate scientists?
7. What is the meaning of Payne's quotes?

You will become equipped to answer these questions by reading the passage. For now, let the prompts guide your reading. Be on the lookout for facts and concepts you could use to respond to the prompts. While reading, you also should think about our two Big Idea questions: Why do whales sing? and What does a whale song sound like?

Direct students to page 3 in their Student Books. Now it's time to read. Where are your eyes while I read? (on text) Where is your pencil? (following along, word for word) Eyes on text, pencil on words. Let's begin. Follow along with your pencil eraser as I read the text. Read the passage aloud.

Guiding Students Toward Independent Reading

While the lessons are written for a teacher read aloud, it is important that your students read as much and as often as they can. Assign readings that meet the needs of your students, based on your observations or data. This is a good opportunity to stretch students, but if they become frustrated, return to the read-aloud method.

Options for reading text:

- Teacher read aloud
- Teacher-led or student-led choral read
- Independent read of small sections with frequent comprehension checks
- Paired read or independent read

An Old Song

Sailors have listened to whale songs for thousands of years. The songs fascinate us. Roger Payne is a scientist who studies whale songs. He wants to uncover the purpose of their songs. Until recently, scientists did not know that whales used songs to communicate. Slowly, they are realizing whale songs are messages, but they still don't know what the different songs mean.

Timer

For confirmation of engagement, take 30 seconds to have students share one thing they learned with their partner. If needed, provide this example for students: While reading, I was realizing that I don't know much about sounds that whales make or the purpose of their songs. This is a fascinating topic. Now it's your turn. Share your thoughts and one thing you learned with your partner. Partners, you should listen carefully and ask questions to check understanding.

Parts of the Song

Some whale songs have many parts. First, the most basic part of a whale song is an element. An element is one sound. Elements can be long groans. They can be low moans, roars, trills, cries, or snores. They can also be growls, whistles, or chirps. Whales emit different elements in a repetitive sequence to compose a *phrase*. Two to four different elements are repeated to create short sound strings called phrases. The last part of a whale's song is the *theme*. Whales repeat the same phrases several times to sing a theme. Whales do not pause between themes. Often they sing for a very long time. Whales sing themes in order, from the first to the last. A song may contain seven or eight themes and last anywhere from 10 to 30 minutes. The songs prove that whales have amazing memories. When a song ends, whales surface to breathe. Then they begin to sing again, starting over with the same sequence of themes.

For confirmation of engagement, take 30 seconds to have students share one thing they learned with their partner. Provide this example for students: While reading, I was feeling confused about the use of the word *element*. I've heard of elements related to chemistry, but this must be a different meaning. Your turn. Switch roles. Share your thoughts and one thing you learned with your partner. Try to use one of the bold vocabulary words. Partners, you should listen carefully and ask questions to check understanding.

Time for Singing

Whales sing when they migrate. They leave the colder waters and swim to the warmer waters of the tropics. They sing as they migrate to warmer waters, and they sing again during their migration back to colder waters. During the early spring or late summer, some whales are silent, but others still sing.

Who Sings?

Not all whales sing. Only males sing the elaborate whale songs. A singing male often swims alone, staying underwater for a long time and remaining in a small area. He comes up to breathe every 8 to 15 minutes and then continues his underwater serenade.

For confirmation of engagement, take 30 seconds to have students share one thing they learned with their partner.

Purposes of Whale Song

Scientists continue to study whale songs and try to understand the different reasons they sing. It appears that whales sing for a variety of reasons. Scientists believe the songs are not just for entertainment. The songs communicate guidelines for a specific group of whales. The role of whale song is similar to that of bird song. It may be a signal for other whales to work together and stop competing. Scientists believe the songs are also used to attract females. They have observed females slapping the water with their fins in response to a male's song. Without the songs, what would happen? Groups of whales could become separated during migration. Feeding and behavior would not be coordinated.

For confirmation of engagement, take 30 seconds to have students share one thing they learned with their partner.

Singing a New Song

Another interesting fact is that whale songs change. Each year's song is a little different. The whales make changes during the singing season. They all change their song at the same time. The changes may be minor, affecting only one or two elements while the basic song pattern remains the same. For example, moans may be altered from a long moan to a short moan, but they are still moans.

Scientists don't know why whales change their songs. They know whales living in different parts of the ocean sing different songs. They have even heard whales begin to sing the same songs as whales living on the other side of the ocean. The new song may be started by a dominant whale, or it may simply interest other whales. Whatever the reason, all of the male whales in the area begin to sing this new song.

Whale songs fascinate many people. Through intensive study, scientists are learning how whales communicate. One day, people and whales may communicate. When that happens, it will probably be with song.

For confirmation of engagement, take 30 seconds to have students share one thing they learned with their partner.

Now that you have read "Whale Song," tell me something you shared with your partner during the reading. Have students share answers.

Unit 7 Lesson 2

Lesson Opener

Before the lesson, choose one of the following activities to write on the board or post on the *LANGUAGE! Live* Class Wall online.

- *List five facts about whales. Compare your list with your partner's list.*
- *Write a sentence about whales using two descriptive words (adjectives).*
- *Define* exclude.

Vocabulary

Objectives

- Determine the meaning of the multiple-meaning word *mean*.
- Demonstrate their understanding by using *mean* in written sentences.

Multiple-Meaning Word: *mean*

Direct students to page 7 in their Student Books.

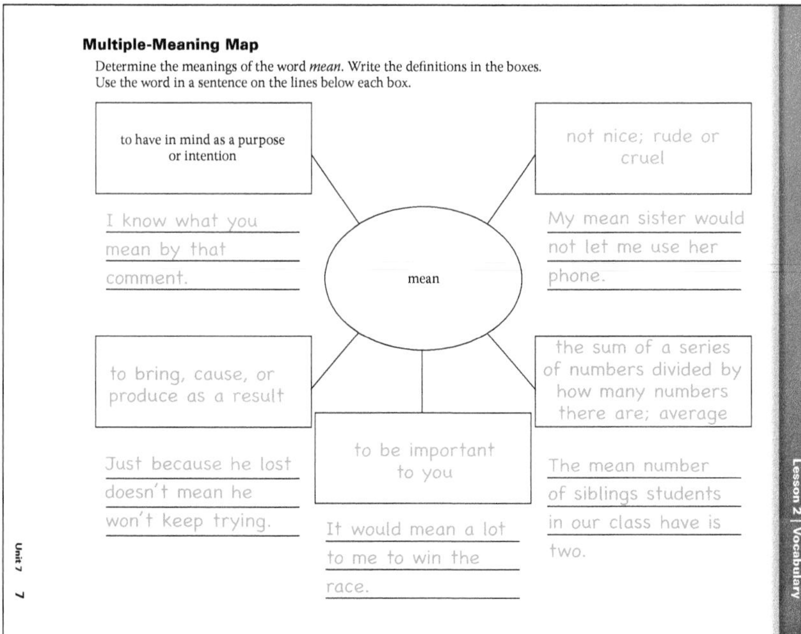
Multiple-Meaning Map

Determine the meanings of the word *mean*. Write the definitions in the boxes. Use the word in a sentence on the lines below each box.

mean
to have in mind as a purpose or intention
I know what you mean by that comment.
not nice; rude or cruel
My mean sister would not let me use her phone.
to bring, cause, or produce as a result
Just because he lost doesn't mean he won't keep trying.
to be important to you
It would mean a lot to me to win the race.
the sum of a series of numbers divided by how many numbers there are; average
The mean number of siblings students in our class have is two.
Unit 7 7
Lesson 2 | Vocabulary

In this unit, we are talking about whales and the songs they sing. Scientists have been studying the songs and sounds of whales to determine what they mean.

Mean is a word that has more than one meaning. The word *mean* can be a noun, a verb, or an adjective. *Mean* is one of the most commonly used multiple-meaning words in the English language. For instance:

Use a worn out novel as a prop.

Pick up a book and hold it close to you. Read the following story, exaggerating the pronunciation of *mean* at each occurrence.

This book *means* a lot to me because it was given to me by a friend. A couple of years ago, we stopped being friends because I hurt her. I didn't *mean* to hurt her, but she said I was *mean* and decided we shouldn't be friends. Just because we are no longer friends doesn't *mean* that I don't still cherish her gift. I am sure she didn't *mean* for it to be a gift that I would keep forever, but it has become very important to me. It is about the *meaning* of life and I read it every year.

I just used the same word six different ways to tell you about a book. So, how do we know which definition of the word is being used? It all depends on how it is used in a sentence. We look for clues around the word to help us.

Lead students in a discussion of the various meanings of the word *mean*. Have them write the meanings and sentences on the Multiple-Meaning Map in their Student Books.

Model

Have you ever heard someone ask *What do you mean?* In this usage, the verb *mean* means "to have in mind as a purpose or intention." Write the definition ***to have in mind as a purpose or intention*** on the board and have students find it on their map. Have students think of a good sentence for this usage and write it below that definition.

Guided Practice

On the board, add four numbers, then divide the total by 4. Circle the result and explain that it is the mean of the four numbers. The mean of 5, 7, 9, and 11 is 8. What is the definition of *mean* in this usage? (the sum of a series of numbers divided by how many there are; average) Write the definition on the board and have students write it on their map. Have students think of a good sentence for this usage and write it below that definition. Continue the process until students' maps are complete. Review the sentences and have students correct as needed.

Note: Base the number of modeled and guided examples on student ability and progress. Challenge them with independent practice when appropriate.

Additional Definitions of *mean*

Noun

- method used to attain a goal (means)
- available resources (means)

Verb

- matter
- stand for

Prepositional Phrase

- *by all means:* certainly
- *by any means:* in any way at all
- *by no means:* in no way; not at all

Idiom

- *mean well:* to have good intentions

Grammar

Objectives

- Demonstrate an understanding of the function of object pronouns in sentences.
- Write sentences using object pronouns in place of a direct object and in place of the object of a preposition.

Object Pronouns

Pronoun poster

Write the following words on the board: *I, we, he, she, they, you.* We use these words to take the place of certain nouns when we write and when we speak. What are these words called? (pronouns) Write the following sentences on the board and read them aloud:

James went to the office. He needed a pass for class.

Who is *he*? (James) What word did *he* replace? (James) What job is the word *James* doing in the first sentence? (It is the subject.) Pronouns that take the place of subjects are called subject pronouns. We should always use a subject pronoun when we need to replace a subject noun.

We have learned that not all nouns are subject nouns. If I want to replace a noun that is not a subject noun, I will have to use a different pronoun. Write the following sentence on the board and read it aloud:

Maria picked Rosa to be on the team.

What is the subject? (Maria) Who was picked? (Rosa) Rosa received the action, so what job is the noun *Rosa* doing in the sentence? (It is the direct object.) If I wanted to replace that noun with a pronoun, I would not use a subject pronoun. Because the noun is the direct object, I need to use an object pronoun. Have students think about the word they would use to replace Rosa.

Direct students to pages 8 and 9 in their Student Books. Read the information on object pronouns. Then, read the example in the box. In this sentence, *Sally* is not the direct object. What job is the noun *Sally* doing? (*Sally* is the object of the preposition.) It's important to know the different jobs words can do in a sentence. In this case, it will help us choose the right replacement.

Direct objects and objects of the preposition are both replaced by object pronouns. Write the following sentence on the board and read it aloud:

Kim buys gum for the boys.

What is the direct object? (gum) What is the object of the preposition? (the boys) Ask students what object pronouns could be used to replace *Kim, gum,* and *the boys.*

Show students how sentences with all subjects and objects replaced with pronouns can be confusing by writing the new sentence with all pronouns:

She buys it for them.

Direct students to Part B and read the instructions.

Model

Model how to determine the correct object pronoun to replace the underlined noun in the example.

Guided Practice

Guide students in completion of the first sentence.

Independent Practice

Read the remaining sentences and have students replace the nouns with object pronouns. Review the answers as a class.

Now that you've practiced using object pronouns, let's practice identifying the type of pronoun used in each sentence. Read the example sentence and explain that *them* is the object of the preposition. Point out the preposition *to* before the pronoun *them*. Guide students in determining the pronoun in the first two sentences. Use questions for subjects and objects to demonstrate how to decide what job the pronoun is doing in each sentence.

Have students determine the job of the pronouns in the remaining sentences independently. Review the answers as a class.

Note: Base the number of modeled and guided examples on student ability and progress. Challenge them with independent practice when appropriate.

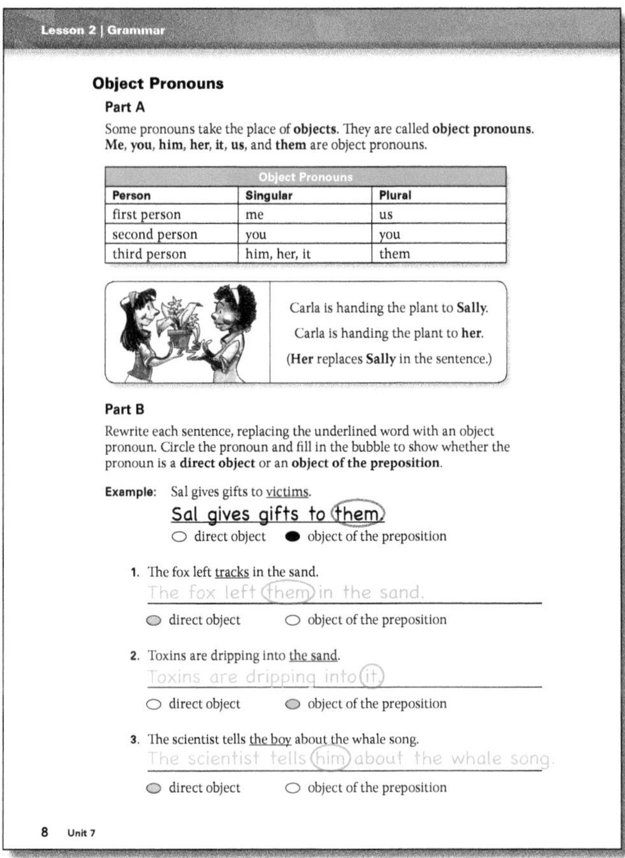

Lesson 2 | Grammar

Object Pronouns

Part A

Some pronouns take the place of **objects**. They are called **object pronouns**. **Me**, **you**, **him**, **her**, **it**, **us**, and **them** are object pronouns.

Object Pronouns		
Person	**Singular**	**Plural**
first person	me	us
second person	you	you
third person	him, her, it	them

Carla is handing the plant to **Sally**.
Carla is handing the plant to **her**.
(**Her** replaces **Sally** in the sentence.)

Part B

Rewrite each sentence, replacing the underlined word with an object pronoun. Circle the pronoun and fill in the bubble to show whether the pronoun is a **direct object** or an **object of the preposition**.

Example: Sal gives gifts to victims.
Sal gives gifts to them.
○ direct object ● object of the preposition

1. The fox left tracks in the sand.
The fox left them in the sand.
● direct object ○ object of the preposition

2. Toxins are dripping into the sand.
Toxins are dripping into it.
○ direct object ● object of the preposition

3. The scientist tells the boy about the whale song.
The scientist tells him about the whale song.
● direct object ○ object of the preposition

8 Unit 7

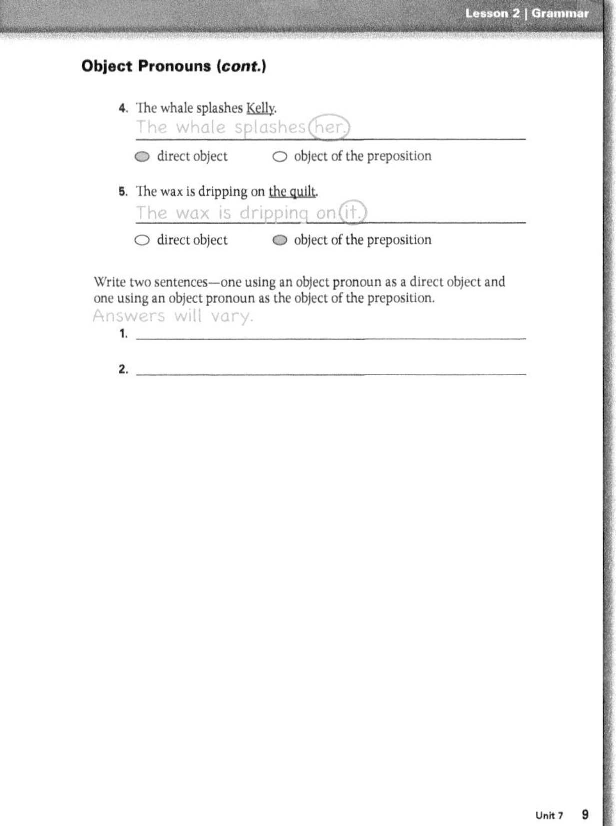

Lesson 2 | Grammar

Object Pronouns (*cont.*)

4. The whale splashes Kelly.
The whale splashes her.
● direct object ○ object of the preposition

5. The wax is dripping on the quilt.
The wax is dripping on it.
○ direct object ● object of the preposition

Write two sentences—one using an object pronoun as a direct object and one using an object pronoun as the object of the preposition.
Answers will vary.

1. ______

2. ______

Unit 7 9

Writing

Objectives

- Demonstrate an understanding of the function of commas and quotation marks in dialogue.
- Use commas and quotation marks correctly in written dialogue.

Punctuate It: Quotation Marks

In this lesson, we continue our examination of punctuation with a focus on clarifying meaning, both for the reader and the writer. When you read, how do you know if someone is actually speaking? There are special punctuation marks that signal conversation, or dialogue. Quotation marks and commas help separate the identity of the speaker from his or her words.

Direct students to pages 10 and 11 in their Student Books. Have students follow along as you read the dialogue.

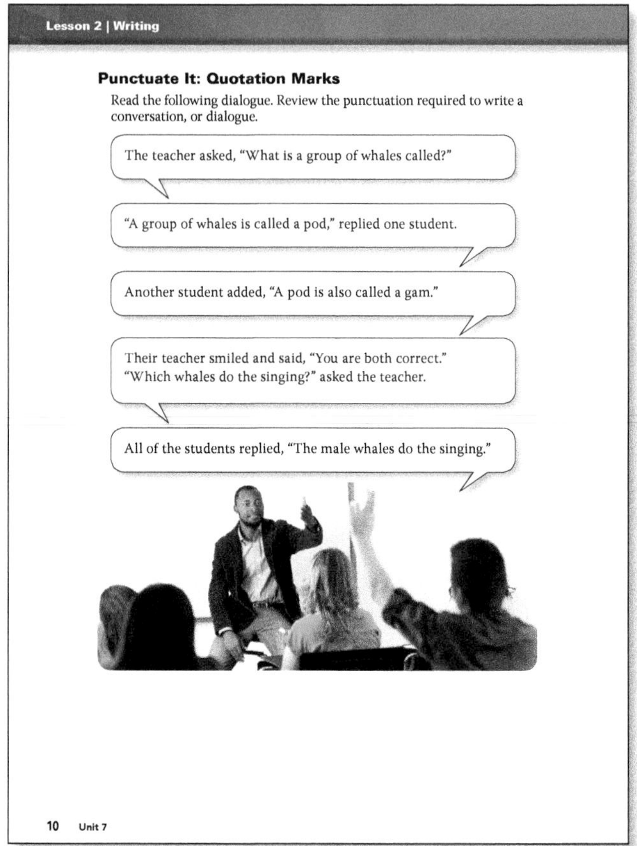
Lesson 2 | Writing

Punctuate It: Quotation Marks

Read the following dialogue. Review the punctuation required to write a conversation, or dialogue.

The teacher asked, "What is a group of whales called?"

"A group of whales is called a pod," replied one student.

Another student added, "A pod is also called a gam."

Their teacher smiled and said, "You are both correct."
"Which whales do the singing?" asked the teacher.

All of the students replied, "The male whales do the singing."

10 Unit 7

Notice that each line of dialogue identifies the speaker and uses the correct punctuation.

Look at the first line. A comma is used to separate the identity of the speaker and the actual words that are spoken.

- Who is the first person to speak? (the teacher)
- What are the exact words spoken by the teacher? (What is a group of whales called?)

Notice that quotation marks are used to frame the spoken words. They are placed before the first word and after the last word.

- Is the question mark inside or outside of the quotation mark? (inside the quotation mark)
- What happens when the sentence begins with the dialogue and ends with the identification of the speaker? Look at the second line of dialogue and tell me who is speaking. (one of the students) A comma is still used to separate the actual words spoken and the identity of the speaker, even though the spoken words come first.
- What words are spoken by the student? (A group of whales is called a pod.) Those are the words framed by the pair of quotation marks.

Continue reading each line of dialogue and comparing the punctuation required when speakers are identified before and after the dialogue. Reinforce correct placement of the quotation marks.

Before we move on to the next dialogue, look for verbs in this dialogue that mean the same thing as *said.* Write the following words on the board:

asked, replied, added, said

What other verbs could be used? (possible answers: shouted, exclaimed, responded, inquired) Keep these words in mind whenever you write dialogue. Try to use a variety of verbs instead of always using *said.*

Now let's look at the next page. After reading the dialogue, we will write it and add the needed punctuation as we identify each speaker.

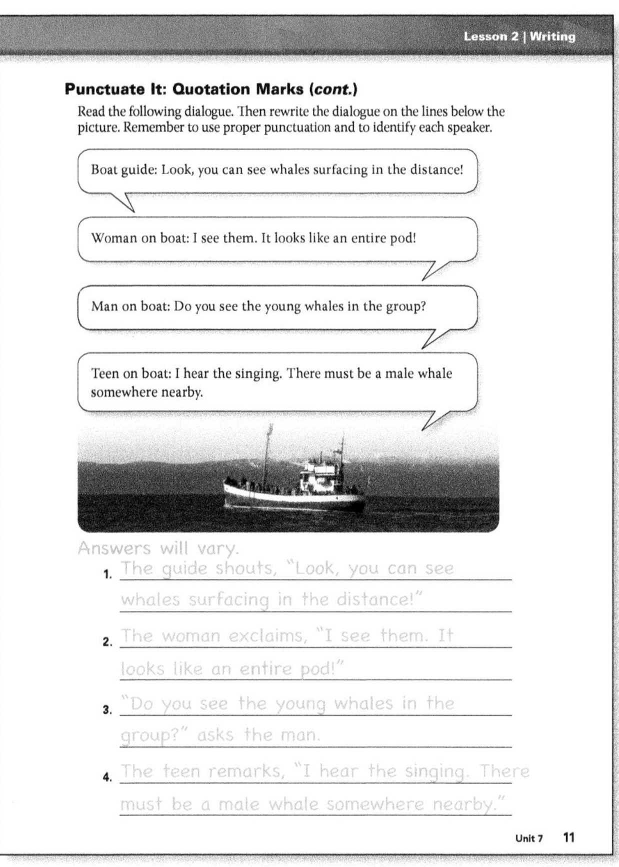

Lesson 2 | Writing

Punctuate It: Quotation Marks (*cont.*)

Read the following dialogue. Then rewrite the dialogue on the lines below the picture. Remember to use proper punctuation and to identify each speaker.

Answers will vary.

1. The guide shouts, "Look, you can see whales surfacing in the distance!"
2. The woman exclaims, "I see them. It looks like an entire pod!"
3. "Do you see the young whales in the group?" asks the man.
4. The teen remarks, "I hear the singing. There must be a male whale somewhere nearby."

Unit 7 11

Model

Read the dialogue and then model how to write the first line using the correct punctuation.

Guided Practice

Guide students in writing subsequent lines, encouraging them to use a verb other than *said.* Review the answers as a class.

Note: Base the number of modeled and guided examples on student ability and progress. Challenge them with independent practice when appropriate.

Lesson 3

Lesson Opener

Before the lesson, choose one of the following activities to write on the board or post on the *LANGUAGE! Live* Class Wall online.

- *Write three sentences using the word* mean, *using a different meaning in each sentence.*
- *Write a sentence about something you own using a possessive noun.*
- *List three things you would like to know about whales.*

Reading

Objective

- Read words to develop fluency.

Word Fluency: First Read

Timer

Follow the Fluency Procedure outlined below. If it is necessary, begin the fluency drill with a choral read of the words as you provide a rhythm (snap your fingers, tap your foot, tap your pencil). Direct students to page 12 in their Student Books and complete the process.

Word Fluency: First Read

Read the words fluently.

	Correct	Errors
1st Try		
2nd Try		

boys	feeling	teeth	fluke	sharp	charted	joy	sting	hang	cloth	10
teeth	fluke	sharp	charted	joy	sting	hang	cloth	spike	lung	20
sharp	charted	joy	sting	hang	cloth	spike	lung	start	quotes	30
joy	sting	hang	cloth	spike	lung	start	quotes	blame	speaking	40
hang	cloth	spike	lung	start	quotes	blame	speaking	toys	marched	50
spike	lung	start	quotes	blame	speaking	toys	marched	things	ploy	60
start	quotes	blame	speaking	feeling	marched	things	ploy	feeling	boys	70
blame	speaking	toys	marched	things	ploy	feeling	boys	fluke	teeth	80
toys	marched	things	ploy	toys	boys	fluke	teeth	charted	sharp	90
things	ploy	feeling	boys	fluke	teeth	charted	sharp	sting	joy	100

Lesson 3 | Reading

12 Unit 7

Fluency Procedure

- Partners switch books, so the recorder is marking errors in the reader's book.
- A timer is set for one minute.
- Readers and recorders move left to right, tracking each word with a pencil.
- As readers read the words aloud, recorders mark errors with a small x above the misread word.
- Recorders place a star to the right of the last word read when time ends.
- If the reader is able to read all words in the allotted time, the reader needs to start over at the beginning. The recorder must indicate this feat by placing two stars to the right of the last word read.
- When both students have read, partners switch books.
- Students calculate total words read, then subtract errors and record.
- Students record information on the progress chart in back of the Student Book.

Vocabulary

Objectives

- Review passage vocabulary.
- Demonstrate an understanding of simple similes.
- Write simple similes.
- Identify similes in popular music.

Review

Direct students to page 2 in their Student Books.

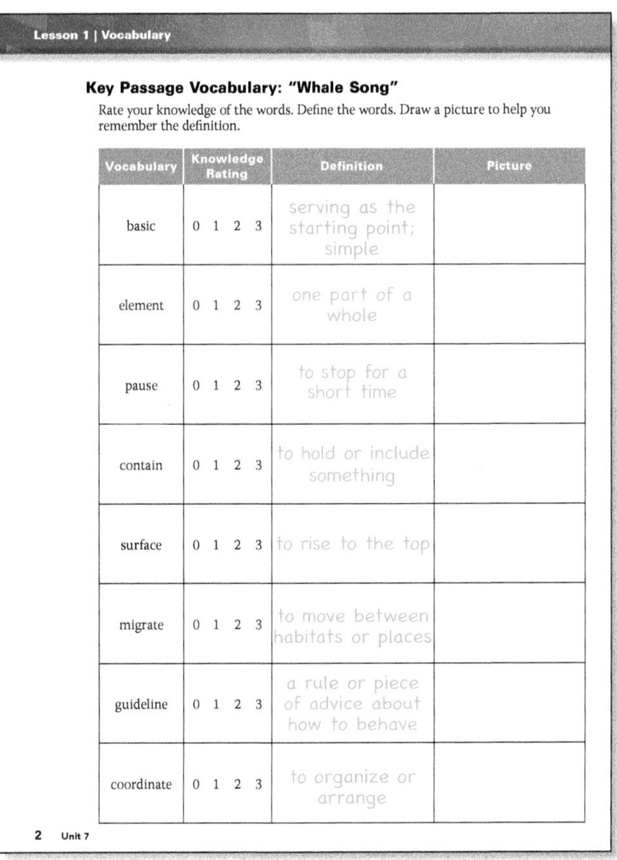

Lesson 1 | Vocabulary

Key Passage Vocabulary: "Whale Song"

Rate your knowledge of the words. Define the words. Draw a picture to help you remember the definition.

Vocabulary	Knowledge Rating	Definition	Picture
basic	0 1 2 3	serving as the starting point; simple	
element	0 1 2 3	one part of a whole	
pause	0 1 2 3	to stop for a short time	
contain	0 1 2 3	to hold or include something	
surface	0 1 2 3	to rise to the top	
migrate	0 1 2 3	to move between habitats or places	
guideline	0 1 2 3	a rule or piece of advice about how to behave	
coordinate	0 1 2 3	to organize or arrange	

2 Unit 7

Review the vocabulary words from the passage "Whale Song." Have students answer each question with a complete sentence.

- Whales do not *pause* between their themes. But do they ever *pause* in their singing? (Yes, whales pause in their singing.) To stop for a short time is to what? (To stop for a short time is to pause.)
- Why do whales *surface*? (Whales are mammals so they surface to breathe.) To rise to the top is to what? (To rise to the top is to surface.)
- Do whales communicate *guidelines* to other whales? (Yes, whales communicate guidelines to other whales.) A rule or piece of advice about something is a what? (A guideline is a rule or piece of advice.)
- Whale songs are *coordinated*. Is their surfacing *coordinated*? (No, their surfacing is not coordinated.) To organize or arrange is to what? (To coordinate is to organize or arrange.)
- Is laughing a *basic* sound for a whale? (No, laughing is not a basic sound for a whale.) If something is simple or the starting point, what is it? (Something that is simple is basic.)
- Is a moan an *element* of a whale song? (Yes, a moan is an element of a whale song.) We say that one part of a whole is what? (An element is one part of a whole.)
- Do whale songs *contain* organized themes? (Yes, whale songs contain organized themes.) To hold or include something is to what? (To contain is to hold or include something.)
- Do whales *migrate* long distances? (Yes, whales migrate long distances.) To move between habitats or places is to what? (To move between places is to migrate.)

Vocabulary Concept: Simile

We have compared literal and figurative language. In literal language, the words mean exactly what they say. If I say "black horse," you can picture a black horse in your mind. Figurative language is more descriptive, and the words may not mean exactly what they say.

In this lesson, we will focus on a kind of figurative language called a *simile*. Similes are used in all kinds of texts, including poems and songs, to make the writing more descriptive and vivid. The word *simile* and the word *similar* both come from a Latin word meaning "a like thing." A simile is a figure of speech in which two unlike things are compared to show how they are similar. A simile often uses exaggeration and the words *like* or *as*.

Find examples of similes to share with students.

Here are some similes you may have heard:

- That lake is *as dry as a bone*. What does this mean? (The lake is very dry.)
- It was like *a slap in the face* when I didn't get invited to my friend's party. *Like a slap in the face* means what? (an insult) When something is compared to a slap in the face, it means that it hurt, just like a slap in the face does. It is a different kind of hurt, though, and that is why in this context, *a slap in the face* is considered figurative language.
- *As quick as lightning*, he closed his computer. *As quick as lightning* means what? (very fast)

Direct students to page 13 in their Student Books.

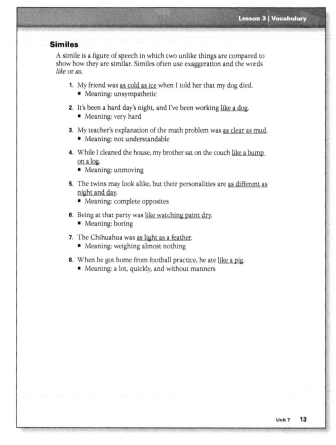

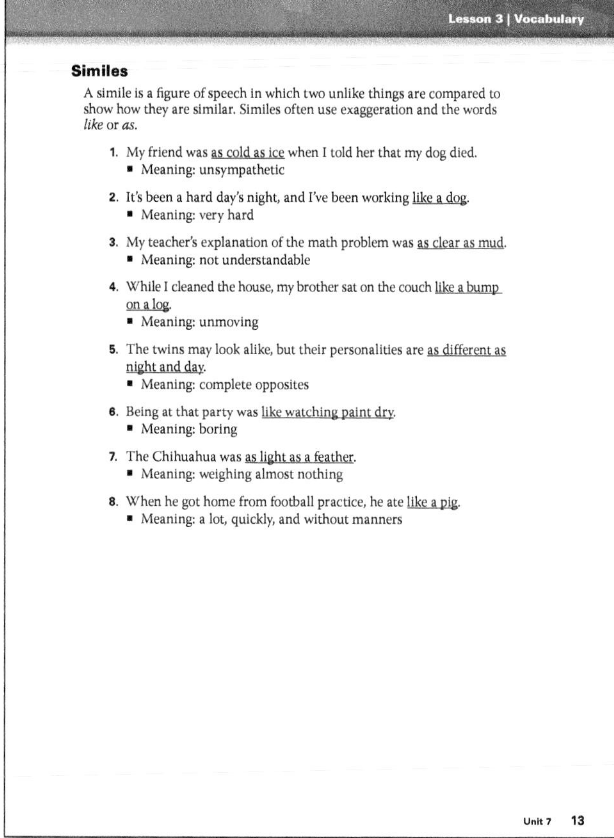
Lesson 3 | Vocabulary

Similes

A simile is a figure of speech in which two unlike things are compared to show how they are similar. Similes often use exaggeration and the words *like* or *as*.

1. My friend was as cold as ice when I told her that my dog died.
   - Meaning: unsympathetic
2. It's been a hard day's night, and I've been working like a dog.
   - Meaning: very hard
3. My teacher's explanation of the math problem was as clear as mud.
   - Meaning: not understandable
4. While I cleaned the house, my brother sat on the couch like a bump on a log.
   - Meaning: unmoving
5. The twins may look alike, but their personalities are as different as night and day.
   - Meaning: complete opposites
6. Being at that party was like watching paint dry.
   - Meaning: boring
7. The Chihuahua was as light as a feather.
   - Meaning: weighing almost nothing
8. When he got home from football practice, he ate like a pig.
   - Meaning: a lot, quickly, and without manners

Unit 7 13

Read the sentences and the meanings of the similes aloud, and offer the following explanations.

Explanations

1. Ice is hard and cold. When someone is caring, we often refer to them as warm or soft. The opposite of caring is cold and hard—like ice.
2. In the past, dogs were used mainly as working animals, helping to herd sheep and hunt. So, when someone is working hard at a chore or a job, we can say they are working like a dog.
3. When mud is smeared on a window, can you see through the window? No. *Clear* has two meanings. It means "can be seen through" and it means that something is "understandable." When you do not understand something, you can compare it to mud and people will know that it isn't clear at all.

4. Logs from trees often have bumps where branches and stems once were. The log, bumps and all, isn't part of a tree any more. It's dead. The bumps don't move at all. So, saying that someone is like a bump on a log is saying that they just sit there and do nothing.
5. Night is dark. Day is light. Night is associated with sleep, while day is associated with activity. Night is cool. Day is warm. Night and day are opposites. When we say that two things are as different as night and day, we are saying that they are total opposites.
6. After people paint something, do they typically sit there and watch while the paint dries? No, that would be boring. The paint doesn't do anything or change in any way. There is nothing to see, hear, or touch. When an event is compared to watching paint dry, that event is not entertaining at all. It is totally boring.
7. If you have ever picked up a feather, you know that feathers are almost weightless. They have to be, or birds wouldn't be able to fly. When we say that something is as light as a feather, we are saying that it weighs very little.
8. Pigs eat anything—and lots of it. Pigs are often fed in a trough. They are given all the scraps and leftover food that other people and animals did not eat or want. They eat quickly and in large quantities. When a person is said to have eaten like a pig, it usually means that he or she ate a lot, very quickly, and without manners.

Creating Similes

Model

Let's create a few similes of our own. A common simile is *as tall as a tree,* which means that something is really tall.
I could also say *as tall as a skyscraper.*

Have students offer other similes comparing height.

Another common simile is *as good as gold.* With a partner, start with the phrase *as good as,* and add things that are good. Have partners create similes and share their answers with the class.

Guided Practice

Direct students to Part A on page 14 in their Student Books.

Here are some examples of similes using the word *like* to compare two things:

The girl runs *like a deer.*
Is she running fast or slowly? (fast)

My friend swims *like a fish.*
Is the swimming good or bad? (good)

Lesson 3 | Vocabulary

Creating Similes

A **simile** is a type of figurative language in which two unlike things are compared using *like* or *as.*

Part A

Read the examples, then write five similes using *like.* Use the verbs in the box to help you. Answers will vary.

Examples:
runs like a deer
swims like a fish

_____ like _____
(verb) (noun)

Verbs:
talks, plays, sleeps, looks, walks, jumps

1. swims like a fish
2. _____ like _____
3. _____ like _____
4. _____ like _____
5. _____ like _____
6. _____ like _____

Part B

Read the examples, then write five similes using *as.* Use the adjectives in the box to help you.

Examples:
as soft as a pillow
as graceful as a swan

as _____ as _____
(adjective) (noun)

Adjectives:
fast, slow, quiet, cute, hard, old, skinny, red, small, light

1. as soft as a pillow
2. as _____ as _____
3. as _____ as _____
4. as _____ as _____
5. as _____ as _____
6. as _____ as _____

14 Unit 7

Independent Practice

Write the following pattern on the board:

_______ *like* _______
(verb) *(noun)*

Read the verbs in the box (talks, plays, sleeps, looks, walks, jumps), but tell students they may use any verb they wish.

Have partners write five similes using *like* in their Student Books. Have volunteers share their similes.

Direct students to Part B.

Here are examples of similes using *as*:

The couch was *as soft as a pillow.*
The couch was very what? (soft)

The dancer was *as graceful as a swan.*
Were the movements of the dancer smooth? (yes)

Write the following pattern on the board:

as _________ *as* _______
(adjective) *(noun)*

Read the adjectives in the box (fast, slow, quiet, cute, hard, old, skinny, red, small, light), but tell students they may use any adjective they wish.

Have partners write five similes using *as.* Have volunteers share their similes.

Note: Base the number of modeled and guided examples on student ability and progress. Challenge them with independent practice when appropriate.

Finding similes in poems and other texts—including songs—is a fun exercise that allows you to deepen your understanding of figurative language and of the text you are reading.

Make a list of similes from popular songs.

Provide examples of similes in popular songs. Then challenge students to listen closely to their favorite songs between now and the end of the unit and compile a list of similes they hear. Offer an incentive for doing so, if possible. On the day they bring the similes to class, guide students to interpret their meanings.

Grammar

Objectives

- Identify singular and plural subject pronouns.
- Identify singular and plural object pronouns.
- Demonstrate an understanding of subject and object pronouns in sentences.

Subject and Object Pronouns

Draw the following chart on the board, leaving the information in parentheses blank:

Subject Pronouns	Singular	Plural
first person	(I)	(we)
second person	(you)	(you)
third person	(he, she, it)	(they)

We've learned that words can be categorized by their function, and that asking questions can help us determine a word's function. Words that take the place of naming words, or nouns, are called pronouns. Nouns do a variety of jobs in a sentence, so pronouns have to do the same kinds of jobs.

- What are some of the different ways a noun can be used in a sentence? (subject, direct object, or object of the preposition)
- What do we call a pronoun that takes the place of a subject noun? (a subject pronoun) The name *subject pronoun* gives us a clue, as long as we understand the job of a subject.

I need your help to fill in the chart on the board.

Ask students to provide pronouns to fill in the chart. Provide pronouns for students if they cannot generate them.

A noun is not always a subject noun. What other jobs can a noun do in a sentence? (direct object or the object of the preposition) Again, the name *object pronoun* gives a clue about the job this type of pronoun does. Draw the following chart on the board, leaving the information in parentheses blank:

Object Pronouns	Singular	Plural
first person	(me)	(us)
second person	(you)	(you)
third person	(him, her, it)	(them)

Ask students to provide pronouns to fill in the chart. Provide pronouns for students if they cannot generate them.

Let's practice some more with subject and object pronouns.

Direct students to page 15 in their Student Books.

Model

Look at the example sentence. What is the pronoun in the example sentence? (me)

Let's figure out what job that pronoun is doing in the sentence. Who is doing the action? (Mel)

Mel is our subject, so can *me* be a subject pronoun? (no) Who was shown, or who received the action? (me) The pronoun *me* is doing the job of the direct object, so it must be an object pronoun. We would write *object pronoun* on the line. Let's take a look at the first sentence.

Lesson 3 | Grammar

Identify It: Subject and Object Pronouns

Read each sentence and underline the pronoun. Identify the pronoun as a **subject pronoun** or an **object pronoun**.

Example: Mel showed me a Web site. object pronoun

1. He collects old baseball caps. subject pronoun
2. Mel tells me stories about the caps. object pronoun
3. Some old players have given caps to him. object pronoun
4. We went to the Web site yesterday. subject pronoun
5. It listed many teams. subject pronoun
6. The majority of them are long gone. object pronoun
7. The caps on the Web site might interest you. object pronoun
8. Mel's sister borrows caps from him. object pronoun
9. She wears caps on the weekends. subject pronoun
10. Some caps fit her well. object pronoun

Unit 7 15

Guided Practice

Follow the same procedure with the first two sentences. Then have a student identify the pronoun in the third sentence. Have students determine whether the pronoun is a subject pronoun or an object pronoun. Follow the same procedure for the fourth sentence, calling on two different students.

Independent Practice

Read the remaining sentences aloud, having students complete the items independently. Then review the answers as a class.

Note: Base the number of modeled and guided examples on student ability and progress. Challenge them with independent practice when appropriate.

Reading

Objectives

- Ask and answer questions to demonstrate an understanding of a text.
- Use inference, interpretation, comparisons, and categorization to analyze a text.

Critical Understandings

Some questions take the form of prompts. Prompts are statements that require a constructed response that can range from a list, to a complete sentence, to a paragraph or an essay. In this unit, we will continue to work with prompts that ask you to recall literal information. We will also move on to more challenging prompts that require you to demonstrate conceptual understanding. Often, these higher level prompts will ask you to find evidence in a text. Evidence is a detail from the text that supports a bigger idea. Evidence can be a single word, a phrase, a sentence, or a group of sentences.

When responding to prompts at the conceptual understanding level, you will recall relevant information from your memory and the text *and* demonstrate understanding of the concepts or ideas related to that information. Conceptual understanding prompts will include verbs such as *categorize, infer, relate, interpret,* and *compare.*

- What level prompt will we study in this unit? (conceptual understanding) Conceptual understanding requires you to recall and understand.
- What will you need to do at this level of comprehension? (recall and understand)

Direction Words: Conceptual Understanding poster

Direct students to the chart on page 16 or refer to the Conceptual Understanding poster if you have it displayed. Have students follow along as you read the information in the Conceptual Understandings section (from Categorize to Compare).

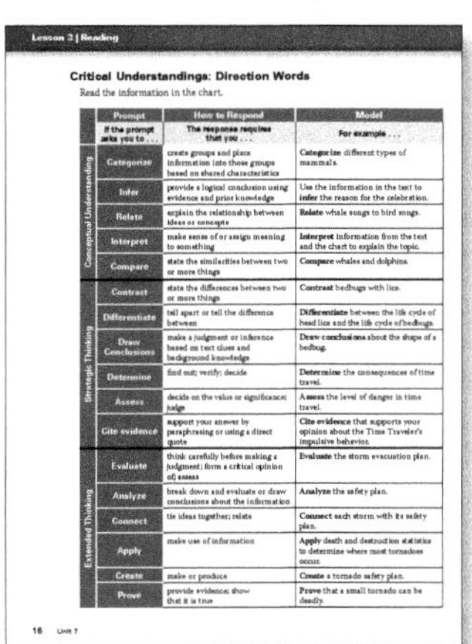

Lesson 3 | Reading

Critical Understandings: Direction Words

Read the information in the chart.

	Prompt	How to Respond	Model
	If the prompt asks you to . . .	The response requires that you . . .	For example . . .
Conceptual Understanding	Categorize	create groups and place information into those groups based on shared characteristics	**Categorize** different types of mammals.
	Infer	provide a logical conclusion using evidence and prior knowledge	Use the information in the text to **infer** the reason for the celebration.
	Relate	explain the relationship between ideas or concepts	**Relate** whale songs to bird songs.
	Interpret	make sense of or assign meaning to something	**Interpret** information from the text and the chart to explain the topic.
	Compare	state the similarities between two or more things	**Compare** whales and dolphins.
Strategic Thinking	Contrast	state the differences between two or more things	**Contrast** bedbugs with lice.
	Differentiate	tell apart or tell the difference between	**Differentiate** between the life cycle of head lice and the life cycle of bedbugs.
	Draw Conclusions	make a judgment or inference based on text clues and background knowledge	**Draw conclusions** about the shape of a bedbug.
	Determine	find out; verify; decide	**Determine** the consequences of time travel.
	Assess	decide on the value or significance; judge	**Assess** the level of danger in time travel.
	Cite evidence	support your answer by paraphrasing or using a direct quote	**Cite evidence** that supports your opinion about the Time Traveler's impulsive behavior.
Extended Thinking	Evaluate	think carefully before making a judgment; form a critical opinion of; assess	**Evaluate** the storm evacuation plan.
	Analyze	break down and evaluate or draw conclusions about the information	**Analyze** the safety plan.
	Connect	tie ideas together; relate	**Connect** each storm with its safety plan.
	Apply	make use of information	**Apply** death and destruction statistics to determine where most tornadoes occur.
	Create	make or produce	**Create** a tornado safety plan.
	Prove	provide evidence; show that it is true	**Prove** that a small tornado can be deadly.

16 Unit 7

Categorize

If the prompt asks you to *categorize,* it is asking you to create groups and place information into those groups based on shared characteristics. Read the example with me. (Categorize different types of mammals.)

Infer

If the prompt asks you to *infer,* you will need to combine what you know with information or evidence in the text to draw a logical conclusion. Sometimes prompts ask you to infer without using the word *infer.* For example, consider this question: Do all mammals have teeth? Although the prompt did not ask me to infer, I answer the question by using logic and drawing a conclusion: if a whale is a mammal, and not all whales have teeth, then not all mammals have teeth. To answer this prompt, you do not need to use the word *infer.* Simply answer the question in a complete sentence: Not all mammals have teeth. Read the example with me. (Use the information in the text to infer the reason for the celebration.)

Relate

If the prompt asks you to *relate*, it is asking you to explain the relationship between ideas or concepts. Read the example with me. (Relate whale songs to bird songs.)

Interpret

If the prompt asks you to *interpret*, it is asking you to make sense of or assign meaning to material that you have read. Read the example with me. (Interpret information from the text and the chart to explain the topic.)

Compare

If the prompt asks you to *compare*, it is asking you to state the similarities between two or more things. Read the example with me. (Compare whales and dolphins.)

It is critical to understand what each kind of prompt is asking and how to respond. We will become automatic with these prompts and learn exactly how to respond at a mastery level. Look at the How to Respond column in the chart. Each prompt requires you to construct a higher level response that uses information from different sources, including your own prior knowledge, the text, charts, and graphs.

Direct students to pages 17 and 18 in their Student Books.

Lesson 3 | Reading

Critical Understandings

Review the conceptual understanding prompts on the chart on page 16. Then read the prompts at the bottom of this page to establish a purpose for reading. Read the passage and respond to the prompts.

Whale Watching

Imagine yourself on a whale-watching trip. Humpback whales surface to the delight of everyone. The guide drops a microphone into the water. What you will hear is just as amazing as what you will see! The whale is huge. It swims past the boat. Inspect it. Its skin is black, and it has a gloss to it. It has a fin on its back. Like an exotic Asian carp, a whale jumps out of the water and lands with a splash. A whale is not some exotic fish, however. In fact, it is not a fish at all. It is a mammal. Fish have gills, but whales have lungs. That is why whale watching is so exciting. They must come up to breathe. And when they do, they are a sight and sound to enjoy.

1. **Infer** why what you hear on a whale-watching trip is just as amazing as what you see.
   In the ocean, you will see whales jump and come close to the boat. You will also hear their amazing songs.
2. **Interpret** the statement, "A whale is not some exotic fish, however."
   A whale is not an exotic fish because a whale is a mammal.
3. **Compare** a whale and a fish.
   Whales and fish both have fins, they both live in water, they both jump, and they both splash.
4. **Relate** whale watching to attending a concert.
   What you hear is as entertaining as what you see in both whale watching and a concert.

Unit 7 17

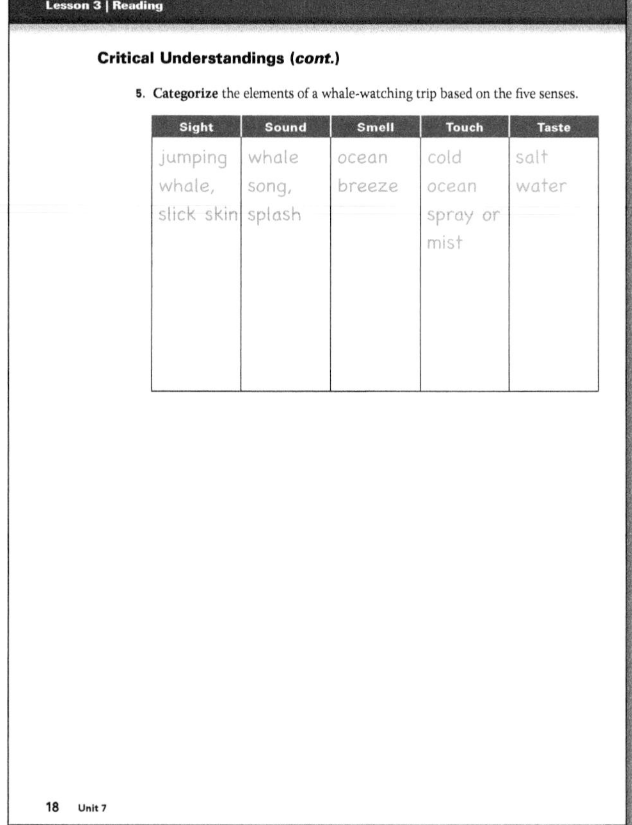

Lesson 3 | Reading

Critical Understandings (*cont.*)

5. **Categorize** the elements of a whale-watching trip based on the five senses.

Sight	Sound	Smell	Touch	Taste
jumping whale, slick skin	whale song, splash	ocean breeze	cold ocean spray or mist	salt water

18 Unit 7

Let's preview some prompts that require conceptual understanding of a short piece of text. I'll read the prompt, and you repeat the direction word in bold.

1. **Infer** why what you hear on a whale-watching trip is just as amazing as what you see. (infer)
2. **Interpret** the statement, "A whale is not some exotic fish, however." (interpret)
3. **Compare** a whale and a fish. (compare)
4. **Relate** whale watching to attending a concert. (relate)
5. **Categorize** the elements of a whale-watching trip based on the five senses. (categorize)

Notice that each of these direction words is the first word in the prompt. This is not always true. Sometimes the direction word is embedded or buried in the middle of the prompt. Prompts may also include a direct quote from the text. When we use exact words from a text, we put quotation marks around those words to show the words are not our own. Which prompt includes a quote from the text? (2) How can you tell that it is a direct quote? (quotation marks)

With eyes on text, listen while I read this short text about whale watching. Use your pencil eraser to follow along. Let's begin. Read the text aloud.

Note: While the lessons are written for a teacher read aloud, it is important that your students read as much and as often as they can. Assign readings that meet the needs of your students, based on your observations or data. This is a good opportunity to stretch students, but if they become frustrated, return to the read-aloud method.

Whale Watching

Imagine yourself on a whale-watching trip. Humpback whales surface to the delight of everyone. The guide drops a microphone into the water. What you will hear is just as amazing as what you will see! The whale is huge. It swims past the boat. Inspect it. Its skin is black, and it has a gloss to it. It has a fin on its back. Like an exotic Asian carp, a whale jumps out of the water and lands with a splash. A whale is not some exotic fish, however. In fact, it is not a fish at all. It is a mammal. Fish have gills, but whales have lungs. That is why whale watching is so exciting. They must come up to breathe. And when they do, they are a sight and sound to enjoy.

Let's check our comprehension of this passage by responding to the prompts that require conceptual understanding of the text. For each prompt, you will need to find evidence in the text to support your answer.

In previous units we worked with question words. We have also learned how to respond to prompts. We are often given prompts instead of questions because teachers want to challenge us and find out what we know. But each prompt is really a question in disguise—and we already know how to answer questions. So, if you are unsure how to respond to a prompt, it can be helpful to turn it into a question. We will practice responding to prompts that require conceptual understanding and recall using evidence from text. Try turning each prompt into a question so that you know exactly how to respond.

Model

Read the first prompt aloud.

1. **Infer** why what you hear on a whale-watching trip is just as amazing as what you see. (infer)

I can change that prompt into a question to determine how to respond. The question would be, Why do you think what you hear on a whale-watching trip is just as amazing as what you see? When we respond, we need to use evidence from the text together with our own logic. We do not have to use the direction word, *infer,* in our response. Write a response with students based on their combined efforts. (Possible response: In the ocean, you will see whales jump and come close to the boat. You will also hear their amazing songs.)

Guided Practice

Read the next prompt aloud.

2. **Interpret** the statement, "A whale is not some exotic fish, however." (interpret)

I can change this prompt into a question to determine how I need to respond. The question would be, What does "A whale is not some exotic fish, however" mean? Before we look at the context for evidence, let's discuss the word *exotic. Exotic* is a word that describes or tells more about the word *fish. Exotic* means "interesting, exciting, or unusual." Whales may be exotic, but are they fish? Have students discuss how *exotic fish* is used in context, write a response, and share it. Remind them to use a complete sentence. (A whale is not an exotic fish because a whale is a mammal.)

Independent Practice

Have partners complete the remaining prompts. Review the answers as a class to ensure that students understand what each prompt is asking.

Note: Base the number of modeled and guided examples on student ability and progress. Challenge them with independent practice when appropriate.

Provide these alternative questions and sentence starters for those who need additional help.

3. How are a whale and a fish the same?

   Whales and fish both ____.

4. How is whale watching similar to attending a concert?

   ________________________________ in both whale watching and a concert.

5. What do you hear, see, feel, smell, and taste on a whale-watching trip?

Unit 7 Lesson 4

Lesson Opener

Before the lesson, choose one of the following activities to write on the board or post on the *LANGUAGE! Live* Class Wall online.

- *Complete the simile and add a sentence telling why: A whale song is as _____ as _____.*
- *Write a sentence about whales using a linking verb.*
- *Write a sentence about whales using an action verb.*

Reading

Objective

- Read phrases to develop fluency.

Sentence Fluency

In this unit, students move from reading phrases to reading sentences for fluency practice. Students will benefit from repeated readings to develop accurate and automatic word recognition. The sentence fluency process is the same as the phrase fluency process.

Timer

Follow the Fluency Procedure outlined below. If it is necessary, begin the fluency drill with a choral read of all sentences. Direct students to page 19 in their Student Books and complete the process.

Fluency Procedure

- Partners switch books, so the recorder is marking errors in the reader's book.
- A timer is set for one minute.
- Readers and recorders move left to right, tracking each word with a pencil.
- As readers read the words aloud, recorders mark errors with a small x above the misread word.
- Recorders place a star to the right of the last word read when time ends.
- If the reader is able to read all words in the allotted time, the reader needs to start over at the beginning. The recorder must indicate this feat by placing two stars to the right of the last word read.
- When both students have read, partners switch books.
- Students calculate total words read, then subtract errors and record.
- Students record information on the progress chart in back of the Student Book.

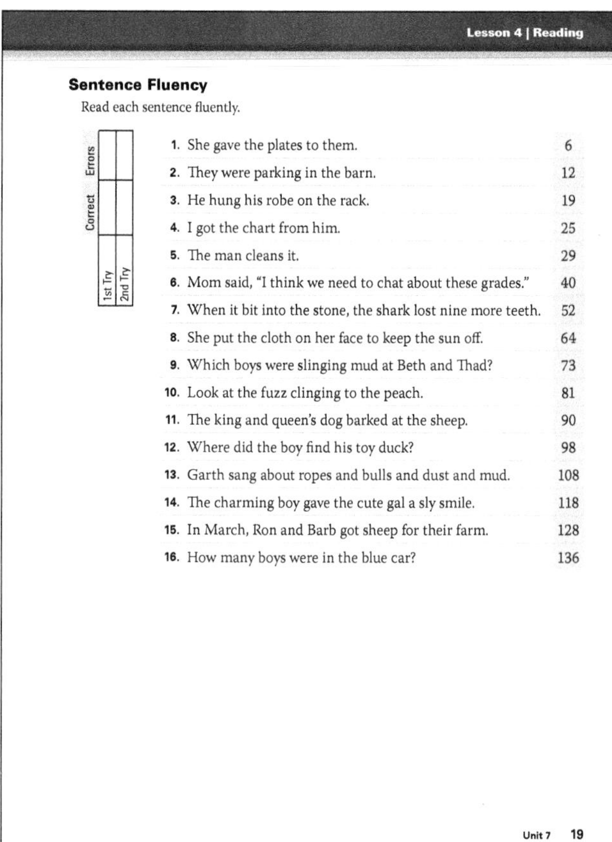

Lesson 4 | Reading

Sentence Fluency

Read each sentence fluently.

	Errors	Correct
1st Try		
2nd Try		

1. She gave the plates to them. 6
2. They were parking in the barn. 12
3. He hung his robe on the rack. 19
4. I got the chart from him. 25
5. The man cleans it. 29
6. Mom said, "I think we need to chat about these grades." 40
7. When it bit into the stone, the shark lost nine more teeth. 52
8. She put the cloth on her face to keep the sun off. 64
9. Which boys were slinging mud at Beth and Thad? 73
10. Look at the fuzz clinging to the peach. 81
11. The king and queen's dog barked at the sheep. 90
12. Where did the boy find his toy duck? 98
13. Garth sang about ropes and bulls and dust and mud. 108
14. The charming boy gave the cute gal a sly smile. 118
15. In March, Ron and Barb got sheep for their farm. 128
16. How many boys were in the blue car? 136

Unit 7 19

Grammar

Objectives

- Listen to oral sentences and accurately write them.
- Demonstrate an understanding of the function of pronouns in sentences.
- Demonstrate an understanding of the function of subject pronouns and object pronouns in sentences.

Object Pronouns, Subject Pronouns

You just read sentences for speed and accuracy. Now, we will look closely at these sentences to reinforce the work we have been doing with subject and object pronouns.

Direct students to Part A on page 20 in their Student Books. Read the instructions and remind students of the procedure for sentence dictation.

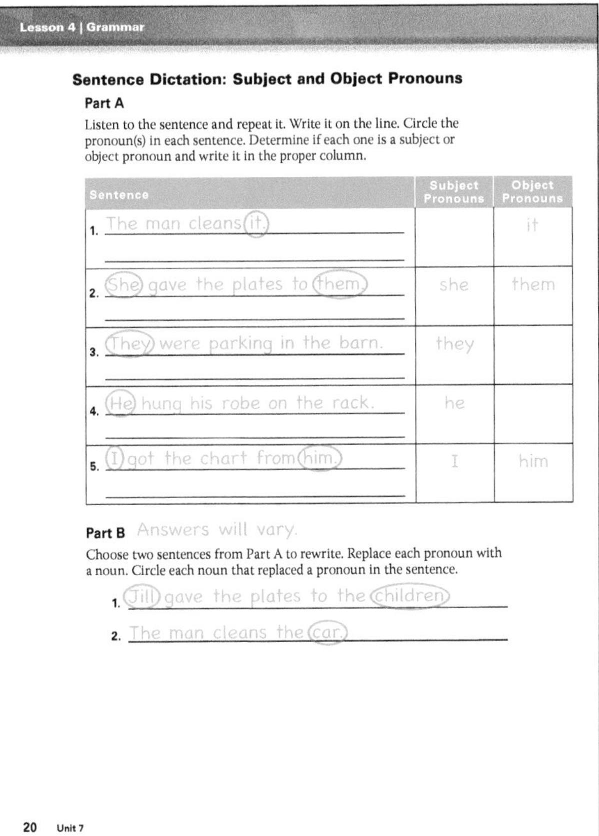
Lesson 4 | Grammar

Sentence Dictation: Subject and Object Pronouns

Part A

Listen to the sentence and repeat it. Write it on the line. Circle the pronoun(s) in each sentence. Determine if each one is a subject or object pronoun and write it in the proper column.

Sentence	Subject Pronouns	Object Pronouns
1. The man cleans (it).		it
2. (She) gave the plates to (them).	she	them
3. (They) were parking in the barn.	they	
4. (He) hung his robe on the rack.	he	
5. (I) got the chart from (him).	I	him

Part B Answers will vary.

Choose two sentences from Part A to rewrite. Replace each pronoun with a noun. Circle each noun that replaced a pronoun in the sentence.

1. (Jill) gave the plates to the (children).
2. The man cleans the (car).

20 Unit 7

Dictation Procedure

- Teacher reads the sentence.
- Students repeat the sentence.
- Students write the sentence.
- Teacher reads the sentence a second time as students check their work.

Read the following sentences aloud twice, allowing repeating and writing time in between:

1. The man cleans it.
2. She gave the plates to them.
3. They were parking in the barn.
4. He hung his robe on the rack.
5. I got the chart from him.

Have students circle each pronoun and then sort them on the chart. Review to make sure students have written the sentences correctly and marked and sorted the pronouns properly.

Write the following sentence on the board:

She went to the beach.

Look at the sentence on the board. The pronoun in this sentence is *she*, so I am going to circle it. I have to rewrite this sentence, replacing the pronoun. I'm going to use a girl's name to replace the pronoun. My new sentence will become: *Mary went to the beach*. Because *Mary* is the noun I've used to replace the pronoun, I'm going to circle it. Circle the noun *Mary*.

Now, you choose two sentences from Part A and replace the pronoun in each sentence with a noun. Write your sentences in your Student Books under Part B. Monitor students' work. Have volunteers share their sentences.

Reading

Objectives

- Read sentence phrases with fluency to support comprehension.
- Preview a text.
- Respond to specific questions to demonstrate an understanding of a text using interpretation, inference, comparison, and categorization to answer questions.

Phrase It

Prosody is a term that refers to phrasing, expression, and the way the voice is used when reading. You can tell whether people understand what they are reading by the way they read. Do they chunk the words into phrases? Do they stop at periods and pause at commas? Do they raise their voice with a question?

Reading with prosody helps with comprehension. Reading in phrases is a part of prosody. A phrase is a group of words with a chunk of meaning. In English we typically see a subject phrase and then a predicate phrase. With this predictable order, we know what is coming. It helps us comprehend what we read.

Read the following phrases, pausing in between for students to create a mental picture.

> The male whale . . . slapped its tail . . . almost overturning . . . our canoe.

The male whale is the subject, and *almost overturning our canoe* is the predicate.

For Phrase It, we scoop phrases using our pencil. When we scoop a phrase, we form an image in our heads. The next phrase we read may add to or change the image. This process is comprehension. The picture of the male whale changes as soon as we read the first part of the predicate—*slapped its tail.* It changes even more when we read the second part of the predicate—*almost overturning.* It changes even more when we read the third part of the predicate—*our canoe.* Seeing the whale almost overturn the canoe changed the feeling of the sentence. The addition of each phrase—not the addition of each word—changes our mental image. That's why we read in chunks.

Direct students to page 21 in their Student Books.

Model

Complete the first item as a model.

Guided Practice

Guide the completion of the next two.

Independent Practice

Read the remaining sentences and have students scoop the phrases. Review the answers as a class.

Note: Base the number of modeled and guided examples on student ability and progress. Challenge them with independent practice when appropriate.

There are various ways the sentences can be broken into phrases. Accept logical answers.

Phrase It

Read each phrase and scoop it with a pencil. As you read each phrase, form an image in your mind. Read the sentence with prosody.

1. Shane's cheek was bleeding from the cuts.
2. Which boys had been at the skate park in the dark?
3. We parked the car in the lot close to the jazz club.
4. Come and eat the peach jam in the jar.
5. To get thin, people need to eat lean meat.
6. Does Josh's dog like to tug on its leash?
7. I used to live east of the park by the red barn.
8. Clark sang the sad tune about those ducks.
9. With a thud, she fell off her bike.
10. His only task was cleaning the cat's teeth.

Critical Understandings

Direction Words: Conceptual Understanding poster

We will continuing responding to prompts at the conceptual understanding level. Remember, you will need to recall relevant knowledge and demonstrate understanding of the concepts or ideas related to that information. You will respond to prompts that include verbs such as *categorize, infer, relate, interpret,* and *compare.* Conceptual understanding requires you to recall and understand. What will you need to do for these prompts? (recall and understand)

Direct students to pages 22 and 23 in their Student Books.

Let's preview some prompts about a short text we will read. Why do we read questions or prompts before we read the text? (to provide a purpose for reading) I'll read the prompt, and you repeat the key word in bold. Ready? Let's begin.

1. Use context to **interpret** the name given to the whales that can swim 30 miles per hour. (interpret)
2. **Categorize** toothed and baleen whales into the personalities of passive and aggressive. (categorize)
3. **Infer** which type of whale is the better hunter. (infer)
4. **Compare** toothed whales and baleen whales. (compare)
5. **Relate** the hunting style of toothed whales and the hunting style of bats. (relate)

Lesson 4 | Reading

Critical Understandings

Read the prompts at the bottom of the page to establish a purpose for reading. Then read the passage and respond to the prompts.

Two Types of Whales

Whales live their entire lives in the ocean, but they are not fish. Like other mammals, all whales are warm-blooded, breathe air, give birth to live babies, and even have a little bit of hair. However, not all whales are the same. There are two main kinds of whales: toothed whales and baleen whales.

As you might guess by their name, toothed whales have teeth, which they use to catch squid, fish, and other sea animals. Some have only two teeth and others have as many as 250 teeth. Toothed whales find their food by sending out high-pitched clicking sounds that bounce off things underwater. When the sounds return, whales can tell the size and position of an object. They can tell if something is a rock, a fish, or a squid. There are more than 60 kinds of toothed whales. Killer whales are members of this group and swim up to 30 miles per hour, which makes them the fastest whales on Earth.

Only 10 kinds of whales belong to the baleen whales group. Baleen whales have no teeth at all. Instead, they have baleen plates, which they use to strain small fish and plankton from the water. Baleen whales take water into their mouths, close their mouths, and then push the water through their baleen plate. This traps the food in their mouths. The blue whale is a member of this group, and it is the largest living animal on Earth.

1. Use context to **interpret** the name given to the whales that can swim 30 miles per hour.
   "Killer whales" means that they are deadly because they are predators and have the ability to move very fast.
2. **Categorize** toothed and baleen whales into the personalities of passive and aggressive.
   Toothed whales are aggressive, whereas baleen whales are passive creatures.

22 Unit 7

Lesson 4 | Reading

Critical Understandings (*cont.*)

3. **Infer** which type of whale is the better hunter.
   Toothed whales are better hunters because they use a strategy to find food.
4. **Compare** toothed whales and baleen whales.
   Toothed whales and baleen whales are both large mammals that live in the ocean and eat fish.
5. **Relate** the hunting style of toothed whales and the hunting style of bats.
   Both animals use sonar/echolocation to find their prey.

Unit 7 23

Keep these prompts in mind as we read the text. Have students follow along as you read the text.

Note: While the lessons are written for a teacher read aloud, it is important that your students read as much and as often as they can. Assign readings that meet the needs of your students, based on your observations or data. This is a good opportunity to stretch students, but if they become frustrated, return to the read-aloud method.

Two Types of Whales

Whales live their entire lives in the ocean, but they are not fish. Like other mammals, all whales are warm-blooded, breathe air, give birth to live babies, and even have a little bit of hair. However, not all whales are the same. There are two main kinds of whales: toothed whales and baleen whales.

As you might guess by their name, toothed whales have teeth, which they use to catch squid, fish, and other sea animals. Some have only two teeth and others have as many as 250 teeth. Toothed whales find their food by sending out high-pitched clicking sounds that bounce off things underwater. When the sounds return, whales can tell the size and position of an object. They can tell if something is a rock, a fish, or a squid. There are more than 60 kinds of toothed whales. Killer whales are members of this group and swim up to 30 miles per hour, which makes them the fastest whales on Earth.

Only 10 kinds of whales belong to the baleen whales group. Baleen whales have no teeth at all. Instead, they have baleen plates, which they use to strain small fish and plankton from the water. Baleen whales take water into their mouths, close their mouths, and then push the water through their baleen plate. This traps the food in their mouths. The blue whale is a member of this group, and it is the largest living animal on Earth.

Let's check our comprehension of this passage by responding to prompts that require conceptual understanding of the text. For each prompt, you will need to use text evidence plus what you already know to demonstrate understanding of the content.

Remember that each prompt is really a question. If you are unsure how to respond to a prompt, turn the prompt into a question. Then you will know exactly how to answer it. We will practice responding to prompts that require conceptual understanding and recall using evidence from text. Try asking yourself a question so you know exactly how to respond.

Model

Read the first prompt aloud.

1. Use context to **interpret** the name given to the whales that can swim 30 miles per hour. (interpret)

I can change this prompt into a question to determine how I need to respond. The question would be: Why do we call the whales that can swim 30 miles per hour "killer whales"? We know that we answer a *why* question with a reason. So I will give the reason they are called "killer whales" in my answer. I know the answer won't be explicitly stated in the text, but I can figure it out. Killer whales are toothed whales, so I know they hunt for food. That is part of the reason they are "killer." But what is unique about this whale that makes it more deadly than others? (They swim fast.) That must make it hard for fish and squid to escape. Use this information to write your response.

Guided Practice

Read the second prompt aloud.

2. **Categorize** toothed and baleen whales into the personalities of passive and aggressive. (categorize)

I can change this prompt into a question to determine how I need to respond. For this prompt, I will actually need to ask myself two questions: What type of whale is aggressive? What type of whale is passive? Before I can answer these questions, I need to make sure I understand the words *passive* and *aggressive*. Have volunteers define the words and correct as needed. Then guide students in a discussion about which whale would likely fit in the aggressive category and which whale would likely fit in the passive category. Have students use the information to write a response in their Student Books.

Independent Practice

Have partners respond to the remaining prompts. Review the answers as a class to ensure that students understand what each prompt is asking.

Note: Base the number of modeled and guided examples on student ability and progress. Challenge them with independent practice when appropriate.

Provide these alternative questions and sentence starters for those who need additional help.

3. What kind of whale is most likely the better hunter?

   ______________________________ are better hunters because ______________________________.

4. How are toothed whales similar to baleen whales?

   Toothed whales and baleen whales are both ______________________________.

5. What is the connection between the hunting style of bats and the hunting style of toothed whales?

   Both animals ______________________________.

Lesson 5

Lesson Opener

Before the lesson, choose one of the following activities to write on the board or post on the *LANGUAGE! Live* Class Wall online.

- *Write sentences using each of the following pronouns:* we, us, he, him.
- *Write a sentence about what whales eat. Write a second sentence using a subject pronoun and an object pronoun.*
- *Use the word* coarse *in a sentence.*

Vocabulary

Objectives

- Review and clarify the meaning of key passage vocabulary.

Recontextualize Passage Vocabulary

Direct students to page 2 in their Student Books.

Lesson 1 | Vocabulary

Key Passage Vocabulary: "Whale Song"

Rate your knowledge of the words. Define the words. Draw a picture to help you remember the definition.

Vocabulary	Knowledge Rating	Definition	Picture
basic	0 1 2 3	serving as the starting point; simple	
element	0 1 2 3	one part of a whole	
pause	0 1 2 3	to stop for a short time	
contain	0 1 2 3	to hold or include something	
surface	0 1 2 3	to rise to the top	
migrate	0 1 2 3	to move between habitats or places	
guideline	0 1 2 3	a rule or piece of advice about how to behave	
coordinate	0 1 2 3	to organize or arrange	

2 Unit 7

Review the Key Passage Vocabulary from "Whale Song."

- To stop for a short time is to what? (pause) When you get to a stop sign, do you *pause* or stop for a long time? (pause) At a stop sign, drivers stop for only a short time to see if it's safe to proceed, which means they *pause*.
- To rise to the top is to what? (surface) After a heavy rain, my son's missing toy *surfaced* from the sandbox. Where was the toy before it *surfaced*? (buried beneath the sand)
- A rule or piece of advice about how to behave is what? (a guideline) Every sport has *guidelines* on how to play fair. Penalties are given when players don't follow the what? (guidelines)
- To organize or arrange is what? (coordinate) I try to *coordinate* our grammar lessons with our writing lessons. I want to make sure they are organized to flow together. What do I do with the lessons? (coordinate them)
- Something serving as the starting point, or something simple, is what? (basic) What is the *basic* ingredient in bread? (flour)

- We say that one part of a whole is a what? (an element) What is one *element* of the Writer's Checklist? (Answers will vary.)
- To hold or include something is to what? (contain it) Turn to your partner and tell three things your bedroom *contains*. Use *contains* in your sentence.
- To move between habitats or places is to what? (migrate) Some animals *migrate* because of the weather. If you could *migrate* anywhere during the hot months or the cold months, where would you *migrate*? Remember that when you *migrate*, you have to return.

Reading

Objectives

- Write questions or prompts about the passage to deepen comprehension.
- Respond to questions or prompts orally.

Guided Reading of "Whale Song": Ask and Answer Questions

Proficient readers reread text slowly and carefully to gain understanding. They monitor their thinking while reading to be sure that each sentence and paragraph make sense. Good readers look for answers to Big Idea questions. In this unit, we are answering the questions Why do whales sing? and What does a whale song sound like?

Direction Words: Conceptual Understanding poster

Direct students to page 16 in their Student Books or refer to the Conceptual Understanding poster if you have it displayed.

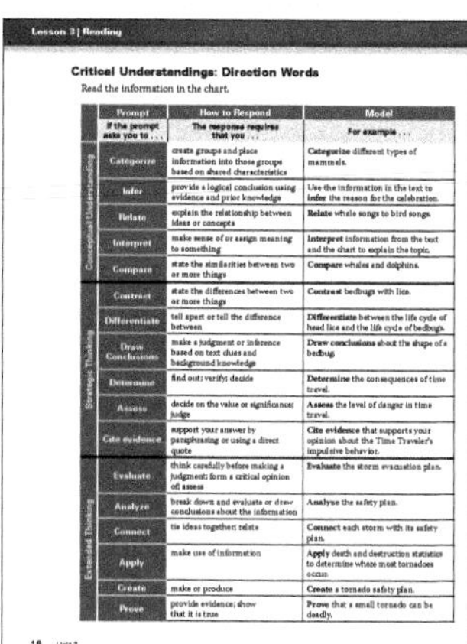
Lesson 3 | Reading

Critical Understandings: Direction Words

Read the information in the chart.

	Prompt	How to Respond	Model
	If the prompt asks you to . . .	**The response requires that you . . .**	**For example . . .**
Conceptual Understanding	Categorize	create groups and place information into those groups based on shared characteristics	**Categorize** different types of mammals.
	Infer	provide a logical conclusion using evidence and prior knowledge	Use the information in the text to **infer** the reason for the celebration.
	Relate	explain the relationship between ideas or concepts	**Relate** whale songs to bird songs.
	Interpret	make sense of or assign meaning to something	**Interpret** information from the text and the chart to explain the topic.
	Compare	state the similarities between two or more things	**Compare** whales and dolphins.
Strategic Thinking	Contrast	state the differences between two or more things	**Contrast** bedbugs with lice.
	Differentiate	tell apart or tell the difference between	**Differentiate** between the life cycle of head lice and the life cycle of bedbugs.
	Draw Conclusions	make a judgment or inference based on text clues and background knowledge	**Draw conclusions** about the shape of a bedbug.
	Determine	find out; verify; decide	**Determine** the consequences of time travel.
	Assess	decide on the value or significance; judge	**Assess** the level of danger in time travel.
	Cite evidence	support your answer by paraphrasing or using a direct quote	**Cite evidence** that supports your opinion about the Time Traveler's impulsive behavior.
Extended Thinking	Evaluate	think carefully before making a judgment; form a critical opinion of; assess	**Evaluate** the storm evacuation plan.
	Analyze	break down and evaluate or draw conclusions about the information	**Analyze** the safety plan.
	Connect	tie ideas together; relate	**Connect** each storm with its safety plan.
	Apply	make use of information	**Apply** death and destruction statistics to determine where most tornadoes occur.
	Create	make or produce	**Create** a tornado safety plan.
	Prove	provide evidence; show that it is true	**Prove** that a small tornado can be deadly.

16 Unit 7

We have been talking about how certain direction words require a specific response or answer. You will review this chart with a partner. Review the Chart Reading Procedure with students.

Chart Reading Procedure

- Group students with partners or in triads.
- Have students count off as 1s or 2s attempting to give all students a chance to be a student leader (1). If working with triads, the third student becomes a 2.
- Student leaders (1s) read the left column (Prompt) in addition to managing the time and turn-taking if working with a triad.
- The 2s explain the middle column of the chart (How to Respond). If working in triads, 2s take turns explaining the middle column.
- The 1s read the model in the right column (Model), and 2s restate the model as a question.
- All students should follow along with their pencil eraser while others are explaining the chart.
- Students must work from left to right, top to bottom in order to benefit from this activity.

Let's practice the first one before you work in your groups.

Have student groups chorally read their part of the chart along with you.

1s: If the prompt asks you to *Categorize . . .*

2s: The response requires that you create groups and place information into those groups based on shared characteristics.

1s: For example: Categorize different types of mammals.

2s: What category does each mammal belong to?

Have student groups or pairs complete the Conceptual Understanding portion of the chart (from Categorize to Compare) in this manner.

This time, when we read "Whale Song" we will ask questions about the text. Doing this will help us understand what is important. We will also answer the questions that we ask, which should clear up any confusion we had during our first read.

Let's reread "Whale Song" with an eye on asking and answering questions.

Remember what you do when you read. Your eyes need to track, or follow, the text while your pencil points to the words. While you're busy looking and pointing to text, your brain is busy looking for patterns and making meaning. While reading, be aware of questions that come to mind and questions that you can ask others.

Direct students to page 3 in their Student Books or have them tear out the extra copy of "Whale Song" from the back of the book.

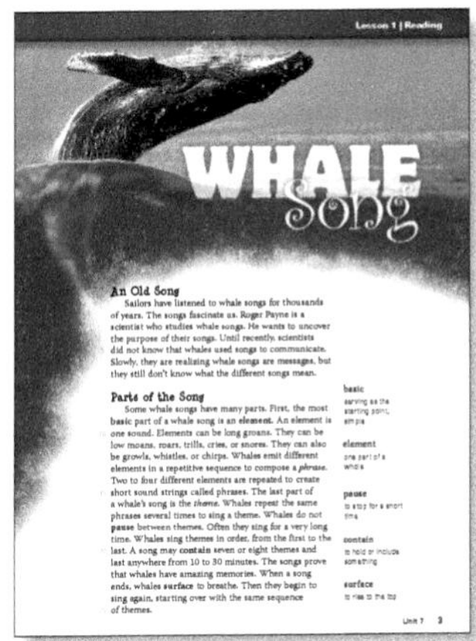

Note: To minimize flipping back and forth between the pages, a copy of each text has been included in the back of the Student Books. Encourage students to tear this out and use it when working on activities that require the use of the text.

Note: While the lessons are written for a teacher read aloud, it is important that your students read as much and as often as they can. Assign readings that meet the needs of your students, based on your observations or data. This is a good opportunity to stretch students, but if they become frustrated, return to the read-aloud method.

Eyes ready? Pencil ready? Let's begin.

Read the first section, An Old Song.

An Old Song

Sailors have listened to whale songs for thousands of years. The songs fascinate us. Roger Payne is a scientist who studies whale songs. He wants to uncover the purpose of their songs. Until recently, scientists did not know that whales used songs to communicate. Slowly, they are realizing whale songs are messages, but they still don't know what the different songs mean.

Direct students to page 24 in their Student Books. Think about the text. What questions do you still have or what should your peers have learned about whale songs in this section?

- Choose one question word or direction word you have learned to begin your question. Consider starting your question with *Who*.
- If you want to challenge yourself to write a prompt, try using *Infer*.
- Write the question or prompt in your Student Books under the heading An Old Song. Be prepared to answer your question or prompt orally. Remember, questions require a question mark. Prompts require a period.

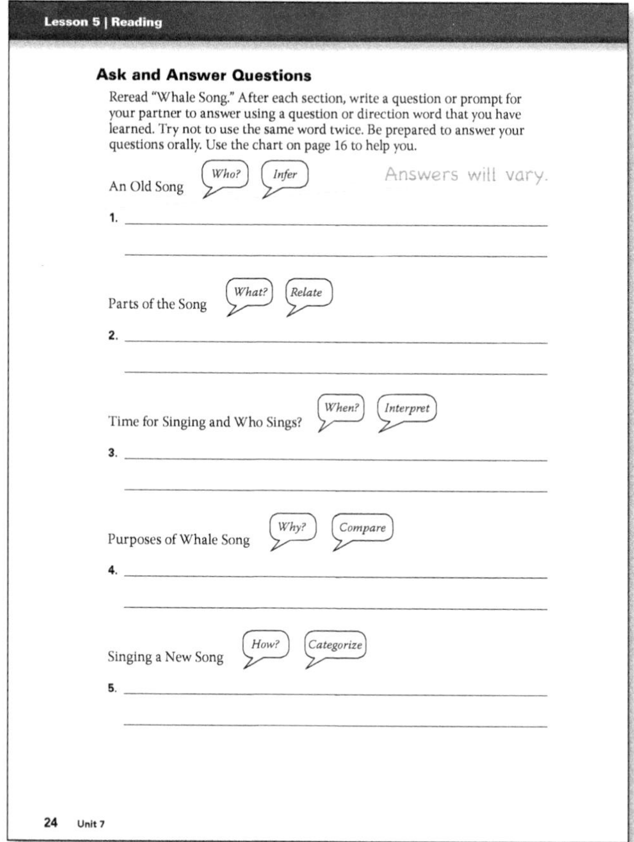
Lesson 5 | Reading

Ask and Answer Questions

Reread "Whale Song." After each section, write a question or prompt for your partner to answer using a question or direction word that you have learned. Try not to use the same word twice. Be prepared to answer your questions orally. Use the chart on page 16 to help you.

An Old Song *Who?* *Infer* Answers will vary.

1. ______

Parts of the Song *What?* *Relate*

2. ______

Time for Singing and Who Sings? *When?* *Interpret*

3. ______

Purposes of Whale Song *Why?* *Compare*

4. ______

Singing a New Song *How?* *Categorize*

5. ______

24 Unit 7

Direct students back to the passage.

Let's read the next section, Parts of the Song. Eyes ready? Pencil ready? Let's begin.

Read the next section.

Parts of the Song

Some whale songs have many parts. First, the most basic part of a whale song is an element. An element is one sound. Elements can be long groans. They can be low moans, roars, trills, cries, or snores. They can also be growls, whistles, or chirps. Whales emit different elements in a repetitive sequence to compose a *phrase*. Two to four different elements are repeated to create short sound strings called phrases. The last part of a whale's song is the *theme*. Whales repeat the same phrases several times to sing a theme. Whales do not pause between themes. Often they sing for a very long time. Whales sing themes in order, from the first to the last. A song may contain seven or eight themes and last anywhere from 10 to 30 minutes. The songs prove that whales have amazing memories. When a song ends, whales surface to breathe. Then they begin to sing again, starting over with the same sequence of themes.

Direct students to page 24 in their Student Books.

- Choose a different direction or question word. Try using *What* or *Relate*.
- Write the question or prompt on the page. Be prepared to provide answers orally.

Direct students back to the passage. Let's read the next two sections, Time for Singing and Who Sings? Eyes ready? Pencil ready? Let's begin.

Read the next two sections.

Time for Singing

Whales sing when they migrate. They leave the colder waters and swim to the warmer waters of the tropics. They sing as they migrate to warmer waters, and they sing again during their migration back to colder waters. During the early spring or late summer, some whales are silent, but others still sing.

Who Sings?

Not all whales sing. Only males sing the elaborate whale songs. A singing male often swims alone, staying underwater for a long time and remaining in a small area. He comes up to breathe every 8 to 15 minutes and then continues his underwater serenade.

Direct students to page 24 in their Student Books.

- Choose a different direction or question word. Try using *When* or *Interpret.*
- Write the question or prompt on the page. Be prepared to provide answers orally.

Direct students back to the passage. Let's read the next section, Purposes of Whale Song. Eyes ready? Pencil ready? Let's begin.

Read the next section.

Purposes of Whale Song

Scientists continue to study whale songs and try to understand the different reasons they sing. It appears that whales sing for a variety of reasons. Scientists believe the songs are not just for entertainment. The songs communicate guidelines for a specific group of whales. The role of whale song is similar to that of bird song. It may be a signal for other whales to work together and stop competing. Scientists believe the songs are also used to attract females. They have observed females slapping the water with their fins in response to a male's song. Without the songs, what would happen? Groups of whales could become separated during migration. Feeding and behavior would not be coordinated.

Direct students to page 24 in their Student Books.

- Choose a different direction or question word. Try using *Why* or *Compare.*
- Write the question or prompt on the page. Be prepared to provide answers orally.

Direct students back to the passage. Let's read the next section, Singing a New Song. Eyes ready? Pencil ready? Let's begin.

Read the last section.

Singing a New Song

Another interesting fact is that whale songs change. Each year's song is a little different. The whales make changes during the singing season. They all change their song at the same time. The changes may be minor, affecting only one or two elements while the basic song pattern remains the same. For example, moans may be altered from a long moan to a short moan, but they are still moans.

Scientists don't know why whales change their songs. They know whales living in different parts of the ocean sing different songs. They have even heard whales begin to sing the same songs as whales living on the other side of the ocean. The new song may be started by a dominant whale, or it may simply interest other whales. Whatever the reason, all of the male whales in the area begin to sing this new song.

Whale songs fascinate many people. Through intensive study, scientists are learning how whales communicate. One day, people and whales may communicate. When that happens, it will probably be with song.

Direct students to page 24 in their Student Books.

- Choose a different direction or question word. Try using *How* or *Categorize*.
- Write the question or prompt on the page. Be prepared to provide answers orally.

Share Questions or Prompts

Have partners read their questions or prompts to each other and answer them orally, correcting each other if needed. Each pair shares with another pair, then those four share with four others if time permits. Have volunteers share their questions or prompts and responses with the class.

Writing

Objectives

- Write responses to prompts to categorize, infer, compare, and interpret information from the passage.
- Support written answers with evidence from text.

Answer It: Direction Words

Direct students to pages 25 and 26 in their Student Books. Now, we will respond to prompts about "Whale Song" for more practice. Some of the prompts may be similar to the prompts you already responded to.

- Read each prompt. Identify and underline the direction word.
- Use the Critical Understandings chart on page 16 or the Conceptual Understanding poster to review the type of information the prompts are asking for.
- Use text headings or other text features to locate the information you need to write a response.
- Reread the section to retrieve exact information to use as text evidence.

Direction Words: Conceptual Understanding poster

Answer It: Direction Words

Underline the direction word(s) in each prompt. Then respond to each prompt using complete sentences. Provide line numbers for the text evidence.

1. Complete the chart to categorize and describe the parts of a whale song.

Categories	Element	Phrase	Theme
Key detail	one sound	2–4 elements	several repeated phrases
Key detail	groan	short string of sound	no pauses in between
Key detail	roar		sung in order from first to last

2. Infer why male whales sing.
Answers will vary. Male whales sing during migration to communicate with their group and attract females.
Text Evidence: Lines 40–45

3. Relate whale songs to migration.
Whale song is important during migration to communicate guidelines about working together as a group.
Text Evidence: Lines 41–42

4. Compare the purpose of whale song and bird song.
Whales and birds both sing to communicate and attract females.
Text Evidence: Lines 43–44

5. Infer what scientists are using as evidence of a whale's good memory.
Scientists feel that whales have a good memory because they sing long songs in the same order over and over.
Text Evidence: Lines 19–22

Look closely at the questions. As we move into the higher level questions that require text evidence as well as information from outside sources, it is imperative to find evidence in the text. This way, you aren't answering the questions with just your opinion. However, since the questions are becoming more complex, you will no longer be expected to copy the evidence from the text. Instead, you can simply provide the line numbers from the passage.

Model

Read the first prompt aloud.

1. Complete the chart to categorize and describe the parts of a whale song.

Let's begin by locating the direction words in the prompt. (categorize and describe) If we change this prompt, we have to ask two questions: What are the parts of a whale song? and What is included in each part?

Direct students to the passage "Whale Song." Next, look at the chart and predict how many parts of a whale song there will be. (three, one for each category)

Go into the text and look for evidence of three parts of a whale song. Provide time to skim text. What are the three parts of a whale song? (element, phrase, theme)

Complete category headings with students.

Next, let's look for details or more information about each part of a whale song.

- What are some details about the elements of a whale song? (one sound, groan, roar) Have students tell you the line numbers in the text. Have students add this information to their charts.
- What are some details about a phrase? (2–4 elements, short string of sound) Have students tell you the line numbers in the text. Have students add this information to their charts.
- What are some details about a theme? (several repeated phrases, no pauses in between, sung in order from first to last) Complete the chart with students. Have students tell you the line numbers in the text.
- What did the prompt ask you to do? (Categorize and describe.) Did you create groups and state details and information about those groups? (yes)

Guided Practice

Read the next prompt aloud.

2. Infer why male whales sing.

- What is the direction word in this prompt? (infer)
- How do we respond to a prompt that begins with *infer*? (Use prior knowledge and evidence from text to draw a logical conclusion). Do we need to use the word *infer* in our answer? (no)
- If we changed this prompt to a question, what would it be? (Why do male whales sing?) What do we need to do next? (Find evidence from text and combine it with what we know.)

Direct students to the passage. Have students tell you the line numbers for the evidence they find in the text. Then write this sentence starter on the board for students to begin their response:

Male whales sing ______________________________.
(logical conclusion)

Have students write their responses in their Student Books.

Independent Practice

Have students use text evidence to answer the remaining questions independently. Create a small group for students who need more assistance, using prompt 3 as additional guided practice. Remind students to make corrections if necessary.

Note: Base the number of modeled and guided examples on student ability and progress. Challenge students with independent practice when appropriate.

Provide these alternative questions and sentence starters for those who need additional help.

3. How are whale songs related to migration?

   Whale song is important during migration ______________________.

4. How is the purpose for whale songs similar to the purpose for bird songs?

   Whales and birds both ______________________.

5. How do scientists know that whales have a good memory?

   Scientists feel that whales have a good memory because ______________________.

6. Why do whales fascinate scientists?

   Whales fascinate scientists because ______________________.

7. What does Payne's quote mean?

Lesson 5 | Writing

Answer It: Direction Words (*cont.*)

6. Use "Whale Song" along with Payne's quotes on pages 4 and 6 to interpret why whales fascinate scientists.

   Answers will vary. Whales fascinate scientists because their songs are a mysterious form of communication.

   Text Evidence: Lines 37–39; 59–60

7. Use context to interpret the meaning of one of Payne's quotes found in the margins on page 4 or page 6. Finish this sentence: Payne felt ________ because ________

   Answers will vary. Payne felt happy because he could hear the humpback whales singing in the sea.
   Payne felt overwhelmed because he could hear echoes of whale song from the deep sea underneath his boat.

   Text Evidence: quotations on pages 4 and 6

26 Unit 7

Reading

Objectives

- Interpret information presented orally.
- Identify structural elements of a poem, including rhythm and rhyme.

Secondary Text: "Dolphin Talk"

Direct students to page 27 in their Student Books.

Another ocean mammal that is well known for its communication skills is the dolphin. Let's read a poem to learn more about dolphins. Listen as I read the poem about how dolphins "talk" to each other. Listen for facts about the ways dolphins communicate. In addition, pay close attention to how the poet's word choice creates a sense of rhythm. Like our work in Masterpiece Sentences, these words seek to create vivid images in the reader's mind.

Read "Dolphin Talk."

Note: While the lessons are written for a teacher read aloud, it is important that your students read as much and as often as they can. Assign readings that meet the needs of your students, based on your observations or data. This is a good opportunity to stretch students, but if they become frustrated, return to the read-aloud method.

Dolphin Talk

Through the glass bottom of my tourist boat
I see the dolphin pod afloat.
I hear whistles as high as the Empire State
And know they are trying to communicate.
Each dolphin has a unique sound
That it wears like a name tag, while swimming around.

Now I hear the sound of a quickly spinning wheel.
It must be a dolphin trying to find its next meal.
In murky water the dolphin's as blind as a bat.
It uses clicks to "see" where it is at.
Using sonar, the sounds bounce off what's near.
Distance, depth, and size are what the dolphin can hear.

Moans and squeaks echo in the abyss.
Dolphins alert each other of danger in their midst.
Atop their heads, the blowholes emit sound
As if beautifully played instruments abound.
In the boat I can hear many sounds from the sea.
The music of the dolphin is like a song written for me.

One way poets create a sense of rhythm is through the use of rhyme. As I read the poem one more time, listen for the rhyme patterns.

Read the poem again. Ask for examples of rhyming words if time permits.

Lesson 6

Lesson Opener

Before the lesson, choose one of the following activities to write on the board or post on the *LANGUAGE! Live* Class Wall online.

- *Turn to your Key Passage Vocabulary chart. Complete your drawings and add information to definitions as needed.*
- *Write three sentences with a subject pronoun and an object pronoun. For example: I see you working.*
- *Use the word* mean *in a sentence about math.*

Writing

Objectives

- Know spelling-sound correspondences for words with the digraph /ng/ with /ă/ and /ŭ/.
- Know spelling-sound correspondences for words with the *oy* vowel team.

Spelling Words

Use this spelling activity to practice or assess the unit's spelling patterns students have learned online.

Direct student to Part A on page 28 in their Student Books. Read the instructions and remind students of the procedure for spelling. Use the spelling reminders to help struggling students.

1. car; My brother got a new car.
2. thick; I put on some thick socks.
3. fangs; My dog showed its fangs.
4. bars; The gorilla rattled the bars of its cage.
5. cling; The baby likes to cling to its mother.
6. toys; Please put your toys away.
7. lungs; I filled my lungs with air.
8. sharp; Be careful, that knife is sharp.
9. soy; I like to drink soy milk.
10. math; I made an A on my math test.

Lesson 6 | Writing

Spelling

Part A

Write the words your teacher dictates.

1. car
2. thick
3. fangs
4. bars
5. cling
6. toys
7. lungs
8. sharp
9. soy
10. math

Part B

Write the sentence your teacher dictates. Check for sentence signals—correct capitalization and end punctuation.

The boy tossed his toy darts into my thin arm.

28 Unit 7

Direct student to Part B on page 28 in their Student Books. Read the instructions and remind students of the procedure for sentence dictation.

The boy tossed his toy darts into my thin arm.

Spelling Words Procedure

- Teacher reads the word.
- Students repeat the word.
- Teacher reads the sentence.
- Students write the word.
- Teacher reads the word a second time as students check their work.

Sentence Dictation Procedure

- Teacher reads the sentence.
- Students repeat the sentence.
- Students write the sentence.
- Teacher reads the sentence a second time as students check their work.

Spelling Reminders

Words with digraph /ng/ with /ă/ and /ŭ/
The digraph *ng* makes the sound /ng/, as in *sing*. Listen carefully to the difference in the words *sang* with the letters *ng* and *sag* with just the letter *g*.

Words with *oy* vowel team
When /oi/ is the last sound in a word or syllable, we spell it *oy*. Remember, like the vowel team *ee* and *ea*, the two letters *oy* spell just one sound. It's a slider vowel.

Vocabulary

Objectives

- Use context to determine the meaning of words in text.
- Demonstrate an understanding of compound words.
- Brainstorm and write compound words.

Define It

Direct students to page 29 in their Student Books.

To define words, we need to understand the words' categories and attributes.

Categories are broad groups. Attributes are things like size, shape, color, texture, and function.

You may complete the activity together or independently, depending on students' abilities. Then review the answers as a group.

Lesson 6 | Vocabulary

Define It

Determine the category and attributes of each word. Then write the definition.

Word		Category		Attributes
theme	=	element of a whale song	+	repetition of phrases; sung in order; several per song

Definition: A theme is one of several parts of a whale song that contains repeated phrases and occurs in sequential order.

Word		Category		Attributes
serenade	=	song	+	performed by an individual or group; for someone specific

Definition: A serenade is a song performed by an individual or group for someone specific.

Word		Category		Attributes
message	=	communication	+	given to another individual or group; with meaning

Definition: A message is a meaningful form of communication given to another individual or group.

Word		Category		Attributes

Definition:

Unit 7 29

Model

Direct students to the second paragraph of "Whale Song." Have them find the word *theme.* We may not know what *theme* means in this case, but we can look at the context around the word to determine its category and attributes. Because it says that the last part of a song is the theme, I know that a theme is a part of a whale song. That is its category. Write *element of a whale song* under Category on the chart.

It also says that "whales repeat the same phrases several times" to create a theme, that they "sing themes in order," and that there are seven or eight themes in a song. So, the attributes of a theme are a repetition of phrases; sung in order; and seven or eight per song. Write these phrases under Attributes. I didn't have to know anything about the word *theme* to figure out what it means. I just had to read closely. Now that I have my category and attributes, I can write my definition. Write the definition on the board and read it aloud:

> *A theme is one of several parts of a whale song that contains repeated phrases and occurs in sequential order.*

Have students write the definition in their Student Books.

Guided and Independent Practice

Dictionaries

Repeat the process for the second word, allowing students to generate the category, attributes, and definition. Then have partners complete the activity. Explain that they may choose and define any unknown word from the passage for the last item. Have partners use a dictionary to verify their definitions and make corrections as needed.

Note: Base the number of modeled and guided examples on student ability and progress. Challenge them with independent practice when appropriate.

Compound Words

Make a list of items that can be put together to create compound words. Use them in a demonstration if possible.

For example:
back pack
chalk board
lip stick
finger nail
note book

A *compound word* is a word made of two or more smaller words. Often the word can be understood from the two smaller words. A house for a dog is a doghouse. A backpack is a pack that goes on your back.

Direct students to page 1 in their Student Books and have them scan the page for a compound word. *Checklist* is a compound word. It is a list that you check.

Direct students to page 2 and have them scan the vocabulary list for a compound word. *Guideline* is a compound word. It is a line that guides your actions or behavior.

Model

Let's look at some more compound words. Write *baseball* on the board. Baseball is a game in which a ball and bases are used. Basketball is what? (a game with a ball and baskets) *Eyeball* is a compound word. Is an eyeball a game? (no) A ballpark is what? (a park where ball is played) Have students call out other compound words with the word *ball*. (football, ballgame, ballpoint, ballroom, cannonball, meatball, snowball, kickball)

Write *headlight* on the board. Is a headlight a head made of light? (no) But, it is a light that you wear on your head. With a partner, think of other compound words with *head*. (headphones, headache, headboard, headrest, headquarters, headset, headstone headdress)

Have volunteers share compound words.

Direct students to page 30 in their Student Books.

Guided Practice

Read the word *bird*. Explain that examples of compound words with *bird* are *bluebird* and *birdcage*, noting that *bird* can come at the beginning or end of the compound. Have students generate other examples. Model writing answers as students give responses. Have students write the compound words using *bird* in their Student Books.

Independent Practice

Have partners generate compound words with the words *side* and *berry*. Have students write answers in their Student Books. Review the answers as a class.

Note: Base the number of modeled and guided examples on student ability and progress. Challenge them with independent practice when appropriate.

Lesson 6 | Vocabulary

Compound Words

A **compound word** is a word made of two or more smaller words. Often the word can be understood from the two smaller words. Write compound words containing each of the smaller words. Answers will vary.

bird

bluebird	hummingbird	redbird
birdcage	blackbird	snowbird
mockingbird	songbird	birdbath
birdseed	birdbrain	birdman
birdcall	firebird	cowbird
lovebird	jailbird	seabird

side

backside	bedside	blindside
broadside	curbside	dockside
downside	graveside	hillside
inside	lakeside	mountainside
outside	ringside	roadside
sidearm	sidebar	sidecar
sidelight	sideline	sideshow
sidewalk	sideways	sidewinder
underside	upside	

berry

blueberry	strawberry	raspberry
blackberry	honeyberry	silverberry

30 Unit 7

Creating Compound Words

Create word cards if necessary.

Direct students to page 31 in their Student Books. Read the instructions and words with students. Model the activity with *skate* and *board*. Model writing the compound word, *skateboard*, on the first line.

Choose an activity from the three below.

Activity 1
Students match small words to create compound words, and write the words in their Student Books.

Activity 2
Using word cards, partners lay the cards out and move them to create compound words. Have students write the compound words in their Student Books.

Activity 3
Using word cards, groups play a matching game similar to Memory. Turn the word cards facedown. Then have students take turns flipping two word cards at a time. If they can match the words to make a compound word, they keep the cards. If they cannot, they replace them, facedown. Have students write the compound words in their Student Books.

Lesson 6 | Vocabulary

Creating Compound Words

Match small words to create compound words. Write the compound words on the lines below. Use each word one time.

air	plane	life	take	side	bag
star	ball	top	gum	ring	sand
ear	ball	up	time	fish	hill
pack	car	base	race	sun	in
shine	sick	back	sea	board	pick
skate	tea	up	cup	set	out
sun	some	lap	one	back	spin

Answers will vary.

skateboard	earring	teacup
gumball	airplane	seasick
racecar	sunset	sunshine
baseball	starfish	pickup
laptop	uphill	sandbag
inside	backpack	takeout
lifetime	backspin	someone

Unit 7 31

Writing

Objective

- Demonstrate an understanding of the conventions of English by editing their writing for punctuation, capitalization, spelling, and word order.

Masterpiece Sentences: Stage 6

Masterpiece Sentences poster

Masterpiece Sentences is a strategy that we use to expand basic sentences and to focus on different elements of sentence structure. Today, we will work with the final stage in the process. Stage 6 gives us the chance to apply final edits, or polish, to our sentences. In this stage, we check for spelling, punctuation, and any other writing conventions that apply to a sentence. Let's review the first five stages.

Direct students to page 32 in their Student Books. Read the information for the first five stages.

You will notice the example for Stage 6 is missing. Let's work on it together. What are some things we need to add? (capitalization, end punctuation, commas within the sentence) Make the edits you think are necessary, and then compare yours with mine. Provide writing time. Then write the following sentence on the board:

During migration, all of the male whales, with the uncanny instinct to communicate, repeatedly sang the same song in the vast icy darkness of the ocean.

As you can see, Stage 6 is all about "polishing" our sentence.

Masterpiece Sentences: Stage 6

Use the provided sentence elements to write a polished sentence in the Stage 6 Examples box.

Stage	Process	Questions to Answer	Examples
Stage 1: Prepare Your Canvas	Choose (identify) a noun for the subject. Choose (identify) a past tense verb for the predicate.	Subject: Who or what did it? Predicate: What did he/she/it/they do? What did he/she/it/they do it to?	Whales sang songs
Stage 2: Paint Your Predicate	Tell more about what happened.	When? Where? How?	when they migrated beneath the ocean's surface constantly
Stage 3: Move the Predicate Painters	Move the Predicate Painters to create a different sentence structure.		When they migrated, whales constantly sang songs beneath the ocean's surface.
Stage 4: Paint Your Subject	Tell more about the subject.	Which one? What kind? How many?	with a message male all
Stage 5: Paint Your Words	Select words or phrases in the sentence and replace them with more descriptive words or phrases.		~~When they migrated~~—During migration; ~~constantly~~—repeatedly; ~~songs~~—the same song; ~~beneath the ocean's surface~~—in the vast icy darkness of the ocean; ~~with a message~~—with the uncanny instinct to communicate
Stage 6: Finishing Touches	Move sentence parts, check spelling, and check punctuation.		During migration, all of the male whales with the uncanny instinct to communicate repeatedly sang the same song in the vast icy darkness of the ocean.

Lesson 6 | Writing

32 Unit 7

Reading

Objectives

- Discuss characteristics of poetry.
- Describe how words and phrases supply rhythm and meaning in a poem.
- Read to identify rhyme and figurative language in a poem.
- Reread a poem for key information.

Poetry and Figurative Language

Direct students to pages 33 and 34 in their Student Books.

We read the poem "Dolphin Talk" in the last lesson. Now we'll have the chance to take an even closer look at its form and content. What is poetry? Remind students of the definition of *poet* they learned in Unit 3. There isn't a simple definition for the word *poetry*, but many poems have distinctive signs or elements. Let's take a look at six elements, or characteristics, of poetry.

Six Elements of Poetry

Review the elements of poetry in the chart below. Then listen to "Dolphin Talk." List examples of similes and rhyming words on the lines.

Thought	Thought is the element that contains the poem's message. One component of thought is the theme, which is often stated as a universal truth—unlimited by time and space.
Imagery	Imagery refers to the poem's creation of mental pictures, or images, for the reader. Metaphor, simile, and personification are examples of techniques that poets use to create imagery.
Mood	Poems evoke emotions and set an atmosphere or a tone for the reader. This element is called mood.
Melody	Melody is the element created by a poet's use of sound. Alliteration, rhyme, assonance, consonance, and onomatopoeia are examples of devices used to create melody in poetry.
Meter	Patterns of stressed and unstressed syllables in a poem create meter or poetic rhythm.
Form	Form is the element that defines the poem's actual structure. Examples of poetic forms include quatrain, sonnet, blank verse, limerick, ballad, and free (open) verse.

Examples of Imagery—Similes:

1. as high as the Empire State—dolphin whistles
2. like a name tag—sound
3. as blind as a bat—dolphin
4. as if beautifully played instruments abound—blowhole sound
5. like a song written for me—music of the dolphin

Thought: A poem has a message, or theme. What would you say is the overall message of "Dolphin Talk"? (possible answer: that dolphins communicate)

Imagery: Imagery is another element of poetry. The words in a poem are typically chosen to create a vivid picture in the reader's mind, one that will help communicate the theme. We have been studying figurative language—specifically, similes—in this unit. Remember, a simile compares two things that do not seem similar at first glance. For example, the desert and a bone can be compared to create an image of extreme dryness. Similes often use exaggeration, and they often use the words *like* or *as*.

Mood: A poet strives to choose words that will create a certain mood or feeling. Some poems are very dark and melancholy, while others are light and playful. What kind of mood do you think the poet tried to create in "Dolphin Talk"? (playful, upbeat)

Melody: Many song lyrics would qualify as poetry. How does spoken language have a melody? The arrangement of words, unusual sentence or phrase structure, and rhyme contribute to the sense of rhythm or melody. This poem uses rhyme patterns to create a sense of melody. When we reread the poem, I will ask you to listen for examples of rhyme.

Meter: In more sophisticated poems, such as sonnets, the poet consciously chooses words to build certain numbers of syllables and units of stress. Meter, or a set pattern of stressed and unstressed syllables, is another way poets create rhythm.

Form: Form refers to the physical structure of the poem. Some poems have set forms while others do not. A poem with a set form would have a certain number of lines, a certain meter, and a certain rhyme scheme. A poem without a set form might have varying line lengths and no rhyme at all.

In this lesson, we will focus on two of these six elements: imagery and melody. I will reread the poem, stopping after each pair of lines. Your job is to listen for two things: similes and rhyming words.

Direct students to page 27 in their Student Books or have them tear out the extra copy of "Dolphin Talk" from the back of the book.

Lesson 6 | Reading

Dolphin Talk

Through the glass bottom of my tourist boat
I see the dolphin pod afloat.
I hear whistles as high as the Empire State
And know they are trying to communicate.
Each dolphin has a unique sound
That it wears like a name tag, while swimming around.

Now I hear the sound of a quickly spinning wheel.
It must be a dolphin trying to find its next meal.
In murky water the dolphin's as blind as a bat.
It uses clicks to "see" where it is at.
Using sonar, the sounds bounce off what's near.
Distance, depth, and size are what the dolphin can hear.

Moans and squeaks echo in the abyss.
Dolphins alert each other of danger in their midst.
Atop their heads, the blowholes emit sound
As if beautifully played instruments abound.
In the boat I can hear many sounds from the sea.
The music of the dolphin is like a song written for me.

Unit 7 27

> **Note:** To minimize flipping back and forth between the pages, a copy of each text has been included in the back of the Student Books. Encourage students to tear this out and use it when working on activities that require the use of the text.

Begin reading:

> Through the glass bottom of my tourist boat
> I see the dolphin pod afloat.

Do you hear a rhyming pattern? (yes, boat and afloat) Circle the words in your text. I don't see any comparisons, or similes, in these lines. Turn to page 34 and write this pair of rhyming words underneath the heading Examples of Melody—Rhyme.

Direct students to the poem. Continue reading:

> I hear whistles as high as the Empire State
> And know they are trying to communicate.

Do you hear a rhyming pattern? (yes, State and communicate) Circle those words. Is anything being compared in these two lines? (The poet compared the high pitch of the dolphins' whistles to the height of a very tall building, the Empire State Building.) Underline "as high as the Empire State." Turn to page 34 and write the second pair of rhyming words under Examples of Melody, then record the simile under Imagery—Similes on page 33. I want you to fill in the appropriate blanks on these pages after we read each pair of lines. As you can see, we will find a total of five similes and nine rhyming pairs.

Direct students back to the poem. Continue reading:

> Each dolphin has a unique sound
> That it wears like a name tag, while swimming around.

Circle the rhyming pattern. What did you mark? (sound, around) Is anything being compared in these two lines? (sound and name tag) Because every dolphin has a unique sound, that sound can be used to identify that dolphin and distinguish it from others. That's what a name tag does for a person: It identifies him or her. Underline "like a name tag." Write the simile and rhyming word pair in the appropriate places on pages 33 and 34.

Direct students back to the poem. Continue reading:

> Now I hear the sound of a quickly spinning wheel.
> It must be a dolphin trying to find its next meal.

What words did you circle to identify the rhyming pattern? (wheel, meal) Are you beginning to predict where the rhyme will occur? (yes, at the end of each line) Although there isn't a simile, the poet creates a vivid image by using the sound of a spinning wheel to describe the sound a dolphin makes while hunting. Have students write the rhyming words on page 34.

Direct students back to the poem and continue reading:

> In murky water the dolphin's as blind as a bat.
> It uses clicks to "see" where it is at.

Circle the rhyming words and underline the simile. Pause. If you circled *bat* and *at*, you're right. The dolphins cannot see in the murky water, so their vision is compared to that of a bat. If you underlined "as blind as a bat," you correctly identified the simile. Have students write the simile and rhyming pair in the appropriate places on pages 33 and 34.

Direct students back to the poem and continue reading:

> Using sonar, the sounds bounce off what's near.
> Distance, depth, and size are what the dolphin can hear.

What words did you circle? (near, hear) Did you find a simile? (no) Have students write the rhyming word pair on page 34.

Direct students back to the poem and continue reading:

> Moans and squeaks echo in the abyss.
> Dolphins alert each other of danger in their midst.

Sometimes a rhyme isn't exact, but it still helps to create rhythm. *Abyss* and *midst* are an example of "near rhyme." *Abyss* may be a word that you don't know. An abyss is a space so deep that it cannot be measured, like the extreme depths of the ocean. It makes me think of a very dark, isolated space. The poet's use of the word *abyss* is an example of creating imagery through precise word choice. Have students write the rhyming word pair on page 34.

Direct students back to the poem and continue reading:

> Atop their heads, the blowholes emit sound
> As if beautifully played instruments abound.

Circle the rhyming words and underline the simile. What did you circle? (sound, abound) What did you underline? (as if beautifully played instruments abound) What is being compared to the beautifully played instruments? (the sounds from the blowhole) Have students write the simile and rhyming word pair in the appropriate places on pages 33 and 34.

Direct students back to the poem and continue reading:

> In the boat I can hear many sounds from the sea.
> The music of the dolphin is like a song written for me.

Circle the rhyming words and look for our final simile. What words did you circle? (sea, me) What is the simile? (like a song written for me) What is "like a song written for me"? (the music of the dolphin)

Have students write down the simile and rhyming word pair in the appropriate places on pages 33 and 34.

Let's take another look at the similes you wrote down. We're going to add the object that is being compared in each simile.

- What is "as high as the Empire State"? (the whistle of the dolphin) Let's write *dolphin whistles* on the first line
- What is "like a name tag"? (the sound each dolphin makes) Okay, let's write *sound* on the second line.
- What is "as blind as a bat"? (a dolphin) Write it down.
- What is "as if beautifully played instruments abound"? (sound from the blowhole) Have students write it on the fourth line.
- What is "like a song written for me"? (the music of the dolphin) Have students write it on the fifth line.

Guided Reading: "Dolphin Talk"

"Dolphin Talk" gave us the opportunity to take a closer look at the elements of a poem. It also provided us with some very useful information about dolphins and how they communicate. There are some striking similarities between dolphins and whales when it comes to communication. When we read "Dolphin Talk" again, our focus will be on information that helps us compare dolphins and whales. Listen for information about dolphins as I read the poem one more time.

Direct students to the poem, "Dolphin Talk," and have them follow along as you read the poem aloud.

> **Note:** While the lessons are written for a teacher read aloud, it is important that your students read as much and as often as they can. Assign readings that meet the needs of your students, based on your observations or data. This is a good opportunity to stretch students, but if they become frustrated, return to the read-aloud method.

Dolphin Talk

Through the glass bottom of my tourist boat
I see the dolphin pod afloat.
I hear whistles as high as the Empire State
And know they are trying to communicate.
Each dolphin has a unique sound
That it wears like a name tag, while swimming around.

Now I hear the sound of a quickly spinning wheel.
It must be a dolphin trying to find its next meal.
In murky water the dolphin's as blind as a bat.
It uses clicks to "see" where it is at.
Using sonar, the sounds bounce off what's near.
Distance, depth, and size are what the dolphin can hear.

Moans and squeaks echo in the abyss.
Dolphins alert each other of danger in their midst.
Atop their heads, the blowholes emit sound
As if beautifully played instruments abound.
In the boat I can hear many sounds from the sea.
The music of the dolphin is like a song written for me.

Writing

Objective

- Take notes of key information in a poem.

Two-Column Notes

Direct students to page 35 in their Student Books.

What are some things you learned about dolphins from the poem? How do they communicate? Have students write information about dolphins in the Two-Column Notes. Guide students in the note-taking process if necessary.

Model

Complete the first note as a model.

Guided Practice

Guide students in finding the information for the second note.

Independent Practice

Have students complete the process independently.

In the next lesson, we will revisit "Whale Song" to help us examine specific qualities of whale communication and how this compares to the communication of dolphins.

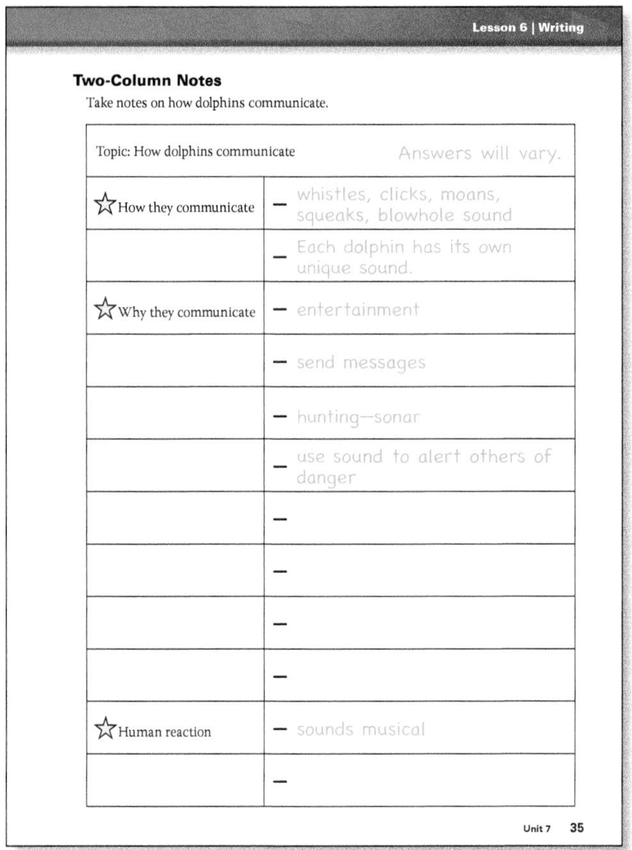

Lesson 6 | Writing

Two-Column Notes

Take notes on how dolphins communicate.

Topic: How dolphins communicate	Answers will vary.
☆How they communicate	– whistles, clicks, moans, squeaks, blowhole sound
	– Each dolphin has its own unique sound.
☆Why they communicate	– entertainment
	– send messages
	– hunting—sonar
	– use sound to alert others of danger
	–
	–
	–
	–
☆Human reaction	– sounds musical
	–

Unit 7 35

Note: Base the number of modeled and guided examples on student ability and progress. Challenge them with independent practice when appropriate.

Unit 7

Lesson 7

Lesson Opener

Before the lesson, choose one of the following activities to write on the board or post on the *LANGUAGE! Live* Class Wall online.

- *Create a list of common attributes of whales and dolphins.*
- *Write three elaborations that help explain this detail: Whales are interesting animals.*
- *Write a Masterpiece Sentence about whales and dolphins.*

Reading

Objectives

- Read with purpose and understanding.
- Answer questions to demonstrate comprehension of text.
- Determine the main ideas of the text.
- Explain explicit details from text.

Guided Highlighting of "Whale Song"

We have been working diligently to become great readers. We preview the text. We reread text slowly and carefully to gain understanding. We practice metacognition, or thinking about our thinking. And we look for answers to the Big Idea questions: Why do whales sing? and What does a whale song sound like?

There are a lot of reasons to become a better reader. Skilled readers can identify an author's purpose, or reason for writing the text. Proficient readers can compare two ideas or concepts and tell how they are alike. Proficient readers can also interpret figurative language, or words that do not mean exactly what they say.

Let's do what skilled readers do and reread "Whale Song."

Green, yellow, and pink highlighters or colored pencils

Have students get out a colored pencil or highlighter.

Direct students to page 36 in their Student Books. We will review the text features of nonfiction, or expository, text. Please use your writing utensil to mark your answer according to my instructions.

Draw a rectangle around the title, "Whale Song."

Listen and mark each bold vocabulary word as I read it aloud. I'm going to pause after every word to give you time to process whether you know the word and its meaning. We will review your ratings from Lesson 1 after we finish.

- basic—*Basic* means "to serve as a starting point or to be simple." Say *basic*. (basic) *Basic* song patterns repeat during whale songs.
- elements—*Elements* are parts of a whole. Say *elements*. (elements) Each *element* of a whale song sounds different.
- pause—*Pause* means "to stop for a short time." Say *pause*. (pause) Whales do not *pause* between themes.
- contain—*Contain* means "to hold or include something." Say *contain*. (contain) A phrase may *contain* two to four elements.
- surface—*Surface* means "to rise to the top." Say *surface*. (surface) Whales *surface* to breathe.
- migrate—*Migrate* means "to move between habitats or places." Say *migrate*. (migrate) The humpback whale will *migrate* to warmer water.
- guideline—A *guideline* is a rule or piece of advice about how to behave. Say *guideline*. (guideline) The *guideline* is communicated through song.
- coordinated—*Coordinated* means "organized or arranged." Say *coordinated*. (coordinated) The dominant male will *coordinate* feeding and behavior through song.

Lesson 7 | Reading

Guided Highlighting

Read the text and complete the tasks.

Whale Song

An Old Song

Sailors have listened to whale songs for thousands of years. The songs fascinate us. Roger Payne is a scientist who studies whale songs. He wants to uncover the purpose of their songs. Until recently, scientists did not know that whales used songs to communicate. Slowly, they are realizing whale songs are messages, but they still don't know what the different songs mean.

- **Write an IVF topic sentence for this section.**
  An Old Song tells that whales have been communicating through song for a long time.

Parts of the Song

Some whale songs have many parts. First, the most **basic** part of a whale song is an **element**. An element is one sound. Elements can be long groans. They can be low moans, roars, trills, cries, or snores. They can also be growls, whistles, or chirps. Whales emit different elements in a repetitive sequence to compose a *phrase*. Two to four different elements are repeated to create short sound strings called phrases. The last part of a whale's song is the *theme*. Whales repeat the same phrases several times to sing a theme. Whales do not **pause** between themes. Often they sing for a very long time. Whales sing themes in order, from the first to the last. A song may **contain** seven or eight themes and last anywhere from 10 to 30 minutes. The songs prove that whales have amazing memories. When a song ends, whales **surface** to breathe. Then they begin to sing again, starting over with the same sequence of themes.

- **Write a number topic sentence for this section. Avoid starting the sentence with *There are*.**
  Whale songs have three parts.

36 Unit 7

With a partner, talk about any vocabulary word that is still confusing for you to read or understand. Share your ratings from Lesson 1 on page 2 of your Student Books. Were you honest about your word knowledge? Now is the time to do something about it!

You will reread the text "Whale Song" one paragraph at a time. After each paragraph, you will monitor your understanding by circling the check mark or the question mark. Remember, good readers are honest about what they don't know and they do something about it. Good readers are metacognitive. Please be sure to draw a question mark over any confusing words, phrases, or sentences. I will provide specific instructions on how to mark the text that will help with your comprehension and writing.

With eyes on text, listen to each section as it is read to you. Use your pencil eraser to follow along.

Note: If you feel your students are capable, instruct them to highlight the main idea of each paragraph or section in green and the supporting details in yellow.

Let's read the first section, An Old Song. Read the paragraph.

Note: While the lessons are written for a teacher read aloud, it is important that your students read as much and as often as they can. Assign readings that meet the needs of your students, based on your observations or data. This is a good opportunity to stretch students, but if they become frustrated, return to the read-aloud method.

An Old Song

Sailors have listened to whale songs for thousands of years. The songs fascinate us. Roger Payne is a scientist who studies whale songs. He wants to uncover the purpose of their songs. Until recently, scientists did not know that whales used songs to communicate. Slowly, they are realizing whale songs are messages, but they still don't know what the different songs mean.

- Circle the check mark or question mark for each paragraph. Draw a question mark over words that confuse you.
- Go to line 1. Mark how long people have been listening to whale songs. (thousands of years) In the same line, mark who has been listening. (sailors)
- Go to line 4. Mark the explanation for why whales make sounds. (to communicate)
- Go to line 6. Mark the word that means "stands for." (mean)
- Mark a detail that explains how whales communicate. (songs are messages)
- Mark a detail about how people feel about whale songs. (they fascinate us)
- What does this tell us about whale sounds? Write your answer in the margin. (whales make sounds that are intriguing and we like to listen to them)
- Write an IVF topic sentence for this section in your Student Books. (An Old Song tells that whales have been communicating through song for a long time.)

Let's read the next section, Parts of the Song. Read the paragraph.

Parts of the Song

Some whale songs have many parts. First, the most basic part of a whale song is an element. An element is one sound. Elements can be long groans. They can be low moans, roars, trills, cries, or snores. They can also be growls, whistles, or chirps. Whales emit different elements in a repetitive sequence to compose a *phrase.* Two to four different elements are repeated to create short sound strings called phrases. The last part of a whale's song is the *theme.* Whales repeat the same phrases several times to sing a theme. Whales do not pause between themes. Often they sing for a very long time. Whales sing themes in order, from the first to the last. A song may contain seven or eight themes and last anywhere from 10 to 30 minutes. The songs prove that whales have amazing memories. When a song ends, whales surface to breathe. Then they begin to sing again, starting over with the same sequence of themes.

- Circle the check mark or question mark for each paragraph. Draw a question mark over words that confuse you.
- Go to line 7. Underline the number topic sentence. Circle the number word. (Some whale songs have many parts. Circle *many.*)
- On the same line, circle the transition word that helps you locate the first part of a whale song. (First)
- Go to line 8. Double underline the definition of *element.* Draw an arrow from *element* to its definition. (one sound)
- Go to line 10. Mark the synonym for *produce* or *release.* (emit)
- Go to line 12. Underline the definition of *phrases.* (short sound strings)
- On the same line, write the numeral 2 above the second part of a whale song. (phrases)
- Go to line 13. Mark the transition words that help you locate the third part of a whale song. (last part)
- Go to lines 13–17. Mark the key details that tell more about a whale theme. (repeat phrases several times, in order, first to last, seven or eight themes, 10 to 30 minutes)
- Mark the sounds whales use to communicate. (moans, roars, trills, cries, snores, growls, whistles, and chirps)
- Write a number topic sentence for this section. Avoid starting the sentence with the words *There are.* (Whale songs have three parts.)

Let's read the next section, Time for Singing. Read the paragraph.

Time for Singing

Whales sing when they migrate. They leave the colder waters and swim to the warmer waters of the tropics. They sing as they migrate to warmer waters, and they sing again during their migration back to colder waters. During the early spring or late summer, some whales are silent, but others still sing.

Guided Highlighting (*cont.*)

Time for Singing

Whales sing when they **migrate**. They leave the colder waters and swim to the warmer waters of the tropics. They sing as they migrate to warmer waters, and they sing again during their migration back to colder waters. During the early spring or late summer, some whales are silent, but others still sing.

Who Sings?

Not all whales sing. Only males sing the elaborate whale songs. A singing male often swims alone, staying underwater for a long time and remaining in a small area. He comes up to breathe every 8 to 15 minutes and then continues his underwater serenade.

Purposes of Whale Song

Scientists continue to study whale songs and try to understand the different reasons they sing. It appears that whales sing for a variety of reasons. Scientists believe the songs are not just for entertainment. The songs communicate **guidelines** for a specific group of whales. The role of whale songs is similar to that of bird songs. It may be a signal for other whales to work together and stop competing. Scientists believe the songs are also used to attract females. They have observed females slapping the water with their fins in response to a male's song. Without the songs, what would happen? Groups of whales could become separated during migration. Feeding and behavior would not be **coordinated**.

- **Write a number topic sentence for this section.**
  Whale songs have many purposes.

- Circle the check mark or question mark for each paragraph. Draw a question mark over words that confuse you.
- Go to lines 21 and 22. Mark the adjectives that are also antonyms. (colder, warmer)
- Go to lines 22 and 23. Mark two words in the same sentence that are related to travel. (migrate, migration)
- On the same lines, mark when whales sing. (when they migrate)

Let's read the next section, Who Sings? Read the paragraph.

Who Sings?

Not all whales sing. Only males sing the elaborate whale songs. A singing male often swims alone, staying underwater for a long time and remaining in a small area. He comes up to breathe every 8 to 15 minutes and then continues his underwater serenade.

- Circle the check mark or question mark for each paragraph. Draw a question mark over words that confuse you.
- Go to line 26. Mark who sings. (male whales)
- Go to line 29. Mark the synonym for *song*. (serenade)

Let's read the next section, Purposes of Whale Song. Read the paragraph.

Purposes of Whale Song

Scientists continue to study whale songs and try to understand the different reasons they sing. It appears that whales sing for a variety of reasons. Scientists believe the songs are not just for entertainment. The songs communicate guidelines for a specific group of whales. The role of whale song is similar to that of bird song. It may be a signal for other whales to work together and stop competing. Scientists believe the songs are also used to attract females. They have observed females slapping the water with their fins in response to a male's song. Without the songs, what would happen? Groups of whales could become separated during migration. Feeding and behavior would not be coordinated.

- Circle the check mark or question mark for each paragraph. Draw a question mark over words that confuse you.
- Go to line 31. Mark the word *variety*.
- Go to lines 32–40. Mark and number the reasons that whales sing. (1. Entertainment, 2. Communicate guidelines, 3. Attract females, 4. Whales could become separated, 5. Feeding and behavior coordinated)
- Write a number topic sentence for this section. (Whale songs have many purposes.)

Let's read the last section, Singing a New Song. Read the section.

Singing a New Song

Another interesting fact is that whale songs change. Each year's song is a little different. The whales make changes during the singing season. They all change their song at the same time. The changes may be minor, affecting only one or two elements while the basic song pattern remains the same. For example, moans may be altered from a long moan to a short moan, but they are still moans.

Scientists don't know why whales change their songs. They know whales living in different parts of the ocean sing different songs. They have even heard whales begin to sing the same songs as whales living on the other side of the ocean. The new song may be started by a dominant whale, or it may simply interest other whales. Whatever the reason, all of the male whales in the area begin to sing this new song.

Whale songs fascinate many people. Through intensive study, scientists are learning how whales communicate. One day, people and whales may communicate. When that happens, it will probably be with song.

- Circle the check mark or question mark for each paragraph. Draw a question mark over words that confuse you.
- Go to line 41. Mark what happens to whale songs every year. (they change)
- Write a number topic sentence for this section. (Scientists have several ideas about why whales change their songs.)

Have partners compare text markings and correct any errors.

Guided Highlighting (*cont.*)

Singing a New Song

Another interesting fact is that whale songs change. Each year's song is a little different. The whales make changes during the singing season. They all change their song at the same time. The changes may be minor, affecting only one or two elements while the basic song pattern remains the same. For example, moans may be altered from a long moan to a short moan, but they are still moans.

Scientists don't know why whales change their songs. They know whales living in different parts of the ocean sing different songs. They have even heard whales begin to sing the same songs as whales living on the other side of the ocean. The new song may be started by a dominant whale, or it may simply interest other whales. Whatever the reason, all of the male whales in the area begin to sing this new song.

Whale songs fascinate many people. Through intensive study, scientists are learning how whales communicate. One day, people and whales may communicate. When that happens, it will probably be with song.

- **Write a number topic sentence for this section.**
  Scientists have several ideas about why whales change their songs.

Unit 7

Lesson 8

Lesson Opener

Before the lesson, choose one of the following activities to write on the board or post on the *LANGUAGE! Live* Class Wall online.

- *Write two similes that describe how fast a dolphin swims and how playful dolphins are.*
- *List three facts about dolphins.*
- *Write two sentences about dolphins using at least one adverb in each.*

Writing

Objectives

- Gather relevant information from notes about the passage.
- Orally review key ideas from the passage.
- Write a clear introductory topic sentence for a comparison piece.
- Write a concluding sentence for a comparison piece.
- Write a comparison paragraph.

Prepare to Write

We need to consider our writing prompt for "Whale Song." Read the prompt aloud.

Have students write the direction words on the line in their Student Books. Ask them what the topic of their paragraph will be. (how whales and dolphins communicate) Have them write the topic on the line.

Direct students to page 39 in their Student Books to introduce the writing prompt. Review the Compare Words in Part B and ask students to think about the topic sentence they will write to compare whales and dolphins.

After we complete our notes, we will come back and write our topic sentence, but I want you to begin formulating your sentence and the commonalities you will choose to write about. We will use our Guided Highlighting of "Whale Song" to take notes on a Two-Column Note template similar to the one we used for note-taking as we read "Dolphin Talk." Because our writing is a comparison of dolphin and whale communication, we will keep the same focus while we take notes.

Lesson 8 | Writing

Prepare to Write

Part A. Study the Prompt

Read the prompt and identify the topic and direction words.

Compare how whales and dolphins communicate. Write a paragraph describing how they are similar.

Direction words: write a paragraph, describe how they are similar

Topic: how whales and dolphins communicate

Part B. Write the Topic Sentence Answers will vary.

Use a word or phrase from the box to write a Compare topic sentence.

Compare Words		
in common	the same	similar
alike	and	also
both	resemble	similarities

As communicators, whales and dolphins have several (three) things in common.

Unit 7 39

Direct students to page 41 in their Student Books and read the categories in the left column.

Have partners review their Guided Highlighting on pages 36–38 and consider what highlighted or marked information needs to be written in the Two-Column Notes on page 41 in their Student Books.

Lesson 8 | Writing

Two-Column Notes

Take notes on how whales communicate.

Topic: How whales communicate	Answers will vary.
☆ How they communicate	– moans, roars, trills, cries, snores, growls, whistles, or chirps
	– sing songs
☆ Why they communicate	– entertainment
	– send messages
	– to stay together as they travel
	– use sound to alert others of danger
	– guidelines for migration
	– coordinate feeding and behavior
	– attract females
	–
☆ Human reaction	– listened for thousands of years
	– fascination

Unit 7 41

Two-Column Notes for Compare Paragraph

Direct students to page 40 in their Student Books. We're going to use Two-Column Notes as a tool to combine the important information in the notes we took on both pieces of writing. You will use the Two-Column Notes from pages 35 and 41 to complete the comparison notes.

Have students write three supporting details in the left column that will help them organize their writing. Explain that these supporting details should be more descriptive and specific than the initial categories used in the notes. They should state three ways that whale and dolphin communication is similar.

Now write specifics that explain the details to use as elaborations. Have students enter the information in their Two-Column Notes format on page 40. Call on several students to share their ideas. Then talk about adding details to the supporting ideas.

Lesson 8 | Writing

Prepare to Write (*cont.*)

Part C. Organize the Information

Use the Two-Column Notes to identify similarities that you will describe in your paragraph.

Answers will vary.

Topic: Similarities in how whales and dolphins communicate	
☆Make sounds to communicate	– moan and whistles
	– sounds like music
☆Communicate for a variety of reasons	– use sound to alert others of danger
	– help others
☆People like listening to them	– listened for thousands of years
	– sound like instruments
	–

Part D. Write the Concluding Sentence

Rearrange your topic sentence and change the wording to write your concluding sentence.

When it comes to communicating, whales and dolphins are alike in many ways.

40 Unit 7

Passage Retell

Direct students to use their Two-Column Notes on page 40 to tell their partners about the similarities they will use in their paragraphs. Review your notes on the similarities between dolphins and whales.

Talk to your partner about your paragraph and ideas for comparing the animals. It's important to use this opportunity for rehearsing what you will write as well as to provide your partner with meaningful feedback. Allow time for partners to retell comparison information.

Compare Statement

Direct students to page 39 in their Student Books. It's time to cement your topic sentence. Look at the words in the Compare Words chart. Read the words and have students repeat them.

We could use a variety of sentence patterns to write a Compare topic sentence. The key to writing this sentence is that we use one of the words from the box to make it clear that we will focus on commonalities between dolphins and whales. Our topic sentence needs to clarify our purpose for writing. Talk with your partner about your ideas, then write your sentence.

Next, restate your topic sentence to create your concluding sentence. Write your concluding sentence on page 40 under Part D.

Circulate as students discuss their sentences, and make sure everyone has written a topic sentence and a concluding sentence. Help any student struggling to get his or her sentence written. If students are struggling with writing, put several choices on the board.

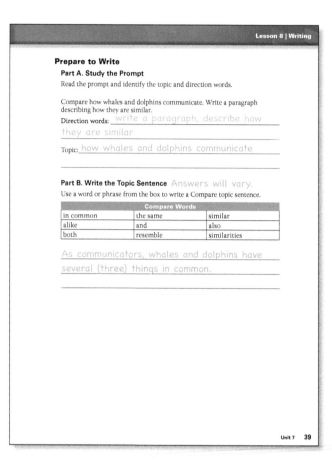

Lesson 8 | Writing

Prepare to Write

Part A. Study the Prompt

Read the prompt and identify the topic and direction words.

Compare how whales and dolphins communicate. Write a paragraph describing how they are similar.

Direction words: write a paragraph, describe how they are similar

Topic: how whales and dolphins communicate

Part B. Write the Topic Sentence Answers will vary.

Use a word or phrase from the box to write a Compare topic sentence.

Compare Words		
in common	the same	similar
alike	and	also
both	resemble	similarities

As communicators, whales and dolphins have several (three) things in common.

Unit 7 39

Write Compare Paragraph

Guide students in the writing process. Have them use their notes from pages 39 and 40.

Notebook paper

Copies of the Blueprint for Writing from the back of the Student Book for students who need additional support

On a clean sheet of paper, write your topic sentence. Then turn your first supporting detail into a sentence. Have volunteers share their sentences.

Now, look at your elaborations. Write sentences for each elaboration, or combine them into one sentence.

Guide students in turning each supporting detail into a complete sentence and then adding one sentence that elaborates. Have students copy their concluding sentence into the paragraph. If time permits, ask a volunteer to read his or her paragraph aloud. Use the example paragraph, if needed.

Example Compare Paragraph

As communicators, whales and dolphins have several things in common. Both creatures use sounds to communicate. Moans and whistles are among the many sounds both animals make. When put together, their noises are like music. Whales and dolphins have a variety of reasons for communicating. Because groups of whales and groups of dolphins travel together, they can use sounds to alert each other of approaching danger and help each other. The sounds of both animals have provided entertainment to people for thousands of years. Dolphins and whales are like musicians, and humans study them in a quest to understand and decipher their lyrics. When it comes to communicating, whales and dolphins are alike in many ways.

Lesson 9

Lesson Opener

Before the lesson, choose one of the following activities to write on the board or post on the *LANGUAGE! Live* Class Wall online.

- *Write sentences with the following verbs:* is, was, wash, washed.
- *Write two sentences with the verb* was. *Use it as a linking verb in the first sentence and as a helping verb in the second sentence.*
- *Write one fact about whale songs and one opinion about whale songs.*

Reading

Objective

- Read words to develop fluency.

Timer

Word Fluency: Second Read

Follow the Fluency Procedure outlined below. If it is necessary, begin the fluency drill with a choral read of the words as you provide a rhythm (snap your fingers, tap your foot, tap your pencil). Direct students to page 42 in their Student Books and complete the process.

Word Fluency: Second Read

Read the words fluently.

	Correct	Errors
1st Try		
2nd Try		

boys	feeling	teeth	fluke	sharp	charted	joy	sting	hang	cloth	10
teeth	fluke	sharp	charted	joy	sting	hang	cloth	spike	lung	20
sharp	charted	joy	sting	hang	cloth	spike	lung	start	quotes	30
joy	sting	hang	cloth	spike	lung	start	quotes	blame	speaking	40
hang	cloth	spike	lung	start	quotes	blame	speaking	toys	marched	50
spike	lung	start	quotes	blame	speaking	toys	marched	things	ploy	60
start	quotes	blame	speaking	feeling	marched	things	ploy	feeling	boys	70
blame	speaking	toys	marched	things	ploy	feeling	boys	fluke	teeth	80
toys	marched	things	ploy	toys	boys	fluke	teeth	charted	sharp	90
things	ploy	feeling	boys	fluke	teeth	charted	sharp	sting	joy	100

Lesson 9 | Reading

42 Unit 7

Fluency Procedure

- Partners switch books, so the recorder is marking errors in the reader's book.
- A timer is set for one minute.
- Readers and recorders move left to right, tracking each word with a pencil.
- As readers read the words aloud, recorders mark errors with a small x above the misread word.
- Recorders place a star to the right of the last word read when time ends.
- If the reader is able to read all words in the allotted time, the reader needs to start over at the beginning. The recorder must indicate this feat by placing two stars to the right of the last word read.
- When both students have read, partners switch books.
- Students calculate total words read, then subtract errors and record.
- Students record information on the progress chart in back of the Student Book.

Vocabulary

Objectives

- Demonstrate an understanding of a word by relating it to its antonyms, synonyms, and related words.
- Write similes.

Four-Square

Direct students to page 43 in their Student Books.

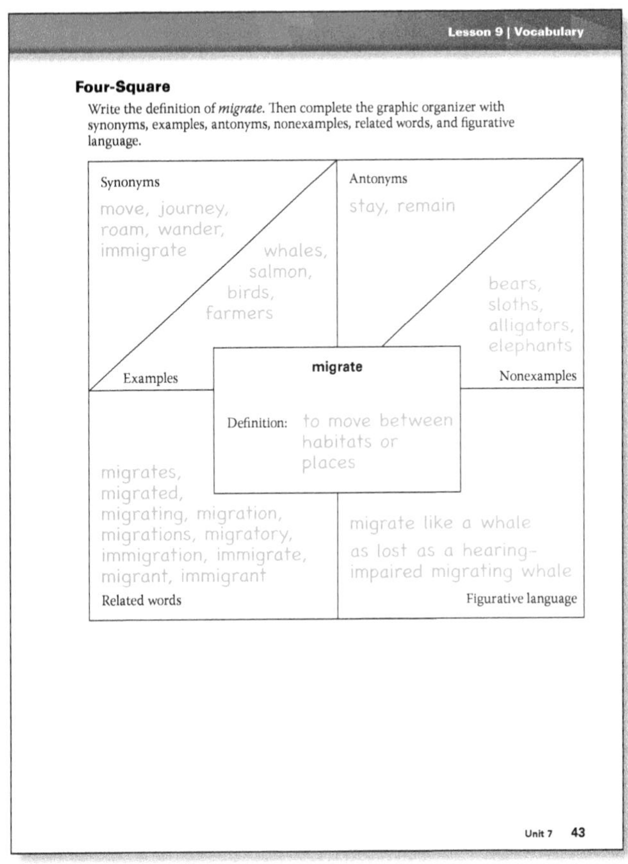

Lesson 9 | Vocabulary
Four-Square
Write the definition of *migrate*. Then complete the graphic organizer with synonyms, examples, antonyms, nonexamples, related words, and figurative language.
Synonyms
move, journey, roam, wander, immigrate
whales, salmon, birds, farmers
Examples
Antonyms
stay, remain
bears, sloths, alligators, elephants
Nonexamples
migrate
Definition: to move between habitats or places
migrates, migrated, migrating, migration, migrations, migratory, immigration, immigrate, migrant, immigrant
Related words
migrate like a whale
as lost as a hearing-impaired migrating whale
Figurative language
Unit 7 43

Review the word *migrate* and its definition.

Read the instructions. Have partners complete the synonyms, examples, antonyms, nonexamples, and related words. Review the answers as a class.

Ask students for examples of similes that include the word *migrate*. Display the simile patterns on the board for guidance.

_______ *like* ________
(verb) *(noun)*

as __________ *as* ________
(adjective) *(noun)*

Let's start with *like*. If we insert *migrate* into the formula, we would have "migrate like." What are some words that would fit into the noun space? (whales, birds, reindeer, salmon) Have students write a simile with *like* in the square, then use it in a sentence. Read the examples aloud.

Examples of Similes with *like*

The Inuit people of Alaska roamed from place to place, migrating like the reindeer they followed.

In my new school, I felt out of place, like a migrating whale in new water for the first time.

Let's look at using *as* in a simile. Because the *as* formula doesn't use a verb, we will have to change the word *migrate* to an adjective or a noun. Let's look at the noun *migration*. What do we know about migration? (It takes a long time; it is usually for food or seasons.) Have partners write a simile with *as* in the square, then use it in a sentence. Read the examples aloud.

Examples of Similes with *as*

> Although the amusement park is near our house, I was so excited that the trip seemed to take as long as an animal migration.
>
> I didn't know what to do, so I followed the guidelines as carefully as a migrating whale going back home.
>
> I was as lost as a hearing-impaired migrating whale.

Writing

Objective

- Revise and edit their paragraphs according to ideas and content and organization.

Writer's Checklist

Now I want you to use the Writer's Checklist to review your paragraph. Direct students to page 44 in their Student Books.

Lesson 9 | Writing

Writer's Checklist

Trait	Yes	No	Did the writer . . . ?
Ideas and Content			focus all sentences on the topic
			provide supporting details for the topic sentence
			include examples, evidence, and/or explanations to develop the supporting detail sentences
Organization			write a topic sentence
			tell things in an order that makes sense
			use transition words and/or phrases
			write a concluding sentence
Voice and Audience Awareness			think about the audience and purpose for writing
			write in a clear and engaging way that makes the audience want to read the work; write so the reader can "hear" the writer speaking
Word Choice			try to find a unique way to say things
			use words that are lively and specific to the content
Sentence Fluency			write complete sentences
			expand some sentences by painting the subject and/or predicate
Conventions			capitalize words correctly:
			capitalize the first word of each sentence
			capitalize proper nouns, including people's names
			punctuate correctly:
			put a period or question mark at the end of each sentence
			put an apostrophe before the *s* for a singular possessive noun
			use a comma after a long adverb phrase at the beginning of a sentence
			use grammar correctly:
			use the correct verb tense
			make sure the verb agrees with the subject in number
			use correct spelling

44 Unit 7

Look at the first trait: Ideas and Content. As we review each aspect of the checklist, I want you to refer to your paragraph. Make any changes you think you need to make and then check it off.

Go through the checklist, reading the items listed for each trait. Give students time to refer to their paragraphs and make any changes they think they need to make.

Six Traits of Writing

Direct students to page 45 in their Student Books to review the Six Traits of Writing.

Now that you've reread your paragraph using the checklist, let's apply two categories of the rubric to our paragraphs. I want you to focus on Ideas and Development and Organization for scoring purposes.

Read the descriptors for the two traits and then read the example paragraph. Have student score the paragraph. Then, score the paragraph yourself and explain your rationale.

Have students reread their paragraphs silently and assign a score for Ideas and Development and Organization.

Six Traits of Writing

	Ideas and Development	Organization	Voice and Audience Awareness	Word Choice	Sentence Fluency	Language Conventions
5	The paper is very clear and well focused. Supporting details make the paper very easy and interesting to understand.	Ideas are very clearly organized. All parts of the essay (introduction, body, and conclusion) work together to support the thesis.	The writer's voice is distinctive and shows an interest in the topic. The writer knows who his or her audience is.	Words are used correctly and are very well chosen. They create pictures in the reader's mind.	Sentences have an easy flow and rhythm. Transitions are very smooth.	There are no grammar errors. There are few or no errors in spelling, capitalization, or punctuation.
4	The paper is clear and well focused. Supporting details make the paper easy to understand.	Ideas are clearly organized. The paper includes all parts of an essay (introduction, body, and conclusion).	The writer's voice is natural and shows an interest in the topic. The writer knows who his or her audience is.	Words are used correctly. Some words may be a bit general.	Sentences are formed correctly and are varied in structure. Transitions are clear.	There are no major grammar errors. There are few errors in spelling, capitalization, or punctuation.
3	The paper has a clear thesis. The ideas are somewhat developed, but there are only a few details.	Ideas are fairly well organized. The paper includes all parts of an essay (introduction, body, and conclusion).	The writer's voice is natural, but the writer is not fully engaged in the topic. At times the writer's viewpoint may be vague.	Most words are used correctly. A few words are too general. Some words are repeated.	Sentences are formed correctly, although they may be similar in structure. Most transitions are clear.	There are a few grammar errors. There are a few errors in spelling, capitalization, or punctuation.
2	The thesis of the paper is unclear. The paper is poorly developed.	Ideas are not clearly organized. The paper may be missing an introduction or a conclusion.	The writer seems somewhat uninterested in the topic and unaware of his or her audience.	Some words are used incorrectly, some are too general, or some words are repeated often.	The sentences do not flow well. They are short and choppy, or long and confusing.	There are many grammar or spelling errors. There are quite a few errors in capitalization and punctuation.
1	The paper is missing a thesis. The paper is very confusing or poorly developed.	The paper has no organization. There is no introduction or conclusion.	The writer is uninterested in the topic and unaware of his or her audience.	Many words are used incorrectly, many words are general, or many words are repeated.	The sentences are not correctly structured, and they do not flow well.	There are many spelling and grammar errors. There are many errors in capitalization and punctuation.

Unit 7 45

Lesson 9 | Writing

Grammar

Objectives

- Demonstrate an understanding of the function of action verbs and linking verbs in sentences by diagramming sentences.
- Demonstrate an understanding of the function of simple subjects and complete subjects in sentences.
- Demonstrate an understanding of the function of simple predicates and complete predicates in sentences.

Diagram It: Action Verbs and Linking Verbs

In addition to showing action, we have learned that verbs can also act like "connectors" in a sentence. They link or connect information back to the subject noun. Consider the work that the verbs are doing in these two sentences.

Model

Write the following sentences on the board:

Dolphins alert each other of danger.

Dolphins are playful.

Read the first sentence aloud. What is the verb in this sentence, or what do dolphins do? (alert) Is this an example of an action verb or a linking verb? (action verb)

Read the second sentence. Is there a verb that tells you what dolphins do? (no) What is the verb in this sentence? (are) What kind of verb is *are*? (linking verb) It links the subject, *dolphin*, to the describing word *playful*. By diagramming sentences, we can show how words are related and how they function in a sentence.

Guided Practice

Direct students to pages 46 and 47 in their Student Books to practice diagramming sentences.

Look at the diagram template for the first sentence. You should be able to tell what kind of verb is in this sentence. Is the verb an action verb or a linking verb? (action verb) How can you tell? (The line separating the verb from what follows it is perpendicular to the baseline. The words following the verb will modify the verb.) What is the verb? (fascinate) What fascinates? (songs) What kind of songs? (whale) Who do they fascinate? (us) Write each word in its proper place on the diagramming template.

Look at the second template. You should notice something different. The angle of the line following the verb is significant. What does it signal? (a linking verb followed by words that modify the subject noun) What is the verb? (is) What is the subject? (Roger Payne) Who is he? (a scientist) Write the words on the template.

Independent Practice

Read the remaining sentences and have students complete the diagrams and categorize the verbs. Review the answers as a class.

> **Note:** Base the number of modeled and guided examples on student ability and progress. Challenge them with independent practice when appropriate.

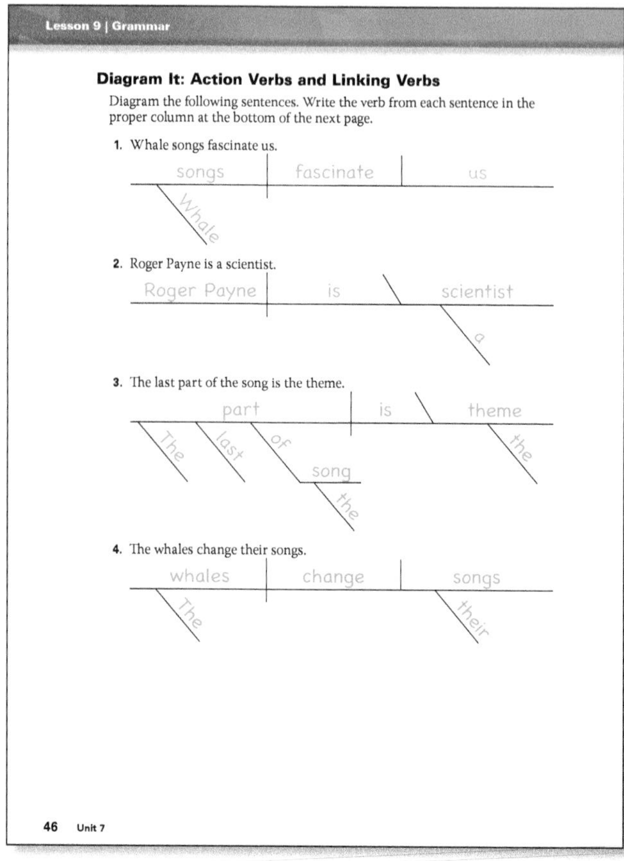

Lesson 9 | Grammar

Diagram It: Action Verbs and Linking Verbs

Diagram the following sentences. Write the verb from each sentence in the proper column at the bottom of the next page.

1. Whale songs fascinate us.

2. Roger Payne is a scientist.

3. The last part of the song is the theme.

4. The whales change their songs.

46 Unit 7

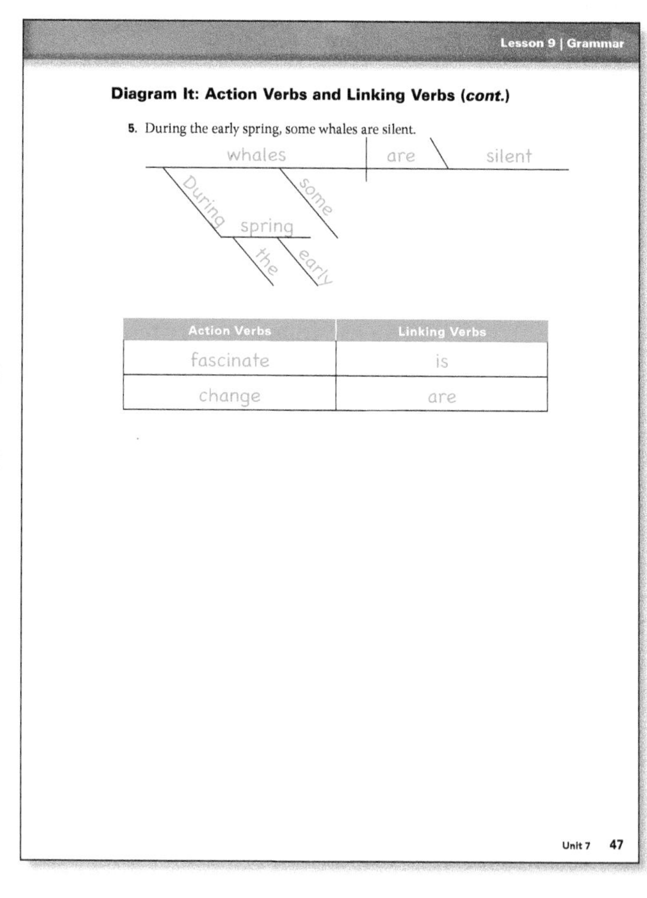

Lesson 9 | Grammar

Diagram It: Action Verbs and Linking Verbs (*cont.*)

5. During the early spring, some whales are silent.

Action Verbs	Linking Verbs
fascinate	is
change	are

Unit 7 47

Simple Subject and Complete Subject

When we talk about subjects and predicates, we sometimes use the words *simple* or *complete*. These terms can be confusing, so let's take a closer look at each of them.

Direct students to page 48 in their Student Books.

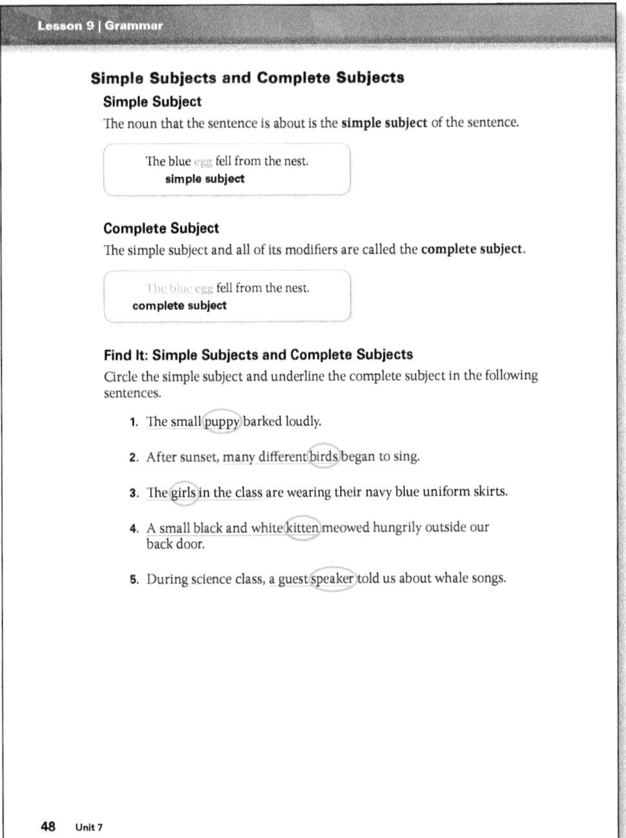
Lesson 9 | Grammar

Simple Subjects and Complete Subjects

Simple Subject

The noun that the sentence is about is the **simple subject** of the sentence.

The blue egg fell from the nest.
simple subject

Complete Subject

The simple subject and all of its modifiers are called the **complete subject**.

The blue egg fell from the nest.
complete subject

Find It: Simple Subjects and Complete Subjects

Circle the simple subject and underline the complete subject in the following sentences.

1. The small puppy barked loudly.
2. After sunset, many different birds began to sing.
3. The girls in the class are wearing their navy blue uniform skirts.
4. A small black and white kitten meowed hungrily outside our back door.
5. During science class, a guest speaker told us about whale songs.

48 Unit 7

Model

Read the definition and example of a simple subject. Then read the definition and example of a complete subject.

Think about the work we do with Masterpiece Sentences. When we prepare the canvas, we have generated a simple subject. The complete subject would include all of the subject painters we added. Sometimes the subject is only one word, and in that case the simple subject and the complete subject are the same.

Look at the first sentence in the Find It activity. Read the directions and then read the first sentence. To find the simple subject, I have to ask myself, What barked? The puppy barked, so I know *puppy* is my simple subject. It is the noun that the sentence is about. I circle *puppy*. To find the complete subject, I ask myself, What else do I know about the puppy? I can answer the *what kind* question. The puppy is *small*. "The small puppy" is the complete subject, so I'll underline those words.

Guided Practice

Be careful when you read the second sentence, as the first naming word or noun is not always the subject noun. Ask yourself, What began to sing? What is the simple subject? (birds) Let's circle that word since it's our simple subject. What else do we know about birds? (many different) Underline "many different birds" as the complete subject. What question does *after sunset* answer? (the *when* question) It is a predicate modifier.

Read the third sentence. Circle the simple subject and underline the complete subject. What did you circle? (girls) What did you underline? (the girls in the class)

Independent Practice

Read the remaining sentences and have students mark them appropriately. Review the answers as a class.

Note: Base the number of modeled and guided examples on student ability and progress. Challenge them with independent practice when appropriate.

Simple Predicate and Complete Predicate

Direct students to page 49 in their Student Books. Just like subjects, sentences have simple and complete predicates. Review the definition and example of a simple predicate. Then read the definition and example of a complete predicate. Again, if you think about the work we do with Masterpiece Sentences, you should have a solid understanding of the difference between simple and complete predicates. When we prepare the canvas, we create our simple predicate. We add predicate painters to create our complete predicate.

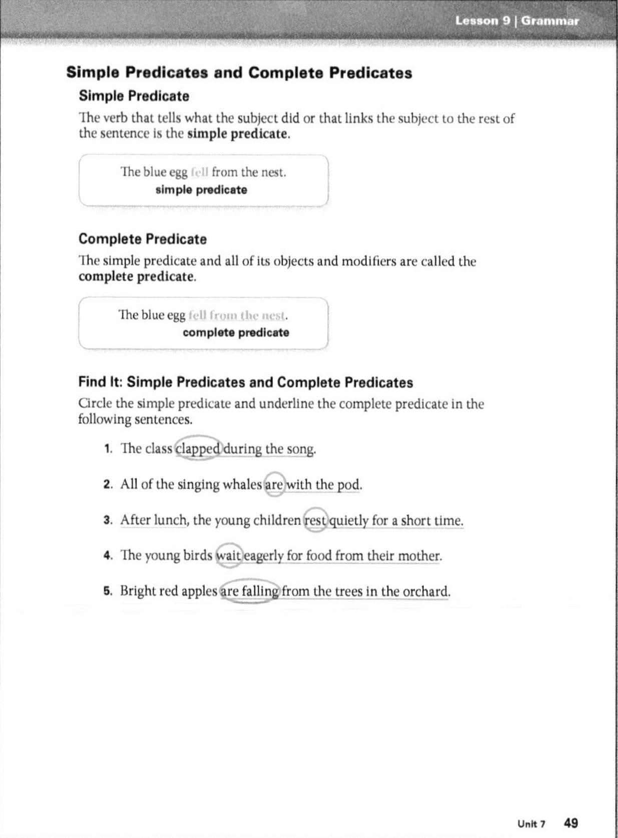
Lesson 9 | Grammar

Simple Predicates and Complete Predicates

Simple Predicate

The verb that tells what the subject did or that links the subject to the rest of the sentence is the **simple predicate**.

The blue egg fell from the nest.
simple predicate

Complete Predicate

The simple predicate and all of its objects and modifiers are called the **complete predicate**.

The blue egg fell from the nest.
complete predicate

Find It: Simple Predicates and Complete Predicates

Circle the simple predicate and underline the complete predicate in the following sentences.

1. The class clapped during the song.
2. All of the singing whales are with the pod.
3. After lunch, the young children rest quietly for a short time.
4. The young birds wait eagerly for food from their mother.
5. Bright red apples are falling from the trees in the orchard.

Unit 7 49

Model

Read the first sentence in the Find It activity.

To find the simple predicate, I ask myself, What did the class do? They clapped, so I will circle *clapped*. What else do I know about the word *clapped*? Have any predicate painters been added to the sentence? Yes, I know they clapped *during the song*, so I know when they clapped. I will underline *clapped during the song*.

Read the second sentence.

In this sentence, we won't find an action verb. We find a verb that links, or connects, the subject with the rest of the sentence. We circle *are* and then look to see what is being said about *are*. The whales are *with the pod*, so we need to underline the phrase *are with the pod*. The words *with the pod* are the predicate painters.

Guided Practice

What about the third sentence? Read the sentence. What do the children do? (rest) Look for predicate painters. When did they rest? (after lunch) How did they rest? (quietly) How long did they rest? (for a short time) All of those painters need to be underlined along with the verb to indicate the complete predicate. Because we are thoughtful about the questions answered by predicate painters, we correctly identify phrases like *after lunch* as part of the complete predicate. We know it's not part of the subject just because it's at the beginning of the sentence.

Independent Practice

Read the remaining sentences and have students mark them appropriately. Review the answers as a class.

> **Note:** Base the number of modeled and guided examples on student ability and progress. Challenge them with independent practice when appropriate.

Let's take a look at the sentence diagrams on page 46 as a tool for determining subject and predicate elements. Diagramming a sentence can help us separate the subject and all of its modifiers from the predicate and all of its modifiers. Notice the vertical line that goes all the way through the baseline. It separates the complete subject from the complete predicate. The simple subject and simple predicate are found on either side of the dividing line. So in number 1, what are the simple subject and simple predicate? (songs, fascinate) What is the complete subject? (Whale songs) What is the complete predicate? (fascinate us) Complete this process for the remaining diagrams, reinforcing how the diagram template helps identify these sentence components.

Simple Subject and Simple Predicate, Complete Subject and Complete Predicate

Make sentence index cards.

Create enough cards for each student to have one index card, but make sure you distribute enough cards to re-create each sentence in full. For each sentence, write the simple subject, the complete subject, the simple predicate, and the complete predicate on separate cards. Display a sign for each category in four distinct places around the room. Students should decide what the words on the card represents and sort themselves accordingly. Once they have moved to the proper section of the room, ask them to read their cards aloud to the class. After the cards have been read, have students with complete subjects go find "the rest of their sentence" in the complete predicate group. Meanwhile, students with simple subject and simple predicate cards should find their elaborated sentences. Students who complete their task first earn bonus points.

Example Sentences

The young kitten meowed loudly for more milk.

- Make the following index cards: The young
kitten
meowed
loudly for more milk

Three red birds flew around our backyard.

Five black cars parked on the driveway.

The restless children talked during nap time.

Writing

Objectives

- Create sentences using a word as a different part of speech in each sentence.
- Ensure pronoun-antecedent agreement in sentences.

Multiple Functions of Words

Have the class form teams. You will give the teams the same word and they are to think of different ways for that word to function in a sentence. Their focus should be function, or part of speech, as opposed to different meanings. Give the class this example to introduce the activity.

I'm going to give you a word. Each time you use the word, I want you to work as a team to use the word in sentences. Its function, or part of speech, should change. Take the word *batted*, for instance. My first thought is that it is a verb because of the *-ed* ending. So, I could say, "He batted for an hour at practice." Is there any other way I could use this word? Yes, I could say, "The batted balls were scattered all over the field." My team would earn two points because we used the word as a verb and then as an adjective.

Timer

Write a new word on the board and set a timer for one minute. Tell students to collaborate with their teams. They need to assign "scribes" within their groups to make sure their sentences are written down. Have teams read their sentences, and assign points for each sentence that uses the word as a different part of speech.

Example Words

ring	exclude	left	paused
migrated	pause	coordinated	excluded
regulate	coordinate	regulated	

Unit 7

Lesson 10

Lesson Opener

Before the lesson, choose one of the following activities to write on the board or post on the *LANGUAGE! Live* Class Wall online.

- *Write four meaningful sentences with the vocabulary words from this unit:* pause, surface, guideline, coordinate, basic, element, contain, migrate. *Each sentence will contain two vocabulary words.*
- *Change each of the following kernel sentences to make a sentence with a complete subject and complete predicate: The dog barks. The man hides.*
- *Write a sentence about whales using a prepositional phrase.*

Vocabulary

Objectives

- Clarify the meaning of key passage vocabulary.
- Demonstrate an understanding of passage vocabulary by using the words in sentences.

Review

Direct students to page 2 in their Student Books. Remind them of the review procedure. Have partners review the Key Passage Vocabulary.

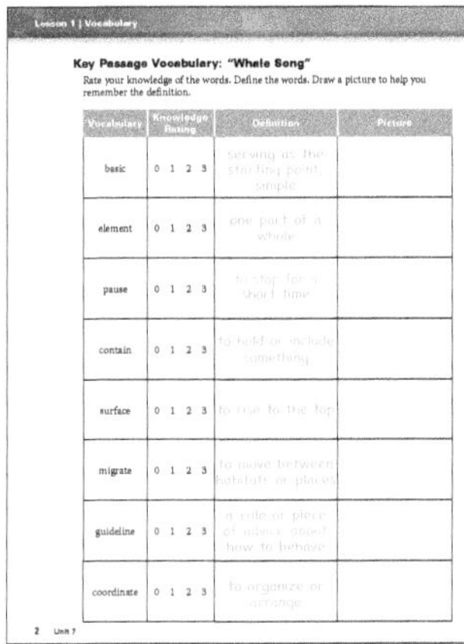

Lesson 1 | Vocabulary

Key Passage Vocabulary: "Whale Song"

Rate your knowledge of the words. Define the words. Draw a picture to help you remember the definition.

Vocabulary	Knowledge Rating	Definition	Picture
basic	0 1 2 3	serving as the starting point; simple	
element	0 1 2 3	one part of a whole	
pause	0 1 2 3	to stop for a short time	
contain	0 1 2 3	to hold or include something	
surface	0 1 2 3	to rise to the top	
migrate	0 1 2 3	to move between habitats or places	
guideline	0 1 2 3	a rule or piece of advice about how to behave	
coordinate	0 1 2 3	to organize or arrange	

2 Unit 7

Review Procedure

- Student A reads the word.
- Student B tells the meaning.
- Students swap roles for each word.

Have students revisit their rating of the words. If they cannot change all ratings to a 3, pull them aside to discuss the vocabulary words they do not know.

Cloze Activity

Now we will read a paragraph. You will determine which vocabulary words are missing and write them on the lines.

Direct students to page 50 in their Student Books. Remind them of the cloze procedure.

Cloze Procedure

- Teacher reads the text aloud, pausing at the blanks for students to write.
- Students fill in the blanks with words from the word bank.
- Teacher rereads the text as students chorally tell the correct word for each blank.
- Students correct errors.

Lesson 10 | Vocabulary

Using New Vocabulary

Fill in the blanks with the appropriate vocabulary words. If you need assistance, use the word bank at the bottom of the page.

Whales amaze us because of their communication through song. __Basic__ song __elements__ such as clicks, whistles, snores, and moans are repeated in phrases. Phrases are contained in a theme. Singing underwater, the whales do not __pause__ between themes. But, they do stop briefly when they __surface__ to breathe. Scientists think the songs __contain__ messages for other whales. The messages are __guidelines__ that help __coordinate__ whales during migration. Whales __migrate__ thousands of miles. Maybe the baby whales use moans and snores to ask the question "Are we there yet?"

Word Bank

elements	basic	contain	pause
surface	guidelines	coordinate	migrate

50 Unit 7

Reading

Objective

- Discuss and answer questions to demonstrate an understanding of the passages' main idea and key details.

Big Idea and Point of View

Direct students to page 1 in their Student Books.

Before we began reading "Whale Song," we answered two Big Idea questions. Take a minute to look over your answers.

Now that we have read the passage thoroughly, has your opinion changed? Have you learned additional facts that support or challenge your opinion? Do you feel differently about whales?

Discuss the questions and answers with the class.

Now, I want you to consider what motivated the authors to write the informational text about whales and the poem about dolphins. Can you guess how each author feels about marine mammals like whales or dolphins? Encourage students to share their thoughts. (Responses should center on authors' positive feelings toward the creatures.) Does knowing that whales and dolphins communicate and look out for each other change your feelings about how we should be caring for our oceans? Have students share their thoughts. What about fishing for whales or dolphins? Does knowing that they communicate make them seem more "human"? Do you think this was part of the authors' purpose for writing? Encourage students to share their thoughts.

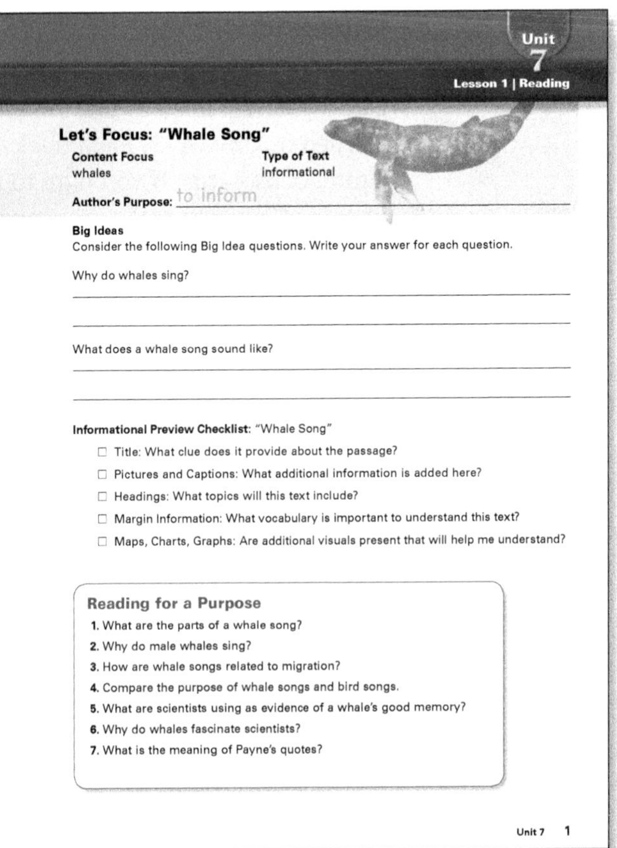

Unit 7

Lesson 1 | Reading

Let's Focus: "Whale Song"

Content Focus
whales

Type of Text
informational

Author's Purpose: to inform

Big Ideas

Consider the following Big Idea questions. Write your answer for each question.

Why do whales sing?

What does a whale song sound like?

Informational Preview Checklist: "Whale Song"

- ☐ Title: What clue does it provide about the passage?
- ☐ Pictures and Captions: What additional information is added here?
- ☐ Headings: What topics will this text include?
- ☐ Margin Information: What vocabulary is important to understand this text?
- ☐ Maps, Charts, Graphs: Are additional visuals present that will help me understand?

Reading for a Purpose

1. What are the parts of a whale song?
2. Why do male whales sing?
3. How are whale songs related to migration?
4. Compare the purpose of whale songs and bird songs.
5. What are scientists using as evidence of a whale's good memory?
6. Why do whales fascinate scientists?
7. What is the meaning of Payne's quotes?

Unit 7 1

Vocabulary

Objective

- Review key passage vocabulary from Units 4–7 by matching words to their definitions.

Game—Go Fish

Create word cards. Create definition cards.

Students will play Go Fish with the vocabulary they have learned in Units 4–7. For this game, you will need a card for each vocabulary word and a card for each definition learned in Units 4–7. Each deck of cards should have 32 words and 32 definitions, for a total of 64 cards. If you plan to have multiple groups, you will need multiple decks of cards. You may make the word cards ahead of time, or have students make them as part of the activity.

The vocabulary words are below. You can find the definitions in the Preteach Vocabulary section of Units 4–7.

Unit 4: recipe, steady, simple, plantation, social, demand, combine, express

Unit 5: spoil, destroy, substance, pollution, modern, device, variety, support

Unit 6: version, specific, appropriate, regulate, interest, permit, coarse, exclude

Unit 7: element, pause, contain, surface, migrate, guideline, coordinate, basic

Organize students in groups of five or six.

In the last four units, we learned 32 vocabulary words. We're going to play a card game with these words. You may want to take a minute and look at the vocabulary lists for all four units to refresh your memories.

Explain the game and have students play.

How to Play

- Students distribute four vocabulary cards to each person in the game. The remaining cards are placed in a stack, facedown in a central location.
- Each player is trying to make matches between vocabulary words and the correct definitions. When a match is made, the player lays the match faceup on his or her desk. Opponents can check for accuracy.
- Players ask the person to their right for the appropriate card. If they have a vocabulary word on their card, they ask for the definition. If they have a definition on their card, they ask for the word.
- Players must give the player the card if it is in their hand. If not, the player must draw from the stack.
- Players who successfully make a match during their turn get to keep asking for cards until they don't make a match. Then play moves to the person on the right.
- The first player to run out of cards wins the game.

Reading

Objective for Content Mastery

- Demonstrate an understanding of how to interpret text through categorization, inference, interpretation, and comparison.

Responding to Prompts: *categorize, infer, relate, interpret, compare*

Follow the procedure outlined below for the Reading Content Mastery questions and prompts.

Content Mastery Procedure

- Teacher reminds students to follow along with their pencils and listen.
- Teacher reads the question.
- Teacher reads each answer choice.
- Students choose the correct answer.
- Teacher repeats the question as students check their answers.

Have students turn to page 51 in their Student Books.

Let's look at the example first. Read the example aloud to students.

Listen: Categorize the uses for whale songs. To answer this prompt, I need to ______.

A create groups and place information into those groups based on shared characteristics

B provide a logical conclusion using evidence and prior knowledge

C explain the relationship between ideas or concepts

D make sense of or assign meaning to something

Fill in the bubble for the correct response. Which bubble did you fill in? You should have filled in A, the bubble for "create groups and place information into those groups based on shared characteristics." That is how you would respond to a question that asks you to categorize something.

Follow along as I read the prompts aloud. Fill in the bubble for your answer choice.

Lesson 10 | Reading Content Mastery

Responding to Prompts

Listen to the sentences and possible answers. Fill in the bubble for your answer choice.

Example: Categorize the uses for whale songs.
To answer this prompt, I need to ____.
Ⓐ create groups and place information into those groups based on shared characteristics
Ⓑ provide a logical conclusion using evidence and prior knowledge
Ⓒ explain the relationship between ideas or concepts
Ⓓ make sense of or assign meaning to something

1. Infer why whales change their songs.
To answer this prompt, I need to _____.
Ⓐ make sense of or assign meaning to something
Ⓑ explain the relationship between ideas or concepts
Ⓒ provide a logical conclusion using evidence and prior knowledge
Ⓓ state the similarities between two or more things

2. Relate whale songs to the music you listen to.
To answer this prompt, I need to _____.
Ⓐ explain the relationship between ideas or concepts
Ⓑ make sense of or assign meaning to something
Ⓒ state the similarities between two or more things
Ⓓ create groups and place information into those groups based on shared characteristics

3. Interpret the following statement: Male whales that are near each other all sing the same song.
To answer this prompt, I need to _____.
Ⓐ state the similarities between two or more things
Ⓑ make sense of or assign meaning to something
Ⓒ create groups and place information into those groups based on shared characteristics
Ⓓ provide a logical conclusion using evidence and prior knowledge

4. Compare a whale's phrase with a whale's theme.
To answer this prompt, I need to _____.
Ⓐ explain the relationship between ideas or concepts
Ⓑ create groups and place information into those groups based on shared characteristics
Ⓒ provide a logical conclusion using evidence and prior knowledge
Ⓓ state the similarities between two or more things

Unit 7 51

Use the following recommendations to reinforce or reteach according to student performance.

If...	Then...
Students miss 1 question	Review the question in a small group or individual setting, offering answer explanations.
Students miss 2 or more questions	Reteach the elements taught in Lesson 3 in a small group or individual setting. Unmarked copies of the student page can be reprinted from the Teacher Resources online.

Vocabulary

Objective for Content Mastery

- Identify similes in sentences.

Similes

Follow the procedure outlined below for the Vocabulary Content Mastery questions and prompts.

Content Mastery Procedure

- Teacher reminds students to follow along with their pencils and listen.
- Teacher reads the question.
- Teacher reads each answer choice.
- Students choose the correct answer.
- Teacher repeats the question as students check their answers.

Have students turn to page 52 in their Student Books.

Let's look at the example first. Read the example aloud to students.

Listen: Her angry words were as sharp as knives. They cut me to the core. Which of these phrases is a simile?

A Her angry words

B They cut me

C angry words were as sharp as knives

D cut me to the core

Which bubble did you fill in? You should have filled in the bubble for C. Remember a simile compares two unlike things to show how they are similar. Similes often use the words *like* or *as*. This simile compares words to knives.

Lesson 10 | Vocabulary Content Mastery

Similes

Listen to the sentences and possible answers. Fill in the bubble for your answer choice.

Example: Her angry words were as sharp as knives. They cut me to the core.
Which of these phrases is a simile?
Ⓐ Her angry words
Ⓑ They cut me
● angry words were as sharp as knives
Ⓓ cut me to the core

1. The ice skater spun like a top and then she made a graceful leap, landing on one foot.
Which of these phrases is the simile in that sentence?
● The ice skater spun like a top
Ⓑ the ice skater spun
Ⓒ she made a graceful leap
Ⓓ landing on one foot

2. That boy eats like a horse, but he's still skinny.
Which of these phrases is the simile in that sentence?
Ⓐ he's still skinny
● That boy eats like a horse
Ⓒ That boy eats
Ⓓ but he's

3. The dancers floated like bubbles on a breeze as they danced across the floor.
Which of these phrases is the simile in that sentence?
Ⓐ bubbles on a breeze
Ⓑ as they danced
● The dancers floated like bubbles
Ⓓ The dancers

4. When Sam had a cold last week, his nose was as red as a cherry.
Which of these phrases is the simile in that sentence?
● his nose was as red as a cherry
Ⓑ When Sam had a cold
Ⓒ Sam had a cold last week
Ⓓ his nose was red

5. I was so tired that the rough, rocky ground felt as soft as a pillow when I sat down.
Which of these phrases is the simile in that sentence?
Ⓐ so tired that the rough, rocky ground
Ⓑ I was so tired that the rough, rocky ground
Ⓒ when I sat down
● the rough, rocky ground felt as soft as a pillow

52 Unit 7

Follow along as I read each sentence and the questions and possible answers aloud. Fill in the bubble for your answer choice.

Use the following recommendations to reinforce or reteach according to student performance.

If...	Then...
Students miss 2 questions	Review the questions in a small group or individual setting, offering answer explanations.
Students miss 3 or more questions	Reteach the elements taught in Lesson 3 in a small group or individual setting. Unmarked copies of the student page can be reprinted from the Teacher Resources online.

Grammar

Objectives for Content Mastery

- Demonstrate an understanding of the function of object pronouns in sentences.
- Identify action and linking verbs in sentences.
- Demonstrate an understanding of the function of action and linking verbs in sentences.
- Demonstrate an understanding of the difference between the simple subject and complete subject in sentences.
- Demonstrate an understanding of the difference between the simple predicate and complete predicate in sentences.

Object Pronouns: *him, her, them, us, it, me*

Follow the procedure outlined below for each of the Grammar Content Mastery questions and prompts.

Content Mastery Procedure

- Teacher reminds students to follow along with their pencils and listen.
- Teacher reads the question.
- Teacher reads each answer choice.
- Students choose the correct answer.
- Teacher repeats the question as students check their answers.

Have students turn to page 53 in their Student Books.

Let's look at the example first. Read the example aloud to students.

Listen: We watched my brother hit a home run. Choose the object pronoun to replace the underlined words in the sentence. Fill in the bubble for your answer.

A her

B him

C it

D them

Which bubble did you fill in? You should have filled in B, the bubble for "him." The object pronoun *him* replaces *my brother* in the sentence: We watched him hit a home run.

Follow along as I read the sentences and possible answers aloud. Fill in the bubble for your answer choice.

Lesson 10 | Grammar Content Mastery

Object Pronouns

Listen to the sentences and possible answers. Fill in the bubble for your answer choice.

Example: We watched my brother hit a home run.
Choose the object pronoun to replace the underlined word in the sentence.
Ⓐ her
Ⓑ him
Ⓒ it
Ⓓ them

1. Whale songs fascinate many people.
Choose the object pronoun to replace the underlined words in the sentence.
Ⓐ they
Ⓑ it
Ⓒ them
Ⓓ you

2. Sometimes female whales slap the water in response to a song.
Choose the object pronoun to replace the underlined words in the sentence.
Ⓐ it
Ⓑ them
Ⓒ they
Ⓓ him

3. All of my family like to go whale watching.
Choose the object pronoun to replace the underlined words in the sentence.
Ⓐ we
Ⓑ us
Ⓒ her
Ⓓ him

4. The shoe salesman handed the bag to Mom.
Choose the object pronoun to replace the underlined word in the sentence.
Ⓐ she
Ⓑ it
Ⓒ him
Ⓓ her

5. Humpback whale songs are inspiring to Roger Payne.
Choose the object pronoun to replace the underlined words in the sentence.
Ⓐ him
Ⓑ it
Ⓒ them
Ⓓ us

Unit 7 53

Use the following recommendations to reinforce or reteach according to student performance.

If...	Then...
Students miss 2 questions	Review the questions in a small group or individual setting, offering answer explanations.
Students miss 3 or more questions	Reteach the elements taught in Lesson 2 in a small group or individual setting. Unmarked copies of the student page can be reprinted from the Teacher Resources online.

Action Verb vs. Linking Verb

Have students turn to page 54 in their Student Books.

Let's look at the example first. Read the example aloud to students.

Listen: Only the male whales ______. Choose the verb that correctly finishes the sentence. Fill in the bubble for your answer.

A sing

B sung

C singed

D singing

Which bubble did you fill in? You should have filled in the bubble for A. The verb *sing* correctly finishes the sentence: Only the male whales sing.

Follow along as I read the sentences and possible answers aloud. Fill in the bubble for your answer choice.

Lesson 10 | Grammar Content Mastery

Action Verb vs. Linking Verb

Listen to the sentences and possible answers. Fill in the bubble for your answer choice.

Example: Only the male whales _____.
Choose the verb that correctly finishes the sentence.
Ⓐ sing
Ⓑ sung
Ⓒ was singed
Ⓓ singing

1. Roger Payne _____ a scientist who studies whales.
Choose the verb that correctly finishes the sentence.
Ⓐ were
Ⓑ are
Ⓒ am
Ⓓ is

2. Whales _____ their songs.
Choose the verb that correctly finishes the sentence.
Ⓐ change
Ⓑ is changing
Ⓒ changes
Ⓓ is

3. Whale songs _____ messages.
Choose the verb that correctly finishes the sentence.
Ⓐ is
Ⓑ are
Ⓒ is singing
Ⓓ was

4. Scientists _____ to understand the whale songs.
Choose the verb that correctly finishes the sentence.
Ⓐ were tried
Ⓑ tries
Ⓒ is
Ⓓ try

5. A singing male often _____ alone.
Choose the verb that correctly finishes the sentence.
Ⓐ were swimming
Ⓑ swim
Ⓒ swims
Ⓓ are

54 Unit 7

Use the following recommendations to reinforce or reteach according to student performance.

If...	Then...
Students miss 2 questions	Review the questions in a small group or individual setting, offering answer explanations.
Students miss 3 or more questions	Reteach the elements taught in Lesson 9 in a small group or individual setting. Unmarked copies of the student page can be reprinted from the Teacher Resources online.

Simple Subject and Complete Subject

Have students turn to page 55 in their Student Books. You will follow along as I read the sentences and answer choices aloud. Then you will identify either the simple subject or the complete subject in the sentence. Fill in the bubble for that answer. Remember, the simple subject is the noun that the sentence is about. The complete subject is the noun and all the words that describe it.

Let's look at the example first. Read the example aloud to students.

Listen: The tall green trees shaded the park. What is the simple subject in this sentence? Fill in the bubble for your answer.

A The tall green trees

B green trees

C trees

D trees shaded

Lesson 10 | Grammar Content Mastery

Simple Subject and Complete Subject

Listen to the sentences and possible answers. Fill in the bubble for your answer choice.

Example: The tall green trees shaded the park.
What is the simple subject in this sentence?
Ⓐ The tall green trees
Ⓑ green trees
Ⓒ trees
Ⓓ trees shaded

1. The girl in the red dress took the corner piece of cake.
What is the simple subject in this sentence?
Ⓐ The girl
Ⓑ The girl in the red dress
Ⓒ girl
Ⓓ girl in the red

2. The pink rose bloomed all winter.
What is the complete subject in this sentence?
Ⓐ The pink rose
Ⓑ rose
Ⓒ rose bloomed
Ⓓ The rose

3. The striped cat had black kittens.
What is the complete subject in this sentence?
Ⓐ The striped cat
Ⓑ cat
Ⓒ cat had kittens
Ⓓ The cat

4. The high school band played at the championship game.
What is the simple subject in this sentence?
Ⓐ band played
Ⓑ high school
Ⓒ The high school band
Ⓓ band

5. The tall man caught the fly ball.
What is the complete subject in this sentence?
Ⓐ man
Ⓑ The tall man
Ⓒ tall
Ⓓ the fly ball

Unit 7 55

Which bubble did you fill in? You should have filled in C for "trees." The simple subject is *trees.* The complete subject, *The tall green trees,* includes the words *The tall green,* that tell all about the trees.

Follow along as I read the sentences and possible answers aloud. Fill in the bubble for your answer choice.

Use the following recommendations to reinforce or reteach according to student performance.

If...	Then...
Students miss 2 questions	Review the questions in a small group or individual setting, offering answer explanations.
Students miss 3 or more questions	Reteach the elements taught in Lesson 9 in a small group or individual setting. Unmarked copies of the student page can be reprinted from the Teacher Resources online.

Simple Predicate and Complete Predicate

Have students turn to page 56 in their Student Books. You will follow along as I read the sentences and answer choices aloud. Then you will select either the simple predicate or the complete predicate in the sentence. Fill in the bubble for that answer. Remember, the simple predicate is the main verb, or action word, in a sentence. The complete predicate is the verb and all the words that modify it, or describe what is going on.

Let's look at the example first. **Read the example aloud to students.**

Listen: Gina shot the winning score. What is the simple predicate in this sentence? Fill in the bubble for your answer.

- A winning score
- B shot the winning score
- C Gina shot
- D shot

Lesson 10 | Grammar Content Mastery

Simple Predicate and Complete Predicate

Listen to the sentences and possible answers. Fill in the bubble for your answer choice.

Example: Gina shot the winning score.
What is the simple predicate in this sentence?
- Ⓐ winning score
- Ⓑ shot the winning score
- Ⓒ Gina shot
- ● shot

1. The dog licked my shoe.
   What is the simple predicate in this sentence?
   - Ⓐ The dog licked
   - Ⓑ licked my shoe
   - ● licked
   - Ⓓ The dog

2. My mom fixed the dryer.
   What is the complete predicate in this sentence?
   - Ⓐ My mom fixed
   - Ⓑ fixed
   - ● fixed the dryer
   - Ⓓ the dryer

3. It rained hard for three days.
   What is the complete predicate in this sentence?
   - Ⓐ for three days
   - Ⓑ rained
   - Ⓒ rained hard
   - ● rained hard for three days

4. My brother slept on the couch.
   What is the simple predicate in this sentence?
   - ● slept
   - Ⓑ slept on the couch
   - Ⓒ My brother
   - Ⓓ on the couch

5. The candles burned brightly.
   What is the complete predicate in this sentence?
   - ● burned brightly
   - Ⓑ burned
   - Ⓒ the candles
   - Ⓓ candles burned

56 Unit 7

Which bubble did you fill in? You should have filled in D for "shot." The simple predicate, or main verb, is *shot*. The complete predicate, *shot the winning score*, tells all about what happened.

Follow along as I read the sentences and possible answers aloud. Fill in the bubble for your answer choice.

Use the following recommendations to reinforce or reteach according to student performance.

If...	Then...
Students miss 2 questions	Review the questions in a small group or individual setting, offering answer explanations.
Students miss 3 or more questions	Reteach the elements taught in Lesson 9 in a small group or individual setting. Unmarked copies of the student page can be reprinted from the Teacher Resources online.

Unit 8 Unit Plan

Primary Text:
"How Bugs Bug Us"

Text type: informational

Secondary Text:
"Bugs in Medicine"

Text type: informational

Lesson 1	Lesson 2
Reading • Determine the topic of the text. • Determine the author's purpose. • Discuss the topic of the text. • Preview the passage. **Vocabulary** • Determine the meaning of key passage vocabulary. **Reading** • Demonstrate an understanding of the text by asking and answering questions and referring to key details in the text.	**Vocabulary** • Determine the meanings of the multiple-meaning words *bug* and *spread*. • Demonstrate an understanding or the words by using them in written sentences. **Grammar** • Demonstrate an understanding of the function of coordinating conjunctions in sentences. **Writing** • Use coordinating conjunctions in written sentences.

Lesson 6	Lesson 7
Writing • Know spelling-sound correspondences for the voiced digraph /th/ as in *that*. • Know spelling-sound correspondences for words in the *–all* word family. • Know spelling-sound correspondences for vowel team /ou/, spelled *ow*. • Know spelling-sound correspondences for *r*-controlled consonant blends. **Vocabulary** • Use context to determine the meaning of words in text. • Demonstrate an understanding of common homophones. **Writing** • Demonstrate an understanding of the conventions of English by editing writing for punctuation, capitalization, spelling, and word order. **Reading** • Reread a text for key information. • Take notes of key information in a text. • Demonstrate an understanding of point of view. • Identify the point of view in a text.	**Reading** • Read with purpose and understanding. • Demonstrate comprehension of text by answering questions. • Identify and explain explicit details from text. • Identify metaphors in a text.

Lesson 3	Lesson 4	Lesson 5
Reading • Read to develop fluency. **Vocabulary** • Review key passage vocabulary. • Demonstrate an understanding of metaphor. • Write simple metaphors. • Identify metaphors in popular music. **Grammar** • Demonstrate an understanding of the difference between verbs and verb phrases. • Demonstrate an understanding of inflectional suffixes. **Reading** • Use critical thinking skills to analyze a text. • Ask and answer questions to demonstrate an understanding of a text.	**Reading** • Read sentences to develop fluency. **Grammar** • Listen to oral sentences and write them accurately. • Demonstrate an understanding of the function of conjunctions in sentences. **Reading** • Read sentence phrases with fluency to support comprehension. • Use critical thinking skills to respond to specific questions about a text. • Interpret information presented in a diagram, and explain how the information contributes to an understanding of the text. • Explain how an author uses reasons and evidence to support particular points in a text. • Integrate information from two texts on the same topic.	**Vocabulary** • Review key passage vocabulary. • Identify metaphors in a text. **Reading** • Write questions or prompts about the passage to deepen comprehension. • Respond orally to specific questions about a text. **Writing** • Use critical and strategic thinking skills to write responses to prompts about the text. • Support written answers with evidence from text. • Interpret information presented in a diagram, and explain how the information contributes to an understanding of the text. **Reading** • Read texts on similar topics.

Lesson 8	Lesson 9	Lesson 10
Writing • Gather relevant information from notes about the passage. • Orally review key ideas from the passage. • Write a paragraph that explains contrasting subject matter. • Write clear introductory topic and concluding sentences. • Develop the paragraph with concrete facts and details. • Strengthen writing by editing for organization, word choice, sentence fluency, and basic writing conventions.	**Reading** • Read words to develop fluency. **Vocabulary** • Demonstrate an understanding of words by relating them to their synonyms, antonyms, and related words. • Demonstrate an understanding of figurative language. • Generate examples of metaphors. **Grammar** • Demonstrate an understanding of the function of conjunctions in sentences. • Use the conjunctions *and, but,* and *or* in written sentences. • Demonstrate an understanding of the function of direct objects, predicate nominatives and predicate adjectives by diagramming sentences. **Writing** • Edit text for basic conventions (punctuation, spelling, capitalization). **Reading** • Read decodable text to develop fluency.	**Vocabulary** • Clarify the meaning of key passage vocabulary. • Demonstrate an understanding of passage vocabulary by using the words in sentences. **Reading** • Discuss and answer questions to demonstrate an understanding of the passages' main ideas and key details. • Discuss and answer questions to demonstrate an understanding of each author's point of view. **Grammar** • Demonstrate an understanding of verb phrases by using them in oral sentences.

Unit 8

Lesson 1

Lesson Opener

Before the lesson, choose one of the following activities to write on the board or post on the *LANGUAGE! Live* Class Wall online.

- *Write two statements using compare words about the similarities between bats and dolphins.*
- *Write a sentence using the word* mean *twice.*
- *Write two sentences about bugs. What do you already know about bugs?*

Reading

Objectives

- Determine the topic of the text.
- Determine the author's purpose.
- Discuss the topic of the text.
- Preview the passage.

Unit Introduction

Direct students to page 57 in their Student Books.

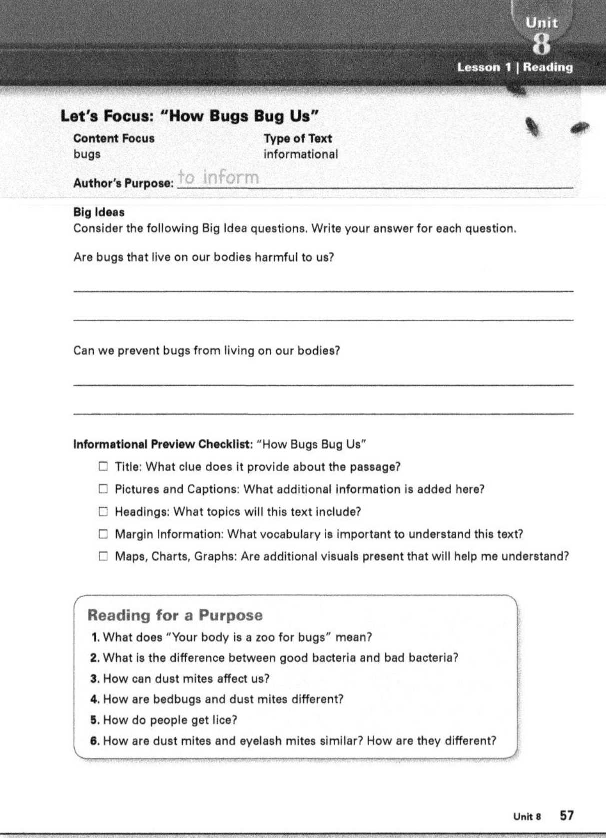
Unit 8

Lesson 1 | Reading

Let's Focus: "How Bugs Bug Us"

Content Focus bugs

Type of Text informational

Author's Purpose: to inform

Big Ideas

Consider the following Big Idea questions. Write your answer for each question.

Are bugs that live on our bodies harmful to us?

Can we prevent bugs from living on our bodies?

Informational Preview Checklist: "How Bugs Bug Us"

- ☐ Title: What clue does it provide about the passage?
- ☐ Pictures and Captions: What additional information is added here?
- ☐ Headings: What topics will this text include?
- ☐ Margin Information: What vocabulary is important to understand this text?
- ☐ Maps, Charts, Graphs: Are additional visuals present that will help me understand?

Reading for a Purpose

1. What does "Your body is a zoo for bugs" mean?
2. What is the difference between good bacteria and bad bacteria?
3. How can dust mites affect us?
4. How are bedbugs and dust mites different?
5. How do people get lice?
6. How are dust mites and eyelash mites similar? How are they different?

Unit 8 57

Discuss the content focus of the unit.

Content Focus

bugs

What do you think you will learn in this passage? (Answers will vary based on prior knowledge of bugs as pests.)

Type of Text

informational

What is another name for informational text? (nonfiction) What does the prefix *non-* mean? (not) Nonfiction text is not made up. It tells about real people, places, things, and events. So, do you think this text will be fact or fiction? (fact) This passage will give us information or facts. What will the information be about? (bugs)

Author's Purpose

The author's purpose is the reason that he or she wrote the text. Authors write for different purposes. Turn to your partner and tell him or her why authors write texts. (to entertain, to persuade, to inform or teach) Have students share reasons. Knowing an author's purpose can help a reader understand text better. "How Bugs Bug Us" was written to inform about bugs that annoy us. Was "How Bugs Bug Us" written to inform or entertain? (inform) Have students write the answer on the line next to "Author's Purpose." Will the author teach you something or entertain you? (teach) We will review author's purpose when we look at the text structure.

Background Information

The title of the text is "How Bugs Bug Us." What does that mean? First, let's look at the word *bugs* in this context. What do you know about bugs? (Answers will vary.) The word *bug* is a generic term that includes insects, spiders, and other creepy crawlers. *Bugs* is a plural noun that means what? (more than one bug) How else is *bug* used in the title? *Bug* can also be an action that means "to bother or irritate." More meanings of *bug* will be addressed in an upcoming lesson.

Next, let's consider all the words in the title, "How Bugs Bug Us." What did it? (bugs) What did they do? (bug or annoy) Who did they do it to? (us) Have you ever considered where bugs live? Where does a fly live? How about a mosquito? Have students share their responses. We will learn about bugs that live on or near our bodies. What do you think those bugs are doing there? (Answers will vary.) Some of them are bugging us!

What is another word for *bug* when used as a verb? I'm looking for a synonym to replace *bug* in the title. Write the title on the board. Underneath the title, make a list of synonyms for *bug* that don't change the meaning of the title. (bother, annoy, irritate, aggravate, etc.) Why do you think the author chose the word *bug* instead of one of these words? (Answers will vary.)

When something or someone is bugging you, does it happen just once and then stop? Think about your little sister or little brother or baby cousin. Do they ever bug you over and over? When bugs bug us, they do it consistently, or over and over. If it happened just once, you might be able to ignore it and move on. When it is consistent, though, we get annoyed, or itchy, or maybe even sick or hurt.

What if people stay home from work or school because they caught a bug? What does that mean? Did they go out with a jar and a net and capture bugs? (No, they got sick.) It means that a germ snuck into their body and made them sick. A virus is one type of germ. A virus is not a living thing and cannot survive long on its own. A bacterium is another type of microscopic germ commonly referred to as a bug. What is one way that we can keep from catching a bug? (We can wash our hands several times a day with hot, soapy water.) We will learn more about bacteria in this unit's text, "How Bugs Bug Us."

Play the Unit 8 Text Training video found in the Teacher Resources online.

Before we read the passage about bugs, we will watch a short video to help build background knowledge. I want you to combine what you just heard with what you are about to watch on this video. Listen for two things you did not know about bugs. You will share this new information with a partner after the video. Play the Unit 8 Text Training video. Have partners discuss what they learned from the video.

Direct students to page 57 in their Student Books. Read the following Big Idea questions aloud:

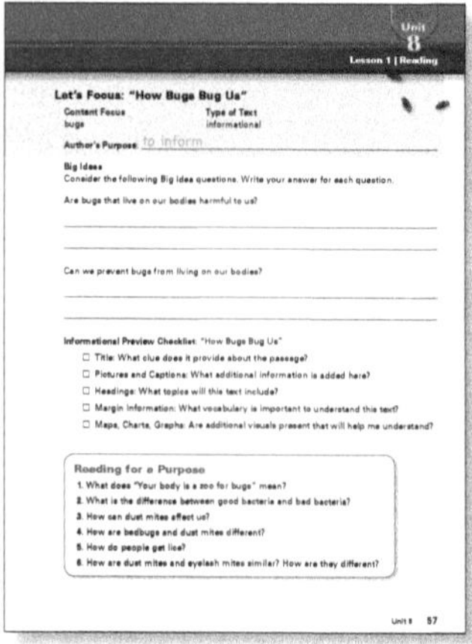

Unit 8

Lesson 1 | Reading

Let's Focus: "How Bugs Bug Us"

Content Focus bugs

Type of Text informational

Author's Purpose to inform

Big Ideas

Consider the following Big Idea questions. Write your answer for each question.

Are bugs that live on our bodies harmful to us?

Can we prevent bugs from living on our bodies?

Informational Preview Checklist: "How Bugs Bug Us"

- ☐ Title: What clue does it provide about the passage?
- ☐ Pictures and Captions: What additional information is added here?
- ☐ Headings: What topics will this text include?
- ☐ Margin Information: What vocabulary is important to understand this text?
- ☐ Maps, Charts, Graphs: Are additional visuals present that will help me understand?

Reading for a Purpose

1. What does "Your body is a zoo for bugs" mean?
2. What is the difference between good bacteria and bad bacteria?
3. How can dust mites affect us?
4. How are bedbugs and dust mites different?
5. How do people get lice?
6. How are dust mites and eyelash mites similar? How are they different?

Unit 8 57

Big Ideas

Are bugs that live on our bodies harmful to us?

Can we prevent bugs from living on our bodies?

As a class, consider the two Big Idea questions. After discussing each question, have students write an answer. We'll come back to these questions after we finish learning about bugs. You will have much more to add to your answers. You can edit your answers as you gain information.

Preview

Good readers preview the features of nonfiction texts independently and automatically. To develop this reading habit, you will preview today's text on your own, and then discuss what you noticed with a partner.

Direct students to pages 59–61 in their Student Books to preview the text. Remind them of the Informational Preview Checklist in their Student Books on page 57. Give them permission to peek at the checklist during the preview if they need a reminder of text features.

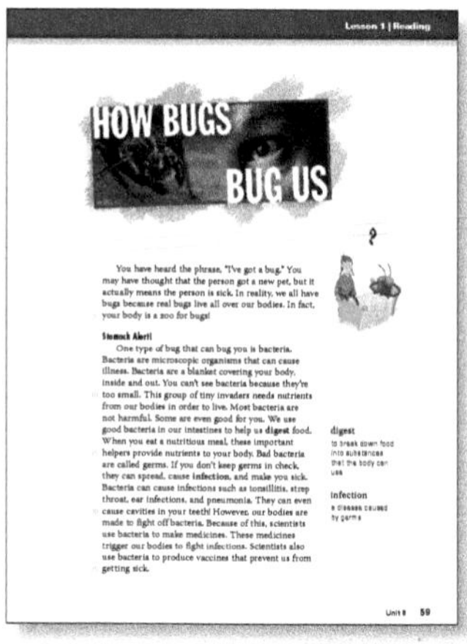

Lesson 1 | Reading

HOW BUGS BUG US

You have heard the phrase, "I've got a bug." You may have thought that the person got a new pet, but it actually means the person is sick. In reality, we all have bugs because real bugs live all over our bodies. In fact, your body is a zoo for bugs!

Stomach Alert!

One type of bug that can bug you is bacteria. Bacteria are microscopic organisms that can cause illness. Bacteria are a blanket covering your body, inside and out. You can't see bacteria because they're too small. This group of tiny invaders needs nutrients from our bodies in order to live. Most bacteria are not harmful. Some are even good for you. We use good bacteria in our intestines to help us **digest** food. When you eat a nutritious meal, these important helpers provide nutrients to your body. Bad bacteria are called germs. If you don't keep germs in check, they can spread, cause **infection**, and make you sick. Bacteria can cause infections such as tonsillitis, strep throat, ear infections, and pneumonia. They can even cause cavities in your teeth! However, our bodies are made to fight off bacteria. Because of this, scientists use bacteria to make medicines. These medicines trigger our bodies to fight infections. Scientists also use bacteria to produce vaccines that prevent us from getting sick.

digest to break down food into substances that the body can use

infection a disease caused by germs

Unit 8 59

Note: Create a small teacher-led group for students who indicated dependence or confusion with the previewing process in Unit 7. New students and truant students should also join this group until they reach independence.

Preview the text using text features. After, you will debrief with your partner, using the checklist as a reminder to be sure that you didn't skip an important text feature.

Have individuals preview the text. After sufficient time, have partners use the checklist to evaluate each other's previewing skills. Gauge individual success as you circulate around the room. Determine which students need extra practice with the skills and provide them with alternative practice sources.

Vocabulary

Objective

- Determine the meaning of key passage vocabulary.

Rate Your Knowledge

Direct students to page 58 in their Student Books.

You will rate your word knowledge. The purpose of this activity is to recognize how familiar you are with this unit's Key Passage Vocabulary.

Vocabulary Rating Scale poster

Review the Vocabulary Rating Scale with students.

Vocabulary Rating Scale

0—I have never heard the word before.

1—I have heard the word, but I'm not sure how to use it.

2—I am familiar with the word, but I'm not sure if I know the correct meaning.

3—I know the meaning of the word and can use it correctly in a sentence.

Lesson 1 | Vocabulary

Key Passage Vocabulary: "How Bugs Bug Us"

Rate your knowledge of the words. Define the words. Draw a picture to help you remember the definition.

Vocabulary	Knowledge Rating	Definition	Picture
digest	0 1 2 3	to break down food into substances that the body can use	
infection	0 1 2 3	a disease caused by germs	
multiply	0 1 2 3	to increase in amount or number	
creature	0 1 2 3	a living person or animal	
victim	0 1 2 3	a person or thing harmed or threatened by another	
scalp	0 1 2 3	the skin on the top, sides, and back of the head	
eliminate	0 1 2 3	to remove or destroy something	
horror	0 1 2 3	a feeling of great fear or disgust	

58 Unit 8

Read the list of words. Have students repeat each word. Provide time for students to rate their knowledge of each word.

Have partners discuss the words they rated as 3s and tell each other the meanings.

Preteach Vocabulary

You've rated your knowledge and talked about what you think the words mean. Now, let's discuss the words.

Preteach Procedure

This activity is intended to take only a short amount of time, so make it an oral exercise if your students aren't capable of writing quickly.

- Introduce each word as indicated on the word card.
- Read the definition and example sentences.
- Ask questions to clarify and deepen understanding.
- If time permits, allow students to share.

* Do not provide instruction time to write definitions or draw pictures, but explain that students should complete both as time permits during the unit.

Note: Research has proven that vocabulary is best learned when students represent their knowledge of words in linguistic and/or nonlinguistic ways. Thus, drawing a picture will help students remember the words. This strategy is especially effective for English language learners.

digest

Let's read the first word together. *Digest.*

Definition: *Digest* means "to break down food into substances that the body can use." To break down food into substances that the body can use is what? (digest)

Example 1: Foods with proteins, such as meat, take longer to *digest* than foods with simple sugars, such as doughnuts.

Example 2: Dogs shouldn't eat chocolate because they have a hard time *digesting* it.

Example 3: When we put food into our mouth and start chewing, *digestion* begins.

Question 1: Does our body use the food we eat before or after *digestion*? (after)

Question 2: If our body didn't *digest* food, would we have energy? (no)

Pair Share: Tell your partner how you think the word *digest* will be used in the passage "How Bugs Bug Us."

infection

Let's read the next word together. *Infection.*

Definition: An *infection* is "a disease caused by germs." A disease caused by germs is what? (an infection)

Example 1: Drinking unclean water causes *infection* to spread.

Example 2: My cut finger is red and hot; it is *infected.*

Example 3: Coughing, itchy eyes, and a runny nose are symptoms of an *infection* we call a cold.

Question 1: Can you get an *infection* from someone else? (yes)

Question 2: Can an *infection* make you feel bad? (yes)

Pair Share: With your partner, tell how you would care for a minor *infection.*

multiply

Let's read the next word together. *Multiply.*

Definition: *Multiply* means "to increase in amount or number." To increase in amount or number is to what? (multiply)

Example 1: To *multiply* the number of cookies the recipe makes, double all of the ingredients.

Example 2: During the summer, my time spent watching TV *multiplies.*

Example 3: When you move from elementary school to junior high, the number of teachers you have *multiplies.*

Question 1: Do workers hope their salary *multiplies* every year? Yes or no? (yes)

Question 2: Can an animal such as a rabbit *multiply*? Yes or no? (yes)

Pair Share: With a partner, describe an example of *multiplying* that does not involve numbers.

creature

Let's read the next word together. *Creature.*

Definition: A *creature* is "a living person or animal." A living person or animal is a what? (a creature)

Example 1: Horses, dogs, cats, and mice are all four-legged *creatures.*

Example 2: When I was little, I used to have dreams about scary *creatures* from outer space.

Example 3: You and I are *creatures* because we are living beings.

Question 1: Are dolphins and whales *creatures*? Yes or no? (yes)

Question 2: Are all *creatures* big enough to see with the human eye? Yes or no? (no)

Pair Share: In Clement Moore's poem "'Twas the Night Before Christmas," one line says, "Not a *creature* was stirring, not even a mouse." With a partner, discuss what that line means.

victim

Let's read the next word together. *Victim.*

Definition: A *victim* is "a person or thing harmed or threatened by another." A person or thing harmed or threatened by another is a what? (a victim)

Example 1: We were the *victims* of theft when someone broke into our car.

Example 2: Four *victims* died in the helicopter crash.

Example 3: I was an innocent *victim* when a shopping cart slammed into me from behind.

Question 1: Is being a *victim* a good or bad thing? (bad)

Question 2: Does a bully pick on *victims*? Yes or no? (yes)

Pair Share: Tell your partner how you think the word *victim* will be used in the passage "How Bugs Bug Us."

scalp

Let's read the next word together. *Scalp.*

Definition: The *scalp* is "the skin on the top, sides, and back of the head." The skin on the top, sides, and back of our heads is the what? (scalp)

Example 1: When I wash my hair, I always massage my *scalp* with my fingertips.

Example 2: Dandruff occurs when the *scalp* sheds too many dead skin cells.

Example 3: When a person is bald, the hair stops growing on the *scalp*.

Question 1: Is your *scalp* made of skin? Yes or no? (yes)

Question 2: Does hair grow on a *scalp*? Yes or no? (yes)

Pair Share: Turn to your partner and tell the difference between a *scalp* and a skull.

eliminate

Let's read the next word together. *Eliminate.*

Definition: *Eliminate* means "to remove or destroy something." To remove or destroy something is to what? (eliminate it)

Example 1: We had mice in our kitchen and needed to *eliminate* them.

Example 2: When my brother shaved his head, he *eliminated* the need for a brush.

Example 3: Digestion starts with chewing and ends when waste is *eliminated* from the body.

Question 1: Does a garbage disposal *eliminate* things? Yes or no? (yes)

Question 2: Can an infection be *eliminated*? Yes or no? (yes)

Pair Share: Turn to your partner and tell what food you love that you should *eliminate* from your diet because it is bad for you.

horror

Let's read the last word together. *Horror.*

Definition: *Horror* is "a feeling of great fear or disgust." A feeling of great fear or disgust is what? (horror)

Example 1: She watched in *horror* as the last of her remaining food fell into the river and floated away.

Example 2: I was filled with *horror* when I dreamed I was lost in a dark forest.

Example 3: I don't watch *horror* movies because I don't like to be scared or disgusted.

Question 1: Have you ever read a *horror* novel? (yes or no)

Question 2: Can a plant experience *horror*? Yes or no? (no)

Pair Share: With your partner, tell why you like or don't like *horror* movies.

Reading

Objective

- Demonstrate an understanding of the text by asking and answering questions and referring to key details in the text.

"How Bugs Bug Us"

Direct students to page 59 in their Student Books.

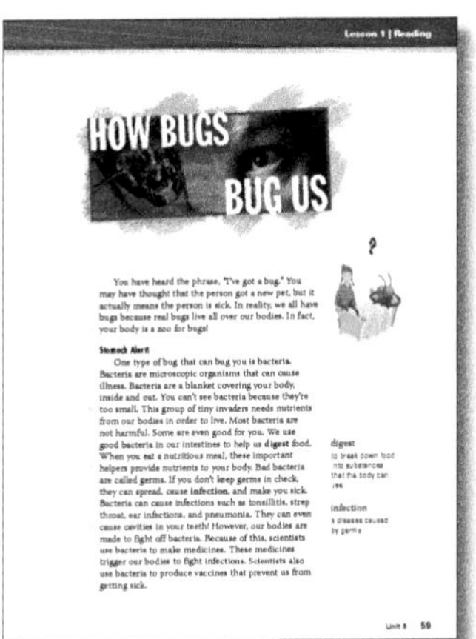

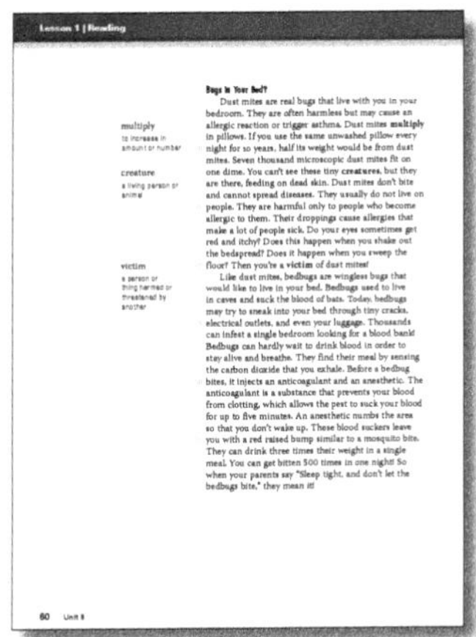

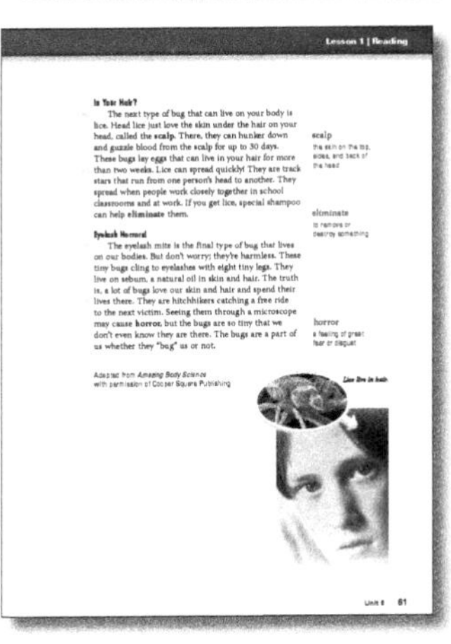

Words to Know

In addition to the vocabulary words, here are some words students might have trouble with:

type a group of things that are the same in some way; kind
cause to make something happen
half one of two equal parts that make up a whole
weight how heavy something is
happen to take place or occur
another one more in addition to the others
special different, better, or more important than normal
cling to hold on tightly or stick to something

You have already previewed the text. Let's discuss some key points before we read.

- Text features can provide readers with information about a text before they begin reading. Often, text features can help readers identify the topic, which is the subject of the passage. What is the topic of this passage? (how bugs bother us)
- Notice the pictures behind the title "How Bugs Bug Us." Use those pictures and the small graphic below it to predict what the text will be about. What do you see in the larger picture? (Answers will vary.) Prompt students to simply name what they see for now. Let's look at the smaller picture in the right margin of page 59. What do you see there? (a confused girl) Is there a caption to explain the picture? (no) Ask a probing question such as one of the following:
  - What do you think the girl is thinking? (Possible response: Why is there a bug in my bed?)
  - Do you relate this picture to the one behind the title in any way? What do they both have? (bugs)
  - Let's look at the picture on page 61. What do you see? (a girl with arrows indicating a bug in her hair) Let's read the caption. They should provide more clues about the text. Read the caption aloud. Turn to your partner and tell how the caption relates to the picture. Have volunteers share explanations with the class.
- Scan the headings. Nonfiction texts often have headings that divide the text into meaningful sections. What do you notice about the topics of the headings?

(They are all related to bugs in different places.) Use these text features to decide which sections will be related to bugs *on* your body. (Bugs in Your Bed?, In Your Hair?, Eyelash Horrors!) Which section will be related to bugs *in* your body? (Stomach Alert!) What else do you notice about the headings? What do they have in common? Look at the punctuation marks. (Each one has a question mark or an exclamation point.) Do headings always have punctuation? (no) In this text, the punctuation in each heading provides a clue about how the author feels about that topic. How does the author feel about the topics that end with a question mark? (surprised, shocked) How does the author feel about the topics that end with an exclamation point? (excited, but also "grossed out") When we read this text, we need to pay attention to the way we feel during each section and see if our feelings match the author's. Which text features did you use to predict how the author feels about each topic? (headings)

Direct students to page 57 in their Student Books. Have students look at the prompts while you read them aloud.

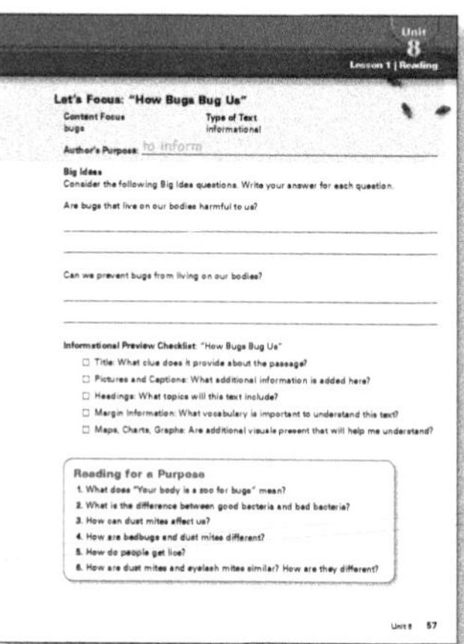

Reading for a Purpose

1. What does "Your body is a zoo for bugs" mean?
2. What is the difference between good bacteria and bad bacteria?
3. How can dust mites affect us?
4. How are bedbugs and dust mites different?
5. How do people get lice?
6. How are dust mites and eyelash mites similar? How are they different?

You will become equipped to answer these questions by reading the passage. For now, let the questions guide your reading. Be on the lookout for facts and concepts you could use to respond to the questions. While reading, you also should think about our two Big Idea questions: Are bugs that live on our bodies harmful to us? and Can we prevent bugs from living on our bodies?

Direct students to page 59 in their Student Books. Now it's time to read. Where are your eyes while I read? (on text) Where is your pencil? (following along, word for word) Eyes on text, pencil on words. Follow along with your pencil eraser as I read the text. Read the passage aloud.

Guiding Students Toward Independent Reading

While the lessons are written for a teacher read aloud, it is important that your students read as much and as often as they can. Assign readings that meet the needs of your students, based on your observations or data. This is a good opportunity to stretch students, but if they become frustrated, return to the read-aloud method.

Options for reading text:

- Teacher read aloud
- Teacher-led or student-led choral read
- Independent read of small sections with frequent comprehension checks
- Paired read or independent read

How Bugs Bug Us

You have heard the phrase, "I've got a bug." You may have thought that the person got a new pet, but it actually means the person is sick. In reality, we all have bugs because real bugs live all over our bodies. In fact, your body is a zoo for bugs!

Timer

For confirmation of engagement, take 30 seconds to have students share one thing they learned with their partner. If needed, provide this example for students: While reading, I was wondering if the last sentence is an example of figurative language. It doesn't use the words *like* or *as*, as we learned in Unit 7, so I'm not sure. Your turn. Share your thoughts and one thing you learned with your partner. Partners, you should listen carefully and ask questions to check understanding.

Stomach Alert!

One type of bug that can bug you is bacteria. Bacteria are microscopic organisms that can cause illness. Bacteria are a blanket covering your body, inside and out. You can't see bacteria because they're too small. This group of tiny invaders needs nutrients from our bodies in order to live. Most bacteria are not harmful. Some are even good for you. We use good bacteria in our intestines to help us digest food. When you eat a nutritious meal, these important helpers provide nutrients to your body. Bad bacteria are called germs. If you don't keep germs in check, they can spread, cause infection, and make you sick. Bacteria can cause infections such as tonsillitis, strep throat, ear infections, and pneumonia. They can even cause cavities in your teeth! However, our bodies are made to fight off bacteria. Because of this, scientists use bacteria to make medicines. These medicines trigger our bodies to fight infections. Scientists also use bacteria to produce vaccines that prevent us from getting sick.

For confirmation of engagement, take 30 seconds to have students share one thing they learned with their partner.

Bugs in Your Bed?

Dust mites are real bugs that live with you in your bedroom. They are often harmless but may cause an allergic reaction or trigger asthma. Dust mites multiply in pillows. If you use the same unwashed pillow every night for 10 years, half its weight would be from dust mites. Seven thousand microscopic dust mites fit on one dime. You can't see these tiny creatures, but they are there, feeding on dead skin. Dust mites don't bite and cannot spread diseases. They usually do not live on people. They are harmful only to people who become allergic to them. Their droppings cause allergies that make a lot of people sick. Do your eyes sometimes get red and itchy? Does this happen when you shake out the bedspread? Does it happen when you sweep the floor? Then you're a victim of dust mites!

For confirmation of engagement, take 30 seconds to have students share one thing they learned with their partner. Provide this example for students: While reading, I was thinking that I want a new pillow! Your turn. Switch roles. Share your thoughts and one thing you learned with your partner. Try to use one of the bold vocabulary words. Partners, you should listen carefully and ask questions to check understanding.

Like dust mites, bedbugs are wingless bugs that would like to live in your bed. Bedbugs used to live in caves and suck the blood of bats. Today, bedbugs may try to sneak into your bed through tiny cracks, electrical outlets, and even your luggage. Thousands can infest a single bedroom looking for a blood bank! Bedbugs can hardly wait to drink blood in order to stay alive and breathe. They find their meal by sensing the carbon dioxide that you exhale. Before a bedbug bites, it injects an anticoagulant and an anesthetic. The anticoagulant is a substance that prevents your blood from clotting, which allows the pest to suck your blood for up to five minutes. An anesthetic numbs the area so that you don't wake up. These blood suckers leave you with a red raised bump similar to a mosquito bite. They can drink three times their weight in a single meal. You can get bitten 500 times in one night! So when your parents say "Sleep tight, and don't let the bedbugs bite," they mean it!

For confirmation of engagement, take 30 seconds to have students share one thing they learned with their partner. While reading, I was thinking I didn't even know that bedbugs were real! I thought it was just a saying that my grandma used to say when she tucked me at night. Your turn. Switch roles. Share your thoughts and one thing you learned with your partner. Try to use one of the bold vocabulary words. Partners, you should listen carefully and ask questions to check understanding.

In Your Hair?

The next type of bug that can live on your body is lice. Head lice just love the skin under the hair on your head, called the scalp. There, they can hunker down and guzzle blood from the scalp for up to 30 days. These bugs lay eggs that can live in your hair for more than two weeks. Lice can spread quickly! They are track stars that run from one person's head to another. They spread when people work closely together in school classrooms and at work. If you get lice, special shampoo can help eliminate them.

For confirmation of engagement, take 30 seconds to have students share one thing they learned with their partner.

Eyelash Horrors!

The eyelash mite is the final type of bug that lives on our bodies. But don't worry; they're harmless. These tiny bugs cling to eyelashes with eight tiny legs. They live on sebum, a natural oil in skin and hair. The truth is, a lot of bugs love our skin and hair and spend their lives there. They are hitchhikers catching a free ride to the next victim. Seeing them through a microscope may cause horror, but the bugs are so tiny that we don't even know they are there. The bugs are a part of us whether they "bug" us or not.

For confirmation of engagement, take 30 seconds to have students share one thing they learned with their partner.

Now that you have read "How Bugs Bug Us," tell me something you shared with your partner during the reading. Have volunteers share answers.

Unit 8 Lesson 2

Lesson Opener

Before the lesson, choose one of the following activities to write on the board or post on the *LANGUAGE! Live* Class Wall online.

- *List five facts about bugs. Compare your list with your partner's list.*
- *Write a sentence about something that was said in your favorite movie. Don't forget to use quotation marks and identify who is speaking.*
- *Write a simile about bugs.*

Vocabulary

Objectives

- Determine the meanings of the multiple-meaning words *bug* and *spread.*
- Demonstrate an understanding or the words by using them in written sentences.

Multiple-Meaning Words: *bug, spread*

In this unit, we are talking about bugs that live on and around us. *Bug* is a word that has more than one meaning. The word *bug* can be a noun or a verb. It all depends on how it is used in a sentence. When we read, how do we know which meaning is being used? We look for clues around the word to help us.

Direct students to page 62 in their Student Books. Lead students in a discussion of the various meanings of the word *bug*. Have them write the meanings and sentences on the Multiple-Meaning Map in their Student Books.

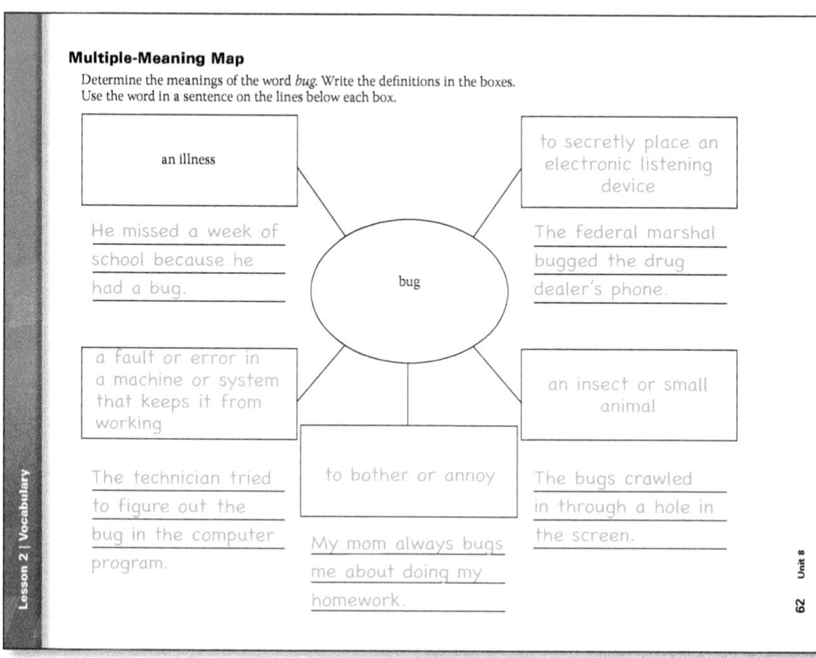

Multiple-Meaning Map

Determine the meanings of the word *bug*. Write the definitions in the boxes. Use the word in a sentence on the lines below each box.

bug

an illness

He missed a week of school because he had a bug.

to secretly place an electronic listening device

The federal marshal bugged the drug dealer's phone.

a fault or error in a machine or system that keeps it from working

The technician tried to figure out the bug in the computer program.

to bother or annoy

My mom always bugs me about doing my homework.

an insect or small animal

The bugs crawled in through a hole in the screen.

Lesson 2 | Vocabulary

62 Unit 8

Model

Have you ever heard someone say that he or she has a bug? Does this mean that person has a little creature in a cage at home? Probably not. It means he or she has some sort of an illness. Write the definition *an illness* on the board and have students find it on their map. Have students think of a good sentence for this usage and write the sentence below that definition.

Guided Practice

Point to your computer or another technological device. My computer crashed yesterday because it has some kind of a bug. What is the definition of *bug* as I am using it? (a fault or error in a machine or system that keeps it from working) Write the definition on the board and have students write it on their map. Have students think of a good sentence for this usage and write the sentence below the definition. Continue the process until the maps are complete. Review the sentences and have students correct as needed.

Additional Definitions of *bug*

Noun

- a microorganism such as bacteria that can cause a disease

Idiom

- *put a bug in someone's ear:* to give someone a hint or suggestion
- *bug off:* to leave or depart rapidly

Direct students to page 63 in their Student Books. Repeat the process with the word *spread.*

Note: Base the number of modeled and guided examples on student ability and progress. Challenge them with independent practice when appropriate.

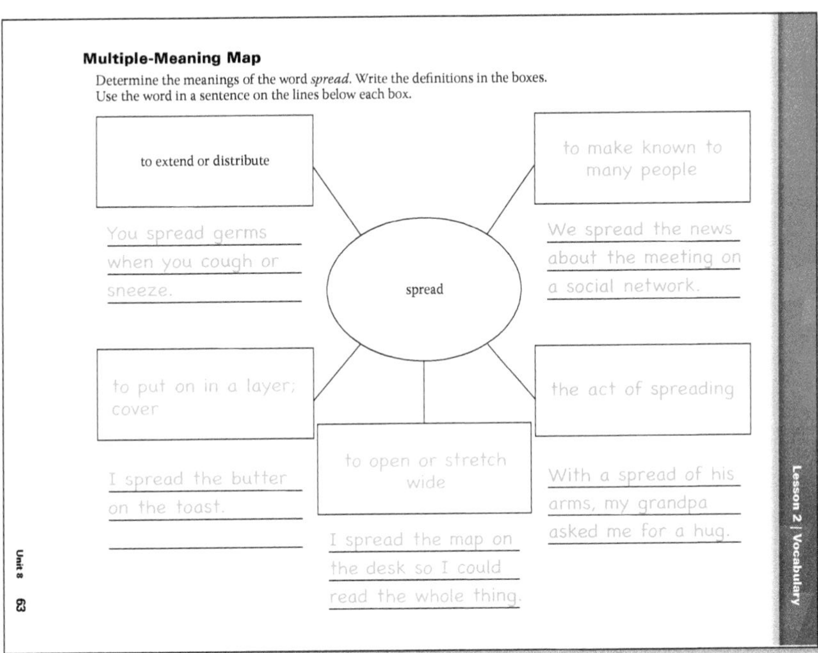

Multiple-Meaning Map
Determine the meanings of the word *spread*. Write the definitions in the boxes.
Use the word in a sentence on the lines below each box.
to extend or distribute
You spread germs when you cough or sneeze.
to make known to many people
We spread the news about the meeting on a social network.
spread
to put on in a layer; cover
I spread the butter on the toast.
to open or stretch wide
I spread the map on the desk so I could read the whole thing.
the act of spreading
With a spread of his arms, my grandpa asked me for a hug.
Unit 8 63
Lesson 2 | Vocabulary

Additional Definitions of *spread*

Noun

- a covering over the sheets on a bed
- a creamy food substance used on bread or crackers

Grammar

Objective

- Demonstrate an understanding of the function of coordinating conjunctions in sentences.

Conjunctions

In this lesson, we will learn about a new category of words. The primary function of these words is to join other words or groups of words. They can join nouns, verbs, and even sentences.

And

Use the items on your desk to complete the following sentence frame: I have ______ *and* ______ on my desk. The word *and* joins the two objects together.

Or

If you have a choice between two things, you often use a different connecting word: I will have pizza *or* a sandwich for lunch. The word *or* signals a choice.

But

Sometimes you need to join contrasting ideas. I wanted to go to the concert, *but* I couldn't afford the ticket. The word *but* signals a change, or contrast, in the outcome.

Direct students to page 64 in their Student Books. These three words—*and*, *or*, and *but*—are conjunctions. Because they join words that have the same job or function, they are called "coordinating conjunctions." **Write *coordinating conjunction* on the board.**

If we look at these words and think about what they mean, we will better understand and remember the label. *Coordinate* was a vocabulary word in the last unit. What does *coordinate* mean? **(to organize or arrange)** When this word is used as an adjective, it means that something "has been arranged to go together." Knowing this helps us remember that these words put other words together.

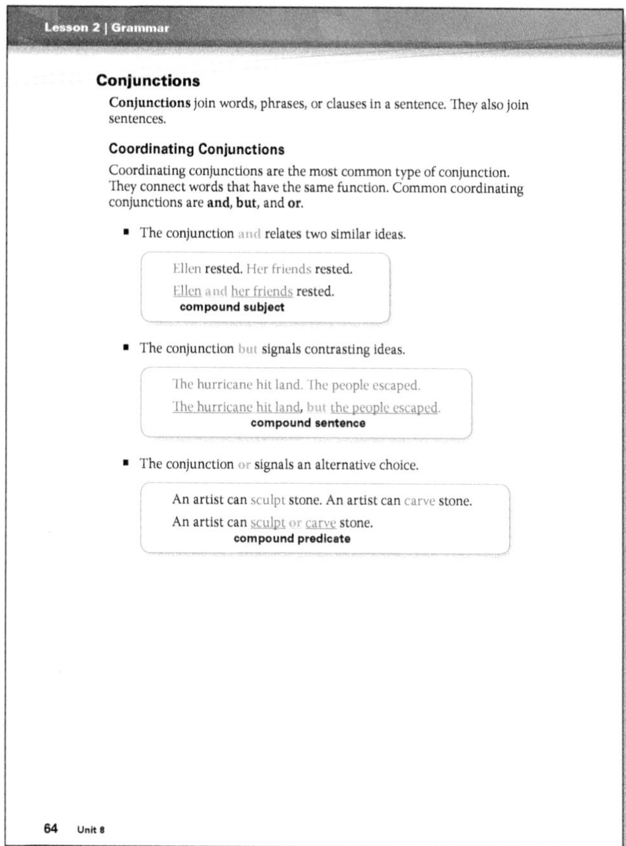

Lesson 2 | Grammar

Conjunctions

Conjunctions join words, phrases, or clauses in a sentence. They also join sentences.

Coordinating Conjunctions

Coordinating conjunctions are the most common type of conjunction. They connect words that have the same function. Common coordinating conjunctions are **and**, **but**, and **or**.

- The conjunction and relates two similar ideas.

  Ellen rested. Her friends rested.
  Ellen and her friends rested.
  compound subject

- The conjunction but signals contrasting ideas.

  The hurricane hit land. The people escaped.
  The hurricane hit land, but the people escaped.
  compound sentence

- The conjunction or signals an alternative choice.

  An artist can sculpt stone. An artist can carve stone.
  An artist can sculpt or carve stone.
  compound predicate

64 Unit 8

Consider the word *conjunction.* **Underline *junction.*** What do you think of when you hear the word *junction*? (Possible answers: where two roads come together, where roads or railroad tracks cross) Yes, *junction* means "a place where two or more things come together or the act of joining." This is exactly what conjunctions do. In your book, you see examples of how these three conjunctions can be used. Review the bulleted information and each example.

Direct students to Part A on page 65 in their Student Books. Read the model and point out that *attack* and *kill* are similar. Read the next sentence. What is the conjunction in this sentence? (or) Is it connecting similar ideas, contrasting ideas, or alternative choices? (alternative choices) Read the remaining sentences aloud and have students circle the conjunction and identify what kinds of ideas it connects. Review the answers as a class. Next, direct students to Part B and read the instructions. Read each sentence, and have students write the correct conjunction. Review the answers as a class.

Lesson 2 | Grammar

Coordinating Conjunctions

Part A

Read each sentence and circle the conjunction. Then identify what kind of ideas the conjunction connects.

	Similar Ideas	Contrasting Ideas	Alternative Choices
The bugs attack crops and kill them.	✓		
1. I will drink water or milk with dinner.			✓
2. Bill picked up the trash, but he forgot to grab the newspaper.		✓	
3. After school, Jill and Betty walked to the gym for practice.	✓		
4. Martin got a part in the play, but he is not the leading man.		✓	
5. She will ride the bus to school, or she will catch a ride with Bill.			✓

Part B

Read each sentence and complete it with the correct conjunction.

1. When we pollute our environment, we kill plants and (similar) animals.
2. To prevent sunburn, you should wear a hat and a long-sleeved shirt or (alternative) use sunscreen.
3. I looked for the missing pet, but (contrast) I did not find it.
4. We tried to catch both the whale show and (similar) the animal parade at the park.
5. My grandmother called the house, but (contrast) I did not get a chance to talk to her.

Unit 8 65

Writing

Objective

- Use coordinating conjunctions in written sentences.

Sentence Combining: Conjunctions

Once we understand how conjunctions impact meaning, we can use them to vary our sentence structure and to prevent repetitive language. Write the following sentences on the board:

We hiked through the woods.

We hiked over the hills.

Consider these two sentences. Would combining the sentences enhance the sentence fluency? If so, what should our new sentence be? (We hiked through the woods and over the hills.)

Direct students to page 66 in their Student Books. In this exercise, you will create new sentences by combining the ideas in each sentence pair. Look for ways to get rid of redundant or repetitive language, and be sure to use the appropriate conjunction. To choose the right conjunction, first decide whether the ideas are similar, contrasting, or alternatives.

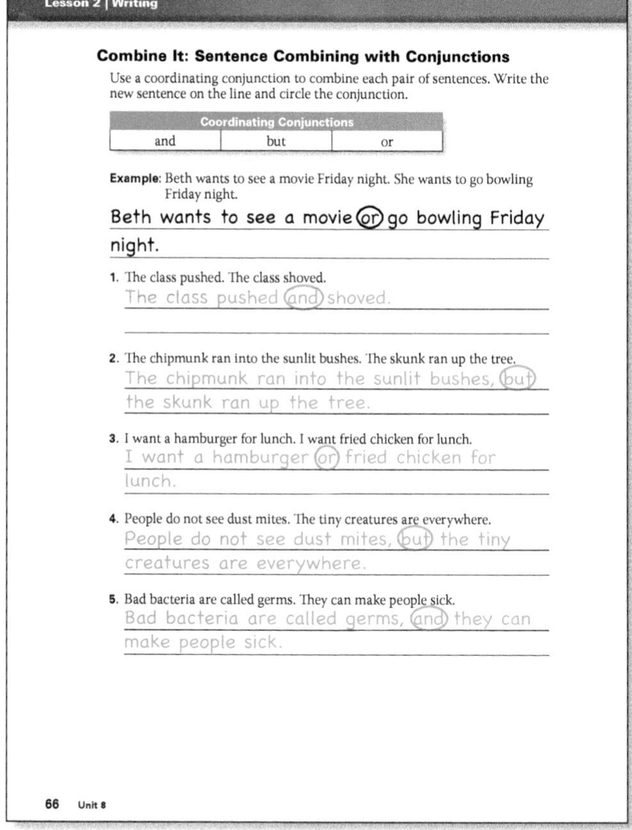
Lesson 2 | Writing

Combine It: Sentence Combining with Conjunctions

Use a coordinating conjunction to combine each pair of sentences. Write the new sentence on the line and circle the conjunction.

Coordinating Conjunctions		
and	but	or

Example: Beth wants to see a movie Friday night. She wants to go bowling Friday night.

Beth wants to see a movie or go bowling Friday night.

1. The class pushed. The class shoved.
   The class pushed and shoved.
2. The chipmunk ran into the sunlit bushes. The skunk ran up the tree.
   The chipmunk ran into the sunlit bushes, but the skunk ran up the tree.
3. I want a hamburger for lunch. I want fried chicken for lunch.
   I want a hamburger or fried chicken for lunch.
4. People do not see dust mites. The tiny creatures are everywhere.
   People do not see dust mites, but the tiny creatures are everywhere.
5. Bad bacteria are called germs. They can make people sick.
   Bad bacteria are called germs, and they can make people sick.

66 Unit 8

Model

Read the instructions and the example sentence.

Guided Practice

Guide students in completion of the first two sentences.

Independent Practice

Have partners complete sentences 3–5. Read the sentences aloud if students need support. Review the answers as a class. If students have made different choices, ask them to explain their thinking. Accept valid responses.

Note: Base the number of modeled and guided examples on student ability and progress. Challenge them with independent practice when appropriate.

Unit 8 Lesson 3

Lesson Opener

Before the lesson, choose one of the following activities to write on the board or post on the *LANGUAGE! Live* Class Wall online.

- *Write three sentences with the word* spread. *Use a different meaning in each sentence.*
- *Write two to three sentences about something or someone that bugs you.*
- *Write two sentences using object pronouns.*

Reading

Objective

- Read words to develop fluency.

Word Fluency: First Read

Timer

Follow the Fluency Procedure below. If it is necessary, begin the fluency drill with a choral read of the words as you provide a rhythm (snap your fingers, tap your foot, tap your pencil). Direct students to page 67 in their Student Books and complete the process.

Word Fluency: First Read

Read the words fluently.

	Correct	Errors
1st Try		
2nd Try		

brings	tall	creeping	hung	parked	now	small	marked	clanging	breach	10
creeping	hung	parked	now	small	marked	clanging	breach	drive	walls	20
parked	now	small	marked	clanging	breach	drive	walls	drowning	froze	30
small	marked	clanging	breach	drive	walls	drowning	froze	grapes	frowned	40
clanging	breach	drive	walls	drowning	froze	grapes	frowned	soy	malls	50
drive	walls	drowning	froze	grapes	frowned	soy	malls	crude	how	60
drowning	froze	grapes	frowned	soy	malls	crude	how	tall	brings	70
grapes	frowned	soy	malls	crude	how	tall	brings	hung	creeping	80
soy	malls	crude	how	tall	brings	hung	creeping	now	parked	90
crude	how	tall	brings	hung	creeping	now	parked	marked	small	100

Unit 8 67

Lesson 3 | Reading

Fluency Procedure

- Partners switch books, so the recorder is marking errors in the reader's book.
- A timer is set for one minute.
- Readers and recorders move left to right, tracking each word with a pencil.
- As readers read the words aloud, recorders mark errors with a small x above the misread word.
- Recorders place a star to the right of the last word read when time ends.
- If the reader is able to read all words in the allotted time, the reader needs to start over at the beginning. The recorder must indicate this feat by placing two stars to the right of the last word read.
- When both students have read, partners switch books.
- Students calculate total words read, then subtract errors and record.
- Students record information on the progress chart in back of the Student Book.

Vocabulary

Objectives

- Review key passage vocabulary.
- Demonstrate an understanding of metaphor.
- Write simple metaphors.
- Identify metaphors in popular music.

Review

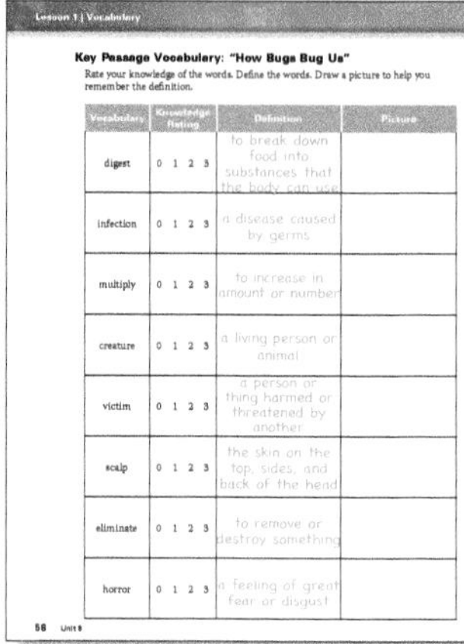

Lesson 1 | Vocabulary

Key Passage Vocabulary: "How Bugs Bug Us"

Rate your knowledge of the words. Define the words. Draw a picture to help you remember the definition.

Vocabulary	Knowledge Rating	Definition	Picture
digest	0 1 2 3	to break down food into substances that the body can use	
infection	0 1 2 3	a disease caused by germs	
multiply	0 1 2 3	to increase in amount or number	
creature	0 1 2 3	a living person or animal	
victim	0 1 2 3	a person or thing harmed or threatened by another	
scalp	0 1 2 3	the skin on the top, sides, and back of the head	
eliminate	0 1 2 3	to remove or destroy something	
horror	0 1 2 3	a feeling of great fear or disgust	

58 Unit 8

Direct students to page 58 in their Student Books.

Review the vocabulary words from the passage "How Bugs Bug Us." Have students answer in complete sentences.

- Dust mites generally do not bite humans, but they can cause red and itchy eyes. Can a person allergic to mites be a *victim*? (Yes, a person allergic to mites can be a victim.) A person or thing harmed or threatened by another is a what? (A victim is a person or thing harmed or threatened by another.)
- Do we need bacteria to help *digest* food? (Yes, we need bacteria to help digest food.) To break down food into substances that the body can use is to what? (To digest is to break down food into substances that the body can use.)
- Do lice suck blood from *scalps* and lay their eggs in hair? (Yes, lice suck blood from scalps and lay eggs in hair.) The skin on the top, sides, and back of the head is what? (The scalp is the skin on the top, sides, and back of our heads.)
- Dust mites *multiply* in pillows, comforters, or bedspreads. As they *multiply*, does the pillow get heavier? (Yes, the pillow gets heavier when dust mites multiply.) To increase in amount or number is to what? (To multiply is to increase in amount or number.)
- What adjective describes the *creatures* we call dust mites? (Dust mites are tiny creatures.) A living person or animal is a what? (A creature is a living person or animal.)
- Do all bacteria cause *infection*? (No, not all bacteria cause infection.) A disease caused by germs is what? (An infection is a disease caused by germs.)
- Can a special shampoo help *eliminate* lice from your head? (Yes, a special shampoo can help eliminate lice from your head.) To remove or destroy something is to what? (To remove or destroy something is to eliminate it.)
- Which fills you with the most *horror*: eyelash mites, dust mites, or lice? (Answers will vary.) A feeling of great fear or disgust is what? (Horror is a feeling of great fear or disgust.)

Vocabulary Concept: Metaphors

Direct students to page 68 in their Student Books.

A metaphor is a type of figurative language, or figure of speech, that describes something by comparing it to something else but does not use *like* or *as*. A metaphor compares two things that are unrelated by saying that one thing *is* something else.

Write the following simile on the board:

The boy is as tall as a skyscraper.

This is a simile comparing a boy to a skyscraper. Skyscrapers and boys are unrelated, but this comparison shows how they are similar: They are both very tall. If we wanted to change this simile to a metaphor, we would simply say, "The boy is a skyscraper." Write the metaphor on the board.

Lesson 3 | Vocabulary

Metaphors

A metaphor is a type of figurative language, or figure of speech, that describes something by comparing it to something else but does not use *like* or *as*. A metaphor compares two things that are unrelated by saying that one thing *is* or *was* something else. Underline the metaphor in each sentence. Write the meaning of each metaphor on the line.

1. My mom's closet is a time capsule.
   - Meaning: old fashioned; out-of-date
2. On my drive home from work, the freeway was a parking lot.
   - Meaning: a lot of cars that aren't moving
3. My little sister is a leech when we go to the mall.
   - Meaning: sticks to you
4. My grandma was the glue that held the family together, and when she organized a family reunion, everyone came.
   - Meaning: connected people; kept things together
5. My brother is a sloth during the summer.
   - Meaning: lazy; barely moves
6. The car was a Monet.
   - Meaning: looks good from far away, but not up close
7. My brother is a tornado destroying everything in his path.
   - Meaning: destructive; out of control
8. Our computer is a dinosaur.
   - Meaning: very old; outdated

68 Unit 8

Read the metaphors on page 68 in the Student Book aloud and have students interpret each one. Provide explanations, and have students write the meanings on the lines.

Explanations

1. A time capsule is where people put things that are popular at the time and bury it to be dug up at a later date. To say that something is a *time capsule* is to say that it is very out-of-date.
2. A parking lot is where cars park and don't move. When a road is compared to a parking lot, it means that the cars are packed together and can't move. It means there is a traffic jam.
3. A leech is a blood-sucking bug that attaches itself to you and is very hard to get rid of. To say that someone is a *leech* is to say that they are attached to you and hard to get rid of.
4. Glue holds things together. To say that someone is *the glue* means that the person keeps everyone connected.
5. A sloth is an animal that barely moves its entire life. When it does move, it moves very slowly. When we compare a person to sloth, it means he or she is very lazy.
6. Monet was an Impressionist painter. His paintings are a series of marks that form a beautiful scene from a distance but look like a bunch of dabs and dashes up close. To say that someone or something is a *Monet* is to say that person or thing looks good from far away but not when you get close.

7. A tornado is very destructive and impossible to control. To say that someone is a *tornado* is to say that he or she is out of control and destroys whatever is in the way.
8. Dinosaurs lived long ago and are now extinct. To say that something is a *dinosaur* is to say that it is extremely outdated and no longer useful.

Creating Simple Metaphors

Write the following pattern on the board:

_____ *is/was* _____
(noun) *(noun)*

Direct students to page 69 in their Student Books.

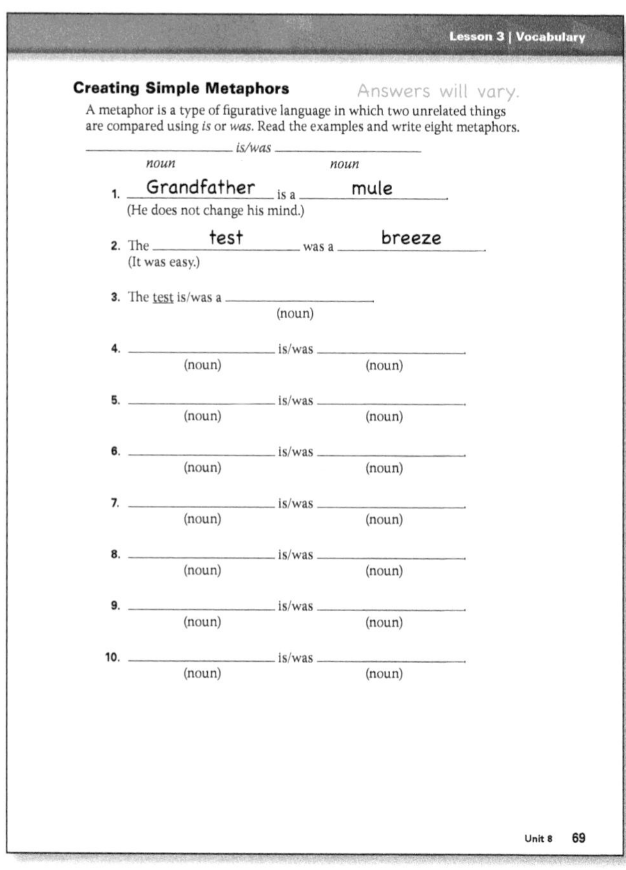

Lesson 3 | Vocabulary

Creating Simple Metaphors Answers will vary.

A metaphor is a type of figurative language in which two unrelated things are compared using *is* or *was*. Read the examples and write eight metaphors.

_____ *is/was* _____
noun *noun*

1. Grandfather is a mule.
(He does not change his mind.)
2. The test was a breeze.
(It was easy.)
3. The test is/was a _____
(noun)
4. _____ is/was _____
(noun) (noun)
5. _____ is/was _____
(noun) (noun)
6. _____ is/was _____
(noun) (noun)
7. _____ is/was _____
(noun) (noun)
8. _____ is/was _____
(noun) (noun)
9. _____ is/was _____
(noun) (noun)
10. _____ is/was _____
(noun) (noun)

Unit 8 69

Model

Discuss the first example. Explain that a mule is a stubborn animal, so the metaphor suggests that Grandfather, too, is stubborn. Grandfather is hard to get along with and difficult to be around. He only wants to hear his ideas. What other animals might describe grandfather? Discuss students' suggestions, explaining why each does or does not create an effective metaphor.

Guided Practice

Have students look at the second example. What two things are being compared? (test, breeze) If students have not heard this metaphor, guide them to understand that a breeze is a light, pleasant wind. What does this say about the test? (It was easy.)

Use the word *test* again, and ask students for a noun they could use to create a metaphor to describe a difficult test. If needed, prompt students to think about harsh winds. (Possible answers: hurricane, tornado) Next, ask students to compare a difficult test to an animal. (Possible answers: bear, snake, lion)

Independent Practice

Have partners complete the remaining metaphors and share them with the class. Ask them to explain metaphors with unclear meanings.

Note: Base the number of modeled and guided examples on student ability and progress. Challenge them with independent practice when appropriate.

Finding metaphors in poems and other texts is a fun exercise that allows you to deepen your understanding of figurative language and of the text you are reading.

Find metaphors in familiar songs.

Provide examples of metaphors in popular songs. Then challenge students to listen closely to their favorite songs between now and the end of the unit and compile a list of metaphors they hear. Offer an incentive for doing so, if possible. On the day they bring the metaphors to class, guide students to interpret their meanings.

Grammar

Objectives

- Demonstrate an understanding of the difference between verbs and verb phrases.
- Demonstrate an understanding of inflectional suffixes.

Verb Phrases

We know that a phrase is a group of words working together. What do you think a *verb phrase* is? (two or more verbs working together) Sometimes it takes more than one verb to express the desired tense—the time when the action in a sentence took place or will take place. Think about a verb that ends in *-ing*. If the word functions as the main verb in a sentence, it has to have help.

For example, I can't say: I singing. To use the verb *singing* correctly, I have to add a helping verb. Write this sentence on the board: *I am singing.*

I'd have to say, I am singing. In this sentence, *am singing* is a verb phrase. We need the main verb and a helping verb.

Direct students to page 70 in their Student Books. Read the instructions aloud.

Model

Let's read the example sentence: Bugs are living all over the house. What are bugs doing? Bugs *are living*. It takes the helping verb plus the main verb to express this ongoing action. This sentence has a verb phrase, so the phrase is circled.

Now, look at the second example: The house is full of them! This sentence has a linking verb but no other verb element. It is a single verb, so it is underlined.

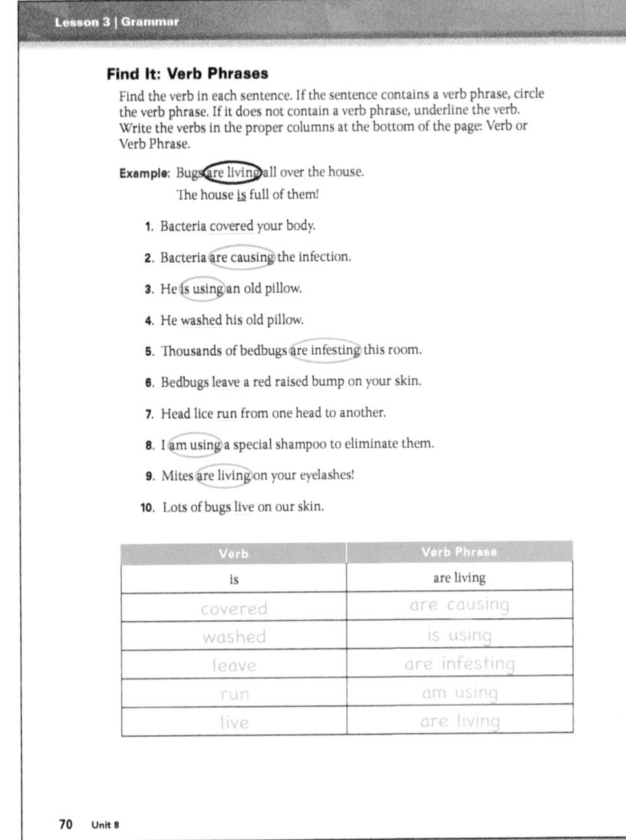

Lesson 3 | Grammar

Find It: Verb Phrases

Find the verb in each sentence. If the sentence contains a verb phrase, circle the verb phrase. If it does not contain a verb phrase, underline the verb. Write the verbs in the proper columns at the bottom of the page: Verb or Verb Phrase.

Example: Bugs are living all over the house.
The house is full of them!

1. Bacteria covered your body.
2. Bacteria are causing the infection.
3. He is using an old pillow.
4. He washed his old pillow.
5. Thousands of bedbugs are infesting this room.
6. Bedbugs leave a red raised bump on your skin.
7. Head lice run from one head to another.
8. I am using a special shampoo to eliminate them.
9. Mites are living on your eyelashes!
10. Lots of bugs live on our skin.

Verb	Verb Phrase
is	are living
covered	are causing
washed	is using
leave	are infesting
run	am using
live	are living

70 Unit 8

Guided Practice

Read the first sentence and guide students in finding the verb.

Independent Practice

Read each remaining sentence aloud, having students find and mark the verb or verb phrase. Review the answers before asking students to sort the verbs. Review the sorted answers as a class.

> **Note:** Base the number of modeled and guided examples on student ability and progress. Challenge them with independent practice when appropriate.

Noun and Verb Endings

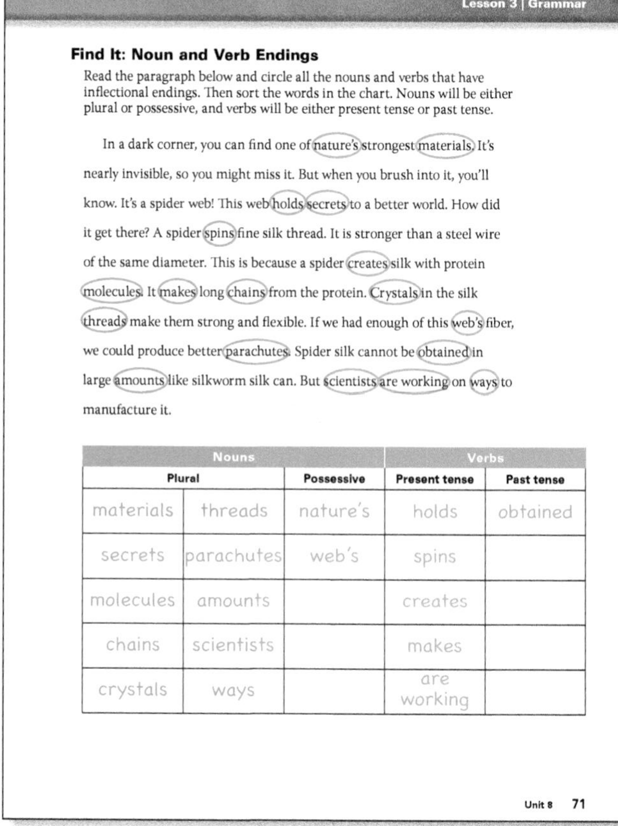

Lesson 3 | Grammar

Find It: Noun and Verb Endings

Read the paragraph below and circle all the nouns and verbs that have inflectional endings. Then sort the words in the chart. Nouns will be either plural or possessive, and verbs will be either present tense or past tense.

In a dark corner, you can find one of nature's strongest materials. It's nearly invisible, so you might miss it. But when you brush into it, you'll know. It's a spider web! This web holds secrets to a better world. How did it get there? A spider spins fine silk thread. It is stronger than a steel wire of the same diameter. This is because a spider creates silk with protein molecules. It makes long chains from the protein. Crystals in the silk threads make them strong and flexible. If we had enough of this web's fiber, we could produce better parachutes. Spider silk cannot be obtained in large amounts like silkworm silk can. But scientists are working on ways to manufacture it.

Nouns			Verbs	
Plural		Possessive	Present tense	Past tense
materials	threads	nature's	holds	obtained
secrets	parachutes	web's	spins	
molecules	amounts		creates	
chains	scientists		makes	
crystals	ways		are working	

Unit 8 71

Most of the verbs in the preceding exercise were formed by adding an ending to the base verb.

For example, we add an *-s* to many verbs to form the third person present tense: He walks. She sits.

To express ongoing action in the present progressive tense, we add *-ing.* He is walking. She is sitting.

To make many nouns plural, meaning more than one, we add an *-s*: pencils, books.

What is added to a noun to show ownership or possession? (*-'s*) Bob's cat, the boy's dog.

Direct students to page 71 in their Student Books. Word endings such as *-s* and *-ing* are called inflectional suffixes. As I read the paragraph, I want you to look for nouns and verbs that have inflectional suffixes. These suffixes are very important because they add a layer of meaning to the base word. In order to fully comprehend text, we need to notice these endings and know how they impact the meaning of words. Have students follow along as you read the paragraph.

Model

Let's reread each sentence, looking for nouns and/or verbs that have an inflectional suffix. Read the first sentence. The first sentence has two nouns with an inflectional suffix. What are they? (nature's and materials) How does the *-'s* impact the meaning of the word *nature*? (It shows ownership or possession.) What does nature own? (materials) How does the *-s* impact the meaning of the base word *material*? (It makes it plural or more than one.) You have to be careful, though, because every *-'s* doesn't necessarily signal ownership. You have to ask yourself if it makes sense.

Guided and Independent Practice

Complete the paragraph, one sentence at a time, asking students to identify the words in the sentences that have inflectional suffixes. Ask how the ending impacts or adds to the meaning of each word. Once all of the words have been identified, have students sort them properly. Review the answers as a class.

Note: Base the number of modeled and guided examples on student ability and progress. Challenge them with independent practice when appropriate.

Reading

Objectives

- Use critical thinking skills to analyze a text.
- Ask and answer questions to demonstrate an understanding of a text.

Critical Understandings

Good readers can answer a variety of questions at a variety of difficulty levels and in a variety of forms. Some questions take the form of prompts. Prompts are statements that ask you to construct a particular kind of response, such as a list, a complete sentence, a paragraph, or an essay. In this lesson we will work with challenging prompts that require you to demonstrate critical thinking. Often, these higher level prompts will ask you to find evidence in the text. Evidence is a detail from the text that supports a bigger idea. Evidence can be a single word, a phrase, a sentence, or a group of sentences.

Proficient readers do more than recall and understand. They are strategic thinkers who make connections between texts, are curious about new learning, and are able to reevaluate their own opinions based on what they read. At the strategic thinking level, you will need to recall, understand, and use advanced strategies to construct responses to prompts that include verbs such as *contrast, differentiate,* and *draw conclusions.* You will need deeper knowledge about the subject matter. What level prompt will we study in this unit? (strategic thinking) What will you need to do to respond to a prompt at this level? (recall, understand, and think strategically)

Direction Words: Strategic Thinking poster

Direct students to the chart on page 16 in their Student Books or refer to the Strategic Thinking poster if you have it displayed.

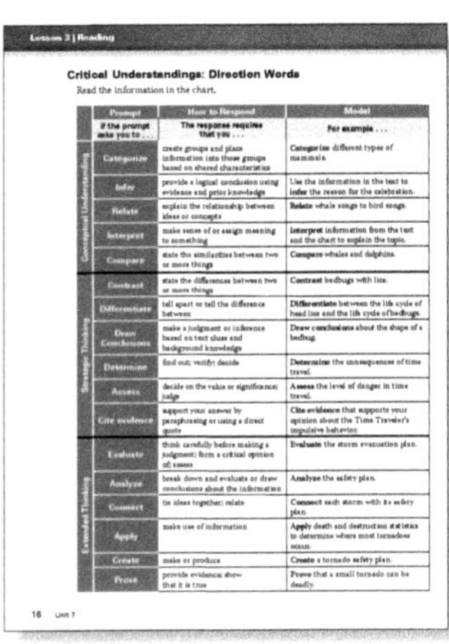
Lesson 3 | Reading

Critical Understandings: Direction Words

Read the information in the chart.

	Prompt	How to Respond	Model
	If the prompt asks you to . . .	The response requires that you . . .	For example . . .
Conceptual Understanding	Categorize	create groups and place information into those groups based on shared characteristics	**Categorize** different types of mammals.
	Infer	provide a logical conclusion using evidence and prior knowledge	Use the information in the text to **infer** the reason for the celebration.
	Relate	explain the relationship between ideas or concepts	**Relate** whale songs to bird songs.
	Interpret	make sense of or assign meaning to something	**Interpret** information from the text and the chart to explain the topic.
	Compare	state the similarities between two or more things	**Compare** whales and dolphins.
Strategic Thinking	Contrast	state the differences between two or more things	**Contrast** bedbugs with lice.
	Differentiate	tell apart or tell the difference between	**Differentiate** between the life cycle of head lice and the life cycle of bedbugs.
	Draw Conclusions	make a judgment or inference based on text clues and background knowledge	**Draw conclusions** about the shape of a bedbug.
	Determine	find out; verify; decide	**Determine** the consequences of time travel.
	Assess	decide on the value or significance; judge	**Assess** the level of danger in time travel.
	Cite evidence	support your answer by paraphrasing or using a direct quote	**Cite evidence** that supports your opinion about the Time Traveler's impulsive behavior.
Extended Thinking	Evaluate	think carefully before making a judgment; form a critical opinion of; assess	**Evaluate** the storm evacuation plan.
	Analyze	break down and evaluate or draw conclusions about the information	**Analyze** the safety plan.
	Connect	tie ideas together; relate	**Connect** each storm with its safety plan.
	Apply	make use of information	**Apply** death and destruction statistics to determine where most tornadoes occur.
	Create	make or produce	**Create** a tornado safety plan.
	Prove	provide evidence; show that it is true	**Prove** that a small tornado can be deadly.

16 Unit 7

Contrast

Earlier, you learned that if the prompt asks you to compare, the response requires you to state the similarities between two or more ideas or concepts. If I asked you to compare whales with dolphins, you would tell me how they are alike. What do you think you will need to do if the prompt asks you to *contrast*? (tell the differences) If the prompt asks you to contrast, it is asking you to state the differences between two or more ideas or concepts. The words *compare* and *contrast* are opposites, or antonyms. The words *similarities* and *differences* are also antonyms. When we compare, we look for similarities to see how two things are alike. When we contrast, we look for differences to see how two things are different. Read the contrast example with me. (Contrast bedbugs with lice.)

Differentiate

If the prompt asks you to *differentiate,* it is asking you to tell apart or tell the difference between. *Differentiate* is a direction word that means "to contrast or tell two things apart." Read the example with me. (Differentiate between the life cycle of head lice and the life cycle of bedbugs.)

Draw Conclusions

What do you think you will need to do if a prompt asks you to *draw a conclusion*? Will you need to draw a picture? (no) The word *draw* has multiple meanings. It can be a verb that means "to sketch." It can also be a verb that means "to infer" or "to get information, ideas, or knowledge from a resource." Remember, when you are asked to infer, you combine what you know with information from the text. Often you won't find the information right in the text. You will need to *read between the lines,* or understand something that isn't explicitly stated. A conclusion is a final decision or judgment. So, to draw a conclusion is to get information or ideas in order to infer, or make a judgment. When you are asked to draw a conclusion, you are asked to read between the lines and infer meaning by combining what you already know with what you read in the text. To do this, you need to think strategically. Read the example with me. (Draw conclusions about the shape of a bedbug.)

At each level, it is critical that you understand what the prompt is asking and how to respond. We will become automatic with these prompts and learn exactly how to respond at a mastery level. Look at the How to Respond column in the Critical Understandings chart. Look at the two sections, Conceptual Understanding and Strategic Thinking. Some direction words have the same or similar meanings.

- Which direction words expect you to infer? (draw conclusions, interpret)
- Which expect you to find similarities? (compare, relate)
- Which expect you to find differences? (contrast, differentiate)

Prompts using these words require you to construct a higher level response using information from different sources, including your own prior knowledge, the text, charts, and graphs. Proficient readers can also identify "gaps" in the text—places where information is not given and must be found in another source. We will practice doing this later in the lesson.

Direct students to pages 72 and 73 in their Student Books.

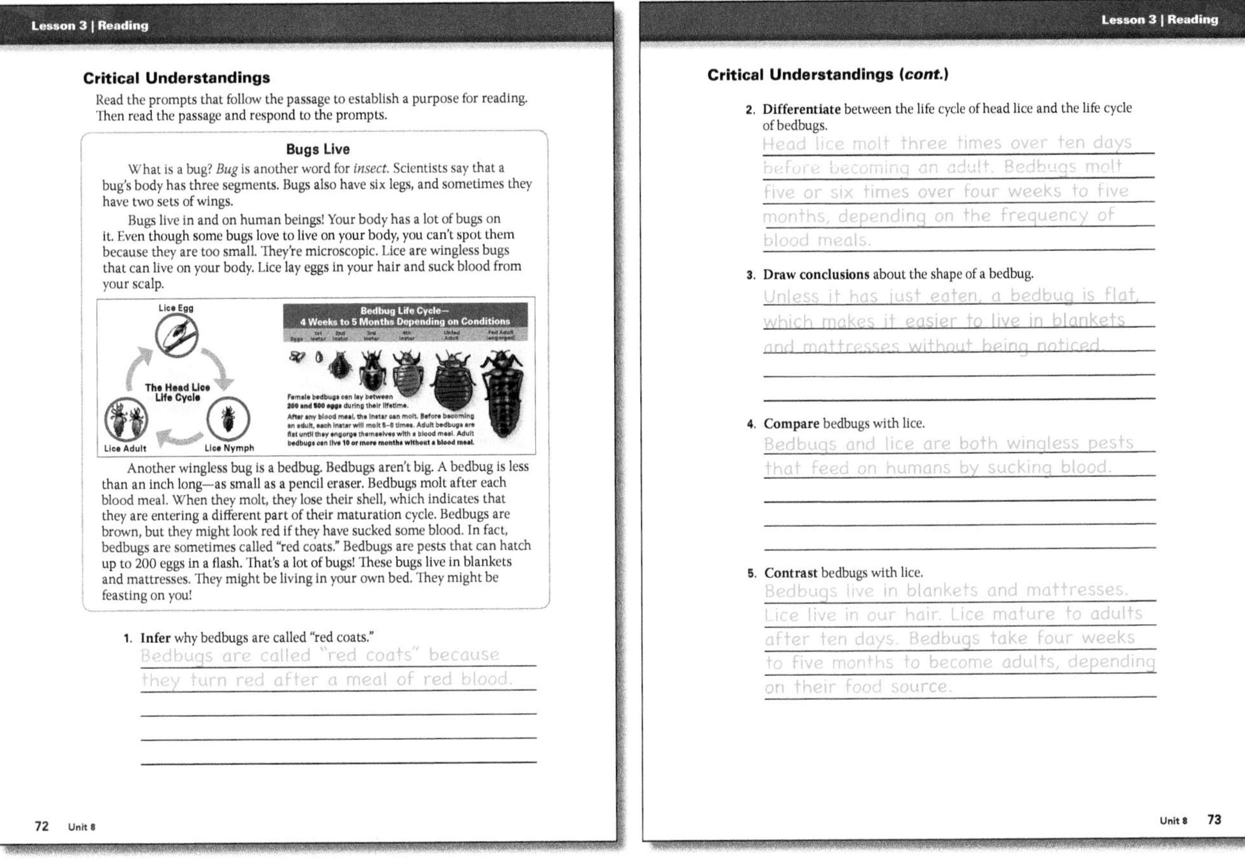

Lesson 3 | Reading

Critical Understandings

Read the prompts that follow the passage to establish a purpose for reading. Then read the passage and respond to the prompts.

Bugs Live

What is a bug? *Bug* is another word for *insect*. Scientists say that a bug's body has three segments. Bugs also have six legs, and sometimes they have two sets of wings.

Bugs live in and on human beings! Your body has a lot of bugs on it. Even though some bugs love to live on your body, you can't spot them because they are too small. They're microscopic. Lice are wingless bugs that can live on your body. Lice lay eggs in your hair and suck blood from your scalp.

Another wingless bug is a bedbug. Bedbugs aren't big. A bedbug is less than an inch long—as small as a pencil eraser. Bedbugs molt after each blood meal. When they molt, they lose their shell, which indicates that they are entering a different part of their maturation cycle. Bedbugs are brown, but they might look red if they have sucked some blood. In fact, bedbugs are sometimes called "red coats." Bedbugs are pests that can hatch up to 200 eggs in a flash. That's a lot of bugs! These bugs live in blankets and mattresses. They might be living in your own bed. They might be feasting on you!

1. **Infer** why bedbugs are called "red coats."
   Bedbugs are called "red coats" because they turn red after a meal of red blood.

72 Unit 8

Lesson 3 | Reading

Critical Understandings (*cont.*)

2. **Differentiate** between the life cycle of head lice and the life cycle of bedbugs.
   Head lice molt three times over ten days before becoming an adult. Bedbugs molt five or six times over four weeks to five months, depending on the frequency of blood meals.
3. **Draw conclusions** about the shape of a bedbug.
   Unless it has just eaten, a bedbug is flat, which makes it easier to live in blankets and mattresses without being noticed.
4. **Compare** bedbugs with lice.
   Bedbugs and lice are both wingless pests that feed on humans by sucking blood.
5. **Contrast** bedbugs with lice.
   Bedbugs live in blankets and mattresses. Lice live in our hair. Lice mature to adults after ten days. Bedbugs take four weeks to five months to become adults, depending on their food source.

Unit 8 73

Let's preview some prompts that require conceptual understanding and strategic thinking. I'll read the prompt, and you repeat the direction word.

1. **Infer** why bedbugs are called "red coats." (infer)
2. **Differentiate** between the life cycle of head lice and the life cycle of bedbugs. (differentiate)
3. **Draw conclusions** about the shape of a bedbug. (draw conclusions)
4. **Compare** bedbugs with lice. (compare)
5. **Contrast** bedbugs with lice. (contrast)

Notice that the direction words are the first word of the prompt. This is not always true. Sometimes a direction word is embedded, or buried, in the sentence.

With eyes on text, listen while I read this short text about bugs. Use your pencil eraser to follow along. Let's begin. Read the text aloud.

Note: While the lessons are written for a teacher read aloud, it is important that your students read as much and as often as they can. Assign readings that meet the needs of your students, based on your observations or data. This is a good opportunity to stretch students, but if they become frustrated, return to the read-aloud method.

Bugs Live

What is a bug? *Bug* is another word for *insect*. Scientists say that a bug's body has three segments. Bugs also have six legs, and sometimes they have two sets of wings.

Bugs live in and on human beings! Your body has a lot of bugs on it. Even though some bugs love to live on your body, you can't spot them because they are too small. They're microscopic. Lice are wingless bugs that can live on your body. Lice lay eggs in your hair and suck blood from your scalp.

Another wingless bug is a bedbug. Bedbugs aren't big. A bedbug is less than an inch long—as small as a pencil eraser. Bedbugs molt after each blood meal. When they molt, they lose their shell, which indicates that they are entering a different part of their maturation cycle. Bedbugs are brown, but they might look red if they have sucked some blood. In fact, bedbugs are sometimes called "red coats." Bedbugs are pests that can hatch up to 200 eggs in a flash. That's a lot of bugs! These bugs live in blankets and mattresses. They might be living in your own bed. They might be feasting on you!

Let's check our comprehension of this passage by responding to the prompts we read earlier. For each prompt, you will need to find evidence in the text to support your answer.

Remember, each prompt is really a question in disguise—and we already know how to answer questions. So, if you are unsure how to respond to a prompt, it can be helpful to turn it into a question. We will practice responding to prompts that require conceptual understanding and strategic thinking based on evidence from text. Try turning each prompt into a question so that you know exactly how to respond.

Model

Read the first prompt aloud.

1. **Infer** why bedbugs are called "red coats."

We need to spend time understanding the prompt before constructing a response.

First, let's change the prompt into a question so we know how to respond. Turn to your neighbor and restate the prompt as a question to show that you understand it. Provide partner time; confirm understanding. The question would be, Why are bedbugs called "red coats"?

To respond, we need to put evidence from the text together with our own thinking. We do not have to use the direction word, *infer*, in our response. However, because the question form of the prompt asks *why*, our response should contain the word *because*. Turn to your partner, and answer the question together. Write a response with students based on their combined efforts. (Answers will vary. Possible response: Bedbugs are called "red coats" because they turn red after a meal of red blood.)

Guided Practice

Read the next prompt aloud.

2. **Differentiate** between the life cycle of head lice and the life cycle of bedbugs.

I can change this prompt into a question to determine how I need to respond. The question would be, How is the life cycle of head lice different from the life cycle of bedbugs? Where can we find the evidence we need to answer this question? (in the text and the diagrams) How many diagrams do we have to study? (two) Have partners use the information from the text and diagrams to write an answer. While students are working, write the following sentence starters on the board:

Head lice molt ______ over ______ before becoming an adult.

Bedbugs molt ______ over ______, depending on ______.

After sufficient time, direct students' attention to the sentence starters. Let's read these sentence starters together. Read them aloud. Your job is to combine information from the text and both charts to fill in the blanks for each sentence starter. Write the complete answer in your Student Book.

Independent Practice

Have partners respond to the remaining prompts. Review the answers as a class to ensure that students understand what each prompt is asking.

Note: Base the number of modeled and guided examples on student ability and progress. Challenge them with independent practice when appropriate.

Provide these alternative questions and sentence starters for those who need additional help.

3. How is the shape of a bedbug significant?

   Unless it has just eaten, a bedbug is ______________________________, which ______________________________.

4. How are bedbugs similar to lice?

   Bedbugs and lice are both ______________________________.

5. How are bedbugs different from lice?

   Bedbugs live in ______________________________.
   Lice live ______________________________.
   Lice mature to adults ______________________________.
   Bedbugs take ______________________________ to become adults, depending on ______________________________.

Unit 8 Lesson 4

Lesson Opener

Before the lesson, choose one of the following activities to write on the board or post on the *LANGUAGE! Live* Class Wall online.

- *Complete the metaphor and add a sentence telling why: A bug is _____.*
- *Write sentences to draw conclusions about the following bugs based on their names: wolf spider, robber fly, assassin bug.*
- *Write a sentence about school using a verb phrase.*

Reading

Objective

- Read sentences to develop fluency.

Sentence Fluency

Timer

Follow the Fluency Procedure outlined below. If it is necessary, begin the fluency drill with a choral read of all sentences. Direct students to page 74 in their Student Books and complete the process.

Fluency Procedure

- Partners switch books, so the recorder is marking errors in the reader's book.
- A timer is set for one minute.
- Readers and recorders move left to right, tracking each word with a pencil.
- As readers read the words aloud, recorders mark errors with a small x above the misread word.
- Recorders place a star to the right of the last word read when time ends.
- If the reader is able to read all words in the allotted time, the reader needs to start over at the beginning. The recorder must indicate this feat by placing two stars to the right of the last word read.
- When both students have read, partners switch books.
- Students calculate total words read, then subtract errors and record.
- Students record information on the progress chart in back of the Student Book.

Lesson 4 | Reading

Sentence Fluency

Read each sentence fluently.

	Correct	Errors
1st Try		
2nd Try		

1. We can start on the bike ride, or we can rest in the shade. 14
2. Grab a snack, and we will sit in the grass to eat. 26
3. I do not like that car, and I do not want a van. 39
4. We can eat at home, or we can grill in the park. 51
5. Rob does well in art, but he likes math best of all. 63
6. Have him check the brakes very well, so you know the car is safe. 77
7. Where in the water did the clown drown? 85
8. Does the after prom bash have a theme? 93
9. She may want to chat with all of her chums online. 104
10. The Smiths went backpacking for five days in Rock Lake Park. 115
11. Would you take me back the other way to the farm? 126
12. Could you keep track of how many people are on the tram? 138

74 Unit 8

Grammar

Objectives

- Listen to oral sentences and write them accurately.
- Demonstrate an understanding of the function of conjunctions in sentences.

Conjunctions

You have just read sentences for speed and accuracy. Now we will look closely at the sentences to reinforce the work we have done with conjunctions.

Direct students to page 75 in their Student Books. Read the instructions and remind students of the procedure for sentence dictation.

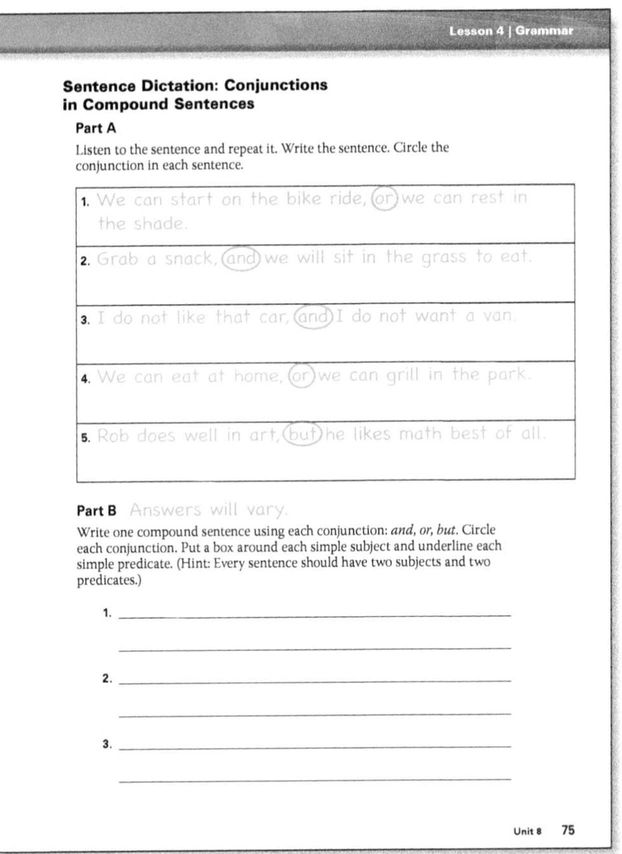
Lesson 4 | Grammar

Sentence Dictation: Conjunctions in Compound Sentences

Part A

Listen to the sentence and repeat it. Write the sentence. Circle the conjunction in each sentence.

1. We can start on the bike ride, (or) we can rest in the shade.
2. Grab a snack, (and) we will sit in the grass to eat.
3. I do not like that car, (and) I do not want a van.
4. We can eat at home, (or) we can grill in the park.
5. Rob does well in art, (but) he likes math best of all.

Part B Answers will vary.

Write one compound sentence using each conjunction: *and, or, but.* Circle each conjunction. Put a box around each simple subject and underline each simple predicate. (Hint: Every sentence should have two subjects and two predicates.)

1. ______
2. ______
3. ______

Unit 8 75

Dictation Procedure

- Teacher reads the sentence.
- Students repeat the sentence.
- Students write the sentence.
- Teacher reads the sentence a second time as students check their work.

Dictate the following sentences:

1. We can start on the bike ride, or we can rest in the shade.
2. Grab a snack, and we will sit in the grass to eat.
3. I do not like that car, and I do not want a van.
4. We can eat at home, or we can grill in the park.
5. Rob does well in art, but he like math best of all.

Have students circle the conjunctions in the sentences. Review the students' sentences to make sure they have been written correctly and the conjunctions have been circled.

Direct students to Part B on page 75 in their Student Books. For the second part of this activity, you will use the three coordinating conjunctions to write compound sentences. We have already worked with compound sentences; we just haven't given them a name. In the preceding unit, we learned about compound words. What is a compound word? (a word made of two shorter words joined together) Knowing what a compound word is will help you understand what a compound sentence is. A compound sentence is two sentences joined together to make one sentence. What is the name of those small words we use to join phrases or sentences together? (conjunctions)

Remember what each conjunction adds to the meaning of the sentence.

- When you want to combine two similar ideas, what conjunction should you use? (and)
- When you want to combine an idea with an alternative idea, what conjunction should you use? (or)
- When you want to contrast one idea with another, what conjunction should you use? (but)

One way to write a compound sentence is to start with two simple sentences that are related and then think of a way to combine them using a conjunction. Consider these two sentences:

I like many colors.

Green is my favorite.

How could I use a conjunction to combine these two ideas? I'm making a contrast between many colors (that I like) and the specific color green (which is my favorite). Because I want to contrast these two ideas, I will use the conjunction *but.* As I write my new sentence, I need to remember to put a comma before the conjunction.

Remind students that in a compound sentence, both sentences are complete and can stand alone. Write the new sentence on the board:

I like many colors, but green is my favorite.

Have students write three compound sentences, one using each conjunction: *and, or,* and *but.* Circulate to monitor student sentences and offer suggestions if students are struggling. Have volunteers read one of their sentences.

Reading

Objectives

- Read sentence phrases with fluency to support comprehension.
- Use critical thinking skills to respond to specific questions about a text.
- Interpret information presented in a diagram, and explain how the information contributes to an understanding of the text.
- Explain how an author uses reasons and evidence to support particular points in a text.
- Integrate information from two texts on the same topic.

Phrase It

Reading in phrases is an important step in becoming a proficient reader. Read the following phrases, pausing in between for students to create a mental picture.

The tiny bug . . . sucked blood . . . from my scalp . . . while I showered.

The tiny bug is the subject, and *sucked blood from my scalp while I showered* is the predicate.

For Phrase It, we scoop phrases using our pencil. When we scoop a phrase, we form an image in our heads. The next phrase we read may add to or change the image. This process is what makes up comprehension. Our mental picture of the tiny bug changes as soon as we read the first part of the predicate—*sucked blood*. It changes again when we read the second part of the predicate—*from my scalp*. It changes yet again when we read the third part of the predicate—*while I showered*. Imagining the small bug on a person's head while showering changed the feeling of the sentence. The addition of each phrase—not the addition of each word—changes our mental image. That's why we read in chunks.

Direct students to page 76 in their Student Books.

Model

Complete the first item as a model.

Guided Practice

Guide the completion of the next two.

Independent Practice

Read the remaining sentences and have students scoop the phrases. Review the answers as a class.

Note: There are various ways the sentences can be broken into phrases. Accept logical answers.

Base the number of modeled and guided examples on student ability and progress. Challenge them with independent practice when appropriate.

Lesson 4 | Reading

Phrase It

Read each phrase and scoop it with a pencil. As you read the phrase, form an image in your mind. Read the sentence with prosody.

1. Some cows will come to graze in the green grass by the barn.
2. I had grit and grime in my teeth from the dust and mud.
3. Who will win the top prize for the big fish?
4. If you drive out by the lake, then you will see the cranes.
5. Do you know if she pressed her green dress for the big day?
6. Should she read the words on the card to them?
7. I got more and more chilled as I sat by the lake.
8. First, they used thick bricks to make the base for the grill.
9. I had a dream about eating two tubs of green ice cream each day.
10. His grim look said he did not do well in the game.

76 Unit 8

Critical Understandings

Direction Words: Strategic Thinking poster

We will continue responding to prompts at the strategic thinking level. You will respond to prompts that include verbs such as *contrast, differentiate*, and *draw conclusions*. What level prompt will we study in this unit? (strategic thinking) At this level of comprehension, you will need to recall information, understand what the information means, and think strategically about new information. What is the base word of *strategic* and *strategically*? (strategy)

Direct students to pages 77 and 78 in their Student Books.

Let's preview some prompts that require strategic thinking about bugs. I'll read each prompt, and you repeat the key word in bold. Ready? Let's begin.

1. Use the text and diagram to **draw conclusions** about the ideal climate for chinch bugs. (draw conclusions)
2. **Differentiate** between a chinch bug and a bedbug. (differentiate)
3. **Draw conclusions** about how you would notice chinch bugs in the grass near your home. (draw conclusions)
4. **Contrast** conditions necessary for bedbugs and chinch bugs to progress from egg to adult. (contrast)
5. **Compare** these bugs: lice, bedbugs, and chinch bugs. (compare)

Lesson 4 | Reading

Critical Understandings

First, read the prompts at the bottom of the page to establish a purpose for reading. Next, read the passage. Finally, respond to the prompts.

Chinch Bugs

Some bugs have an appetite for grass. One such bug is the chinch bug. It is a pest that lives in sod. This pest is bad for grass. Why? When hot months come, chinch bugs drop eggs in the sod. The eggs hatch, and many of the small bugs live. These bugs kill grass. How? They attack grass stems and suck on them. The grass wilts, and this kills the grass.

1. Use the text and diagram to **draw conclusions** about the ideal climate for chinch bugs.
   Because chinch bugs feed on grass, the ideal climate would be warm and wet year-round.
2. **Differentiate** between a chinch bug and a bedbug.
   A chinch bug lives in sod and sucks on grass stems. A bedbug lives in blankets and mattresses and sucks on human blood.
3. **Draw conclusions** about how you would notice chinch bugs in the grass near your home.
   If there were chinch bugs in the grass, I would notice dead patches of grass or see bugs sucking on grass stems during warm weather.

Unit 8 77

Lesson 4 | Reading

Critical Understandings (*cont.*)

4. **Contrast** conditions necessary for bedbugs and chinch bugs to progress from egg to adult.
   Bedbugs need blood meals to grow from egg to adult. Chinch bugs need warm weather and grass to feed on.
5. **Compare** these bugs: lice, bedbugs, and chinch bugs.
   Lice, bedbugs, and chinch bugs are all pests because they feed on other things and are a nuisance.

78 Unit 8

Have students follow along as you read the text.

Note: While the lessons are written for a teacher read aloud, it is important that your students read as much and as often as they can. Assign readings that meet the needs of your students, based on your observations or data. This is a good opportunity to stretch students, but if they become frustrated, return to the read-aloud method.

Chinch Bugs

Some bugs have an appetite for grass. One such bug is the chinch bug. It is a pest that lives in sod. This pest is bad for grass. Why? When hot months come, chinch bugs drop eggs in the sod. The eggs hatch, and many of the small bugs live. These bugs kill grass. How? They attack grass stems and suck on them. The grass wilts, and this kills the grass.

Let's check our comprehension of this passage and the diagram by responding to some prompts that require strategic thinking. For each prompt, you will need to find evidence to support your answer. Remember, try turning the prompt into a question to help you decide how to respond.

Model

Read the first prompt aloud.

1. Use the text and diagram to **draw conclusions** about the ideal climate for chinch bugs.

I can change this prompt into a question to determine how I need to respond. The question would be, What is most likely the ideal climate for a chinch bug?

My first thought is to review the text to see if it contains information that will help with the answer. I see information about a cinch bug's favorite food, but nothing about climate. I will have to use my prior knowledge about climate to answer the question. From the text, I know that chinch bugs live where grass grows. So, I can ask myself, What does grass need to grow? With this knowledge, I should be able to infer the ideal climate for a chinch bug. Have students use their prior knowledge to answer the question. (Because chinch bugs feed on grass, the ideal climate would be warm and wet year-round.)

Guided Practice

Read the second prompt aloud.

2. **Differentiate** between a chinch bug and a bedbug.

I can change this prompt into a question to determine how best to respond. The question would be, What is the difference between a chinch bug and a bedbug?

Where should I first look for evidence to include in my response? (the text) Which text? ("Chinch Bugs" from this lesson and "Bugs Live" from Lesson 3.) Right. To answer this question, we need to make a text-to-text connection. Provide time for partners to gather information from both texts.

While students are working, write the sentence frames below on the board:

A chinch bug lives _____ *and sucks* _____.

A bedbug lives _____ *and sucks* _____.

Work with students to formulate their answer and record it in their Student Books on page 77.

I was once told that chinch bugs and bedbugs were the same thing! This text does not mention bedbugs. Does that mean that what I heard is not true? (no) Do we have enough information to answer our new question? (no) What will we have to do? (more research) If possible, offer extra points for students who do additional research and write an explanation.

Independent Practice

Have partners complete the remaining prompts. Review the answers as a class to ensure that students understand what each prompt is asking.

Note: Base the number of modeled and guided examples on student ability and progress. Challenge them with independent practice when appropriate.

Provide these alternative questions and sentence starters for those who need additional help.

3. How would you know there were chinch bugs in grass near your home?

   If there were chinch bugs in the grass, I would notice _____________________.

4. How are bedbugs and chinch bugs different in terms of what they need to grow from egg to adult?

   Bedbugs need ______________________________ to grow from egg to adult.
   Chinch bugs need ______________________________________.

5. How are lice, bedbugs, and chinch bugs similar?

   Lice, bedbugs, and chinch bugs are all ___________________________.

Lesson 5

Lesson Opener

Before the lesson, choose one of the following activities to write on the board or post on the *LANGUAGE! Live* Class Wall online.

- *Write compound sentences using each of the following conjunctions:* and, or, but.
- *Write sentences to draw conclusions about the following bugs based on their names: vampire moth, hickory-horned devil, killer bee.*
- *Write a sentence contrasting you and your best friend. How are you different?*

Vocabulary

Objectives

- Review key passage vocabulary.
- Identify metaphors in a text.

Recontextualize Passage Vocabulary

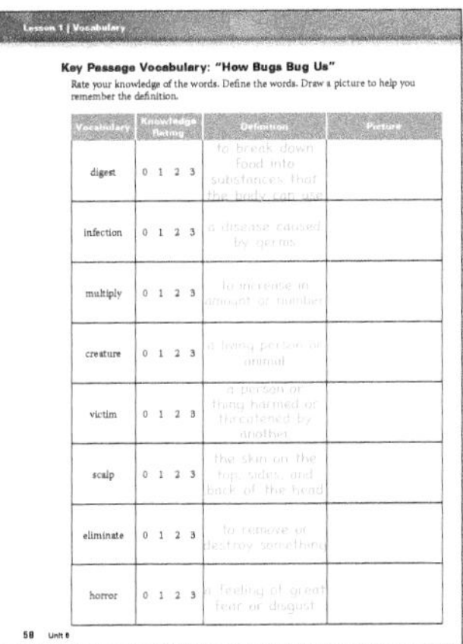

Lesson 1 | Vocabulary

Key Passage Vocabulary: "How Bugs Bug Us"

Rate your knowledge of the words. Define the words. Draw a picture to help you remember the definition.

Vocabulary	Knowledge Rating	Definition	Picture
digest	0 1 2 3	to break down food into substances that the body can use	
infection	0 1 2 3	a disease caused by germs	
multiply	0 1 2 3	to increase in amount or number	
creature	0 1 2 3	a living person or animal	
victim	0 1 2 3	a person or thing harmed or threatened by another	
scalp	0 1 2 3	the skin on the top, sides, and back of the head	
eliminate	0 1 2 3	to remove or destroy something	
horror	0 1 2 3	a feeling of great fear or disgust	

58 Unit 8

Direct students to page 58 in their Student Books.

Review the Key Passage Vocabulary from "How Bugs Bug Us."

- A person or thing harmed or threatened by another is a what? (a victim) If I am a thief and I steal from you, what are you? (the victim)
- To break down food into substances that the body can use is what? (to digest) If your body doesn't break down the food, you have no energy. So what is an important function if you want to have energy to make it through the day? (digestion)
- The skin on top, sides, and back of your head is the what? (scalp) Touch your *scalp* and say the word. (scalp)
- To increase in amount or number is to what? (multiply) Every time you read a book, what happens to your knowledge? (It multiplies.)
- A living person or an animal is a what? (a creature) A plant is living, but it isn't a *creature*. What does something have to be, to be a *creature*? (a person or an animal)
- A disease caused by germs is what? (an infection) Some *infections* have cures and some do not. If you want to avoid an *infection*, you need to avoid what? (germs)
- To remove or destroy something is to what? (eliminate it) I do not want bedbugs in my room. What can I do to *eliminate* them? (Answers will vary.)
- A feeling of great fear or disgust is what? (horror) I fear snakes, rats, and spiders. What do they cause me? (horror)

Metaphors

Direct students to "How Bugs Bug Us."

Review the metaphors from the text. Read the following metaphors aloud.

> In fact, your body is a zoo for bugs!
>
> Bacteria are a blanket covering your body.
>
> They are track stars that run from one person's head to another.
>
> They are hitchhikers catching a free ride to the next victim.

Direct students to "Bugs in Medicine."

Read the metaphor from the text aloud.

> But doctors realized that this use of the vampires of the bug world rarely helped patients, so the use of leeches stopped.

If students struggle understanding the metaphor, explain that the typical metaphor pattern is not used, but the sentence is saying that leeches *are* vampires, which fits the definition of a metaphor: comparing two things that are unrelated by saying that one this *is* something else.

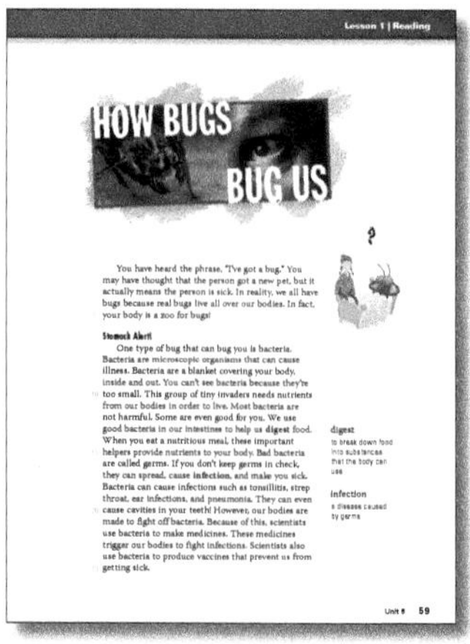

Lesson 1 | Reading

HOW BUGS BUG US

You have heard the phrase, "I've got a bug." You may have thought that the person got a new pet, but it actually means the person is sick. In reality, we all have bugs because real bugs live all over our bodies. In fact, your body is a zoo for bugs!

Stomach Alert

One type of bug that can bug you is bacteria. Bacteria are microscopic organisms that can cause illness. Bacteria are a blanket covering your body, inside and out. You can't see bacteria because they're too small. This group of tiny invaders needs nutrients from our bodies in order to live. Most bacteria are not harmful. Some are even good for you. We use good bacteria in our intestines to help us **digest** food. When you eat a nutritious meal, these important helpers provide nutrients to your body. Bad bacteria are called germs. If you don't keep germs in check, they can spread, cause **infection**, and make you sick. Bacteria can cause infections such as tonsillitis, strep throat, ear infections, and pneumonia. They can even cause cavities in your teeth! However, our bodies are made to fight off bacteria. Because of this, scientists use bacteria to make medicines. These medicines trigger our bodies to fight infections. Scientists also use bacteria to produce vaccines that prevent us from getting sick.

digest to break down food into substances that the body can use

infection a disease caused by germs

Unit 8 59

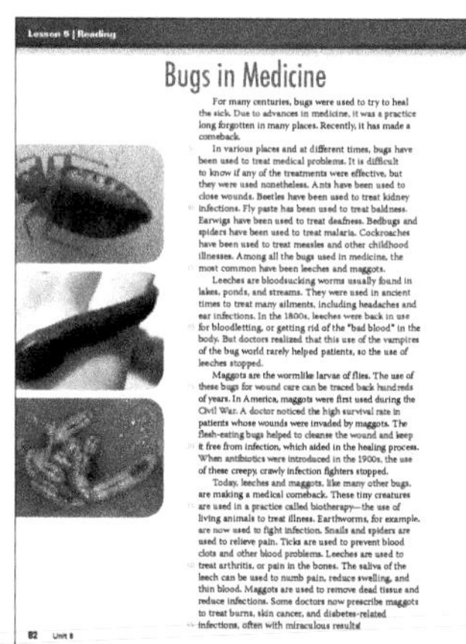

Lesson 5 | Reading

Bugs in Medicine

For many centuries, bugs were used to try to heal the sick. Due to advances in medicine, it was a practice long forgotten in many places. Recently, it has made a comeback.

In various places and at different times, bugs have been used to treat medical problems. It is difficult to know if any of the treatments were effective, but they were used nonetheless. Ants have been used to close wounds. Beetles have been used to treat kidney infections. Fly paste has been used to treat baldness. Earwigs have been used to treat deafness. Bedbugs and spiders have been used to treat malaria. Cockroaches have been used to treat measles and other childhood illnesses. Among all the bugs used in medicine, the most common have been leeches and maggots.

Leeches are bloodsucking worms usually found in lakes, ponds, and streams. They were used in ancient times to treat many ailments, including headaches and ear infections. In the 1800s, leeches were back in use for bloodletting, or getting rid of the "bad blood" in the body. But doctors realized that this use of the vampires of the bug world rarely helped patients, so the use of leeches stopped.

Maggots are the wormlike larvae of flies. The use of these bugs for wound care can be traced back hundreds of years. In America, maggots were first used during the Civil War. A doctor noticed the high survival rate in patients whose wounds were invaded by maggots. The flesh-eating bugs helped to cleanse the wound and keep it free from infection, which aided in the healing process. When antibiotics were introduced in the 1900s, the use of these creepy, crawly infection fighters stopped.

Today, leeches and maggots, like many other bugs, are making a medical comeback. These tiny creatures are used in a practice called biotherapy—the use of living animals to treat illness. Earthworms, for example, are now used to fight infection. Snails and spiders are used to relieve pain. Ticks are used to prevent blood clots and other blood problems. Leeches are used to treat arthritis, or pain in the bones. The saliva of the leech can be used to numb pain, reduce swelling, and thin blood. Maggots are used to remove dead tissue and reduce infections. Some doctors now prescribe maggots to treat burns, skin cancer, and diabetes-related infections, often with miraculous results!

82 Unit 8

Reading

Objectives

- Write questions or prompts about the passage to deepen comprehension.
- Respond orally to specific questions about a text.

Guided Reading of "How Bugs Bug Us": Ask and Answer Questions

I already pointed out that skilled readers preview the text for text features such as headings and graphics. Proficient readers also reread text slowly and carefully to gain understanding. They monitor their thinking while reading to be sure that each sentence and paragraph make sense. Good readers look for answers to Big Idea questions. In this unit we are answering the questions, Are bugs that live on our bodies harmful to us? and Can we prevent bugs from living on our bodies?

Good readers also ask themselves and others questions about their reading. Challenging questions require readers to combine what they already know with information in the text and charts or maps. Proficient readers understand that asking questions improves their comprehension. They ask themselves new questions after they hear others' questions.

Direction Words: Strategic Thinking poster

Direct students to the chart on page 16 in their Student Books or refer to the Strategic Thinking poster if you have it displayed.

We have been talking about how certain direction words require a specific response or answer. You will review this chart with a partner. Review the Chart Reading Procedure with students.

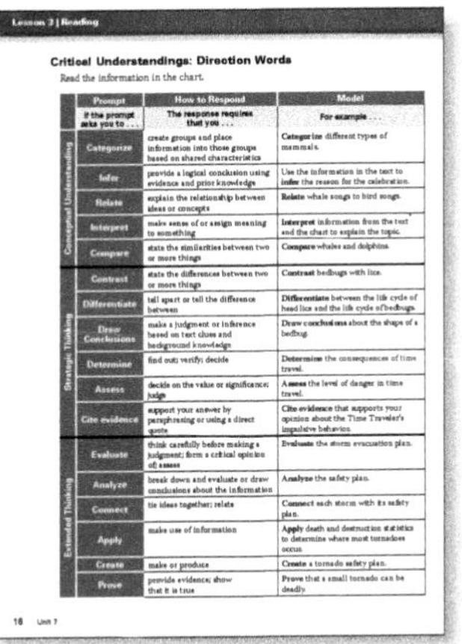

Lesson 3 | Reading

Critical Understandings: Direction Words

Read the information in the chart.

	Prompt	How to Respond	Model
	If the prompt asks you to . . .	The response requires that you . . .	For example . . .
Conceptual Understanding	Categorize	create groups and place information into those groups based on shared characteristics	**Categorize** different types of mammals.
	Infer	provide a logical conclusion using evidence and prior knowledge	Use the information in the text to **infer** the reason for the celebration.
	Relate	explain the relationship between ideas or concepts	**Relate** whale songs to bird songs.
	Interpret	make sense of or assign meaning to something	**Interpret** information from the text and the chart to explain the topic.
	Compare	state the similarities between two or more things	**Compare** whales and dolphins.
Strategic Thinking	Contrast	state the differences between two or more things	**Contrast** bedbugs with lice.
	Differentiate	tell apart or tell the difference between	**Differentiate** between the life cycle of head lice and the life cycle of bedbugs.
	Draw Conclusions	make a judgment or inference based on text clues and background knowledge	**Draw conclusions** about the shape of a bedbug.
	Determine	find out; verify; decide	**Determine** the consequences of time travel.
	Assess	decide on the value or significance; judge	**Assess** the level of danger in time travel.
	Cite evidence	support your answer by paraphrasing or using a direct quote	**Cite evidence** that supports your opinion about the Time Traveler's impulsive behavior.
Extended Thinking	Evaluate	think carefully before making a judgment; form a critical opinion of; assess	**Evaluate** the storm evacuation plan.
	Analyze	break down and evaluate or draw conclusions about the information	**Analyze** the safety plan.
	Connect	tie ideas together; relate	**Connect** each storm with its safety plan.
	Apply	make use of information	**Apply** death and destruction statistics to determine where most tornadoes occur.
	Create	make or produce	**Create** a tornado safety plan.
	Prove	provide evidence; show that it is true	**Prove** that a small tornado can be deadly.

16 Unit 7

Chart Reading Procedure

- Group students with partners or in triads.
- Have students count off as 1s or 2s attempting to give all students a chance to be a student leader (1). If working with triads, the third student becomes a 2.
- Student leaders (1s) read the left column (Prompt) in addition to managing the time and turn-taking if working with a triad.
- The 2s explain the middle column of the chart (How to Respond). If working in triads, 2s take turns explaining the middle column.
- The 1s read the model in the right column (Model), and 2s restate the model as a question.
- All students should follow along with their pencil eraser while others are explaining the chart.
- Students must work from left to right, top to bottom in order to benefit from this activity.

Have student groups or pairs complete the top half of the Strategic Thinking section of the Critical Understandings chart (from Contrast to Draw Conclusions) in this manner.

This time, when we read "How Bugs Bug Us" we will ask questions about the text. Doing this will help us understand what is important. We will also answer the questions that we ask, which should clear up any confusion we had during our first read.

Direct students to page 59 in their Student Books or have them tear out the extra copy of "How Bugs Bug Us" from the back of their book.

Lesson 1 | Reading

HOW BUGS BUG US

You have heard the phrase, "I've got a bug." You may have thought that the person got a new pet, but it actually means the person is sick. In reality, we all have bugs because real bugs live all over our bodies. In fact, your body is a zoo for bugs!

Stomach Alert!

One type of bug that can bug you is bacteria. Bacteria are microscopic organisms that can cause illness. Bacteria are a blanket covering your body, inside and out. You can't see bacteria because they're too small. This group of tiny invaders needs nutrients from our bodies in order to live. Most bacteria are not harmful. Some are even good for you. We use good bacteria in our intestines to help us **digest** food. When you eat a nutritious meal, these important helpers provide nutrients to your body. Bad bacteria are called germs. If you don't keep germs in check, they can spread, cause **infection**, and make you sick. Bacteria can cause infections such as tonsillitis, strep throat, ear infections, and pneumonia. They can even cause cavities in your teeth! However, our bodies are made to fight off bacteria. Because of this, scientists use bacteria to make medicines. These medicines trigger our bodies to fight infections. Scientists also use bacteria to produce vaccines that prevent us from getting sick.

digest
to break down food into substances that the body can use

infection
a disease caused by germs

Unit 8 59

Note: To minimize flipping back and forth between the pages, a copy of each text has been included in the back of the Student Books. Encourage students to tear this out and use it when working on activities that require the use of the text.

Let's do what good readers do and reread "How Bugs Bug Us" with our minds on asking and answering questions.

Remember what you do when you read. Your eyes need to track, or follow, the text while your pencil points to the words. While you're busy looking and pointing to text, your brain is busy looking for patterns and making meaning. While listening, be aware of questions that come to your mind and questions that you can ask others.

Note: While the lessons are written for a teacher read aloud, it is important that your students read as much and as often as they can. Assign readings that meet the needs of your students, based on your observations or data. This is a good opportunity to stretch students, but if they become frustrated, return to the read-aloud method.

Eyes ready? Pencil ready? Let's begin.

Read the introduction and first section, Stomach Alert!

You have heard the phrase, "I've got a bug." You may have thought that the person got a new pet, but it actually means the person is sick. In reality, we all have bugs because real bugs live all over our bodies. In fact, your body is a zoo for bugs!

Stomach Alert!

One type of bug that can bug you is bacteria. Bacteria are microscopic organisms that can cause illness. Bacteria are a blanket covering your body, inside and out. You can't see bacteria because they're too small. This group of tiny invaders needs nutrients from our bodies in order to live. Most bacteria are not harmful. Some are even good for you. We use good bacteria in our intestines to help us digest food. When you eat a nutritious meal, these important helpers provide nutrients to your body. Bad bacteria are called germs. If you don't keep germs in check, they can spread, cause infection, and make you sick. Bacteria can cause infections such as tonsillitis, strep throat, ear infections, and pneumonia. They can even cause cavities in your teeth! However, our bodies are made to fight off bacteria. Because of this, scientists use bacteria to make medicines. These medicines trigger our bodies to fight infections. Scientists also use bacteria to produce vaccines that prevent us from getting sick.

Direct students to page 79 in their Student Books. Think about the text. What questions do you still have or what should your peers have learned about bugs from this section?

- Choose one question word or prompt we have learned. Consider starting your question with *What.* If you want to challenge yourself to write a prompt, try using *Draw conclusions.*
- Write the question or prompt on the page. Be prepared to answer your question or prompt orally. Remember, questions require a question mark. Prompts require a period.

Ask and Answer Questions Answers will vary.

Reread "How Bugs Bug Us." After each section, write a question or prompt for your partner to answer using a question or direction word that you have learned. Try not to use the same word twice. Be prepared to answer your questions orally. Use the chart on page 16 to help you.

Introduction and Stomach Alert! *What?* *Draw conclusions*

1. ______________________________

Bugs in Your Bed? *How?* *Differentiate*

2. ______________________________

In Your Hair? *Where?* *Contrast*

3. ______________________________

Eyelash Horrors! *Who?* *Interpret*

4. ______________________________

Direct students back to the passage. Let's read the next section. Eyes ready? Pencil ready? Let's begin.

Read the next section, Bugs in Your Bed?

Bugs in Your Bed?

Dust mites are real bugs that live with you in your bedroom. They are often harmless but may cause an allergic reaction or trigger asthma. Dust mites multiply in pillows. If you use the same unwashed pillow every night for 10 years, half its weight would be from dust mites. Seven thousand microscopic dust mites fit on one dime. You can't see these tiny creatures, but they are there, feeding on dead skin. Dust mites don't bite and cannot spread diseases. They usually do not live on people. They are harmful only to people who become allergic to them. Their droppings cause allergies that make a lot of people sick. Do your eyes sometimes get red and itchy? Does this happen when you shake out the bedspread? Does it happen when you sweep the floor? Then you're a victim of dust mites!

Like dust mites, bedbugs are wingless bugs that would like to live in your bed. Bedbugs used to live in caves and suck the blood of bats. Today, bedbugs may try to sneak into your bed through tiny cracks, electrical outlets, and even your luggage. Thousands can infest a single bedroom looking for a blood bank! Bedbugs can hardly wait to drink blood in order to stay alive and breathe. They find their meal by sensing the carbon dioxide that you exhale. Before a bedbug bites, it injects an anticoagulant and an anesthetic. The anticoagulant is a substance that prevents your blood from clotting, which allows the pest to suck your blood for up to five minutes. An anesthetic numbs the area so that you don't wake up. These blood suckers leave you with a red raised bump similar to a mosquito bite. They can drink three times their weight in a single meal. You can get bitten 500 times in one night! So when your parents say "Sleep tight, and don't let the bedbugs bite," they mean it!

Direct students to page 79 in their Student Books.

- Choose a different question or direction word. Try using *How* or *Differentiate*.
- Write the question or prompt on the page. Be prepared to provide an answer orally.

Direct students back to the passage. Let's read the next section. Eyes ready? Pencil ready? Let's begin.

Read the next section, In Your Hair?

In Your Hair?

The next type of bug that can live on your body is lice. Head lice just love the skin under the hair on your head, called the scalp. There, they can hunker down and guzzle blood from the scalp for up to 30 days. These bugs lay eggs that can live in your hair for more than two weeks. Lice can spread quickly! They are track stars that run from one person's head to another. They spread when people work closely together in school classrooms and at work. If you get lice, special shampoo can help eliminate them.

Direct students to page 79 in their Student Books.

- Choose a different question or direction word. Try using *Where* or *Contrast*.
- Write the question or prompt on the page. Be prepared to provide an answer orally.

Direct students back to the passage. Let's read the next section. Eyes ready? Pencil ready? Let's begin.

Read the last section, Eyelash Horrors!

Eyelash Horrors!

The eyelash mite is the final type of bug that lives on our bodies. But don't worry; they're harmless. These tiny bugs cling to eyelashes with eight tiny legs. They live on sebum, a natural oil in skin and hair. The truth is, a lot of bugs love our skin and hair and spend their lives there. They are hitchhikers catching a free ride to the next victim. Seeing them through a microscope may cause horror, but the bugs are so tiny that we don't even know they are there. The bugs are a part of us whether they "bug" us or not.

Direct students to page 79 in their Student Books.

- Choose a different question or direction word. Try using *Who* or *Interpret*.
- Write the question or prompt on the page. Be prepared to provide an answer orally.

Share Questions or Prompts

Have partners read their questions or prompts to each other and answer them orally, correcting each other if needed. Each pair shares with another pair, then those four share with four others if time permits. Have volunteers share their questions or prompts and responses with the class.

Writing

Objectives

- Use critical and strategic thinking skills to write responses to prompts about the text.
- Support written answers with evidence from text.
- Interpret information presented in a diagram, and explain how the information contributes to an understanding of the text.

Answer It: Direction Words

Direction Words: Strategic Thinking poster

Direct students to page 80 in their Student Books. Now, we will respond to prompts about "How Bugs Bug Us" for more practice. Some of the prompts may be similar to the prompts you already responded to.

- Read each prompt. Identify and underline the direction word.
- Use the Critical Understandings chart on page 16 or the Strategic Thinking poster to review the type of information the prompts are asking for.
- Use text headings or other text features to locate the information you need to write a response.
- Reread the section to retrieve exact information to use as text evidence.

Lesson 5 | Writing

Answer It: Direction Words Answers will vary.

Underline the direction word in each prompt. Then respond to each prompt using a complete sentence. Provide line numbers for text evidence.

1. Use context and illustrations to interpret this quote from the text: "Your body is a zoo for bugs."
   "Your body is a zoo for bugs" is a metaphor that compares a person's body to a zoo. Since a zoo is a home for animals, the quotation means that a person's body is a home for bugs.
   Text Evidence: Line 4
2. Differentiate between good bacteria and bad bacteria.
   Good bacteria help us digest food in our intestines. Bad bacteria, or germs, can cause infection and make us sick or cause cavities in our teeth.
   Text Evidence: Lines 13, 17–20
3. Draw conclusions about how dust mites can affect us.
   Dust mites affect people who are allergic to their droppings. If you are allergic, dust mites can make you sneeze, have an asthma attack, or get itchy eyes.
   Text Evidence: Lines 36–38
4. Contrast bedbugs with dust mites.
   Bedbugs are different from dust mites because they bite anyone they can. Dust mites don't bite and only aggravate people with allergies. Bedbugs leave welts like a mosquito bite. Dust mites cause itchy eyes and may cause an asthma attack.
   Text Evidence: Lines 35–38, 47–48, 54–55

80 Unit 8

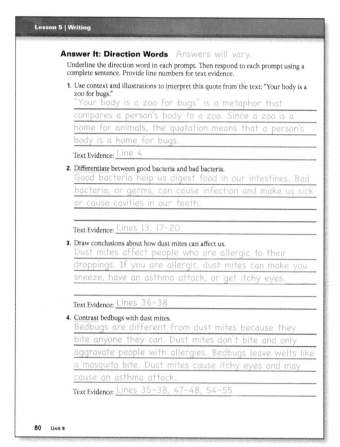

Remember, the Six Traits writing rubric is no longer a part of the activity. At this point, your sentence writing should be where it needs to be. We also changed the way we do text evidence. As we move into the higher level questions that require text evidence as well as information from outside sources, it is imperative to find evidence in the text. This way, you aren't just answering the questions with your opinion. However, because the questions are becoming more complex, you will no longer be expected to copy the evidence from the text. Instead, you may simply provide line numbers from the passage.

Model

Read the first prompt aloud.

1. Use context and illustrations to interpret this quote from the text: "Your body is a zoo for bugs."

- What is the direction word? (interpret)
- How do we respond to a prompt that asks us to interpret? (make sense of the quote by assigning meaning) In this case, the quote is a metaphor so we will need to read between the lines to determine the meaning of the metaphor.
- If I change this to a question, it would be, What does "Your body is a zoo for bugs" mean?

Let's use the quote as our sentence starter. While writing the quote in your Student Book, be sure to use quotation marks to show that the words come straight from the text. Write the sentence starters on the board:

"Your body is a zoo for bugs" is a metaphor that compares ______.
Since a zoo is a ______, the quotation means that a person's body is a ______.

Now it is time to finish our thought by combining what we know about metaphors with specific information from the text. What two things are being compared in this metaphor? (body and zoo) How can we use our understanding of this metaphor to answer the question? What does the metaphor mean?

Point out that the text evidence is in the line directly before the metaphor, in line 4.

Guided Practice

Read the next prompt aloud.

2. Differentiate between good bacteria and bad bacteria.

- What is the direction word in this prompt? (differentiate)
- How do we respond to a prompt that begins with *differentiate*? (tell apart or tell the difference between)
- If I change this to a question, it would be, What is the difference between good bacteria and bad bacteria?

Write the following sentence starters on the board:

Good bacteria help us ______. Bad bacteria, or ______, can cause ______.

- What do we need to do next? (Find evidence from the text that contrasts good and bad bacteria.) Have students complete the sentence starter and identify the line numbers of the text evidence.

Independent Practice

Have students find and use text evidence to answer the remaining prompts independently. Create a small group for students who need more assistance, using prompt 3 as additional guided practice. If students struggle to complete the Venn diagram in prompt 6, guide them as needed.

Note: Base the number of modeled and guided examples on student ability and progress. Challenge students with independent practice when appropriate.

Lesson 5 | Writing

Answer It: Direction Words (*cont.*)

5. Use information gained from the text and the illustration on page 55 to draw conclusions about how you could get lice.
I could get lice by working closely with someone who has lice. Because lice spread quickly, I could get lice by sharing hats, combs, brushes, or headbands.

Text Evidence: Lines 66–68

6. Compare and contrast dust mites and eyelash mites. Complete the Venn diagram, then use the diagram to compare and contrast the two types of bugs. Write your answer in complete sentences.

Dust Mites	Both	Eyelash Mites
live in pillows feed on dead skin live near your body cause allergies	harmless—don't bite microscopic don't spread disease	live on eyelashes feed on oil in skin and hair live on your body

Dust mites and eyelash mites are similar because they are both microscopic, harmless bugs. They don't bite, and they don't spread disease. Dust mites live in pillows, feed on dead skin, cause allergies, and live near your body. In contrast, eyelash mites live on eyelashes, feed on oils in skin, and live on your body.

Text Evidence: Lines 26–40, 70–79

Unit 8 81

Provide these alternative questions and sentence starters for those who need additional help.

3. How can dust mites affect us?

   Dust mites affect people __________.

4. How are bedbugs different from dust mites?

   Bedbugs are different from dust mites because __________.
   Dust mites __________.
   Bedbugs __________.
   Dust mites __________.

5. How could you get lice? Combine information from the reading and the illustration on page 55 to determine how you could get lice.

   I could get lice by __________.
   Because lice spread quickly, I could get lice by __________.

6. How are dust mites and eyelash mites similar? How are dust mites and eyelash mites different? Complete the Venn diagram, then use the diagram to answer the question in complete sentences.

   Dust mites and eyelash mites are similar because __________.
   Dust mites __________.
   In contrast, eyelash mites __________.

Reading

Objective

- Read texts on similar topics.

Secondary Text: "Bugs in Medicine"

Direct students to page 82 in their Student Books. We will read another text that gives us a different perspective on bugs. As we read, notice how this text makes you feel about bugs. Follow along as I read the text. Mark confusing paragraphs with a question mark and paragraphs that you understand with a check mark. Also, don't forget to draw a question mark over any words, phrases, or sentences you find confusing. Read the text.

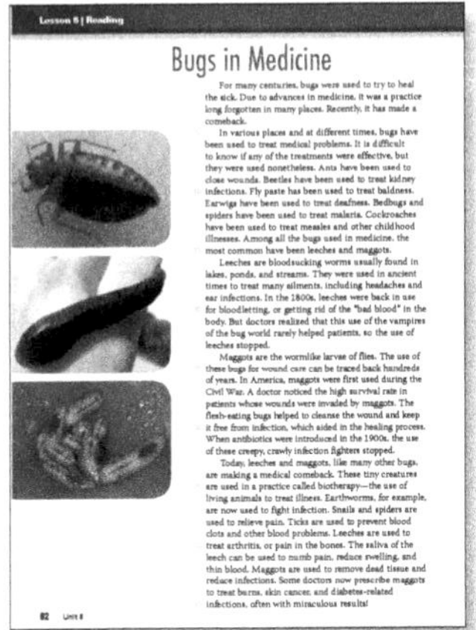

Lesson 5 | Reading

Bugs in Medicine

For many centuries, bugs were used to try to heal the sick. Due to advances in medicine, it was a practice long forgotten in many places. Recently, it has made a comeback.

In various places and at different times, bugs have been used to treat medical problems. It is difficult to know if any of the treatments were effective, but they were used nonetheless. Ants have been used to close wounds. Beetles have been used to treat kidney infections. Fly paste has been used to treat baldness. Earwigs have been used to treat deafness. Bedbugs and spiders have been used to treat malaria. Cockroaches have been used to treat measles and other childhood illnesses. Among all the bugs used in medicine, the most common have been leeches and maggots.

Leeches are bloodsucking worms usually found in lakes, ponds, and streams. They were used in ancient times to treat many ailments, including headaches and ear infections. In the 1800s, leeches were back in use for bloodletting, or getting rid of the "bad blood" in the body. But doctors realized that this use of the vampires of the bug world rarely helped patients, so the use of leeches stopped.

Maggots are the wormlike larvae of flies. The use of these bugs for wound care can be traced back hundreds of years. In America, maggots were first used during the Civil War. A doctor noticed the high survival rate in patients whose wounds were invaded by maggots. The flesh-eating bugs helped to cleanse the wound and keep it free from infection, which aided in the healing process. When antibiotics were introduced in the 1900s, the use of these creepy, crawly infection fighters stopped.

Today, leeches and maggots, like many other bugs, are making a medical comeback. These tiny creatures are used in a practice called biotherapy—the use of living animals to treat illness. Earthworms, for example, are now used to fight infection. Snails and spiders are used to relieve pain. Ticks are used to prevent blood clots and other blood problems. Leeches are used to treat arthritis, or pain in the bones. The saliva of the leech can be used to numb pain, reduce swelling, and thin blood. Maggots are used to remove dead tissue and reduce infections. Some doctors now prescribe maggots to treat burns, skin cancer, and diabetes-related infections, often with miraculous results!

82 Unit 8

Note: While the lessons are written for a teacher read aloud, it is important that your students read as much and as often as they can. Assign readings that meet the needs of your students, based on your observations or data. This is a good opportunity to stretch students, but if they become frustrated, return to the read-aloud method.

Bugs in Medicine

For many centuries, bugs were used to try to heal the sick. Due to advances in medicine, it was a practice long forgotten in many places. Recently, it has made a comeback.

In various places and at different times, bugs have been used to treat medical problems. It is difficult to know if any of the treatments were effective, but they were used nonetheless. Ants have been used to close wounds. Beetles have been used to treat kidney infections. Fly paste has been used to treat baldness. Earwigs have been used to treat deafness. Bedbugs and spiders have been used to treat malaria. Cockroaches have been used to treat measles and other childhood illnesses. Among all the bugs used in medicine, the most common have been leeches and maggots.

Leeches are bloodsucking worms usually found in lakes, ponds, and streams. They were used in ancient times to treat many ailments, including headaches and ear infections. In the 1800s, leeches were back in use for bloodletting, or getting rid of the "bad blood" in the body. But doctors realized that this use of the vampires of the bug world rarely helped patients, so the use of leeches stopped.

Maggots are the wormlike larvae of flies. The use of these bugs for wound care can be traced back hundreds of years. In America, maggots were first used during the Civil War. A doctor noticed the high survival rate in patients whose wounds were invaded by maggots. The flesh-eating bugs helped to cleanse the wound and keep it free from infection, which aided in the healing process. When antibiotics were introduced in the 1900s, the use of these creepy, crawly infection fighters stopped.

Today, leeches and maggots, like many other bugs, are making a medical comeback. These tiny creatures are used in a practice called biotherapy—the use of living animals to treat illness. Earthworms, for example, are now used to fight infection. Snails and spiders are used to relieve pain. Ticks are used to prevent blood clots and other blood problems. Leeches are used to treat arthritis, or pain in the bones. The saliva of the leech can be used to numb pain, reduce swelling, and thin blood. Maggots are used to remove dead tissue and reduce infections. Some doctors now prescribe maggots to treat burns, skin cancer, and diabetes-related infections, often with miraculous results!

Discuss the text if time permits. Have students imagine themselves as biotherapy patients and predict their response to the treatment.

Unit 8

Lesson 6

Lesson Opener

Before the lesson, choose one of the following activities to write on the board or post on the *LANGUAGE! Live* Class Wall online.

- *Turn to your Key Passage Vocabulary chart. Complete your drawings and add information to definitions as needed.*
- *Use the word* infection *in a sentence.*
- *Write two sentences with a possessive noun and a verb phrase in each.*

Writing

Objectives

- Know spelling-sound correspondences for the voiced digraph /th/ as in *that*.
- Know spelling-sound correspondences for words in the *-all* word family.
- Know spelling-sound correspondences for vowel team /ou/, spelled *ow*.
- Know spelling-sound correspondences for *r*-controlled consonant blends.

Spelling Words

Use this spelling activity to practice or assess the unit's spelling patterns students have learned online.

Direct student to Part A on page 83 in their Student Books. Read the instructions and remind students of the procedure for spelling. Use the spelling reminders to help struggling students.

1. small; Her feet are very small.
2. those; How much are those tickets?
3. brown; I wore my brown hat.
4. crab; The crab crawled on the sand.
5. bow; He took a bow after he sang.
6. dress; That is my favorite dress.
7. tall; My dad is so tall.
8. this; May I have this cookie?
9. now; I need to go home now.
10. grade; I hope I get a good grade on my test.

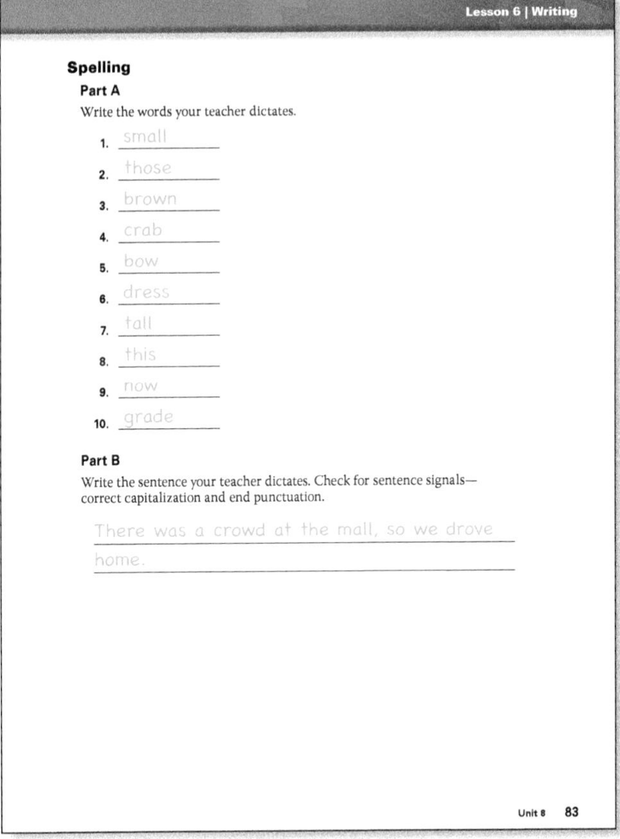
Lesson 6 | Writing

Spelling

Part A

Write the words your teacher dictates.

1. small
2. those
3. brown
4. crab
5. bow
6. dress
7. tall
8. this
9. now
10. grade

Part B

Write the sentence your teacher dictates. Check for sentence signals—correct capitalization and end punctuation.

There was a crowd at the mall, so we drove home.

Unit 8 83

Direct student to Part B on page 83 in their Student Books. Read the instructions and remind students of the procedure for sentence dictation.

There was a crowd at the mall, so we drove home.

Spelling Words Procedure

- Teacher reads the word.
- Students repeat the word.
- Teacher reads the sentence.
- Students write the word.
- Teacher reads the word a second time as students check their work.

Sentence Dictation Procedure

- Teacher reads the sentence.
- Students repeat the sentence.
- Students write the sentence.
- Teacher reads the sentence a second time as students check their work.

Spelling Reminders

The *-all* Word Family
A common word ending is *-a* followed by *-ll.* The *all* combination is pronounced /awl/.

The *ou* Vowel Team
The phoneme /ou/ is spelled *-ow* at the ends of words and often before *-n.* Remember, the two letters spell just one sound. It's a slider vowel.

Consonant *-r* Blends
You know that a blend is two consonant sounds in the same syllable. Blends with *r* are tricky: the /r/ sound can get lost. There are quite a few consonant-*r* blends: *br, cr, dr, fr, gr, pr,* and *tr.* Remember to listen carefully for all the sounds in a word.

Vocabulary

Objectives

- Use context to determine the meaning of words in text.
- Demonstrate an understanding of common homophones.

Define It

Direct students to page 84 in their Student Books.

To define words we need to understand the words' categories and attributes.

Categories are broad groups. Attributes are things like size, shape, color, texture, and function.

Lesson 6 | Vocabulary

Define It

Determine the category and attributes of each word. Then write the definition.

Word		Category		Attributes
bacteria	=	bug	+	live on/in our bodies; cause infection and illness; too small to see; most bacteria aren't harmful; help digest food; used in medicines to prevent sickness

Definition: Bacteria are invisible bugs on our bodies that can cause infection or help us digest food or prevent sickness.

Word		Category		Attributes
intestines	=	body part	+	help with digestion; where good bacteria live

Definition: Intestines are a body part used for digestion of food where good bacteria live.

Word		Category		Attributes
lice	=	insect	+	wingless; spread disease; feed on skin and blood; inhabit scalp; attach to hair; pale beige to dark gray; egg called a nit

Definition: Lice are wingless insects that attach to hair and feed on skin and blood.

Word		Category		Attributes

Definition:

84 Unit 8

Model

Direct students to the second paragraph of "How Bugs Bug Us" and have them find the word *bacteria*. We may not know what *bacteria* means, but we can look at the context around the word to determine its category and attributes. Because the text says that bacteria are a type of bug that bugs us, I know that *bacteria* fits into the category *bugs*. Bacteria are bugs.

Now I will read the entire paragraph to see if I can find some attributes of bacteria. Because the text is about bugs on our bodies, I know where bacteria live. It also says that they cause infection and illness, that they are too small to see, that most bacteria aren't harmful, that they help digest food, and that they are used in medicines to prevent sickness.

These are all attributes of bacteria. I didn't have to know anything about bacteria; I just had to read closely. Now that I have my category and attributes, I can write a definition. Write the definition on the board and read it aloud. *Bacteria are invisible bugs on our bodies that can cause infection or help us digest food or prevent sickness.* Have students write the definition in their Student Books.

Guided and Independent Practice

Dictionaries

Repeat the process for the second word, allowing students to provide the category, attributes, and definition for you. Then, have partners complete the activity. Explain that they may choose and define any unknown word from the passage for the last item. Have partners use a dictionary to verify their definitions and make corrections as needed.

> **Note:** Base the number of modeled and guided examples on student ability and progress. Challenge them with independent practice when appropriate.

Homophones

Homophones are words that sound the same but have different meanings and different spellings.

Words that sound the same but have different meanings and different spellings are called what? (homophones)

Write the following sets of homophones on the board and have students tell you what each word means. Correct as needed. Use the various meanings in sentences.

two, too, to	*there, their, they're*
write, right	*red, read*
won, one	*for, four*
plain, plane	

Direct students to page 85 in their Student Books.

Model

Let's talk about some words from "How Bugs Bug Us" that have homophones. *Pain* is when something hurts. Write *pain* on the board.

There is another word that sounds exactly the same, but it is spelled differently. Write *pane* on the board. This kind of pane is the glass in a window. Words that sound the same but have different meanings and different spellings are called what? (homophones)

Guided Practice

The next word is *know.* To know something is to understand it. Can you think of a different word that has the same pronunciation? (no) Write *know* and *no* on the board.

Know and *no* are what? (homophones)

Lesson 6 | Vocabulary

Homophones

Homophones are words that sound the same but have different meanings and different spellings. Choose the correct homophones to complete the sentences.

1. pain: hurting — pane: piece of glass
   The saliva of a leech can be used to numb __pain__.
2. no: not any; don't agree — know: to understand something
   It is difficult to __know__ if the treatments were effective.
3. hair: thin strand that grows — hare: rabbit
   I love nice clean __hair__.
4. real: actual — reel: a tool for winding fishing line
   There are __real__ bugs that live all over your body.
5. sea: a body of salt water — see: to view with your eyes
   You can't __see__ bacteria.
6. heal: to get well — heel: a part of the foot
   Bugs have been used to __heal__ the sick.
7. aunts: sisters of your mom or dad — ants: small insects
   __Ants__ bit my foot when I stepped on the mound.
8. eight: the number 8 — ate: past tense of the verb *eat*
   Mites cling to your eyelashes with __eight__ tiny legs.

Unit 8 85

Independent Practice

Read aloud each remaining homophone and meaning. Then read the sentence frame. Have students choose the correct spelling and write it on the line in their Student Books.

Writing

Objective

- Demonstrate an understanding of the conventions of English by editing writing for punctuation, capitalization, spelling, and word order.

Masterpiece Sentences

Masterpiece Sentences poster

We have worked on all six stages of the Masterpiece Sentences strategy. Direct students to page 86 in their Student Books. Review the Masterpiece Sentence stages. Look at the Masterpiece Sentences chart and you will see that the first five stages have been completed for you. Notice the canvas has been prepared with a kernel sentence: Bugs ate the leaves.

Have students identify the subject, predicate, and direct object. Then, read the Process, Questions to Answer, and Examples for Stages 2–5.

The predicate painters have been provided, which is part of Stage 2, and they have been upgraded, a part of Stage 5. The subject painters have also been provided and a few of them upgraded—Stages 4 and 5.

Use all of the components to create your final sentence. You should focus on two things: sensible word order and proper punctuation. Also, make sure your spelling is accurate.

After you finish writing your sentence, share your sentence with your partner. Check each other's sentences to make sure they are "polished."

Write the final version of your sentence in the Example column for Stage 6. Have volunteers share their sentences with the class if time permits.

Masterpiece Sentences: Stage 6

Use the provided sentence elements to write a polished sentence in the Stage 6 Examples box.

Stage	Process	Questions to Answer	Examples
Stage 1: Prepare Your Canvas	Choose (identify) a noun for the subject. Choose (identify) a past tense verb for the predicate.	Subject: Who or what did it? Predicate: What did he/she/it/they do? Direct Object: What did he/she/it/they do it to?	Bugs ate the leaves.
Stage 2: Paint Your Predicate	Tell more about what happened.	When? Where? How?	this summer on the blueberry bush completely
Stage 3: Move the Predicate Painters	Move the Predicate Painters to create a different sentence structure.		This summer, bugs completely ate the leaves on the blueberry bush.
Stage 4: Paint Your Subject	Tell more about the subject.	Which one? What kind? How many?	with an appetite hungry many
Stage 5: Paint Your Words	Select words or phrases in the sentence and replace them with more descriptive words or phrases.		~~this summer~~—by the end of summer; ~~ate~~—devoured; ~~many~~—a horde; ~~hungry~~—ravenous; with an insatiable appetite
Stage 6: Finishing Touches	Move sentence parts, check spelling, and check punctuation.		By the end of summer, a horde of ravenous bugs with an insatiable appetite had completely devoured the leaves on the blueberry bush.

Lesson 6 | Writing

86 Unit 8

Reading

Objectives

- Reread a text for key information.
- Take notes of key information in a text.
- Demonstrate an understanding of point of view.
- Identify the point of view in a text.

Guided Reading: "Bugs in Medicine"

Direct students to Part A on page 94 in their Student Books and read the prompt aloud.

> Bugs impact our lives in significantly different ways. Write a paragraph contrasting the beneficial uses and harmful effects of bugs.

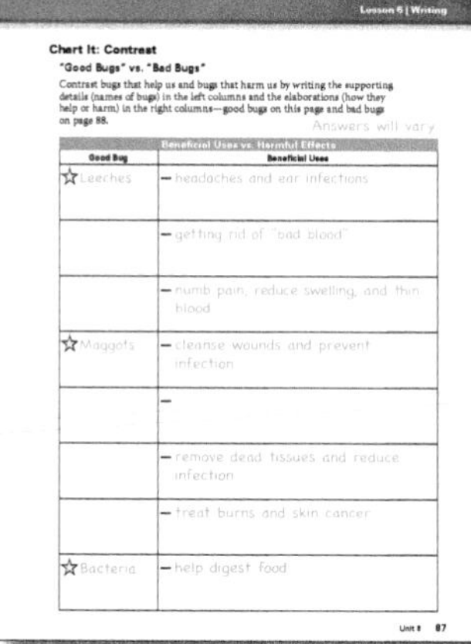

Explain that they will need to use both texts ("How Bugs Bug Us" and "Bugs in Medicine") to respond to the prompt. Then, direct them to page 87 to review the Chart It template they will use as they read.

Direct students to page 82 in their Student Books or have them tear out the extra copy of "Bugs in Medicine" from the back of their book.

> **Note:** To minimize flipping back and forth between the pages, a copy of each text has been included in the back of the Student Books. Encourage students to tear this out and use it when working on activities that require the use of the text.

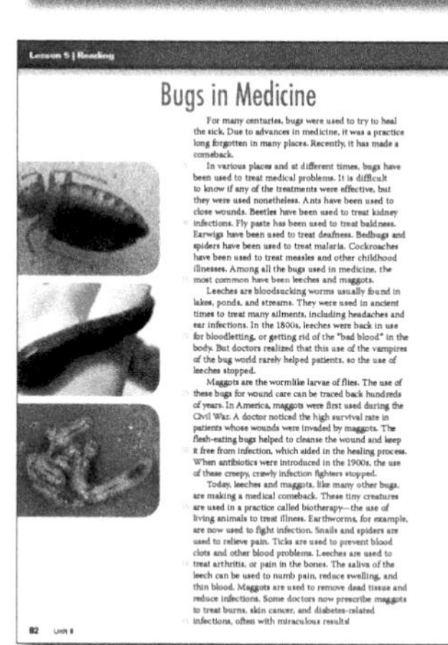

As we reread "Bugs in Medicine," our focus will be on the beneficial uses of bugs. This is what you need to look for as you read. Finding the beneficial uses of bugs will help you with your writing assignment.

This reading may also answer any questions you had when we read the text in the preceding lesson. If not, we will stop to answer your questions, then clear up any remaining confusion when we finish.

Now, follow along with your pencil as I read.

Read the title and the first two paragraphs.

Note: While the lessons are written for a teacher read aloud, it is important that your students read as much and as often as they can. Assign readings that meet the needs of your students, based on your observations or data. This is a good opportunity to stretch students, but if they become frustrated, return to the read-aloud method.

Bugs in Medicine

For many centuries, bugs were used to try to heal the sick. Due to advances in medicine, it was a practice long forgotten in many places. Recently, it has made a comeback.

In various places and at different times, bugs have been used to treat medical problems. It is difficult to know if any of the treatments were effective, but they were used nonetheless. Ants have been used to close wounds. Beetles have been used to treat kidney infections. Fly paste has been used to treat baldness. Earwigs have been used to treat deafness. Bedbugs and spiders have been used to treat malaria. Cockroaches have been used to treat measles and other childhood illnesses. Among all the bugs used in medicine, the most common have been leeches and maggots.

The second paragraph mentions many different bugs but offers very few details. Let's continue reading and see if we can find more in-depth information about specific bugs and their use in medicine.

Read the next paragraph, then pause to discuss.

Leeches are bloodsucking worms usually found in lakes, ponds, and streams. They were used in ancient times to treat many ailments, including headaches and ear infections. In the 1800s, leeches were back in use for bloodletting, or getting rid of the "bad blood" in the body. But doctors realized that this use of the vampires of the bug world rarely helped patients, so the use of leeches stopped.

What is the focus of this paragraph? (how leeches were used to treat people) What are some ways leeches have been used? (Leeches have been used to treat headaches and ear infections. They have also been used to get rid of "bad blood.") This is something we need to make note of.

Lesson 6 | Writing

Chart It: Contrast

"Good Bugs" vs. "Bad Bugs"

Contrast bugs that help us and bugs that harm us by writing the supporting details (names of bugs) in the left columns and the elaborations (how they help or harm) in the right columns—good bugs on this page and bad bugs on page 88.

Answers will vary.

Beneficial Uses vs. Harmful Effects	
Good Bug	**Beneficial Uses**
☆Leeches	– headaches and ear infections
	– getting rid of "bad blood"
	– numb pain, reduce swelling, and thin blood
☆Maggots	– cleanse wounds and prevent infection
	–
	– remove dead tissues and reduce infection
	– treat burns and skin cancer
☆Bacteria	– help digest food

Unit 8 87

Lesson 6 | Writing

Chart It: Contrast (*cont.*)

Beneficial Uses vs. Harmful Effects	
Bad Bug	**Harmful Effects**
☆Bacteria	– bad bacteria (germs): spread, cause illnesses
	–
☆Dust Mites	– cause allergic reactions, asthma
	– live in old pillows
☆Bedbugs	– bite leaves a red raised bump; someone can be bitten up to 500 times in a night
	– live in blankets and mattresses
☆Lice	– live on scalp up to 30 days
	– spread quickly; run from person to person
	– need special shampoo to kill them

88 Unit 8

Direct students to the Chart It template on pages 87 and 88 and have them write the information about leeches in the chart. If students struggle to take notes independently, guide them in the process.

Let's write *leeches* by the star in the Good Bug column and make a few notes about their medicinal uses. Give students time to do so, or guide them to do so as needed. What other bug, along with leeches was most commonly used? (maggots) Let's write *maggots* by the next star in the Good Bug column, and then see what we learn about maggots in the next paragraph.

Direct students back to the passage and have them find their place in the text.

Read the paragraph beginning on line 24, then stop to discuss.

Maggots are the wormlike larvae of flies. The use of these bugs for wound care can be traced back hundreds of years. In America, maggots were first used during the Civil War. A doctor noticed the high survival rate in patients whose wounds were invaded by maggots. The flesh-eating bugs helped to cleanse the wound and keep it free from infection, which aided in the healing process. When antibiotics were introduced in the 1900s, the use of these creepy, crawly infection fighters stopped.

Did we learn more about the use of maggots in this paragraph? (yes) I predicted that we would learn more about maggots in this paragraph based on the last sentence of the second paragraph: "Among all the bugs used in medicine, the most common have been leeches and maggots." Engaged readers look for clues and anticipate information. Have students record several phrases that tell how maggots were used in the chart.

Direct students back to the passage and have them find their place in the text.

Read the final paragraph, then stop to discuss.

> Today, leeches and maggots, like many other bugs, are making a medical comeback. These tiny creatures are used in a practice called biotherapy—the use of living animals to treat illness. Earthworms, for example, are now used to fight infection. Snails and spiders are used to relieve pain. Ticks are used to prevent blood clots and other blood problems. Leeches are used to treat arthritis, or pain in the bones. The saliva of the leech can be used to numb pain, reduce swelling, and thin blood. Maggots are used to remove dead tissue and reduce infections. Some doctors now prescribe maggots to treat burns, skin cancer, and diabetes-related infections, often with miraculous results!

What is the use of living animals to treat illness called? (biotherapy) Think about that word for a minute and you'll probably find some clues to its meaning. *Bio* means "living" or "life" and *therapy* means "a course of treatment." Can you imagine being treated with maggots or leeches? Under both *leeches* and *maggots*, have students add a few notes regarding contemporary uses of these bugs. If your focus is on note-taking, have students add other good bugs mentioned in the text to the chart.

Point of View

Let's think for a minute about the author's point of view in this passage. Direct students to page 89 in their Student Books.

First Person

Sometimes an author uses the words *I* and *me* in reference to himself or herself. Look at the chart. You'll see that when authors do this, they are writing in what is known as first-person point of view.

Second Person

When the author speaks directly to the audience with the pronouns *you* and *yours*, he or she is using second-person point of view. When does the narrator typically use second person? (when he or she is writing to explain something to someone)

Third Person

Look at the chart. When an author is writing about a person, place, thing, or idea, what pronouns are typically used? (he, she, they) Informational or expository text is usually written in third person. This point of view keeps the reader's attention on the information, not on the author. It presents the information in a clear and objective manner.

In Unit 6 we read the letter to the congressman that was written in first person. Writers use first person when they want to be personal and persuasive. The author of the letter to the congressman wrote in first person to make her experiences and frustrations more emotional.

Model

Read the first passage aloud and point out clues that help you determine the point of view. Discuss the answer and have students write it on the page in their Student Books.

Guided Practice

Read the second passage aloud and have students identify clues that help them determine the point of view. Have students write the answer on the page.

Independent Practice

Read each remaining passage aloud and have students determine its point of view independently. Review the answers as a class.

Note: Base the number of modeled and guided examples on student ability and progress. Challenge them with independent practice when appropriate.

Point of View

The position of the author or narrator in relation to other people and events in a story or text is called **point of view**. Point of view can be first person, second person, or third person.

Person	Pronoun Forms				Used . . .
first person	I me mine my	we us our, ours			when author is writing about himself or herself.
second person	you your yours				when author is writing to explain something to someone.
third person	she her hers	he him his	it it its	they them their theirs	when author is writing about a person, place, thing, or idea.

Read each passage and determine if it is written in the first person, second person, or third person. Write the answer on the line.

1. Yesterday, Carlos and I were hiding in the closet. I heard footsteps and my heart started pounding. I could tell Carlos heard them too because he looked nervous. I hoped she wouldn't open the door. The footsteps got quieter and I began to calm down. "She didn't find us. Let's get out of here," I said.

   first person

2. "This is too shallow," said Meg. She glanced around the swamp. She had never seen the water this low. It made her feel sad. Todd was worried too. He stared at the wood duck digging for food with its beak. Its ducklings were paddling close behind. "It is almost completely drained. The animals will not survive without more water."

   third person

Point of View (*cont.*)

3. Monarch butterflies are orange and black. Their wings are often referred to as a thing of beauty. Each year, monarchs migrate from the north to Mexico. This great migration is amazing to see. Thousands of butterflies make the journey from the cold climates of the north to the warmer climate of Mexico. Butterfly enthusiasts often make the journey as well, occupying many of Mexico's resorts during this time of year.

   third person

4. The rain forest is fascinating. You should spend some time visiting one if you haven't already. There are exotic animals and plants, as well as other amazing elements of nature for you to see. You can be inside the canopy and not feel a single drop of rain when it is raining cats and dogs. But make sure you take an umbrella.

   second person

5. As citizens of the world, each of us is responsible for the health of our planet. Our choices and our actions contribute to the well being or deterioration of the environment. It's our earth, the only one we have. If we don't care about the environment, who will?

   first person

6. Have you ever thought about how your choices affect the earth's well being and how you can minimize the impact you and your family make on the environment? From the cars you drive to the products you consume, every choice you make on a daily basis has a consequence for the environment. It is up to you to make the right choices.

   second person

Unit 8 Lesson 7

Lesson Opener

Before the lesson, choose one of the following activities to write on the board or post on the *LANGUAGE! Live* Class Wall online.

- *Tell three ways bugs have been used in medicine.*
- *Contrast leeches and maggots. How are they different?*
- *Compare leeches and maggots. How are they similar?*

Reading

Objectives

- Read with purpose and understanding.
- Demonstrate comprehension of text by answering questions.
- Identify and explain explicit details from text.
- Identify metaphors in a text.

Guided Highlighting of "How Bugs Bug Us"

Green, yellow, and pink highlighters or colored pencils

We have been working diligently to become great readers.

There are a lot of good reasons to become a better reader. Skilled readers can identify the author's purpose, or reason for writing a text. They can then make judgments about the author's point of view by assessing his or her claims, reasoning, and evidence. Proficient readers can compare two ideas or concepts and tell how they are alike. They can also interpret figurative language, or language that does not mean exactly what it says.

Let's do what skilled readers do and reread "How Bugs Bug Us."

Have students get out a colored pencil or a highlighter.

Direct students to page 91 in their Student Books. We will review the text features of nonfiction, or expository text. Please use your writing utensil to mark the text according to my instructions.

- Draw a rectangle around the title, "How Bugs Bug Us."
- Circle the headings.

Listen and mark each bold vocabulary word as I read it aloud. I will pause after every word to give you time to process whether you know the word and its meaning. We will review your ratings from Lesson 1 after we finish.

Lesson 7 | Reading

Guided Highlighting

Read the text and complete the tasks.

How Bugs Bug Us

You have heard the phrase, "I've got a bug." You may have thought that the person got a new pet, but it actually means the person is sick. In reality, we all have bugs because real bugs live all over our bodies. In fact, your body is a zoo for bugs!

Stomach Alert!

One type of bug that can bug you is bacteria. Bacteria are microscopic organisms that can cause illness. Bacteria are a blanket covering your body, inside and out. You can't see bacteria because they're too small. This group of tiny invaders needs nutrients from our bodies in order to live. Most bacteria are not harmful. Some are even good for you. We use good bacteria in our intestines to help us **digest** food. When you eat a nutritious meal, these important helpers provide nutrients to your body. Bad bacteria are called germs. If you don't keep germs in check, they can spread, cause **infection**, and make you sick. Bacteria can cause infections such as tonsillitis, strep throat, ear infections, and pneumonia. They can even cause cavities in your teeth! However, our bodies are made to fight off bacteria. Because of this, scientists use bacteria to make medicines. These medicines trigger our bodies to fight infections. Scientists also use bacteria to produce vaccines that prevent us from getting sick.

- **Rewrite the metaphor in line 6 as a simile with the words *like* or *as*. Circle the two nouns being compared.**

  Bacteria are like a blanket covering your body, inside and out.

Unit 8 91

- digest—*Digest* means "to break down food into substances that the body can use." Say *digest.* (digest) Good bacteria help us *digest* our food.
- infection—An *infection* is a disease caused by germs. Say *infection.* (infection) An *infection* caused by bacteria requires an antibiotic treatment.
- multiply—*Multiply* means "to increase in amount or number." Say *multiply.* (multiply) If you wash your hands with hot soap and water, germs cannot *multiply.*
- creatures—*Creatures* are living persons or animals. In other words, a *creature* is anything that lives and is not a plant. Say *creatures.* (creatures) A bedbug is an annoying *creature.*
- victim—A *victim* is a person or thing harmed or threatened by another. Say *victim.* (victim) The *victim* of the car crash was in the hospital for several weeks.
- scalp—*Scalp* is the skin on the top, sides, and back of your head. Say *scalp.* (scalp) Touch your *scalp.* Some bald men wear a hat to cover their *scalps.*
- eliminate—*Eliminate* means "to remove or destroy something." Say *eliminate.* (eliminate) Exterminators *eliminate* bugs.
- horror—*Horror* is a feeling of great fear or disgust. Say *horror.* (horror) I felt *horror* during the last scene of the scary movie.

Talk with your partner about any vocabulary word that is still confusing for you to read or understand. Share your ratings from Lesson 1. Were you honest about your word knowledge? Now is the time to do something about it!

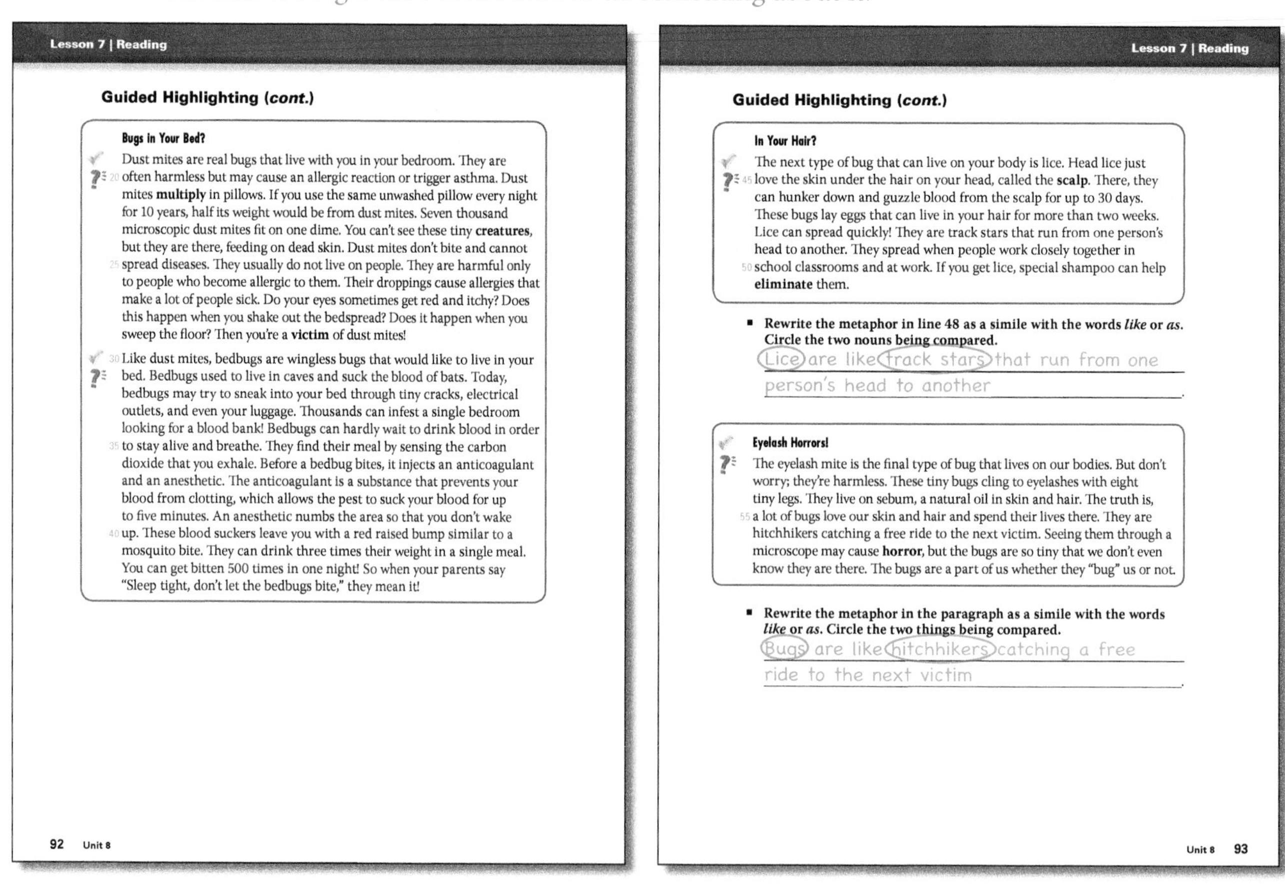
Lesson 7 | Reading

Guided Highlighting (*cont.*)

Bugs in Your Bed?

Dust mites are real bugs that live with you in your bedroom. They are often harmless but may cause an allergic reaction or trigger asthma. Dust mites **multiply** in pillows. If you use the same unwashed pillow every night for 10 years, half its weight would be from dust mites. Seven thousand microscopic dust mites fit on one dime. You can't see these tiny **creatures**, but they are there, feeding on dead skin. Dust mites don't bite and cannot spread diseases. They usually do not live on people. They are harmful only to people who become allergic to them. Their droppings cause allergies that make a lot of people sick. Do your eyes sometimes get red and itchy? Does this happen when you shake out the bedspread? Does it happen when you sweep the floor? Then you're a **victim** of dust mites!

Like dust mites, bedbugs are wingless bugs that would like to live in your bed. Bedbugs used to live in caves and suck the blood of bats. Today, bedbugs may try to sneak into your bed through tiny cracks, electrical outlets, and even your luggage. Thousands can infest a single bedroom looking for a blood bank! Bedbugs can hardly wait to drink blood in order to stay alive and breathe. They find their meal by sensing the carbon dioxide that you exhale. Before a bedbug bites, it injects an anticoagulant and an anesthetic. The anticoagulant is a substance that prevents your blood from clotting, which allows the pest to suck your blood for up to five minutes. An anesthetic numbs the area so that you don't wake up. These blood suckers leave you with a red raised bump similar to a mosquito bite. They can drink three times their weight in a single meal. You can get bitten 500 times in one night! So when your parents say "Sleep tight, don't let the bedbugs bite," they mean it!

92 Unit 8

Lesson 7 | Reading

Guided Highlighting (*cont.*)

In Your Hair?

The next type of bug that can live on your body is lice. Head lice just love the skin under the hair on your head, called the **scalp**. There, they can hunker down and guzzle blood from the scalp for up to 30 days. These bugs lay eggs that can live in your hair for more than two weeks. Lice can spread quickly! They are track stars that run from one person's head to another. They spread when people work closely together in school classrooms and at work. If you get lice, special shampoo can help **eliminate** them.

- **Rewrite the metaphor in line 48 as a simile with the words *like* or *as*. Circle the two nouns being compared.**

Lice are like track stars that run from one person's head to another.

Eyelash Horrors!

The eyelash mite is the final type of bug that lives on our bodies. But don't worry; they're harmless. These tiny bugs cling to eyelashes with eight tiny legs. They live on sebum, a natural oil in skin and hair. The truth is, a lot of bugs love our skin and hair and spend their lives there. They are hitchhikers catching a free ride to the next victim. Seeing them through a microscope may cause **horror**, but the bugs are so tiny that we don't even know they are there. The bugs are a part of us whether they "bug" us or not.

- **Rewrite the metaphor in the paragraph as a simile with the words *like* or *as*. Circle the two things being compared.**

Bugs are like hitchhikers catching a free ride to the next victim.

Unit 8 93

It's time to reread the text the way proficient readers do. You will reread the text "How Bugs Bug Us" one paragraph at a time. After each paragraph, you will monitor your understanding by circling the check mark or the question mark. Remember, good readers are honest about what they don't know and they do something about it. Good readers are metacognitive. Please be sure to draw a question mark over any confusing words, phrases, or sentences. I will provide specific instructions on how to mark the text that will help with your comprehension and writing.

With eyes on text, listen to each section as it is read to you. Use your pencil eraser to follow along.

Note: If you feel your students are capable, instruct them to highlight the main idea of each paragraph or section in green, and the supporting details in yellow. Then make all additional marks in another color.

Let's read the first paragraph. Read the paragraph.

Note: While the lessons are written for a teacher read aloud, it is important that your students read as much and as often as they can. Assign readings that meet the needs of your students, based on your observations or data. This is a good opportunity to stretch students, but if they become frustrated, return to the read-aloud method.

You have heard the phrase, "I've got a bug." You may have thought that the person got a new pet, but it actually means the person is sick. In reality, we all have bugs because real bugs live all over our bodies. In fact, your body is a zoo for bugs!

- Circle the check mark or question mark for this paragraph. Draw a question mark over words that confuse you.
- Go to line 2. Mark the word that means "got a bug." (sick)
- Go to line 4. Underline the metaphor in the paragraph. Circle the two nouns being compared. (Your body is a zoo for bugs; body, zoo)

Let's read the next section, Stomach Alert! Read the paragraph.

Stomach Alert!

One type of bug that can bug you is bacteria. Bacteria are microscopic organisms that can cause illness. Bacteria are a blanket covering your body, inside and out. You can't see bacteria because they're too small. This group of tiny invaders needs nutrients from our bodies in order to live. Most bacteria are not harmful. Some are even good for you. We use good bacteria in our intestines to help us digest food. When you eat a nutritious meal, these important helpers provide nutrients to your body. Bad bacteria are called germs. If you don't keep germs in check, they can spread, cause infection, and make you sick. Bacteria can cause infections such as tonsillitis, strep throat, ear infections, and pneumonia. They can even cause cavities in your teeth! However, our bodies are made to fight off bacteria. Because of this, scientists use bacteria to make medicines. These medicines trigger our bodies to fight infections. Scientists also use bacteria to produce vaccines that prevent us from getting sick.

- Circle the check mark or question mark for this paragraph. Draw a question mark over words that confuse you.
- Go to lines 5 and 6. Use context clues to underline the definition of *bacteria*. (microscopic organisms that can cause illness)
- Go to line 9. Mark what we learned about most bacteria. (not harmful)
- Go to line 10. Mark how bacteria can help you. (digest food)
- Go to line 12. Mark another name for bad bacteria. (germs)
- On the same line, mark the phrase that means "under control." (in check)
- Mark three things that bad bacteria can do. (spread, cause infection, make you sick)
- Mark the infections that bacteria can cause. (tonsillitis, strep throat, ear infections, pneumonia, cavities)
- Identify the metaphor in line 6. Circle the two nouns being compared. (Bacteria are a blanket; bacteria, blanket)
- Rewrite the metaphor as a simile using *like* or *as*. (Bacteria are like a blanket covering your body, inside and out.)

Let's read the next section, Bugs in Your Bed? Read the paragraphs.

Bugs in Your Bed?

Dust mites are real bugs that live with you in your bedroom. They are often harmless but may cause an allergic reaction or trigger asthma. Dust mites multiply in pillows. If you use the same unwashed pillow every night for 10 years, half its weight would be from dust mites. Seven thousand microscopic dust mites fit on one dime. You can't see these tiny creatures, but they are there, feeding on dead skin. Dust mites don't bite and cannot spread diseases. They usually do not live on people. They are harmful only to people who become allergic to them. Their droppings cause allergies that make a lot of people sick. Do your eyes sometimes get red and itchy? Does this happen when you shake out the bedspread? Does it happen when you sweep the floor? Then you're a victim of dust mites!

Like dust mites, bedbugs are wingless bugs that would like to live in your bed. Bedbugs used to live in caves and suck the blood of bats. Today, bedbugs may try to sneak into your bed through tiny cracks, electrical outlets, and even your luggage. Thousands can infest a single bedroom looking for a blood bank! Bedbugs can hardly wait to drink blood in order to stay alive and breathe. They find their meal by sensing the carbon dioxide that you exhale. Before a bedbug bites, it injects an anticoagulant and an anesthetic. The anticoagulant is a substance that prevents your blood from clotting, which allows the pest to suck your blood for up to five minutes. An anesthetic numbs the area so that you don't wake up. These blood suckers leave you with a red raised bump similar to a mosquito bite. They can drink three times their weight in a single meal. You can get bitten 500 times in one night! So when your parents say "Sleep tight, and don't let the bedbugs bite," they mean it!

- Circle the check mark or question mark for each paragraph. Draw a question mark over words that confuse you.
- Go to line 20. Mark the word that means "without harm." Circle the suffix that means "without." (harmless; -less)
- On the same line, mark the negative effects of dust mites. (cause an allergic reaction; trigger asthma)
- Go to line 21. Mark the place most dust mites live. (pillows)
- On the same line, mark the word that means "not washed." Circle the prefix in that word that means "not." (unwashed; circle -un)
- Go to line 25. Mark the antonym of *harmless*. (harmful)
- Go to line 28. Draw an arrow to the event the pronoun *this* refers to in the preceding sentence. (eyes get red and itchy)
- On the same line, draw an arrow to the event the pronoun *it* refers to. (eyes get red and itchy)

- Go to line 30. Mark the transition phrase that connects the paragraphs. (Like dust mites)
- Go to line 32. Mark where bedbugs live. (bed)
- Go to line 33. Mark the verb that means "invade in large numbers." (infest)
- On the same line, mark the synonym for *one.* (single)
- Go to line 34. Mark what bedbugs do to stay alive. (drink blood)
- Go to line 40. Mark the evidence you would see if you had been bitten by a bedbug. (red raised bump)
- Go to line 42. Mark how many times a person can be bitten in one night. (500 times)
- Review lines 30–41. Mark each noun, noun phrase, and pronoun that renames *bedbug.* (wingless bugs, they, it, the pest, blood suckers, they)

Let's read the next section, In Your Hair? Read the paragraph.

In Your Hair?

The next type of bug that can live on your body is lice. Head lice just love the skin under the hair on your head, called the scalp. There, they can hunker down and guzzle blood from the scalp for up to 30 days. These bugs lay eggs that can live in your hair for more than two weeks. Lice can spread quickly! They are track stars that run from one person's head to another. They spread when people work closely together in school classrooms and at work. If you get lice, special shampoo can help eliminate them.

- Circle the check mark or question mark for each paragraph. Draw a question mark over words that confuse you.
- Go to line 44. Mark the transition phrase that connects the paragraphs. (The next type)
- Go to line 45. Use context clues to underline the definition of *scalp.* (the skin under the hair on your head)
- On the same line, mark where lice live. (scalp)
- Go to line 46. Mark what lice eat. (blood)
- On the same line, mark the idiom that means "stubbornly stay in one place." (hunker down)
- On the same line, mark the synonym for *gulp.* (guzzle)
- Go to lines 47–49. Mark what makes lice so difficult to manage. (Lice can spread quickly!)
- In the same lines, mark how they spread. (run)
- In line 50, mark the way you get rid of lice. (special shampoo)
- Go to line 51. Mark the word that means "get rid of." (eliminate)

- Identify the metaphor in the paragraph. Circle the two nouns being compared. You may have to look back to the sentence before. (They are track stars that run from one person's head to another. lice, track stars)
- Rewrite the metaphor as a simile using *like* or *as.* (Lice are like track stars that run from one person's head to another.)

Let's read the last section, Eyelash Horrors! Read the section.

Eyelash Horrors!

The eyelash mite is the final type of bug that lives on our bodies. But don't worry; they're harmless. These tiny bugs cling to eyelashes with eight tiny legs. They live on sebum, a natural oil in skin and hair. The truth is, a lot of bugs love our skin and hair and spend their lives there. They are hitchhikers catching a free ride to the next victim. Seeing them through a microscope may cause horror, but the bugs are so tiny that we don't even know they are there. The bugs are a part of us whether they "bug" us or not.

- Circle the check mark or question mark for each paragraph. Draw a question mark over words that confuse you.
- Go to line 52. Circle the transition that connects ideas between paragraphs. (the final type)
- Go to line 53. Mark the reason that we don't need to worry about eyelash mites. (they're harmless)
- Go to line 54. Use context clues to mark the definition of *sebum.* (a natural oil in skin and hair)
- Identify the metaphor in the paragraph. Circle the two nouns being compared. You may have to look back to the sentence before. (They are hitchhikers catching a free ride to the next victim. bugs, hitchhikers)
- Rewrite the metaphor as a simile using *like* or *as.* (Bugs are like hitchhikers catching a free ride to the next victim.)

Have partners compare text markings and correct any errors.

Unit 8

Lesson 8

Lesson Opener

Before the lesson, choose one of the following activities to write on the board or post on the *LANGUAGE! Live* Class Wall online.

- *What kind of bug bothers you the most? Why does it bother you?*
- *Use the word* bacteria *in a sentence.*
- *Write a sentence with a simple subject and a simple predicate. Then rewrite the sentence with a complete subject and a complete predicate.*

Writing

Objectives

- Gather relevant information from notes about the passage.
- Orally review key ideas from the passage.
- Write a paragraph that explains contrasting subject matter.
- Write clear introductory topic and concluding sentences.
- Develop the paragraph with concrete facts and details.
- Strengthen writing by editing for organization, word choice, sentence fluency, and basic writing conventions.

Prepare to Write

Let's review our writing prompt for "How Bugs Bug Us." Direct students to page 94 in their Student Books to review the writing prompt. Have students identify the topic and direction words and write them on the page.

Review the compare words from Unit 7 and introduce the contrast words. In our last unit, we focused on how whales and dolphins are similar, but in this unit our writing assignment focuses on the differences among bugs. Some bugs have harmful effects on us, whereas other bugs have beneficial uses. We have already taken some notes on how the medical world has explored some beneficial uses of bugs.

Now, we will use our Guided Highlighting of "How Bugs Bug Us" to look for specific bugs that have a harmful effect or beneficial use. We will take a few notes on each bug to help us describe how they help us or hurt us.

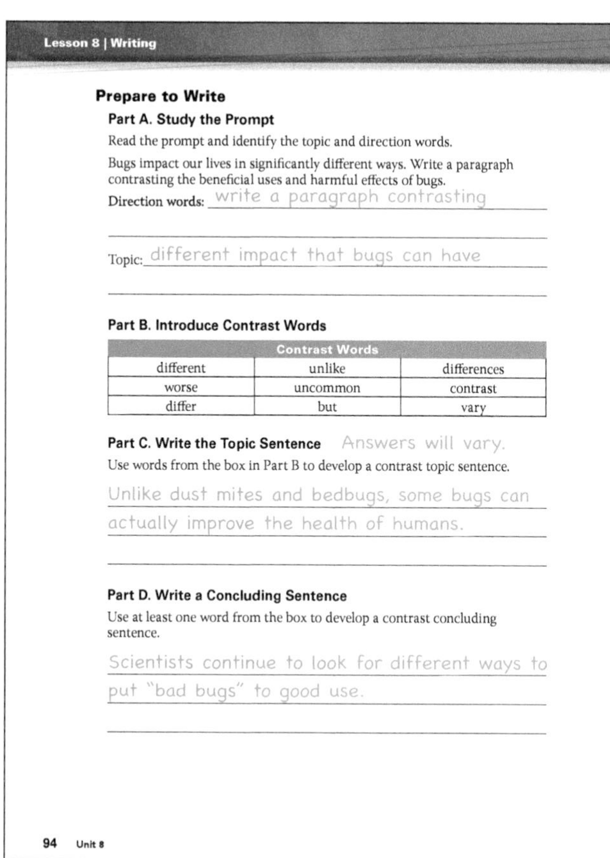

Lesson 8 | Writing

Prepare to Write

Part A. Study the Prompt

Read the prompt and identify the topic and direction words.

Bugs impact our lives in significantly different ways. Write a paragraph contrasting the beneficial uses and harmful effects of bugs.

Direction words: write a paragraph contrasting

Topic: different impact that bugs can have

Part B. Introduce Contrast Words

Contrast Words		
different	unlike	differences
worse	uncommon	contrast
differ	but	vary

Part C. Write the Topic Sentence Answers will vary.

Use words from the box in Part B to develop a contrast topic sentence.

Unlike dust mites and bedbugs, some bugs can actually improve the health of humans.

Part D. Write a Concluding Sentence

Use at least one word from the box to develop a contrast concluding sentence.

Scientists continue to look for different ways to put "bad bugs" to good use.

94 Unit 8

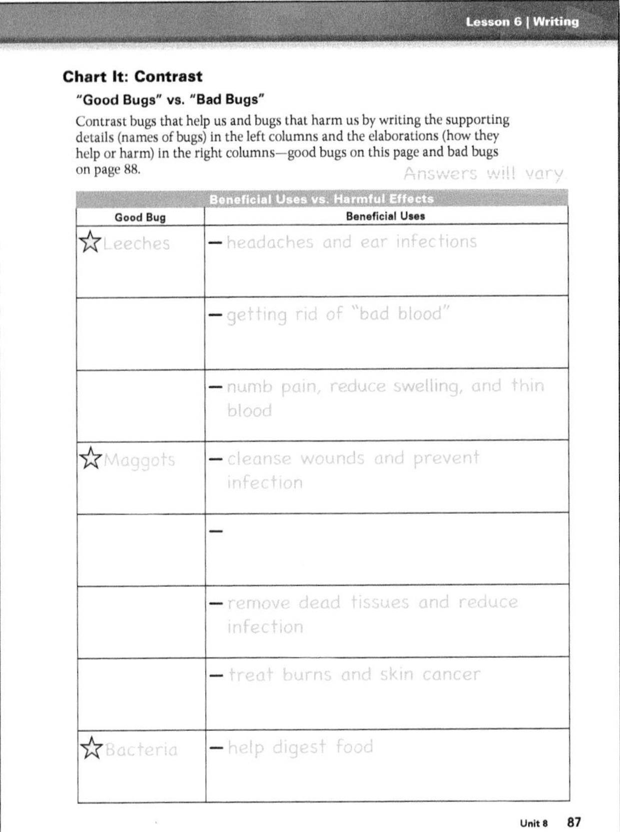

Chart It: Contrast

"Good Bugs" vs. "Bad Bugs"

Contrast bugs that help us and bugs that harm us by writing the supporting details (names of bugs) in the left columns and the elaborations (how they help or harm) in the right columns—good bugs on this page and bad bugs on page 88.

Answers will vary

Beneficial Uses vs. Harmful Effects	
Good Bug	**Beneficial Uses**
☆Leeches	– headaches and ear infections
	– getting rid of "bad blood"
	– numb pain, reduce swelling, and thin blood
☆Maggots	– cleanse wounds and prevent infection
	–
	– remove dead tissues and reduce infection
	– treat burns and skin cancer
☆Bacteria	– help digest food

Chart It: Contrast *(cont.)*

Beneficial Uses vs. Harmful Effects	
Bad Bug	**Harmful Effects**
☆Bacteria	– bad bacteria (germs): spread, cause illnesses
	–
☆Dust Mites	– cause allergic reactions, asthma
	– live in old pillows
☆Bedbugs	– bite leaves a red raised bump; someone can be bitten up to 500 times in a night
	– live in blankets and mattresses
☆Lice	– live on scalp up to 30 days
	– spread quickly; run from person to person
	– need special shampoo to kill them

Direct students to Chart It on pages 87 and 88. Have them add the bugs to the chart along with notes about each bug's effects. Remind students that they will not include eyelash mites in their chart because they are neither beneficial, nor harmful. We are only looking for bugs that harm us or help us. If they don't do either, they don't belong on the chart.

Note: If necessary, guide students in identifying the beneficial and harmful bugs to put in the left columns of the chart.

Two-Column Notes for Contrast Paragraph

Let's review the notes we have taken for both good bugs and bad bugs. We focused on three bugs—leeches, maggots, and bacteria—for our notes on beneficial uses of bugs because the passages provide a good deal of information about them. We focused on four bugs—bacteria, dust mites, bedbugs, and lice—for our notes on harmful effects of bugs because the passages provide a good deal of information about them.

For our writing, let's choose two bugs that help us and two bugs that hurt us. Take a moment and choose the two bugs you want to include from each side of the chart. Circle them in your chart and read over your notes. Read all of the notes from both passages aloud.

Passage Retell

Now that we've reviewed our notes and you've made some decisions about your paragraph, I want you to do a little "oral rehearsal." Turn to your partner and present your paragraph orally. Use your notes to present the information and think about some of the words you want to use when you begin writing your paragraph. Give each other feedback on the way ideas have been developed.

Turn Prompt into Topic Sentence

Now that you have a really good idea of the information you want to include in your paragraph, let's cement our topic sentence. **Direct students to page 94 in their Student Books.**

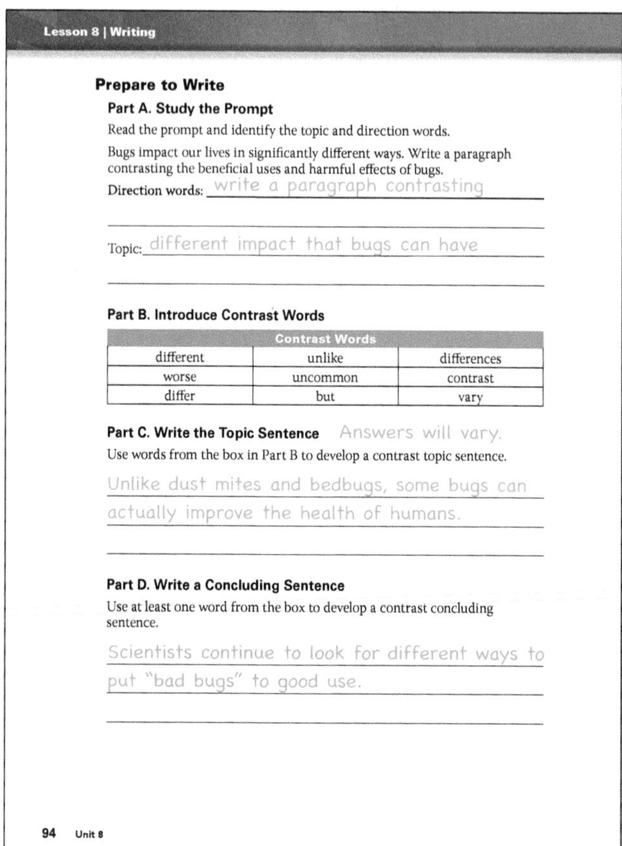
Lesson 8 | Writing

Prepare to Write

Part A. Study the Prompt

Read the prompt and identify the topic and direction words.

Bugs impact our lives in significantly different ways. Write a paragraph contrasting the beneficial uses and harmful effects of bugs.

Direction words: write a paragraph contrasting

Topic: different impact that bugs can have

Part B. Introduce Contrast Words

Contrast Words		
different	unlike	differences
worse	uncommon	contrast
differ	but	vary

Part C. Write the Topic Sentence Answers will vary.

Use words from the box in Part B to develop a contrast topic sentence.

Unlike dust mites and bedbugs, some bugs can actually improve the health of humans.

Part D. Write a Concluding Sentence

Use at least one word from the box to develop a contrast concluding sentence.

Scientists continue to look for different ways to put "bad bugs" to good use.

94 Unit 8

As you develop your topic sentence, consider the bugs you have chosen to include in your paragraph. Review the words in the Contrast Words chart that convey contrasting ideas. Choose one of these words to use in your sentence. **Pause to give students time to review the words.**

Your sentence can be either a general statement about the beneficial uses and harmful effects of bugs, or it can include specific names of bugs. **Read the following sentences as examples:**

Many bugs have harmful effects, but the world of medicine has found ways to put bugs to good use.

Unlike dust mites and bedbugs, some bugs can actually improve the health of humans.

Have students write a topic sentence and share it with the class. Direct students to Part D and have them restate their topic sentence as a concluding sentence. Have volunteers share their concluding sentences.

Write Contrast Paragraph

Notebook paper

Copies of the Blueprint for Writing from the back of the Student Book for students who need additional support

Have students write their paragraph on a sheet of notebook paper. Students should begin with their topic sentence, use their notes to develop the body of their paragraph, and end with their concluding sentence. Remind students they will have time to refine their paragraph with the help of the Writer's Checklist. If students struggle or need additional support in developing their paragraph, use the following paragraph as a model.

Example Contrast Paragraph

Unlike dust mites and bedbugs, some bugs can actually improve the health of humans. Dust mites and bedbugs live in pillows and mattresses and disrupt many households. Many people are allergic to dust mites, and they have red, puffy eyes to prove it. Living in mattresses, bedbugs can bite up to 500 times in a single night. Their bites leave red raised bumps. On the other hand, some bugs are helpful. Although leeches and maggots may look like gross bugs, doctors have used them for centuries to treat sick people. Current science is looking for ways to use living organisms in medicine. Some doctors advocate using maggots to remove dead tissues and reduce infection in wounds. Leeches are being used to numb pain, reduce swelling, and thin blood. Scientists continue to look for different ways to put "bad bugs" to good use.

Writer's Checklist

Once students have written their paragraphs, direct them to the Writer's Checklist on page 95 in their Student Books. Use the checklist to edit your paragraph. Make changes that you think will improve your paragraph.

Lesson 8 | Writing

Writer's Checklist

Trait	Yes	No	Did the writer . . .?
Ideas and Content			focus all sentences on the topic
			provide supporting details for the topic sentence
			include examples, evidence, and/or explanations to develop the supporting detail sentences
Organization			write a topic sentence
			tell things in an order that makes sense
			use transition words and/or phrases
			write a concluding sentence
Voice and Audience Awareness			think about the audience and purpose for writing
			write in a clear and engaging way that makes the audience want to read the work; write so the reader can "hear" the writer speaking
Word Choice			try to find a unique way to say things
			use words that are lively and specific to the content
Sentence Fluency			write complete sentences
			expand some sentences by painting the subject and/or predicate
Conventions			capitalize words correctly:
			capitalize the first word of each sentence
			capitalize proper nouns, including people's names
			punctuate correctly:
			put a period or question mark at the end of each sentence
			put an apostrophe before the *s* for a singular possessive noun
			use a comma after a long adverb phrase at the beginning of a sentence
			use grammar correctly:
			use the correct verb tense
			make sure the verb agrees with the subject in number
			use correct spelling

Unit 8 95

Six Traits of Writing

Direct students to page 96 in their Student Books. For this writing assignment, you will work with your partner to apply the Six Traits rubric to your paragraphs. Review each trait, then have students work with their partners to apply the rubric to "score" their paragraphs. Circulate and provide support as students review their writing.

Six Traits of Writing

	Ideas and Development	Organization	Voice and Audience Awareness	Word Choice	Sentence Fluency	Language Conventions
5	The paper is very clear and well focused. Supporting details make the paper very easy and interesting to understand.	Ideas are very clearly organized. All parts of the essay (introduction, body, and conclusion) work together to support the thesis.	The writer's voice is distinctive and shows an interest in the topic. The writer knows who his or her audience is.	Words are used correctly and are very well chosen. They create pictures in the reader's mind.	Sentences have an easy flow and rhythm. Transitions are very smooth.	There are no grammar errors. There are few or no errors in spelling, capitalization, or punctuation.
4	The paper is clear and well focused. Supporting details make the paper easy to understand.	Ideas are clearly organized. The paper includes all parts of an essay (introduction, body, and conclusion).	The writer's voice is natural and shows an interest in the topic. The writer knows who his or her audience is.	Words are used correctly. Some words may be a bit general.	Sentences are formed correctly and are varied in structure. Transitions are clear.	There are no major grammar errors. There are few errors in spelling, capitalization, or punctuation.
3	The paper has a clear thesis. The ideas are somewhat developed, but there are only a few details.	Ideas are fairly well organized. The paper includes all parts of an essay (introduction, body, and conclusion).	The writer's voice is natural, but the writer is not fully engaged in the topic. At times the writer's viewpoint may be vague.	Most words are used correctly. A few words are too general. Some words are repeated.	Sentences are formed correctly, although they may be similar in structure. Most transitions are clear.	There are a few grammar errors. There are a few errors in spelling, capitalization, or punctuation.
2	The thesis of the paper is unclear. The paper is poorly developed.	Ideas are not clearly organized. The paper may be missing an introduction or a conclusion.	The writer seems somewhat uninterested in the topic and unaware of his or her audience.	Some words are used incorrectly, some are too general, or some words are repeated often.	The sentences do not flow well. They are short and choppy or long and confusing.	There are many grammar or spelling errors. There are quite a few errors in capitalization and punctuation.
1	The paper is missing a thesis. The paper is very confusing or poorly developed.	The paper has no organization. There is no introduction or conclusion.	The writer is uninterested in the topic and unaware of his or her audience.	Many words are used incorrectly, many words are general, or many words are repeated.	The sentences are not correctly structured, and they do not flow well.	There are many spelling and grammar errors. There are many errors in capitalization and punctuation.

Lesson 8 | Writing

96 Unit 8

Lesson 9

Lesson Opener

Before the lesson, choose one of the following activities to write on the board or post on the *LANGUAGE! Live* Class Wall online.

- *Write sentences with the following verb phrases:* am going, was waxing, is telling.
- *Write a metaphor about your best friend.*
- *Write two sentences with linking verbs. The first sentence should contain a predicate nominative (a naming word). The second sentence should contain a predicate adjective (a descriptive word).*

Reading

Objective

- Read words to develop fluency.

Word Fluency: Second Read

Timer

Follow the Fluency Procedure outlined below. If it is necessary, begin the fluency drill with a choral read of the words as you provide a rhythm (snap your fingers, tap your foot, tap your pencil). Direct students to page 97 in their Student Books and complete the process.

Word Fluency: Second Read

Read the words fluently.

	Correct	Errors
1st Try		
2nd Try		

brings	tall	creeping	hung	parked	now	small	marked	clanging	breach	10
creeping	hung	parked	now	small	marked	clanging	breach	drive	walls	20
parked	now	small	marked	clanging	breach	drive	walls	drowning	froze	30
small	marked	clanging	breach	drive	walls	drowning	froze	grapes	frowned	40
clanging	breach	drive	walls	drowning	froze	grapes	frowned	soy	malls	50
drive	walls	drowning	froze	grapes	frowned	soy	malls	crude	how	60
drowning	froze	grapes	frowned	soy	malls	crude	how	tall	brings	70
grapes	frowned	soy	malls	crude	how	tall	brings	hung	creeping	80
soy	malls	crude	how	tall	brings	hung	creeping	now	parked	90
crude	how	tall	brings	hung	creeping	now	parked	marked	small	100

Unit 8 97

Lesson 9 | Reading

Fluency Procedure

- Partners switch books, so the recorder is marking errors in the reader's book.
- A timer is set for one minute.
- Readers and recorders move left to right, tracking each word with a pencil.
- As readers read the words aloud, recorders mark errors with a small x above the misread word.
- Recorders place a star to the right of the last word read when time ends.
- If the reader is able to read all words in the allotted time, the reader needs to start over at the beginning. The recorder must indicate this feat by placing two stars to the right of the last word read.
- When both students have read, partners switch books.
- Students calculate total words read, then subtract errors and record.
- Students record information on the progress chart in back of the Student Book.

Vocabulary

Objectives

- Demonstrate an understanding of words by relating them to their synonyms, antonyms, and related words.
- Demonstrate an understanding of figurative language.
- Generate examples of metaphors.

Four-Square

Review the word *infection* and its definition.

Direct students to page 98 in their Student Books. Read the instructions. Have partners complete the synonyms, examples, antonyms, nonexamples, and related words. Review the answers as a class.

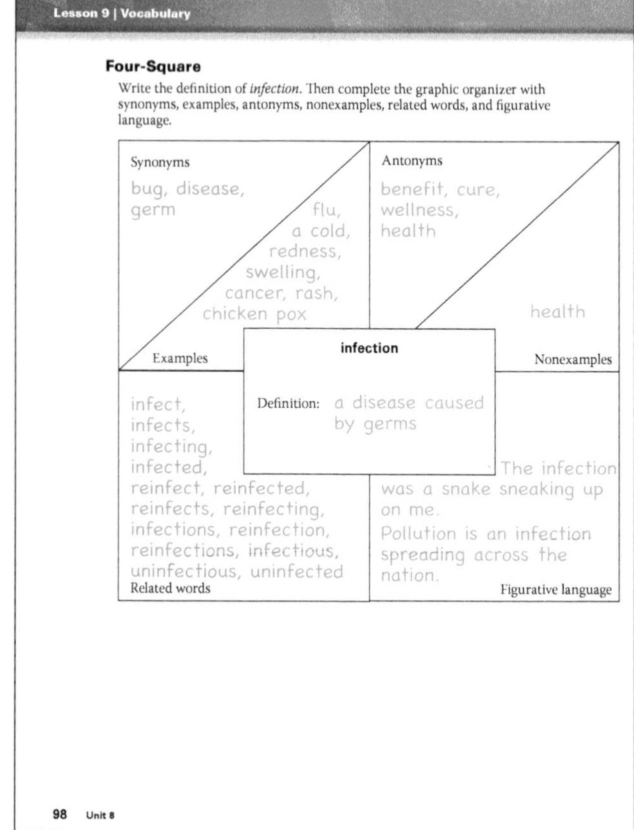

Ask students for examples of metaphors that include the word *infection* or a related word. Write the following metaphor pattern on the board for guidance.

___________ *is/was* ___________
(noun) *(noun)*

Let's put the word *infection* in the first blank and see if we can come up with anything that an infection could be compared to. Sometimes infections sneak up on us and we aren't prepared for them. What could we compare that type of infection to? (a snake, a thief in the night, etc.) Have students write a metaphor using *infection* in the first blank and use it in a sentence.

Now, let's put the word *infection* in the second blank. We know that an infection is a disease that causes harm. So if we compare something to an infection, we are saying that it is like a disease that spreads. What can we put in the first blank to compare to an infection? (pollution, laziness, etc.) Have students write a metaphor with *infection* in the first blank and use it in a sentence.

Grammar

Objectives

- Demonstrate an understanding of the function of conjunctions in sentences.
- Use the conjunctions *and, but,* and *or* in written sentences.
- Demonstrate an understanding of the function of direct objects, predicate nominatives, and predicate adjectives by diagramming sentences.

Using Conjunctions

Direct students to page 99 in their Student Books. Assign each partner one of the pictures. Then, assign each pair a coordinating conjunction: *and, but,* or *or*. Explain the procedure for the activity.

- One partner writes a Masterpiece Sentence for the top picture.
- One partner writes a Masterpiece Sentence for the bottom picture.
- Partners build a compound sentence using the assigned coordinating conjunction.

Remember, if you have the conjunction *and*, you will both want to write about similar ideas that logically would be linked with the word *and*.

If you have the conjunction *or*, each of your sentences should present a different choice, or alternative.

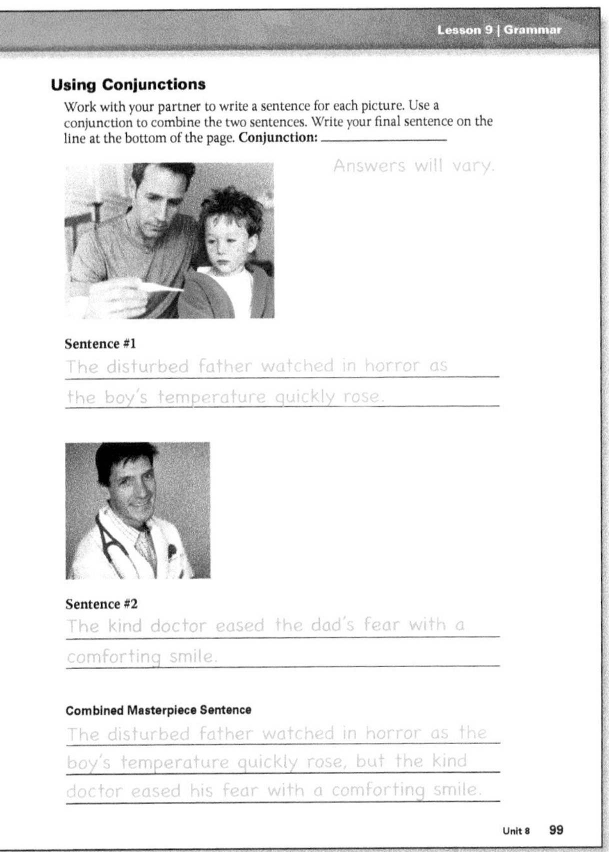

Lesson 9 | Grammar

Using Conjunctions

Work with your partner to write a sentence for each picture. Use a conjunction to combine the two sentences. Write your final sentence on the line at the bottom of the page. **Conjunction:** ________

Answers will vary.

Sentence #1

The disturbed father watched in horror as the boy's temperature quickly rose.

Sentence #2

The kind doctor eased the dad's fear with a comforting smile.

Combined Masterpiece Sentence

The disturbed father watched in horror as the boy's temperature quickly rose, but the kind doctor eased his fear with a comforting smile.

Unit 8 99

If you have the conjunction *but*, your sentences should express contrasting ideas to show what you expected to happen didn't happen.

Depending on the conjunction you've been given, you may have to revise or change the sentences you first come up with. Your main goal is to use the conjunction in a way that joins your sentences logically.

Have partners complete the process. If necessary, follow these steps to guide them.

1. Look at your pictures and commit to your simple subject and simple predicate.
2. Next, develop the sentence by answering the Painter questions. Turn to the chart on page 86 if you need to. Answer at least one of the Stage 2 questions and one of the Stage 4 questions.
3. Replace words with more descriptive ones.
4. Finally, move your words around.
5. Now, work with your partner to combine your sentences, if necessary, revising them to make the compound sentence meaningful.

Remind students to use appropriate pronouns as needed. Have volunteers share their combined sentences.

Diagram It: Direct Objects and Predicate Nominatives and Adjectives

Let's recall what we know about sentence structure and verbs. We've learned that the verb drives a sentence. In a previous lesson, we started with the kernel sentence *Bugs ate leaves.* What is the verb in this sentence? (ate) What did the bugs eat? (leaves) What is the category or label for words like *leaves* that answer the question, What did they do it to? (direct objects)

The diagram template for a sentence with a direct object has a distinctive pattern. It has a special line that signals a direct object is a part of the sentence structure.

Direct students to pages 100 and 101 in their Student Books and point out the line that comes after *leaves* in sentence 1. In this sentence, the word *leaves* is an action verb: The bite of a bedbug *leaves* a red raised bump. The direct object is *a red raised bump.*

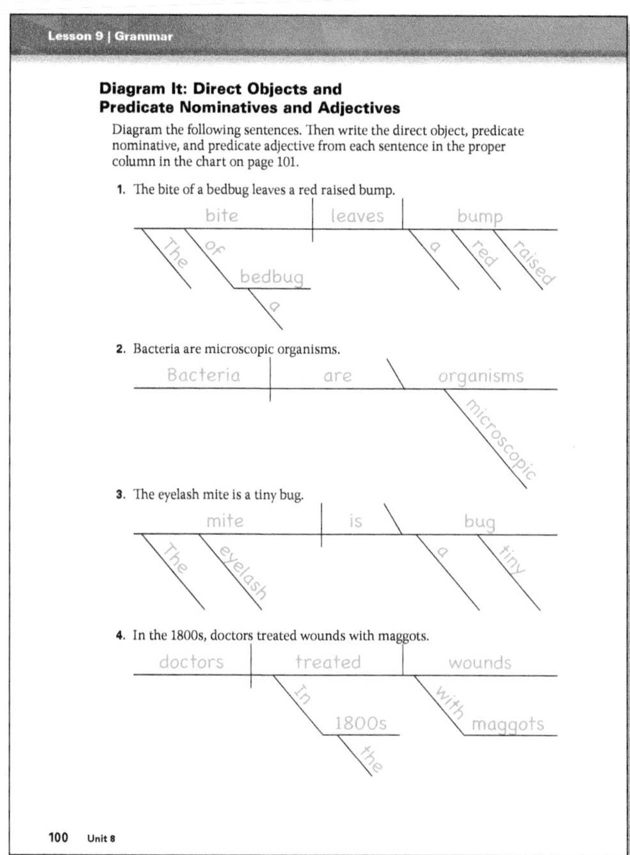

Lesson 9 | Grammar

Diagram It: Direct Objects and Predicate Nominatives and Adjectives

Diagram the following sentences. Then write the direct object, predicate nominative, and predicate adjective from each sentence in the proper column in the chart on page 101.

1. The bite of a bedbug leaves a red raised bump.
2. Bacteria are microscopic organisms.
3. The eyelash mite is a tiny bug.
4. In the 1800s, doctors treated wounds with maggots.

100 Unit 8

However, not every sentence we write or read has an action verb in it. Sometimes the verb links describing words back to the subject, as in the sentences *I am a teacher* and *I am happy.* Write these sentences on the board.

In these sentences, the words *teacher* and *happy* describe the subject, *I*. The describing word *teacher* is a noun. Since it is a part of the predicate, we call it a predicate nominative. In the second sentence, the describing word *happy* is an adjective. It, too, is part of the predicate. We call it a predicate adjective. In both sentences, the describing words are connected to the subject, *I*, by the linking verb *am.*

We will practice diagramming sentences with direct objects, predicate nominatives, and predicate adjectives. Diagramming is like drawing a picture of how the words in a sentence are related or connected to each other. When you diagram a sentence correctly, you show that you understand the job each word does in the sentence.

Guided Practice

Read the instructions and have students guide you in diagramming the first sentence.

Independent Practice

Read the remaining sentences and have students diagram them independently. When they have finished diagramming the sentences, have them complete the chart with the direct objects, predicate nominatives, and predicate adjectives from the sentences. Review all of the diagrams and the chart with the class.

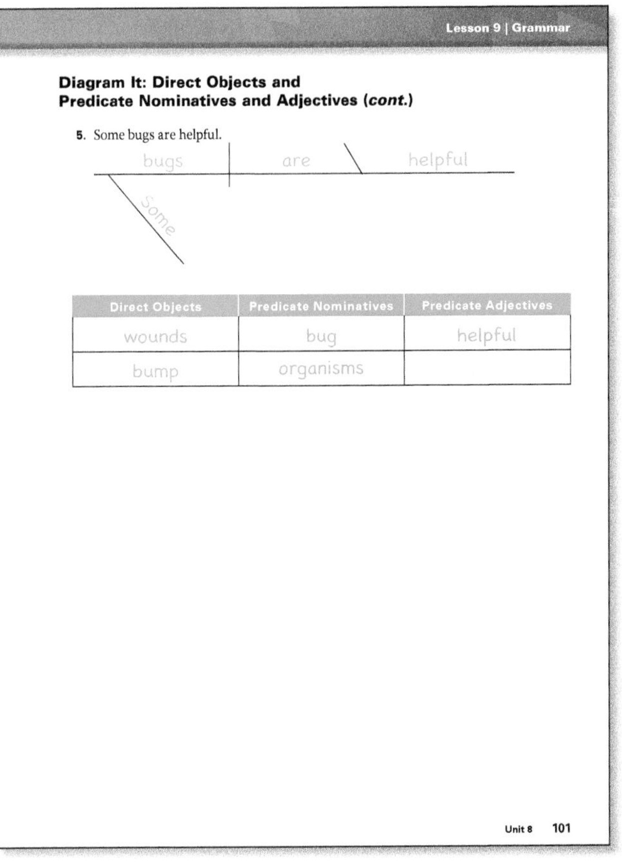
Lesson 9 | Grammar

Diagram It: Direct Objects and Predicate Nominatives and Adjectives (*cont.*)

5. Some bugs are helpful.

Direct Objects	Predicate Nominatives	Predicate Adjectives
wounds	bug	helpful
bump	organisms	

Unit 8 101

Note: Base the number of modeled and guided examples on student ability and progress. Challenge them with independent practice when appropriate.

Writing

Objective

- Edit text for basic conventions (punctuation, spelling, capitalization).

Revise It

Direct students to pages 102 and 103 in their Student Books. Listen and follow along as I read this text. I'll warn you ahead of time: it's a complete mess. After I read the passage, you will work with your partner to read it again and make the necessary revisions. As you revise, focus mainly on writing conventions, or errors in spelling and punctuation.

Lesson 9 | Writing

Revise It: Focus on Spelling and Punctuation

Read the paragraph. Find mistakes in the paragraph, and use editing marks to fix them. Then rewrite the paragraph, correcting the errors.

jill and rosa had to cross some gulches to git to the cabin on the bluff, as they walked, the branches of sum bushes stuck Rosas leg. "Ouch cried Rosa. "that bush has thorns! They rested on too fallen logs. A big black disgusting bug landed on Jills cup. "That is so gross, cried Jill. When they reached the rustic cabin, it was dusk. big bugs buzzed on the front steps. Did you bring any bug spray? asked Rosa. Jill smiled as she pulled the spray from her backpak. The cabin was dark and rosa was glad she had packed matches. She lit the stove and began to unpack the food The old mattresses looked dirty. rosa remembered reading about bedbugs and pulled out her sleeping bag. The floor looked better than the beds! camping wasn't as much fun as they had hoped.

Jill and Rosa had to cross some gulches to get to the cabin on the bluff. As they walked, the branches of some bushes stuck Rosa's leg. "Ouch," cried Rosa. "That bush has thorns!" They rested on two fallen logs. A big, black, disgusting bug landed on Jill's cup. "That is so gross," cried Jill. When they reached the rustic cabin, it was dusk. Big bugs buzzed on the front steps. "Did you bring any bug spray?" asked Rosa. Jill smiled as she pulled the spray from her backpack. The cabin was dark, and Rosa was glad she had packed matches. She lit the stove and began to unpack the food. The old mattresses looked dirty. Rosa remembered reading

102 Unit 8

Lesson 9 | Writing

Revise It: Focus on Spelling and Punctuation (*cont.*)

about bedbugs and pulled out her sleeping bag. The floor looked better than the beds! Camping wasn't as much fun as they had hoped.

Editor's Marks

^	add or change text
℘	delete text
⬭→	move text
¶	new paragraph
≡	capitalize
/	lowercase
⊙	insert period
⬭	check spelling or spell out word

Unit 8 103

Note: Grammatically, each time the speaker changes, it should occur in a new paragraph. However, for simplicity sake, do not monitor that skill at this time. You are only checking the spelling and punctuation. Monitor the progress of your students, and mention it if you feel they are ready.

Review the changes in the paragraph as a class.

Reading

Objective

- Read decodable text to develop fluency.

Reading for Fluency

Direct students to pages 104 and 105 in their Student Books. The following passage is decodable text. You have learned almost all the letters, sounds, and sight words that appear in it. Reading this passage will help you improve your fluency. Have students read the passage independently or with partners.

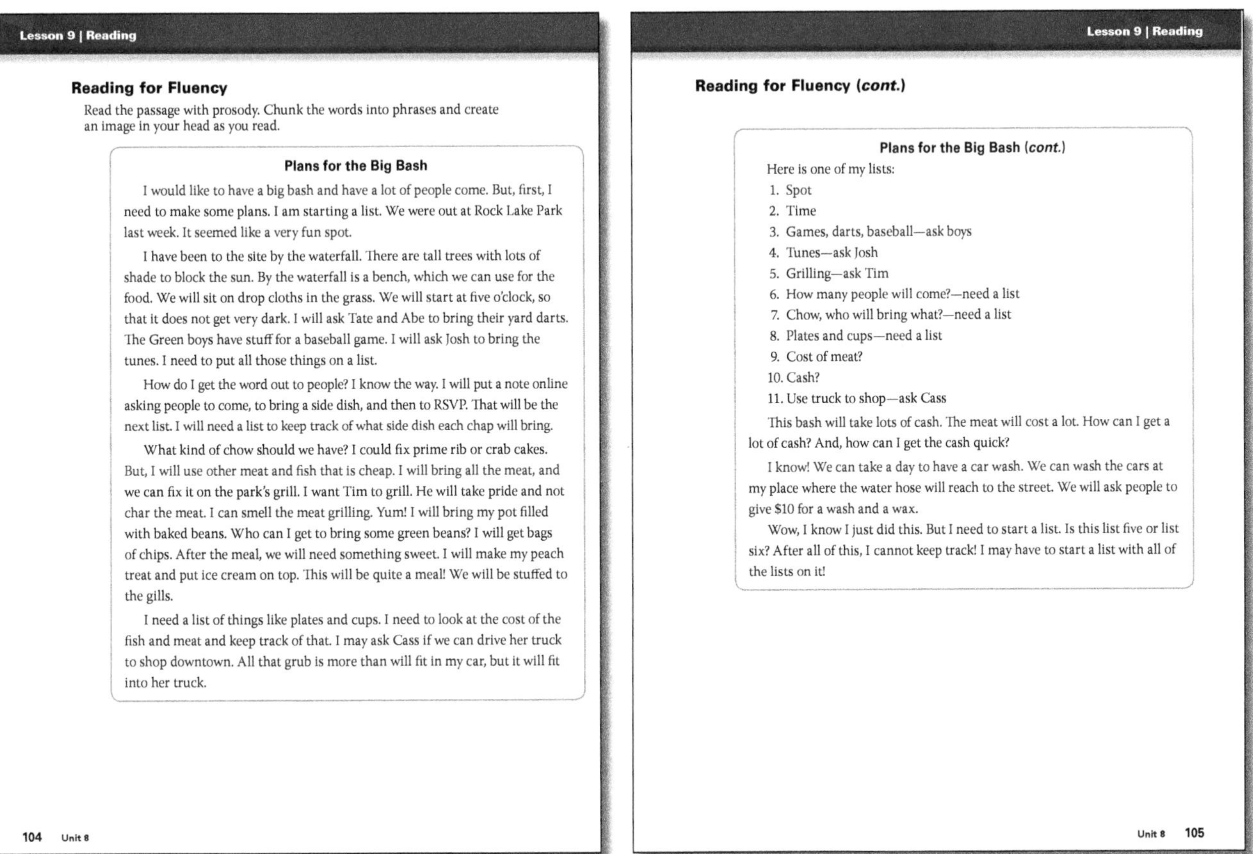

Lesson 9 | Reading

Reading for Fluency

Read the passage with prosody. Chunk the words into phrases and create an image in your head as you read.

Plans for the Big Bash

I would like to have a big bash and have a lot of people come. But, first, I need to make some plans. I am starting a list. We were out at Rock Lake Park last week. It seemed like a very fun spot.

I have been to the site by the waterfall. There are tall trees with lots of shade to block the sun. By the waterfall is a bench, which we can use for the food. We will sit on drop cloths in the grass. We will start at five o'clock, so that it does not get very dark. I will ask Tate and Abe to bring their yard darts. The Green boys have stuff for a baseball game. I will ask Josh to bring the tunes. I need to put all those things on a list.

How do I get the word out to people? I know the way. I will put a note online asking people to come, to bring a side dish, and then to RSVP. That will be the next list. I will need a list to keep track of what side dish each chap will bring.

What kind of chow should we have? I could fix prime rib or crab cakes. But, I will use other meat and fish that is cheap. I will bring all the meat, and we can fix it on the park's grill. I want Tim to grill. He will take pride and not char the meat. I can smell the meat grilling. Yum! I will bring my pot filled with baked beans. Who can I get to bring some green beans? I will get bags of chips. After the meal, we will need something sweet. I will make my peach treat and put ice cream on top. This will be quite a meal! We will be stuffed to the gills.

I need a list of things like plates and cups. I need to look at the cost of the fish and meat and keep track of that. I may ask Cass if we can drive her truck to shop downtown. All that grub is more than will fit in my car, but it will fit into her truck.

104 Unit 8

Lesson 9 | Reading

Reading for Fluency (*cont.*)

Plans for the Big Bash (*cont.*)

Here is one of my lists:

1. Spot
2. Time
3. Games, darts, baseball—ask boys
4. Tunes—ask Josh
5. Grilling—ask Tim
6. How many people will come?—need a list
7. Chow, who will bring what?—need a list
8. Plates and cups—need a list
9. Cost of meat?
10. Cash?
11. Use truck to shop—ask Cass

This bash will take lots of cash. The meat will cost a lot. How can I get a lot of cash? And, how can I get the cash quick?

I know! We can take a day to have a car wash. We can wash the cars at my place where the water hose will reach to the street. We will ask people to give $10 for a wash and a wax.

Wow, I know I just did this. But I need to start a list. Is this list five or list six? After all of this, I cannot keep track! I may have to start a list with all of the lists on it!

Unit 8 105

After reading, ask students the following comprehension questions.

- Do you think the party will be well organized? Why or why not? (Answers will vary.)
- Did the narrator miss anything that might be needed for the party? (drinks, eating utensils; Answers will vary.)
- What is the problem in the story? Is the plan to resolve it a good one? (limited money; Answers will vary.)
- Discuss the author's lists: Were they needed? Did it seem like they were organized? How would you plan the party differently? (Answers will vary.)
- Do you think this will be a fun party? Why or why not? (Answers will vary.)

Lesson 10

Lesson Opener

Before the lesson, choose one of the following activities to write on the board or post on the *LANGUAGE! Live* Class Wall online.

- *Write four meaningful sentences with the vocabulary words from this unit. Each sentence will contain two vocabulary words* (victim, digest, scalp, multiply, creature, infection, eliminate, horror).
- *Write three sentences: one in the first-person point of view, one in the second-person point of view, and one in the third-person point of view.*
- *Do you think bugs should be used in medicine? Explain your answer.*

Vocabulary

Objectives

- Clarify the meaning of key passage vocabulary.
- Demonstrate an understanding of passage vocabulary by using the words in sentences.

Review

Direct students to page 58 in their Student Books. Remind them of the review procedure. Have partners review the Key Passage Vocabulary.

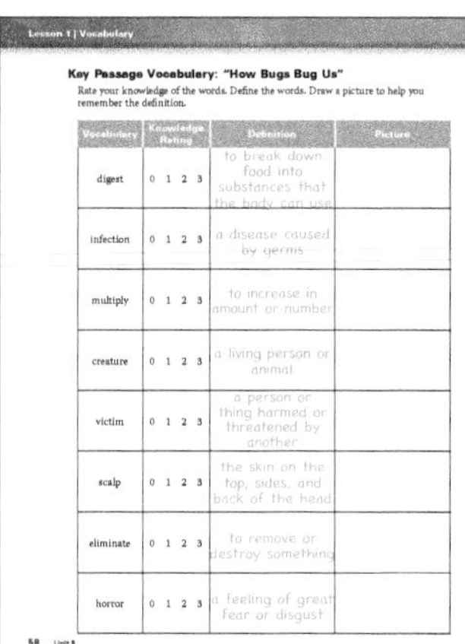

Lesson 1 | Vocabulary

Key Passage Vocabulary: "How Bugs Bug Us"

Rate your knowledge of the words. Define the words. Draw a picture to help you remember the definition.

Vocabulary	Knowledge Rating	Definition	Picture
digest	0 1 2 3	to break down food into substances that the body can use	
infection	0 1 2 3	a disease caused by germs	
multiply	0 1 2 3	to increase in amount or number	
creature	0 1 2 3	a living person or animal	
victim	0 1 2 3	a person or thing harmed or threatened by another	
scalp	0 1 2 3	the skin on the top, sides, and back of the head	
eliminate	0 1 2 3	to remove or destroy something	
horror	0 1 2 3	a feeling of great fear or disgust	

58 Unit 8

Review Procedure

- Student A reads the word.
- Student B tells the meaning.
- Students swap roles for each word.

Have students revisit their rating of the words. If they cannot change all ratings to a 3, pull them aside to discuss the vocabulary words they do not know.

Cloze Activity

Now we will read a paragraph. You will determine which vocabulary words are missing and write them on the lines. Direct students to page 106 in their Student Books. Remind them of the cloze procedure.

Cloze Procedure

- Teacher reads the text aloud, pausing at the blanks for students to write.
- Students fill in the blanks with words from the word bank.
- Teacher rereads the text as students chorally tell the correct word for each blank.
- Students correct errors.

Lesson 10 | Vocabulary

Using New Vocabulary

Fill in the blanks with the appropriate vocabulary words. If you need assistance, use the word bank at the bottom of the page.

Have you ever felt __horror__ as some tiny __creature__ crawled up the back of your neck and attached itself to your __scalp__?

If you have been the __victim__ of a tick bite, you know what it feels like. The spider-like bugs crawl to a place they can't be detected and fasten themselves under your hair. Ticks suck your blood, which can introduce tick-borne __infections__ such as Lyme Disease and Rocky Mountain Spotted Fever. Symptoms include body aches, fever, and problems with __digesting__ food.

Tick bites cannot be __eliminated__, but you can avoid them by using insect repellent and wearing light-colored clothing that covers your body. Precautions should __multiply__ if you are in woody areas with bushes and tall grasses. This is where ticks live and breed.

Word Bank

multiply	digesting	eliminated	scalp
victim	horror	creature	infections

106 Unit 8

Reading

Objectives

- Discuss and answer questions to demonstrate an understanding of the passages' main ideas and key details.
- Discuss and answer questions to demonstrate an understanding of each author's point of view.

Big Idea and Point of View

Direct students to page 57 in their Student Books. Before we began reading "How Bugs Bug Us," we answered two Big Idea questions. Take a minute to look over your answers. Now that we have read the passage thoroughly and learned about medical uses for bugs, has your opinion changed? Have you learned additional facts that support or challenge your original ideas? Do you feel differently about bugs?

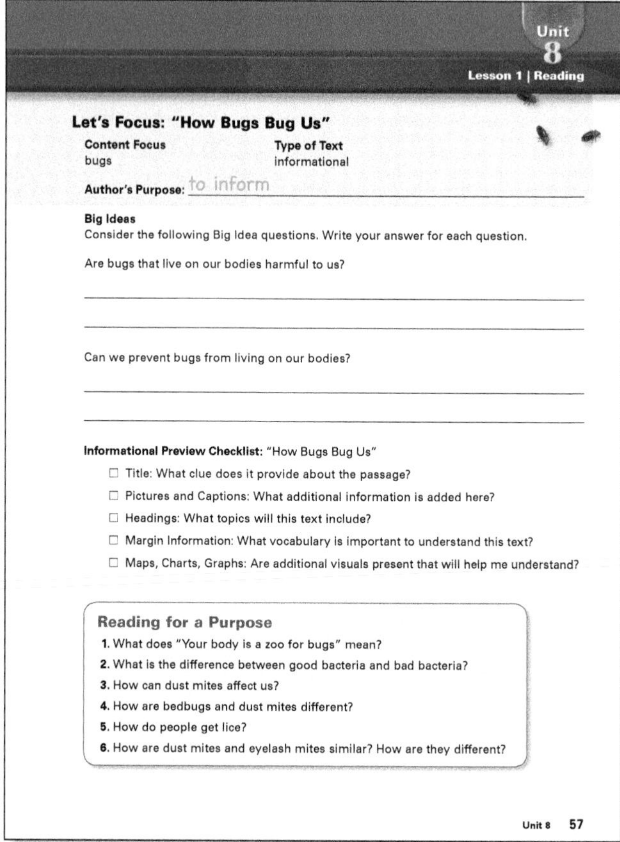

Unit 8

Lesson 1 | Reading

Let's Focus: "How Bugs Bug Us"

Content Focus bugs

Type of Text informational

Author's Purpose: to inform

Big Ideas

Consider the following Big Idea questions. Write your answer for each question.

Are bugs that live on our bodies harmful to us?

Can we prevent bugs from living on our bodies?

Informational Preview Checklist: "How Bugs Bug Us"

- ☐ Title: What clue does it provide about the passage?
- ☐ Pictures and Captions: What additional information is added here?
- ☐ Headings: What topics will this text include?
- ☐ Margin Information: What vocabulary is important to understand this text?
- ☐ Maps, Charts, Graphs: Are additional visuals present that will help me understand?

Reading for a Purpose

1. What does "Your body is a zoo for bugs" mean?
2. What is the difference between good bacteria and bad bacteria?
3. How can dust mites affect us?
4. How are bedbugs and dust mites different?
5. How do people get lice?
6. How are dust mites and eyelash mites similar? How are they different?

Unit 8 57

Discuss the questions and answers with the class. We will continue to examine our interaction with nature and think about the impact humans have on the natural world. One question that comes to my mind now is this: Do you think the pesticides we use to kill insects have negative consequences for other creatures, including "good bugs"? Encourage student responses.

Now, consider the point of view used in each passage. What pronouns did each writer use? In "How Bugs Bug Us," the author "speaks" directly to the reader. The pronoun *you* is used frequently. Does that make you feel more connected to the author? Encourage student responses with reasons.

What about "Bugs in Medicine"? If we look back at that passage, we won't find first- or second-person pronouns. It is written in the third person. It is a much more straightforward passage. How do you think the use of first- or second-person pronouns would have changed the article? Encourage students to support their responses with reasons.

Have students identify each author's feelings about bugs. Then, guide them to discuss the authors' possible purposes for writing. Both authors want to inform their readers. Might they want to persuade their readers too? Of what? Have students relate each author's purposes to the point of view used in the passage.

Grammar

Objective

- Demonstrate an understanding of verb phrases by using them in oral sentences.

Verb Phrases

Direct students to page 107 in their Student Books and read the instructions for playing tic-tac-toe. Have partners play the game. As they play, circulate to ensure students correctly use each verb phrase before initialing a square on the board.

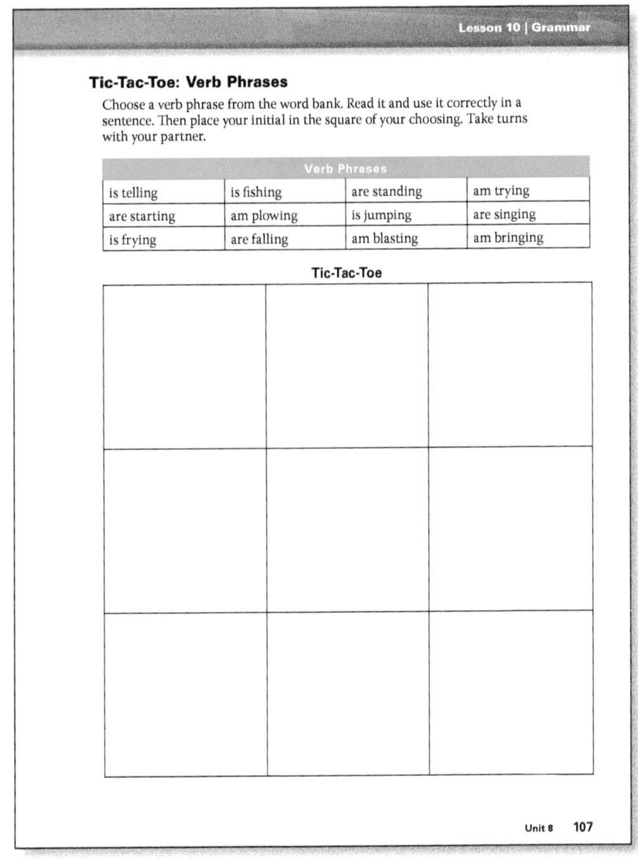

Lesson 10 | Grammar

Tic-Tac-Toe: Verb Phrases

Choose a verb phrase from the word bank. Read it and use it correctly in a sentence. Then place your initial in the square of your choosing. Take turns with your partner.

Verb Phrases			
is telling	is fishing	are standing	am trying
are starting	am plowing	is jumping	are singing
is frying	are falling	am blasting	am bringing

Tic-Tac-Toe

Unit 8 107

Reading

Objectives for Content Mastery

- Demonstrate an understanding of how to interpret text by drawing conclusions, contrasting, and differentiating.
- Demonstrate an understanding of first-person, second-person, and third-person points of view in text.

Responding to Prompts: *draw conclusions, contrast, differentiate*

Follow the procedure outlined below for each of the Reading Content Mastery questions and prompts.

Content Mastery Procedure

- Teacher reminds students to follow along with their pencils and listen.
- Teacher reads the question.
- Teacher reads each answer choice.
- Students choose the correct answer.
- Teacher repeats the question as students check their answers.

Have students turn to page 108 in their Student Books.

Let's look at the example first. Read the example aloud to students.

Listen: Draw conclusions about how dangerous dust mites are. To answer this prompt, I need to _____.

A make an inference based on text clues and background knowledge

B state the differences between dust mites

C state the similarities between dust mites

D make sense of or assign meaning to dust mites

Fill in the bubble for the correct response. Which bubble did you fill in? You should have filled in A, the bubble for "make an inference based on text clues and background knowledge." That is how you would respond to a question that asks you to draw conclusions about something.

Lesson 10 | Reading Content Mastery

Responding to Prompts

Listen to the sentences and possible answers. Fill in the bubble for your answer choice.

Example: Draw conclusions about how dangerous dust mites are.
To answer this prompt, I need to _____.
Ⓐ make an inference based on text clues and background knowledge
Ⓑ state the differences between dust mites
Ⓒ state the similarities between dust mites
Ⓓ make sense of or assign meaning to dust mites

1. Contrast dust mites and bedbugs.
To answer this prompt, I need to _____.
Ⓐ state the differences between dust mites and bedbugs
Ⓑ state the similarities between dust mites and bedbugs
Ⓒ make a judgment about dust mites based on text clues and background knowledge
Ⓓ create groups and place information about dust mites and bedbugs into those groups

2. Differentiate between good bacteria and bad bacteria.
To answer this prompt, I need to _____.
Ⓐ make an inference about bacteria based on text clues and background knowledge
Ⓑ explain the relationship between good bacteria and bad bacteria
Ⓒ tell the differences between good bacteria and bad bacteria
Ⓓ state the similarities of bacteria

3. Draw conclusions about how common bedbugs are.
To answer this prompt, I need to _____.
Ⓐ make sense of or assign meaning to the idea that bedbugs are common
Ⓑ state the differences between kinds of bedbugs
Ⓒ provide a logical conclusion using evidence and prior knowledge of bedbugs
Ⓓ make a judgment based on text and background knowledge about how common bedbugs are

4. Contrast dust mites with eyelash mites.
To answer this prompt, I need to _____.
Ⓐ make an inference about mites based on text and background knowledge
Ⓑ state the similarities between dust mites and eyelash mites
Ⓒ state the differences between dust mites and eyelash mites
Ⓓ create groups and place information about dust mites and eyelash mites into those groups

108 Unit 8

Follow along as I read aloud the questions and prompts. Fill in the bubble for your answer choice.

Use the following recommendations to reinforce or reteach according to student performance.

If...	Then...
Students miss 1 question	Review the question in a small group or individual setting, offering answer explanations.
Students miss 2 or more questions	Reteach the elements taught in Lessons 3 and 4 in a small group or individual setting. Unmarked copies of the student page can be reprinted from the Teacher Resources online.

Point of View

Have students turn to page 109 in their Student Books.

Let's look at the example first. Read the example aloud to students.

Listen: I hate head lice.

Choose the point of view for the sentence. Fill in the bubble for your answer.

A first person

B second person

C third person

Which bubble did you fill in? You should have filled in A, the bubble for "first person." The use of the pronoun *I* is a clue. It tells you that the author has written the sentence from his or her point of view.

Follow along as I read aloud the sentences and possible answers. Fill in the bubble for your answer choice.

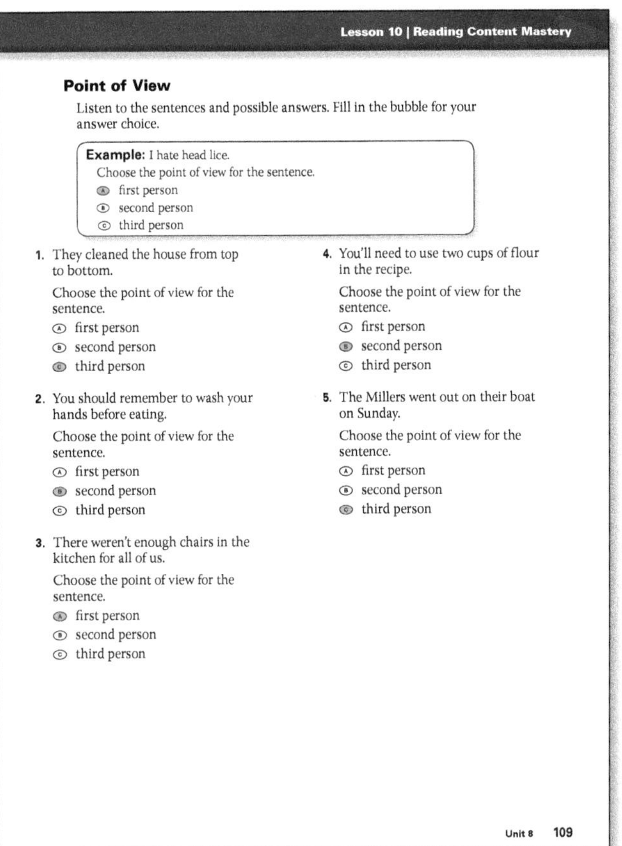

Lesson 10 | Reading Content Mastery

Point of View

Listen to the sentences and possible answers. Fill in the bubble for your answer choice.

Example: I hate head lice.
Choose the point of view for the sentence.
Ⓐ first person
Ⓑ second person
Ⓒ third person

1. They cleaned the house from top to bottom.
Choose the point of view for the sentence.
Ⓐ first person
Ⓑ second person
Ⓒ third person

2. You should remember to wash your hands before eating.
Choose the point of view for the sentence.
Ⓐ first person
Ⓑ second person
Ⓒ third person

3. There weren't enough chairs in the kitchen for all of us.
Choose the point of view for the sentence.
Ⓐ first person
Ⓑ second person
Ⓒ third person

4. You'll need to use two cups of flour in the recipe.
Choose the point of view for the sentence.
Ⓐ first person
Ⓑ second person
Ⓒ third person

5. The Millers went out on their boat on Sunday.
Choose the point of view for the sentence.
Ⓐ first person
Ⓑ second person
Ⓒ third person

Unit 8 109

Use the following recommendations to reinforce or reteach according to student performance.

If...	Then...
Students miss 2 questions	Review the questions in a small group or individual setting, offering answer explanations.
Students miss 3 or more questions	Reteach the elements taught in Lesson 6 in a small group or individual setting. Unmarked copies of the student page can be reprinted from the Teacher Resources online.

Vocabulary

Objective for Content Mastery

- Identify metaphors in sentences.

Metaphors

Follow the procedure outlined below for the Vocabulary Content Mastery questions and prompts.

Content Mastery Procedure

- Teacher reminds students to follow along with their pencils and listen.
- Teacher reads the question.
- Teacher reads each answer choice.
- Students choose the correct answer.
- Teacher repeats the question as students check their answers.

Have students turn to page 110 in their Student Books.

Let's look at the example first. Read the example aloud to students.

Listen: Which sentence contains a metaphor?

A The woman picks a blooming flower.

B The woman smells like a blooming flower.

C The woman's perfume smells wonderful.

D The woman is a blooming flower.

Which bubble did you fill in? You should have filled in the bubble for D. Remember, a metaphor compares two things that are unrelated by saying that one *is* or *was* something else. Metaphors do not use the words *like* or *as*.

Follow along as I read aloud each sentence. Fill in the bubble for your answer choice.

Lesson 10 | Vocabulary Content Mastery

Metaphors

Listen to the sentences and possible answers. Fill in the bubble for your answer choice.

Example: Which sentence contains a metaphor?

- Ⓐ The woman picks a blooming flower.
- Ⓑ The woman smells like a blooming flower.
- Ⓒ The woman's perfume smells wonderful.
- ● The woman is a blooming flower.

1. Which sentence contains a metaphor?
   - Ⓐ The sun is like a blazing furnace.
   - ● The sun is a blazing furnace.
   - Ⓒ The sun is as hot as a blazing furnace.
   - Ⓓ The sun is shining into the blazing furnace.
2. Which sentence contains a metaphor?
   - Ⓐ The box was as flat as a pancake.
   - Ⓑ The box was like a pancake after I sat on it.
   - Ⓒ I sat on the box and ate a pancake.
   - ● The box was a pancake after I sat on it.
3. Which sentence contains a metaphor?
   - Ⓐ My math final was like a nightmare.
   - ● My math final was a nightmare.
   - Ⓒ I had a nightmare about my math final.
   - Ⓓ Even a nightmare wasn't as bad as my math final.
4. Which sentence contains a metaphor?
   - ● The baby is a rag doll when she sleeps.
   - Ⓑ The baby sleeps like a rag doll.
   - Ⓒ The baby is as relaxed as a rag doll.
   - Ⓓ The baby has a rag doll.
5. Which sentence contains a metaphor?
   - Ⓐ The train was like a roaring lion.
   - Ⓑ The train was as loud as a roaring lion.
   - ● The train was a roaring lion.
   - Ⓓ The train carried a roaring lion.

110 Unit 8

Use the following recommendations to reinforce or reteach according to student performance.

If...	Then...
Students miss 2 questions	Review the questions in a small group or individual setting, offering answer explanations.
Students miss 3 or more questions	Reteach the elements taught in Lesson 3 in a small group or individual setting. Unmarked copies of the student page can be reprinted from the Teacher Resources online.

Grammar

Objective for Content Mastery

- Demonstrate an understanding of how the conjunctions *and, but,* and *or* are used in sentences.

Conjunctions: *and, but, or*

Follow the procedure outlined below for the Grammar Content Mastery questions and prompts.

Content Mastery Procedure

- Teacher reminds students to follow along with their pencils and listen.
- Teacher reads the question.
- Teacher reads each answer choice.
- Students choose the correct answer.
- Teacher repeats the question as students check their answers.

Have students turn to page 111 in their Student Books.

Let's look at the example first. Read the example aloud to students.

Listen: Some bacteria are good for us. Some bacteria make us sick.

Choose the best conjunction to combine these two sentences. Fill in the bubble for your answer.

A and

B but

C or

Which bubble did you fill in? You should have filled in the bubble for B, "but." These two sentences have contrasting ideas so we use the conjunction *but* to combine them: Some bacteria are good for use, *but* some make us sick.

Follow along as I read aloud the sentences and possible answers. Fill in the bubble for your answer choice.

Lesson 10 | Grammar Content Mastery

Conjunctions

Listen to the sentences and possible answers. Fill in the bubble for your answer choice.

Example: Some bacteria are good for us. Some bacteria make us sick.
Choose the best conjunction to combine these two sentences.
Ⓐ and
● but
Ⓒ or

1. I will go for a walk on Sunday. I will finish my homework on Sunday.
Choose the best conjunction to combine these two sentences.
● and
Ⓑ but
Ⓒ or

2. Dust mites are harmless to most people. Some people are allergic to them.
Choose the best conjunction to combine these two sentences.
Ⓐ and
● but
Ⓒ or

3. Mom can help me with my homework. My sister can help me with my homework.
Choose the best conjunction to combine these two sentences.
Ⓐ and
Ⓑ but
● or

4. Joe went to dig up clams. Joe went to collect driftwood.
Choose the best conjunction to combine these two sentences.
● and
Ⓑ but
Ⓒ or

5. Linda could catch the bus at 11:00. Linda could catch the bus at 11:20.
Choose the best conjunction to combine these two sentences.
Ⓐ and
Ⓑ but
● or

Unit 8 111

Use the following recommendations to reinforce or reteach according to student performance.

If...	Then...
Students miss 2 questions	Review the questions in a small group or individual setting, offering answer explanations.
Students miss 3 or more questions	Reteach the elements taught in Lesson 2 in a small group or individual setting. Unmarked copies of the student page can be reprinted from the Teacher Resources online.

Unit 9

Unit Plan

Primary Text:
"The Time Machine"

Text type: narrative

Lesson 1	Lesson 2	
Reading • Determine the topic of the text. • Discuss differences between nonfiction and narrative fiction. • Determine the author's purpose. • Discuss the topic of the text. Vocabulary • Determine the meaning of key passage vocabulary. Reading • Preview the passage by reviewing text features. • Read a narrative text. • Demonstrate an understanding of the text by asking and answering questions and referring to key details in the text.	Vocabulary • Determine the meanings of the multiple-meaning word *test.* • Demonstrate an understanding of the word by using them in written sentences. Grammar • Demonstrate an understanding of the function of compound sentences and conjunctions used in sentences. Reading • Demonstrate an understanding of the elements of a narrative, including setting, characters, plot, climax, and resolution.	

Lesson 6	Lesson 7	
Writing • Know spelling-sound correspondences for words with /ü/ spelled *oo*. • Know spelling-sound correspondences for words ending in *-ed*. • Know spelling-sound correspondences for words with /ō/ spelled *ow*. Vocabulary • Use context to determine the meaning of words in text. • Use common Greek and Latin affixes and roots as clues to the meaning of a word. • Consult reference materials to clarify the precise meaning of key words. • Demonstrate an understanding of simple word analogies. Reading • Discuss how authors use characterization in stories. • Describe the traits of characters in a story by drawing on specific details in the story. • Read a folk tale from Fiji. • Discuss the significance of point-of-view in a story.	Reading • Read with purpose and understanding. • Identify and explain explicit details from text. • Take notes on a text. • Identify idioms in text. Writing • Write sentences using concrete words and phrases and sensory details to convey experiences and events precisely.	

Lesson 3	Lesson 4	Lesson 5
Reading • Read to develop fluency. **Vocabulary** • Review key passage vocabulary. • Demonstrate an understanding of metaphors and similes. • Write simple metaphors and similes. **Grammar** • Demonstrate an understanding of the difference between past, present, and future tense. • Write sentences using the future tense. • Identify the use of past, present, or future tense in sentences. **Reading** • Use critical thinking skills to analyze a text. • Ask and answer questions and prompts using strategic thinking skills to demonstrate an understanding of a text.	**Reading** • Read sentences to develop fluency. **Grammar** • Listen to oral sentences and write them accurately. • Demonstrate an understanding of the function of future tense in sentences. **Reading** • Read sentence phrases with fluency to support comprehension. • Use critical thinking skills to respond to specific questions about a text.	**Vocabulary** • Review key passage vocabulary. **Reading** • Write questions or prompts about the passage to deepen comprehension. • Respond orally to specific questions about a text. **Writing** • Use critical and strategic thinking skills to write responses to prompts about the text. • Support written answers with evidence from text.

Lesson 8	Lesson 9	Lesson 10
Writing • Read and examine a personal narrative. • Orally review key ideas from the passage. • Write clear introductory topic and concluding sentences. **Reading** • Review the main elements of a narrative (setting, character traits, plot). • Demonstrate an understanding of the key elements of a narrative. **Writing** • Gather relevant information from notes. • Write a personal narrative. • Develop the paragraph with details.	**Reading** • Read words to develop fluency. **Vocabulary** • Demonstrate an understanding of words by relating them to their synonyms, antonyms, and related words. • Demonstrate an understanding of figurative language by generating examples of similes and metaphors. • Identify and define idioms. **Grammar** • Demonstrate an understanding of the function of verb phrases in sentences. • Identify words with multiple functions (noun, verb, adjective) in sentences. **Writing** • Develop and strengthen writing by editing for descriptive details. • Edit for basic written conventions. • Edit to produce clear and coherent writing in which the development and organization are appropriate to the audience.	**Vocabulary** • Clarify the meaning of key passage vocabulary. • Demonstrate an understanding of passage vocabulary by using them in sentences. **Reading** • Discuss and answer questions to demonstrate an understanding of an author's or narrator's point of view in a story. • Discuss and answer questions to demonstrate an understanding of the passages' main idea and key details. **Grammar** • Demonstrate an understanding of inflectional endings by using words with different endings in sentences. **Reading** • Review the elements of a narrative: setting, characters, plot, and resolution. **Vocabulary** • Use key vocabulary from Units 1–9 to tell a story. • Demonstrate an understanding of narrative structure through cooperative storytelling.

Unit 9

Lesson 1

Lesson Opener

Before the lesson, choose one of the following activities to write on the board or post on the *LANGUAGE! Live* Class Wall online.

- *Write a simile about a cute puppy. Write a simile about a boring party. Write a metaphor about a fat cat.*
- *Describe your favorite day.*
- *Write two sentences about your best friend. In the first sentence use a predicate nominative and in the second sentence use a predicate adjective.*

Reading

Objectives

- Determine the topic of the text.
- Discuss differences between nonfiction and narrative fiction.
- Determine the author's purpose.
- Discuss the topic of the text.

Unit Introduction

Direct students to page 113 in their Student Books.

Discuss the content focus of the unit.

Content Focus
time travel

What do you think you will read about in this passage? (Answers will vary based on prior knowledge of time machines.)

Type of Text
narrative

There are different types of texts, or reading selections. The texts we have read so far have been expository, or informational. Recall that informational text is also called *nonfiction,* which means "not fiction," or "not made up." Today we will read a text that belongs to a category called *literature.* Literature consists of stories, poems, and creatively written prose. The text we will read today is a story. It comes from a longer work of fiction called a novel. Remember, a work of fiction is one whose events, characters, and details are made-up, or not factual. Fictional works that tell a story are narratives. Is a fictional work made-up or based on real life? (made-up)

Unit 9
Lesson 1 | Reading

Let's Focus: "The Time Machine"

Content Focus
time travel

Type of Text
narrative—science fiction

Author's Purpose: to entertain

Big Ideas
Consider the following Big Idea questions. Write your answer for each question.

Why are people fascinated by the possibility of time travel?

What would be the consequences of knowing what's in the future?

Narrative Preview Checklist: "The Time Machine"

- ☐ Title: What clue does it provide about the passage?
- ☐ Pictures: What additional information is added here?
- ☐ Margin Information: What vocabulary is important to understand this text?

Reading for a Purpose

1. Why does the Time Traveler think his time machine has failed?
2. How does the Time Traveler know time is speeding by when he pulls the lever a second time?
3. Why does the window grow dark, then brighten, then darken again?
4. What does the Time Traveler think about time travel?
5. What are the consequences of time travel into the future?

Unit 9 113

So, what will today's text contain, facts from real life or made-up characters, events, and details? (made-up characters, events, and details) Will the text tell a story? (yes) What is a work that tells a story? (a narrative) What will the story be about? (a time machine)

Today's story is a work of fiction, and it is a narrative. It also falls into the category of imaginative literature. Imaginative literature includes myth, fantasy, legend, fairy tales, and science fiction. Which of these do you think a story about time travel will be? (science fiction) Science fiction is futuristic; it takes place years in the future. The purpose of science fiction is to entertain, comment on current society, or imagine future science and technology. In general, science fiction explores the question, What if? What type of narrative will we read? (science fiction) Will the story be set in the present, past, or future? (future)

Author's Purpose

The author's purpose is the reason that he or she wrote the text. Authors write for different purposes. Why do authors write texts? (to entertain, to persuade, or to inform or teach) Knowing an author's purpose can help a reader understand a text better. "The Time Machine" was written to entertain us. Was "The Time Machine" written to inform or to entertain? (entertain) Will the author teach you something or entertain you? (entertain) Have students write the answer on the page in their Student Books.

Have we read any other works of literature whose author's purpose was to entertain? (the poem "Dolphin Talk") Like the novel, poetry is a form of literature.

Background Information

"The Time Machine" is an adaptation of the novel *The Time Machine* by H.G. Wells. What does that mean? First, let's determine who wrote the original novel, *The Time Machine*. (H.G. Wells) Do you think we are reading the original story? (no) We will read an adapted version. An adaptation is a reworking, or retelling, of the original text. Have you heard of *The Time Machine* before? Provide response time.

At one time this science fiction work was so popular that it was turned into films, television shows, and comic books. As a matter of fact, H.G. Wells is credited for coining the term *time machine* to mean "a vehicle that allows an operator to travel in time." What is the name of the machine that travels in time? (time machine) Are time machines real? (no) Is the main character, the Time Traveler, real? (no)

Note: The complete unabridged text is available as a free download at http://www.gutenberg.org/ebooks/35.

Play the Unit 9 Text Training video found in the Teacher Resources online.

Before we read "The Time Machine," we will watch a short video to help build background knowledge. Combine what you just heard with what you are about to watch on this video. Listen for two things you did not know about time. You will share this new information with a partner after the video. Play the Unit 9 Text Training video. Have partners discuss what they learned from the video.

Direct students to page 113 in their Student Books. Read the following Big Idea questions aloud:

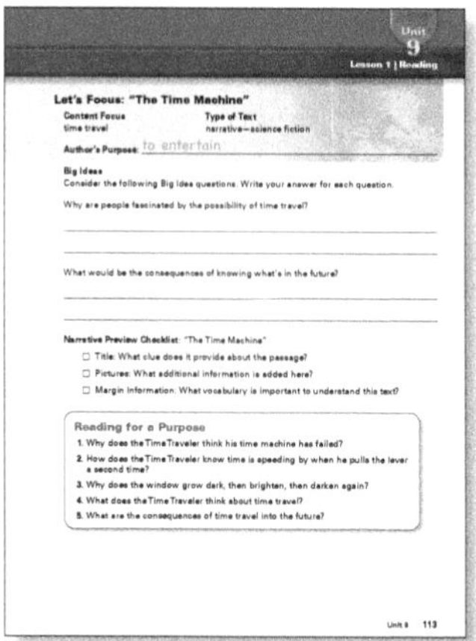
Unit 9
Lesson 1 | Reading

Let's Focus: "The Time Machine"

Content Focus
time travel

Type of Text
narrative—science fiction

Author's Purpose: to entertain

Big Ideas
Consider the following Big Idea questions. Write your answer for each question.

Why are people fascinated by the possibility of time travel?

What would be the consequences of knowing what's in the future?

Narrative Preview Checklist: "The Time Machine"

- ☐ Title: What clue does it provide about the passage?
- ☐ Pictures: What additional information is added here?
- ☐ Margin Information: What vocabulary is important to understand this text?

Reading for a Purpose

1. Why does the Time Traveler think his time machine has failed?
2. How does the Time Traveler know time is speeding by when he pulls the lever a second time?
3. Why does the window grow dark, then brighten, then darken again?
4. What does the Time Traveler think about time travel?
5. What are the consequences of time travel into the future?

Unit 9 113

Big Ideas

Why are people fascinated by the possibility of time travel?

What would be the consequences of knowing what's in the future?

As a class, consider the two Big Idea questions. After discussing each question, have students write an answer. We'll come back to these questions after we finish learning about time travel. You will have much more to add to your answers. You can edit your answers as you gain information.

Preview

Direct students to page 115 in their Student Books to preview the text. Remind them of the Narrative Preview Checklist in their Student Books on page 113. Give students permission to look at the checklist during the preview if they need a reminder of text features.

Lesson 1 | Reading

THE TIME MACHINE

By H.G. Wells
Based on an adaptation by Les Martin

What is time? Is time travel possible? For centuries, these questions have **intrigued** mystics, **philosophers**, and scholars. H.G. Wells, a science teacher and science fiction writer, also became interested in the idea. He published a novel called *The Time Machine* in 1895, and it quickly became famous. In this story of one man's **attempt** to travel through time, the protagonist builds a "black and polished brass" Time Machine and launches it into the future. After a series of harrowing adventures, he returns to the present to **relate** to his friends the **consequences** of seeing things to come.

The following passage, adapted from *The Time Machine*, describes how H.G. Wells's protagonist, the Time Traveler, takes his first flight in the machine he has invented.

intrigue
to stir up interest; fascinate; make curious

philosopher
a person who studies life's unanswered questions and problems

attempt
a try

relate
to tell

consequence
a result or outcome of an event or action

Unit 9 115

Note: Create a small teacher-led group for students who indicated dependence or confusion with the previewing process in Unit 8. New students and truant students should also join this group until they reach independence.

Preview the text using text features. Before we preview the text, let's consider the difference between expository text and narrative text. In previous lessons, when we previewed expository text, we found features such as headings, charts, and graphs. Do you think a narrative text will have the same text features? (no) Good readers quickly determine the type of text they are about to read by noticing certain features. In this case, you will notice that the features of a story, or narrative, are very different from those of an expository, or nonfiction, text. Let's look at the text features together. What do you notice? (no headings, graphs, charts) What do you notice about the color of the text? (It changes from black to purple.)

While reading, we will have to determine why the color changes.

Have students preview the text and predict what will happen in the story. After sufficient time, have partners use the checklist to evaluate each other's previewing skills. Gauge individual success as you circulate around the room. Determine which students need extra practice with the skills and provide them with alternative practice sources.

Vocabulary

Objective

- Determine the meaning of key passage vocabulary.

Rate Your Knowledge

Direct students to page 114 in their Student Books.

You will rate your word knowledge. The purpose of this activity is to recognize how familiar you are with this unit's Key Passage Vocabulary.

Vocabulary Rating Scale poster

Review the Vocabulary Rating Scale with students.

Vocabulary Rating Scale

0—I have never heard the word before.

1—I have heard the word, but I'm not sure how to use it.

2—I am familiar with the word, but I'm not sure if I know the correct meaning.

3—I know the meaning of the word and can use it correctly in a sentence.

Lesson 1 | Vocabulary

Key Passage Vocabulary: "The Time Machine"

Rate your knowledge of the words. Define the words. Draw a picture to help you remember the definition.

Vocabulary	Knowledge Rating	Definition	Picture
intrigue	0 1 2 3	to stir up interest; fascinate; make curious	
philosopher	0 1 2 3	a person who studies life's unanswered questions and problems	
attempt	0 1 2 3	a try	
relate	0 1 2 3	to tell	
consequence	0 1 2 3	a result or outcome of an event or action	
slight	0 1 2 3	small; minor	
moment	0 1 2 3	the time when something happens	
vanish	0 1 2 3	to pass out of sight; disappear	

114 Unit 9

Read the list of words. Have students repeat each word. Provide time for students to rate their knowledge of each word.

Have partners discuss the words they rated as 3s and tell each other the meanings.

Preteach Vocabulary

You've rated your knowledge and talked about what you think the words mean. Now, let's discuss the words.

Preteach Procedure

This activity is intended to take only a short amount of time, so make it an oral exercise if your students aren't capable of writing quickly.

- Introduce each word as indicated on the word card.
- Read the definition and example sentences.
- Ask questions to clarify and deepen understanding.
- If time permits, allow students to share.

* Do not provide instruction time to write definitions or draw pictures, but explain that students should complete both as time permits during the unit.

Note: Research has proven that vocabulary is best learned when students represent their knowledge of words in linguistic and/or nonlinguistic ways. Thus, drawing a picture will help students remember the words. This strategy is especially effective for English language learners.

intrigue

Let's read the first word together. *Intrigue.*

Definition: *Intrigue* means "to stir up the interest of, fascinate, or make curious." To stir up the interest of, fascinate, or make curious is what? (to intrigue)

Example 1: In 1969, Neil Armstrong's walk on the moon *intrigued* people around the world.

Example 2: Because the novel *intrigued* me, I was still reading long after midnight.

Example 3: It *intrigues* me, though it is hard to understand, how far stars really are from Earth.

Question 1: Do the same things *intrigue* all people? Yes or no? (No, but answers will vary.)

Question 2: Can watching a bug *intrigue* someone? Yes or no? (yes)

Pair Share: Turn to your partner and tell two futuristic ideas that *intrigue* you.

philosopher

Let's read the next word together. *Philosopher.*

Definition: A *philosopher* is "a person who studies life's unanswered questions and problems." A person who studies life's unanswered questions and problems is a what? (a philosopher)

Example 1: The *philosopher* Socrates asked questions to lead his students to think logically about difficult or unanswerable questions such as, Who am I?

Example 2: Some questions studied by *philosophers* are moral or ethical questions, such as, Should the rich help the poor?

Example 3: A question a modern *philosopher* might study is, What limits should we put on technology?

Question 1: Does a *philosopher* study easy or hard questions? (hard)

Question 2: Does a *philosopher* use logic and reason? Yes or no? (yes)

Pair Share: With your partner, discuss this question a *philosopher* might study: Is it ever okay to tell a lie? Why?

attempt

Let's read the next word together. *Attempt.*

Definition: An *attempt* is "a try." A try is a what? (an attempt)

Example 1: Our family makes an *attempt* to clean the house on Saturday mornings so we can have fun in the afternoon.

Example 2: Many people have made *attempts* to climb Mt. Everest. Some have succeeded.

Example 3: My *attempt* to become a hip-hop dancer was a failure. I don't know why I even tried.

Question 1: Is an *attempt* an action? Yes or no? (yes)

Question 2: Is an *attempt* purposeful? Yes or no? (yes)

Pair Share: Tell your partner about something you have recently *attempted* and succeeded at.

relate

Let's read the next word together. *Relate.*

Definition: To *relate* means "to tell." To tell is to what? (relate)

Example 1: Each student *related* his or her version of the event to the principal.

Example 2: Dad asked me to *relate* the message that dinner would be ready at 6:30.

Example 3: During an oral test, it is important to accurately *relate* information to the teacher.

Question 1: Can a fish *relate* a message? Yes or no? (no)

Question 2: To *relate* a message, what is the minimum number of people needed? (two)

Pair Share: Turn to your partner and *relate* your most recent act of kindness.

consequence

Let's read the next word together. *Consequence.*

Definition: A *consequence* means "a result or outcome of an event or action." A result or outcome of an event or action is a what? (a consequence)

Example 1: I knew I was speeding, and one *consequence* of this choice was a speeding ticket.

Example 2: I chose to stay out past my curfew and knew that I would be grounded as a *consequence.*

Example 3: I studied hard, and the *consequence* was a good grade on the test.

Question 1: Is a *consequence* always bad? Yes or no? (no)

Question 2: Does a *consequence* involve an action? Yes or no? (yes)

Pair Share: Turn to your partner and relate the dangerous *consequences* of texting while driving.

slight

Let's read the next word together. *Slight.*

Definition: *Slight* means "small; minor." Something small and minor is what? (slight)

Example 1: On an electronic tablet you only need a *slight* touch to get the icons to move.

Example 2: The road was slick, and I was afraid even a *slight* skid would send me into the ditch.

Example 3: I have studied well, so I am not the *slightest* bit worried about the test.

Question 1: When you wink an eye, is that a *slight* movement? Yes or no? (yes)

Question 2: Can a person have a *slight* headache? Yes or no? (yes)

Pair Share: Turn to your partner and differentiate between massive and *slight.*

moment

Let's read the next word together. *Moment.*

Definition: A *moment* means "the time when something happens." The time when something happens is the what? (moment)

Example 1: The Civil War was a defining *moment* in American history.

Example 2: The quarterback released the ball a *moment* before he was tackled.

Example 3: The *moment* my head hit the pillow, I was sound asleep.

Question 1: Can a *moment* be a second? (yes) Can a *moment* be a minute? (yes)

Question 2: Is a *moment* related to time? Yes or no? (yes)

Pair Share: With your partner, relate a defining *moment* in your life.

vanish

Let's read the last word together. *Vanish.*

Definition: *Vanish* means "to pass out of sight or disappear." To pass out of sight or disappear is what? (to vanish)

Example 1: I had just finished my report when it *vanished* from my computer.

Example 2: Dinosaurs *vanished* from the planet about 65 million years ago.

Example 3: I took an aspirin and my headache *vanished.*

Question 1: Can a magician seem to make something *vanish*? Yes or no? (yes)

Question 2: Can a thief make your car *vanish*? Yes or no? (yes)

Pair Share: Tell your partner about a moment you wished you could have *vanished.*

Reading

Objectives

- Preview the passage by reviewing text features.
- Read a narrative text.
- Demonstrate an understanding of the text by asking and answering questions and referring to key details in the text.

"The Time Machine"

Direct students to page 115 in their Student Books.

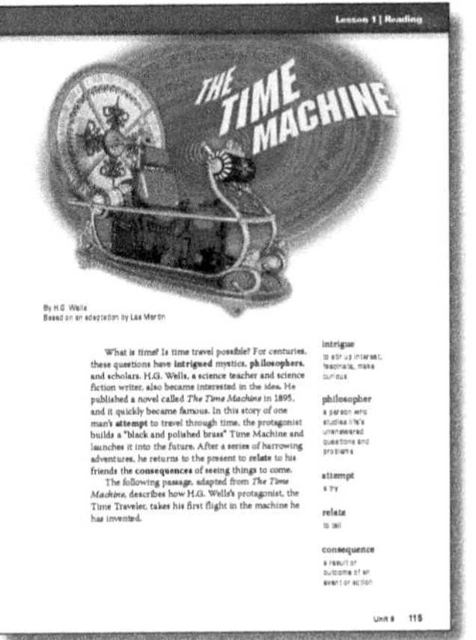

Lesson 1 | Reading

THE TIME MACHINE

By H.G. Wells
Based on an adaptation by Lee Martin

What is time? Is time travel possible? For centuries, these questions have **intrigued** mystics, **philosophers**, and scholars. H.G. Wells, a science teacher and science fiction writer, also became interested in the idea. He published a novel called *The Time Machine* in 1895, and it quickly became famous. In this story of one man's **attempt** to travel through time, the protagonist builds a "black and polished brass" Time Machine and launches it into the future. After a series of harrowing adventures, he returns to the present to **relate** to his friends the **consequences** of seeing things to come.

The following passage, adapted from *The Time Machine*, describes how H.G. Wells's protagonist, the Time Traveler, takes his first flight in the machine he has invented.

intrigue to stir up interest; fascinate; make curious

philosopher a person who studies life's unanswered questions and problems

attempt a try

relate to tell

consequence a result or outcome of an event or action

Unit 9 115

Lesson 1 | Reading

H.G. Wells

It was almost four in the morning, and I had finished my work, so I measured the levers one last time, and now, only one thing was left to do. I had to give the Time Machine its first test.

I sat down in the seat of the Time Machine and looked at my pocket watch; it said nineteen minutes after four. I held my breath as I gripped the lever and pulled it down a tiny bit. How can I say what it felt like? Only that it felt like falling; it felt like falling through endless space. My stomach was trying to squeeze into my throat, and my mouth was open; it looked like the mouth of a fish—a fish gasping in air.

Quickly, I pulled the stop lever and felt a **slight** bump and the machine came to a stop. I looked around and my heart sank.

My tools were exactly where I had laid them, my coat still hung over a chair, and my workshop was just as I had left it; my machine was a failure.

slight small, minor

116 Unit 9

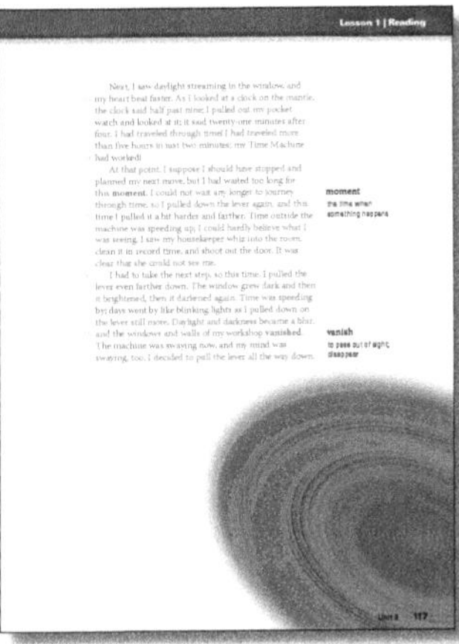

Lesson 1 | Reading

Next, I saw daylight streaming in the window, and my heart beat faster. As I looked at a clock on the mantle, the clock said half past nine; I pulled out my pocket watch and looked at it; it said twenty-one minutes after four. I had traveled through time! I had traveled more than five hours in just two minutes; my Time Machine had worked!

At that point, I suppose I should have stopped and planned my next move, but I had waited too long for this **moment**. I could not wait any longer to journey through time, so I pulled down the lever again, and this time I pulled it a bit harder and farther. Time outside the machine was speeding up; I could hardly believe what I was seeing. I saw my housekeeper whiz into the room, clean it in record time, and shoot out the door. It was clear that she could not see me.

I had to take the next step, so this time, I pulled the lever even farther down. The window grew dark and then it brightened, then it darkened again. Time was speeding by; days went by like blinking lights as I pulled down on the lever still more. Daylight and darkness became a blur, and the windows and walls of my workshop **vanished**. The machine was swaying now, and my mind was swaying, too. I decided to pull the lever all the way down.

moment the time when something happens

vanish to pass out of sight; disappear

Unit 9 117

Lesson 1 | Reading

The next thing I saw around me was a world of wonders. Huge buildings were rising taller and taller; skies were changing from dark gray to bright blue; the countryside grew greener and greener. What a fantastic show! It was hard to turn my eyes away, and when I did, I looked at the dials. They told me how fast and far I was traveling. I was shocked; I had gone much faster and farther than I thought. I was in the year AD 802,701. Those huge numbers made me lose my head, and I was in a panic; I yanked hard on the stop lever.

At last, I paid the price because the stop was too sharp and the machine tipped over. I was thrown from my seat. Stunned, I lay on soft green grass. I heard a very loud thunderclap, and a shower of hailstones stung my face. It was impossible to see. "A fine welcome," I muttered, "a man travels over 800,000 years for a visit, and this is the greeting he gets!" Then the hail thinned, the sun shone through a break in the clouds, and I got my first good look at the world of the future.

H.G. Wells published The Time Machine in 1895.

118 Unit 9

Words to Know

In addition to the vocabulary words, here are some words students might have trouble with:

possible able to happen or be done

century a period of 100 years

harrowing very upsetting or disturbing

scholars people who have great knowledge about a subject

failure something that does not work or succeed

suppose to believe that something is true but without strong feeling

hardly almost not; barely

panic a sudden strong feeling of fear or anger that causes people to act without thinking carefully

We reviewed the differences between text features of fiction and nonfiction text. Let's discuss some key points before we read.

- Text features provide information about a text before we read it. Text features can sometimes help us identify the topic, which is the subject of the passage. What is the topic of "The Time Machine"? (time travel or time machine)
- Notice the picture next to the title "The Time Machine." How would you describe the picture? (Answers will vary.) Is this a vehicle that exists today? (No, it is futuristic.) Ask probing questions such as:
  - How many people can fit in the time machine? (one)
  - What is the large round disc on the back of the time machine? (Answers will vary.)

- Let's look at the picture on the next page. What do you see? (a photograph of the author, H.G. Wells) What is he doing? (He is writing with an old-fashioned pen.) What do the first two graphics have in common? (both have a red and purple swirl design) What do you think the swirl is meant to suggest? (time travel)
- Turn to the picture on page 118. What do you see? (A man is riding the time machine with the same red and purple swirl in the background. The man looks like H.G. Wells.) Is the time machine exactly the same as the one on page 115? (no) Note a few differences.

  Describe the sky in the picture. (The sky is blue with stars and short lines that could be rain or could be showing movement.)

Direct students to page 113 in their Student Books. Have students look at the prompts while you read them aloud.

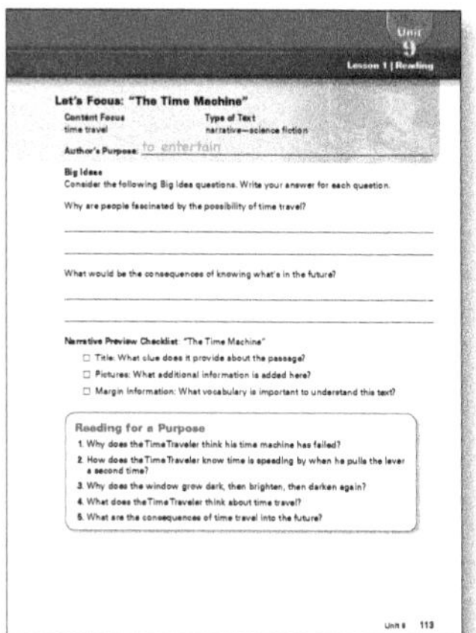

Reading for a Purpose

1. Why does the Time Traveler think his time machine has failed?
2. How does the Time Traveler know time is speeding by when he pulls the lever a second time?
3. Why does the window grow dark, then brighten, then darken again?
4. What does the Time Traveler think about time travel?
5. What are the consequences of time travel into the future?

You will become equipped to answer these questions by reading the passage. For now, let the questions guide your reading. Be on the lookout for information you could use to respond to them. While reading, you also should think about our two Big Idea questions: Why are people fascinated by the possibility of time travel? and What would be the consequences of knowing what's in the future?

Direct students to page 115 in their Student Books. Now it's time to read. Where are your eyes while I read? (on text) Where is your pencil? (following along, word for word) Eyes on text, pencil on words. Follow along with your pencil eraser as I read the text. Read the passage aloud.

Guiding Students Toward Independent Reading

While the lessons are written for a teacher read aloud, it is important that your students read as much and as often as they can. Assign readings that meet the needs of your students, based on your observations or data. This is a good opportunity to stretch students, but if they become frustrated, return to the read-aloud method.

Options for reading text:

- Teacher read aloud
- Teacher-led or student-led choral read
- Independent read of small sections with frequent comprehension checks
- Paired read or independent read

The Time Machine

What is time? Is time travel possible? For centuries, these questions have intrigued mystics, philosophers, and scholars. H.G. Wells, a science teacher and science fiction writer, also became interested in the idea. He published a novel called *The Time Machine* in 1895, and it quickly became famous. In this story of one man's attempt to travel through time, the protagonist builds a "black and polished brass" Time Machine and launches it into the future. After a series of harrowing adventures, he returns to the present to relate to his friends the consequences of seeing things to come.

The following passage, adapted from *The Time Machine*, describes how H.G. Wells's protagonist, the Time Traveler, takes his first flight in the machine he has invented.

Timer

For confirmation of engagement, take 30 seconds to have students share one thing they learned with their partner. If needed, provide this example for students: While reading the introduction, I was thinking that it would be scary to travel into the future by myself. I would want my best friend with me. Your turn. Share your thoughts about time travel with your partner. Partners, you should listen carefully and ask questions to check understanding. Provide sharing time.

Let's continue by reading an excerpt from the book *The Time Machine*. Follow along with your pencil eraser as I read the text. Read the entire excerpt without interruption.

It was almost four in the morning, and I had finished my work, so I measured the levers one last time, and now, only one thing was left to do. I had to give the Time Machine its first test.

I sat down in the seat of the Time Machine and looked at my pocket watch; it said nineteen minutes after four. I held my breath as I gripped the lever and pulled it down a tiny bit. How can I say what it felt like? Only that it felt like falling; it felt like falling through endless space. My stomach was trying to squeeze into my throat, and my mouth was open; it looked like the mouth of a fish—a fish gasping in air.

Quickly, I pulled the stop lever and felt a slight bump and the machine came to a stop. I looked around and my heart sank.

My tools were exactly where I had laid them, my coat still hung over a chair, and my workshop was just as I had left it; my machine was a failure.

Next, I saw daylight streaming in the window, and my heart beat faster. As I looked at a clock on the mantle, the clock said half past nine; I pulled out my pocket watch and looked at it; it said twenty-one minutes after four. I had traveled through time! I had traveled more than five hours in just two minutes; my Time Machine had worked!

At that point, I suppose I should have stopped and planned my next move, but I had waited too long for this moment. I could not wait any longer to journey through time, so I pulled down the lever again, and this time I pulled it a bit harder and farther. Time outside the machine was speeding up; I could hardly believe what I was seeing. I saw my housekeeper whiz into the room, clean it in record time, and shoot out the door. It was clear that she could not see me.

I had to take the next step, so this time, I pulled the lever even farther down. The window grew dark and then it brightened, then it darkened again. Time was speeding by; days went by like blinking lights as I pulled down on the lever still more. Daylight and darkness became a blur, and the windows and walls of my workshop vanished. The machine was swaying now, and my mind was swaying, too. I decided to pull the lever all the way down.

The next thing I saw around me was a world of wonders. Huge buildings were rising taller and taller; skies were changing from dark gray to bright blue; the countryside grew greener and greener. What a fantastic show! It was hard to turn my eyes away, and when I did, I looked at the dials. They told me how fast and far I was traveling. I was shocked; I had gone much faster and farther than I thought. I was in the year AD 802,701. Those huge numbers made me lose my head, and I was in a panic; I yanked hard on the stop lever.

At last, I paid the price because the stop was too sharp and the machine tipped over. I was thrown from my seat. Stunned, I lay on soft green grass. I heard a very loud thunderclap, and a shower of hailstones stung my face. It was impossible to see. "A fine welcome," I muttered, "a man travels over 800,000 years for a visit, and this is the greeting he gets!" Then the hail thinned, the sun shone through a break in the clouds, and I got my first good look at the world of the future.

For confirmation of engagement, take 30 seconds to have students share one thing they learned with their partner. While reading, I was wondering about the consequences of time travel and thinking the Time Traveler was rather impulsive to keep pulling the lever without stopping to think first. Your turn. Switch roles. Share your thoughts about this time travel story with your partner. Partners, you should listen carefully and ask questions to check understanding.

Now that you have read "The Time Machine," tell me something about the Time Machine or the Time Traveler. Have students share answers.

Unit 9

Lesson 2

Lesson Opener

Before the lesson, choose one of the following activities to write on the board or post on the *LANGUAGE! Live* Class Wall online.

- *Write a sentence about what you plan to do this weekend using a coordinating conjunction.*
- *How does the main character know he has successfully traveled through time?*
- *If you could travel to the future, at what age would you like to see yourself? Why?*

Vocabulary

Objectives

- Determine the meanings of the multiple-meaning word *test*.
- Demonstrate an understanding of the word by using it in a written sentence.

Multiple-Meaning Word: *test*

In this unit, we are talking about a time machine created by an inventor. Inventors spend much of their time coming up with ideas and creating things. Then, they *test* each invention over and over it to see if it works.

Test is a word that has more than one meaning. The word *test* can be a noun, an adjective, or a verb. It all depends on how it is used in a sentence. When we read, how do we know which meaning is being used? We look for clues around the word to help us.

Direct students to page 119 in their Student Books. Lead students in a discussion of the various meanings of the word *test*. Have them write the meanings and sentences on the Multiple-Meaning Map.

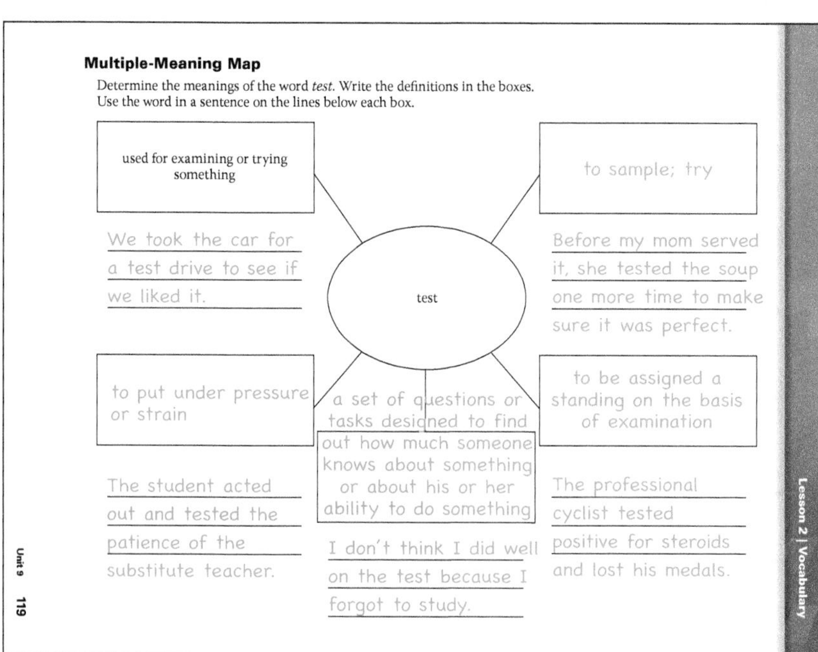

Multiple-Meaning Map
Determine the meanings of the word test. Write the definitions in the boxes. Use the word in a sentence on the lines below each box.
used for examining or trying something
We took the car for a test drive to see if we liked it.
to sample; try
Before my mom served it, she tested the soup one more time to make sure it was perfect.
test
to put under pressure or strain
The student acted out and tested the patience of the substitute teacher.
a set of questions or tasks designed to find out how much someone knows about something or about his or her ability to do something
I don't think I did well on the test because I forgot to study.
to be assigned a standing on the basis of examination
The professional cyclist tested positive for steroids and lost his medals.
Unit 9 119
Lesson 2 | Vocabulary

Model

Have you ever gone with someone to buy a car? Before people decide whether they want to buy a car, they go on a *test* drive. This is an example of the word *test* being used as an adjective. It tells what kind of drive it is. In a test drive, people *test* a vehicle to see if they like it. The definition of the word *test* in this usage is "used for testing or revealed by testing." Write the definition on the board and have students find it on their map. Have students think of a good sentence for this usage and write it below the definition.

Guided Practice

I have a difficult student who really *tests* my patience. He is constantly off task, out of his seat, and bothering other students. What is the definition of the word *test* in this case? (to put under pressure or strain) Write the definition on the board and have students write it on their map. Have students think of a good sentence for this usage and write it below the definition. Continue the process until the maps are complete. Review the sentences and have students correct as needed.

Note: Base the number of modeled and guided examples on student ability and progress. Challenge them with independent practice when appropriate.

Additional Definitions of *test*

Noun

- an examination or experiment to find out what something is, what it is made up of, or how good it is

Verb

- to apply a criteria for analysis

Grammar

Objective

- Demonstrate an understanding of the function of compound sentences and conjunctions used in sentences.

Compound Sentences and Conjunctions

In the previous unit, we worked with words that help us join ideas in our speaking *and* writing. In fact, I just used a joining word. What joining word did I use? (and)

We can use joining words to talk about more than one thing *or* more than one action. I just used another one! I used it to show a choice. What word did I use? (or)

We can also use these special words to join complete sentences, *but* we have to remember to punctuate the new sentence correctly. I just used the third joining word to contrast the idea of punctuating the sentence correctly when we write. What was it? (but) What do we call words like *and, but,* and *or*? (conjunctions)

Write the following sentences on the board:

Beth or Robert will pick you up.

Sam washed and dried the dishes.

I needed tape to finish the project, but I had used all of it.

Read each sentence and have students identify the conjunctions. Underline each conjunction. Then have students identify what parts of each sentence have been "compounded": the subjects, the predicates, or two complete sentences. Circle the subject in the first sentence, the predicate in the second sentence, and the two complete sentences in the third.

Direct students to page 120 in their Student Books.

Model

Read the instructions and the example with students. Complete the first item as a model.

Guided and Independent Practice

Then read each remaining sentence, asking students to identify the conjunction and decide what parts of the sentence have been "compounded." Review the answers as a class.

Note: Base the number of modeled and guided examples on student ability and progress. Challenge them with independent practice when appropriate.

Lesson 2 | Grammar

Find It: Conjunctions

Read each sentence. Underline the conjunction. Determine whether the conjunction creates a compound subject, a compound predicate, or a compound sentence and write your answer on the line.

Example: Their tent and raft passed the test. compound subject

1. I sat down in the seat of the Time Machine and looked at my pocket watch. compound predicate
2. It was almost morning, and I had finished my work. compound sentence
3. I live in modern times, but I visited historic times. compound sentence
4. I gripped the lever and pulled it down slowly. compound predicate
5. My stomach was in my throat, and my mouth was opened like a fish. compound sentence
6. My tools and my jacket were still in the same place. compound subject
7. I felt a slight bump, and the machine came to a stop. compound sentence
8. The windows and walls of my workshop vanished. compound subject
9. The machine was swaying, and my mind was swaying, too. compound sentence
10. Many people study time, but few understand it. compound sentence

120 Unit 9

Reading

Objective

- Demonstrate an understanding of the elements of a narrative, including setting, characters, plot, climax, and resolution.

Story Elements

Direct students to page 121 in their Student Books. Let's think for a minute about the types of text we have worked with in this program. We have read informational text in each unit. What other types of writing have we read? (persuasive letter, poem)

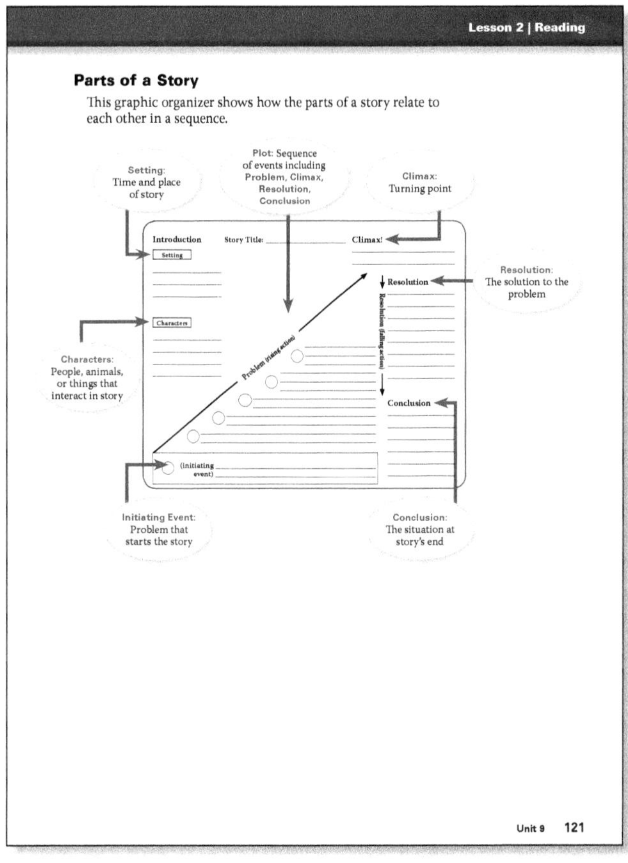
Lesson 2 | Reading

Parts of a Story

This graphic organizer shows how the parts of a story relate to each other in a sequence.

Unit 9 121

In the unit on censorship, we read two different text selections. What was the second type of text we read? (a letter) We learned how one mother felt about inappropriate messages in the media. In her letter, she expressed opinions, which made the text different from the expository texts we had read. It was persuasive.

What kind of non-informational writing did we explore in the unit on whales? (a poem about dolphins) We learned how poetry differs from informational text in form and in its reliance on descriptive and figurative language.

In this unit, we are reading an entirely different kind of literary text: a story, or narrative, taken from a longer fictional work called a novel. The features of narrative texts, or stories, are different from those of expository texts. Look at the diagram in your book as we talk about the different features, or elements, of a story.

Setting

Stories take place in a certain time and place. This time and place is referred to as a story's setting. Do you think a story can have more than one setting? (yes) Does "The Time Machine" include different places and times? (yes) Is the story from modern times? (No, it was written in 1895.) "It was almost four in the morning, and I had finished my work," the Time Traveler says at the beginning of the story. Where does it sound like he is? (his lab) So, when the story opens, the setting is around the year 1895, in an inventor's lab.

Characters

Stories also have characters, some more important than others. In the excerpt from "The Time Machine," we meet only one character. Who is it? (the Time Traveler) This character is telling his story to someone. To whom is he telling it? (his friends)

Problem

Most stories include a problem, or initiating event, that sets other events in motion. Even though we've read only an excerpt of a longer novel, this excerpt introduces us to the central problem that drives the main character to act. What is it? (He wants the machine he built to travel through time.) This may not be the main problem of the novel, but it is the main problem for the short excerpt we are reading. We can only imagine other problems the character will encounter as he travels through time!

Climax

All stories have a plot, or a sequence of events that happen as a result of the problem. As these events unfold, tension builds. The reader grows more eager to see what will happen. Finally, the story reaches a turning point, or climax.

Resolution and Conclusion

Often, a resolution, or wrap-up, follows the turning point. The resolution ties up all the story threads in a neat conclusion. Sometimes a conclusion gives clues that another story, or sequel, is coming. Alert readers stay on the lookout for such clues—especially if they liked the story and hope there is more to come.

Let's choose a story you know well and identify its story elements. Ask students about movies they have seen and choose one to work with.

Example of Story Elements for *The Hunger Games*

Setting:	District 12 in Panem, a country in the future on the continent of North America
Characters:	Katniss, her family (mother and sister Prim), Peeta, Gale, Haymitch, President Snow, Effie
Problem:	surviving the Hunger Games, an event designed to keep the districts loyal and remind them of the price they will pay if they revolt
Climax:	when Peeta and Katniss threaten to eat the poisonous berries and rob the Hunger Games of a victor
Resolution:	The rules of the game are changed and both Katniss and Peeta are declared winners.
Conclusion:	riding the train home, understanding what has been "put in play" by challenging the rules of the game; sets up further action in a sequel

If time permits, choose a fairy tale or fable that all students know, for example, "Little Red Riding Hood" or "The Tortoise and the Hare." Have partners identify the story elements. Review the answers as a class. Write correct answers on the board.

Unit 9

Lesson 3

Lesson Opener

Before the lesson, choose one of the following activities to write on the board or post on the *LANGUAGE! Live* Class Wall online.

- *Describe your avatar's outfit today using a compound sentence.*
- *Write three sentences with the word* test, *using a different meaning in each sentence.*
- *Describe your setting right now. Remember to include time and place.*

Reading

Objective

- Read words to develop fluency.

Word Fluency: First Read

Timer

Follow the Fluency Procedure outlined below. If it is necessary, begin the fluency drill with a choral read of the words as you provide a rhythm (snap your fingers, tap your foot, tap your pencil). Direct students to page 122 in their Student Books and complete the process.

Word Fluency: First Read

Read the words fluently.

	Correct	Errors
1st Try		
2nd Try		

called	booted	bowls	soon	booth	stalling	toyed	herded	march	show	10
bowls	soon	booth	stalling	toyed	herded	march	show	jerked	sport	20
booth	stalling	toyed	herded	march	show	jerked	sport	drowned	germs	30
toyed	herded	march	show	jerked	sport	drowned	germs	thorns	formed	40
march	show	jerked	sport	drowned	germs	thorns	formed	snow	sorted	50
jerked	sport	drowned	germs	thorns	formed	snow	sorted	torched	crowded	60
drowned	germs	thorns	formed	snow	sorted	torched	crowded	booted	called	70
thorns	formed	snow	sorted	torched	crowded	booted	called	soon	bowls	80
snow	sorted	torched	crowded	booted	called	soon	bowls	stalling	toyed	90
torched	crowded	booted	called	soon	bowls	stalling	booth	herded	march	100

Lesson 3 | Reading

122 Unit 9

Fluency Procedure

- Partners switch books, so the recorder is marking errors in the reader's book.
- A timer is set for one minute.
- Readers and recorders move left to right, tracking each word with a pencil.
- As readers read the words aloud, recorders mark errors with a small x above the misread word.
- Recorders place a star to the right of the last word read when time ends.
- If the reader is able to read all words in the allotted time, the reader needs to start over at the beginning. The recorder must indicate this feat by placing two stars to the right of the last word read.
- When both students have read, partners switch books.
- Students calculate total words read, then subtract errors and record.
- Students record information on the progress chart in back of the Student Book.

Vocabulary

Objectives

- Review key passage vocabulary.
- Demonstrate an understanding of metaphors and similes.
- Write simple metaphors and similes.

Review

Direct students to page 114 in their Student Books.

Lesson 1 | Vocabulary

Key Passage Vocabulary: "The Time Machine"

Rate your knowledge of the words. Define the words. Draw a picture to help you remember the definition.

Vocabulary	Knowledge Rating	Definition	Picture
intrigue	0 1 2 3	to stir up interest; fascinate; make curious	
philosopher	0 1 2 3	a person who studies life's unanswered questions and problems	
attempt	0 1 2 3	a try	
relate	0 1 2 3	to tell	
consequence	0 1 2 3	a result or outcome of an event or action	
slight	0 1 2 3	small; minor	
moment	0 1 2 3	the time when something happens	
vanish	0 1 2 3	to pass out of sight; disappear	

114 Unit 9

Review the vocabulary words from the passage "The Time Machine." Have students answer with a complete sentence.

- In "The Time Machine," the Time Traveler is very interested in traveling to the future; it fascinates him. What does time travel do to him? (Time travel intrigues him.) To stir up interest, fascinate, or make curious is what? (To stir up interest, fascinate, or make curious is to intrigue.)
- For centuries, time travel has interested people who want to answer the question, Is time travel possible? What kind of professional studies this question? (A philosopher asks the question, Is time travel possible?) A person who studies life's unanswered questions and problems is a what? (A philosopher is a person who studies life's unanswered questions and problems.)
- Is there a *consequence* when the Time Traveler pulls the levers on the Time Machine? (Yes, the consequence is traveling through time.) A result or outcome of an event or action is a what? (A consequence is a result of an action.)
- When the Time Traveler travels to the future, his workshop is no longer visible. What happens to the workshop? (The workshop vanishes as he travels to the future.) To pass out of sight or disappear means to what? (To pass out of sight or disappear is to vanish.)
- At first glance, the Time Traveler thinks that his first effort to travel through time is a failure. What really happens on this try? Use the word *attempt* in your answer. (His first attempt is a success.) A try is a what? (A try is an attempt.)
- The Time Traveler plans to tell his friends all about his experiences traveling through time. How will he tell them the story? (He will relate the story to his friends.) To tell is to what? (To tell is to relate.)
- When the machine comes to a stop the first time, it does not throw him from the machine, or come to a crashing stop. There is a subtle bump. What kind of movement is it? (He experiences a slight bump when the machine stops.) Something that is small or minor is what? (It is slight.)
- The Time Traveler experiences a long-awaited time when he pulls the lever. What has he been waiting for? Use the word *moment* in your answer. (He has been waiting for the moment he will travel in time.) The time when something happens is a what? (The time when something happens is a moment.)

Vocabulary Concept: Metaphors and Similes

Model

A metaphor is a figure of speech that describes something by comparing it to something else but does not use the words *like* or *as*. A metaphor compares two things that are unrelated. Write the following metaphor on the board:

The boy is a beanpole.

A simile is a figure of speech in which two unlike things are compared to show how they are similar. Simile often uses exaggeration and the words *like* or *as*. Write the following similes on the board:

The boy is as skinny as a rail.

The boy is built like a toothpick.

The metaphor and the similes all mean the same thing. What do they mean? (The boy is skinny.) Good writers use figurative language to make ideas come to life. Figurative language helps us paint mental pictures that in turn help us comprehend what we read.

Direct students to Part A on page 123 in their Student Books and read the instructions.

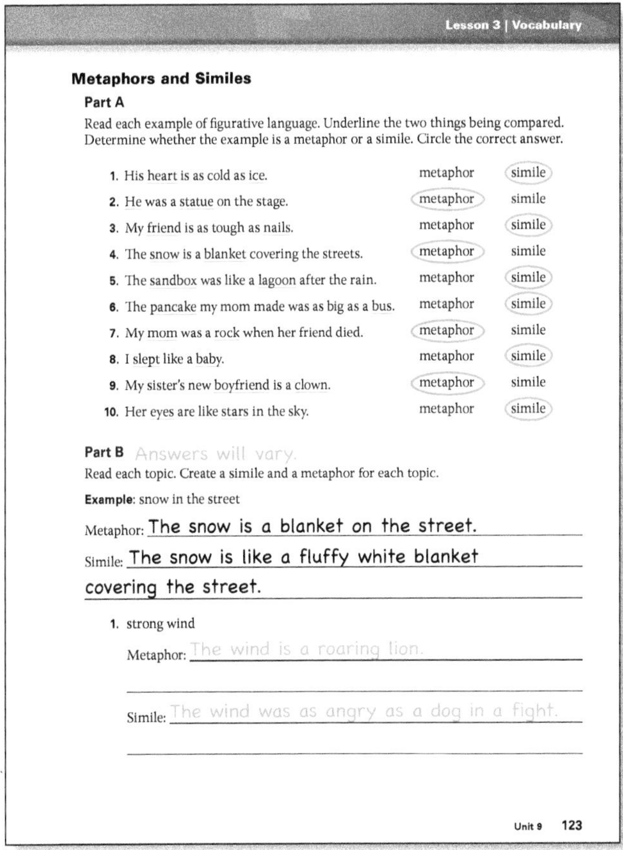

Lesson 3 | Vocabulary

Metaphors and Similes

Part A

Read each example of figurative language. Underline the two things being compared. Determine whether the example is a metaphor or a simile. Circle the correct answer.

1. His heart is as cold as ice. metaphor (simile)
2. He was a statue on the stage. (metaphor) simile
3. My friend is as tough as nails. metaphor (simile)
4. The snow is a blanket covering the streets. (metaphor) simile
5. The sandbox was like a lagoon after the rain. metaphor (simile)
6. The pancake my mom made was as big as a bus. metaphor (simile)
7. My mom was a rock when her friend died. (metaphor) simile
8. I slept like a baby. metaphor (simile)
9. My sister's new boyfriend is a clown. (metaphor) simile
10. Her eyes are like stars in the sky. metaphor (simile)

Part B Answers will vary.

Read each topic. Create a simile and a metaphor for each topic.

Example: snow in the street

Metaphor: The snow is a blanket on the street.

Simile: The snow is like a fluffy white blanket covering the street.

1. strong wind

   Metaphor: The wind is a roaring lion.

   Simile: The wind was as angry as a dog in a fight.

Unit 9 123

Guided Practice

Guide students in completing the first two examples of figurative language. Discuss the meaning of the simile and the metaphor.

Independent Practice

Read the remaining sentences and have students identify what is being compared and whether it is an example of a metaphor or a simile. Review the answers as a class. During the review, have volunteers tell the meaning of each metaphor and simile. Allow students to correct or add to the meanings.

Note: Base the number of modeled and guided examples on student ability and progress. Challenge them with independent practice when appropriate.

Direct students to Part B on pages 123 and 124 in their Student Books and read the instructions.

Model

Write the patterns for creating similes and metaphors on the board and review them. Explain that these simple patterns are not the only way to create metaphors and similes, but they are good ways to get started.

Simile pattern with *like*

______ *like* ______
(verb) *(noun)*

Simile pattern with *as*

as ________ *as* ______
(adjective) *(noun)*

Simple metaphor pattern

______ *is/was* ______
(noun) *(noun)*

Lesson 3 | Vocabulary

Metaphors and Similes (*cont.*)

2. calm nerves

Metaphor: His nerves are steel.

Simile: His nerves are as calm as a lake on a windless day.

3. an old computer

Metaphor: The computer is a dinosaur.

Simile: The computer is as old as the hills.

4. time moving slowly

Metaphor: The minutes were lava slowly creeping down the volcano.

Simile: Time dragged on like a movie in slow motion.

5. time moving rapidly

Metaphor: The time at the amusement park was a speeding bullet.

Simile: The time flew by like a 757 traveling at warp speed.

124 Unit 9

Read the example. Have students note that a topic, such as *snow in the street,* can become a simile or a metaphor.

Direct students' attention to the first topic, *strong wind.* Use the patterns on the board to guide you as you complete the metaphor and simile.

I will use the metaphor pattern. When I think of a *strong wind* I imagine a storm or perhaps a tornado. I write *wind* in the noun spot. I will compare it to something, which will also be a noun. Maybe I will compare it to an animal. Animals that are strong include bears, tigers, and lions. I like lion, so I write *lion* in the blank. I want to make it a little more descriptive, so I add an adjective: *a roaring lion.* And, there is my metaphor. Write the metaphor on the board and read it aloud:

The wind is a roaring lion.

The process is similar in creating a simile. I will use the *as* simile pattern. I write *angry* in the adjective spot because a strong wind can be described as *angry.* I will compare the wind to something, which will be a noun. An animal that can be angry is a dog in a fight. I like that so I write *dog in a fight* in the blank. And there is my simile. Write the metaphor on the board and read it aloud:

The wind was as angry as a dog in a fight.

Now I will use the simile pattern with *like.* I am comparing *wind* to something, so I write *wind* in the noun spot. The wind is like something. Maybe this time, I will compare the wind to an object instead of an animal. The wind in a tornado spins. A top spins. I like the idea of a top. So, I could say, "the wind was spinning like a top."

That is good. But I can also change the words. I like the word *whirling.* Write the simile on the board and read it aloud:

The wind was whirling like a spinning top.

Guided Practice

Guide students in creating a simile and metaphor for the topic *calm nerves.*

Independent Practice

Read the remaining topics, and have partners create a metaphor and simile for each one. Review students' answers as a class.

Note: Base the number of modeled and guided examples on student ability and progress. Challenge them with independent practice when appropriate.

Grammar

Objectives

- Demonstrate an understanding of the difference between past, present, and future tense.
- Write sentences using the future tense.
- Identify the use of past, present, or future tense in sentences.

Tense Timeline: Future

Tense Timeline poster

Present tense talks about today, and past tense talks about yesterday. How do we refer to tomorrow? Direct students to page 125 in their Student Books.

We have two verbs working together to express an action of the future: *will* + the verb. Look at the examples on the tense timeline: I will vote. They will vote. Did you notice that we don't have to change the form of *will* when we change the pronoun? Future tense is easy to recognize and relatively easy to use when we write because of the consistency of the helping verb. Look at the chart that illustrates the use of future tense with singular and plural pronouns for first, second, and third person.

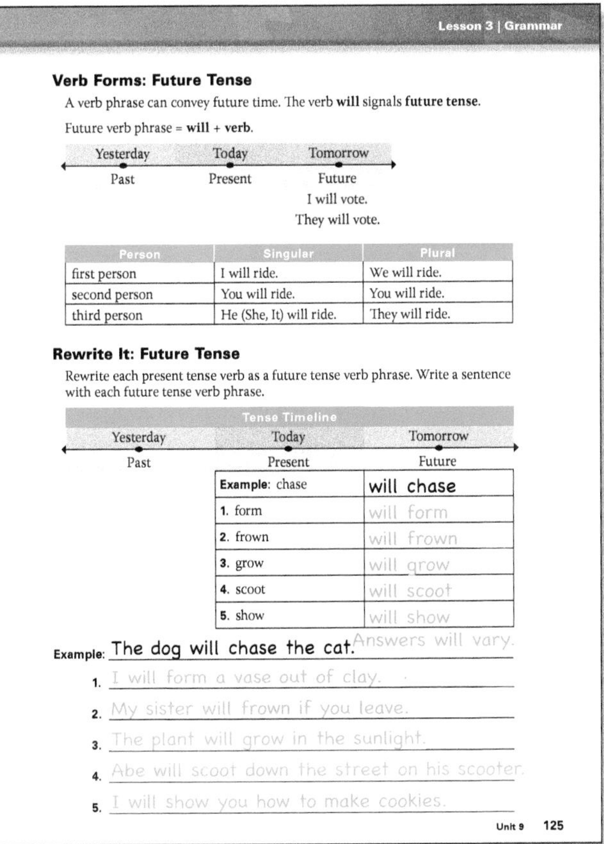

Lesson 3 | Grammar

Verb Forms: Future Tense

A verb phrase can convey future time. The verb **will** signals **future tense.**

Future verb phrase = **will** + **verb.**

Yesterday	Today	Tomorrow
Past	Present	Future
		I will vote. They will vote.

Person	Singular	Plural
first person	I will ride.	We will ride.
second person	You will ride.	You will ride.
third person	He (She, It) will ride.	They will ride.

Rewrite It: Future Tense

Rewrite each present tense verb as a future tense verb phrase. Write a sentence with each future tense verb phrase.

Tense Timeline

Yesterday	Today	Tomorrow
Past	Present	Future
	Example: chase	will chase
	1. form	will form
	2. frown	will frown
	3. grow	will grow
	4. scoot	will scoot
	5. show	will show

Answers will vary.

Example: The dog will chase the cat.

1. I will form a vase out of clay.
2. My sister will frown if you leave.
3. The plant will grow in the sunlight.
4. Abe will scoot down the street on his scooter.
5. I will show you how to make cookies.

Unit 9 125

Model

Read the chart aloud, then read the instructions for the activity. Point out that the goal is to move from present tense to future. Read the model aloud. Have students complete the chart and write sentences. Review the answers in the chart and have volunteers share sentences.

Direct students to page 126 in their Student Books.

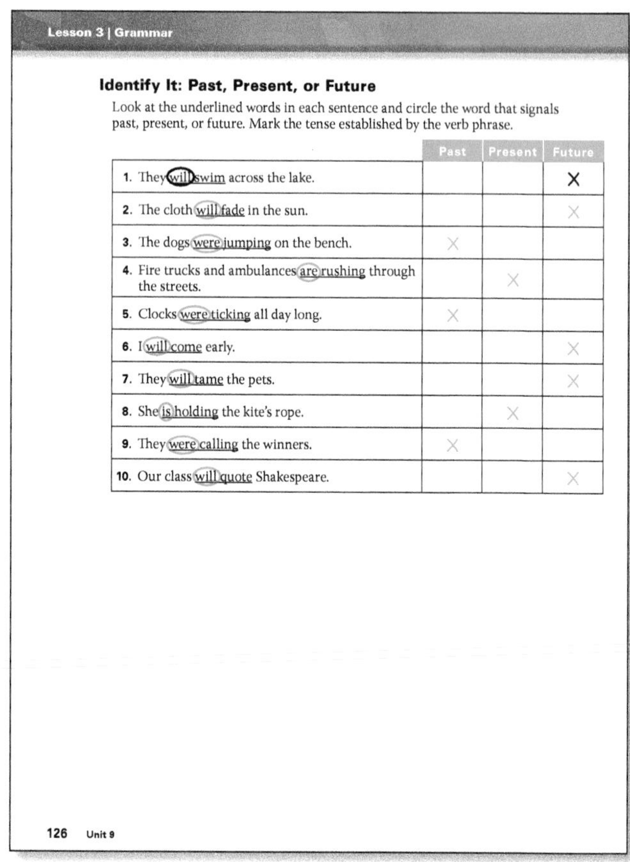

Lesson 3 | Grammar

Identify It: Past, Present, or Future

Look at the underlined words in each sentence and circle the word that signals past, present, or future. Mark the tense established by the verb phrase.

	Past	Present	Future
1. They will swim across the lake.			X
2. The cloth will fade in the sun.			X
3. The dogs were jumping on the bench.	X		
4. Fire trucks and ambulances are rushing through the streets.		X	
5. Clocks were ticking all day long.	X		
6. I will come early.			X
7. They will tame the pets.			X
8. She is holding the kite's rope.		X	
9. They were calling the winners.	X		
10. Our class will quote Shakespeare.			X

126 Unit 9

Guided Practice

Now let's practice identifying the tense in context. Read the instructions and the example. Guide students in completing the first item.

Independent Practice

Read the remaining sentences and have students mark their responses. Review the answers as a class.

Note: Base the number of modeled and guided examples on student ability and progress. Challenge them with independent practice when appropriate.

Reading

Objectives

- Use critical thinking skills to analyze a text.
- Ask and answer questions and prompts using strategic thinking skills to demonstrate an understanding of a text.

Critical Understandings

Direction Words: Strategic Thinking poster

Direct students to the chart on page 16 in their Student Books or refer to the Strategic Thinking poster if you have it displayed.

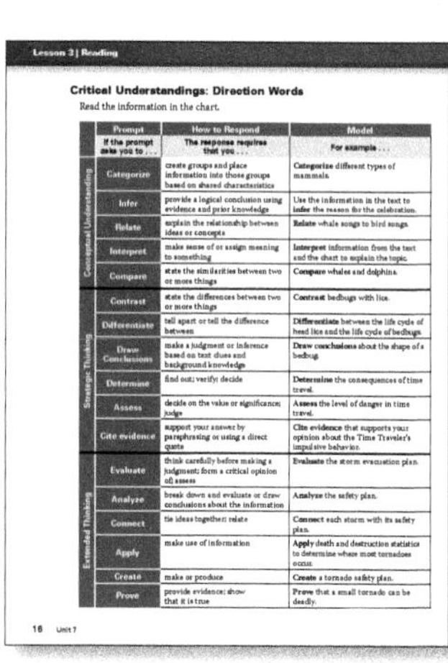

Lesson 3 | Reading

Critical Understandings: Direction Words

Read the information in the chart.

	Prompt	How to Respond	Model
	If the prompt asks you to . . .	The response requires that you . . .	For example . . .
Conceptual Understanding	Categorize	create groups and place information into those groups based on shared characteristics	**Categorize** different types of mammals.
	Infer	provide a logical conclusion using evidence and prior knowledge	Use the information in the text to **infer** the reason for the celebration.
	Relate	explain the relationship between ideas or concepts	**Relate** whale songs to bird songs.
	Interpret	make sense of or assign meaning to something	**Interpret** information from the text and the chart to explain the topic.
	Compare	state the similarities between two or more things	**Compare** whales and dolphins.
Strategic Thinking	Contrast	state the differences between two or more things	**Contrast** bedbugs with lice.
	Differentiate	tell apart or tell the difference between	**Differentiate** between the life cycle of head lice and the life cycle of bedbugs.
	Draw Conclusions	make a judgment or inference based on text clues and background knowledge	**Draw conclusions** about the shape of a bedbug.
	Determine	find out; verify; decide	**Determine** the consequences of time travel.
	Assess	decide on the value or significance; judge	**Assess** the level of danger in time travel.
	Cite evidence	support your answer by paraphrasing or using a direct quote	**Cite evidence** that supports your opinion about the Time Traveler's impulsive behavior.
Extended Thinking	Evaluate	think carefully before making a judgment; form a critical opinion of; assess	**Evaluate** the storm evacuation plan.
	Analyze	break down and evaluate or draw conclusions about the information	**Analyze** the safety plan.
	Connect	tie ideas together; relate	**Connect** each storm with its safety plan.
	Apply	make use of information	**Apply** death and destruction statistics to determine where most tornadoes occur.
	Create	make or produce	**Create** a tornado safety plan.
	Prove	provide evidence; show that it is true	**Prove** that a small tornado can be deadly.

16 Unit 7

We have been responding to higher level prompts that require you to recall information or find evidence in the text. Evidence can be a single word, a phrase, a sentence, or a group of sentences.

Proficient readers are strategic thinkers who make connections between texts, are curious about new information, and are able to reevaluate their own opinions based on what they read. At the strategic thinking level, you will need to recall, understand,

and use advanced strategies to construct responses to prompts. You will need deeper knowledge about the subject matter. At this level of comprehension, you will need to recall information, understand what the information means, and think strategically about new information.

You have already learned how to respond to three different prompts at the strategic thinking level: those that ask you to *contrast*, *differentiate*, and *draw conclusions*. Today we will learn to respond to three more prompts at the strategic thinking level: those that ask you to *determine*, *assess*, and *cite evidence*.

Determine

If a prompt asks you to *determine*, you are being asked to find out, verify, or decide something. For example, if I asked you to determine the consequences of time travel, you would have to find out or decide what would happen if you traveled through time. How will you respond if a prompt asks you to determine something? (find out, verify, or decide)

Assess

If the prompt asks you to *assess*, it is asking you to determine or decide on the value or significance of something. If the prompt asks you to assess, you will need to judge something. Read the example with me. (Assess the level of danger in time travel.) When you assess the level of danger in time travel, you are determining the amount of danger based on what you read and what you already know.

Cite Evidence

If the prompt asks you to *cite evidence*, the response requires that you support your answer by paraphrasing or using a direct quote from the text. Read the example with me. (Cite evidence that supports your opinion about the Time Traveler's impulsive behavior.) When you cite evidence, you are giving credit to the writer by providing proof from the text for your answer. It is important to credit your sources when citing evidence to avoid plagiarism. Plagiarism is copying, stealing, or illegally using other writers' words or ideas. To avoid plagiarism, use quotation marks to differentiate, or set apart, other writers' words or ideas from your own.

At each level, it is critical to understand what the prompt is asking and how to respond. We will become automatic with these prompts and learn exactly how to respond at a mastery level.

Look at the How to Respond column in the Critical Understandings chart. Look at the two sections, Conceptual Understanding and Strategic Thinking. Some prompts have the same or similar meanings. Which prompts ask you to decide or judge? (determine and assess) Which prompt expects you to give credit to others for their work? (cite evidence)

Each conceptual understanding and strategic thinking prompt requires you to construct a higher level response by using information from different sources, including your own prior knowledge, the text, charts, and graphs. Proficient readers can also determine when the text leaves matters uncertain and how to "fill in the blanks" with additional information from another source. We will practice identifying examples of text that does not provide enough information and requires additional research.

Direct students to page 128 in their Student Books. Let's preview some prompts that require strategic thinking about a short piece of text. I'll read the prompt, and you repeat the bold direction words.

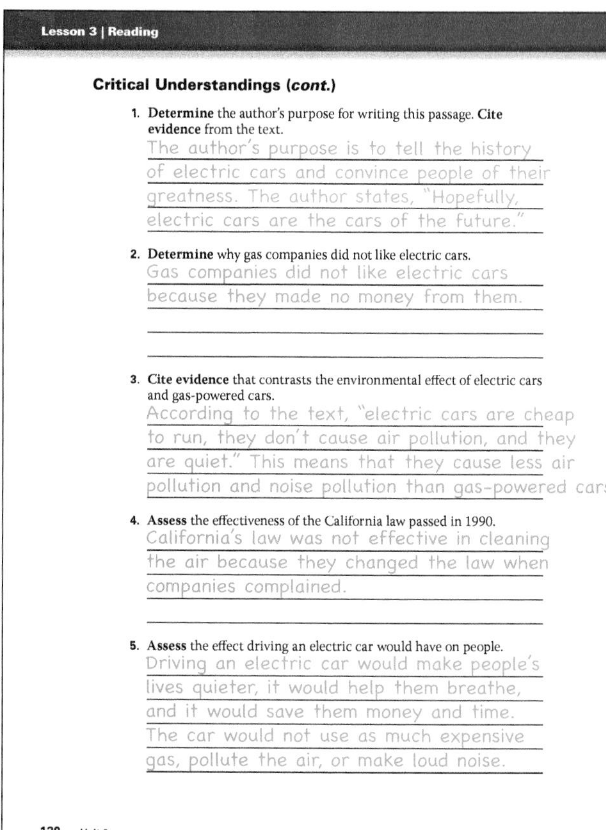

Lesson 3 | Reading
Critical Understandings (cont.)
1. Determine the author's purpose for writing this passage. Cite evidence from the text.
The author's purpose is to tell the history of electric cars and convince people of their greatness. The author states, "Hopefully, electric cars are the cars of the future."
2. Determine why gas companies did not like electric cars.
Gas companies did not like electric cars because they made no money from them.
3. Cite evidence that contrasts the environmental effect of electric cars and gas-powered cars.
According to the text, "electric cars are cheap to run, they don't cause air pollution, and they are quiet." This means that they cause less air pollution and noise pollution than gas-powered cars.
4. Assess the effectiveness of the California law passed in 1990.
California's law was not effective in cleaning the air because they changed the law when companies complained.
5. Assess the effect driving an electric car would have on people.
Driving an electric car would make people's lives quieter, it would help them breathe, and it would save them money and time. The car would not use as much expensive gas, pollute the air, or make loud noise.
128 Unit 9

Notice that direction words often come at the beginning of a prompt. Sometimes the prompt can have more than one direction. Which prompt includes more than one direction? (number 1) Some prompts require you to include a direct quote from the text. When we use someone else's exact words, we put quotation marks around the sentence to credit the writer for his or her words or ideas. Which prompts require a direct quote from the text? (1 and 3) What are the direction words that ask you to provide a direct quote? (cite evidence)

Direct students to page 127 in their Student Books. With eyes on text, listen while I read this short text about the cars of the future. Use your pencil eraser to follow along. Let's begin. Read the text aloud.

Note: While the lessons are written for a teacher read aloud, it is important that your students read as much and as often as they can. Assign readings that meet the needs of your students, based on your observations or data. This is a good opportunity to stretch students, but if they become frustrated, return to the read-aloud method.

Cars of the Future?

An electric car is run by electricity instead of gas. Electric cars are cheap to run, they don't cause air pollution, and they are quiet. Owners plug cars into electrical outlets to make them run, so they save money on gas. People who have owned electric cars love them. But there are few electric cars around today.

Back in the 1890s, electric cars ruled the road. Only one car in every ten was run by gas. All cars were made by hand. But when factories started making cars, they responded to the need for cars that could make longer trips in shorter amounts of time and built cars that ran on gas. Soon, gas stations sprang up across the United States and gas-powered cars flooded streets and highways. The production of electric cars came to a halt.

In the late 1960s and early 1970s, people became worried about air pollution and gas prices. In 1990, California decided to clean up its dirty air and passed a law requiring car makers to make cleaner cars. Two percent of new cars would have to be electric by 1998. Ten percent of new cars would have to be electric by 2003.

Car companies began building a few electric cars by hand. The people who drove them liked them. But there were others who were against electric cars. Gas companies did not like them. Car companies claimed that not enough people wanted to buy them. They persuaded California to change the 1990 law.

Car companies quit building electric cars again. They went so far as to crush their electric cars, even though fans asked them not to.

Today, people still worry about gas prices and air pollution. There are some electric cars being made. Hybrid cars that run partly on electricity and partly on gas have become popular. Some people think electric cars will someday rule the road again. Hopefully, electric cars are the cars of the future.

Let's check our comprehension of this passage by responding to some prompts that require conceptual understanding of the text. For each prompt, you will need to find evidence in the text to support your answer.

If you struggle to remember how to respond to a prompt, it can be helpful to turn the prompt into a question so you know exactly how to answer it. We will practice responding to prompts that require conceptual understanding and strategic thinking using evidence from text. Try asking yourself a question so that you know exactly how to respond.

Model

Read the first prompt aloud.

1. **Determine** the author's purpose for writing this passage. **Cite evidence** from the text.

We can change this prompt into a question to determine how best to respond. Turn to your neighbor and restate the prompt as a question to demonstrate your understanding of it. Provide time; confirm understanding. The question would be, What is the author's purpose for writing this text?

Because the prompt also asks us to cite evidence, our response will need to include a direct quote from the text. Before we respond, we need to find out, verify, or decide by considering the text. With your partner, write your sentence starter by restating the prompt. When you are happy with your sentence starter, discuss and then answer the question together. Write a response with students based on their combined efforts. (Answers will vary. Possible response: The author's purpose is to tell the history of electric cars and convince people of their greatness. The author states, "Hopefully, electric cars are the cars of the future.")

Guided Practice

Read the next prompt aloud.

2. **Determine** why gas companies did not like electric cars.

We can change this prompt into a question to determine how best to respond. Have students do so. The question would be, Why didn't gas companies like electric cars?

Have partners answer the question. Then offer sentence starters for those who are struggling. While students work, write the following sentence starter on the board:

Gas companies did not like electric cars because ______.

Independent Practice

Have partners complete the remaining prompts. Review the answers as a class to ensure students understand what each prompt is asking.

Note: Base the number of modeled and guided examples on student ability and progress. Challenge them with independent practice when appropriate.

Provide these alternative questions and sentence starters for those who need additional help.

3. How is the environmental effect of electric cars different from the environmental effect of gas-powered cars? Support your answer with a quote from the text.

   According to the text, ______________________________.
   This means that they ______________________________.

4. How effective was the California law passed in 1990? Explain.

   California's law ______________________________
   because ______________________________.

5. How would driving an electric car affect people? Explain.

   Driving an electric car would ______________________________.
   The car would not ______________________________.

Unit 9

Lesson 4

Lesson Opener

Before the lesson, choose one of the following activities to write on the board or post on the *LANGUAGE! Live* Class Wall online.

- *Suppose you have time traveled to this classroom in the year 2056. Describe the setting and the main character (me).*
- *Write a simile and a metaphor to describe the main character: The Time Traveler is as ______ as a ______. The Time Traveler is a ______.*
- *Change the following sentences to future tense: I have traveled back in time. The Time Machine is ready to go. The Time Traveler waited for the perfect time.*

Reading

Objective

- Read sentences to develop fluency.

Sentence Fluency

Timer

Follow the Fluency Procedure below. If it is necessary, begin the fluency drill with a choral read of all sentences. Direct students to page 129 in their Student Books and complete the process.

Fluency Procedure

- Partners switch books, so the recorder is marking errors in the reader's book.
- A timer is set for one minute.
- Readers and recorders move left to right, tracking each word with a pencil.
- As readers read the words aloud, recorders mark errors with a small x above the misread word.
- Recorders place a star to the right of the last word read when time ends.
- If the reader is able to read all words in the allotted time, the reader needs to start over at the beginning. The recorder must indicate this feat by placing two stars to the right of the last word read.
- When both students have read, partners switch books.
- Students calculate total words read, then subtract errors and record.
- Students record information on the progress chart in back of the Student Book.

Lesson 4 | Reading

Sentence Fluency

Read each sentence fluently.

	Correct	Errors
1st Try		
2nd Try		

1.	Will you show me the tool room?	7
2.	Will the large fork work?	12
3.	We will bowl even if it snows.	19
4.	Will you hand me another little spoon?	26
5.	He will blow the horn to tell people of the storm.	37
6.	We are parked in the right spot.	44
7.	Because of the game at noon, it is crowded in town.	55
8.	He formed large loops with the small cords.	63
9.	Are there any other brooms to pick from?	71
10.	The roof on the old porch may fall in at any time.	83
11.	The clerk shorted me when she gave me my cash back.	94
12.	We had a great time with the little kids at the pool.	106
13.	He jerked and snorted in his sleep right before he woke up.	118
14.	I like the sports of baseball and bowling.	126
15.	I need to fill out another form before I start work.	137

Unit 9 129

Grammar

Objectives

- Listen to oral sentences and write them accurately.
- Demonstrate an understanding of the function of future tense in sentences.

Future Tense

You have just read sentences for speed and accuracy. Now we will look closely at those sentences to reinforce what we have learned about verbs in the future tense.

Direct students to page 130 in their Student Books. Read the instructions and remind students of the procedure for sentence dictation.

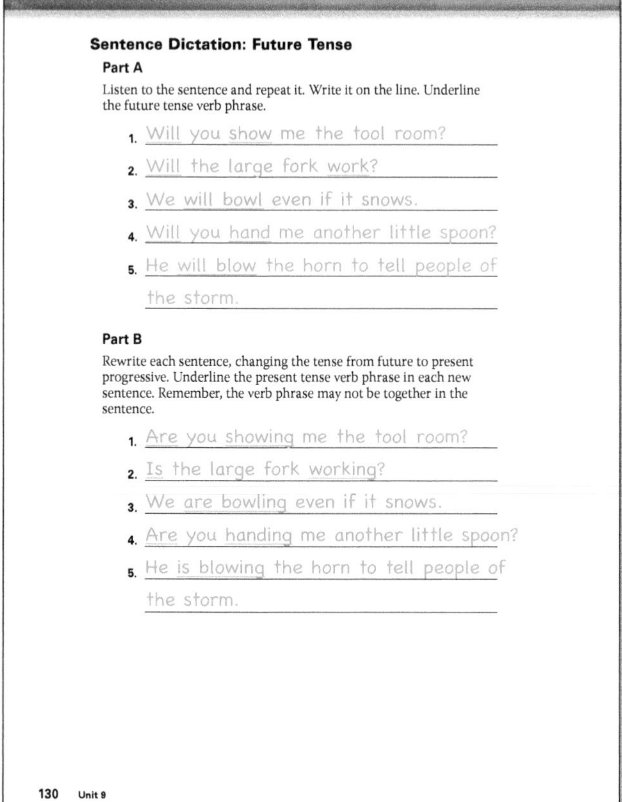

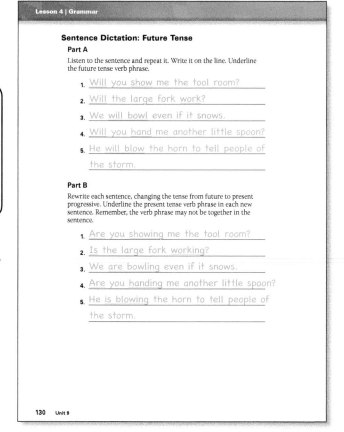

Lesson 4 | Grammar

Sentence Dictation: Future Tense

Part A

Listen to the sentence and repeat it. Write it on the line. Underline the future tense verb phrase.

1. Will you show me the tool room?
2. Will the large fork work?
3. We will bowl even if it snows.
4. Will you hand me another little spoon?
5. He will blow the horn to tell people of the storm.

Part B

Rewrite each sentence, changing the tense from future to present progressive. Underline the present tense verb phrase in each new sentence. Remember, the verb phrase may not be together in the sentence.

1. Are you showing me the tool room?
2. Is the large fork working?
3. We are bowling even if it snows.
4. Are you handing me another little spoon?
5. He is blowing the horn to tell people of the storm.

130 Unit 9

Dictation Procedure

- Teacher reads the sentence.
- Students repeat the sentence.
- Students write the sentence.
- Teacher reads the sentence a second time as students check their work.

Dictate the following sentences:

1. Will you show me the tool room?
2. Will the large fork work?
3. We will bowl even if it snows.
4. Will you hand me another little spoon?
5. He will blow the horn to tell people of the storm.

Have students underline the future tense verbs in the sentences. Review the sentences to make sure they have been written correctly and the future tense verbs have been underlined.

For the second part of this activity, you will rewrite the dictated sentences, changing the verb from future to present progressive. When we add *-ing* to a verb along with a form of *be* as a helping verb, we have created the present progressive tense.

Model

Look at number 1. The verb phrase is *will show.* We know we will add *-ing* to create the verb *showing.* Now we have to decide on the form of *be* to add for the pronoun *you*. We say *you are*, so our verb phrase will be *are showing.* If we plug that into the sentence frame our new question is, Are you showing me the tool room?

Guided and Independent Practice

What about the second sentence? What is the verb phrase? (will work) What will the verb *work* become? (working) Now we have to ask what form of *be* we will use with our subject, *fork*. What form will we use? (is) What is our new question? (Is the large fork working?) Have partners complete the remaining sentences. Review the answers as a class.

> **Note:** Base the number of modeled and guided examples on student ability and progress. Challenge them with independent practice when appropriate.

Reading

Objectives

- Read sentence phrases with fluency to support comprehension.
- Use critical thinking skills to respond to specific questions about a text.

Phrase It

Reading in phrases is a part of prosody. A phrase is a group of words with a chunk of meaning. In English we typically see a subject phrase followed by a predicate phrase. With this predictable order, we know what is coming next, which helps us understand what we read. Read the following phrases, pausing in between for students to create a mental picture.

> The intrigued boy . . . sneakily pulled the lever . . . on the time machine . . . when I turned my back.

The intrigued boy is the subject, and *sneakily pulled the lever on the time machine when I turned my back* is the predicate.

For Phrase It, we scoop phrases using our pencil. When we scoop a phrase, we form an image in our heads. The next phrase we read may add to or change the image. This process is comprehension. The picture of the intrigued boy changes as soon as we read the first part of the predicate—*sneakily pulled the lever.* It changes again when we read the second part of the predicate—*on the time machine.* It changes yet again when we read the third part of the predicate—*when I turned my back.* Imagining that the boy pulled the lever of the time machine when the narrator's back was turned changes the feeling of the sentence. The addition of each *phrase*—not the addition of each *word*—changes our mental image. That's why we read in chunks.

Direct students to page 131 in their Student Books.

Model

Complete the first item as a model.

Guided Practice

Guide the completion of the next two.

Independent Practice

Read the remaining sentences and have students scoop the phrases. Review the answers as a class.

Note: Base the number of modeled and guided examples on student ability and progress. Challenge them with independent practice when appropriate.

There are various ways the sentences can be broken into phrases. Accept logical answers.

Lesson 4 | Reading

Phrase It

Read each phrase and scoop it with a pencil. As you read the phrase, form an image in your mind. Read the sentence with prosody.

1. I am following the herd of cows to the green gate.
2. She tooted her horn and called to the cowboys.
3. Do we have time to eat before the show?
4. After the low falls, the creek flows through the cracked rocks.
5. The short stools are good for the little kids.
6. He mowed around Mom's roses and the little trees.
7. How many years has the old clown been around?
8. I sorted the forks and spoons into piles.
9. The black crows were perched on the short wall.
10. I stooped down to reach the little boy.

Unit 9 131

Critical Understandings

Direction Words: Strategic Thinking poster

We will continue responding to prompts at the strategic thinking level. You will respond to prompts that include verbs such as *determine*, *assess*, and *cite evidence*. What level prompt will we study in this unit? (strategic thinking) At this level of comprehension, you will need to recall information, understand what the information means, and think strategically about new information. What is the base word of *strategic* and *strategically*? (strategy) In this class you are learning strategies that can help you comprehend text. These strategies will help you throughout life. What will you need to do at this level of comprehension? (recall, understand, and think strategically) Do these strategies work in other classes? (yes)

Direct students to pages 132 and 133 in their Student Books.

Let's preview some prompts that require more strategic thinking about the electric cars that we read about yesterday. I'll read each prompt, and you repeat the key word in bold. Ready? Let's begin.

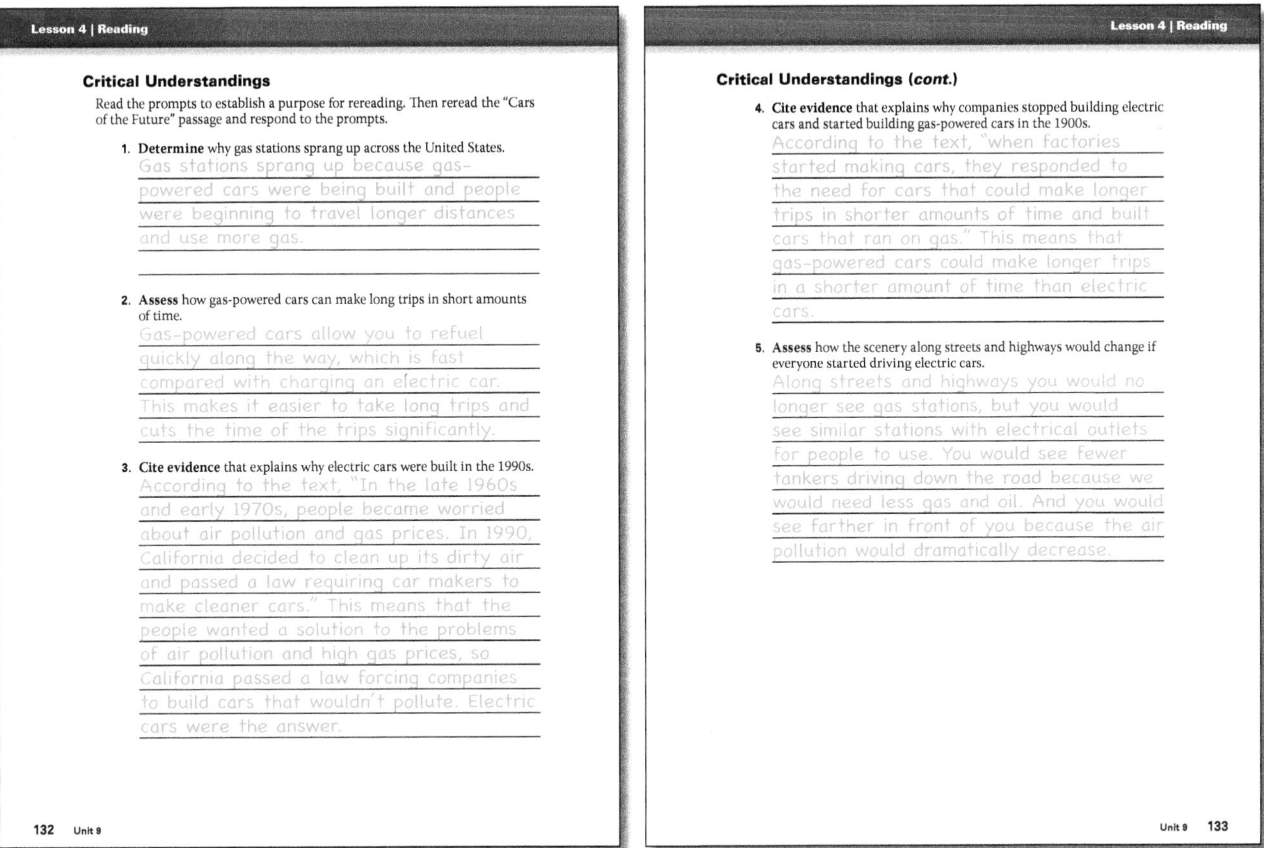

Lesson 4 | Reading

Critical Understandings

Read the prompts to establish a purpose for rereading. Then reread the "Cars of the Future" passage and respond to the prompts.

1. **Determine** why gas stations sprang up across the United States.
Gas stations sprang up because gas-powered cars were being built and people were beginning to travel longer distances and use more gas.

2. **Assess** how gas-powered cars can make long trips in short amounts of time.
Gas-powered cars allow you to refuel quickly along the way, which is fast compared with charging an electric car. This makes it easier to take long trips and cuts the time of the trips significantly.

3. **Cite evidence** that explains why electric cars were built in the 1990s.
According to the text, "In the late 1960s and early 1970s, people became worried about air pollution and gas prices. In 1990, California decided to clean up its dirty air and passed a law requiring car makers to make cleaner cars." This means that the people wanted a solution to the problems of air pollution and high gas prices, so California passed a law forcing companies to build cars that wouldn't pollute. Electric cars were the answer.

132 Unit 9

Lesson 4 | Reading

Critical Understandings (*cont.*)

4. **Cite evidence** that explains why companies stopped building electric cars and started building gas-powered cars in the 1900s.
According to the text, "when factories started making cars, they responded to the need for cars that could make longer trips in shorter amounts of time and built cars that ran on gas." This means that gas-powered cars could make longer trips in a shorter amount of time than electric cars.

5. **Assess** how the scenery along streets and highways would change if everyone started driving electric cars.
Along streets and highways you would no longer see gas stations, but you would see similar stations with electrical outlets for people to use. You would see fewer tankers driving down the road because we would need less gas and oil. And you would see farther in front of you because the air pollution would dramatically decrease.

Unit 9 133

The prompts on this page refer to the text we read in Lesson 3. **Direct students to page 127 in their Student Books.** Let's reread the text. Proficient readers reread text to gain deeper understanding. With eyes on text, listen while I reread this short text about future cars. Use your pencil eraser to follow along. Let's begin. **Read the text aloud.**

Note: While the lessons are written for a teacher read aloud, it is important that your students read as much and as often as they can. Assign readings that meet the needs of your students, based on your observations or data. This is a good opportunity to stretch students, but if they become frustrated, return to the read-aloud method.

Cars of the Future?

An electric car is run by electricity instead of gas. Electric cars are cheap to run, they don't cause air pollution, and they are quiet. Owners plug cars into electrical outlets to make them run, so they save money on gas. People who have owned electric cars love them. But there are few electric cars around today.

Back in the 1890s, electric cars ruled the road. Only one car in every ten was run by gas. All cars were made by hand. But when factories started making cars, they responded to the need for cars that could make longer trips in shorter amounts of time and built cars that ran on gas. Soon, gas stations sprang up across the United States and gas-powered cars flooded streets and highways. The production of electric cars came to a halt.

In the late 1960s and early 1970s, people became worried about air pollution and gas prices. In 1990, California decided to clean up its dirty air and passed a law requiring car makers to make cleaner cars. Two percent of new cars would have to be electric by 1998. Ten percent of new cars would have to be electric by 2003.

Car companies began building a few electric cars by hand. The people who drove them liked them. But there were others who were against electric cars. Gas companies did not like them. Car companies claimed that not enough people wanted to buy them. They persuaded California to change the 1990 law.

Car companies quit building electric cars again. They went so far as to crush their electric cars, even though fans asked them not to.

Today, people still worry about gas prices and air pollution. There are some electric cars being made. Hybrid cars that run partly on electricity and partly on gas have become popular. Some people think electric cars will someday rule the road again. Hopefully, electric cars are the cars of the future.

Direct students back to pages 132 and 133. Let's check our comprehension of this passage by responding to some prompts that require strategic thinking about the text. For each prompt, you will need to find evidence in the text to support your answer.

Remember, a prompt can be turned into a question to help clarify how you should respond. Write a complete response to each prompt on pages 132 and 133 in the Student Book.

Have partners respond to the prompts. Review the answers as a class to ensure students understand what each prompt is asking.

Provide these alternative questions and sentence starters for those who need additional help.

1. Why did gas stations spring up across the United States?

   Gas stations sprang up because ________________________________.

2. How can gas-powered cars make long trips in short amounts of time?

   Gas-powered cars ________________________________.
   This makes it ________________________________.

3. Why were electric cars built in the 1990s? Support your answer with a quote from the text.

   According to the text, ________________________________.
   This means ________________________________.

4. Why did companies stop building electric cars and start building gas-powered cars in the 1900s? Support your answer with a quote from the text.

   According to the text, ________________________________.
   This means ________________________________.

5. How would the scenery along streets and highways change if everyone started driving electric cars? Explain.

   Along streets and highways you would no longer see ________________,
   but you would see ________________________________.
   You would see ________________________________
   because ________________________________.
   And you would see ________________________________.

Unit 9

Lesson 5

Lesson Opener

Before the lesson, choose one of the following activities to write on the board or post on the *LANGUAGE! Live* Class Wall online.

- *If you could time travel back to your favorite day, but had no guarantee that it would turn out the same way, would you do it? Why or why not?*
- *Add inflectional endings to* test *and use each in a sentence:* -s, -'s, -ing, -ed.
- *Use the word* test *twice in a sentence using a different meaning of the word each time.*

Vocabulary

Objectives

- Review key passage vocabulary.

Recontextualize Passage Vocabulary

Direct students to page 114 in their Student Books.

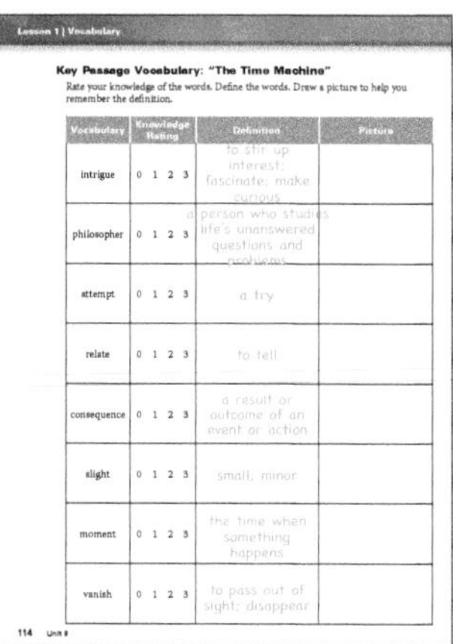

Lesson 1 | Vocabulary

Key Passage Vocabulary: "The Time Machine"

Rate your knowledge of the words. Define the words. Draw a picture to help you remember the definition.

Vocabulary	Knowledge Rating	Definition	Picture
intrigue	0 1 2 3	to stir up interest; fascinate; make curious	
philosopher	0 1 2 3	a person who studies life's unanswered questions and problems	
attempt	0 1 2 3	a try	
relate	0 1 2 3	to tell	
consequence	0 1 2 3	a result or outcome of an event or action	
slight	0 1 2 3	small; minor	
moment	0 1 2 3	the time when something happens	
vanish	0 1 2 3	to pass out of sight; disappear	

114 Unit 9

Review the Key Passage Vocabulary from "The Time Machine."

- If I told you that there was a green leprechaun dancing in the hallway, you would probably want to come look for yourself. You would be what? (intrigued) To stir up the interest of, fascinate, or make curious is to what? (intrigue)
- A person who studies life's unanswered questions and problems is a what? (a philosopher) You may take a philosophy class in college. Your professor, or teacher, for this class will likely be what? (a philosopher)
- A result or an outcome of an event or action is a what? (a consequence) The Time Traveler relates the *consequences* of seeing the future to his friends, but this part is not included in the passage. With your partner, describe what those *consequences* might be. (Answers will vary.)
- To pass out of sight or disappear is to what? (vanish) I came out of the bathroom at a party once, and I had toilet paper stuck to my shoe. I was embarrassed and wished people couldn't see me. What did I wish I could do? (vanish)
- A try is a what? (an attempt) There is an old saying: "If at first you don't succeed, try, try again." What is the first try called? (an attempt)
- To tell is to what? (relate) With your partner, *relate* what you are doing after school today.
- Something small or minor is what? (slight) Turn to your partner and demonstrate a *slight* wave of your hand. Now, show your partner a big wave.
- The time when something happens is a what? (a moment) At this very *moment*, I would like you to relate your favorite *moment* in school to your partner and use the word *moment* in your sentence.

Reading

Objectives

- Write questions or prompts about the passage to deepen comprehension.
- Respond orally to specific questions about a text.

Guided Reading of "The Time Machine": Ask and Answer Questions

I already pointed out that skilled readers preview the text for text features. We learned that text features for narratives do not include headings, charts, and graphs, but often include pictures or graphics. Proficient readers also reread text slowly and carefully to gain understanding. They monitor their thinking while reading to be sure that each sentence and paragraph make sense. Good readers look for answers to Big Idea questions. In this unit, we are answering these questions: Why are people fascinated by the possibility of time travel? and What might be some consequences of knowing what's in the future?

Good readers also ask themselves and others questions about their reading. Challenging questions require readers to combine what they already know with information in the text and the illustrations that go with it. Proficient readers understand that asking questions improves their own comprehension. They ask themselves new questions after they hear others' questions.

Direction Words: Strategic Thinking poster

Direct students to the chart on page 16 in their Student Books or refer to the Strategic Thinking poster if you have it displayed.

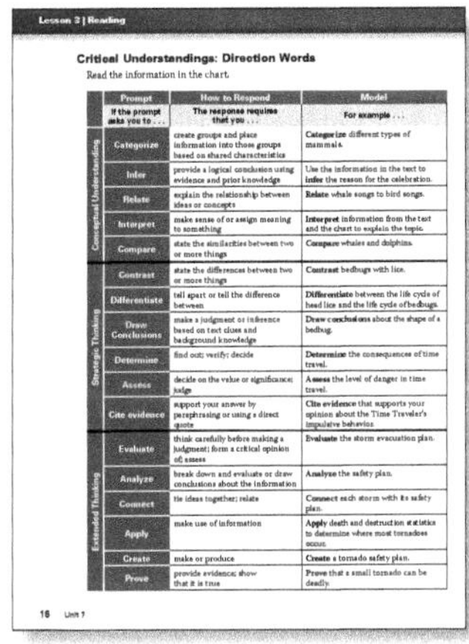

Lesson 3 | Reading

Critical Understandings: Direction Words

Read the information in the chart.

	Prompt	How to Respond	Model
	If the prompt asks you to . . .	The response requires that you . . .	For example . . .
Conceptual Understanding	Categorize	create groups and place information into those groups based on shared characteristics	**Categorize** different types of mammals.
	Infer	provide a logical conclusion using evidence and prior knowledge	Use the information in the text to **infer** the reason for the celebration.
	Relate	explain the relationship between ideas or concepts	**Relate** whale songs to bird songs.
	Interpret	make sense of or assign meaning to something	**Interpret** information from the text and the chart to explain the topic.
	Compare	state the similarities between two or more things	**Compare** whales and dolphins.
Strategic Thinking	Contrast	state the differences between two or more things	**Contrast** bedbugs with lice.
	Differentiate	tell apart or tell the difference between	**Differentiate** between the life cycle of head lice and the life cycle of bedbugs.
	Draw Conclusions	make a judgment or inference based on text clues and background knowledge	**Draw conclusions** about the shape of a bedbug.
	Determine	find out; verify; decide	**Determine** the consequences of time travel.
	Assess	decide on the value or significance; judge	**Assess** the level of danger in time travel.
	Cite evidence	support your answer by paraphrasing or using a direct quote	**Cite evidence** that supports your opinion about the Time Traveler's impulsive behavior.
Extended Thinking	Evaluate	think carefully before making a judgment; form a critical opinion of; assess	**Evaluate** the storm evacuation plan.
	Analyze	break down and evaluate or draw conclusions about the information	**Analyze** the safety plan.
	Connect	tie ideas together; relate	**Connect** each storm with its safety plan.
	Apply	make use of information	**Apply** death and destruction statistics to determine where most tornadoes occur.
	Create	make or produce	**Create** a tornado safety plan.
	Prove	provide evidence; show that it is true	**Prove** that a small tornado can be deadly.

16 Unit 7

We have been talking about how certain question words require a specific response or answer. You will review this chart with a partner. Review the Chart Reading Procedure with students.

Chart Reading Procedure

- Group students with partners or in triads.
- Have students count off as 1s or 2s attempting to give all students a chance to be a student leader (1). If working with triads, the third student becomes a 2.
- Student leaders (1s) read the left column (Prompt) in addition to managing the time and turn-taking if working with a triad.
- The 2s explain the middle column of the chart (How to Respond). If working in triads, 2s take turns explaining the middle column.
- The 1s read the model in the right column (Model), and 2s restate the model as a question.
- All students should follow along with their pencil eraser while others are explaining the chart.
- Students must work from left to right, top to bottom in order to benefit from this activity.

Have students review the Strategic Thinking portion of the chart as instructed (from Determine to Cite Evidence).

This time when we read "The Time Machine," we will ask questions about the text. Doing this will help us understand what is important. We will also answer the questions that we ask, which should help clear up any confusion we had during our first read.

Direct students to page 115 in their Student Books or have them tear out the extra copy of "The Time Machine" from the back of their book.

Note: To minimize flipping back and forth between the pages, a copy of each text has been included in the back of the Student Books. Encourage students to tear this out and use it when working on activities that require the use of the text.

Let's do what good readers do and reread "The Time Machine" with our minds on asking and answering questions.

Remember to track the text while your pencil points to the words. While reading, be aware of questions that come to mind and questions that you can ask others.

Eyes ready? Pencil ready? Let's begin.

Read the first two paragraphs, lines 1–15.

Note: While the lessons are written for a teacher read aloud, it is important that your students read as much and as often as they can. Assign readings that meet the needs of your students, based on your observations or data. This is a good opportunity to stretch students, but if they become frustrated, return to the read-aloud method.

The Time Machine

What is time? Is time travel possible? For centuries, these questions have intrigued mystics, philosophers, and scholars. H.G. Wells, a science teacher and science fiction writer, also became interested in the idea. He published a novel called *The Time Machine* in 1895, and it quickly became famous. In this story of one man's attempt to travel through time, the protagonist builds a "black and polished brass" Time Machine and launches it into the future. After a series of harrowing adventures, he returns to the present to relate to his friends the consequences of seeing things to come.

The following passage, adapted from *The Time Machine,* describes how H.G. Wells's protagonist, the Time Traveler, takes his first flight in the machine he has invented.

Direct students to page 134 in their Student Books. Think about the text. What questions do you still have or what should your peers have learned during this section?

- Choose one question word or prompt we have learned. Consider starting your question with *When.*
- If you want to challenge yourself to write a prompt, try using *Determine.*
- Write the question or prompt on the page. Be prepared to answer your question or prompt orally. Remember, questions require a question mark. Prompts require a period.

Lesson 5 | Reading

Ask and Answer Questions Answers will vary.

Reread "The Time Machine." After each section, write a question or prompt for your partner to answer using question or direction words that you have learned so far. Try not to use the same word twice. Be prepared to answer your questions orally. Use the Critical Understandings chart or the poster to help you.

Introduction, Lines 1–15 *When?* *Determine*

1. ______________________

Lines 16–33 *What?* *Infer*

2. ______________________

Lines 34–57 *How?* *Assess*

3. ______________________

Lines 58–76 *Why?* *Cite evidence*

4. ______________________

134 Unit 9

Direct students back to the passage. Let's read the next four paragraphs. Eyes ready? Pencil ready? Let's begin.

Read the next four paragraphs, lines 16–33.

It was almost four in the morning, and I had finished my work, so I measured the levers one last time, and now, only one thing was left to do. I had to give the Time Machine its first test.

I sat down in the seat of the Time Machine and looked at my pocket watch; it said nineteen minutes after four. I held my breath as I gripped the lever and pulled it down a tiny bit. How can I say what it felt like? Only that it felt like falling; it felt like falling through endless space. My stomach was trying to squeeze into my throat, and my mouth was open; it looked like the mouth of a fish—a fish gasping in air.

Quickly, I pulled the stop lever and felt a slight bump and the machine came to a stop. I looked around and my heart sank.

My tools were exactly where I had laid them, my coat still hung over a chair, and my workshop was just as I had left it; my machine was a failure.

Direct students to page 134 in their Student Books.

- Choose a different direction or question word. Try using *What* or *Infer.*
- Write the question or prompt on the page. Be prepared to provide answers orally.

Direct students back to the passage. Let's read the next three paragraphs. Eyes ready? Pencil ready? Let's begin.

Read the next three paragraphs, lines 34–57.

> Next, I saw daylight streaming in the window, and my heart beat faster. As I looked at a clock on the mantle, the clock said half past nine; I pulled out my pocket watch and looked at it; it said twenty-one minutes after four. I had traveled through time! I had traveled more than five hours in just two minutes; my Time Machine had worked!
>
> At that point, I suppose I should have stopped and planned my next move, but I had waited too long for this moment. I could not wait any longer to journey through time, so I pulled down the lever again, and this time I pulled it a bit harder and farther. Time outside the machine was speeding up; I could hardly believe what I was seeing. I saw my housekeeper whiz into the room, clean it in record time, and shoot out the door. It was clear that she could not see me.
>
> I had to take the next step, so this time, I pulled the lever even farther down. The window grew dark and then it brightened, then it darkened again. Time was speeding by; days went by like blinking lights as I pulled down on the lever still more. Daylight and darkness became a blur, and the windows and walls of my workshop vanished. The machine was swaying now, and my mind was swaying, too. I decided to pull the lever all the way down.

Direct students to page 134 in their Student Books.

- Choose a different direction or question word. Try using *How* or *Assess*.
- Write the question or prompt on the page. Be prepared to provide answers orally.

Direct students back to the passage. Now we will read the next two paragraphs. Eyes ready? Pencil ready? Let's begin.

Read the last two paragraphs, lines 58–76.

The next thing I saw around me was a world of wonders. Huge buildings were rising taller and taller; skies were changing from dark gray to bright blue; the countryside grew greener and greener. What a fantastic show! It was hard to turn my eyes away, and when I did, I looked at the dials. They told me how fast and far I was traveling. I was shocked; I had gone much faster and farther than I thought. I was in the year AD 802,701. Those huge numbers made me lose my head, and I was in a panic; I yanked hard on the stop lever.

At last, I paid the price because the stop was too sharp and the machine tipped over. I was thrown from my seat. Stunned, I lay on soft green grass. I heard a very loud thunderclap, and a shower of hailstones stung my face. It was impossible to see. "A fine welcome," I muttered, "a man travels over 800,000 years for a visit, and this is the greeting he gets!" Then the hail thinned, the sun shone through a break in the clouds, and I got my first good look at the world of the future.

Direct students to page 134 in their Student Books.

- Choose a different direction or question word. Try using *Why* or *Cite evidence.*
- Write the question or prompt on the page. Be prepared to provide answers orally.

Share Questions or Prompts

Have partners read their questions or prompts to each other and answer them orally, correcting each other if needed. Each pair shares with another pair, then those four share with four others if time permits. Have volunteers share their questions or prompts and responses with the class.

Writing

Objectives

- Use critical and strategic thinking skills to write responses to prompts about the text.
- Support written answers with evidence from text.

Answer It: Direction Words

Direct students to page 135 in their Student Books. Now, we will respond to prompts about "The Time Machine" for more practice. Some of the prompts may be similar to the prompts you already responded to.

- Read each prompt. Identify and underline the direction word.
- Use the Critical Understandings chart on page 16 or the Strategic Thinking poster to review the information different prompts are asking for.
- Locate the information you need to answer the question. Reread the section to retrieve exact information to use as text evidence.
- Use the direction word to formulate a response.

Direction Words: Strategic Thinking poster

Lesson 5 | Writing

Answer It: Direction Words

Underline the direction word in each prompt. Then respond to each prompt using a complete sentence. Provide line numbers for the text evidence.

1. Determine why the Time Traveler thinks his time machine has failed. Cite evidence from the text to support your answer.

   The Time Traveler thinks that his time machine has failed because when he stops the machine for the first time, the Time Traveler says, "My tools were exactly where I had laid them, my coat still hung over a chair, and my workshop was just as I had left it; my machine was a failure."

   Text Evidence: Lines 31–33

2. Assess how the Time Traveler knows time is speeding by when he pulls the lever a second time.

   The Time Traveler knows time is speeding because he watches his housekeeper clean in record time and shoot out the door. Hours of work happen in a few seconds.

   Text Evidence: Lines 47–48

Unit 9 135

Model

Read the first prompt aloud.

1. Determine why the Time Traveler thinks his time machine has failed. Cite evidence from the text to support your answer.

What is the direction word? (determine) Is there another direction word or phrase? (cite evidence) How do we respond to a prompt that asks us to determine? (find out, verify, or decide)

What else do we have to do? (support our answer with a quote from the text) If I change this to a question, it would be, Why does the Time Traveler think his time machine failed? What evidence from the text supports the answer?

Let's use part of the prompt as our sentence starter. Have students help you write the sentence starter. Write the sentence starter on the board:

The Time Traveler thinks that his time machine has failed because ______.

Next, we need to go into the text and find a quote that supports our answer. What is the evidence? ("My tools were exactly where I had laid them, my coat still hung over a chair, and my workshop was just as I had left it; my machine was a failure.") When writing the quote on your page, be sure to use quotation marks to show that the words belong to the author. **Write the quote on the board using quotation marks.** Verify that you have used quotation marks correctly by comparing your work with my example.

> *The Time Traveler thinks that his time machine has failed because when he stops the machine for the first time, the Time Traveler says, "My tools were exactly where I had laid them, my coat still hung over a chair, and my workshop was just as I had left it; my machine was a failure."*

Guided Practice

Read the next prompt aloud.

> 2. Assess how the Time Traveler knows time is speeding by when he pulls the lever a second time.

What is the direction word in this prompt? (assess) How do we respond to a prompt that begins with *assess*? (Decide on the value/significance or judge.)

Have students change the prompt into a question. (How does the Time Traveler know time is speeding by when he pulls the lever a second time?) **Have a volunteer provide a sentence starter. Write the sentence starter on the board:**

> *The Time Traveler knows time is speeding because _____.*

What do we need to do next? (Find evidence from text that provides key details.) **Have students complete the answer on the page.** (The Time Traveler knows time is speeding because he watches his housekeeper clean in record time and shoot out the door. Hours of work happen in a few seconds.)

Answer It: Direction Words (*cont.*)

3. Determine what is happening in this sentence: *"The window grew dark and then it brightened, then it darkened again."*

The Time Traveler is racing at an ever faster rate into the future, all the way to AD 802,701.

Text Evidence: Lines 52–54, 65

4. Determine the character's point of view regarding time travel. Cite evidence from the text to support your answer.

The Time Traveler begins thinking time travel is a dream come true but changes his point of view. He refers to his time travel as a "harrowing adventure" and returns to share the "consequences of seeing the future." Although he is a scientist and inventor, he describes time travel as traumatic and having consequences, or costs.

Text Evidence: Lines 9–11

Answer It: Direction Words (*cont.*)

5. Assess the consequences of time travel into the future.

Answers will vary. Consequences of time travel into the future may include spoiling life's surprises and making everything predictable and eventually boring.

6. Imagine that a person from the ancient past traveled into the present time. Determine what he or she would find shocking.

Answers will vary. Visitors might be shocked by airplanes, space travel, refrigeration, modern music, movies, television, computers, tablets, smart phones, electronic books, etc.

7. Determine similarities the visitor might notice between people of long ago and people of today.

Answers will vary. Visitors from the past would find human emotions and behaviors such as love, hate, greed, generosity, intelligence, and honesty to be the same.

Independent Practice

Have students find and use text evidence to answer the remaining questions independently. Create a small group for students who need more assistance, using question 3 as additional guided practice.

Note: Base the number of modeled and guided examples on student ability and progress. Challenge students with independent practice when appropriate.

Provide these alternative questions and sentence starters for those who need additional help.

3. What is happening in this sentence?
   "The window grew dark and then it brightened, then it darkened again."

   The Time Traveler is ________________________________.

4. What is the character's point of view regarding time travel? Support your answer with a quote from the text.

   The Time Traveler begins thinking ____________, but ______________.
   He refers to his time travel as ______________________________.
   Although he is a scientist and inventor, ______________________.

5. What are the consequences of time travel into the future?

   Consequences of time travel into the future ____________________.

6. Imagine that a person from the ancient past traveled into the present time. What would he or she find shocking?

   Visitors might be shocked by ______________________________.

7. What similarities would a visitor from the past notice between people of long ago and people of today?

   Visitors from the past would find __________________________.

Lesson 6

Lesson Opener

Before the lesson, choose one of the following activities to write on the board or post on the *LANGUAGE! Live* Class Wall online.

- *Turn to your Key Passage Vocabulary chart. Complete your drawings and add information to definitions as needed.*
- *Write a sentence about your avatar using a predicate adjective.*
- *Use the word* attempt *in a sentence about your future.*

Writing

Objectives

- Know spelling-sound correspondences for words with /ū/ spelled *oo*.
- Know spelling-sound correspondences for words ending in *-ed*.
- Know spelling-sound correspondences for words with /ō/ spelled *ow*.

Spelling Words

Use this spelling activity to practice or assess the unit's spelling patterns students have learned online.

Direct students to Part A on page 138 in their Student Books. Read the instructions and remind students of the procedure for spelling. Use the spelling reminders to help struggling students.

1. teacher; My teacher is great.
2. cool; It feels cool outside today.
3. heated; This swimming pool is heated.
4. grow; This plant will grow quickly.
5. pork; I love to eat pork chops.
6. crow; The black crow sat on the fence.
7. spoon; I fed the baby with a spoon.
8. sports; I like to watch sports on TV.
9. mashed; Please pass the mashed potatoes.
10. drilled; The dentist drilled into my tooth.

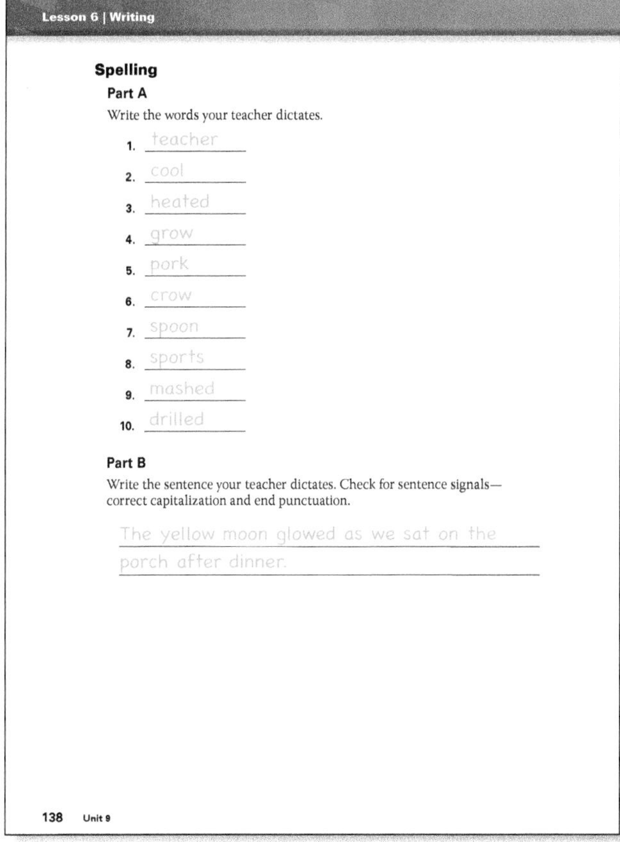

Lesson 6 | Writing

Spelling

Part A

Write the words your teacher dictates.

1. teacher
2. cool
3. heated
4. grow
5. pork
6. crow
7. spoon
8. sports
9. mashed
10. drilled

Part B

Write the sentence your teacher dictates. Check for sentence signals—correct capitalization and end punctuation.

The yellow moon glowed as we sat on the porch after dinner.

138 Unit 9

Direct students to Part B on page 138 in their Student Books. Read the instructions and remind students of the procedure for sentence dictation.

The yellow moon glowed as we sat on the porch after dinner.

Spelling Words Procedure

- Teacher reads the word.
- Students repeat the word.
- Teacher reads the sentence.
- Students write the word.
- Teacher reads the word a second time as students check their work.

Sentence Dictation Procedure

- Teacher reads the sentence.
- Students repeat the sentence.
- Students write the sentence.
- Teacher reads the sentence a second time as students check their work.

Spelling Reminders

Words with /ū/ spelled *oo*
You learned that long *u* sometimes makes the sound /oo/. However, when /oo/ is plain, without /y/, it is usually written with the double *o* pattern, *oo*, as in *moon.*

Words ending in *-ed*
When the inflectional ending *-ed* is added to a verb, it usually means that the action took place in the past. The inflectional ending *-ed* is always spelled the same way, even though it has three different pronunciations, as in *spotted, tossed,* and *hummed.*

Words with /ō/ spelled *ow*
When /ō/ is the last sound in a word, such as *snow* or *crow,* we often use the letters *ow* to spell the sound. We also use *ow* before *n,* as in the words *grown* and *flown.*

Vocabulary

Objectives

- Use context to determine the meaning of words in text.
- Use common Greek and Latin affixes and roots as clues to the meaning of a word.
- Consult reference materials to clarify the precise meaning of key words.
- Demonstrate an understanding of simple word analogies.

Define It

Direct students to page 139 in their Student Books.

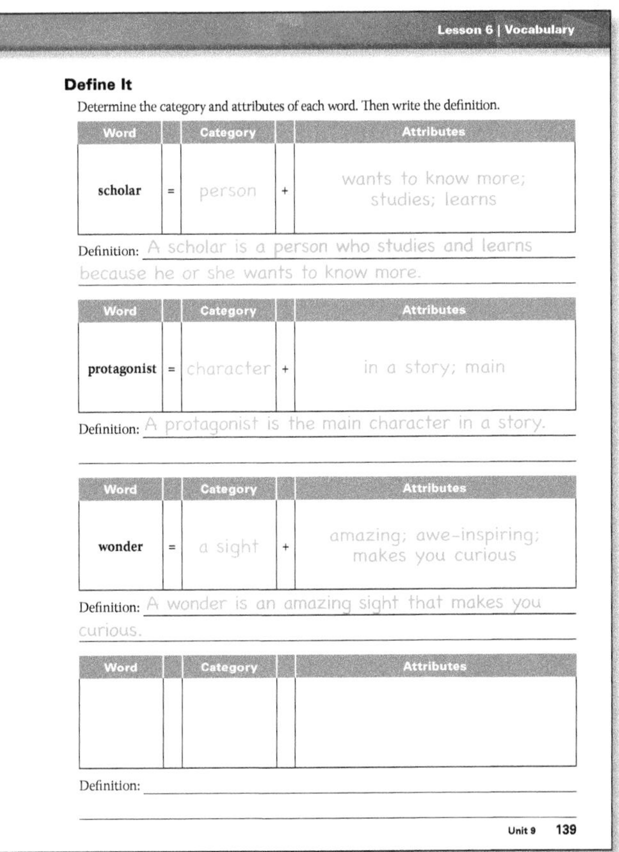
Lesson 6 | Vocabulary

Define It

Determine the category and attributes of each word. Then write the definition.

Word		Category		Attributes
scholar	=	person	+	wants to know more; studies; learns

Definition: A scholar is a person who studies and learns because he or she wants to know more.

Word		Category		Attributes
protagonist	=	character	+	in a story; main

Definition: A protagonist is the main character in a story.

Word		Category		Attributes
wonder	=	a sight	+	amazing; awe-inspiring; makes you curious

Definition: A wonder is an amazing sight that makes you curious.

Word		Category		Attributes

Definition:

Unit 9 139

To define words we need to understand the words' categories and attributes.

Categories are broad groups. Attributes are things like size, shape, color, texture, and function.

Model

Direct students to the first paragraph of "The Time Machine" and have them find the word *scholars.* We may not know what *scholars* means, but we can look at the context around the word to determine the category and attributes. Because the word appears in a series with the word *philosophers,* and we know that a philosopher is a person who studies life's unanswered questions, I will put *scholars* in the broad category of *person.* Looking at the remainder of the sentence, I can see that this person was intrigued, which means he wanted to know more. I will make that an attribute. It doesn't really say anything else about scholars in the text, so I will look at the word itself. Write *scholars* on the board. Underline *schol.*

Look at this word part. Does it look like a word you are familiar with? It should. What if I add an *o*? So, let's think about the word *school* to see if we can deduce anything about the word *scholar.* What do we do at school? (study, learn) Because it has the same root, let's add those words to our attributes. Write the definition on the board and read it aloud.

> *A scholar is a person who studies and learns because he or she wants to know more.*

Have students write the definition in their Student Books.

Guided and Independent Practice

Dictionaries

Repeat the process for the second word, allowing students to provide the category, attributes, and definition for you. Then have partners complete the activity. Explain that they may choose and define any unknown word from the passage for the last item. Have partners verify their definitions in a dictionary and make corrections as needed.

> **Note:** Base the number of modeled and guided examples on student ability and progress. Challenge them with independent practice when appropriate.

Antonym Analogies

An analogy is a logic problem based on two pairs of words that have the same relationship. Write the following analogy on the board:

bats : caves :: rabbits : holes

As you read the analogy, point to each element on the board. Bats are to caves as rabbits are to holes. How are bats and caves related or connected? (Caves are where bats live.) How are rabbits and holes related or connected? (Holes are where rabbits live.)

There are various types of analogies. We will begin with antonym analogies. What is an antonym? (opposite)

- The antonym of black is what? (white)
- The antonym of cold is what? (hot)

An antonym analogy is a comparison of two sets of words that are opposites. An example would be black is to white as hot is to cold. Black and white are opposite colors, and hot and cold are opposite temperatures. Write the analogy on the board:

black : white :: hot : cold

Two pairs of words that share the same relationship are called what? (analogies)

Words that are opposites are called what? (antonyms)

A word problem made up of two pairs of antonyms is called what? (an antonym analogy)

Direct students to page 140 in their Student Books and read the instructions aloud.

Lesson 6 | Vocabulary

Antonym Analogies

Part A

An antonym analogy is a comparison of two pairs of words that are opposites. Read the incomplete antonym analogies. Identify the missing word from the word bank and write it on the line.

Word Bank

clean	right	hate	start	closed	day	many

1. sad : happy :: dirty : clean
2. above : below :: few : many
3. finish : start :: begin : end
4. open : closed :: love : hate
5. day : night :: left : right

Part B

Look for words that are antonyms. Finish the antonym analogies by filling in the blanks.

Word Bank

large	little	thick	sleep	up	push	thin	stop	out	wet
yes	long	dull	sharp	down	slow	after	on	before	first

1. wake : sleep :: big : little
2. off : on :: pull : push
3. large : small :: first : last
4. dry : wet :: out : in
5. stop : go :: fast : slow
6. no : yes :: short : long
7. dull : sharp :: before : after
8. thin : thick :: down : up

140 Unit 9

Model

Then direct students' attention to the first item. Model completing the item as follows.

Sad is to *happy*. *Sad* and *happy* are antonyms. *Dirty* needs to be compared to another word in the same way. That means that I need to find the opposite of *dirty*. I see the word *clean* in the word bank, and I know *dirty* and *clean* are antonyms. Therefore, the word *clean* will complete this antonym analogy. The colon between *sad* and *happy* tells us that these two words are connected. The colon between *dirty* and *clean* tells us that those two words are connected. The double colons between the pairs of words tell us that the words in each pair are connected in the same way. In this case, both pairs are antonyms. We would read the analogy like this: *sad* is to *happy* as *dirty* is to *clean*.

Have students repeat the analogy.

Guided Practice

Direct students' attention to the second item.

Have a volunteer read the first part of the analogy using the phrase *is to*. *Above* and *below* are opposites. What is the opposite of *few*? (many) Have students complete the analogy in their Student Books.

Independent Practice

Have partners complete the remaining analogies. Review the answers as a class.

Note: Base the number of modeled and guided examples on student ability and progress. Challenge them with independent practice when appropriate.

Direct students to Part B and read the instructions aloud.

Model

Let's look for more antonyms to create analogies.

Wake. The opposite of *wake* is *sleep*. I see the word *sleep* in the word bank, so I will write it on the line. *Wake* is to *sleep* as *big* is to . . . What is the opposite of *big*? I see *little* in the word bank, so I will write it on the line. *Wake* is to *sleep* as *big* is to *little*.

Guided Practice

What is the opposite of *off*? (on) What is the opposite of *pull*? (push) Have students say the analogy using the pattern. (Off is to on as pull is to push.)

Independent Practice

Have students complete the remaining analogies. Encourage them to cross out words in the box as they use them. Explain that the final two analogies will be made with words that haven't yet been used. Review the answers as a class.

Note: Base the number of modeled and guided examples on student ability and progress. Challenge them with independent practice when appropriate.

Reading

Objectives

- Discuss how authors use characterization in stories.
- Describe the traits of characters in a story by drawing on specific details in the story.
- Read a folktale from Fiji.
- Discuss the significance of point of view in a story.

Story Elements: Characterization and Point of View

Characters are one of the story elements we identified earlier in this unit. Good writers develop characters that are complex and believable. They help us "see" the character through descriptive language and help us get to know the character through dialogue and action. When we talk about the personality of a character, we are talking about his or her traits. A character might be generous, funny, grumpy, lazy, smart, or any combination of such traits.

Think for a minute about people you know and how you know them. How do we know if someone is generous? It's not just what he or she says, but what that person does. Actions really do speak louder than words. This is especially true in stories. Authors know they need to do more than say a character is funny or rude. They have to include examples of behavior that illustrate the trait.

Direct students to pages 141 and 142 in their Student Books. Follow along as I read "Butterfly's Bet." Think about how the story develops and what you are learning about the characters.

Lesson 6 | Reading

Characterization

Read the story and pay close attention to the characters, their traits, and their motivations.

Butterfly's Bet
A folktale from Fiji retold by Holly Melton

It was a beautiful day in the Fiji Islands. Heron stood on his long stick legs in the white sands of his favorite lagoon. He closed his eyes lazily and thought about his next meal. "Maybe I'll have jumbo shrimp," he thought. "Or I might catch a juicy crab." Thinking about food was Heron's favorite pastime.

Just then something very light bounced off his head and landed on his bill. Heron's eyes snapped open. There, flapping her wings and staring at him thoughtfully, was a small butterfly.

"What do you think you're doing?" Heron asked crossly.

"Resting," said Butterfly. "I'm on my way to Tonga, to visit my cousins."

"You'll never make it to Tonga!" said Heron. "You're too small and weak, and the island is too far away!"

Butterfly knew that she was small and that Tonga was far away. She also knew that Heron was large and strong.

Butterfly had a plan.

"I may be small, but I'm fast," she said. "I bet I could beat you in a race to Tonga!"

"Why should I go to Tonga?" Heron asked.

"Because Tonga has the largest and tastiest seafood in the world," answered Butterfly.

Heron was very proud of his flying ability. And he was very fond of large and tasty seafood.

"I accept your challenge," he said.

The race was on!

With a few powerful beats of his wings, Heron rose into the air. He felt the wind ruffle his feathers as he flew through the skies.

Unit 9 141

Lesson 6 | Reading

Characterization (*cont.*)

Butterfly's Bet (*cont.*)

He did *not*, however, feel the small butterfly perched lightly on his back, hitching a free ride.

Heron flew along, thinking about mud lobsters and other tasty tidbits. Suddenly, Butterfly seemed to appear from nowhere. As she streaked ahead of him, she shouted, "What a slowpoke you are! You'll never get to Tonga!"

Heron flew faster and passed Butterfly. "I could beat you with one wing tied behind my back!" he shouted.

He did not realize that Butterfly had once again settled lightly and comfortably onto that very back.

Time passed, and Heron grew tired. But each time he slowed down, Butterfly appeared out of nowhere to tell him she was winning. Each time, Heron flew faster and passed her up. And each time, Butterfly hitched a free ride when he wasn't looking. At sunset, the sun began to sink toward the sea like a big red ball. Heron was so exhausted that he began to sink toward the sea too.

Butterfly saw that Heron was in trouble. Quickly she rose from his back and flew beside him. "We're almost there, Heron!" she said. "Come on, you can make it!"

Heron was too tired to ask where she'd come from. He beat his wings weakly as Butterfly fluttered about his head, encouraging him.

Butterfly and Heron reached the island together, so no one won the race. They didn't mind, though. Butterfly had a good visit with her cousins. As for Heron, he decided that the seafood of Tonga was, indeed, the largest and tastiest he'd ever eaten.

142 Unit 9

Note: While the lessons are written for a teacher read aloud, it is important that your students read as much and as often as they can. Assign readings that meet the needs of your students, based on your observations or data. This is a good opportunity to stretch students, but if they become frustrated, return to the read-aloud method.

Butterfly's Bet

A folktale from Fiji retold by Holly Melton

It was a beautiful day in the Fiji Islands. Heron stood on his long stick legs in the white sands of his favorite lagoon. He closed his eyes lazily and thought about his next meal. "Maybe I'll have jumbo shrimp," he thought. "Or I might catch a juicy crab." Thinking about food was Heron's favorite pastime.

Just then something very light bounced off his head and landed on his bill. Heron's eyes snapped open. There, flapping her wings and staring at him thoughtfully, was a small butterfly.

"What do you think you're doing?" Heron asked crossly.

"Resting," said Butterfly. "I'm on my way to Tonga, to visit my cousins."

"You'll never make it to Tonga!" said Heron. "You're too small and weak, and the island is too far away!"

Butterfly knew that she was small and that Tonga was far away. She also knew that Heron was large and strong.

Butterfly had a plan.

"I may be small, but I'm fast," she said. "I bet I could beat you in a race to Tonga!"

"Why should I go to Tonga?" Heron asked.

"Because Tonga has the largest and tastiest seafood in the world," answered Butterfly.

Heron was very proud of his flying ability. And he was very fond of large and tasty seafood.

"I accept your challenge," he said.

The race was on!

With a few powerful beats of his wings, Heron rose into the air. He felt the wind ruffle his feathers as he flew through the skies.

He did *not*, however, feel the small butterfly perched lightly on his back, hitching a free ride.

Heron flew along, thinking about mud lobsters and other tasty tidbits. Suddenly, Butterfly seemed to appear from nowhere. As she streaked ahead of him, she shouted, "What a slowpoke you are! You'll never get to Tonga!"

Heron flew faster and passed Butterfly. "I could beat you with one wing tied behind my back!" he shouted.

He did not realize that Butterfly had once again settled lightly and comfortably onto that very back.

Time passed, and Heron grew tired. But each time he slowed down, Butterfly appeared out of nowhere to tell him she was winning. Each time, Heron flew faster and passed her up. And each time, Butterfly hitched a free ride when he wasn't looking. At sunset, the sun began to sink toward the sea like a big red ball. Heron was so exhausted that he began to sink toward the sea too.

Butterfly saw that Heron was in trouble. Quickly she rose from his back and flew beside him. "We're almost there, Heron!" she said. "Come on, you can make it!"

Heron was too tired to ask where she'd come from. He beat his wings weakly as Butterfly fluttered about his head, encouraging him.

Butterfly and Heron reached the island together, so no one won the race. They didn't mind, though. Butterfly had a good visit with her cousins. As for Heron, he decided that the seafood of Tonga was, indeed, the largest and tastiest he'd ever eaten.

Setting

Where does the story take place? (The story begins in the Fiji islands and ends on the island of Tonga.) It is very common for stories to have multiple settings, particularly as the story progresses. In this case, the change in setting is actually part of the story's plot.

Characters

Direct students to page 143 in their Student Books. Who are the characters in the story? (Butterfly and Heron) Write the names in the Character Traits template. What did you learn about the characters in this story? Discuss the characters with your partner. Focus on their characteristics as opposed to what happened. Have students share a few of their ideas about Butterfly and Heron with the class.

Let's take a closer look at the text to find clues about the traits of these two characters. I'll read one paragraph at a time, and you tell me what we learned about the characters from that paragraph. We'll write down the information in our chart.

Read the first paragraph. What does the last sentence tell us about Heron? (He likes to eat.) Let's put that in our template as a trait: *likes to eat*. How do we know that? Did we have to figure it out or did the text tell us? (The text told us.)

Lesson 6 | Reading

Identify It: Character Traits

Determine the character traits of Heron and Butterfly. Explain how you discovered each trait.

Answers will vary.

Character: Heron

Trait	How do you know? (In the text or inferred)
likes to eat	-text—tells us favorite pastime
proud of flying ability	-text—tells us he is proud -infer—quick to criticize Butterfly for being weak and small
strong	-text—a few powerful beats of his wings
competitive	-text—flies harder every time Butterfly catches up

Character: Butterfly

Trait	How do you know? (In the text or inferred)
ambitious	-text—wants to go visit cousins even though it's far away
has plan	-text—challenges Heron to a race in order to "hitch" a ride
knows how to motivate	-text—tells Heron about the food in Tonga -text and infer—appeals to his pride
compassionate	-infer—encourages Heron to keep going, even though it means no one wins the race
intelligent	-text—devises a sound plan to accomplish her task
manipulative	-text—gets Heron to help her without thinking he is helping

Unit 9 143

Use the Character Traits template to guide students through each paragraph and pull out details about the two characters. Help students see that characters grow over time and their actions help define them, even when the motivation behind the action is not readily apparent.

Point of View

Let's think for a minute about point of view. Does one of the characters tell this story? (no) Think about how pronouns are used in the story. When the characters are speaking, they use first-person pronouns like *I*, but when the text refers to a character, third-person pronouns are used. The author seems to know about both characters equally. How would the story change if one of the characters were telling it? (Answers will vary.)

Heron never really figures out that Butterfly "hitches" a ride. How would we as readers have figured that out if Heron were the storyteller? By using third person, the author can "clue us in" as readers. This makes it easier for us to appreciate the characters' strengths and weaknesses. Point of view affects the reader. Therefore, authors choose a point of view carefully and consciously.

Unit 9

Lesson 7

Lesson Opener

Before the lesson, choose one of the following activities to write on the board or post on the *LANGUAGE! Live* Class Wall online.

- *If you could time travel, would you take a trip to the past or the future? Explain your answer.*
- *Describe the Time Machine.*
- *Use the word* wonder *in a sentence.*

Reading

Objectives

- Read with purpose and understanding.
- Identify and explain explicit details from text.
- Take notes on a text.
- Identify idioms in text.

Guided Highlighting of "The Time Machine"

Highlighters or colored pencils

We have been working diligently to become great readers. We preview the text. We reread text slowly and carefully to gain understanding. We practice metacognition. And we look for answers to Big Idea questions. In this unit, we are looking for answers to these questions: Why are people fascinated by the possibility of time travel? and What might be some consequences of knowing what's in the future?

There are a lot of good reasons to become a better reader. Proficient readers can recognize the features of narrative and expository texts. They understand figurative language such as idioms, similes, and metaphors. They can identify and use figurative language when speaking, listening, and writing. Skilled readers can also identify an author's purpose, or reason for writing a text. They can then make judgments about the author's point of view by assessing his or her claims, reasoning, and evidence. Proficient readers compare and contrast an author's point of view with their own when encouraged to take some kind of action on an issue. If readers agree with the author's point of view, they are more likely to be persuaded or influenced to take some action.

Let's do what skilled readers do and reread "The Time Machine."

Have students get out a colored pencil or highlighter.

Direct students to pages 144 and 145 in their Student Books. We will review the features of narrative text. Please use your writing utensil to mark your answer according to my instructions.

- Draw a rectangle around the title, "The Time Machine."

Listen and mark each bold vocabulary word as I read it aloud. I will pause after every word to give you time to process whether you know the word and its meaning. We will review your ratings from Lesson 1 after we finish.

- intrigued—*Intrigued* means "stirred up the interest of, fascinated, or made curious." Say *intrigued.* (intrigued) Time travel has *intrigued* many philosophers.
- philosophers—*Philosophers* are people who study life's unanswered questions or problems. Say *philosophers.* (philosophers) The *philosopher* studied the possibility of time travel.
- attempt—An *attempt* is a try. Say *attempt.* (attempt) His *attempt* to travel through time was not a failure.
- relate—*Relate* means "to tell." Say *relate.* (relate) *Relate* one thing that you learned about the Time Traveler.
- consequences—*Consequences* are results or outcomes of an event or action. Say *consequences.* (consequences) The *consequences* of time travel are unknown.
- slight—*Slight* means "small or minor." Say *slight.* (slight) A *slight* push of the lever can transport a time traveler to the future.
- moment—*Moment* means "the time when something happens." Say *moment.* (moment) I'll be with you in just a *moment.*
- vanished—*Vanished* means "passed out of sight or disappeared." Say *vanished.* (vanished) My coat and chair *vanished* before my eyes.

Talk with a partner about any vocabulary word that is still confusing for you to read or understand. Share your ratings from Lesson 1. Were you honest about your word knowledge? Now is the time to do something about it!

You will reread the text "The Time Machine" one paragraph at a time. Please be sure to draw a question mark over any confusing words, phrases, or sentences. I will provide specific instructions on how to mark the text that will help with your comprehension and writing.

Let's read each section. Use your pencil eraser to follow along.

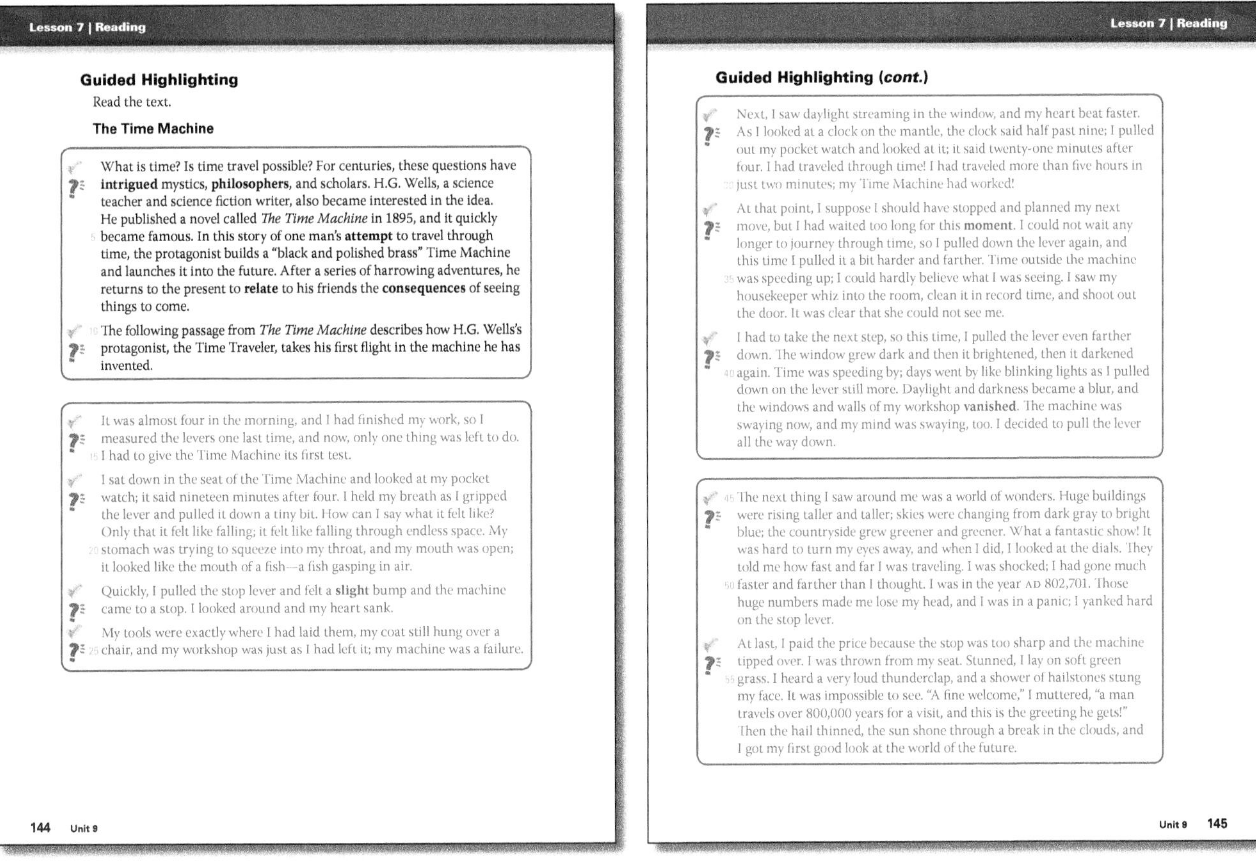
Lesson 7 | Reading

Guided Highlighting

Read the text.

The Time Machine

What is time? Is time travel possible? For centuries, these questions have **intrigued** mystics, **philosophers**, and scholars. H.G. Wells, a science teacher and science fiction writer, also became interested in the idea. He published a novel called *The Time Machine* in 1895, and it quickly became famous. In this story of one man's **attempt** to travel through time, the protagonist builds a "black and polished brass" Time Machine and launches it into the future. After a series of harrowing adventures, he returns to the present to **relate** to his friends the **consequences** of seeing things to come.

The following passage from *The Time Machine* describes how H.G. Wells's protagonist, the Time Traveler, takes his first flight in the machine he has invented.

It was almost four in the morning, and I had finished my work, so I measured the levers one last time, and now, only one thing was left to do. I had to give the Time Machine its first test.

I sat down in the seat of the Time Machine and looked at my pocket watch; it said nineteen minutes after four. I held my breath as I gripped the lever and pulled it down a tiny bit. How can I say what it felt like? Only that it felt like falling; it felt like falling through endless space. My stomach was trying to squeeze into my throat, and my mouth was open; it looked like the mouth of a fish—a fish gasping in air.

Quickly, I pulled the stop lever and felt a **slight** bump and the machine came to a stop. I looked around and my heart sank.

My tools were exactly where I had laid them, my coat still hung over a chair, and my workshop was just as I had left it; my machine was a failure.

144 Unit 9

Lesson 7 | Reading

Guided Highlighting (*cont.*)

Next, I saw daylight streaming in the window, and my heart beat faster. As I looked at a clock on the mantle, the clock said half past nine; I pulled out my pocket watch and looked at it; it said twenty-one minutes after four. I had traveled through time! I had traveled more than five hours in just two minutes; my Time Machine had worked!

At that point, I suppose I should have stopped and planned my next move, but I had waited too long for this **moment**. I could not wait any longer to journey through time, so I pulled down the lever again, and this time I pulled it a bit harder and farther. Time outside the machine was speeding up; I could hardly believe what I was seeing. I saw my housekeeper whiz into the room, clean it in record time, and shoot out the door. It was clear that she could not see me.

I had to take the next step, so this time, I pulled the lever even farther down. The window grew dark and then it brightened, then it darkened again. Time was speeding by; days went by like blinking lights as I pulled down on the lever still more. Daylight and darkness became a blur, and the windows and walls of my workshop **vanished**. The machine was swaying now, and my mind was swaying, too. I decided to pull the lever all the way down.

The next thing I saw around me was a world of wonders. Huge buildings were rising taller and taller; skies were changing from dark gray to bright blue; the countryside grew greener and greener. What a fantastic show! It was hard to turn my eyes away, and when I did, I looked at the dials. They told me how fast and far I was traveling. I was shocked; I had gone much faster and farther than I thought. I was in the year AD 802,701. Those huge numbers made me lose my head, and I was in a panic; I yanked hard on the stop lever.

At last, I paid the price because the stop was too sharp and the machine tipped over. I was thrown from my seat. Stunned, I lay on soft green grass. I heard a very loud thunderclap, and a shower of hailstones stung my face. It was impossible to see. "A fine welcome," I muttered, "a man travels over 800,000 years for a visit, and this is the greeting he gets!" Then the hail thinned, the sun shone through a break in the clouds, and I got my first good look at the world of the future.

Unit 9 145

Let's read the introduction. Read the introduction.

Note: While the lessons are written for a teacher read aloud, it is important that your students read as much and as often as they can. Assign readings that meet the needs of your students, based on your observations or data. This is a good opportunity to stretch students, but if they become frustrated, return to the read-aloud method.

The Time Machine

What is time? Is time travel possible? For centuries, these questions have intrigued mystics, philosophers, and scholars. H.G. Wells, a science teacher and science fiction writer, also became interested in the idea. He published a novel called *The Time Machine* in 1895, and it quickly became famous. In this story of one man's attempt to travel through time, the protagonist builds a "black and polished brass" Time Machine and launches it into the future. After a series of harrowing adventures, he returns to the present to relate to his friends the consequences of seeing things to come.

The following passage, adapted from *The Time Machine*, describes how H.G. Wells's protagonist, the Time Traveler, takes his first flight in the machine he has invented.

- Circle the check mark or question mark for each paragraph. Draw a question mark over any confusing words or phrases.
- Go to line 1. Mark the word that means "hundreds of years." (centuries)
- Go to line 6. Mark the word that means "main character in a story." (protagonist)
- Go to line 7. Mark the time period that the man is traveling to. (future)
- On the same line, mark the synonym for *traumatic*. (harrowing)
- Go to line 8. Look at the word *consequences*. Use your knowledge of the word to write *benefit* or *problem* under the word. Is the author saying it is good or bad?
- Think about the protagonist. Mark all the action words in the text that show what the protagonist did. (attempt, builds, launches)

Let's read the next four paragraphs, lines 13–25. **Read the paragraphs.**

It was almost four in the morning, and I had finished my work, so I measured the levers one last time, and now, only one thing was left to do. I had to give the Time Machine its first test.

I sat down in the seat of the Time Machine and looked at my pocket watch; it said nineteen minutes after four. I held my breath as I gripped the lever and pulled it down a tiny bit. How can I say what it felt like? Only that it felt like falling; it felt like falling through endless space. My stomach was trying to squeeze into my throat, and my mouth was open; it looked like the mouth of a fish—a fish gasping in air.

Quickly, I pulled the stop lever and felt a slight bump and the machine came to a stop. I looked around and my heart sank.

My tools were exactly where I had laid them, my coat still hung over a chair, and my workshop was just as I had left it; my machine was a failure.

- Circle the check mark or question mark for each paragraph. Draw a question mark over any confusing words or phrases.
- Go to line 14. Mark the text that proves the Time Traveler was diligent. (measured the levers one last time)
- Go to line 17. Mark the proof that the Time Traveler was nervous. (I held my breath)
- Go to lines 19–23. Underline the words or phrases that describe how the protagonist looked or felt. (falling; stomach was trying to squeeze into my throat; mouth was open; heart sank)
- Identify the simile in lines 20 and 21. Circle the two nouns being compared. You may have to look in the previous line. (it looked like the mouth of a fish; circle my mouth, mouth of a fish.)
- Go to line 23. Mark the phrase that means the Time Traveler was disappointed. (my heart sank)
- Go to line 25. Mark the setting of this part of the story. (workshop)

- On the same line, mark the reason why the Time Traveler's heart sank. (machine was a failure)

Let's read the next three paragraphs, lines 26–44. Read the paragraphs.

Next, I saw daylight streaming in the window, and my heart beat faster. As I looked at a clock on the mantle, the clock said half past nine; I pulled out my pocket watch and looked at it; it said twenty-one minutes after four. I had traveled through time! I had traveled more than five hours in just two minutes; my Time Machine had worked!

At that point, I suppose I should have stopped and planned my next move, but I had waited too long for this moment. I could not wait any longer to journey through time, so I pulled down the lever again, and this time I pulled it a bit harder and farther. Time outside the machine was speeding up; I could hardly believe what I was seeing. I saw my housekeeper whiz into the room, clean it in record time, and shoot out the door. It was clear that she could not see me.

I had to take the next step, so this time, I pulled the lever even farther down. The window grew dark and then it brightened, then it darkened again. Time was speeding by; days went by like blinking lights as I pulled down on the lever still more. Daylight and darkness became a blur, and the windows and walls of my workshop vanished. The machine was swaying now, and my mind was swaying, too. I decided to pull the lever all the way down.

- Circle the check mark or question mark for each paragraph. Draw a question mark over any confusing words or phrases.
- Go to line 26. Mark the evidence that proves the Time Traveler was excited. (my heart beat faster)
- Go to line 27. Mark the phrase that means "9:30." (half past nine)
- Go to line 30. Mark the phrase that describes why his heart beat faster. (Time Machine had worked)
- In the middle paragraph, highlight the sentence that proves the Time Traveler was impulsive. (I could not wait any longer to journey through time, so I pulled down the lever again, and this time I pulled it a bit harder and farther.)
- Circle each instance that the Time Traveler pulled the lever. (I pulled down the lever again; I pulled the lever even farther down; I pulled down on the lever still more; I decided to pull the lever all the way down.)
- Go to line 36. Mark how the Time Traveler knows the machine is working. (whiz; clean in record time)
- On the same line, mark the synonym for *speed* or *rush*. (whiz)
- Number the visual representations of day and night that relate to the speed of the Time Machine. (the window grew dark, then it brightened; days went by like blinking lights; daylight and darkness became a blur)
- Go to line 40. Mark the simile; circle two things being compared. (days went by

like blinking lights; circle days, blinking lights)

- Go to line 42. Mark the synonym for *disappeared.* (vanished)
- Go to line 44. Mark the proof that the Time Traveler was dizzy. (my mind was swaying, too)

Let's read the next two paragraphs, lines 45–59. Read the paragraphs.

The next thing I saw around me was a world of wonders. Huge buildings were rising taller and taller; skies were changing from dark gray to bright blue; the countryside grew greener and greener. What a fantastic show! It was hard to turn my eyes away, and when I did, I looked at the dials. They told me how fast and far I was traveling. I was shocked; I had gone much faster and farther than I thought. I was in the year AD 802,701. Those huge numbers made me lose my head, and I was in a panic; I yanked hard on the stop lever.

At last, I paid the price because the stop was too sharp and the machine tipped over. I was thrown from my seat. Stunned, I lay on soft green grass. I heard a very loud thunderclap, and a shower of hailstones stung my face. It was impossible to see. "A fine welcome," I muttered, "a man travels over 800,000 years for a visit, and this is the greeting he gets!" Then the hail thinned, the sun shone through a break in the clouds, and I got my first good look at the world of the future.

- Circle the check mark or question mark for each paragraph. Draw a question mark over any confusing words or phrases.
- Go to line 45. Mark the evidence that the Time Traveler was amazed by what he saw. (a world of wonders)
- What does he see out the window that describes the world of the future? (huge buildings; blue skies; green countryside)
- Go to line 49. Mark the synonym for *surprised.* (shocked)
- Go to line 50. Mark why the Time Traveler was shocked. (I had gone much faster and farther than I thought.)
- On the same line, mark the year in the future when the Time Traveler landed. (802,701)
- Go to line 51. Mark the figurative language that means "confused." (lose my head)
- Go to line 53. Mark the figurative language that means "suffered." (paid the price)
- Go to line 54. Mark the synonym for *shocked.* (stunned)
- On the same line, mark what happened to the Time Traveler when he stopped. (I was thrown from my seat.)
- Go to line 55. Highlight what the weather is like in the future. (shower of hailstones)
- Go to line 56. Mark the sarcastic comment. (A fine welcome)

Have partners compare text markings and correct any errors.

Writing

Objective

- Write sentences using concrete words and phrases and sensory details to convey experiences and events precisely.

Masterpiece Sentences

Masterpiece Sentences poster

In this lesson we will use the Sentence Builder Chart to work on the stages of Masterpiece Sentences and practice expanding a kernel sentence. Direct students to page 146 in their Student Books and review the stages.

Sentence Builder Chart Answers will vary.

Use the stages of Masterpiece Sentences to answer the questions in the chart. Write the complete sentences below the chart.

	How many? Which ones? What kind? (adjectives)	Who? What? (noun)	Is/was doing, feeling, thinking (verb)	What did they do it to? (noun phrase—direct object)	Where? When? How? Why? (adverbs/prepositional phrases)
Stage 1	A	man	invented	a machine	
Stages 2–4	brilliant				in his laboratory to travel through time
Stage 5		scientist			
Stage 1	The	man	traveled		
Stages 2–4	intrigued				easily to 802,701 with the push of a lever to see what the future held
Stage 5		adventurer	journeyed		

In his laboratory, a brilliant scientist invented a machine to travel through time.

With the push of a lever, the intrigued adventurer easily journeyed to 802,701 to see what the future held.

We've been working with an excerpt from "The Time Machine," so let's use what we know from the story to improve our base sentence: A man invented a machine.

Have students identify the subject, predicate, and direct object. Then, read the questions in the column heads for Stages 2–5.

Model

Let's start by answering the *what kind* question for the first sentence. Solicit student ideas for answers. (Possible answers: clever, determined, smart) Write them on the board as the students brainstorm. Okay, now choose your favorite answer and write it in the box below the question for Stages 2–4.

What about *invented*? We know what he invented, but we don't know where, when, how, or why. Where did he build this machine? Solicit student responses and write them on the board. Have students choose their favorite response and write it in the box. (Possible answers: in his laboratory, basement, workshop)

Why did he build the machine? Solicit student responses and write them on the board. Have students choose their favorite response and write it in the box. (Possible answers: He wanted to see the future; he wanted to travel through time.) Let's add that to the same box.

Do we know the answer to *when* or *how*? (no) It's possible that because this is an excerpt, that information was in an earlier part of the novel. So, we will leave those questions unanswered.

Working on different painters and their position in the sentence is the work of the first four stages. Stage 5 encourages us to improve our word choice. Can you think of a more descriptive word for our subject, *man*? **Solicit student responses and write them on the board. Have students choose their favorite response and write it in the box.** (Possible answers: scientist, inventor, creator)

Have students make any other changes they think are needed. Now, combine the parts to create your final version of the sentence and write it on the first line below the chart.

Guided and Independent Practice

With your partner, repeat the process for the second kernel sentence. Make sure you write your final sentence below the chart. **Have volunteers share their sentences.**

Note: Base the number of modeled and guided examples on student ability and progress. Challenge them with independent practice when appropriate.

Lesson 8

Lesson Opener

Before the lesson, choose one of the following activities to write on the board or post on the *LANGUAGE! Live* Class Wall online.

- *If you could travel back in time, who would you want to visit? Explain your answer.*
- *Write two sentences: one with a compound subject and one with a compound predicate.*
- *Use a pair of homophones in one sentence about school.*

Writing

Objectives

- Read and examine a personal narrative.
- Orally review key ideas from the passage.
- Write clear introductory topic and concluding sentences.

Introduction to Personal Narrative

In this unit, we will be completing a different kind of writing. We will be writing a personal narrative. A personal narrative is an expressive form of writing. Direct students to page 147 in their Student Books. Introduce personal narratives by reading and discussing the bulleted examples.

Now, let's spend some time exploring the structure of a personal narrative.

Lesson 8 | Writing

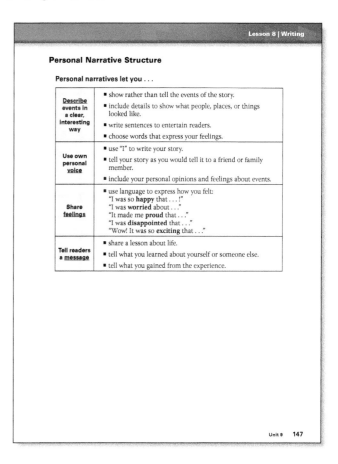

Personal Narrative Structure

Personal narratives let you . . .

Describe events in a clear, interesting way	▪ show rather than tell the events of the story. ▪ include details to show what people, places, or things looked like. ▪ write sentences to entertain readers. ▪ choose words that express your feelings.
Use own personal voice	▪ use "I" to write your story. ▪ tell your story as you would tell it to a friend or family member. ▪ include your personal opinions and feelings about events.
Share feelings	▪ use language to express how you felt: "I was so **happy** that . . . !" "I was **worried** about . . ." "It made me **proud** that . . ." "I was **disappointed** that . . ." "Wow! It was so **exciting** that . . ."
Tell readers a message	▪ share a lesson about life. ▪ tell what you learned about yourself or someone else. ▪ tell what you gained from the experience.

Unit 9 147

Direct students to page 148 in their Student Books. Follow along as I read this example of a personal narrative. As we go, we will examine how this type of writing is structured. First, I will read the narrative without stopping or asking questions. Then we'll reread the passage and take a closer look at its elements.

Read the passage once; then reread, stopping after the title, the introduction, the beginning of the story, the middle of the story, the end of the story, and the conclusion. Have students label each part as you reread it.

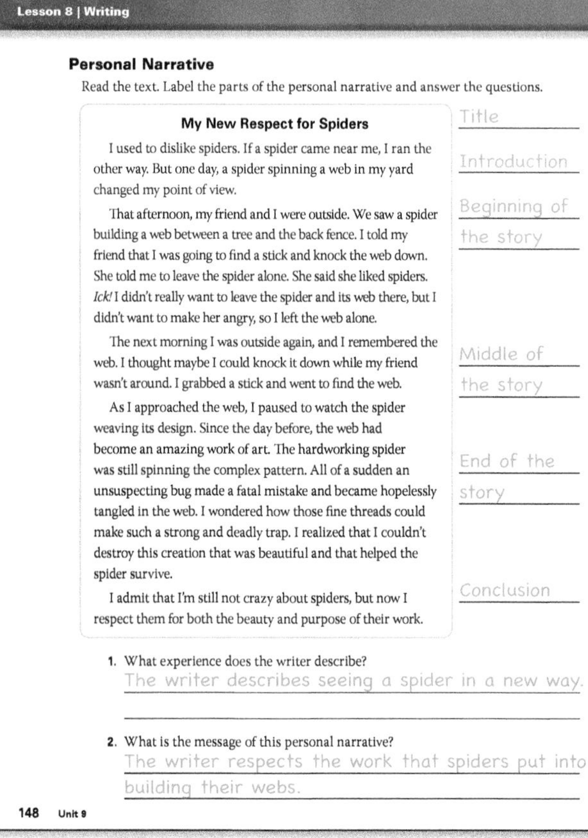
Lesson 8 | Writing

Personal Narrative

Read the text. Label the parts of the personal narrative and answer the questions.

My New Respect for Spiders	Title
I used to dislike spiders. If a spider came near me, I ran the other way. But one day, a spider spinning a web in my yard changed my point of view.	Introduction
That afternoon, my friend and I were outside. We saw a spider building a web between a tree and the back fence. I told my friend that I was going to find a stick and knock the web down. She told me to leave the spider alone. She said she liked spiders. *Ick!* I didn't really want to leave the spider and its web there, but I didn't want to make her angry, so I left the web alone.	Beginning of the story
The next morning I was outside again, and I remembered the web. I thought maybe I could knock it down while my friend wasn't around. I grabbed a stick and went to find the web.	Middle of the story
As I approached the web, I paused to watch the spider weaving its design. Since the day before, the web had become an amazing work of art. The hardworking spider was still spinning the complex pattern. All of a sudden an unsuspecting bug made a fatal mistake and became hopelessly tangled in the web. I wondered how those fine threads could make such a strong and deadly trap. I realized that I couldn't destroy this creation that was beautiful and that helped the spider survive.	End of the story
I admit that I'm still not crazy about spiders, but now I respect them for both the beauty and purpose of their work.	Conclusion

1. What experience does the writer describe?
The writer describes seeing a spider in a new way.

2. What is the message of this personal narrative?
The writer respects the work that spiders put into building their webs.

148 Unit 9

My New Respect for Spiders

I used to dislike spiders. If a spider came near me, I ran the other way. But one day, a spider spinning a web in my yard changed my point of view.

That afternoon, my friend and I were outside. We saw a spider building a web between a tree and the back fence. I told my friend that I was going to find a stick and knock the web down. She told me to leave the spider alone. She said she liked spiders. *Ick!* I didn't really want to leave the spider and its web there, but I didn't want to make her angry, so I left the web alone.

The next morning I was outside again, and I remembered the web. I thought maybe I could knock it down while my friend wasn't around. I grabbed a stick and went to find the web.

As I approached the web, I paused to watch the spider weaving its design. Since the day before, the web had become an amazing work of art. The hardworking spider was still spinning the complex pattern. All of a sudden an unsuspecting bug made a fatal mistake and became hopelessly tangled in the web. I wondered how those fine threads could make such a strong and deadly trap. I realized that I couldn't destroy this creation that was beautiful and that helped the spider survive.

I admit that I'm still not crazy about spiders, but now I respect them for both the beauty and purpose of their work.

Discuss the questions following the narrative. Then use them as a springboard to discuss students' ideas for their personal narrative.

Now, let's think about the parts of "The Time Machine." How does the Time Traveler feel about time at the beginning of the passage? (Possible responses: He thinks it's worth exploring and sees value in traveling through time. He sees it as an adventure, something that needs to be explored, like space or the depths of the ocean. He doesn't imagine any negative consequences.)

At the end of the novel, the Time Traveler will feel differently about time. Based on the introduction, we know that he thought there were consequences to knowing the future. With that in mind, will he think time should be left alone, or will he feel even more strongly about the value of exploring time? (He will think time should be left alone.)

Talk about what the Time Traveler might have seen or experienced in the future that would affect his attitude about time. Encourage responses that express different viewpoints.

Example Questions

- What do *you* think about time travel?
- Would you want to know what will happen in the future?
- What are some possible positives and negatives for doing this?
- Discuss these questions with your partner.

Note: Student discussions of what might have happened will guide them in development of their narrative. If you think it would help them, have them take notes during the discussion.

Two-Sentence Introduction and Conclusion

Let's look at strategies for developing strong introductions and conclusions. Direct students to pages 149 and 150 in their Student Books. Read the instructions. Then read about each personal narrative, having students circle the topic and underline words that relate to the message. Discuss the answers to the questions that follow each example.

Now let's use this knowledge to write the introduction and conclusion for our own personal narrative.

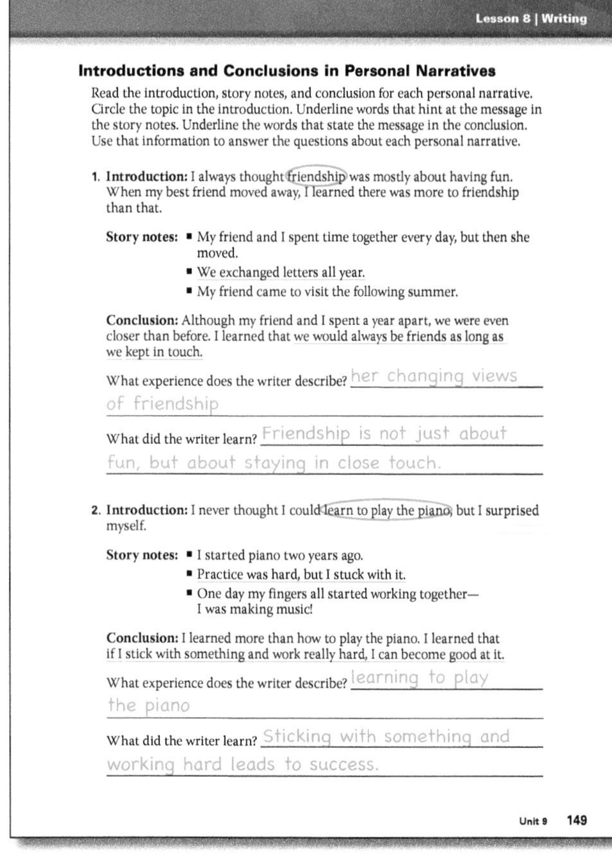

Lesson 8 | Writing

Introductions and Conclusions in Personal Narratives

Read the introduction, story notes, and conclusion for each personal narrative. Circle the topic in the introduction. Underline words that hint at the message in the story notes. Underline the words that state the message in the conclusion. Use that information to answer the questions about each personal narrative.

1. **Introduction:** I always thought friendship was mostly about having fun. When my best friend moved away, I learned there was more to friendship than that.

   Story notes:
   - My friend and I spent time together every day, but then she moved.
   - We exchanged letters all year.
   - My friend came to visit the following summer.

   Conclusion: Although my friend and I spent a year apart, we were even closer than before. I learned that we would always be friends as long as we kept in touch.

   What experience does the writer describe? her changing views of friendship

   What did the writer learn? Friendship is not just about fun, but about staying in close touch.

2. **Introduction:** I never thought I could learn to play the piano, but I surprised myself.

   Story notes:
   - I started piano two years ago.
   - Practice was hard, but I stuck with it.
   - One day my fingers all started working together—I was making music!

   Conclusion: I learned more than how to play the piano. I learned that if I stick with something and work really hard, I can become good at it.

   What experience does the writer describe? learning to play the piano

   What did the writer learn? Sticking with something and working hard leads to success.

Unit 9 149

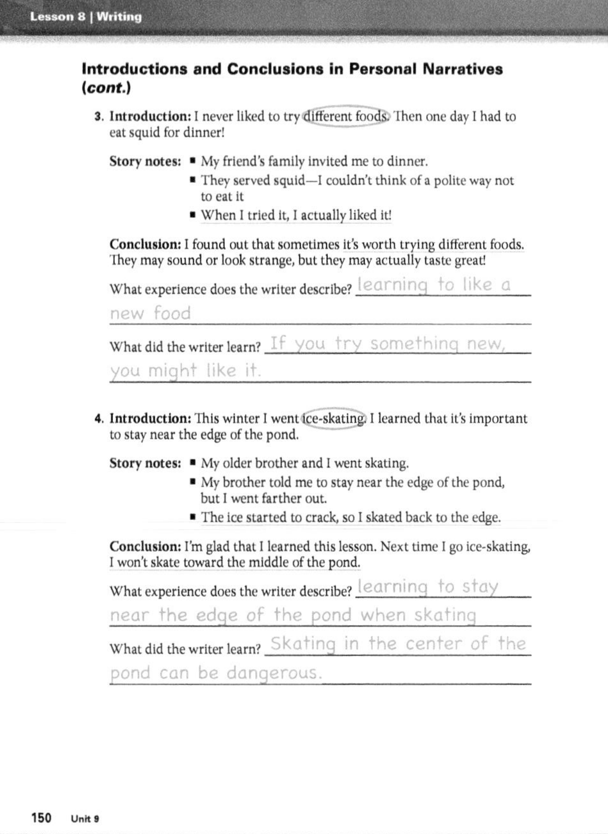

Lesson 8 | Writing

Introductions and Conclusions in Personal Narratives (*cont.*)

3. **Introduction:** I never liked to try different foods. Then one day I had to eat squid for dinner!

   Story notes:
   - My friend's family invited me to dinner.
   - They served squid—I couldn't think of a polite way not to eat it
   - When I tried it, I actually liked it!

   Conclusion: I found out that sometimes it's worth trying different foods. They may sound or look strange, but they may actually taste great!

   What experience does the writer describe? learning to like a new food

   What did the writer learn? If you try something new, you might like it.

4. **Introduction:** This winter I went ice-skating. I learned that it's important to stay near the edge of the pond.

   Story notes:
   - My older brother and I went skating.
   - My brother told me to stay near the edge of the pond, but I went farther out.
   - The ice started to crack, so I skated back to the edge.

   Conclusion: I'm glad that I learned this lesson. Next time I go ice-skating, I won't skate toward the middle of the pond.

   What experience does the writer describe? learning to stay near the edge of the pond when skating

   What did the writer learn? Skating in the center of the pond can be dangerous.

150 Unit 9

Prepare to Write

Direct students to page 151 in their Student Books. Read the prompt and have students identify the topic, directions, and purpose for writing.

Prepare to Write

Part A. Study the Prompt Answers will vary.

Read the prompt and identify the topic, directions, and purpose for writing.

Imagine yourself as the Time Traveler in H.G. Wells's "The Time Machine." Write a personal narrative about traveling through time and tell how the experience changed your ideas about time.

Topic: traveling through time

Directions: write personal narrative

Purpose for writing: tell how experience of time travel changed thinking about time; entertain

Part B. Write the Topic Sentence: Two-Sentence Introduction

Write a sentence that introduces the experience. Write an additional sentence that suggests what you learned.

I have always been fascinated with the idea of traveling through time. Realizing a lifelong dream certainly made a difference in how I look at time.

Part C. Write a Concluding Sentence: Two-Sentence Conclusion

Reorganize your topic sentence to write a concluding sentence.

The idea of time travel still thrills me. Based on my personal experiences, the potential benefits of such travel exceed my wildest dreams.

Now that you know what you will be writing, we will read "The Time Machine" again. It is an example of a well-written narrative, and exposing yourself to good writing is the best way to become a proficient writer.

We will use our Guided Highlighting notes to outline specific information that will help us write our narrative.

Direct students to page 151 in their Student Books to reexamine the prompt and develop their two-sentence introduction. How will you feel after traveling through time? You have to figure this out, and then develop details that support these feelings. If you feel even more strongly about the value of traveling through time, what happened to confirm and strengthen its value? If you now think time travel has dangerous consequences, what happened to change your mind?

You need to state your position in the two-sentence introduction. Regardless of which position you develop, your first sentence can state your interest or fascination with time. Write the following sentence on the board:

I have always been fascinated with the idea of traveling through time.

We could use our second sentence to set up the direction of the narrative without "tipping our hand." Write the following sentence on the board:

Realizing a lifelong dream certainly made a difference in how I look at time.

Have students write these two sentences as their introduction. Allow them to modify the sentences if they have another idea about developing their introduction. Check their sentences to make sure they set up the narrative sufficiently.

Let's look back at the conclusion in the example narrative to get an idea about writing our own conclusion. Reread the final sentence in the Personal Narrative on page 148 and discuss how it further defines the writer's attitude toward spiders. Write the following sentence on the board:

The idea of time travel still thrills me.

Now we can add another sentence to express either negative or positive feelings about time. Write the following sentences on the board:

> *Based on my personal experiences, though, the negative consequences certainly outweigh any possible benefits.*
>
> *Based on my personal experiences, the potential benefits of such travel exceed my wildest dreams.*

Explain to students that combining the first sentence with one of these sentences would create a strong conclusion, but that each expresses a very different perspective on time travel.

Reading

Objectives

- Review the main elements of a narrative (setting, character traits, plot).
- Demonstrate an understanding of the key elements of a narrative.

Direct students to page 152 in their Student Books and review the elements that make up the Story Elements Map.

To write our narrative, we will need to look at the Time Traveler's character traits, since the narrative we write will be from his point of view and we want to remain true to his character. We will need to understand the plot of the story. We also need to look at the setting, including the year he travels to, and what he sees when he lands. This will help us continue the narrative where it left off.

Have partners complete the Story Elements Map using information from the Guided Highlighting activity. Then, have students identify other information they will use in their writing and examples of descriptive language and figurative language that the author uses.

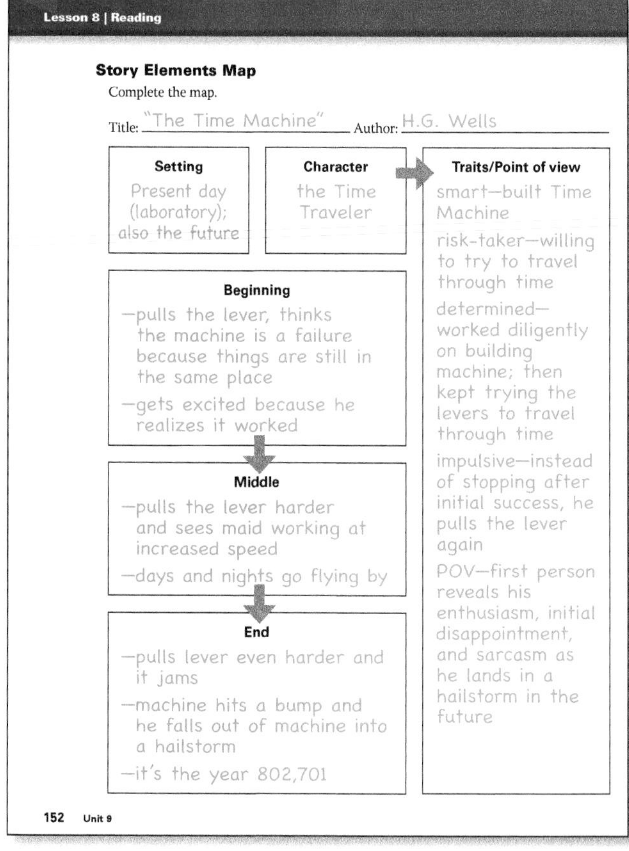
Lesson 8 | Reading

Story Elements Map

Complete the map.

Title: "The Time Machine" Author: H.G. Wells

Setting: Present day (laboratory); also the future

Character: the Time Traveler

Traits/Point of view: smart—built Time Machine; risk-taker—willing to try to travel through time; determined—worked diligently on building machine; then kept trying the levers to travel through time; impulsive—instead of stopping after initial success, he pulls the lever again; POV—first person reveals his enthusiasm, initial disappointment, and sarcasm as he lands in a hailstorm in the future

Beginning: —pulls the lever, thinks the machine is a failure because things are still in the same place —gets excited because he realizes it worked

Middle: —pulls the lever harder and sees maid working at increased speed —days and nights go flying by

End: —pulls lever even harder and it jams —machine hits a bump and he falls out of machine into a hailstorm —it's the year 802,701

152 Unit 9

Note: If necessary, guide students in completion of the story map using the complete map as a guide for discussion points.

Writing

Objectives

- Gather relevant information from notes.
- Write a personal narrative.
- Develop the paragraph with details.

The Body of the Narrative

We now have our introduction and conclusion written. Let's transfer them to our Personal Narrative Planner and then focus on developing the story.

Direct students to the Personal Narrative Planner on page 153 in their Student Books. We can refer to our Story Elements Map as a reminder of how the story develops. Let's complete the Beginning section with information from the text. Guide students in completion of this section.

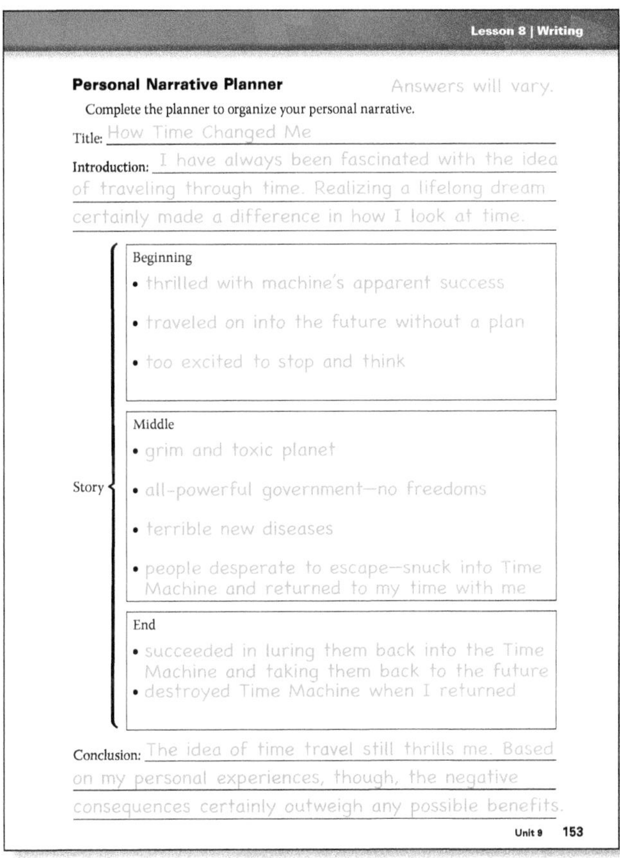
Lesson 8 | Writing

Personal Narrative Planner Answers will vary.

Complete the planner to organize your personal narrative.

Title: How Time Changed Me

Introduction: I have always been fascinated with the idea of traveling through time. Realizing a lifelong dream certainly made a difference in how I look at time.

Story

Beginning
- thrilled with machine's apparent success
- traveled on into the future without a plan
- too excited to stop and think

Middle
- grim and toxic planet
- all-powerful government—no freedoms
- terrible new diseases
- people desperate to escape—snuck into Time Machine and returned to my time with me

End
- succeeded in luring them back into the Time Machine and taking them back to the future
- destroyed Time Machine when I returned

Conclusion: The idea of time travel still thrills me. Based on my personal experiences, though, the negative consequences certainly outweigh any possible benefits.

Unit 9 153

Based on your concluding sentence, you will have to add more details to the chart to defend your conclusion. This will go in the Middle and End sections. But first, turn back to the Story Elements Map on page 152 and review your notes with your partner. Talk about what the Time Traveler might have seen or experienced in the future that would affect his attitude about time. After giving students a few minutes to talk, have them complete the Personal Narrative Planner. Explain that everyone's beginning will be the same, but that the middle and ending details will be different, based on the conclusion they chose.

Notebook paper

Have students use the bulleted ideas in the Personal Narrative Planner to write a rough draft for the body of the narrative on a clean sheet of paper.

Example Personal Narrative

I have always been fascinated with the idea of traveling through time. Realizing a lifelong dream certainly made a difference in how I look at time. When I pulled the lever and my time machine actually traveled through time, I felt an incredible sense of gratification. All of my hard work and long hours had paid off! I willingly hurled myself into the future without stopping to develop a plan.

I pulled the lever to stop the machine and as I rolled out onto the ground, I realized I had not thought about anything except getting to the future. A grim, gray world greeted me.

The landscape was bare and a haze hung in the air. I heard stern voices in the background and hid in a clump of thorny bushes. Soldiers appeared on the road with what appeared to be a group of prisoners. Panic settled over me as they disappeared from sight. What kind of a world was this?

A voice whispered in my ear, and I almost screamed out in fear and surprise. Frightened and desperate, a young man told me about his life. An all-powerful government had taken away every freedom people had once enjoyed. Friends and family members were dying of incurable diseases caused by the polluted environment. I had landed in a nightmare and all I wanted to do was escape.

Without hesitating or looking around, I ran back to my machine. I threw the lever, desperate to be back in my own time. When I landed back in my laboratory, I realized I had not traveled back through time alone.

A small band of sickly stowaways had clung to the outside of the machine and now they were standing in my laboratory. They did not move or say a word. I knew our science and medicine was no match for their diseases. I had brought the equivalent of the Black Plague back from the future.

Desperate to lure them into the machine, I began to tell them of an even more wonderful place in time. I took them to a time beyond their own, hoping the people had taken back control of their world. I landed in a beautiful green meadow this time. My stowaways looked up at the blue skies and eagerly walked out into the meadow. As quick as a wink, I pulled the lever and sent myself back through time.

My laboratory had never looked so welcoming. The idea of time travel still thrills me, but I will not be rebuilding my machine. Based on my personal experiences, the negative consequences certainly outweigh any possible benefits.

Have students write their final narrative on a separate sheet of paper.

Unit 9

Lesson 9

Lesson Opener

Before the lesson, choose one of the following activities to write on the board or post on the *LANGUAGE! Live* Class Wall online.

- *Assess the similarities between you and the Time Traveler. Write two sentences about how you are alike.*
- *Write two sentences with each of the following words, using each first as a verb and then as an adjective:* cashed, parked.
- *Write three sentences about the online word training. Tell me the last lesson you completed, the lesson you are on right now, and when you think you will begin the next lesson.*

Reading

Objective

- Read words to develop fluency.

Word Fluency: Second Read

Timer

Follow the Fluency Procedure outlined below. If it is necessary, begin the fluency drill with a choral read of the words as you provide a rhythm (snap your fingers, tap your foot, tap your pencil). Direct students to page 154 in their Student Books and complete the process.

Word Fluency: Second Read

Read the words fluently.

	Correct	Errors
1st Try		
2nd Try		

called	booted	bowls	soon	booth	stalling	toyed	herded	march	show	10
bowls	soon	booth	stalling	toyed	herded	march	show	jerked	sport	20
booth	stalling	toyed	herded	march	show	jerked	sport	drowned	germs	30
toyed	herded	march	show	jerked	sport	drowned	germs	thorns	formed	40
march	show	jerked	sport	drowned	germs	thorns	formed	snow	sorted	50
jerked	sport	drowned	germs	thorns	formed	snow	sorted	torched	crowded	60
drowned	germs	thorns	formed	snow	sorted	torched	crowded	booted	called	70
thorns	formed	snow	sorted	torched	crowded	booted	called	soon	bowls	80
snow	sorted	torched	crowded	booted	called	soon	bowls	stalling	toyed	90
torched	crowded	booted	called	soon	bowls	stalling	booth	herded	march	100

Lesson 9 | Reading

154 Unit 9

Fluency Procedure

- Partners switch books, so the recorder is marking errors in the reader's book.
- A timer is set for one minute.
- Readers and recorders move left to right, tracking each word with a pencil.
- As readers read the words aloud, recorders mark errors with a small x above the misread word.
- Recorders place a star to the right of the last word read when time ends.
- If the reader is able to read all words in the allotted time, the reader needs to start over at the beginning. The recorder must indicate this feat by placing two stars to the right of the last word read.
- When both students have read, partners switch books.
- Students calculate total words read, then subtract errors and record.
- Students record information on the progress chart in back of the Student Book.

Vocabulary

Objectives

- Demonstrate an understanding of words by relating them to their synonyms, antonyms, and related words.
- Demonstrate an understanding of figurative language by generating examples of similes and metaphors.
- Identify and define idioms.

Four-Square

Review the word *failure* and its definition.

Direct students to page 155 in their Student Books. Read the instructions. Have partners complete the synonyms, examples, antonyms, nonexamples, and related words. Review the answers as a class.

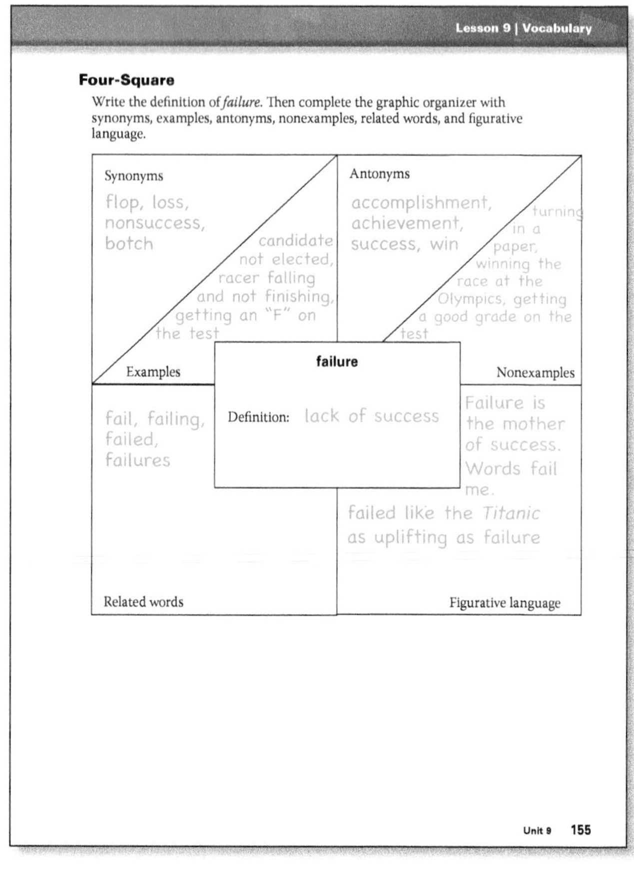

Ask students for examples of metaphors or similes that include the word *failure* or a related word. Then have partners create another metaphor or simile, if possible.

Write these patterns on the board for guidance:

______ *like* _______
(verb) *(noun)*

as ________ *as* ______
(adjective) *(noun)*

______ *is/was* ______
(noun) *(noun)*

Failure is a noun. Our first model asks for a verb. Look at the word *failure*, and tell me the verb that the word comes from. (fail) Let's put the word *failed* in the verb spot and see if we can think of something that was a huge failure. The *Titanic* was supposed to be an unsinkable ship, but it sank on its first voyage. I would say that was a huge failure. So, our simile could be *failed like the Titanic.* Have students write a simile with *fail* in the verb spot and use it in a sentence.

Let's move on to the next simile type. Now, let's put the word *failure* in the noun spot. What adjective can we think of that describes a failure or how a failure feels? (disappointing, heartbreaking, challenging, etc.) Or you can also come up with an adjective that is the opposite of how a failure makes you feel. Sometimes sarcasm is used in similes. (uplifting, soothing, etc.) Have students write another simile with *failure* in the noun spot and use it in a sentence.

If time allows, repeat the process with the metaphor pattern.

Grammar

Objectives

- Demonstrate an understanding of the function of verb phrases in sentences.
- Identify words with multiple functions (noun, verb, adjective) in sentences.

Verb Phrases

Present Tense

We've learned about verb endings, verb tense, action verbs, and linking verbs. We've also learned that verbs sometimes work alone and sometimes get some help.

When a sentence contains a main verb and a helping verb, we call that a verb phrase. Consider the verb *sing*.

I *sing* in the choir.

Sing is the main verb and it works alone.

I *am singing* in the choir.

Does that sentence have a verb phrase? (yes) What is it? (am singing) What tense is the verb in both sentences? (present)

Future Tense

What is required to make the verb show future tense? (the word *will* before the verb) To express future tense, we have to use a verb phrase. Do we have to use a verb phrase to show present tense? (no) **Prompt students for examples.** Do we have to use a verb phrase to show past tense? (no) **Prompt students for examples.** Let's look at the sentences we worked on in Lesson 6 and change the tense to future tense. After we change the verbs to future tense, what will the sentences contain? (verb phrases)

Direct students to Part A on page 156 in their Student Books. Read the instructions and the example aloud. Have students complete the activity. Review the answers as a class. Read the instructions aloud for Part B. Have partners write sentences and share them.

Lesson 9 | Grammar

Change It: Verb Phrases

Part A Answers will vary.

Copy the two sentences from the Sentence Builder Chart on page 146 on the lines below. Change the tense in each sentence to future tense. Underline the verb phrase in each new sentence.

Example: The young bird chirped hungrily in its nest.
Revised: The young bird will chirp hungrily in its nest.

1. In his laboratory, a brilliant scientist invented a machine to travel through time.
Revised: In his laboratory, a brilliant scientist will invent a machine to travel through time.

2. With the push of a lever, the intrigued adventurer easily journeyed to 802,701 to see what the future held.
Revised: With the push of a lever, the intrigued adventurer will easily journey to 802,701 to see what the future holds.

Part B

What other phrases can you build using the future tense verbs from the above sentences?

1. The student will invent a homework machine to do the tedious work for him.

2. With his new hybrid car, the environmentally conscientious man will easily journey to work and back each day of the week.

156 Unit 9

Multiple Functions of Words

In addition to learning that verbs can work alone or with another verb, we have also learned that many words can do multiple jobs. That is, they can be verbs or nouns or adjectives based on how they are used in a sentence. Think about the word *stands*.

She *stands* in the bleachers. What question does *stands* answer in that sentence? (What is she doing?) Yes, it is working as a verb in that sentence.

The *stands* are filled with cheering fans. What question does *stands* answer in that sentence? (What?) Right; it is doing the work of a noun.

Direct students to pages 157 and 158 in their Student Books.

Model

Let's do some more practice in identifying the work certain words do in sentences. Read the instructions and the example aloud, modeling the questions that need to be asked to determine the part of speech.

Guided Practice

Read the sentences for number 1 and have students tell you the correct answers.

Independent Practice

Read the next pair of sentences and have students write their answers independently, and then review the answers. Complete the remainder of the activity in this manner.

Note: Base the number of modeled and guided examples on student ability and progress. Challenge them with independent practice when appropriate.

Lesson 9 | Grammar

Identify It: Multiple Functions of Words

Identify the function, or job, of the underlined word in each sentence. The word may be a noun (naming word), a verb (action word), or an adjective (describing word). Write the correct answer on the line following each sentence.

Example: Because he did not prepare thoroughly, he failed the exam. verb

The failed rocket launch was a setback for the entire research team. adjective

1. Because of the warning signs, we will park in the right place. verb

   We will plan a trip to explore the historic park. noun

2. Because of the storm, people are going inside. noun

   Soon, we will move to the storm shelter. adjective

3. To make sure the machine works according to the plan, they test it repeatedly. verb

   After studying all night, I overslept and missed the test. noun

4. We walk through the open door. adjective

   My dad likes to open the door for my mom. verb

5. We bowl every Friday night with our friends. verb

   The bowl was filled with fresh fruit and vegetables from the garden. noun

6. They show me to my seat at the movie theater. verb

   I sit down to watch the show. noun

Unit 9 157

Lesson 9 | Grammar

Identify It: Multiple Functions of Words (*cont.*)

Challenge:

7. She attempts to open the treasure chest. verb

   After three attempts, she quit. noun

8. The white tigers intrigue the visitors to the zoo. verb

   The intrigue fades after several months. noun

9. The slight movement made me jump. adjective

   The server did not slight me, but gave me a large piece of cake. verb

10. The boy related the events of the fire to the officer. verb

    The related events happened one after another. adjective

158 Unit 9

Writing

Objectives

- Develop and strengthen writing by editing for descriptive details.
- Edit for basic written conventions.
- Edit to produce clear and coherent writing in which the development and organization are appropriate to the audience.

Review and Revise

Direct students to the Writer's Checklist on page 159 in their Student Books. Have them use the checklist to review and revise their personal narratives. Allow them to work independently for about five minutes. Circulate to monitor student work and answer any questions.

Direct students to page 160. Have them work with their partners to apply the Six Traits of Writing to their narratives. Have students focus on Voice. Read the criteria for Voice and Audience Awareness to the class and then give students several minutes to "score" their writing. When time expires, ask for volunteers to share their insights.

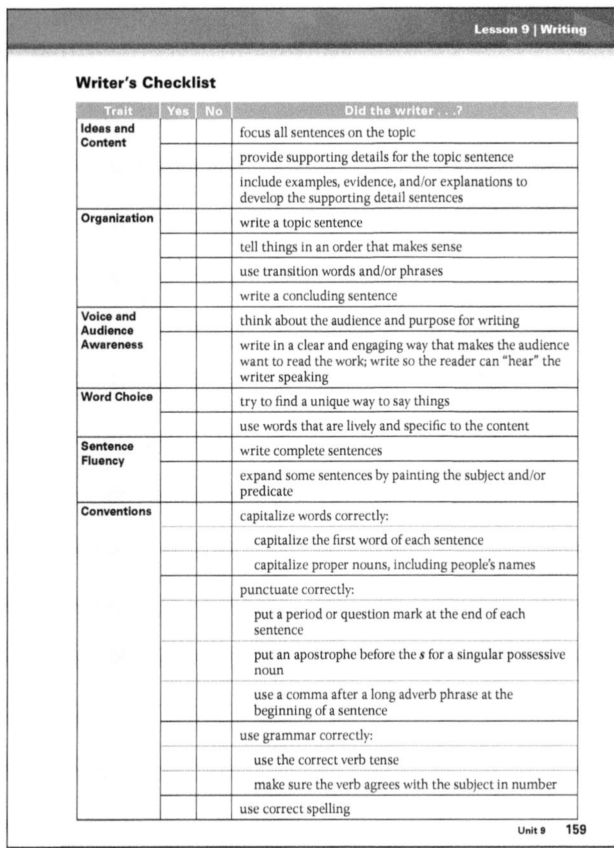
Lesson 9 | Writing

Writer's Checklist

Trait	Yes	No	Did the writer . . . ?
Ideas and Content			focus all sentences on the topic
			provide supporting details for the topic sentence
			include examples, evidence, and/or explanations to develop the supporting detail sentences
Organization			write a topic sentence
			tell things in an order that makes sense
			use transition words and/or phrases
			write a concluding sentence
Voice and Audience Awareness			think about the audience and purpose for writing
			write in a clear and engaging way that makes the audience want to read the work; write so the reader can "hear" the writer speaking
Word Choice			try to find a unique way to say things
			use words that are lively and specific to the content
Sentence Fluency			write complete sentences
			expand some sentences by painting the subject and/or predicate
Conventions			capitalize words correctly:
			capitalize the first word of each sentence
			capitalize proper nouns, including people's names
			punctuate correctly:
			put a period or question mark at the end of each sentence
			put an apostrophe before the *s* for a singular possessive noun
			use a comma after a long adverb phrase at the beginning of a sentence
			use grammar correctly:
			use the correct verb tense
			make sure the verb agrees with the subject in number
			use correct spelling

Unit 9 159

Six Traits of Writing: Personal Narrative

	Criteria				Value	
Trait	4	3	2	1		Comments
Ideas and Content	Tells a single story using anecdotes/events to develop the message/lesson learned. Includes substantial description and detail. No irrelevant material.	Tells a single story developed with some anecdotes/events. Includes some description. Message/lesson learned may be unclear. Limited irrelevant material.	No clear sense of a single story. Details/description may be absent or unrelated to the message/lesson learned. Too repetitious or too much irrelevant material.	Does not address prompt and/or lacks focus on the topic. Does not tell a story that includes related anecdotes/events. Little or no description and detail.	___	
Organization	Introductory paragraph hints at the message. Three body paragraphs contain the story's beginning, middle, and end. Story transitions connect anecdotes/events. Concluding paragraph explains the message/lesson learned.	Introductory paragraph hints at the message. Three body paragraphs contain story's beginning, middle, and end. Some story transitions may be unclear or missing. Contains a concluding paragraph that explains the message/lesson learned.	Introductory paragraph missing or unrelated to the message. Body paragraphs do not tell a story's beginning, middle, and end. Story transitions are missing, as is a concluding paragraph that explains the message/lesson learned.	No evident structure. Lack of organization seriously interferes with meaning.	___	
Voice and Audience Awareness	Strong sense of person and purpose behind the words. Brings story to life.	Some sense of person and purpose behind the words.	Little sense of person and purpose behind the words.	No sense of person or purpose behind the words.	___	
Word Choice	Words are specific, accurate, and vivid. Word choice enhances meaning and reader's enjoyment.	Words are correctly used but may be somewhat general and unspecific.	Word choice limited. Words may be used inaccurately or repetitively.	Extremely limited range of words. Restricted vocabulary impedes message.	___	
Sentence Fluency	Writes complete sentences, some of which are expanded.	Writes complete sentences with some expansion.	Writes mostly simple and/or awkwardly constructed sentences. May include some run-ons and fragments.	Numerous run-ons and/or sentence fragments interfere with meaning.	___	
Conventions	*Capitalization & Punctuation* 0–1 error. Indents paragraphs.	*Capitalization & Punctuation* 2 errors. Indents paragraphs.	*Capitalization & Punctuation* 3 errors. May not indent paragraphs.	*Capitalization & Punctuation* 4+ errors. May not indent paragraphs.	___	
	Grammar/Usage 0–1 error	*Grammar/Usage* 2 errors	*Grammar/Usage* 3 errors	*Grammar/Usage* 4+ errors	___	
	Spelling 0–1 error	*Spelling* 2 errors	*Spelling* 3 errors	*Spelling* 4+ errors	___	

Lesson 9 | Writing

160 Unit 9

Unit 9 Lesson 10

Lesson Opener

Before the lesson, choose one of the following activities to write on the board or post on the *LANGUAGE! Live* Class Wall online.

- *Is time travel a good idea? Why or why not?*
- *Write four meaningful sentences using vocabulary words from this unit. Each sentence will contain two vocabulary words* (intrigue, philosopher, consequence, vanish, attempt, relate, slight, moment).
- *Write a sentence using the word* time *as a noun and as a verb.*

Vocabulary

Objectives

- Clarify the meaning of key passage vocabulary.
- Demonstrate an understanding of passage vocabulary by using them in sentences.

Review

Direct students to page 114 in their Student Books. Remind them of the review procedure. Have partners review the Key Passage Vocabulary.

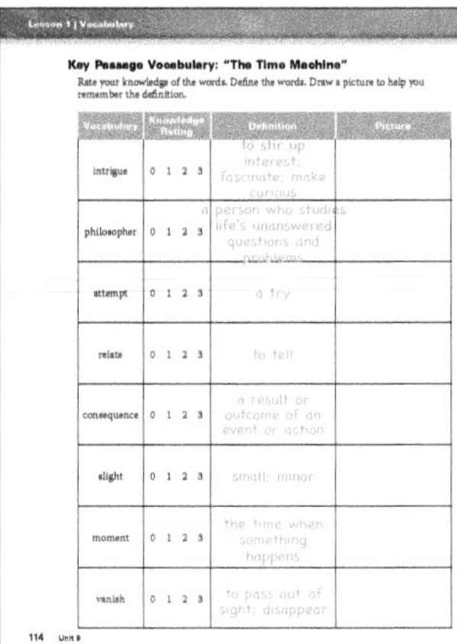
Lesson 1 | Vocabulary

Key Passage Vocabulary: "The Time Machine"

Rate your knowledge of the words. Define the words. Draw a picture to help you remember the definition.

Vocabulary	Knowledge Rating	Definition	Picture
intrigue	0 1 2 3	to stir up interest; fascinate; make curious	
philosopher	0 1 2 3	a person who studies life's unanswered questions and problems	
attempt	0 1 2 3	a try	
relate	0 1 2 3	to tell	
consequence	0 1 2 3	a result or outcome of an event or action	
slight	0 1 2 3	small; minor	
moment	0 1 2 3	the time when something happens	
vanish	0 1 2 3	to pass out of sight; disappear	

114 Unit 9

Review Procedure

- Student A reads the word.
- Student B tells the meaning.
- Students swap roles for each word.

Have students revisit their rating of the words. If they cannot change all ratings to a 3, pull them aside to discuss the vocabulary words they do not know.

Cloze Activity

Now we will read a paragraph. You will determine which vocabulary words are missing and write them on the lines. Direct students to page 161 in their Student Books. Remind them of the cloze procedure.

Cloze Procedure

- Teacher reads the text aloud, pausing at the blanks for students to write.
- Students fill in the blanks with words from the word bank.
- Teacher rereads the text as students chorally tell the correct word for each blank.
- Students correct errors.

Lesson 10 | Vocabulary

Using New Vocabulary

Fill in the blanks with the appropriate vocabulary words. If you need assistance, use the word bank at the bottom of the page.

Time travel ___intrigues___ many people. Inventors who are fascinated with the idea have made many ___attempts___ to create a way to ___vanish___ from the present time and appear in the future. This idea was ___related___ to readers in the novel *A Christmas Carol*. In that story, the protagonist travels to the future and sees how people are affected by his ___slight___ cruelty. The ___consequence___ of his trip to the future is an immediate change in behavior the ___moment___ he returns to the present.

Though seeing the future was beneficial for Scrooge, ___philosophers___ wonder whether knowing the future would be wise or not. It is possible that knowing the future would not only make life boring, but also lead to fear and anxiety over what's to come.

Word Bank

consequence	moment	slight	intrigues
related	philosophers	attempts	vanish

Unit 9 161

Reading

Objectives

- Discuss and answer questions to demonstrate an understanding of an author's or narrator's point of view in a story.
- Discuss and answer questions to demonstrate an understanding of the passages' main idea and key details.

Character Point of View vs. Personal Point of View

In this unit, you considered the merits of time travel through a character's eyes and through your own. Do you feel the same way about time as the Time Traveler does? It is possible that your point of view is different, which makes your story different. Many stories would have a very different slant if they were told from another character's perspective. Some authors have written comical versions of well-known fairy tales by changing the author's point of view. Think about how differently a story would feel if it were told from the villain's point of view. What about "The Three Little Pigs"? How would that story be different if it were told from the wolf's perspective? Encourage discussion. Encourage students to consider other familiar stories that would be dramatically different if told from another perspective.

History often influences our point of view on an event. For example, as Americans, we might view our role in a given war differently than other countries may view it. *All Quiet on the Western Front* is a novel about World War I. It provides painful insights into the tragedy of war from the point of view of a young German soldier. Being aware of the power of point of view and using it to your advantage will make you a much better writer.

Big Idea

Direct students to page 113 in their Student Books.

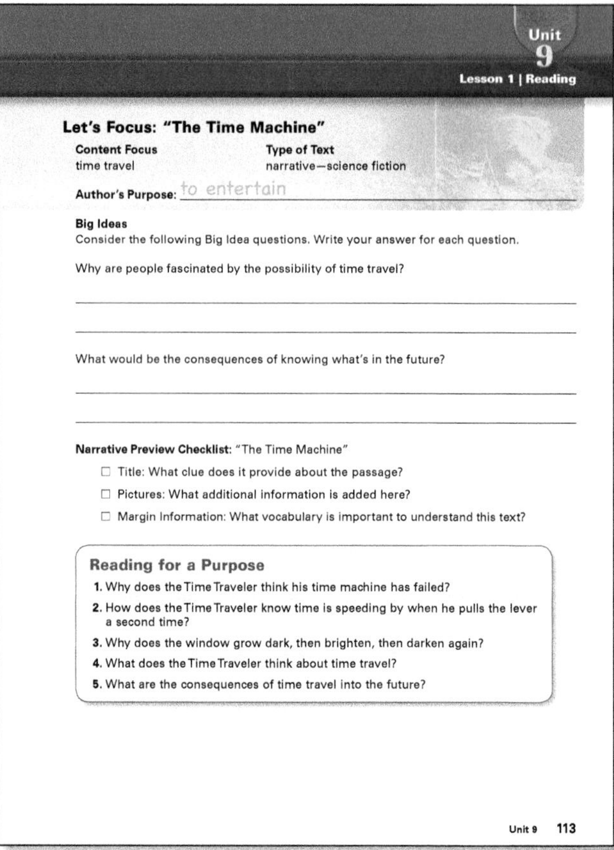

Unit 9

Lesson 1 | Reading

Let's Focus: "The Time Machine"

Content Focus
time travel

Type of Text
narrative—science fiction

Author's Purpose: to entertain

Big Ideas

Consider the following Big Idea questions. Write your answer for each question.

Why are people fascinated by the possibility of time travel?

What would be the consequences of knowing what's in the future?

Narrative Preview Checklist: "The Time Machine"

- ☐ Title: What clue does it provide about the passage?
- ☐ Pictures: What additional information is added here?
- ☐ Margin Information: What vocabulary is important to understand this text?

Reading for a Purpose

1. Why does the Time Traveler think his time machine has failed?
2. How does the Time Traveler know time is speeding by when he pulls the lever a second time?
3. Why does the window grow dark, then brighten, then darken again?
4. What does the Time Traveler think about time travel?
5. What are the consequences of time travel into the future?

Unit 9 113

Before we began reading "The Time Machine," we answered two Big Idea questions. Take a minute to look over your answers. Now that we have read the passage thoroughly and even practiced looking at time through the Time Traveler's eyes, have your original ideas changed? Have you learned anything that supports or challenges your ideas? Do you feel differently about time?

Discuss the questions and answers with the class. Time travel is one topic that stirs up controversy among the scientists who think about it. In the last unit, we read about some controversial and unorthodox medical treatments involving maggots and leeches. Can you think of other areas of scientific research that have stirred up controversy? (Possible topics: cloning, defense/weapons development, biological warfare) Encourage a wide variety of student responses.

Grammar

Objective

- Demonstrate an understanding of inflectional endings by using words with different endings in sentences.

Inflectional Endings

Prepare index cards.

Write the words from the word bank on index cards. Then have the class form two teams. Divide the word cards between teams. Direct students to page 162 in their Student Books.

- Have teams work together to fill in the blanks in the paragraph.
- Ask the teams to decide whether they have the word that goes in the first blank. If they do, they must read the word and tell the meaning of the inflectional ending.
- Players earn two points for their team by reading the correct word and properly identifying the meaning of the inflectional ending.

Lesson 10 | Grammar

Inflectional Endings

Choose the best word for each blank from the word bank. Write the word in the blank. Some words fit in more than one blank, but each word fits **best** into only one of the blanks.

Tom's car smokes as he steps away. It was a short ride. He gazes at the landscape. He knows he is not in his town, but where is he? The people seem odd. They are alone, but talking to someone. Who?

Two boys are flying on disks. Other people are walking. He gets close to one woman and sees a small blue device on her right ear. He chases her. She shows him the thing on her ear. Inside the blue thing, he hears a sound. A man is speaking. Who is it? Is he little? Is the man stuck in the device? What is going on with the new town's people? Are some smaller than a pin?

Tom looks at the crowd. They look like him, but they do not act like him.

Tom is wishing to go back to his simple life in 1952.

Word Bank

town's	gazes	knows	chases	shows
Tom's	flying	smokes	disks	
speaking	wishing	walking	looks	

162 Unit 9

Reading

Objective

- Review the elements of a narrative: setting, characters, plot, and resolution.

Review Story Elements

Direct students to the Story Elements Diagram on page 163 in their Student Books. Review the story elements to set up the Story Path game.

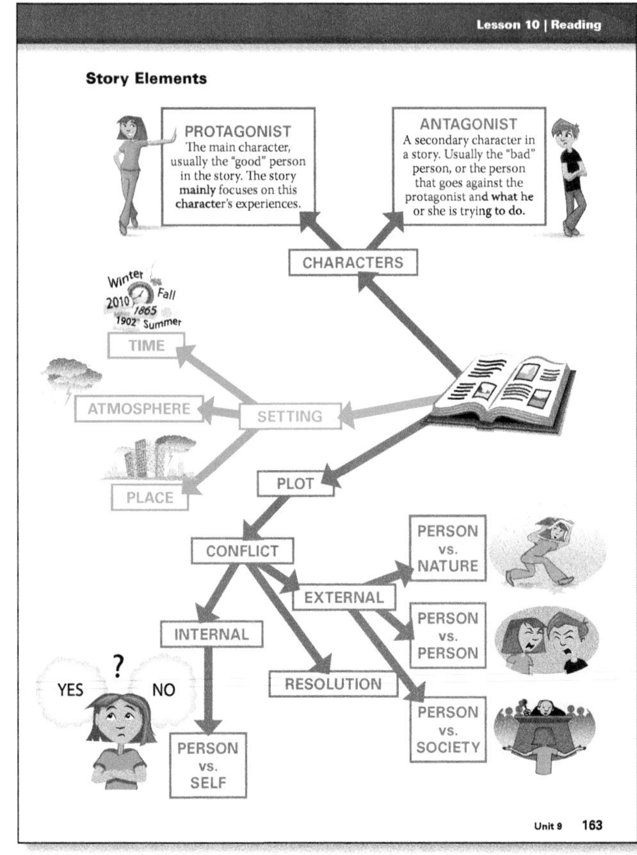

Vocabulary

Objectives

- Use key vocabulary from Units 1–9 to tell a story.
- Demonstrate an understanding of narrative structure through cooperative storytelling.

Game—Story Path

Markers for game board

Prepare vocabulary index cards.

Use index cards to make a set of vocabulary cards for each group, or have students do so.

Unit 1: connect, vision, sonar, colony, danger, interfere, ignorance, negligence

Unit 2: desert, emerge, pulley, port, precise, create, fragile, display

Unit 3: constellation, pattern, ancient, poet, devoted, mortal, expert, brilliant

Unit 4: recipe, steady, simple, plantation, social, demand, combine, express

Unit 5: spoil, destroy, substance, pollution, modern, device, variety, support

Unit 6: version, specific, appropriate, regulate, interest, permit, coarse, exclude

Unit 7: element, pause, contain, surface, migrate, guideline, coordinate, basic

Unit 8: digest, infection, multiply, creature, victim, scalp, eliminate, horror

Unit 9: intrigue, philosopher, attempt, relate, consequence, slight, moment, vanish

In the last nine units, we have learned 72 vocabulary words. We will play a game with many of these words. You may want to take some time and look at the vocabulary lists for all nine units to refresh your memory. We will use our vocabulary words along with what we know about story elements to tell a story.

Direct students to pages 164 and 165 in their Student Books. Story Path is a collaborative narrative creation game. It requires advanced knowledge of the words and how they can be used in sentences.

How to Play

- Up to six students can play.
- Students divide a deck of word cards between them, so all cards are distributed.
- An object is placed on the board to show which prompt they are on.
- Using the prompt at each space on the board, students take turns creating a part of the story using one of the words in their hand. Story parts should be one to three sentences.
- Students place their card down once they have given a story part.
- Each consecutive student builds on the narrative using the next prompt. At certain points, a student may choose between optional paths.
- The goal of the game is to complete the narrative as a group.
- If a student gets stuck or misuses a word, the student to that player's left exchanges a card with him or her. Other students can assist openly in the creation process, as well.

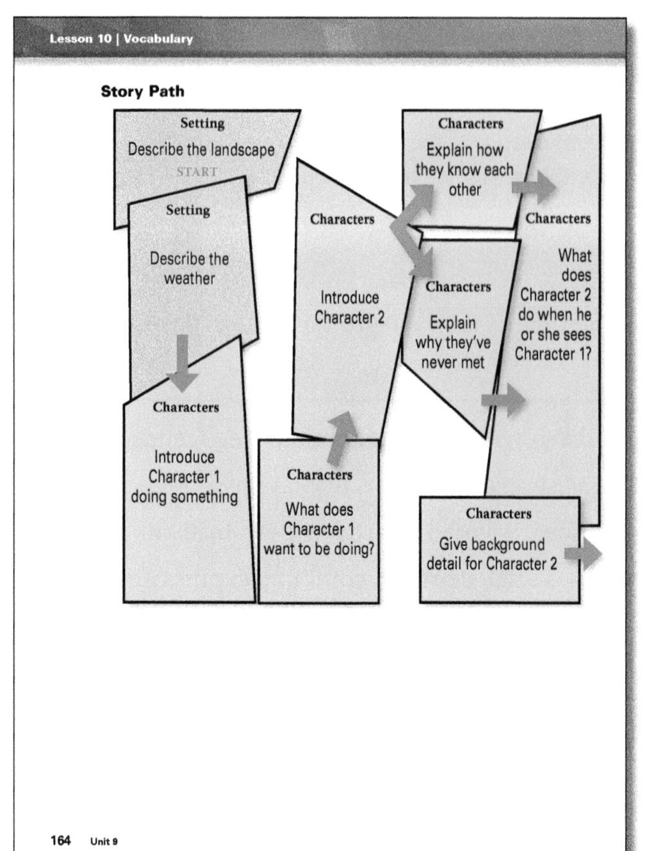
Lesson 10 | Vocabulary
Story Path
Setting
Describe the landscape
START
Setting
Describe the weather
Characters
Introduce Character 1 doing something
Characters
Introduce Character 2
Characters
What does Character 1 want to be doing?
Characters
Explain how they know each other
Characters
Explain why they've never met
Characters
What does Character 2 do when he or she sees Character 1?
Characters
Give background detail for Character 2
164 Unit 9

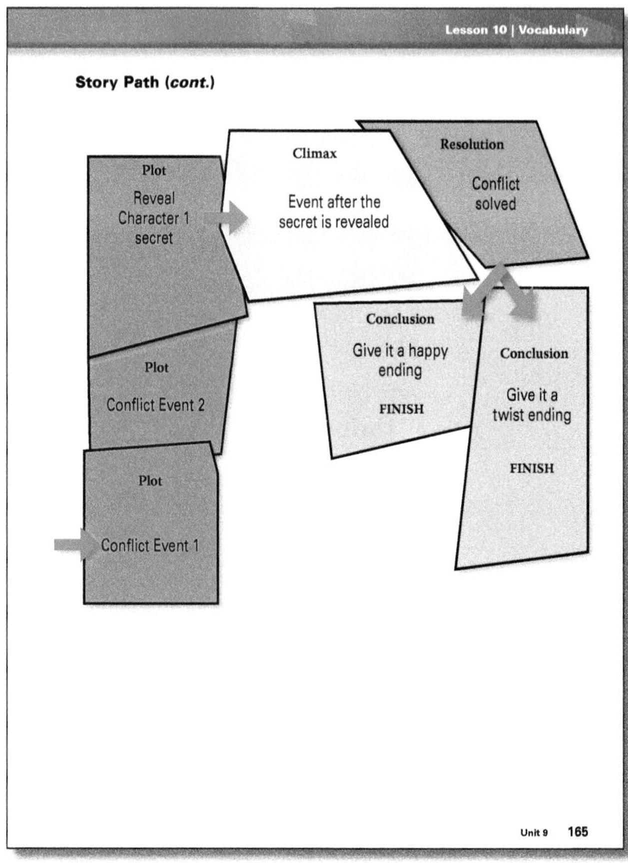
Lesson 10 | Vocabulary
Story Path (cont.)
Plot
Reveal Character 1 secret
Climax
Event after the secret is revealed
Resolution
Conflict solved
Plot
Conflict Event 2
Plot
Conflict Event 1
Conclusion
Give it a happy ending
FINISH
Conclusion
Give it a twist ending
FINISH
Unit 9 165

Reading

Objectives for Content Mastery

- Demonstrate an understanding of how to use strategic thinking skills to interpret text.
- Demonstrate an understanding of story elements in a narrative.

Responding to Prompts: *assess, determine, cite evidence*

Follow the procedure outlined below for each of the Reading Content Mastery questions and prompts.

Content Mastery Procedure

- Teacher reminds students to follow along with their pencils and listen.
- Teacher reads the question.
- Teacher reads each answer choice.
- Students choose the correct answer.
- Teacher repeats the question as students check their answers.

Have students turn to page 166 in their Student Books.

Let's look at the example first. Read the example aloud to students.

Listen: Assess how efficient electric cars are. To answer this prompt, I need to ______.

A find out, verify, and decide on information about electric cars

B support my answer by paraphrasing information or using a direct quote about electric cars

C decide on the value or significance of the efficiency of electric cars

D tell the differences between electric cars and gas-powered cars

Fill in the bubble for the correct response. Which bubble did you fill in? You should have filled in C, the bubble for "decide on the value or significance of the efficiency of electric cars." That is how you would respond to a question that asks you to *assess* something.

Follow along as I read aloud the questions and prompts. Fill in the bubble for your answer choice.

Lesson 10 | Reading Content Mastery

Responding to Prompts

Listen to the sentences and possible answers. Fill in the bubble for your answer choice.

Example: Assess how efficient electric cars are.
To answer this prompt, I need to ____.
- Ⓐ find out, verify, and decide on information about electric cars
- Ⓑ support my answer by paraphrasing information or using a direct quote about electric cars
- Ⓒ decide on the value or significance of the efficiency of electric cars
- Ⓓ tell the differences between electric cars and gas-powered cars

1. Determine if time travel is possible.
To answer this prompt, I need to ____.
   - Ⓐ verify if time travel is possible
   - Ⓑ support my answer by paraphrasing information or using a direct quote about time travel
   - Ⓒ decide on the value of time travel
   - Ⓓ State the differences between time travel and traveling by plane

2. Cite evidence that electric cars are practical.
To answer this prompt, I need to ____.
   - Ⓐ find out more about electric cars
   - Ⓑ support my answer by paraphrasing or using a direct quote about the practicality of electric cars
   - Ⓒ decide on the value or significance of electric cars
   - Ⓓ make a judgment about electric cars based on text clues and background knowledge

3. Assess the value of electric cars in reducing air pollution.
To answer this prompt, I need to ____.
   - Ⓐ use a direct quote to support my answer about how electric cars reduce air pollution
   - Ⓑ make a judgment about whether electric cars reduce air pollution
   - Ⓒ verify that electric cars reduce air pollution
   - Ⓓ state the differences between the air pollution caused by electric cars and by gas-powered cars

4. Determine why all new cars aren't electric.
To answer this prompt, I need to ____.
   - Ⓐ state the similarities between new cars and old cars
   - Ⓑ support my answer by using a direct quote about why all cars aren't electric
   - Ⓒ decide on the value or significance of why all new cars aren't electric
   - Ⓓ verify and decide why all cars aren't electric

166 Unit 9

Use the following recommendations to reinforce or reteach according to student performance.

If...	Then...
Students miss 1 question	Review the question in a small group or individual setting, offering answer explanations.
Students miss 2 or more questions	Reteach the elements taught in Lessons 3 and 4 in a small group or individual setting. Unmarked copies of the student page can be reprinted from the Teacher Resources online.

Story Elements

Have students turn to page 167 in their Student Books.

Let's look at the example first. Read the example aloud to students.

Listen: What part of a story does this phrase describe: the time and place of a story. Fill in the bubble for your answer.

A setting

B characters

C problem

D climax

Which bubble did you fill in? You should have filled in A, the bubble for "setting." The time and place of a story is called the *setting*.

Follow along as I read aloud the definitions and possible answers. Fill in the bubble for your answer choice.

Lesson 10 | Reading Content Mastery

Story Elements

Listen to the questions and possible answers. Fill in the bubble for your answer choice.

Example: What part of a story does this phrase describe?
the time and place of a story
- A setting
- B characters
- C problem
- D climax

1. What part of a story does this phrase describe?
   the people, animals, or things that interact in a story
   - A resolution
   - B problem
   - C climax
   - D characters

2. What part of a story does this phrase describe?
   the event that sets other events in motion
   - A conclusion
   - B climax
   - C resolution
   - D problem

3. What part of a story does this phrase describe?
   the turning point
   - A resolution
   - B climax
   - C conclusion
   - D setting

4. What part of a story does this phrase describe?
   the solution to the problem
   - A resolution
   - B conclusion
   - C setting
   - D characters

5. What part of a story does this phrase describe?
   clues that another story, or *sequel*, is coming
   - A characters
   - B setting
   - C conclusion
   - D problem

Unit 9 167

Use the following recommendations to reinforce or reteach according to student performance.

If...	Then...
Students miss 2 questions	Review the questions in a small group or individual setting, offering answer explanations.
Students miss 3 or more questions	Reteach the elements taught in Lesson 2 in a small group or individual setting. Unmarked copies of the student page can be reprinted from the Teacher Resources online.

Vocabulary

Objective for Content Mastery

- Identify metaphors and similes in sentences.

Metaphors and Similes

Follow the procedure outlined below for the Vocabulary Content Mastery questions and prompts.

Content Mastery Procedure

- Teacher reminds students to follow along with their pencils and listen.
- Teacher reads the question.
- Teacher reads each answer choice.
- Students choose the correct answer.
- Teacher repeats the question as students check their answers.

Have students turn to page 168 in their Student Books.

Let's look at the example first. Read the example aloud to students.

Listen: Which of these sentences contains a metaphor?

A Her teeth are like pearls.

B Her teeth are pearls.

C Her teeth are pearly.

D Her teeth are as white as pearls.

Which bubble did you fill in? You should have filled in the bubble for B. Remember, a metaphor compares two things that are unrelated by saying that one *is* or *was* something else. Similes, however, use the words *like* or *as* to compare two unlike things.

Follow along as I read aloud each sentence that could be a metaphor or a simile. Fill in the bubble for your answer choice.

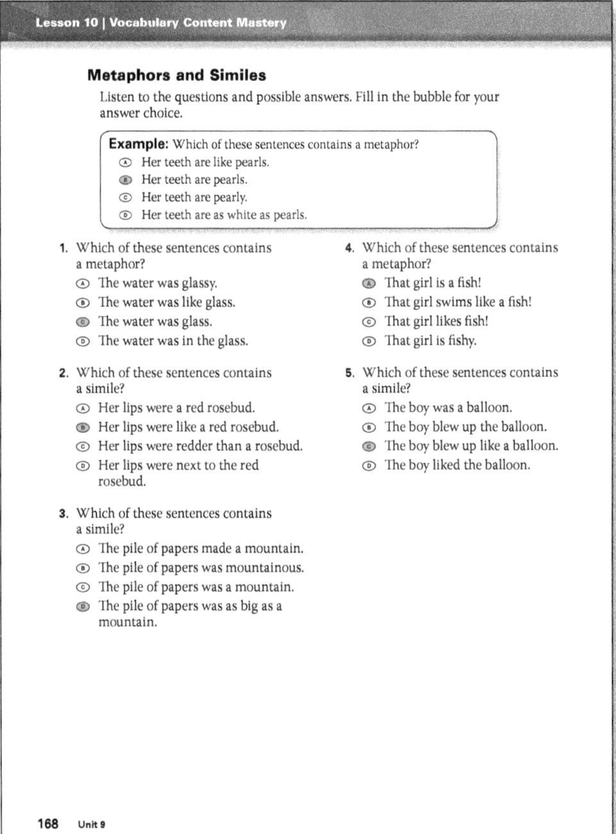

Lesson 10 | Vocabulary Content Mastery

Metaphors and Similes

Listen to the questions and possible answers. Fill in the bubble for your answer choice.

Example: Which of these sentences contains a metaphor?
- A Her teeth are like pearls.
- B Her teeth are pearls.
- C Her teeth are pearly.
- D Her teeth are as white as pearls.

1. Which of these sentences contains a metaphor?
   - A The water was glassy.
   - B The water was like glass.
   - C The water was glass.
   - D The water was in the glass.
2. Which of these sentences contains a simile?
   - A Her lips were a red rosebud.
   - B Her lips were like a red rosebud.
   - C Her lips were redder than a rosebud.
   - D Her lips were next to the red rosebud.
3. Which of these sentences contains a simile?
   - A The pile of papers made a mountain.
   - B The pile of papers was mountainous.
   - C The pile of papers was a mountain.
   - D The pile of papers was as big as a mountain.
4. Which of these sentences contains a metaphor?
   - A That girl is a fish!
   - B That girl swims like a fish!
   - C That girl likes fish!
   - D That girl is fishy.
5. Which of these sentences contains a simile?
   - A The boy was a balloon.
   - B The boy blew up the balloon.
   - C The boy blew up like a balloon.
   - D The boy liked the balloon.

168 Unit 9

Use the following recommendations to reinforce or reteach according to student performance.

If...	Then...
Students miss 2 questions	Review the questions in a small group or individual setting, offering answer explanations.
Students miss 3 or more questions	Reteach the elements taught in Lesson 3 in a small group or individual setting. Unmarked copies of the student page can be reprinted from the Teacher Resources online.

Grammar

Objectives for Content Mastery

- Demonstrate an understanding of future tense verb phrases.
- Demonstrate an understanding of inflectional endings.

Future Tense

Follow the procedure outlined below for each of the Grammar Content Mastery questions and prompts.

Content Mastery Procedure

- Teacher reminds students to follow along with their pencils and listen.
- Teacher reads the question.
- Teacher reads each answer choice.
- Students choose the correct answer.
- Teacher repeats the question as students check their answers.

Have students turn to page 169 in their Student Books.

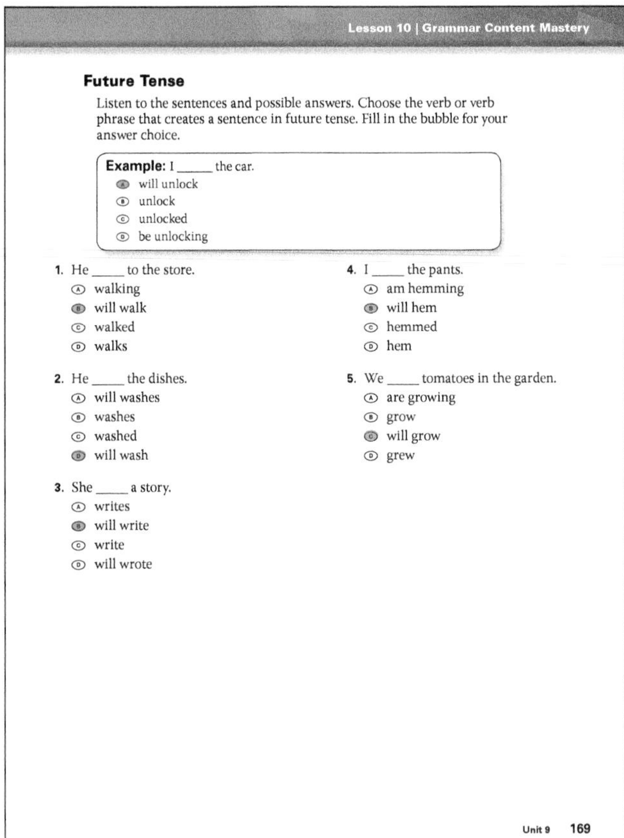
Lesson 10 | Grammar Content Mastery

Future Tense

Listen to the sentences and possible answers. Choose the verb or verb phrase that creates a sentence in future tense. Fill in the bubble for your answer choice.

Example: I _____ the car.
- Ⓐ will unlock
- Ⓑ unlock
- Ⓒ unlocked
- Ⓓ be unlocking

1. He _____ to the store.
   - Ⓐ walking
   - Ⓑ will walk
   - Ⓒ walked
   - Ⓓ walks
2. He _____ the dishes.
   - Ⓐ will washes
   - Ⓑ washes
   - Ⓒ washed
   - Ⓓ will wash
3. She _____ a story.
   - Ⓐ writes
   - Ⓑ will write
   - Ⓒ write
   - Ⓓ will wrote
4. I _____ the pants.
   - Ⓐ am hemming
   - Ⓑ will hem
   - Ⓒ hemmed
   - Ⓓ hem
5. We _____ tomatoes in the garden.
   - Ⓐ are growing
   - Ⓑ grow
   - Ⓒ will grow
   - Ⓓ grew

Unit 9 169

Let's look at the example first. Read the example aloud to students.

Listen: I ______ the car.

Choose the verb or verb phrase that creates a sentence in future tense.

A will unlock

B unlock

C unlocked

D be unlocking

Which bubble did you fill in? You should have filled in the bubble for A, "will unlock." The verb phrase *will unlock* forms the future tense of *unlock*: *I will unlock the car.*

Follow along as I read aloud the sentences and possible answers. Choose the verb or verb phrase that creates a sentence in future tense. Fill in the bubble for your answer choice.

Use the following recommendations to reinforce or reteach according to student performance.

If...	Then...
Students miss 2 questions	Review the questions in a small group or individual setting, offering answer explanations.
Students miss 3 or more questions	Reteach the elements taught in Lessons 3 and 4 in a small group or individual setting. Unmarked copies of the student page can be reprinted from the Teacher Resources online.

Inflectional Endings

Have students turn to page 170 in their Student Books.

Let's look at the example first. Read the example aloud to students.

Listen: Tom is ______ far into the past.

Choose the word with the correct ending to fill the blank. Fill in the bubble for your answer.

A travel

B travels

C traveled

D traveling

Which bubble did you fill in? You should have filled in the bubble for D, "traveling." The word *traveling* correctly completes the sentence.

Follow along as I read aloud the sentences and possible answers. Choose the word with the correct ending to fill the blank. Fill in the bubble for your answer choice.

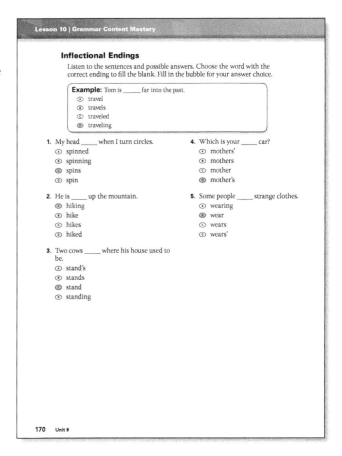

Lesson 10 | Grammar Content Mastery

Inflectional Endings

Listen to the sentences and possible answers. Choose the word with the correct ending to fill the blank. Fill in the bubble for your answer choice.

Example: Tom is _____ far into the past.
- Ⓐ travel
- Ⓑ travels
- Ⓒ traveled
- Ⓓ traveling

1. My head _____ when I turn circles.
   - Ⓐ spinned
   - Ⓑ spinning
   - Ⓒ spins
   - Ⓓ spin
2. He is _____ up the mountain.
   - Ⓐ hiking
   - Ⓑ hike
   - Ⓒ hikes
   - Ⓓ hiked
3. Two cows _____ where his house used to be.
   - Ⓐ stand's
   - Ⓑ stands
   - Ⓒ stand
   - Ⓓ standing
4. Which is your _____ car?
   - Ⓐ mothers'
   - Ⓑ mothers
   - Ⓒ mother
   - Ⓓ mother's
5. Some people _____ strange clothes.
   - Ⓐ wearing
   - Ⓑ wear
   - Ⓒ wears
   - Ⓓ wears'

170 Unit 9

Use the following recommendations to reinforce or reteach according to student performance.

If...	Then...
Students miss 2 questions	Review the questions in a small group or individual setting, offering answer explanations.
Students miss 3 or more questions	Reteach the elements taught in Lesson 3 in a small group or individual setting. Unmarked copies of the student page can be reprinted from the Teacher Resources online.

Unit 10

Unit Plan

Primary Text:
"Hurricane!"

Text type: informational

Lesson 1	Lesson 2
Reading • Determine the topic of the text. • Determine the author's purpose. • Discuss the topic of the text. • Preview the text. Vocabulary • Determine the meaning of key passage vocabulary. Reading • Review text features. • Read an informational text. • Demonstrate an understanding of the text by asking and answering questions and referring to key details in the text.	Vocabulary • Use discussion and context to determine the meanings of the multiple-meaning words *season* and *band*. • Demonstrate an understanding of words by using them in written sentences. Grammar • Demonstrate an understanding of forming and using possessive and plural possessive words. • Identify singular, plural, and possessive nouns. • Demonstrate an understanding of the function of compound sentences and conjunctions by using them in sentences. Writing • Demonstrate command of the conventions of standard English capitalization and punctuation (comma).

Lesson 6	Lesson 7
Writing • Know spelling-sound correspondences for words with digraph *wh*. • Know spelling-sound correspondences for words ending in *-es*. • Know spelling-sound correspondences for words with /ng/ spelled *-n*. • Know spelling-sound correspondences for words with nasal blends. Vocabulary • Use context to determine the meaning of words in text. • Consult reference materials to clarify the precise meaning of words. • Demonstrate an understanding of synonym word analogies. • Write synonym word analogies. Writing • Write sentences using concrete words and phrases and sensory details to convey information precisely. Reading • Review text features in a text. • Draw evidence from a graph and a chart to answer questions.	Reading • Read with purpose and understanding. • Identify and explain explicit details from text. • Take notes on a text. • Identify idioms in text.

Lesson 3	Lesson 4	Lesson 5
Reading • Read to develop fluency. **Vocabulary** • Review key passage vocabulary. • Demonstrate an understanding of metaphors and similes and the meanings of specific metaphors and similes. • Write simple metaphors and similes. **Grammar** • Form and use the past, present, and future tenses of the verb *be* with various pronouns. • Understand the difference between action verbs, linking verbs, and helping verbs. **Reading** • Use critical thinking skills to analyze a text. • Ask and answer questions and prompts using extended thinking skills to demonstrate an understanding of a text.	**Reading** • Read sentences to develop fluency. **Grammar** • Listen to oral sentences and write them accurately. • Demonstrate an understanding of how to write future tense verbs in sentences. • Understand the function of action verbs and linking verbs in sentences. **Reading** • Read sentence phrases with fluency to support comprehension. • Read an informational text. • Use critical thinking skills to respond to specific questions about a text.	**Vocabulary** • Review key passage vocabulary. **Reading** • Write questions or prompts about text to deepen comprehension. • Use critical thinking skills to respond orally to specific questions about a text. **Writing** • Use critical and extended thinking skills to write responses to prompts about a text. • Support written answers with evidence from text.

Lesson 8	Lesson 9	Lesson 10
Writing • Gather relevant information from notes about a text. • Organize information from a text into notes. • Write clear introductory topic and concluding sentences. • Write a constructed response to a prompt. • Develop the written response with concrete facts and details and inferential thinking. • Edit text for basic conventions. • Strengthen writing by editing for voice.	**Reading** • Read words to develop fluency. **Vocabulary** • Demonstrate an understanding of words by relating them to their synonyms, antonyms, and related words. • Demonstrate an understanding of figurative language by generating examples of similes and metaphors. • Identify and define an idiom related to the word *powerful*. **Grammar** • Demonstrate an understanding of direct objects and predicate modifiers as they relate to action verbs and linking verbs. • Demonstrate an understanding of how past, present, and future tense verbs are used in sentences. • Demonstrate an understanding of how subject and object pronouns and possessive nouns are used in text. **Reading** • Read a text to develop fluency. • Demonstrate comprehension by answering specific questions about a text.	**Vocabulary** • Clarify the meaning of key passage vocabulary. • Demonstrate an understanding of passage vocabulary by using words in sentences. **Reading** • Discuss and answer questions to demonstrate an understanding of an author's or narrator's point of view in a text. • Discuss and answer questions to demonstrate an understanding of the passages' main idea and key details. **Writing** • Discuss the value of specific details in creating imagery. • Discuss the value of using strong verbs in writing.

Unit 10 Lesson 1

Lesson Opener

Before the lesson, choose one of the following activities to write on the board or post on the *LANGUAGE! Live* Class Wall online.

- *Write three sentences: one with a compound subject, one with a compound predicate, and one compound sentence.*
- *Describe a character in your favorite movie. Describe his or her physical traits as well as his or her personality traits.*
- *Describe the setting in your bedroom. Use descriptive language.*

Reading

Objectives

- Determine the topic of the text.
- Determine the author's purpose.
- Discuss the topic of the text.
- Preview the text.

Unit Introduction

Direct students to page 171 in their Student Books.

Discuss the content focus for the unit.

Content Focus

hurricanes

What do you think you will learn in this passage? (Answers will vary based on prior knowledge of hurricanes.)

Type of Text

informational

Informational text is also called nonfiction. *Non-* is a prefix, or word part, that means "not." Therefore, *nonfiction* means "not fiction." Remember, fiction is imaginative writing with made-up details. Does nonfiction contain made-up details? (no) So, do you think this passage will contain facts or imagined details? (facts) This passage will give us information, or facts. What will the information be about? (hurricanes)

Unit 10

Lesson 1 | Reading

Let's Focus: "Hurricane!"

Content Focus
hurricanes

Type of Text
informational

Author's Purpose: to inform

Big Ideas
Consider the following Big Idea questions. Write your answer for each question.

How are hurricanes formed?

How are hurricanes different from other storms?

Informational Preview Checklist: "Hurricane!"

- ☐ Title: What clue does it provide about the passage?
- ☐ Pictures and Captions: What additional information is added here?
- ☐ Headings: What topics will this text include?
- ☐ Margin Information: What vocabulary is important to understand this text?
- ☐ Maps, Charts, Graphs: Are additional visuals present that will help me understand?

Reading for a Purpose

1. Is the name given to the violent storms a valid name?
2. Why are hurricanes absent in the Arctic Ocean?
3. How are hurricanes related to the seasons of the year?
4. How does the wall of a hurricane relate to property damage?
5. How does a tropical depression turn into a hurricane?
6. Why was hurricane naming changed recently and was it a good change?

Unit 10 171

Author's Purpose

The author's purpose is the reason that he or she wrote the text. Authors write for different purposes. Why do authors write texts? (to entertain, to persuade, and to inform or teach) Knowing an author's purpose can help a reader understand a text better. This text was written to inform others about how hurricanes form and why they are dangerous. Was "Hurricane!" written to inform or entertain? (inform) Is the author going to teach you something or entertain you? (teach) Have students write the answer on the page in their Student Books.

Background Information

Hurricanes. What do you know about hurricanes? Have students share knowledge. Do you know another word that means the same as *hurricane*? (cyclone) Hurricanes, also called cyclones, are a type of natural disaster. A hurricane is a weather-related natural disaster. Natural disasters cause fascination as well as fear in most people. Why do you think we are fascinated by something that we fear? (Answers will vary.)

Hurricanes start out as ordinary storms and then build enough strength to cause a disaster. Many people remember Hurricane Katrina for its 175-mile-per-hour winds and the disastrous loss of life and property it caused in 2005. People from New Orleans were forced to evacuate, and some never returned. More than 1,800 people died in that natural disaster. It was the costliest natural disaster and one of the five deadliest hurricanes in the United States. More recently, Hurricane Sandy demolished portions of the northeastern United States, especially in New Jersey and New York. Its effects will be felt for a long time—just like those of Hurricane Katrina.

Play the Unit 10 Text Training video found in the Teacher Resources online.

Before we read the passage about hurricanes, we will watch a short video to help build background knowledge. I want you to combine what you just heard with what you are about to watch on this video. Listen for two things you did not know about. You will share this new information with a partner after the video. Play the Unit 10 Text Training video. Have partners discuss what they learned from the video.

Direct students to page 171 in their Student Books. Read the following Big Idea questions aloud:

Big Ideas

How are hurricanes formed?

How are hurricanes different from other storms?

As a class, consider the two Big Idea questions. After discussing each question, have students write an answer. We'll come back to these questions after we finish learning about hurricanes. You will have much more to add to your answers. You can edit your answers as you gain information.

Preview

Good readers preview text features automatically, every time they begin to read. To develop this reading habit, you will preview today's text on your own, and then discuss what you noticed with a partner.

Direct students to page 173 in their Student Books to preview the text. Remind them of the Informational Preview Checklist on page 171. Give them permission to refer to the checklist during the preview if they need a reminder of text features.

Lesson 1 | Reading

HURRICANE!

It's summer, and hurricane season is here! Hurricanes, otherwise known as tropical cyclones, are powerful storms that twist and spin. They can become very large, some covering an area hundreds of miles wide. These storms are feared because their strong winds, high tides, and heavy rains **threaten** life and **property**.

Hurricane season begins on June 1st and runs through November 30th. Warm, tropical water is necessary for hurricane development. The surface temperature of an ocean must be at least 80 degrees Fahrenheit, or 26 degrees Centigrade. However, hurricanes need more than warm water to develop. Low air pressure, moist ocean air, tropical winds, and warm air temperatures must come together to set the stage for hurricane development.

threaten
to be a possible source of danger or discomfort

property
land or objects owned by someone

Number of Tropical Cyclones per 100 Years

The official hurricane season for the Atlantic Basin (the Atlantic Ocean, the Caribbean Sea, and the Gulf of Mexico) is from June 1st to November 30th.

Unit 10 173

Note: Create a small teacher-led group for students who displayed dependence or confusion with the previewing process in the preceding unit. New students and truant students should also join this group until they reach independence.

Have individuals preview the text. After sufficient time, have partners use the checklist to evaluate each other's previewing skills. Gauge individual success as you circulate around the room. Determine which students need extra practice with the skills, and provide them with alternative practice sources.

Vocabulary

Objective

- Determine the meaning of key passage vocabulary.

Vocabulary Rating Scale poster

Rate Your Knowledge

Direct students to page 172 in their Student Books.

You will rate your word knowledge. The purpose of this activity is to recognize how familiar you are with this unit's Key Passage Vocabulary.

Review the Vocabulary Rating Scale with students.

Vocabulary Rating Scale

0—I have never heard the word before.

1—I have heard the word, but I'm not sure how to use it.

2—I am familiar with the word, but I'm not sure if I know the correct meaning.

3—I know the meaning of the word and can use it correctly in a sentence.

Lesson 1 | Vocabulary

Key Passage Vocabulary: "Hurricane!"

Rate your knowledge of the words. Define the words. Draw a picture to help you remember the definition.

Vocabulary	Knowledge Rating	Definition	Picture
threaten	0 1 2 3	to be a possible source of danger or discomfort	
property	0 1 2 3	land or objects owned by someone	
definite	0 1 2 3	firm and clear; exact	
sustained	0 1 2 3	kept going for a period of time	
ordinary	0 1 2 3	not special or different in any way	
intense	0 1 2 3	very great or strong	
surroundings	0 1 2 3	the things or conditions around a person or place	
scale	0 1 2 3	a numbered system or device used to measure something	

172 Unit 10

Read the list of words. Have students repeat each word. Provide time for students to rate their knowledge of each word.

Have partners discuss the words they rated as 3s and tell each other the meanings.

Preteach Vocabulary

You've rated your knowledge and talked about what you think the words mean. Now, let's discuss the words.

Preteach Procedure

This activity is intended to take only a short amount of time, so make it an oral exercise if your students aren't capable of writing quickly.

- Introduce each word as indicated on the word card.
- Read the definition and example sentences.
- Ask questions to clarify and deepen understanding.
- If time permits, allow students to share.

* Do not provide instruction time to write definitions or draw pictures, but explain that students should complete both as time permits during the unit.

Note: Research has proven that vocabulary is best learned when students represent their knowledge of words in linguistic and/or nonlinguistic ways. Thus, drawing a picture will help students remember the words. This strategy is especially effective for English language learners.

threaten

Let's read the first word together. *Threaten.*

Definition: *Threaten* means "to be a possible source of danger or discomfort." To be a possible source of danger or discomfort means to what? (threaten)

Example 1: If a thunderstorm with lightning *threatens*, it is wise to go indoors.

Example 2: Wildfires can *threaten* homes, people, and animals.

Example 3: The swine flu epidemic *threatened* students and teachers, so the school closed for a few days.

Question 1: Can an outbreak of a disease *threaten* people? Yes or no? (yes)

Question 2: Are humans typically *threatened* by butterflies? Yes or no? (no)

Pair Share: Tell your partner a story in which someone is *threatened* by impending danger.

property

Let's read the next word together. *Property.*

Definition: *Property* means "land or objects owned by someone." Objects or land owned by someone are what? (property)

Example 1: I own a car. It is my *property.*

Example 2: The clothes and shoes in your locker are your *property*, but the books you keep there belong to the school.

Example 3: Parks are not owned by an individual, so you can walk on the grass. But you are not permitted to walk in someone's yard because it is his or her private *property.*

Question 1: Is *property* something people own? Yes or no? (yes)

Question 2: If you rent an apartment or house, is it your *property*? Yes or no? (no)

Pair Share: Turn to your partner and determine whether you have similar *property* in your lockers.

definite

Let's read the next word together. *Definite.*

Definition: *Definite* means "firm and clear, or exact." Something firm and clear, or exact, is what? (definite)

Example 1: There is a set pattern to haiku poetry. The first and last lines always have five syllables, and the second line always has seven syllables. It never changes. The pattern is *definite.*

Example 2: My friends and I chose a *definite* time and place to meet before the game.

Example 3: The teacher gave *definite* step-by-step instructions for completing the science experiment.

Question 1: Is the future *definite*? Yes or no? (no)

Question 2: Is there a *definite* answer to the math problem 2 + 2? (yes)

Pair Share: Tell your partner a *definite* part of your morning routine that never changes.

sustained

Let's read the next word together. *Sustained.*

Definition: *Sustained* "means kept going for a period of time." Something that kept going for a period of time is what? (sustained)

Example 1: *Sustained* oxygen is needed for life on our planet. If the flow of oxygen is disrupted, we will die.

Example 2: *Sustained* conversation is difficult when only one person is talking.

Example 3: To *sustain* high grades you must turn in all homework and study for all tests.

Question 1: Does a baby learning to walk need *sustained* balance? Yes or no? (yes)

Question 2: Does an airplane need *sustained* speed to stay in the air? Yes or no? (yes)

Pair Share: Turn to your partner and discuss the effects of *sustained* rain.

ordinary

Let's read the next word together. *Ordinary.*

Definition: *Ordinary* means "not special or different in any way." Something that is not special or different in any way is what? (ordinary)

Example 1: On an *ordinary* school day, I get ready, drive to school, teach my classes, drive home, and then make dinner.

Example 2: Do you prefer an *ordinary* hamburger or one with extras, like cheese, mushrooms, and bacon?

Example 3: What is *ordinary* clothing to us might not be *ordinary* in a small village in Africa. Our clothing might stand out.

Question 1: Do you prefer *ordinary* vanilla or a fancy flavor of ice cream? (Answers will vary.)

Question 2: Is purple hair *ordinary*? (no) Are brown eyes *ordinary*? (yes)

Pair Share: Tell your partner one thing about yourself that is *ordinary* and one thing that is extraordinary, or special.

intense

Let's read the next word together. *Intense.*

Definition: *Intense* means "very great or strong." Something that is very great or strong is what? (intense)

Example 1: The most *intense* wind gust ever recorded was on Mt. Washington, New Hampshire, at 231 mph.

Example 2: The heat from the fire was so *intense* that all the firefighters could do was watch the building burn.

Example 3: The athletes' training schedules became more *intense* as the Olympic games approached.

Question 1: Can hot sauce be *intense*? (yes)

Question 2: Is strolling in the park *intense*? Yes or no? (no)

Pair Share: Turn to your partner and describe an *intense* moment you recently saw on TV.

surroundings

Let's read the next word together. *Surroundings.*

Definition: *Surroundings* means "the things or conditions around a person or place." The things or conditions around a person or place are what? (surroundings)

Example 1: When I look at my *surroundings*, I see desks and students.

Example 2: When I walked into the haunted house, my *surroundings* terrified me.

Example 3: The pond's *surroundings* include pine trees and cottonwood trees.

Question 1: If you are in the cafeteria, what do you see in your *surroundings*? (tables, food, students)

Question 2: Do whales and dolphins have water in their *surroundings*? Yes or no? (yes)

Pair Share: Tell your partner your perfect vacation *surroundings*.

scale

Let's read the last word together. *Scale.*

Definition: A *scale* means "a numbered system or device used to measure something." A numbered system or device used to measure something is a what? (scale)

Example 1: The *scale* that measures the intensity of tornadoes is called the Fujita scale and is numbered from one to six.

Example 2: When I stepped on the *scale* to weigh myself, I found I had gained two pounds over the holidays.

Example 3: A ruler typically has two *scales*, one in inches and one in centimeters.

Question 1: Does a musical *scale* involve numbers? Yes or no? (no)

Question 2: Does a thermometer have a *scale*? Yes or no? (yes)

Pair Share: On a piece of scratch paper, draw a *scale* using your thumb as a unit of measurement.

Reading

Objectives

- Review text features.
- Read an informational text.
- Demonstrate an understanding of the text by asking and answering questions and referring to key details in the text.

"Hurricane!"

Direct students to page 173 in their Student Books.

HURRICANE!

Words to Know

In addition to the vocabulary words, here are some words students might have trouble with:

powerful very strong

pressure a steady force upon something

moisture tiny drops of water in the air or on a surface

organized arranged in a certain way

system a group of things or parts that work together as a whole

destruction a great amount of harm, injury, or damage

eventually after a period of time; in the end

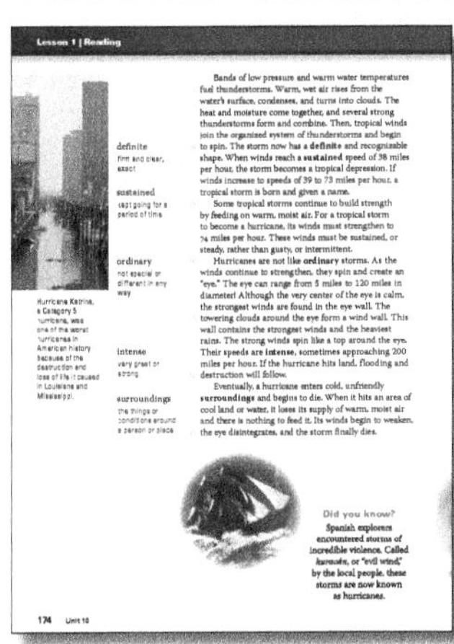

You have already previewed the text. Let's discuss some key points before we read.

- Notice the picture behind the title "Hurricane!" What do you see in the picture? I'll give you a hint: this is an aerial photograph taken from a satellite. (Answers will vary.) Guide students to notice the clouds forming above the ocean.
- What do you notice at the bottom of the page? (graph showing the number of hurricanes and tropical storms by month)
- Turn to the picture on the next page. What do you see? (a ship on the ocean) Discuss the origin of the word *hurricane* and why locals might have called hurricanes "evil winds." (Hurricanes were probably called evil winds because they caused destruction and even death.)
- Look at the photograph on page 174. What does it show? (flooding and damage from Hurricane Katrina)
- Scan for headings. How many do you see? (one) Nonfiction texts often have headings that divide the text into meaningful sections. What does the author want you to learn in this section? (how hurricanes are categorized) What are the headings of the chart? (Category, Wind Speed, and Description of Damage)

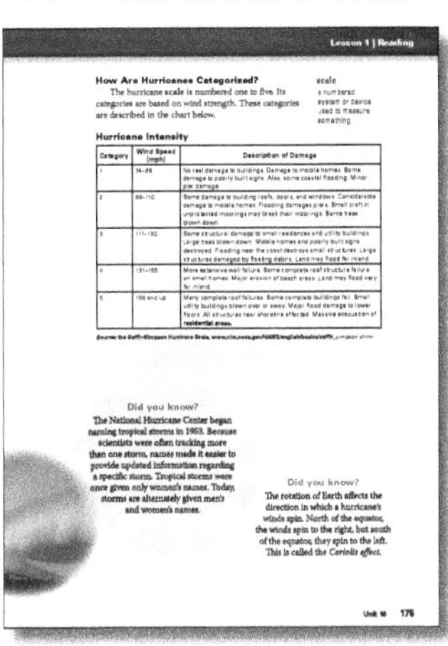

Direct students to page 171 in their Student Books. Have students look at the prompts while you read them aloud.

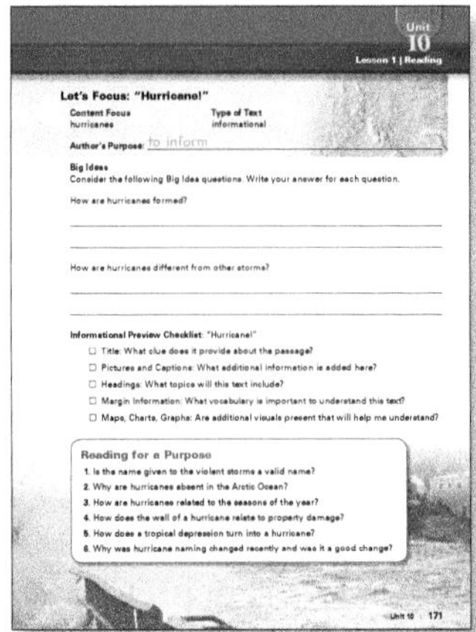

Reading for a Purpose

1. Is the name given to the violent storms a valid name?
2. Why are hurricanes absent in the Arctic Ocean?
3. How are hurricanes related to the seasons of the year?
4. How does the wall of a hurricane relate to property damage?
5. How does a tropical depression turn into a hurricane?
6. Why was hurricane naming changed recently and was it a good change?

You will become equipped to answer these questions by reading the passage. For now, let the prompts guide your reading. Be on the lookout for facts and concepts you could use to respond to the prompts. While reading, you also should think about our two Big Idea questions: How are hurricanes formed? and How are hurricanes different from other storms?

Direct students to page 173 in their Student Books. Now it's time to read. Where are your eyes while I read? (on text) Where is your pencil? (following along, word for word) Eyes on text, pencil on words.

Let's begin. Follow along with your pencil eraser as I read the text. Read the passage aloud.

Guiding Students Toward Independent Reading

While the lessons are written for a teacher read aloud, it is important that your students read as much and as often as they can. Assign readings that meet the needs of your students, based on your observations or data. This is a good opportunity to stretch students, but if they become frustrated, return to the read-aloud method.

Options for reading text:

- Teacher read aloud
- Teacher-led or student-led choral read
- Independent read of small sections with frequent comprehension checks
- Paired read or independent read

Hurricane!

It's summer, and hurricane season is here! Hurricanes, otherwise known as tropical cyclones, are powerful storms that twist and spin. They can become very large, some covering an area hundreds of miles wide. These storms are feared because their strong winds, high tides, and heavy rains threaten life and property.

Hurricane season begins on June 1st and runs through November 30th. Warm, tropical water is necessary for hurricane development. The surface temperature of an ocean must be at least 80 degrees Fahrenheit, or 26 degrees Centigrade. However, hurricanes need more than warm water to develop. Low air pressure, moist ocean air, tropical winds, and warm air temperatures must come together to set the stage for hurricane development.

Timer

For confirmation of engagement, take 30 seconds to have students share one thing they learned with their partner. If needed, provide this example for students: While reading, I was thinking that hurricane season is quite long! Your turn. Share your thoughts and one thing you learned with your partner. Try to use one of the bold vocabulary words. Partners, you should listen carefully and ask questions to check understanding.

Bands of low pressure and warm water temperatures fuel thunderstorms. Warm, wet air rises from the water's surface, condenses, and turns into clouds. The heat and moisture come together, and several strong thunderstorms form and combine. Then, tropical winds join the organized system of thunderstorms and begin to spin. The storm now has a definite and recognizable shape. When winds reach a sustained speed of 38 miles per hour, the storm becomes a tropical depression. If winds increase to speeds of 39 to 73 miles per hour, a tropical storm is born and given a name.

For confirmation of engagement, take 30 seconds to have students share one thing they learned with their partner. While reading, I noticed the phrase "a tropical storm is born." That sounds like a figure of speech to me because storms are not human and can't really be born. Your turn. Switch roles. Share your thoughts and one thing you learned with your partner. Try to use one of the bold vocabulary words. Partners, you should listen carefully and ask questions to check understanding.

Some tropical storms continue to build strength by feeding on warm, moist air. For a tropical storm to become a hurricane, its winds must strengthen to 74 miles per hour. These winds must be sustained, or steady, rather than gusty, or intermittent.

Hurricanes are not like ordinary storms. As the winds continue to strengthen, they spin and create an "eye." The eye can range from 5 miles to 120 miles in diameter! Although the very center of the eye is calm, the strongest winds are found in the eye wall. The towering clouds around the eye form a wind wall. This wall contains the strongest winds and the heaviest rains. The strong winds spin like a top around the eye. Their speeds are intense, sometimes approaching 200 miles per hour. If the hurricane hits land, flooding and destruction will follow.

For confirmation of engagement, take 30 seconds to have students share one thing they learned with their partner. Provide this example for students: While reading, I noticed that the author gives the storm human characteristics; storms cannot really feed on or eat warm, moist air. Your turn. Switch roles. Share your thoughts and one thing you learned with your partner. Try to use one of the bold vocabulary words. Partners, you should listen carefully and ask questions to check understanding.

Eventually, a hurricane enters cold, unfriendly surroundings and begins to die. When it hits an area of cool land or water, it loses its supply of warm, moist air and there is nothing to feed it. Its winds begin to weaken, the eye disintegrates, and the storm finally dies.

For confirmation of engagement, take 30 seconds to have students share one thing they learned with their partner. While reading, I noticed another human characteristic given to the storm: its dying. Your turn. Switch roles. Share your thoughts and one thing you learned with your partner. Partners, you should listen carefully and ask questions to check understanding.

How Are Hurricanes Categorized?

The hurricane scale is numbered one to five. Its categories are based on wind strength. These categories are described in the chart below.

Hurricane Intensity

Category	Wind Speed (mph)	Description of Damage
1	74–95	No real damage to buildings. Damage to mobile homes. Some damage to poorly built signs. Also, some coastal flooding. Minor pier damage.
2	96–110	Some damage to building roofs, doors, and windows. Considerable damage to mobile homes. Flooding damages piers. Small craft in unprotected moorings may break their moorings. Some trees blown down.
3	111–130	Some structural damage to small residences and utility buildings. Large trees blown down. Mobile homes and poorly built signs destroyed. Flooding near the coast destroys small structures. Large structures damaged by floating debris. Land may flood far inland.
4	131–155	More extensive wall failure. Some complete roof structure failure on small homes. Major erosion of beach areas. Land may flood very far inland.
5	156 and up	Many complete roof failures. Some complete buildings fail. Small utility buildings blown over or away. Major flood damage to lower floors. All structures near shoreline affected. Massive evacuation of residential areas.

Source: the Saffir-Simpson Hurricane Scale, www.nhc.noaa.gov/HAW2/english/basics/saffir_simpson.shtml

For confirmation of engagement, take 30 seconds to have students share one thing they learned with their partner. While reading, I was thinking that Katrina must have been categorized as a 5 since winds were as high as 175 miles per hour. Your turn. Switch roles. Share your thoughts and one thing that you learned with your partner. Partners, you should listen carefully and ask questions to check understanding.

Now that you have read "Hurricane!," tell me something you shared with your partner during the reading. Have students share answers.

Unit 10 Lesson 2

Lesson Opener

Before the lesson, choose one of the following activities to write on the board or post on the *LANGUAGE! Live* Class Wall online.

- *What is the most active month for hurricanes and how did you learn that information?*
- *Write a sentence with a compound predicate about the last two books you have read.*
- *Keeping in mind your personality traits, write three sentences to describe how you would react during a hurricane.*

Vocabulary

Objectives

- Use discussion and context to determine the meanings of the multiple-meaning words *season* and *band*.
- Demonstrate an understanding of words by using them in written sentences.

Multiple-Meaning Words: *season, band*

In this unit, we are learning about hurricanes—how they form and when they form. We now know that there is a certain time of year that is considered hurricane season.

Season is a word that has more than one meaning. The word *season* can be an adjective, a noun, or a verb.

So, how do we know which definition of the word is being used? It all depends on how it is used in a sentence. We look for clues around the word to help us.

Direct students to page 176 in their Student Books.

Lead students in a discussion of the various meanings of the word *season*. Have them write the meanings and sentences on the Multiple-Meaning Map in their Student Books.

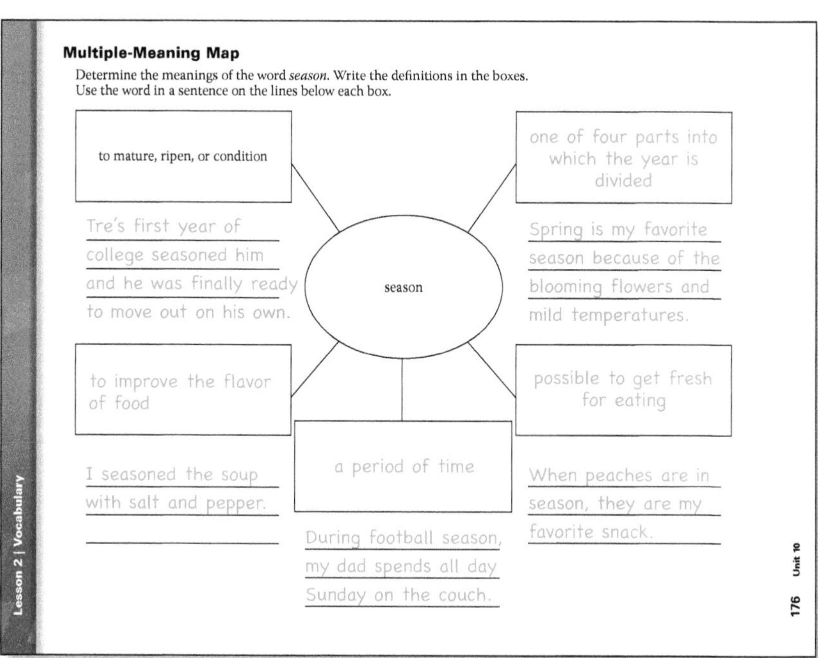
Multiple-Meaning Map

Determine the meanings of the word *season*. Write the definitions in the boxes. Use the word in a sentence on the lines below each box.

season
to mature, ripen, or condition
Tre's first year of college seasoned him and he was finally ready to move out on his own.
one of four parts into which the year is divided
Spring is my favorite season because of the blooming flowers and mild temperatures.
to improve the flavor of food
I seasoned the soup with salt and pepper.
a period of time
During football season, my dad spends all day Sunday on the couch.
possible to get fresh for eating
When peaches are in season, they are my favorite snack.
Lesson 2 | Vocabulary
176
Unit 10

Model

Have you ever heard someone refer to a person as *seasoned*? We often say that experiences over time can *season* people. Professional baseball players with years of experience are called *seasoned*. If you live on the coast and have dealt with hurricanes your whole life, you are a seasoned storm survivor. You know exactly what to do to stay safe. Listen to this sentence: I was terrified when I heard about the coming storm, but my grandmother was calm because living in Florida her whole life has seasoned her.

Write the definition *to mature, ripen, or condition* on the board and have students find it on their map. Have students think of a good sentence for this usage and write it below the definition.

Guided Practice

I love to cook. I usually season my food with salt, pepper, and cumin—my favorite spice. What is the definition of *season* in this usage? (to improve the flavor of food) Write the definition on the board and have students write it on their map. Have students think of a good sentence for this usage and write it below the definition.

Independent Practice

Continue the process until the maps are complete. Review the sentences and correct as needed.

Additional Definitions of *season*

Adjective

- matured; experienced (seasoned)

Idiom

- *for a season:* for a time
- *in season/out of season:* possible to get fresh for eating

Direct students to page 177 in their Student Books. Repeat the process with the word *band*.

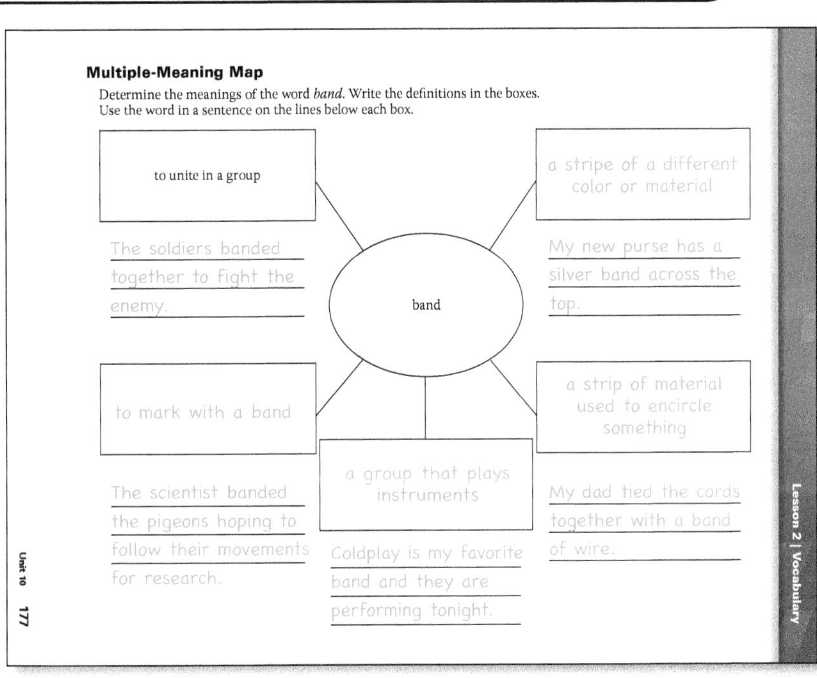

Multiple-Meaning Map
Determine the meanings of the word band. Write the definitions in the boxes. Use the word in a sentence on the lines below each box.
to unite in a group
The soldiers banded together to fight the enemy.
a stripe of a different color or material
My new purse has a silver band across the top.
band
to mark with a band
The scientist banded the pigeons hoping to follow their movements for research.
a group that plays instruments
Coldplay is my favorite band and they are performing tonight.
a strip of material used to encircle something
My dad tied the cords together with a band of wire.
Unit 10 177
Lesson 2 | Vocabulary

Additional Definitions of *band*

Noun

- a group joining together

Idiom

- *one-man band:* a person who does all the work and has all the responsibility

Note: Base the number of modeled and guided examples on student ability and progress. Challenge them with independent practice when appropriate.

Grammar

Objectives

- Demonstrate an understanding of forming and using possessive and plural possessive words.
- Identify singular, plural, and possessive nouns.
- Demonstrate an understanding of the function of compound sentences and conjunctions by using them in sentences.

Plural Possessives

Write the following sentence on the board:

The cat's dish is on the porch.

An apostrophe can do one of several jobs. One of its jobs is to indicate ownership, or possession. Look at the sentence on the board and tell me how the *-'s* adds meaning to the noun *cat.* (It adds the idea of ownership. It means the dish belongs to the cat.)

Direct students to page 178 in their Student Books. Read through the examples on the chart, stressing the change in meaning that results from the placement of the apostrophe before or after the *-s*.

Now let's practice forming plural possessive nouns. The first step is to make a singular noun plural. How will we make the noun plural? (by adding *-s*) How would we write the word cat if we wanted to talk about more than one cat? (cats)

Next, we will make our plural noun possessive. How will we make it possessive? (by adding an apostrophe after the *-s*) How would we write the word cats to show ownership? (cats') The final step is to think of something that could belong to the noun and add it as the next word. Rewrite the sentence on the board so it reads:

The cats' dishes are on the porch.

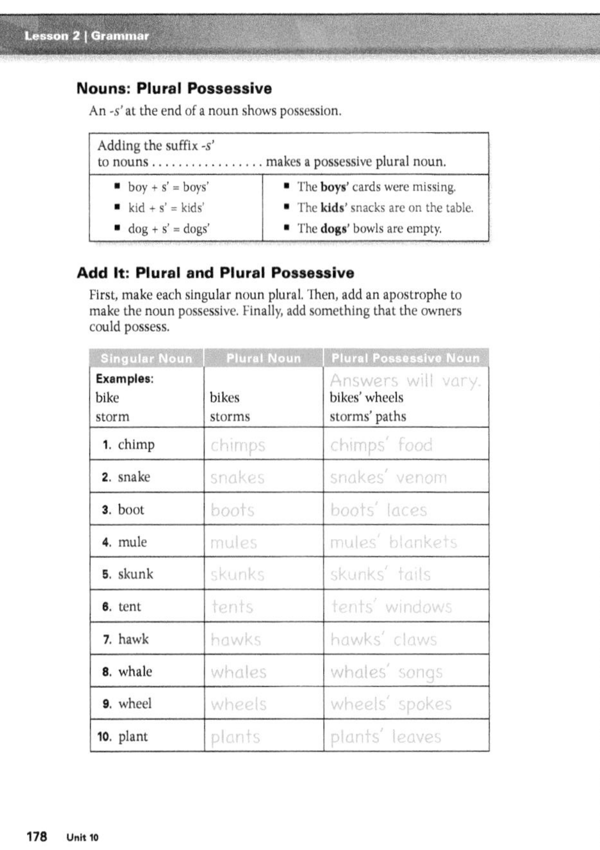

Lesson 2 | Grammar

Nouns: Plural Possessive

An *-s'* at the end of a noun shows possession.

Adding the suffix *-s'* to nouns .... makes a possessive plural noun.	
▪ boy + s' = boys' ▪ kid + s' = kids' ▪ dog + s' = dogs'	▪ The **boys'** cards were missing. ▪ The **kids'** snacks are on the table. ▪ The **dogs'** bowls are empty.

Add It: Plural and Plural Possessive

First, make each singular noun plural. Then, add an apostrophe to make the noun possessive. Finally, add something that the owners could possess.

Singular Noun	Plural Noun	Plural Possessive Noun
Examples: bike storm	 bikes storms	Answers will vary. bikes' wheels storms' paths
1. chimp	chimps	chimps' food
2. snake	snakes	snakes' venom
3. boot	boots	boots' laces
4. mule	mules	mules' blankets
5. skunk	skunks	skunks' tails
6. tent	tents	tents' windows
7. hawk	hawks	hawks' claws
8. whale	whales	whales' songs
9. wheel	wheels	wheels' spokes
10. plant	plants	plants' leaves

178 Unit 10

Model

On the board, model making each of the example nouns plural and then possessive.

Guided Practice

Guide students to complete the first two rows.

Independent Practice

Have students complete items 3 through 10. Review the answers as a class.

When we read, we have to pay close attention to how words end, because subtle differences in word endings can impact meaning. Let's practice distinguishing among singular, plural, and possessive nouns.

Direct students to page 179 in their Student Books. Read the instructions and examples aloud. Have partners

Lesson 2 | Grammar

Identify It: Singular, Plural, or Possessive Nouns

Read each sentence. Decide whether the underlined noun is singular, plural, singular possessive, or plural possessive, and place an X in that column.

Sentence	Singular Noun	Plural Noun	Singular Possessive Noun	Plural Possessive Noun
Examples: The fan broke.	X			
The fans broke.		X		
The fan's blade broke.			X	
The fans' blades broke.				X
1. The wind's gusts bent the branches.			X	
2. The tribes' lands are vast.				X
3. Scott picked up the birds' nest.				X
4. The hurricane's strength was not predicted.	X			
5. The car's brakes did not pass the test.		X		
6. Kites' shapes and sizes can be changed.				X
7. The wind lifts kites up into the sky.	X			
8. The plane's wings shone in the sun.			X	
9. The picnic was held on the pond's banks.			X	
10. We thought Juan's peaches were the best.		X		

Unit 10 179

complete the activity. Review the answers as a class. Encourage students to ask questions if they are struggling.

Note: Base the number of modeled and guided examples on student ability and progress. Challenge them with independent practice when appropriate.

Compound Sentences with Conjunctions

In writing, a *redundancy* is a repeated word, phrase, or idea. One way to reduce redundancies in writing is to combine sentences that contain similar ideas. We have worked on combining two subjects, two predicates, and two complete sentences. What kind of words help us combine sentence parts? (conjunctions)

In this activity, we will combine two complete sentences. To do this, we will have to choose the correct conjunction. Remember, each conjunction carries a different meaning: *and* relates two similar ideas, *but* signals contrasting ideas, and *or* signals a choice.

Direct students to page 180 in their Student Books.

Lesson 2 | Grammar

Combine It: Using Conjunctions

Use a conjunction to combine each pair of sentences. Write the new sentence on the line.

Conjunctions		
and	but	or

1. Jill went to the play. Mark did not go with her.
   Jill went to the play, but Mark did not go with her.
2. The grass needs to be cut. The weeds need to be pulled.
   The grass needs to be cut, and the weeds need to be pulled.
3. We can dine at home. We can eat at Bill's Food Cave.
   We can dine at home, or we can eat at Bill's Food Cave.
4. Beth ran fast. She did not win.
   Beth ran fast, but she did not win.
5. The class got the prize for reading the most words. They made a plan to read even more next time.
   The class got the prize for reading the most words, and they made a plan to read even more next time.

180 Unit 10

Model and Guided Practice

Let's look at the first two sentences. Read the sentences aloud. Jill went to the play. Mark did not go with her.

Jill and Mark did not do the same thing, so the actions are not similar; therefore, we cannot join the sentence with the word *and*. The two sentences also do not express a choice, so we can't use *or* to join them. The two sentences *do* express a contrast between Jill's and Mark's actions, so what conjunction would work best here? (The conjunction *but* works best.) Repeat this process with the second set of sentences.

Independent Practice

Have students complete the remaining items independently. Review the answers as a class. Encourage students to ask questions if they struggled to use the correct conjunctions.

Note: Base the number of modeled and guided examples on student ability and progress. Challenge them with independent practice when appropriate.

Writing

Objective

- Demonstrate command of the conventions of standard English capitalization and punctuation (comma).

Punctuation and Capitalization

Knowing how to punctuate our writing is an important skill. We may not always think about it, but punctuation and other conventions, such as capital letters, directly impact meaning.

Punctuation

An end mark shows where one thought ends and another begins. Commas not only tell us to pause, but they also create units of meaning within a sentence.

Capitalization

Capitalizing the first word in a sentence is another important signal that a new thought has begun. And capitalizing a proper noun signals a specific person or thing.

Direct students to page 181 in their Student Books and read the instructions. You read this passage in a previous unit to work on your fluency. Today you will read this passage again, looking for errors in capitalization and punctuation. Because you are focusing only on these two areas, you will use only two editor's marks. Review the marks and their meanings.

Have students edit the passage and compare edits with a partner. Read the passage one sentence at a time as you review the answers as a class.

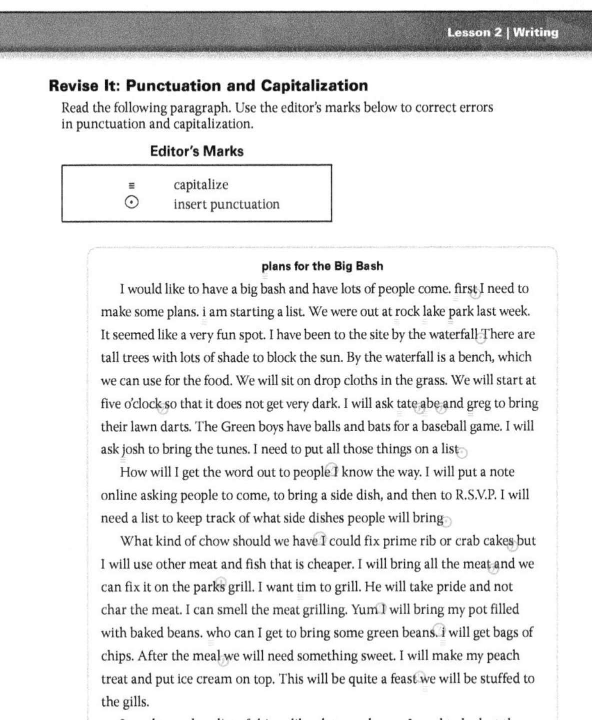

Lesson 2 | Writing

Revise It: Punctuation and Capitalization

Read the following paragraph. Use the editor's marks below to correct errors in punctuation and capitalization.

Editor's Marks

≡	capitalize
⊙	insert punctuation

plans for the Big Bash

I would like to have a big bash and have lots of people come. first I need to make some plans. i am starting a list. We were out at rock lake park last week. It seemed like a very fun spot. I have been to the site by the waterfall There are tall trees with lots of shade to block the sun. By the waterfall is a bench, which we can use for the food. We will sit on drop cloths in the grass. We will start at five o'clock so that it does not get very dark. I will ask tate abe and greg to bring their lawn darts. The Green boys have balls and bats for a baseball game. I will ask josh to bring the tunes. I need to put all those things on a list

How will I get the word out to people I know the way. I will put a note online asking people to come, to bring a side dish, and then to R.S.V.P. I will need a list to keep track of what side dishes people will bring

What kind of chow should we have I could fix prime rib or crab cakes but I will use other meat and fish that is cheaper. I will bring all the meat and we can fix it on the parks grill. I want tim to grill. He will take pride and not char the meat. I can smell the meat grilling. Yum I will bring my pot filled with baked beans. who can I get to bring some green beans. i will get bags of chips. After the meal we will need something sweet. I will make my peach treat and put ice cream on top. This will be quite a feast we will be stuffed to the gills.

I need to make a list of things like plates and cups. I need to look at the cost of the fish and meat and keep track of that I may ask cass if we can drive her truck to shop downtown. all that food is more than will fit in my car but it will fit into her truck

Unit 10 181

Unit 10 Lesson 3

Lesson Opener

Before the lesson, choose one of the following activities to write on the board or post on the *LANGUAGE! Live* Class Wall online.

- *Write three sentences with the word* band, *using a different meaning in each sentence.*
- *If you were in your house and you received a late warning that a hurricane was coming, what is the one thing you would save from destruction and why?*
- *Change your avatar's appearance. How would your avatar look if a hurricane was coming? Title the outfit "Hurricane."*

Reading

Objective

- Read words to develop fluency.

Word Fluency: First Read

Timer

Follow the Fluency Procedure outlined below. If it is necessary, begin the fluency drill with a choral read of the words as you provide a rhythm (snap your fingers, tap your foot, tap your pencil). Direct students to page 182 in their Student Books and complete the process.

Word Fluency: First Read

Read the words fluently.

	Correct	Errors
1st Try		
2nd Try		

hawk	landed	thinks	thawing	blanks	stinking	harmed	drank	hinted	honked	10
thinks	thawing	blanks	stinking	harmed	drank	hinted	honked	tromped	beaches	20
blanks	stinking	harmed	drank	hinted	honked	tromped	beaches	classes	chimps	30
harmed	drank	hinted	honked	tromped	beaches	classes	chimps	wheels	tents	40
hinted	honked	tromped	beaches	classes	chimps	wheels	tents	boxes	whales	50
tromped	beaches	classes	chimps	wheels	tents	boxes	whales	buzzes	spending	60
classes	chimps	wheels	tents	boxes	whales	buzzes	spending	landed	hawk	70
wheels	tents	boxes	whales	buzzes	spending	landed	hawk	thawing	thinks	80
boxes	whales	buzzes	spending	landed	hawk	thawing	thinks	stinking	blanks	90
buzzes	spending	landed	hawk	thawing	thinks	stinking	blanks	drank	harmed	100

Lesson 3 | Reading

182 Unit 10

Fluency Procedure

- Partners switch books, so the recorder is marking errors in the reader's book.
- A timer is set for one minute.
- Readers and recorders move left to right, tracking each word with a pencil.
- As readers read the words aloud, recorders mark errors with a small x above the misread word.
- Recorders place a star to the right of the last word read when time ends.
- If the reader is able to read all words in the allotted time, the reader needs to start over at the beginning. The recorder must indicate this feat by placing two stars to the right of the last word read.
- When both students have read, partners switch books.
- Students calculate total words read, then subtract errors and record.
- Students record information on the progress chart in back of the Student Book.

Vocabulary

Objectives

- Review key passage vocabulary.
- Demonstrate an understanding of metaphors and similes and the meanings of specific metaphors and similes.
- Write simple metaphors and similes.

Review

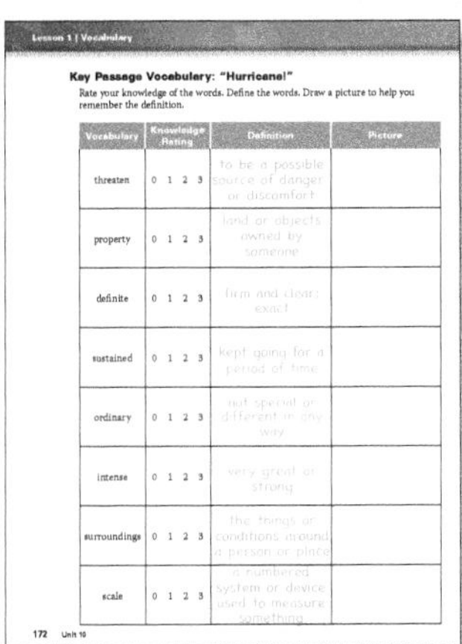

Lesson 1 | Vocabulary

Key Passage Vocabulary: "Hurricane!"

Rate your knowledge of the words. Define the words. Draw a picture to help you remember the definition.

Vocabulary	Knowledge Rating	Definition	Picture
threaten	0 1 2 3	to be a possible source of danger or discomfort	
property	0 1 2 3	land or objects owned by someone	
definite	0 1 2 3	firm and clear; exact	
sustained	0 1 2 3	kept going for a period of time	
ordinary	0 1 2 3	not special or different in any way	
intense	0 1 2 3	very great or strong	
surroundings	0 1 2 3	the things or conditions around a person or place	
scale	0 1 2 3	a numbered system or device used to measure something	

172 Unit 10

Direct students to page 172 in their Student Books.

Review the vocabulary words from the passage "Hurricane!" Have students answer in complete sentences.

- Land or objects owned by someone are what? (Land or objects owned by someone are property.) A hurricane can destroy the things you own. What can a hurricane destroy? (A hurricane can destroy your property.)
- Are hurricanes *ordinary* storms? (No, hurricanes are not ordinary storms.) If something is not special or different in any way, it is what? (Something is ordinary if it is not special or different in any way.)
- Is there a *definite* wind speed when a tropical storm becomes a hurricane? (Yes, a definite wind speed of 74 mph must be reached for a tropical storm to become a hurricane.) Something firm and clear, or exact, is what? (Something firm and clear is definite.)
- Hurricanes are measured using what? (Hurricanes are measured using a scale.) A numbered system or device used to measure something is a what? (A scale is a numbered system or device used to measure something.)
- When a hurricane is coming, you might be in danger. A hurricane can make you feel what? (A hurricane can make you feel threatened.) To be a possible source of danger or discomfort is to what? (To be a possible source of danger or discomfort is to threaten.)
- A hurricane dies when its *surroundings* become colder. The area around something is its what? (The area around something is its surroundings.)
- Could you stand without help in *sustained* winds of 100 mph? (No, I could not stand without help in sustained winds of 100 mph.) Something kept going for a period of time is what? (Something kept going is sustained.)
- What things are *intense* in a hurricane? (Wind and rain are intense in a hurricane.) Something that is very great or strong is what? (Something that is very great or strong is intense.)

Vocabulary Concept: Metaphors and Similes

Find examples of metaphors and similes in popular songs to share with students. These can be in sound clips or text.

Model

We have been discussing two specific types of figurative language: metaphors and similes. A metaphor is a figure of speech that describes something by comparing it to something else but does not use *like* or *as*. Let's look at some metaphors found in songs.

Write the following metaphors from songs on the board:

And know my heart's a stereo that only plays for you.

She had a heart of glass.

She's a hurricane blowing; She's the calm after the storm.

I got this icebox where my heart used to be.

Have students identify the two things being compared in each metaphor and then interpret its meaning. Have volunteers offer other examples from songs they know.

A simile is a figure of speech in which two unlike things are compared to show how they are similar. A simile often uses exaggeration and the word *like* or *as*. Let's look at some similes found in songs.

Write the following similes from songs on the board:

You played through my mind like a symphony.

Shake it like a Polaroid picture.

She's as cold as ice.

Have students identify the two things being compared in each simile and then interpret its meaning. Have volunteers offer other examples from songs they know.

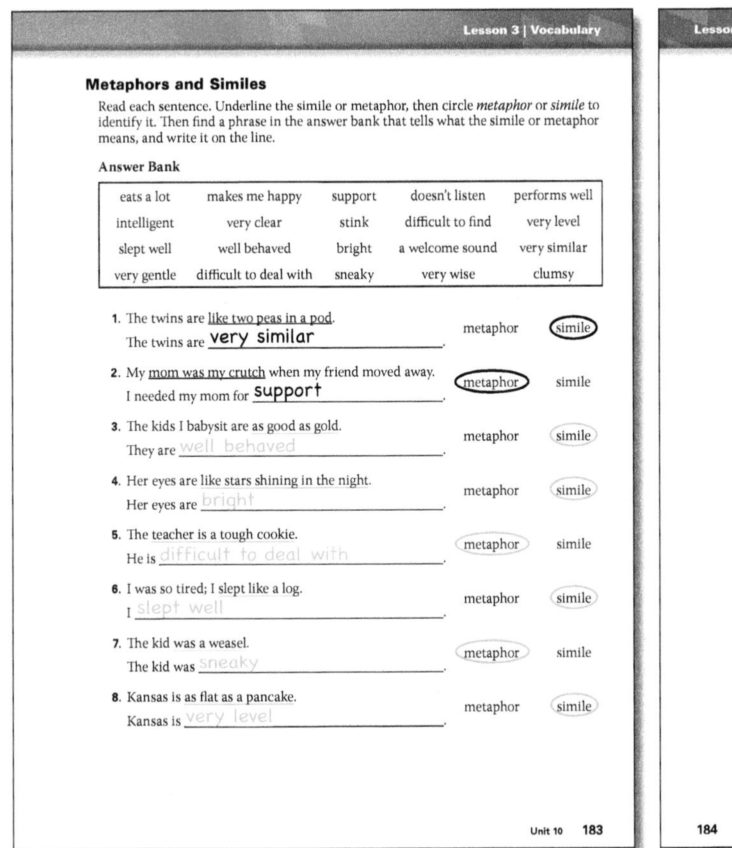
Lesson 3 | Vocabulary

Metaphors and Similes

Read each sentence. Underline the simile or metaphor, then circle *metaphor* or *simile* to identify it. Then find a phrase in the answer bank that tells what the simile or metaphor means, and write it on the line.

Answer Bank

eats a lot	makes me happy	support	doesn't listen	performs well
intelligent	very clear	stink	difficult to find	very level
slept well	well behaved	bright	a welcome sound	very similar
very gentle	difficult to deal with	sneaky	very wise	clumsy

1. The twins are like two peas in a pod.
The twins are very similar. — metaphor — (simile)
2. My mom was my crutch when my friend moved away.
I needed my mom for support. — (metaphor) — simile
3. The kids I babysit are as good as gold.
They are well behaved. — metaphor — (simile)
4. Her eyes are like stars shining in the night.
Her eyes are bright. — metaphor — (simile)
5. The teacher is a tough cookie.
He is difficult to deal with. — (metaphor) — simile
6. I was so tired; I slept like a log.
I slept well. — metaphor — (simile)
7. The kid was a weasel.
The kid was sneaky. — (metaphor) — simile
8. Kansas is as flat as a pancake.
Kansas is very level. — metaphor — (simile)

Unit 10 183

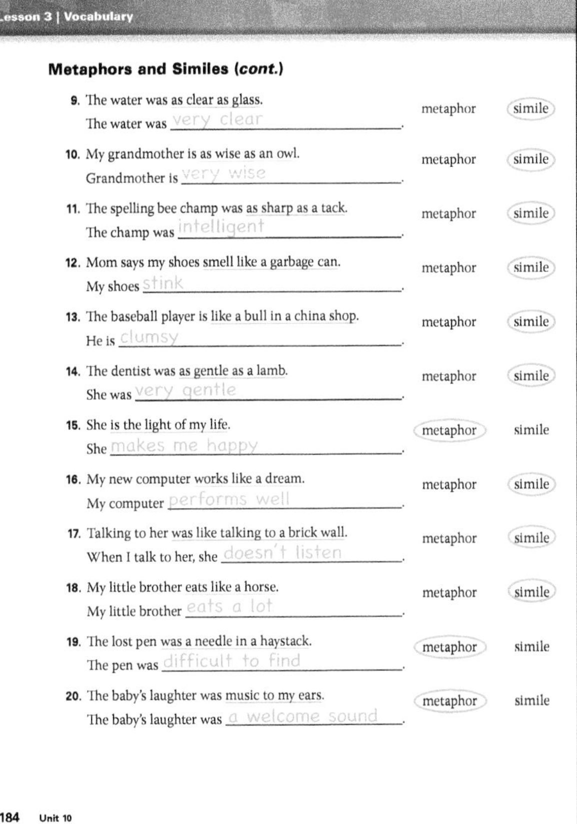
Lesson 3 | Vocabulary

Metaphors and Similes *(cont.)*

9. The water was as clear as glass.
The water was very clear. — metaphor — (simile)
10. My grandmother is as wise as an owl.
Grandmother is very wise. — metaphor — (simile)
11. The spelling bee champ was as sharp as a tack.
The champ was intelligent. — metaphor — (simile)
12. Mom says my shoes smell like a garbage can.
My shoes stink. — metaphor — (simile)
13. The baseball player is like a bull in a china shop.
He is clumsy. — metaphor — (simile)
14. The dentist was as gentle as a lamb.
She was very gentle. — metaphor — (simile)
15. She is the light of my life.
She makes me happy. — (metaphor) — simile
16. My new computer works like a dream.
My computer performs well. — metaphor — (simile)
17. Talking to her was like talking to a brick wall.
When I talk to her, she doesn't listen. — metaphor — (simile)
18. My little brother eats like a horse.
My little brother eats a lot. — metaphor — (simile)
19. The lost pen was a needle in a haystack.
The pen was difficult to find. — (metaphor) — simile
20. The baby's laughter was music to my ears.
The baby's laughter was a welcome sound. — (metaphor) — simile

184 Unit 10

Direct students to pages 183 and 184 in their Student Books.

Guided Practice

Read the first two sentences. Have students identify the metaphor or simile in each sentence and tell what makes it a metaphor or simile. Guide students in determining what is being compared and what the simile or metaphor means.

Independent Practice

Read the remaining sentences. Have students identify the simile or metaphor and its meaning.

Note: Base the number of modeled and guided examples on student ability and progress. Challenge them with independent practice when appropriate.

Creating Metaphors and Similes

Direct students to page 185 in their Student Books.

Guided Practice

Read the instructions and the first description. Guide the class in creating sentences that include a metaphor and a simile describing "a pretty person." Write the sentences on the board and label the figurative language for students to use as a guide.

Independent Practice

Read the remaining descriptions aloud. Have students write a sentence containing a simile or a metaphor for each one. Have volunteers share their figurative language and identify what type it is.

Note: Base the number of modeled and guided examples on student ability and progress. Challenge them with independent practice when appropriate.

Lesson 3 | Vocabulary

Creating Metaphors and Similes

Choose six of the following descriptions. Write a sentence using a simile or a metaphor that enhances the mental image.

Answers will vary.

1. a pretty person My mother was a beautiful flower when she was young. She was as pretty as a song.
2. a bright light After I sat in the dark room for an hour, the lamp light was as bright as the sun.
3. a tall person Steve is a skyscraper reaching high above the crowd.
4. an old house The dinosaur of a house is filled with outdated furniture.
5. a strange object That flying disk is as weird as a purple cow.
6. a fast car My dad's new car is like lightning.
7. an easy contest The ring toss was as simple as two plus two.
8. a mean person Jeff was as mean as a snake to his little brother.
9. a funny person Sue is a clown, constantly cracking jokes and playing tricks on people.
10. a smart dog Our dog Spot is as smart as a straight-A student.

Unit 10 185

Grammar

Objectives

- Form and use the past, present, and future tenses of the verb *be* with various pronouns.
- Understand the difference between action verbs, linking verbs, and helping verbs.

Action Verbs and Linking Verbs

Verb Forms: Be poster

Let's review what we know about the verb *be*. It can function several different ways in a sentence and it can take many different forms. Direct students to page 186 in their Student Books.

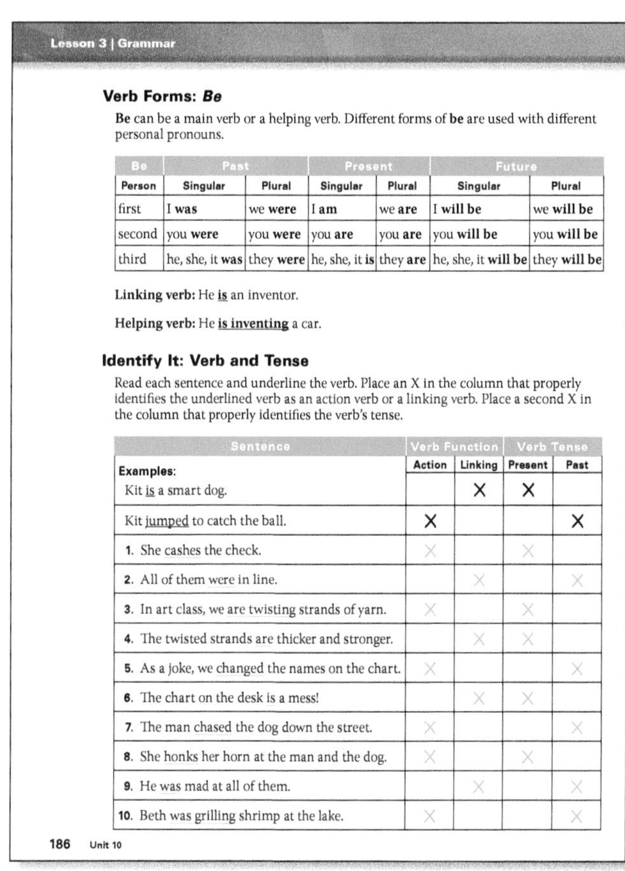

Lesson 3 | Grammar

Verb Forms: *Be*

Be can be a main verb or a helping verb. Different forms of **be** are used with different personal pronouns.

Be	Past		Present		Future	
Person	Singular	Plural	Singular	Plural	Singular	Plural
first	I **was**	we **were**	I **am**	we **are**	I **will be**	we **will be**
second	you **were**	you **were**	you **are**	you **are**	you **will be**	you **will be**
third	he, she, it **was**	they **were**	he, she, it **is**	they **are**	he, she, it **will be**	they **will be**

Linking verb: He <u>is</u> an inventor.

Helping verb: He <u>is inventing</u> a car.

Identify It: Verb and Tense

Read each sentence and underline the verb. Place an X in the column that properly identifies the underlined verb as an action verb or a linking verb. Place a second X in the column that properly identifies the verb's tense.

Sentence	Verb Function		Verb Tense	
	Action	Linking	Present	Past
Examples: Kit <u>is</u> a smart dog.		X	X	
Kit <u>jumped</u> to catch the ball.	X			X
1. She cashes the check.	X		X	
2. All of them were in line.		X		X
3. In art class, we are twisting strands of yarn.	X		X	
4. The twisted strands are thicker and stronger.		X	X	
5. As a joke, we changed the names on the chart.	X			X
6. The chart on the desk is a mess!		X	X	
7. The man chased the dog down the street.	X			X
8. She honks her horn at the man and the dog.	X		X	
9. He was mad at all of them.		X		X
10. Beth was grilling shrimp at the lake.	X			X

186 Unit 10

We use different forms of a verb depending on who or what is doing the action and when the action takes place. Look at the past tense section of the chart. You'll see only two different forms of the verb: *was* and *were*. I'm going to read each pronoun, and I want you to say the correct past tense form of the verb.

- I (was).
- You (were).
- She (was).
- We (were).
- They (were).

Review present and future tenses in the same way. Point out that future tense is the same no matter what the subject is.

Linking Verb

When a form of *be* is the only verb in the sentence, we call it a linking verb. When *be* works as a linking verb, it connects the subject with a word that describes or renames the subject. This word can be a noun or an adjective. Look at the example in your book: He is an inventor. What is he? (an inventor) Is *inventor* a noun or an adjective? (noun) Have students call out the past and present linking verbs as you provide additional oral sentence frames.

Examples

You *were* a baby once.	I *was* a student.
I *am* a teacher.	You *are* a student.
We *are* a group.	She *is* fun.
He *is* loud.	

Helping Verb

When a form of *be* is paired with another verb, it is a helping verb. The two verbs together work as an action verb. Look at the example in your book: He is inventing a car. Have students change the pronoun and the present tense helping verb to create other sentences.

Now, let's use past tense helping verbs. Listen to this sentence: I was waiting in the hall for you. Turn to your partner and take turns finishing a sentence about people at a class, party, dance, or assembly that happened in the past. Use *were* or *was* as a helping verb. Have volunteers share their sentences with the class.

Model

Direct students to the Identify It activity and read the instructions aloud. Read both examples.

Guided Practice

Read the first sentence and ask students what word should be underlined and what columns should be marked.

Independent Practice

Read the second sentence and ask students to underline the verb and mark the proper columns. Ask students how they marked the sentence. If students are not struggling, have them complete the remaining sentences independently. If they seem to be struggling, continue to guide them with the activity. Review the answers as a class.

Note: Base the number of modeled and guided examples on student ability and progress. Challenge them with independent practice when appropriate.

Reading

Objectives

- Use critical thinking skills to analyze a text.
- Ask and answer questions and prompts using extended thinking skills to demonstrate an understanding of a text.

Critical Understandings

Good readers demonstrate what they learned from a text when they answer questions and prompts. In this lesson, we will work with more challenging prompts that require you to demonstrate critical thinking. Often, these higher level prompts will ask you to find evidence in the text. Evidence is a detail from the text that supports a bigger, more general idea. Evidence can be a single word, a phrase, a sentence, or a group of sentences.

Proficient readers need to do more than recall and understand. Proficient readers are strategic thinkers who make connections between ideas in texts, are curious about new learning, and are able to reevaluate their opinions based on what they read. At the strategic thinking level, you need deeper knowledge about the subject matter.

Today, we will move on to the extended thinking level of comprehension. What level of comprehension will we study in this unit? (extended thinking) At this level, you will need to recall information, understand what the information means, think strategically about new information, and take time for extended, higher order thinking. That means that answers to prompts may be in the text, or may require that we combine information from the text with knowledge from other texts or classes.

Direction Words: Extended Thinking poster

Direct students to the chart on page 16 in their Student Books or refer to the Extended Thinking poster if you have it displayed.

Prompts that ask you to respond at the extended thinking level can include one of three verbs: *evaluate, analyze,* or *connect.*

Evaluate

If a prompt asks you to *evaluate,* it is asking you to think carefully about something before making a judgment about it. Read the example with me. (Evaluate the storm evacuation plan.) When you evaluate, you are forming an educated opinion about something you read, heard, or saw.

Analyze

If a prompt asks you to *analyze,* it is asking you to break down and evaluate or draw conclusions about the information. Read the example with me. (Analyze the safety plan.) When you analyze something, you are breaking it down into smaller parts and then using information from the text and from your own knowledge to draw new conclusions about it.

Connect

If a prompt asks you to *connect,* it is asking you to tie ideas together, or relate them to previous learning. For example, if I asked you to connect each storm to its safety plan, you would have to differentiate between storms and then tell how a different safety plan is connected to each type of storm. How will you respond if a prompt asks you to connect something? **(tie ideas together, relate to previous learning)**

At each level, it is critical that you understand what the prompt is asking and how to respond. We will become automatic with these prompts and learn exactly how to respond at a mastery level.

Look at the How to Respond column in the chart for Conceptual Understanding, Strategic Thinking, and Extended Thinking. Some direction words have the same or similar meanings. Which direction words expect you to decide or judge? **(assess, evaluate)** Which direction words expect you to consider the relationship between concepts or ideas? **(relate, connect)**

Each direction word asks you to construct a higher level response using information from different sources, including your own prior knowledge, text, charts, and graphs. Proficient readers can also identify "gaps" in the text—places where information is not given and must be found in another source. At the extended thinking level, you may find it necessary to confirm your answer with an outside source such as another book, a Web site, or an Internet search.

Direct students to pages 187 and 188 in their Student Books. Let's preview some prompts that require extended thinking using a short piece of text. I'll read the prompt, and you repeat the direction word in bold.

Critical Understandings

Review the extended thinking prompts on the chart on page 16. Read the prompts that follow the passage to establish a purpose for reading. Then read the passage and respond to the prompts.

Tsunami

A huge earthquake took place in the Pacific Ocean on March 11, 2011. The earthquake set off a tsunami, which was even worse. A tsunami is a series of powerful ocean waves. At a top speed of 500 miles per hour, the waves can flood an acre of ground in mere seconds. The surge of water can reach up to 100 feet high. With its combination of speed and size, a tsunami can damage everything for miles inland. It can destroy whole towns, including buildings, bridges, and property. A tsunami can kill thousands of people and animals.

Many earthquakes and tsunamis happen in the Pacific Ocean. The earth shakes when rocks shift along its cracks. Many of these cracks, also called faults, are below the Pacific Ocean. When the earth shifts along one of these faults, the movement pushes the water in the ocean up. This creates an enormous wave.

The tsunami of March 11, 2011, poured over northern Japan. It took days to determine that the wild waves had killed more than 11,000 people. In some cases, entire villages were washed away. Farmland was destroyed. It was the worst natural disaster in Japan in nearly 100 years.

A group called the Tsunami Warning System (TWS) checks conditions in the Pacific every day. When an earthquake or cyclone occurs, the TWS reports the data. It urges governments to take every precaution. When a tsunami is on the way, people must travel a long way inland to find safe shelter.

This is difficult for two reasons. First, a tsunami can hit islands like Japan or Hawaii minutes after the earthquake sets it off. This leaves little time to run for safety. Second, all tsunamis are created in deep ocean water, where they might be invisible to the TWS. They can only be seen when they reach shallow water. By then, the warning can come too late.

A volcanic eruption can also set off a tsunami. This happened in 1883 on the tropical island of Krakatau. Together, the explosion and the tsunami killed more than 35,000 people.

1. **Analyze** the job of the TWS. Answers will vary.
The TWS monitors the conditions in the Pacific Ocean and encourages governments to take precautions when tsunamis are forming. The TWS saves lives, property, and money.

Critical Understandings *(cont.)*

Answers will vary.

2. **Evaluate** the effectiveness of the TWS in March 2011.
In my opinion, the TWS was not effective in March 2011. While the TWS could not have helped villages from being washed away and property damage from happening, the alerts of the TWS can always save lives. The fact that 11,000 people died indicates that the TWS was not very effective.

3. **Analyze** the risk of living near the Pacific Ocean.
Living near the Pacific Ocean comes with the risk of losing all of your belongings . . . and possibly your life. The Pacific Ocean has many tsunamis because it has many cracks/faults. These cracks cause earthquakes. When earthquakes happen underwater, a tsunami can result.

4. **Connect** volcanic eruptions and earthquakes.
Volcanic eruptions and earthquakes are both causes of tsunamis.

5. **Connect** Japan, Hawaii, and tsunamis.
Japan and Hawaii are both Pacific islands that can suffer great damage from tsunamis. Tsunamis can hit these islands minutes after an earthquake, making it difficult to issue warnings. This means that people aren't given enough time to take precautions and evacuate, leading to great destruction and loss of life.

Now, with eyes on text, listen while I read this short passage about a different kind of natural disaster. Use your pencil eraser to follow along. Let's begin. Read the text aloud.

Note: While the lessons are written for a teacher read aloud, it is important that your students read as much and as often as they can. Assign readings that meet the needs of your students, based on your observations or data. This is a good opportunity to stretch students, but if they become frustrated, return to the read-aloud method.

Tsunami

A huge earthquake took place in the Pacific Ocean on March 11, 2011. The earthquake set off a tsunami, which was even worse. A tsunami is a series of powerful ocean waves. At a top speed of 500 miles per hour, the waves can flood an acre of ground in mere seconds. The surge of water can reach up to 100 feet high. With its combination of speed and size, a tsunami can damage everything for miles inland. It can destroy whole towns, including buildings, bridges, and property. A tsunami can kill thousands of people and animals.

Many earthquakes and tsunamis happen in the Pacific Ocean. The earth shakes when rocks shift along its cracks. Many of these cracks, also called faults, are below the Pacific Ocean. When the earth shifts along one of these faults, the movement pushes the water in the ocean up. This creates an enormous wave.

The tsunami of March 11, 2011, poured over northern Japan. It took days to determine that the wild waves had killed more than 11,000 people. In some cases, entire villages were washed away. Farmland was destroyed. It was the worst natural disaster in Japan in nearly 100 years.

A group called the Tsunami Warning System (TWS) checks conditions in the Pacific every day. When an earthquake or cyclone occurs, the TWS reports the data. It urges governments to take every precaution. When a tsunami is on the way, people must travel a long way inland to find safe shelter.

This is difficult for two reasons. First, a tsunami can hit islands like Japan or Hawaii minutes after the earthquake sets it off. This leaves little time to run for safety. Second, all tsunamis are created in deep ocean water, where they might be invisible to the TWS. They can only be seen when they reach shallow water. By then, the warning can come too late.

A volcanic eruption can also set off a tsunami. This happened in 1883 on the tropical island of Krakatau. Together, the explosion and the tsunami killed more than 35,000 people.

Let's check our comprehension of this passage by responding to some prompts that require extended thinking. For each prompt, you will need to use information from sources other than this text to support your answer.

Remember, each prompt is really a question—and we already know how to answer questions. If you struggle to remember how to respond to a prompt, it can be helpful to turn the prompt into a question. We will practice responding to prompts that require extended thinking using evidence from this text and from other sources. Try asking yourself a question so that you know exactly how to respond.

Model

Read the first prompt aloud.

1. **Analyze** the job of the TWS.

It is important to fully understand a prompt before constructing a response. Turn to your neighbor and restate the prompt as a question to demonstrate your understanding of it. Provide partner time; confirm understanding. The question would be, What is the job of the TWS and how is it important?

When we respond, we need to use evidence in the text along with our own background knowledge to write a response. Turn to your partner and discuss how to begin writing your answer by restating the prompt. When you are happy with your sentence starter, answer the question together. Write a response with students based on their combined efforts. (The TWS monitors the conditions in the Pacific Ocean and encourages governments to take precautions when tsunamis are forming. The TWS saves lives, property, and money.)

Guided Practice

Read the next prompt aloud.

2. **Evaluate** the effectiveness of the TWS in March 2011.

We can change this prompt into a question to determine how best to respond. Have volunteers do so. The question would be, Was the TWS effective in March 2011? Why or why not? Begin your answer by restating the prompt. While students work, write the sentence starter on the board:

In my opinion, the TWS ______.

Work with students to formulate the answer and have students write it on their Student Book page. (In my opinion, the TWS was not effective in March 2011. While the TWS could not have helped villages from being washed away and property damage from happening, the alerts of the TWS can always save lives. The fact that 11,000 people died indicates that the TWS was not very effective.)

Independent Practice

Have partners complete the remaining prompts. Review their answers as a class to ensure students understand what each prompt is asking.

Note: Base the number of modeled and guided examples on student ability and progress. Challenge them with independent practice when appropriate.

Provide these alternative questions and sentence starters for those who need additional help.

3. What are the risks of living near the Pacific Ocean?

Living near the Pacific Ocean comes with the risk of ______________________.

4. How are volcanic eruptions and earthquakes related?

Volcanic eruptions and earthquakes are both ______________________.

5. What is the connection between Japan, Hawaii, and tsunamis?

Japan and Hawaii ______________________.
Tsunamis ______________________.
This means ______________________.

Unit 10 Lesson 4

Lesson Opener

Before the lesson, choose one of the following activities to write on the board or post on the *LANGUAGE! Live* Class Wall online.

- *Write a simile and a metaphor to describe a hurricane: A hurricane is a _____ . A hurricane is like a _____.*
- *Think about your neighborhood. Describe the setting after a hurricane has just blown through.*
- *Write two sentences with plural possessives.*

Reading

Objective

- Read sentences to develop fluency.

Sentence Fluency

Timer

Follow the Fluency Procedure outlined below. If it is necessary, begin the fluency drill with a choral read of all sentences. Direct students to page 189 in their Student Books and complete the process.

Fluency Procedure

- Partners switch books, so the recorder is marking errors in the reader's book.
- A timer is set for one minute.
- Readers and recorders move left to right, tracking each word with a pencil.
- As readers read the words aloud, recorders mark errors with a small x above the misread word.
- Recorders place a star to the right of the last word read when time ends.
- If the reader is able to read all words in the allotted time, the reader needs to start over at the beginning. The recorder must indicate this feat by placing two stars to the right of the last word read.
- When both students have read, partners switch books.
- Students calculate total words read, then subtract errors and record.
- Students record information on the progress chart in back of the Student Book.

Lesson 4 | Reading

Sentence Fluency

Read each sentence fluently.

	Errors	Correct
1st Try		
2nd Try		

	Sentence	Words
1.	His sheep was the grand champ at the farm show.	10
2.	Shawn stands in line at the shark tank.	18
3.	That man is the clerk who dumped the bag of change.	29
4.	She is drinking a cup of green tea.	37
5.	The fawns are sitting on the lawn below the pond.	47
6.	She is following every move the hawk makes.	55
7.	We sat in the grandstands that are away from the street.	66
8.	Is there any time between the game and the show when we can take a picture?	82
9.	I spent all of my change on the cool drink.	92
10.	The air is filled with smoke because of the fires around the state.	105
11.	Is that the right kind of font for the thank-you cards you are sending?	120
12.	Is there a different path through the park than this one?	131
13.	She passes the pawn shop as she pushes the dishes in the cart.	144

Unit 10 189

Grammar

Objectives

- Listen to oral sentences and write them accurately.
- Demonstrate an understanding of how to write future tense verbs in sentences.
- Understand the function of action verbs and linking verbs in sentences.

Action Verbs and Linking Verbs

Verb Forms: Be poster

You have just read sentences for speed and accuracy. Now we will look closely at those sentences to reinforce what we have learned about action verbs and linking verbs.

Direct students to page 190 in their Student Books. Read the instructions and remind students of the procedure for sentence dictation.

Dictation Procedure

- Teacher reads the sentence.
- Students repeat the sentence.
- Students write the sentence.
- Teacher reads the sentence a second time as students check their work.

Lesson 4 | Grammar

Sentence Dictation: Action Verbs and Linking Verbs

Part A

Listen to each sentence and then repeat it. Write the sentence in the chart below. Underline the verb or verb phrase in the sentence. Place an X in the correct column to identify the type of verb in the sentence.

Sentence	Action Verb	Linking Verb
1. His sheep was the grand champ at the farm show.		X
2. Shawn stands in line at the shark tank.	X	
3. That man is the clerk who dumped the bag of change.		X
4. She is drinking a cup of green tea.	X	
5. The fawns are sitting on the lawn below the pond.	X	

Part B

Rewrite each sentence above using the tense shown in parentheses.

1. (present) His sheep is the grand champ at the farm show.
2. (future) Shawn will stand in line at the shark tank.
3. (past) That man was the clerk who dumped the bag of change.
4. (past) She was drinking a cup of green tea.
5. (past) The fawns were sitting on the lawn below the pond.

190 Unit 10

Dictate the following sentences:

1. His sheep was the grand champ at the farm show.
2. Shawn stands in line at the shark tank.
3. That man is the clerk who dumped the bag of change.
4. She is drinking a cup of green tea.
5. The fawns are sitting on the lawn below the pond.

Have students underline the verbs and place an X in the proper column to identify the verbs. Review students' answers as a class.

Write the following sentence on the board:

She is a teacher.

Look at the sentence on the board. What is the verb? (is) What is the past tense of *is*? (was) How would we restate the sentence to express it in past tense? (She was a teacher.)

Write the following sentence on the board:

She is teaching him.

Look at this sentence. What is the verb phrase in this sentence? (is teaching) What tense is it? (present tense) What would we have to do to make it happen in the past? The helping verb is *is*. What is the past tense of *is*? (was)

Direct students to Part B. To complete the remainder of the assignment, rewrite each sentence, changing the tense. The tense has been identified for you in parentheses. For the first sentence, you are to change the tense to the present. How would you say that sentence, changing the tense to the present? (His sheep is the grand champ at the farm show.) Now, write it. For each sentence, identify the tense for the students and have students write it. Review the answers as a class.

Reading

Objectives

- Read sentence phrases with fluency to support comprehension.
- Read an informational text.
- Use critical thinking skills to respond to specific questions about a text.

Phrase It

Reading in phrases is an important step in becoming a proficient reader. Read the following phrases, pausing in between for students to create a mental picture.

> The hurricane . . . destroyed our two-story house . . . and blew the neighbor's fence . . . into our swimming pool.

The hurricane is the subject, and *destroyed our two-story house and blew the neighbor's fence into our swimming pool* is the predicate.

For Phrase It, we scoop phrases using our pencil. When we scoop a phrase, we form an image in our heads. The next phrase we read may add to or change the image. This process is what we refer to as comprehension. The picture of the hurricane changes as soon as we read the first part of the predicate—*destroyed our two-story house.* It changes again when we read the second part of the predicate—*and blew the neighbor's fence.* It changes yet again when we read the third part of the predicate—*into our swimming pool.* Imagining the destruction caused by the hurricane changed the feeling of the sentence. The addition of each *phrase*—not the addition of each *word*—changes our mental image. That's why we read in chunks.

Direct students to page 191 in their Student Books.

Model

Complete the first item as a model.

Guided Practice

Guide the completion of the next two.

Independent Practice

Read the remaining sentences and have students scoop the phrases. Review the answers as a class.

Note: Base the number of modeled and guided examples on student ability and progress. Challenge them with independent practice when appropriate.

There are various ways the sentences can be broken into phrases. Accept logical answers.

Phrase It

Read each phrase and scoop it with a pencil. As you read the phrase, form an image in your mind. Read the sentence with prosody.

1. That grump farms wheat on his land in the country.
2. As we went into the show, they stamped everyone's hand.
3. Will you tell me again why he chose the white pants?
4. Before he went for a ride in the country, Clint pumped his tank full.
5. She is fond of the blond chimp, which lives at the zoo.
6. I am on the brink of spending all my cash.
7. I fell trying to jump past the stump.
8. We like to tromp through the trees in the park.
9. She wore a pink tank top and a white mink.

Direction Words: Extended Thinking poster

Critical Understandings

We will continue responding to prompts at the extended thinking level. You will respond to prompts that include verbs such as *connect, analyze,* and *evaluate.* What level prompt are we studying in this unit? (extended thinking) What will you need to do at this level of comprehension? (recall, understand, think strategically, and extend thinking) Do these strategies work in other classes? (yes)

Direct students to pages 192 and 193 in their Student Books.

Let's preview some prompts that require extended thinking about a scientific process called cloud seeding. I'll read each prompt, and you repeat the key word in bold.

Lesson 4 | Reading

Critical Understandings

Read the prompts below the passage to establish a purpose for rereading. Then read the passage and respond to the prompts.

Cloud Seeding

Have you ever wished you could control the weather? People have had that wish throughout history. In the past, rain dances were used to help ward off dry summers. Today, a more scientific method is used to bring farmers needed rain and skiers desired snow. This method is called cloud seeding.

In cloud seeding, scientists put granules into clouds. The granules are usually made of a salt mixture or of dry ice (solid carbon dioxide). Sometimes, the granules are shot up into the clouds from a machine on the ground. Other times, the granules are dropped down into the clouds from an airplane. Water vapor in the clouds grabs onto these granules and eventually condenses into rainfall or snowfall.

Cloud seeding was invented in 1946. It is used worldwide today. However, it is still not a perfect science. It is impossible to predict with 100 percent certainty just how effective a "seeding" will be. For example, scientists have noticed that cloud seeding seems to work differently in different climates and in different seasons. However, they have not been able to measure and work with these differences very well. There are also concerns that creating rainfall in one place may reduce it in another.

Questions and concerns aside, experiments in cloud seeding are likely to continue. More is being learned about the various ways cloud seeding may be effective at controlling the weather. Scientists have discovered that cloud seeding can do more than create rain and snow. It can also reduce the size of hail, disperse thick fog, and even clean pollution from the air.

1. **Evaluate** the success of cloud seeding.
   Cloud seeding has been around for more than sixty years and is used worldwide, which means it is successful. However, because scientists can't predict its effectiveness or determine why it is affected by the climate, there is still room for improvement.

192 Unit 10

Lesson 4 | Reading

Critical Understandings (*cont.*)

2. **Connect** dry ice to rainfall.
   Dry ice is put into clouds to create rain.

3. **Analyze** scientists' motivations to seed clouds.
   Scientists are motivated to cloud seed by problems with drought, flooding, fog, storms, and pollution. These problems wreak havoc on people and economies. If scientists can find a way to control this, they will be helping many people.

4. **Evaluate** the possible benefits of cloud seeding.
   Cloud seeding can help farmers' crops flourish, which will help the economy and feed the hungry. Cloud seeding can also keep people safe from damaging storms, floods, and droughts. Finally, it can help people breathe better by reducing pollution in the air.

5. **Connect** scientists to nature.
   Some scientists study nature and learn from it. Other scientists look for ways to manipulate and change nature.

Unit 10 193

Have students follow along as you read the text aloud.

Note: While the lessons are written for a teacher read aloud, it is important that your students read as much and as often as they can. Assign readings that meet the needs of your students, based on your observations or data. This is a good opportunity to stretch students, but if they become frustrated, return to the read-aloud method.

Cloud Seeding

Have you ever wished you could control the weather? People have had that wish throughout history. In the past, rain dances were used to help ward off dry summers. Today, a more scientific method is used to bring farmers needed rain and skiers desired snow. This method is called cloud seeding.

In cloud seeding, scientists put granules into clouds. The granules are usually made of a salt mixture or of dry ice (solid carbon dioxide). Sometimes, the granules are shot up into the clouds from a machine on the ground. Other times, the granules are dropped down into the clouds from an airplane. Water vapor in the clouds grabs onto these granules and eventually condenses into rainfall or snowfall.

Cloud seeding was invented in 1946. It is used worldwide today. However, it is still not a perfect science. It is impossible to predict with 100 percent certainty just how effective a "seeding" will be. For example, scientists have noticed that cloud seeding seems to work differently in different climates and in different seasons. However, they have not been able to measure and work with these differences very well. There are also concerns that creating rainfall in one place may reduce it in another.

Questions and concerns aside, experiments in cloud seeding are likely to continue. More is being learned about the various ways cloud seeding may be effective at controlling the weather. Scientists have discovered that cloud seeding can do more than create rain and snow. It can also reduce the size of hail, disperse thick fog, and even clean pollution from the air.

Let's check our comprehension of this passage by responding to some prompts that require extended thinking about the text. For each prompt, you will need to use evidence from the text plus your own knowledge to support your answer.

Remember, each prompt is a question in disguise—and we already know how to answer questions. If you struggle to remember how to respond to a prompt, try turning it into a question.

Read the first prompt aloud.

1. **Evaluate** the success of cloud seeding.

We can change this prompt into a question to determine how best to respond. The question would be, Is cloud seeding successful? Why or why not?

Work with your partner to respond to the prompt. Write a sentence starter before you return to the text to find evidence. While students work, write the sentence starter on the board:

Cloud seeding ______. However, because ______.

Work with students to formulate the answer and have students write it on their Student Book page. (Cloud seeding has been around for more than sixty years and is used worldwide, which means it is successful. However, because scientists can't predict its effectiveness or determine why it is affected by the climate, there is still room for improvement.)

Read the second prompt aloud.

2. **Connect** dry ice to rainfall.

Have students change the prompt into a question. (How is dry ice connected to rainfall?) Work with your partner to respond to the prompt. Write a sentence starter before you return to the text for text evidence.

While students work, write this sentence frame on the board:

Dry ice ______.

Work with students to formulate the answer and have them write it on their Student Book page. (Dry ice is put into clouds to create rain.)

Have partners complete the remaining prompts. Review the answers as a class to ensure students understand what each prompt is asking.

Provide these alternative questions and sentence starters for those who need additional help.

3. What motivates scientists to seed clouds?

   Scientists are motivated to cloud seed by ______________________.

4. What are the possible benefits of cloud seeding and why are they important?

   Cloud seeding can help ______________________,
   which will help ______________________.
   Cloud seeding can also ______________________.
   Finally, it can help ______________________.

5. How are scientists connected to nature?

   Some scientists ______________________.
   Other scientists ______________________.

Lesson 5

Lesson Opener

Before the lesson, choose one of the following activities to write on the board or post on the *LANGUAGE! Live* Class Wall online.

- *Write sentences using the following verb phrases:* is seasoning, are seasoning, was seasoning, were seasoning.
- *Write a compound sentence about hurricanes and tsunamis.*
- *Write two sentences about your school day. In the first sentence, use a* be *verb to explain what you were doing during the previous class. In the second sentence, use a* be *verb to explain what you will be doing in the next class.*

Vocabulary

Objective

- Review key passage vocabulary.

Recontextualize Passage Vocabulary

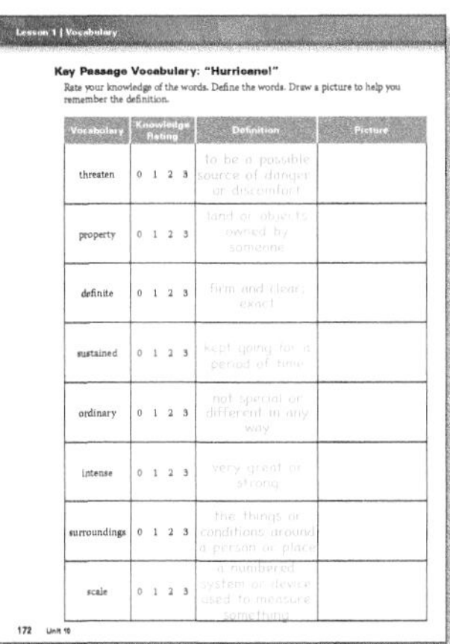

Direct students to page 172 in their Student Books.

Review the Key Passage Vocabulary from "Hurricane!"

- Land or objects owned by someone are what? (property) With your partner, use the words *property, hurricane,* and *vanish* in a sentence. (Answers will vary.)
- Not special or different in any way is what? (ordinary) I saw a house that was shaped like a shoe; it was very different from the other houses in the neighborhood. Houses made of brick or wood with a peaked roof are very common. What are they? (ordinary)
- Firm and clear, or exact, is what? (definite) I am not good at finding my way. If you don't give me exact directions to a place, I will not get there. What kind of directions to I need? (definite)
- A numbered system or device used to measure something is a what? (a scale) Tell your partner one way you use a *scale* in math class.
- To be a possible source of danger or discomfort is to what? (threaten) Sometimes people get angry and tell someone they will harm or injure him or her. What do they do to the person? (threaten him or her)
- The things or conditions around a person or place are what? (surroundings) Are your *surroundings* important to you if you want to go skiing? (yes)
- If something is kept going for a period of time it is what? (sustained) Let's practice *sustained* snapping for 10 seconds. Remember, don't quit . . . because we have to keep it going for a period of time.
- Something that is very great or strong is what? (intense) *Intense* words can often cause pain. We must keep our words what? (gentle)

Reading

Objectives

- Write questions or prompts about text to deepen comprehension.
- Use critical thinking skills to respond orally to specific questions about a text.

Guided Reading of "Hurricane!": Ask and Answer Questions

Remember, proficient readers reread text slowly and carefully to gain understanding. They monitor their thinking to be sure that each sentence and paragraph make sense. Good readers look for answers to Big Idea questions. In this unit, we are answering these questions: How are hurricanes formed? and How are hurricanes different from other storms?

Good readers also ask themselves and others questions about their reading. Challenging questions require readers to combine text and information in charts or maps with what they already know. Proficient readers understand that asking questions improves their own comprehension.

Direction Words: Extended Thinking poster

Direct students to the chart on page 16 in their Student Books or refer to the Extended Thinking poster if you have it displayed.

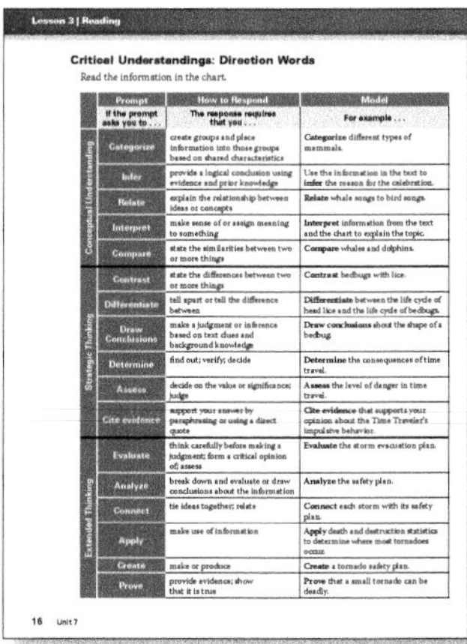
Lesson 3 | Reading

Critical Understandings: Direction Words

Read the information in the chart.

	Prompt If the prompt asks you to . . .	How to Respond The response requires that you . . .	Model For example . . .
Conceptual Understanding	Categorize	create groups and place information into those groups based on shared characteristics	**Categorize** different types of mammals.
	Infer	provide a logical conclusion using evidence and prior knowledge	Use the information in the text to **infer** the reason for the celebration.
	Relate	explain the relationship between ideas or concepts	**Relate** whale songs to bird songs.
	Interpret	make sense of or assign meaning to something	**Interpret** information from the text and the chart to explain the topic.
	Compare	state the similarities between two or more things	**Compare** whales and dolphins.
Strategic Thinking	Contrast	state the differences between two or more things	**Contrast** bedbugs with lice.
	Differentiate	tell apart or tell the difference between	**Differentiate** between the life cycle of head lice and the life cycle of bedbugs.
	Draw Conclusions	make a judgment or inference based on text clues and background knowledge	**Draw conclusions** about the shape of a bedbug.
	Determine	find out; verify; decide	**Determine** the consequences of time travel.
	Assess	decide on the value or significance; judge	**Assess** the level of danger in time travel.
	Cite evidence	support your answer by paraphrasing or using a direct quote	**Cite evidence** that supports your opinion about the Time Traveler's impulsive behavior.
Extended Thinking	Evaluate	think carefully before making a judgment; form a critical opinion of; assess	**Evaluate** the storm evacuation plan.
	Analyze	break down and evaluate or draw conclusions about the information	**Analyze** the safety plan.
	Connect	tie ideas together; relate	**Connect** each storm with its safety plan.
	Apply	make use of information	**Apply** death and destruction statistics to determine where most tornadoes occur.
	Create	make or produce	**Create** a tornado safety plan.
	Prove	provide evidence; show that it is true	**Prove** that a small tornado can be deadly.

16 Unit 7

We have been talking about how certain direction words require a specific response or answer. Your job is to review this chart with a partner. Remember how your roles are defined. Review the Chart Reading Procedure with students.

Chart Reading Procedure

- Group students with partners or in triads.
- Have students count off as 1s or 2s attempting to give all students a chance to be a student leader (1). If working with triads, the third student becomes a 2.
- Student leaders (1s) read the left column (Prompt) in addition to managing the time and turn-taking if working with a triad.
- The 2s explain the middle column of the chart (How to Respond). If working in triads, 2s take turns explaining the middle column.
- The 1s read the model in the right column (Model), and 2s restate the model as a question.
- All students should follow along with their pencil eraser while others are explaining the chart.
- Students must work from left to right, top to bottom in order to benefit from this activity.

Have student groups or pairs complete the Extended Thinking part of the chart (from Evaluate to Connect) in this manner.

This time, when we read "Hurricane!," we will ask questions about the text. Doing this will help us understand what is important. We will also answer the questions that we ask, which should clear up any confusion we had during the first read.

Direct students to page 173 in their Student Books or have them tear out the extra copy of "Hurricane!" from the back of their book.

Note: To minimize flipping back and forth between the pages, a copy of each text has been included in the back of the Student Books. Encourage students to tear this out and use it when working on activities that require the use of the text.

Let's do what good readers do and reread "Hurricane!" with our minds on asking and answering questions.

Remember what you do when you read. Your eyes need to track, or follow, the text while your pencil points to the words. While you're busy looking and pointing to text, your brain is busy looking for patterns and making meaning. While reading, be aware of questions that come to your mind and questions that you might ask others.

Eyes ready? Pencil ready? Let's begin.

Note: While the lessons are written for a teacher read aloud, it is important that your students read as much and as often as they can. Assign readings that meet the needs of your students, based on your observations or data. This is a good opportunity to stretch students, but if they become frustrated, return to the read-aloud method.

Read the first two paragraphs, lines 1–23.

Hurricane!

It's summer, and hurricane season is here! Hurricanes, otherwise known as tropical cyclones, are powerful storms that twist and spin. They can become very large, some covering an area hundreds of miles wide. These storms are feared because their strong winds, high tides, and heavy rains threaten life and property.

Hurricane season begins on June 1st and runs through November 30th. Warm, tropical water is necessary for hurricane development. The surface temperature of an ocean must be at least 80 degrees Fahrenheit, or 26 degrees Centigrade. However, hurricanes need more than warm water to develop. Low air pressure, moist ocean air, tropical winds, and warm air temperatures must come together to set the stage for hurricane development.

Direct students to page 194 in their Student Books. Think about the text. What questions do you still have? What should your peers have learned about hurricanes from this section?

- Choose one question word or prompt we have learned. Consider starting your question with *When*.
- If you want to challenge yourself to write a prompt, try using *Analyze*.
- Write the question or prompt on the page. Be prepared to answer your question or prompt orally. Remember, questions require a question mark. Prompts require a period.

Direct students back to the passage. Let's read the next paragraph. Eyes ready? Pencil ready? Let's begin.

Read the next paragraph, lines 23–34.

Lesson 5 | Reading

Ask and Answer Questions

Reread "Hurricane!" After each section, write a question or prompt for your partner to answer using question or direction words that you have learned so far. Try not to use the same word twice. Be prepared to answer your questions orally. Use the Critical Understandings chart or the poster to help you with the prompts.

Answers will vary.

First two paragraphs (lines 1–23) *When?* *Analyze*

1. ______________________________

Third paragraph (lines 24–34) *How?* *Evaluate*

2. ______________________________

Fourth and fifth paragraphs (lines 35–50) *What?* *Connect*

3. ______________________________

Sixth paragraph (lines 51–55) *Where?* *Determine*

4. ______________________________

How Are Hurricanes Categorized? (text and chart) *Compare* *Contrast* *Interpret*

5. ______________________________

194 Unit 10

Bands of low pressure and warm water temperatures fuel thunderstorms. Warm, wet air rises from the water's surface, condenses, and turns into clouds. The heat and moisture come together, and several strong thunderstorms form and combine. Then, tropical winds join the organized system of thunderstorms and begin to spin. The storm now has a definite and recognizable shape. When winds reach a sustained speed of 38 miles per hour, the storm becomes a tropical depression. If winds increase to speeds of 39 to 73 miles per hour, a tropical storm is born and given a name.

Direct students to page 194 in their Student Books.

- Choose a different question or direction word. Try using *How* or *Evaluate.*
- Write the question or prompt on the page. Be prepared to provide answers orally.

Direct students back to the passage. Let's read the next two paragraphs. Eyes ready? Pencil ready? Let's begin.

Read the next two paragraphs, lines 35–50.

Some tropical storms continue to build strength by feeding on warm, moist air. For a tropical storm to become a hurricane, its winds must strengthen to 74 miles per hour. These winds must be sustained, or steady, rather than gusty, or intermittent.

Hurricanes are not like ordinary storms. As the winds continue to strengthen, they spin and create an "eye." The eye can range from 5 miles to 120 miles in diameter! Although the very center of the eye is calm, the strongest winds are found in the eye wall. The towering clouds around the eye form a wind wall. This wall contains the strongest winds and the heaviest rains. The strong winds spin like a top around the eye. Their speeds are intense, sometimes approaching 200 miles per hour. If the hurricane hits land, flooding and destruction will follow.

Direct students to page 194 in their Student Books.

- Choose a different question or direction word. Try using *What* or *Connect.*
- Write the question or prompt on the page. Be prepared to provide answers orally.

Direct students back to the passage. Let's read the next paragraph. Eyes ready? Pencil ready? Let's begin.

Read the next paragraph, lines 51–55.

Eventually, a hurricane enters cold, unfriendly surroundings and begins to die. When it hits an area of cool land or water, it loses its supply of warm, moist air and there is nothing to feed it. Its winds begin to weaken, the eye disintegrates, and the storm finally dies.

Direct students to page 194 in their Student Books.

- Choose a different question or direction word. Try using *Where* or *Determine.*
- Write the question or prompt on the page. Be prepared to provide answers orally.

Direct students back to the passage. Let's read the last section. Eyes ready? Pencil ready? Let's begin.

Read the last section, How Are Hurricanes Categorized?, along with the chart.

How Are Hurricanes Categorized?

The hurricane scale is numbered one to five. Its categories are based on wind strength. These categories are described in the chart below.

Hurricane Intensity

Category	Wind Speed (mph)	Description of Damage
1	74–95	No real damage to buildings. Damage to mobile homes. Some damage to poorly built signs. Also, some coastal flooding. Minor pier damage.
2	96–110	Some damage to building roofs, doors, and windows. Considerable damage to mobile homes. Flooding damages piers. Small craft in unprotected moorings may break their moorings. Some trees blown down.
3	111–130	Some structural damage to small residences and utility buildings. Large trees blown down. Mobile homes and poorly built signs destroyed. Flooding near the coast destroys small structures. Large structures damaged by floating debris. Land may flood far inland.
4	131–155	More extensive wall failure. Some complete roof structure failure on small homes. Major erosion of beach areas. Land may flood very far inland.
5	156 and up	Many complete roof failures. Some complete buildings fail. Small utility buildings blown over or away. Major flood damage to lower floors. All structures near shoreline affected. Massive evacuation of residential areas.

Source: the Saffir-Simpson Hurricane Scale, www.nhc.noaa.gov/HAW2/english/basics/saffir_simpson.shtml

Direct students to page 194 in their Student Books.

- Choose a different question or direction word. Try using *Compare, Contrast,* or *Interpret.*
- Write the question or prompt on the page. Be prepared to provide answers orally.

Share Questions or Prompts

Have partners read their questions or prompts to each other and answer them orally, correcting each other if needed. Each pair shares with another pair, then those four share with four others if time permits. Have volunteers share their questions or prompts and responses with the class.

Writing

Objectives

- Use critical and extended thinking skills to write responses to prompts about a text.
- Support written answers with evidence from text.

Answer It: Direction Words

Direct students to pages 195 and 196 in their Student Books. Now, we will respond to prompts about "Hurricane!" for more practice. Some of the prompts may be similar to the prompts you already responded to.

- Read each prompt. Identify and underline the direction word.
- Use the Critical Understandings chart on page 16 or the Extended Thinking poster to review the information different types of prompts are asking for.
- Use text headings or other text features to locate the information you need to respond.
- Reread the section to retrieve exact information to use as text evidence. Use the direction word to formulate a response.

Don't forget to cite the line numbers from the passage to show where you found your evidence.

Direction Words: Extended Thinking poster

Lesson 5 | Writing

Answer It: Direction Words

Underline the direction word in each prompt. Then respond to each prompt using a complete sentence. Provide line numbers for the text evidence.

1. Evaluate the meaning of the name Spanish explorers gave to the violent storms they encountered in the Pacific Ocean.

   Answers will vary. Spanish explorers called the violent storms huracán, which means "evil wind." While the winds are definitely bad and cause great harm, in my opinion, the name is not a good one. Evil is something bad done on purpose. Hurricanes are a freak of nature, and therefore not done on purpose.

   Text Evidence: Bottom of page 176

2. Analyze the absence of hurricanes in the Arctic Ocean.

   Hurricanes are not prevalent in the Arctic Ocean because air and land temperatures do not allow for the water temperature to reach 80 degrees, which is the breeding temperature for hurricanes.

   Text Evidence: Lines 12–16

3. Connect hurricanes to seasons of the year.

   Hurricanes occur during the warm seasons of summer and fall.

   Text Evidence: Lines 8–15

Unit 10 195

Model

Read the first prompt aloud.

1. Evaluate the meaning of the name Spanish explorers gave to the violent storms they encountered in the Pacific Ocean.

What is the direction word? (evaluate) How do we respond to a prompt that asks us to *evaluate*? (think carefully before making a judgment)

Dictionary

I can change this prompt into a question to determine how best to respond. I would ask myself, Is the name given to the violent storms a valid name? Next, I need to look back in the text to see what Spanish explorers called the violent storms. I see they called them "evil winds." Before I make a judgment, I want to know the exact definition of *evil*. Have a volunteer find the definition in a dictionary.

Together, construct a response that evaluates the relationship between "evil wind" and a hurricane. (Spanish explorers called the violent storms *huracán*, which means "evil wind." While the winds are definitely bad and cause great harm, in my opinion, the name is not a good one. Evil is something bad done on purpose. Hurricanes are a freak of nature, and therefore not done on purpose.)

Guided Practice

Read the next prompt aloud.

2. Analyze the absence of hurricanes in the Arctic Ocean.

What is the direction word in this prompt? (analyze) How do we respond to a prompt that begins with *analyze*? (break information down, then draw a conclusion)

Have students change the prompt into a question and write the question on the board:

Why are hurricanes absent in the Arctic Ocean?

Work with your partner to respond to the prompt. Write a sentence starter before you return to the text for text evidence. While students work, write the sentence frame below on the board:

Hurricanes are not prevalent in the Arctic Ocean because ______.

Work with students to formulate the answer and have them write it on their Student Book page. (Hurricanes are not prevalent in the Arctic ocean because air and land temperatures do not allow for the water temperature to reach 80 degrees, which is the breeding temperature for hurricanes.)

What do we need to do next? (Find text evidence.)

Explain that the text does not mention the Arctic Ocean, but it does mention what is needed for a hurricane to develop. Students must put this information together with what they know about the Arctic to determine the answer. Provide work time before sharing the answer with students.

Independent Practice

Have students answer the remaining questions independently. Remind them to support their responses with evidence from the text. Create a small group for students who need more assistance, using prompt 3 as additional guided practice.

Note: Base the number of modeled and guided examples on student ability and progress. Challenge students with independent practice when appropriate.

Lesson 5 | Writing

Answer It: Direction Words (*cont.*) Answers will vary.

4. Connect the wall of a hurricane to property damage.

The wall of a hurricane contains the strongest winds and the heaviest rains. This means that property damage is more severe in the path of the wall.

Text Evidence: Lines 46–47

5. Analyze a storm's shift from tropical depression to hurricane.

When the spinning winds of a tropical depression increase to 39 miles per hour, the depression becomes a tropical storm. When the winds increase to 74 miles per hour, the storm becomes a hurricane. Hurricanes have stronger winds and heavier rains and cause more damage than a depression.

Text Evidence: Lines 31–50

6. Evaluate the recent change in hurricane naming.

Since 1953, hurricanes were given women's names. Recently, hurricane naming was changed to include male names as well. This change was good because it is more fair to have both women's and men's names.

Text Evidence: Bottom of page 177

196 Unit 10

Provide these alternative questions and sentence starters for those who need additional help.

3. How are hurricanes related to the seasons of the year?

   Hurricanes occur during ________________________.

4. How does the wall of a hurricane relate to property damage?

   The wall of a hurricane contains ________________________.
   This means that property damage ________________________.

5. How does a tropical depression turn into a hurricane?

   When the spinning winds of a tropical depression ____________,
   the depression becomes a ________________________.
   When the winds increase to 74 miles per hour, ________________.

6. Why was hurricane naming changed recently and was it a good change?

   Since 1953, hurricanes ________________________.
   Recently, hurricane naming was changed to include ____________.
   This change ________________________.

Unit 10

Lesson 6

Lesson Opener

Before the lesson, choose one of the following activities to write on the board or post on the *LANGUAGE! Live* Class Wall online.

- *Turn to your Key Passage Vocabulary chart. Complete your drawings and add information to definitions as needed.*
- *Write a compound sentence indicating the difference between a tropical depression and a tropical storm.*
- *Write two sentences about hurricanes using action verbs. In the second sentence, use a synonym for the action verb you used in the first sentence.*

Writing

Objectives

- Know spelling-sound correspondences for words with digraph *wh*.
- Know spelling-sound correspondences for words ending in *-es*.
- Know spelling-sound correspondences for words with /ng/ spelled *-n*.
- Know spelling-sound correspondences for words with nasal blends.

Spelling Words

Use this spelling activity to practice or assess the unit's spelling patterns students have learned online.

Direct students to Part A on page 197 in their Student Books. Read the instructions and remind students of the procedure for spelling. Use the spelling reminders to help struggling students.

1. which; Which kitten do you like best?
2. teaches; My mom teaches first grade.
3. claw; The cat's claw was sharp.
4. pink; Pink is my favorite color.
5. bank; Let's cash the check at the bank.
6. mint; I like to chew mint gum.
7. hands; I put lotion on my hands.
8. flosses; She flosses every night.
9. paw; The dog licked its paw.
10. white; We painted the room white.

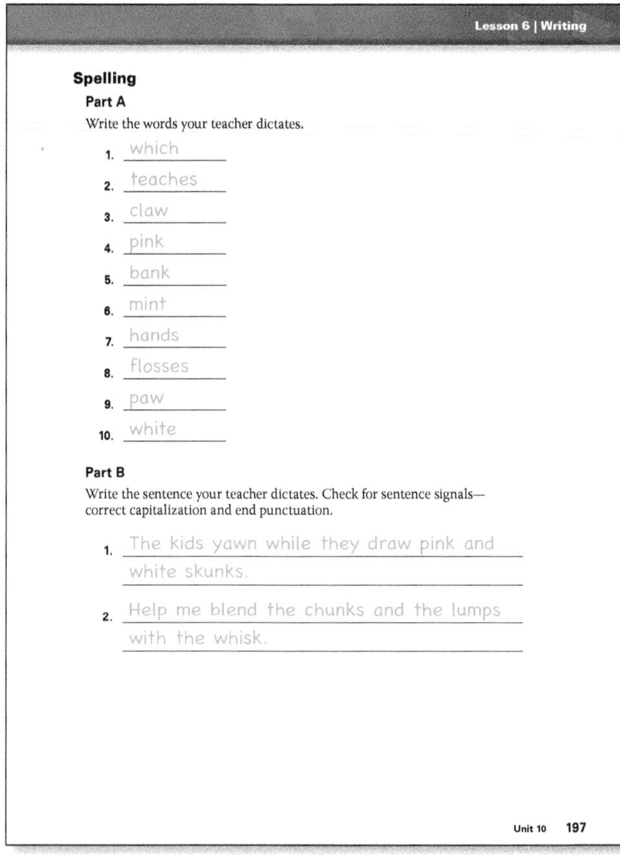
Lesson 6 | Writing

Spelling

Part A

Write the words your teacher dictates.

1. which
2. teaches
3. claw
4. pink
5. bank
6. mint
7. hands
8. flosses
9. paw
10. white

Part B

Write the sentence your teacher dictates. Check for sentence signals—correct capitalization and end punctuation.

1. The kids yawn while they draw pink and white skunks.
2. Help me blend the chunks and the lumps with the whisk.

Unit 10 197

Direct students to Part B on page 197 in their Student Books. Read the instructions and remind students of the procedure for sentence dictation.

The kids yawn while they draw pink and white skunks.

Help me blend the chunks and the lumps with the whisk.

Spelling Words Procedure

- Teacher reads the word.
- Students repeat the word.
- Teacher reads the sentence.
- Students write the word.
- Teacher reads the word a second time as students check their work.

Sentence Dictation Procedure

- Teacher reads the sentence.
- Students repeat the sentence.
- Students write the sentence.
- Teacher reads the sentence a second time as students check their work.

Spelling Reminders

Words with the Digraph *wh*
The digraph *wh* stands for /wh/, a sound that most of us don't say anymore in modern American English. It is very similar to /w/, so you need to listen carefully to determine which spelling pattern to use.

Word Ending in *-es*
When words end in hissy sounds, such as /s/, /ks/, /z/, /ch/, or /sh/, you add the syllable *-es* to make the words plural, and so you can say the ending and have other people hear it. Listen to how it is pronounced: *kisses, wishes, benches.* Remember to listen for the hissy sound before the final sound to make sure you are using the correct ending.

Words with /ng/ Spelled *-n*
The /ng/ sound is spelled with an *n* when it comes before the phoneme /k/, such as in words with the patterns *-ink, -ank, -onk,* and *-unk.* In these words, /k/ is usually spelled with the letter *k.*

Words with Nasal Blends
Remember, a blend is two or more consonants before or after a vowel in a syllable. Some consonant blends have nasal sounds, such as *mp, nd,* and *nt.* Remember to listen carefully for all the sounds in a word.

Vocabulary

Objectives

- Use context to determine the meaning of words in text.
- Consult reference materials to clarify the precise meaning of words.
- Demonstrate an understanding of synonym word analogies.
- Write synonym word analogies.

Define It

Direct students to page 198 in their Student Books.

To define a word we need to understand the word's category and attributes.

Categories are broad groups. Attributes are things like size, shape, color, texture, and function. In this lesson we will define three types of storms. This is a great way to help you understand the differences in the storms.

Lesson 6 | Vocabulary

Define It

Determine the category and attributes of each word. Then write the definition.

Word		Category		Attributes
tropical depression	=	storm	+	system of thunderstorms; over water; tropical winds; sustained speed of 38 mph

Definition: A tropical depression is a storm over water created by a system of thunderstorms and tropical winds with a sustained speed of 38 miles per hour.

Word		Category		Attributes
tropical storm	=	storm	+	system of thunderstorms; over water; tropical winds; sustained speed of 39–73 mph; given a name

Definition: A tropical storm is a named storm over water created by a system of thunderstorms and tropical winds with a sustained speed of 39 to 73 miles per hour.

Word		Category		Attributes
hurricane	=	storm	+	system of thunderstorms; over water; tropical winds; sustained speed of 74 mph or greater; with an eye in the center; causes flooding and destruction

Definition: A hurricane is a destructive storm over water created by a system of thunderstorms and tropical winds with a sustained speed of 74 miles per hour or greater.

Word		Category		Attributes

Definition:

198 Unit 10

Model

Direct students to the third paragraph of "Hurricane!" and have them find the words *tropical depression.* We may not know what a *tropical depression* is, but we can look at the context around the term to determine its category and attributes. Because the preceding sentence talks about a storm, I know that the category *tropical depression* fits into is *storm.* A tropical depression is a storm.

Now I will read the entire paragraph to see if I can come up with attributes of a *tropical depression.* The text says that it is a system of thunderstorms. It occurs over water. It has fast tropical winds, and these winds have a sustained speed of 38 miles per hour. If its winds are faster than that, it becomes another type of storm.

These are all attributes of a *tropical depression.* I didn't need any prior knowledge about the term to figure out its meaning. I just had to read closely. Now that I have identified the term's category and attributes, I can write a definition for it. Write the definition on the board and read it aloud:

> *A tropical depression is a storm over water created by a system of thunderstorms and tropical winds with a sustained speed of 38 miles per hour.*

Have students write the definition in their Student Books.

Guided and Independent Practice

Dictionaries

Repeat the process for the second word, allowing students to provide the category, attributes, and definition for you. Then have partners complete the activity. Explain that they may choose and define any vocabulary word from the passage for the last item. Have partners verify their definitions in a dictionary and make corrections as needed.

> **Note:** Base the number of modeled and guided examples on student ability and progress. Challenge them with independent practice when appropriate.

Synonym Analogies

An analogy is a logic problem based on two pairs of words that have the same relationship. Write the following antonym analogy on the board:

sad : happy :: dirty : clean

There are various types of analogies. In the last unit, we studied antonym analogies, which compared sets of words that are opposites. Point to the analogy on the board and read it: Sad is to happy as dirty is to clean. Point to the symbols as you say the corresponding words. The colon between *sad* and *happy* tells us that they are connected. The colon between *dirty* and *clean* tells us they are connected. The double colons between the pairs of words tell us that the word pairs are connected in the same way.

Today we will learn about a different type of analogy: synonym analogies. What are synonyms? (words with a similar meaning) A synonym of *near* is what? (close) A synonym of *angry* is what? (mad) A synonym analogy compares two pairs of words that are synonyms. An example would be: *happy is to joyful as pretty is to beautiful. Happy* and *joyful* are synonyms, and *pretty* and *beautiful* are synonyms. The first two words describe positive feelings, and the second two words describe something pleasing to the eye.

A word problem showing two pairs of words that have the same relationship is called a what? (an analogy)

Words that are similar are called what? (synonyms)

A word problem made up of two pairs of synonyms is called a what? (a synonym analogy)

Direct students to page 199 in their Student Books and read the instructions aloud.

Model

Then direct students' attention to the first item.

Let's look at the first item. *Correct* is to *right*. *Correct* and *right* are synonyms. This means that the second pair of words will also be synonyms. I see that the first word in that pair is *begin*, so I will need to find a word that means almost the same as *begin*. I see the word *start* in the word bank, and I know *begin* and *start* are synonyms. Together they would complete the first synonym analogy. Both sets of words are synonyms. We would read the analogy this way: Correct is to right as begin is to start.

Have students say the analogy using the pattern. (Correct is to right as begin is to start.)

Synonym Analogies

Read the incomplete synonym analogies. Identify the missing word from the word bank and write it on the line.

Word Bank

closed	jog	fast	sharp	rich	smile	middle	spoiled
mug	form	last	quit	shut	thin	loud	windy
grin	pal	shape	sly	speak	ill	smart	
little	sick	end	cup	hop	jump	start	
lid	cap	big	wet	damp	grand	supper	

1. correct : right :: begin : start
2. large : big :: intelligent : smart
3. stroll : walk :: loud : noisy
4. windy : breezy :: dinner : supper
5. spoiled : ruined :: center : middle
6. wealthy : rich :: friend : pal
7. pointed : sharp :: run : jog
8. thin : slim :: little : small
9. quick : fast :: quit : stop
10. speak : talk :: sneaky : sly

Challenge:

11. shape : form :: last : end
12. closed : shut :: smile : grin
13. sick : ill :: cup : mug
14. cap : lid :: hop : jump
15. wet : damp :: big : grand

Guided Practice

Direct students to the second item. Have a volunteer read the first part of the analogy using the words *is to*. *Large* and *big* are synonyms. The next word is *intelligent*. What is a synonym of *intelligent*? (smart) Have students complete the analogy on the page.

Independent Practice

Have partners complete the remaining analogies through number 10. Review the answers as a class.

Explain that the last five analogies will be made with words that haven't yet been used. Challenge students to write analogies using words from the bank. Review the answers as a class.

Note: Base the number of modeled and guided examples on student ability and progress. Challenge them with independent practice when appropriate.

Writing

Objective

- Write sentences using concrete words and phrases and sensory details to convey information precisely.

Masterpiece Sentences

Masterpiece Sentences poster

Direct students to pages 200 and 201 in their Student Books. You are going to work through all six stages of Masterpiece Sentences. Review the stages of Masterpiece Sentences.

I have a challenge for you. Your goal is to describe a picture so vividly that anyone could match your sentence with the picture. Choose one picture on this page as your writing prompt. Work through each stage of Masterpiece Sentences, writing your ideas next to the painter questions. Write your final sentence on the line at the bottom of the page.

Have students write their Masterpiece Sentence. Explain that each student will try to match his or her sentence to the correct picture in a later lesson.

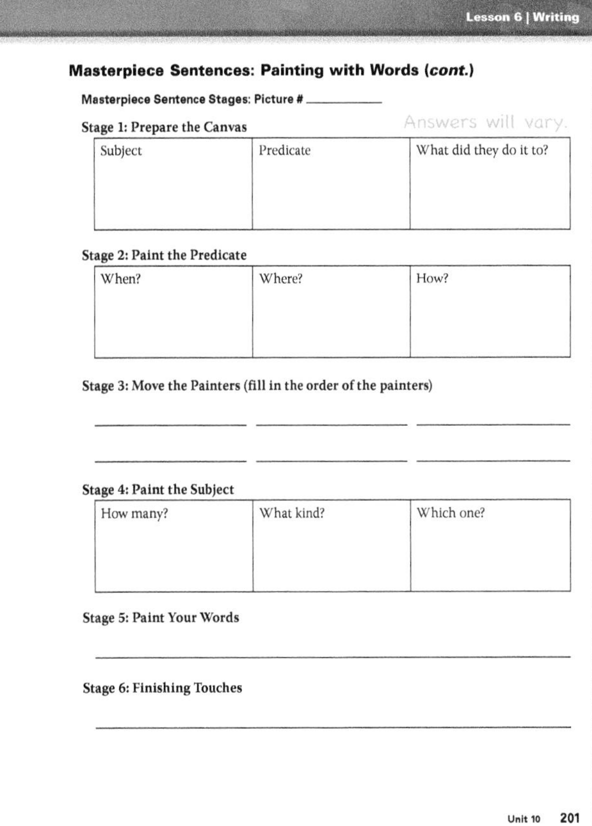

Reading

Objectives

- Review text features in a text.
- Draw evidence from a graph and a chart to answer questions.

Informational Text Features

In every unit we have examined the features of the texts we've read. We've focused on section headers, boldfaced words, and captions that go with pictures. In this unit, our selection gives a great deal of information in charts and graphs. Charts and graphs help us understand a text more deeply by offering information in a clear and visual way.

Direct students to the "Hurricane!" text on page 173 in their Student Books or have them tear out the extra copy of "Hurricane!" from the back of their book.

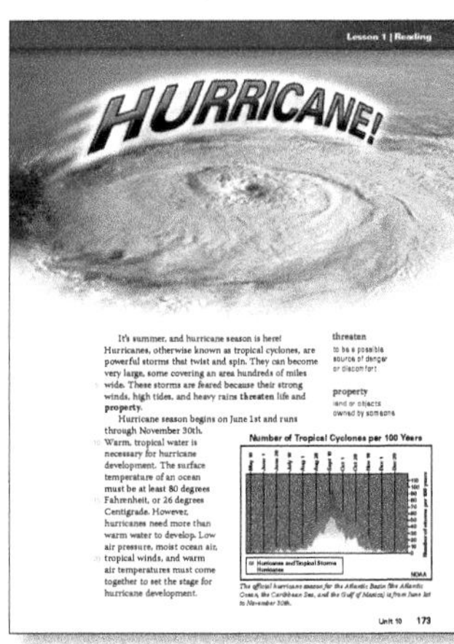

Note: To minimize flipping back and forth between the pages, a copy of each text has been included in the back of the Student Books. Encourage students to tear this out and use it when working on activities that require the use of the text.

Let's take a closer look at these features in "Hurricane!" Look at the graph on page 173. With just one glance at this graph, we can easily see the most active months for hurricane development. Don't forget to pay attention to the captions. They often elaborate or clarify the visual images.

Next, have students turn to the Hurricane Intensity chart on page 175. Review the features of the chart. Remind them of the differences between a chart and a graph. Now, I want you to use information from either the graph on page 173 or the chart on this page to answer some questions.

Have one student in each pair turn to page 202 in their Student Books, while the other remains on the text page. Read each question and have students answer it aloud before writing the answer in their books. For each question, ask students where they found the information. Remind them that each answer needs to be written in a complete sentence. Review the answers as a class.

Lesson 6 | Reading

Answer It: Using Visuals

Use the graph and the chart in the passage "Hurricane!" to answer the following questions in complete sentences.

1. Historically, what month has the most number of tropical cyclones, or hurricanes?
   Historically, September has the most hurricanes.
2. What are the dates for the hurricane season in the Atlantic Basin?
   The hurricane season for the Atlantic Basin runs from June 1st to November 30th.
3. What are the wind speeds of a Category 3 hurricane?
   A Category 3 hurricane has wind speeds of 111–130 mph.
4. Is a storm with winds of 69 mph considered a hurricane?
   No, a storm with winds of 69 mph would not be classified as a hurricane.
5. If a hurricane had sustained winds of 175 mph, what category would it be?
   A hurricane with winds of 175 mph would be a Category 5.

202 Unit 10

Unit 10

Lesson 7

Lesson Opener

Before the lesson, choose one of the following activities to write on the board or post on the *LANGUAGE! Live* Class Wall online.

- *Finish and/or revise your Masterpiece Sentence describing one of the storm pictures.*
- *If your home was destroyed by a hurricane, who would come help you clean up? Why do you think they would come?*
- *Write a compound sentence with an action verb and a linking verb.*

Reading

Objectives

- Read with purpose and understanding.
- Identify and explain explicit details from text.
- Take notes on a text.
- Identify idioms in text.

Guided Highlighting of "Hurricane!"

We have been working diligently to become great readers. We preview the text. We reread text slowly and carefully to gain understanding. And we look for answers to Big Idea questions. In this unit, we've been exploring answers to the questions, How are hurricanes formed? and How are hurricanes different from other storms?

There are a lot of reasons to become a better reader. Proficient readers recognize and understand figurative language such as idioms, similes, and metaphors. They can identify and use figurative language when speaking, listening, and writing. Skilled readers can also identify an author's purpose, or reason for writing text. They can then make judgments about the author's point of view by assessing his or her claims, reasoning, and evidence. Proficient readers can also make connections between information in a text and information learned from other sources.

Let's do what skilled readers do and reread "Hurricane!"

Green, yellow, and pink highlighters or colored pencils

Have students get out a colored pencil or highlighter.

Direct students to pages 203–205 in their Student Books. We will review the text features of nonfiction or expository text. Please use your writing utensil to mark your text according to my instructions.

- Draw a rectangle around the title, "Hurricane!"
- Circle the chart.

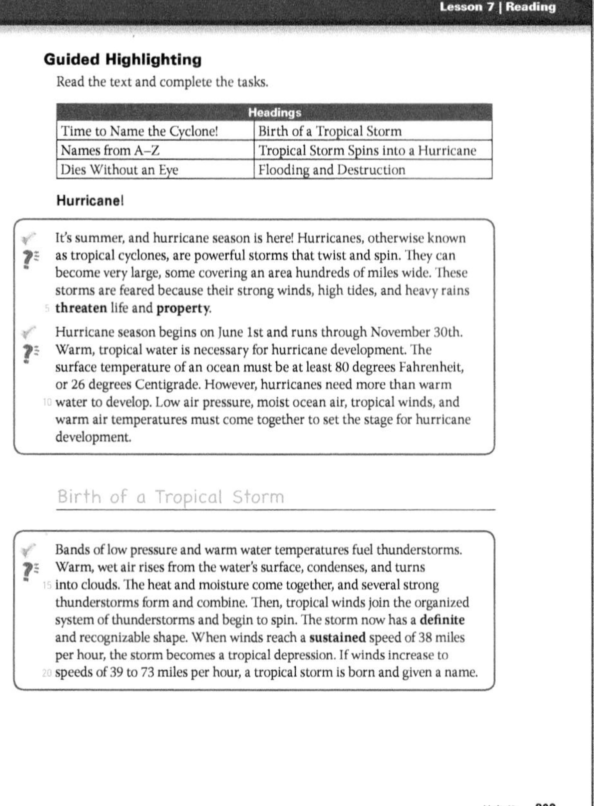

Lesson 7 | Reading

Guided Highlighting

Read the text and complete the tasks.

Headings	
Time to Name the Cyclone!	Birth of a Tropical Storm
Names from A–Z	Tropical Storm Spins into a Hurricane
Dies Without an Eye	Flooding and Destruction

Hurricane!

It's summer, and hurricane season is here! Hurricanes, otherwise known as tropical cyclones, are powerful storms that twist and spin. They can become very large, some covering an area hundreds of miles wide. These storms are feared because their strong winds, high tides, and heavy rains **threaten** life and **property**.

Hurricane season begins on June 1st and runs through November 30th. Warm, tropical water is necessary for hurricane development. The surface temperature of an ocean must be at least 80 degrees Fahrenheit, or 26 degrees Centigrade. However, hurricanes need more than warm water to develop. Low air pressure, moist ocean air, tropical winds, and warm air temperatures must come together to set the stage for hurricane development.

Birth of a Tropical Storm

Bands of low pressure and warm water temperatures fuel thunderstorms. Warm, wet air rises from the water's surface, condenses, and turns into clouds. The heat and moisture come together, and several strong thunderstorms form and combine. Then, tropical winds join the organized system of thunderstorms and begin to spin. The storm now has a **definite** and recognizable shape. When winds reach a **sustained** speed of 38 miles per hour, the storm becomes a tropical depression. If winds increase to speeds of 39 to 73 miles per hour, a tropical storm is born and given a name.

Unit 10 203

Listen and mark each bold vocabulary word as I read it aloud. I'm going to pause after every word to give you time to process whether you know the word and its meaning. We will review your ratings from Lesson 1 after we finish.

- threaten—*Threaten* means "to be a source of danger or discomfort." Say *threaten*. (threaten) Ordinary storms do not *threaten* our life or property.
- property—*Property* means "land or objects owned by someone." Say *property*. (property) Our *property* was secured before the storm.
- definite—*Definite* means "firm and clear, or exact." Say *definite*. (definite) The hurricane has a *definite* path.
- sustained—*Sustained* means "kept going for a period of time." Say *sustained*. (sustained) The *sustained* winds strengthen throughout the storm.
- ordinary—*Ordinary* means "not special or different in any way." Say *ordinary*. (ordinary) A hurricane starts out as an *ordinary* storm.
- intense—*Intense* means "very great or strong." Say *intense*. (intense) *Intense* storms require a safety plan.
- surroundings—*Surroundings* describes "the things or conditions around a person or place." Say *surroundings*. (surroundings) The *surroundings* were evacuated because of the storm.
- scale—A *scale* is "a numbered system or device used to measure something." Say *scale*. (scale) The hurricane *scale* goes from one to five.

With a partner talk about any vocabulary word that is still confusing for you to read or understand. Share your ratings from Lesson 1. Were you honest about your word knowledge? Now is the time to do something about it!

Give students time to discuss their understanding of the vocabulary words with a partner.

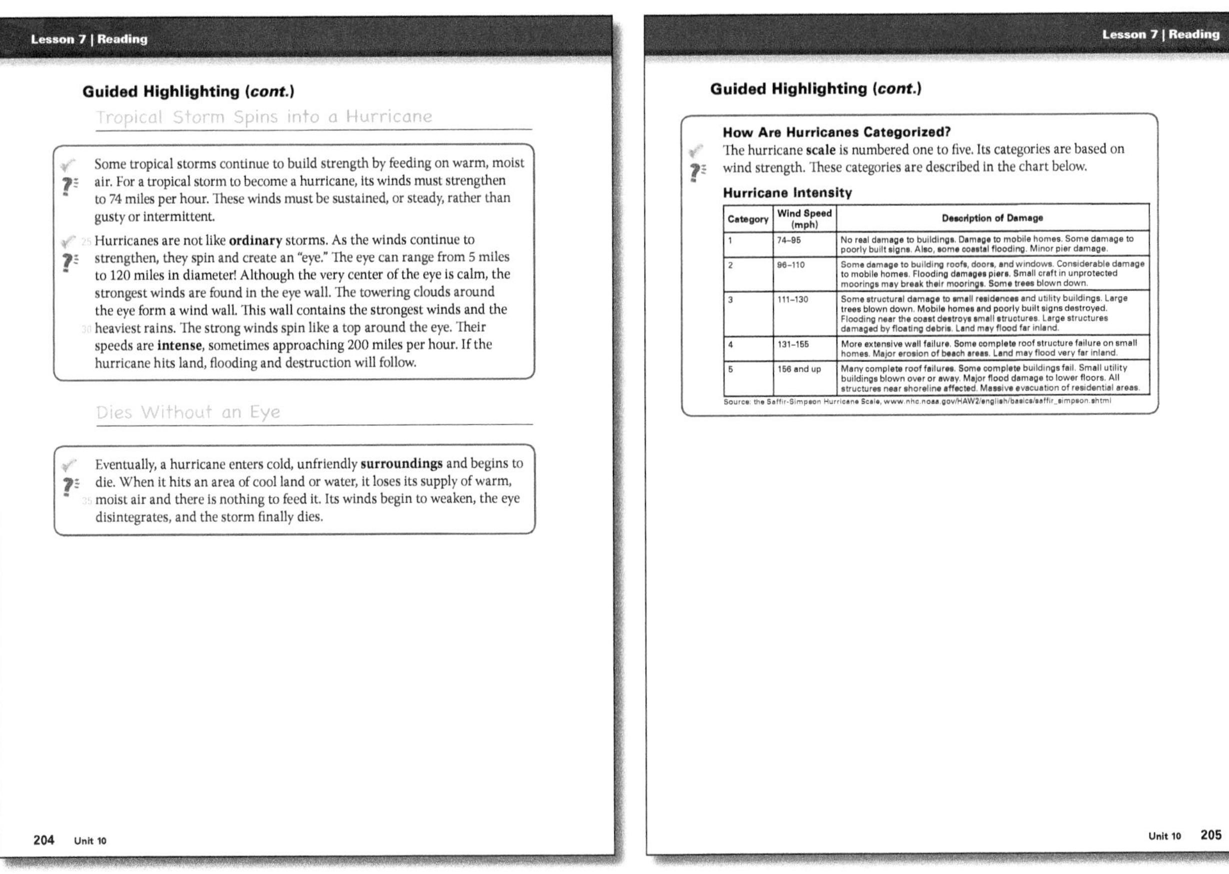

Lesson 7 | Reading

Guided Highlighting (*cont.*)

Tropical Storm Spins into a Hurricane

Some tropical storms continue to build strength by feeding on warm, moist air. For a tropical storm to become a hurricane, its winds must strengthen to 74 miles per hour. These winds must be sustained, or steady, rather than gusty or intermittent.

Hurricanes are not like **ordinary** storms. As the winds continue to strengthen, they spin and create an "eye." The eye can range from 5 miles to 120 miles in diameter! Although the very center of the eye is calm, the strongest winds are found in the eye wall. The towering clouds around the eye form a wind wall. This wall contains the strongest winds and the heaviest rains. The strong winds spin like a top around the eye. Their speeds are **intense**, sometimes approaching 200 miles per hour. If the hurricane hits land, flooding and destruction will follow.

Dies Without an Eye

Eventually, a hurricane enters cold, unfriendly **surroundings** and begins to die. When it hits an area of cool land or water, it loses its supply of warm, moist air and there is nothing to feed it. Its winds begin to weaken, the eye disintegrates, and the storm finally dies.

204 Unit 10

Lesson 7 | Reading

Guided Highlighting (*cont.*)

How Are Hurricanes Categorized?

The hurricane **scale** is numbered one to five. Its categories are based on wind strength. These categories are described in the chart below.

Hurricane Intensity

Category	Wind Speed (mph)	Description of Damage
1	74–95	No real damage to buildings. Damage to mobile homes. Some damage to poorly built signs. Also, some coastal flooding. Minor pier damage.
2	96–110	Some damage to building roofs, doors, and windows. Considerable damage to mobile homes. Flooding damages piers. Small craft in unprotected moorings may break their moorings. Some trees blown down.
3	111–130	Some structural damage to small residences and utility buildings. Large trees blown down. Mobile homes and poorly built signs destroyed. Flooding near the coast destroys small structures. Large structures damaged by floating debris. Land may flood far inland.
4	131–155	More extensive wall failure. Some complete roof structure failure on small homes. Major erosion of beach areas. Land may flood very far inland.
5	156 and up	Many complete roof failures. Some complete buildings fail. Small utility buildings blown over or away. Major flood damage to lower floors. All structures near shoreline affected. Massive evacuation of residential areas.

Source: the Saffir-Simpson Hurricane Scale, www.nhc.noaa.gov/HAW2/english/basics/saffir_simpson.shtml

Unit 10 205

It's time to reread the text the way proficient readers do. You will read the text "Hurricane!" one section at a time. After each section, you will monitor your understanding by circling the check mark or the question mark. Remember, good readers are honest about what they don't know and they do something about it. Please be sure to draw a question mark over any confusing words, phrases, or sentences. I will provide specific instructions on how to mark the text that will help with your comprehension and writing.

With eyes on text, listen to each section as it is read to you. Use your pencil eraser to follow along.

Note: If you feel your students are capable, instruct them to highlight the main idea of each paragraph or section in green, and the supporting details in yellow. Then make all additional marks in another color.

Let's read the first two paragraphs, lines 1–12. Read the paragraphs.

Note: While the lessons are written for a teacher read aloud, it is important that your students read as much and as often as they can. Assign readings that meet the needs of your students, based on your observations or data. This is a good opportunity to stretch students, but if they become frustrated, return to the read-aloud method.

Hurricane!

It's summer, and hurricane season is here! Hurricanes, otherwise known as tropical cyclones, are powerful storms that twist and spin. They can become very large, some covering an area hundreds of miles wide. These storms are feared because their strong winds, high tides, and heavy rains threaten life and property.

Hurricane season begins on June 1st and runs through November 30th. Warm, tropical water is necessary for hurricane development. The surface temperature of an ocean must be at least 80 degrees Fahrenheit, or 26 degrees Centigrade. However, hurricanes need more than warm water to develop. Low air pressure, moist ocean air, tropical winds, and warm air temperatures must come together to set the stage for hurricane development.

- Circle the check mark or question mark for each paragraph. Draw a question mark over any confusing words or phrases.
- Go to line 2. Mark the phrase that means the same as *hurricanes*. (tropical cyclones)
- Go to lines 2–5. Underline the key details that describe hurricanes. (powerful storms, twist and spin, very large, covering an area hundreds of miles wide, strong winds, high tides and heavy rains, threaten life and property)
- Go to line 6. Mark the phrase that answers *when* hurricane season occurs. (June 1st and runs through November 30th)
- Review lines 9 and 10. Number five conditions that make a hurricane possible or likely. (1. warm water; 2. low air pressure; 3. moist ocean air; 4. tropical winds; 5. warm air temperatures)
- Go to line 11. Mark the idiom that means "make it possible or likely." (set the stage)

Let's read the next paragraph, lines 13–20. Read the paragraph.

Bands of low pressure and warm water temperatures fuel thunderstorms. Warm, wet air rises from the water's surface, condenses, and turns into clouds. The heat and moisture come together, and several strong thunderstorms form and combine. Then, tropical winds join the organized system of thunderstorms and begin to spin. The storm now has a definite and recognizable shape. When winds reach a sustained speed of 38 miles per hour, the storm becomes a tropical depression. If winds increase to speeds of 39 to 73 miles per hour, a tropical storm is born and given a name.

- Circle the check mark or question mark for the paragraph. Draw a question mark over any confusing words or phrases.
- Go to line 13. Mark the word that means "provide energy for." (fuel)
- Go to lines 16 and 17. Mark what joins the thunderstorm that causes it to spin. (tropical winds)
- Choose a heading for this section from the Headings text bank. Record the heading on the line above this section. (Birth of a Tropical Storm)

Let's read the next two paragraphs, lines 21–32. Read the paragraphs.

Some tropical storms continue to build strength by feeding on warm, moist air. For a tropical storm to become a hurricane, its winds must strengthen to 74 miles per hour. These winds must be sustained, or steady, rather than gusty, or intermittent.

Hurricanes are not like ordinary storms. As the winds continue to strengthen, they spin and create an "eye." The eye can range from 5 miles to 120 miles in diameter! Although the very center of the eye is calm, the strongest winds are found in the eye wall. The towering clouds around the eye form a wind wall. This wall contains the strongest winds and the heaviest rains. The strong winds spin like a top around the eye. Their speeds are intense, sometimes approaching 200 miles per hour. If the hurricane hits land, flooding and destruction will follow.

- Circle the check mark or question mark for each paragraph. Draw a question mark over any confusing words or phrases.
- Go to lines 21–26. Number four conditions of a hurricane. (1. winds strengthen; 2. warm, moist air feeds it; 3. sustained winds of at least 74 mph; 4. strong winds spin around the eye)
- Go to line 24. Mark the antonym of *sustained.* (intermittent)
- Go to line 27. Mark the adjective that describes the center of the eye. (calm)
- Go to line 28. Mark the synonym for *tall.* (towering)
- In lines 28 and 29, mark what is created by clouds around the eye. (wind wall)

- Mark what happens in this wind wall. (the strongest winds and the heaviest rains)
- Go to line 30. Mark the simile. Circle two things that are being compared. (spin like a top; circle winds, top)
- Go to line 32. Mark the word that means "arrives on." (hits)
- On the same line, mark the effects of a hurricane that hits land. (flooding and destruction)
- Choose a heading for this section from the Headings text bank. Record the heading on the line above this section. (Tropical Storm Spins into a Hurricane)

Let's read the next paragraph, lines 33–36. Read the paragraph.

> Eventually, a hurricane enters cold, unfriendly surroundings and begins to die. When it hits an area of cool land or water, it loses its supply of warm, moist air and there is nothing to feed it. Its winds begin to weaken, the eye disintegrates, and the storm finally dies.

- Circle the check mark or question mark for the paragraph. Draw a question mark over any confusing words or phrases.
- Go to line 33. Mark the transition that means "sooner or later." (eventually)
- Mark the reason that hurricanes begin to die. (enters cold, unfriendly surroundings)
- Mark the reason the hurricane goes hungry and weakens. (it loses its supply of warm, moist air)
- Number the three things that happen once a hurricane hits an area of cool land or water. (1. winds begin to weaken; 2. the eye disintegrates; 3. the storm finally dies)
- Choose a heading for this section from the Headings text bank. Record the heading on the line above this section. (Dies Without an Eye)

Let's read the last paragraph, How Are Hurricanes Categorized? Read the section and the information in the chart.

How Are Hurricanes Categorized?

The hurricane scale is numbered one to five. Its categories are based on wind strength. These categories are described in the chart below.

Hurricane Intensity

Category	Wind Speed (mph)	Description of Damage
1	74–95	No real damage to buildings. Damage to mobile homes. Some damage to poorly built signs. Also, some coastal flooding. Minor pier damage.
2	96–110	Some damage to building roofs, doors, and windows. Considerable damage to mobile homes. Flooding damages piers. Small craft in unprotected moorings may break their moorings. Some trees blown down.
3	111–130	Some structural damage to small residences and utility buildings. Large trees blown down. Mobile homes and poorly built signs destroyed. Flooding near the coast destroys small structures. Large structures damaged by floating debris. Land may flood far inland.
4	131–155	More extensive wall failure. Some complete roof structure failure on small homes. Major erosion of beach areas. Land may flood very far inland.
5	156 and up	Many complete roof failures. Some complete buildings fail. Small utility buildings blown over or away. Major flood damage to lower floors. All structures near shoreline affected. Massive evacuation of residential areas.

Source: the Saffir-Simpson Hurricane Scale, www.nhc.noaa.gov/HAW2/english/basics/saffir_simpson.shtml

- Circle the check mark or question mark for the section. Draw a question mark over any confusing words or phrases.
- Go to line 38. Mark the synonym for *intensity.* (strength)
- Look at the chart heading. Mark the synonym for *destruction.* (damage)
- Look at the description of damage for each category. Mark what happens to buildings. (1: no real damage; 2: damage to roofs, doors, and windows; 3: structural damage to small residences and buildings; 4: extensive wall failure and some complete roof structure failure on small homes; 5: many complete roof failures; some complete buildings fail)

Have partners compare text markings and correct any errors.

Unit 10 Lesson 8

Lesson Opener

Before the lesson, choose one of the following activities to write on the board or post on the *LANGUAGE! Live* Class Wall online.

- *Complete the analogies:* Spin : whirl :: season : _____; Intense : weak :: definite : _____.
- *Write a Masterpiece Sentence about a hurricane that wrecked your neighborhood.*
- *Evaluate your avatar's connection to the real you.*

Writing

Objectives

- Gather relevant information from notes about a text.
- Organize information from a text into notes.
- Write clear introductory topic and concluding sentences.
- Write a constructed response to a prompt.
- Develop the written response with concrete facts and details and inferential thinking.
- Edit text for basic conventions.
- Strengthen writing by editing for voice.

Prepare to Write

Direct students to page 206 in their Student Books. Read the prompt aloud. Let's analyze our prompt and see where we need to focus as we take notes on "Hurricane!"

What is our topic? (hurricane's appearance, potential threat, and aftermath) We will need to look for specific information about these elements in our Guided Highlighting notes. The prompt also asks us to focus on a specific category of storm, so you need to choose a Category 3 or higher storm to describe.

Lesson 8 | Writing

Prepare to Write

Part A. Study the Prompt Answers will vary.

Read the prompt and identify the topic, directions, and purpose.

Write a constructed response that evaluates the appearance, potential threat, and aftermath of a major hurricane making landfall. Designate a specific category for the storm, and include details from the text in your evaluation.

Topic: hurricane's appearance, potential threat, and aftermath

Directions: write a constructed response; evaluate; specific category

Purpose for writing: think deeply about hurricanes and their impact

Part B. Write the Topic Sentence: Two-Sentence Introduction

Write a sentence that introduces the topic and a second sentence that sets the scope of your response.

Hurricanes have distinctive features and characteristics. If a Category 4 hurricane makes landfall, it leaves destruction and disruption in its path.

Part C. Write the Concluding Sentence: Two-Sentence Conclusion

Write a two-sentence conclusion that paraphrases your introduction and summarizes your response.

Hurricanes are unique and dangerous storms. Long after the storm has passed, people are struggling to put their lives back together.

206 Unit 10

Two-Column Notes

Direct students to pages 207 and 208. On page 207, at the top of the Two-Column Notes template, you see the word *Topic*. Use the information from the prompt to fill in that section.

What are the three things we're going to evaluate about a hurricane? (appearance, potential threat, and aftermath) Let's write those in the left-hand column of the template, leaving space for notes about each aspect of a hurricane.

Have partners use their Guided Highlighting notes on pages 203–205 to complete the Two-Column Notes.

If necessary, use the following to guide students.

- What words or phrases in the first section are noteworthy or related to our prompt? (Possible descriptors: large, spinning storm with strong winds, heavy rains, and high tides.) Where should you write notes about the storm's appearance? (on the Two-Column Notes next to the word Appearance)
- What's in the next section that is noteworthy? (Tropical winds cause the storm to spin.)
- Where will you write these notes? (next to Appearance)
- What's in the third section that is noteworthy? (eye wall, the description of the spinning motion, flooding, and destruction)
- Does the final paragraph contain any information related to our topic? (Possible response: eye disintegrates and storm weakens once it hits cool land.)
- Decide what category of storm you are going to describe, and write notes on the Two-Column

Lesson 8 | Writing

Two-Column Notes: "Hurricane!"

Take notes about the elements of the category of storm you have chosen.

Topic: Appearance, potential threat, and aftermath of a Category ___ hurricane	
☆Appearance	– large, spinning storm with strong winds, heavy rains, high tides
	– tropical winds create the spinning movement—spins like a top
	– spinning winds create eye—strongest winds in the wall around the eye—eye can range from 5–120 miles in diameter
	– on cool land, winds diminish and eye disintegrates—becomes more like a regular, ordinary storm
☆Potential threat	– Notes will vary according to the strength of the storm students are writing about.
	– flooding
	– tidal surge related to tide schedule and wind strength
	– winds ranging from ___ to ___

Unit 10 207

Lesson 8 | Writing

Two-Column Notes: "Hurricane!" ***(cont.)***

	– structural damage
	–
☆Aftermath—disruptions (outside of text)	– shelter—cannot live in home, living with family—several households in one home—may even be in another town
	– basic services—electricity, water
	– normal routines—school, work, getting around
	– supplies at local stores

208 Unit 10

Notes. Have students share what category of storm they have chosen and the kind of damage that storm can do.

We will consider another aspect of the storm not discussed in the text of "Hurricane!" Think about peoples' lives. What are some examples of daily routines, or things people do every day? (Possible responses: go to work, go to the store, go to school, prepare meals, watch TV or use the computer, use electronics for entertainment, visit people)

How does a storm affect peoples' lives after the storm is over? I want you to look at the damage and analyze it. What effect would this damage have on people in the days or weeks following a storm?

We have been responding to direction words that require us to use outside information. This is no different. Encourage students to brainstorm examples of disrupted routines and write them on the board. Have students choose details they want to incorporate into their response and write them in the aftermath section of the Two-Column Notes template on page 208 of their Student Books.

Write a Topic Sentence

Now that we've taken all of our notes for the writing assignment, let's work on our topic sentence. Direct students to page 206 in their Student Books and discuss possible topic sentences. Use the following two-sentence topic sentence as a guide to prompt student sentences.

Hurricanes have distinctive features and characteristics. If a Category 4 hurricane makes landfall, it leaves destruction and disruption in its path.

Now that we've written our topic sentence, we need to write our conclusion. It should be a restatement of our introduction. Use the following conclusion as a guide to prompt students to write their own conclusions.

Hurricanes are unique and dangerous storms. Long after the storm has passed, people are struggling to put their lives back together.

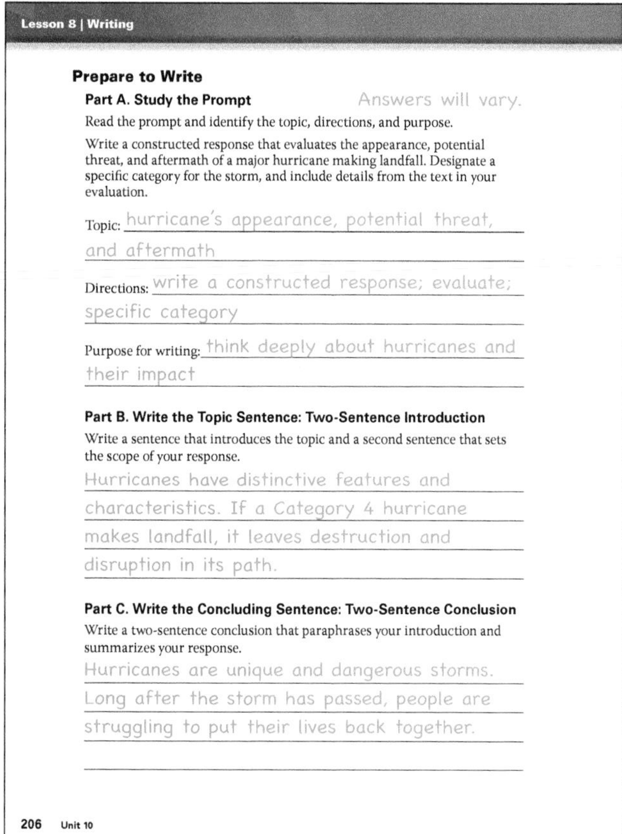
Lesson 8 | Writing

Prepare to Write

Part A. Study the Prompt Answers will vary.

Read the prompt and identify the topic, directions, and purpose.

Write a constructed response that evaluates the appearance, potential threat, and aftermath of a major hurricane making landfall. Designate a specific category for the storm, and include details from the text in your evaluation.

Topic: hurricane's appearance, potential threat, and aftermath

Directions: write a constructed response; evaluate; specific category

Purpose for writing: think deeply about hurricanes and their impact

Part B. Write the Topic Sentence: Two-Sentence Introduction

Write a sentence that introduces the topic and a second sentence that sets the scope of your response.

Hurricanes have distinctive features and characteristics. If a Category 4 hurricane makes landfall, it leaves destruction and disruption in its path.

Part C. Write the Concluding Sentence: Two-Sentence Conclusion

Write a two-sentence conclusion that paraphrases your introduction and summarizes your response.

Hurricanes are unique and dangerous storms. Long after the storm has passed, people are struggling to put their lives back together.

206 Unit 10

Write a Constructed Response

Notebook paper

Steps for Paragraph Writing poster

Like two bookends, we have now written the beginning and end of our constructed response. Look over your notes and plan the body of the paragraph. Remember to use the three topics on the left side of your Two-Column Notes to help you in planning. Provide time to plan.

Write the paragraph or paragraphs that describe what a hurricane looks like, the damage it does, and what life is like afterward. Have students write the body of their constructed response. Suggest that they write one paragraph for each of the three subtopics—appearance, threat, and aftermath.

Share what you have written with your partner and offer feedback. Have students share and discuss.

Use the feedback from your discussions to finish your rough draft. Allow students to work independently for the remainder of the time. Circulate to monitor student progress and answer any questions they may have as they write their rough drafts. Remind them to use descriptive language and Masterpiece Sentences in their writing.

Example Constructed Response

Hurricanes have distinctive features and characteristics. If a Category 4 hurricane makes landfall, it leaves destruction and disruption in its path.

The tropical winds that create the storm also contribute to its spinning motion and fuel it with moisture and warm air. In a Category 4 hurricane, the winds around the eye range from 131 to 155 miles per hour. Winds of this strength pull roofs off houses, cause extensive damage to small buildings, and completely destroy some structures. Objects are flung through the air and often do even more structural damage.

Flooding is a huge concern for coastal communities as well as locations far inland. A wall of wind and water sweeps over the coast as the storm makes landfall. As the storm travels over land, it loses its source of energy and begins to deteriorate.

With this level of destruction, every daily routine is interrupted. People living in these areas often evacuate and wait days for roads to reopen. Even if they can remain in their homes, they are without electricity and often have no running water. When businesses try to open, their employees often cannot get to work and business supplies cannot be delivered. Schools cannot open because they serve as public shelters.

Hurricanes are unique and dangerous storms. Long after the storm has passed, people are struggling to put their lives back together.

Writer's Checklist

Once students have written their paragraphs, direct them to page 209 in their Student Books. Use the checklist to edit your paragraph. Make changes that you think will improve your paragraph.

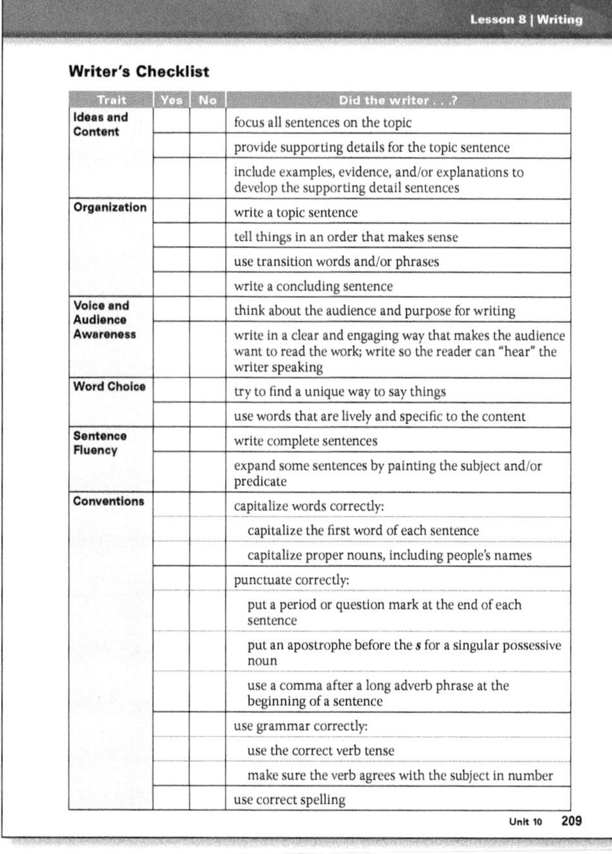
Lesson 8 | Writing

Writer's Checklist

Trait	Yes	No	Did the writer . . .?
Ideas and Content			focus all sentences on the topic
			provide supporting details for the topic sentence
			include examples, evidence, and/or explanations to develop the supporting detail sentences
Organization			write a topic sentence
			tell things in an order that makes sense
			use transition words and/or phrases
			write a concluding sentence
Voice and Audience Awareness			think about the audience and purpose for writing
			write in a clear and engaging way that makes the audience want to read the work; write so the reader can "hear" the writer speaking
Word Choice			try to find a unique way to say things
			use words that are lively and specific to the content
Sentence Fluency			write complete sentences
			expand some sentences by painting the subject and/or predicate
Conventions			capitalize words correctly:
			capitalize the first word of each sentence
			capitalize proper nouns, including people's names
			punctuate correctly:
			put a period or question mark at the end of each sentence
			put an apostrophe before the *s* for a singular possessive noun
			use a comma after a long adverb phrase at the beginning of a sentence
			use grammar correctly:
			use the correct verb tense
			make sure the verb agrees with the subject in number
			use correct spelling

Unit 10 209

Six Traits of Writing

Look over your rough draft and see whether you want to make any more edits to your constructed response.

Direct students to page 210 in their Student Books. Now work with your partner to examine the voice in your writing. Focus on the Voice section in the rubric and see if you can help each other evaluate and possibly improve this trait. When time expires, ask students to share their thoughts about this writing trait.

Six Traits of Writing

	Ideas and Development	Organization	Voice and Audience Awareness	Word Choice	Sentence Fluency	Language Conventions
5	The paper is very clear and well focused. Supporting details make the paper very easy and interesting to understand.	Ideas are very clearly organized. All parts of the essay (introduction, body, and conclusion) work together to support the thesis.	The writer's voice is distinctive and shows an interest in the topic. The writer knows who his or her audience is.	Words are used correctly and are very well chosen. They create pictures in the reader's mind.	Sentences have an easy flow and rhythm. Transitions are very smooth.	There are no grammar errors. There are few or no errors in spelling, capitalization, or punctuation.
4	The paper is clear and well focused. Supporting details make the paper easy to understand.	Ideas are clearly organized. The paper includes all parts of an essay (introduction, body, and conclusion).	The writer's voice is natural and shows an interest in the topic. The writer knows who his or her audience is.	Words are used correctly. Some words may be a bit general.	Sentences are formed correctly and are varied in structure. Transitions are clear.	There are no major grammar errors. There are few errors in spelling, capitalization, or punctuation.
3	The paper has a clear thesis. The ideas are somewhat developed, but there are only a few details.	Ideas are fairly well organized. The paper includes all parts of an essay (introduction, body, and conclusion).	The writer's voice is natural, but the writer is not fully engaged in the topic. At times the writer's viewpoint may be vague.	Most words are used correctly. A few words are too general. Some words are repeated.	Sentences are formed correctly, although they may be similar in structure. Most transitions are clear.	There are a few grammar errors. There are a few errors in spelling, capitalization, or punctuation.
2	The thesis of the paper is unclear. The paper is poorly developed.	Ideas are not clearly organized. The paper may be missing an introduction or a conclusion.	The writer seems somewhat uninterested in the topic and unaware of his or her audience.	Some words are used incorrectly, some are too general, or some words are repeated often.	The sentences do not flow well. They are short and choppy, or long and confusing.	There are many grammar or spelling errors. There are quite a few errors in capitalization and punctuation.
1	The paper is missing a thesis. The paper is very confusing or poorly developed.	The paper has no organization. There is no introduction or conclusion.	The writer is uninterested in the topic and unaware of his or her audience.	Many words are used incorrectly, many words are general, or many words are repeated.	The sentences are not correctly structured and they do not flow well.	There are many spelling and grammar errors. There are many errors in capitalization and punctuation.

Lesson 8 | Writing

210 Unit 10

Unit 10

Lesson 9

Lesson Opener

Before the lesson, choose one of the following activities to write on the board or post on the *LANGUAGE! Live* Class Wall online.

- *Diagram the following sentences:* She is waiting in the hall. She is a good waitress.
- *Draw a pie graph that shows how you spend your time on Saturdays. Be sure to make each piece of pie the correct size for the percentage of time spent.*
- *Write a technical (step-by-step) paragraph about what to do when a hurricane is coming.*

Reading

Objective

- Read words to develop fluency.

Word Fluency: Second Read

Timer

Follow the Fluency Procedure outlined below. If it is necessary, begin the fluency drill with a choral read of the words as you provide a rhythm (snap your fingers, tap your foot, tap your pencil). Direct students to page 211 in their Student Books and complete the process.

Word Fluency: Second Read

Read the words fluently.

	Correct	Errors
1st Try		
2nd Try		

hawk	landed	thinks	thawing	blanks	stinking	harmed	drank	hinted	honked	10
thinks	thawing	blanks	stinking	harmed	drank	hinted	honked	tromped	beaches	20
blanks	stinking	harmed	drank	hinted	honked	tromped	beaches	classes	chimps	30
harmed	drank	hinted	honked	tromped	beaches	classes	chimps	wheels	tents	40
hinted	honked	tromped	beaches	classes	chimps	wheels	tents	boxes	whales	50
tromped	beaches	classes	chimps	wheels	tents	boxes	whales	buzzes	spending	60
classes	chimps	wheels	tents	boxes	whales	buzzes	spending	landed	hawk	70
wheels	tents	boxes	whales	buzzes	spending	landed	hawk	thawing	thinks	80
boxes	whales	buzzes	spending	landed	hawk	thawing	thinks	stinking	blanks	90
buzzes	spending	landed	hawk	thawing	thinks	stinking	blanks	drank	harmed	100

Unit 10 211

Lesson 9 | Reading

Fluency Procedure

- Partners switch books, so the recorder is marking errors in the reader's book.
- A timer is set for one minute.
- Readers and recorders move left to right, tracking each word with a pencil.
- As readers read the words aloud, recorders mark errors with a small x above the misread word.
- Recorders place a star to the right of the last word read when time ends.
- If the reader is able to read all words in the allotted time, the reader needs to start over at the beginning. The recorder must indicate this feat by placing two stars to the right of the last word read.
- When both students have read, partners switch books.
- Students calculate total words read, then subtract errors and record.
- Students record information on the progress chart in back of the Student Book.

Vocabulary

Objectives

- Demonstrate an understanding of words by relating them to their synonyms, antonyms, and related words.
- Demonstrate an understanding of figurative language by generating examples of similes and metaphors.
- Identify and define an idiom related to the word *powerful.*

Four-Square

Review *powerful* and its definition.

Direct students to page 212 in their Student Books. Read the instructions. Have partners complete the synonyms, examples, antonyms, nonexamples, and related words. Review the answers as a class.

Ask students for examples of metaphors that include the word *powerful* or a related word.

Using the prompts, have students write two similes and a metaphor related to *powerful.*

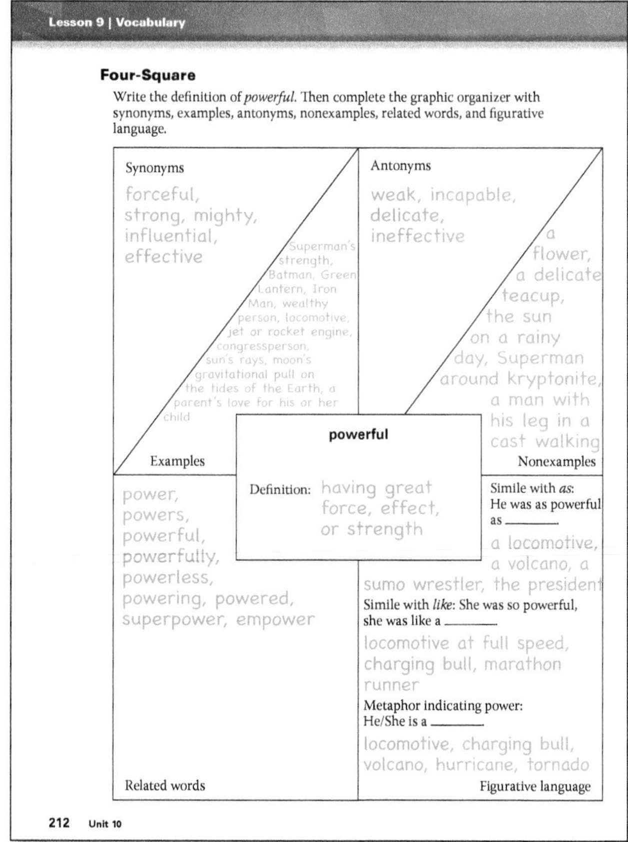

Lesson 9 | Vocabulary

Four-Square

Write the definition of *powerful.* Then complete the graphic organizer with synonyms, examples, antonyms, nonexamples, related words, and figurative language.

Synonyms: forceful, strong, mighty, influential, effective

Examples: Superman's strength, Batman, Green Lantern, Iron Man, wealthy person, locomotive, jet or rocket engine, congressperson, sun's rays, moon's gravitational pull on the tides of the Earth, a parent's love for his or her child

Antonyms: weak, incapable, delicate, ineffective

Nonexamples: a flower, a delicate teacup, the sun on a rainy day, Superman around kryptonite, a man with his leg in a cast walking

powerful

Definition: having great force, effect, or strength

Related words: power, powers, powerful, powerfully, powerless, powering, powered, superpower, empower

Figurative language:

Simile with *as:* He was as powerful as ______ a locomotive, a volcano, a sumo wrestler, the president

Simile with *like:* She was so powerful, she was like a ______ locomotive at full speed, charging bull, marathon runner

Metaphor indicating power: He/She is a ______ locomotive, charging bull, volcano, hurricane, tornado

212 Unit 10

Example Idiom

Powers that be: the people in charge

Grammar

Objectives

- Demonstrate an understanding of direct objects and predicate modifiers as they relate to action verbs and linking verbs.
- Demonstrate an understanding of how past, present, and future tense verbs are used in sentences.
- Demonstrate an understanding of how subject and object pronouns and possessive nouns are used in text.

Direct Objects and Predicate Modifiers

Have students generate examples of action verbs and linking verbs. Prompt students to generate some verb phrases as examples of action verbs.

We have learned that we need to think carefully about how words function within a sentence, and often the verb gives us important clues. The same words and phrases can function differently, depending on whether the verb they follow is an action verb or a linking verb.

Direct students to page 213 in their Student Books and read the instructions.

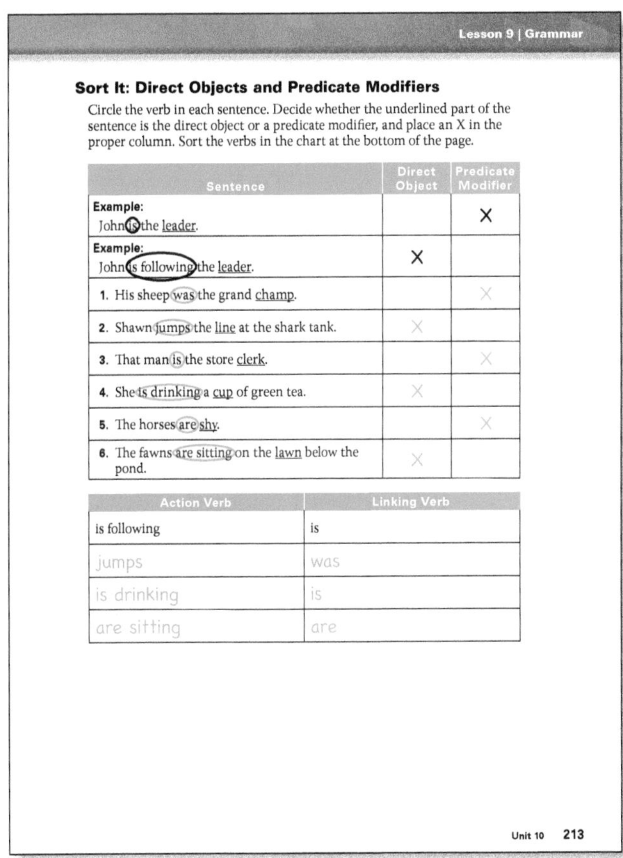

Lesson 9 | Grammar

Sort It: Direct Objects and Predicate Modifiers

Circle the verb in each sentence. Decide whether the underlined part of the sentence is the direct object or a predicate modifier, and place an X in the proper column. Sort the verbs in the chart at the bottom of the page.

Sentence	Direct Object	Predicate Modifier
Example: John is the leader.		X
Example: John is following the leader.	X	
1. His sheep was the grand champ.		X
2. Shawn jumps the line at the shark tank.	X	
3. That man is the store clerk.		X
4. She is drinking a cup of green tea.	X	
5. The horses are shy.		X
6. The fawns are sitting on the lawn below the pond.	X	

Action Verb	Linking Verb
is following	is
jumps	was
is drinking	is
are sitting	are

Unit 10 213

In this activity, your job is to determine whether the underlined word in each sentence is receiving the action—a direct object—or describing the subject—a predicate modifier.

The first thing you will need to do is find the verb and decide whether it's an action verb or a linking verb. If it's a linking verb, then the underlined word will be a predicate modifier. If it's an action verb, you will need to ask, What is receiving the action?

Model

Let's look at the two examples. Our first step is to read the sentence and find the verb: John is the leader. What is the verb? (is) Is it a linking verb or an action verb? (linking verb) What is *leader*? I know it can't be receiving any action because there is no action, so it must be a predicate modifier. The underlined word *leader* gives us more information about John, but it doesn't tell us anything about what he's doing.

Diagram the sentence on the board to illustrate how *leader* modifies the subject noun *John.*

John is the leader.

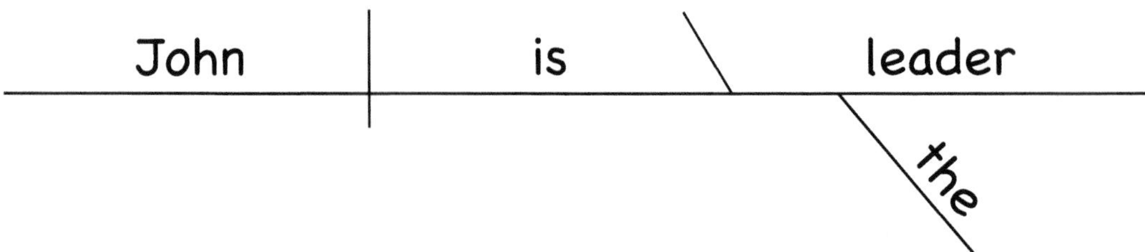

Guided Practice

Let's read the second sentence together. **Read the sentence chorally.** What is the verb? (is following) Is this something that John is doing? (yes) Who is he following? (the leader) Because we can answer the question, Who is John following?, we know the word *leader* is a direct object. **Diagram the sentence on the board to show how *leader* is functioning as a direct object.**

John is following the leader.

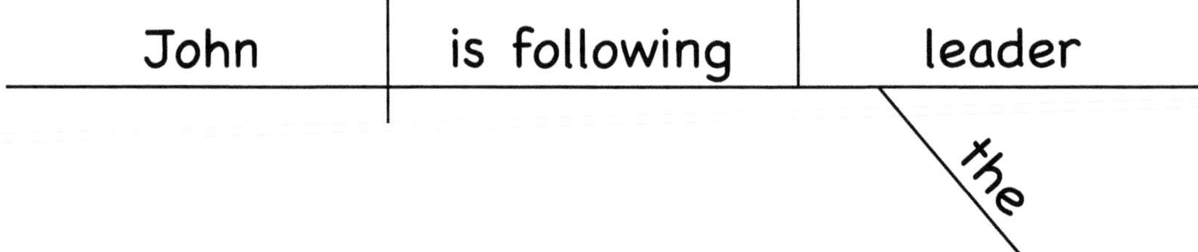

Notice how the underlined word is the same in each sentence, but the different verbs cause it to function differently. Let's read the first sentence together. **Read the sentence chorally.** What is the verb? (was) What kind of verb is it? (linking verb) What is *champ*? (It is a predicate modifier.) **Diagram the sentence on the board to show how *champ* is the predicate modifier.**

1. *His sheep was the grand champ.*

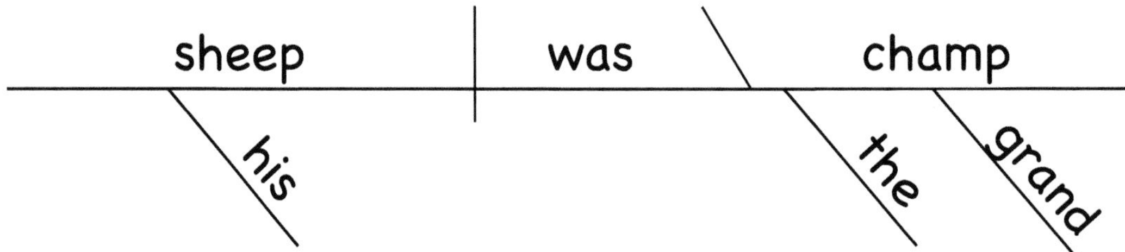

Independent Practice

Have students complete the remaining sentences independently. Review answers by diagramming each sentence on the board. Then have students sort the verbs in the bottom chart. Review the answers as a class.

Note: Base the number of modeled and guided examples on student ability and progress. Challenge them with independent practice when appropriate.

2. Shawn jumps the line at the shark tank.

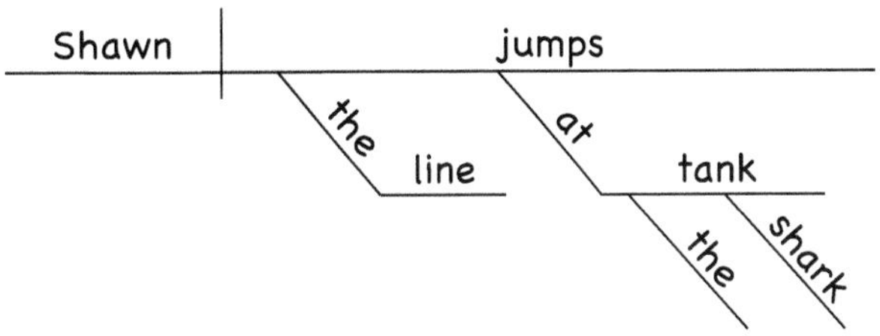

3. That man is the store clerk.

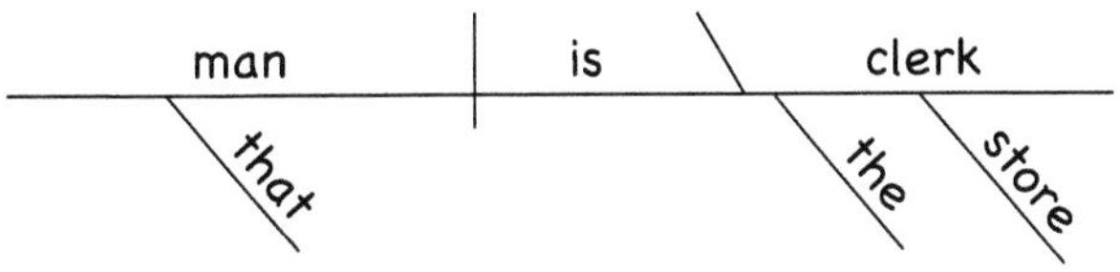

4. She is drinking a cup of green tea.

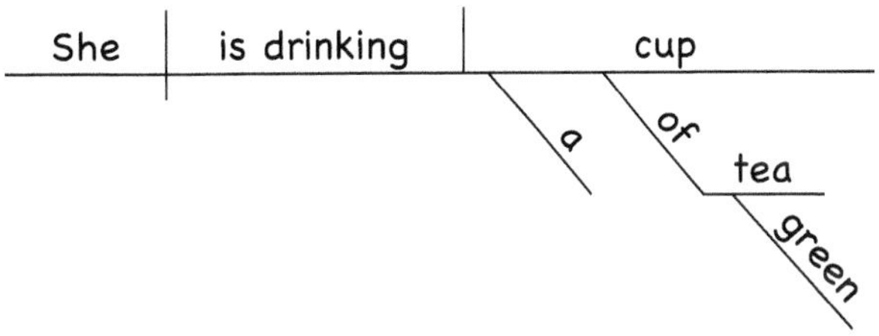

5. The horses are shy.

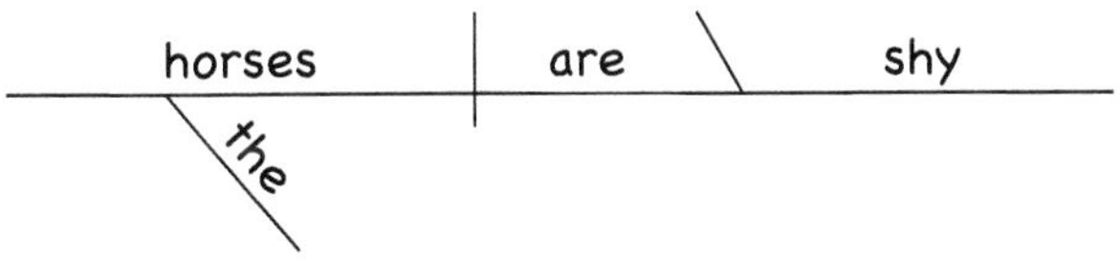

6. The fawns are sitting on the lawn below the pond.

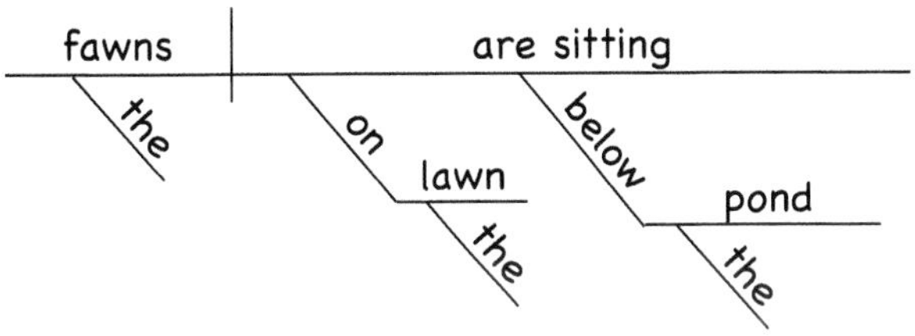

Tense Timeline: Past, Present, Future

Model

Tense Timeline poster

Let's look at some sentences to review what we know about verb tense. What is another word we think of when we hear the word *tense*? (*Time* is another word for *tense*.) Reread each sentence from page 213 in the Student Book, and have students identify the verb tense in each one. Draw the tense timeline on the board, and place each verb in the correct category on the timeline. For each sentence, ask students to change the tense and create new sentences. Write the new verbs in the proper category on the timeline.

Past	Present	Future
was	is	will be
jumped	jumps	will jump
was	is	will be
was drinking/drank*	is drinking	will drink (will be drinking**)
were	are	will be
were sitting/sat*	are sitting	will sit (will be sitting**)

*Students may generate this irregular verb as a response. If so, write it on the board and point out that there's much more to learn about verbs.

**Students may generate this future progressive verb as a response. If so, write it on the board and note that they'll learn more about this kind of verb phrase in a later unit.

Direct students to page 214 in their Student Books and read the instructions.

Guided Practice

Guide students to complete the first two items.

Independent Practice

Read the remaining sentences aloud. Have students underline the verb(s) in each sentence and write them in the correct columns. Review the answers as a class.

Note: Base the number of modeled and guided examples on student ability and progress. Challenge them with independent practice when appropriate.

Lesson 9 | Grammar

Tense Timeline: Past, Present, Future

Underline the verb(s) in each sentence. Sort the verbs according to tense.

1. We will track the coming storm.
2. Beth is using a map to plot its track.
3. Mother remembered a hurricane from her childhood.
4. She often tells stories about the storm.
5. We were plotting the hurricane on the map.
6. She was going to the store for supplies.
7. We will prepare for the storm.
8. We moved the lawn furniture to the shed.
9. The storm is coming and we are ready.
10. We will remember this hurricane for a very long time.

Past (Yesterday)	Present (Today)	Future (Tomorrow)
remembered	is using	will track
were plotting	tells	will prepare
was going	is coming	will remember
moved	are	

214 Unit 10

Pronouns

Pronoun poster

To review what we've learned about pronouns, I'm going to read a passage aloud and you're going to find the pronouns in the text. First, let's review the pronouns we've studied. We've worked with subject and object pronouns. What is the job of a pronoun? (It takes the place of a noun in a sentence.)

Subject Pronouns

What kind of noun does a subject pronoun replace? (the subject noun) Listen to this sentence: Beth is waiting in the hall. Who is waiting? (Beth) What is the job of the noun, *Beth,* in this sentence? (It is the subject noun.) What subject pronoun would work well to replace this noun? (She) What's our new sentence? (She is waiting in the hall.)

Draw a T-chart on the board for subject and object pronouns. Under subject pronouns, write *she*. Have students identify other subject pronouns they have learned (we, you, he, it, they, I). Write these on the board.

Object Pronouns

We know nouns can do more than name the subject. A noun can be the "receiver" of an action, or a direct object. A noun can also appear in a prepositional phrase. In this case, the noun's contextual meaning is tied to the preposition, so it is called an object of the preposition. What kind of noun does an object pronoun replace? (the direct object or the object of a preposition) Listen to this sentence: I met Beth after class. Whom did I meet? (Beth) What is the job of this noun in the sentence? (It is receiving the action, so it is a direct object.) Would I use the same pronoun for *Beth* in this sentence? (no) That's right; I would not say "I met she in the hall." What would I say? (I met her in the hall.) *Her* is an object pronoun. What are the other object pronouns? (me, you, him, it, us, you, them) Write these in the chart on the board. There are other categories of pronouns, but for now, we're focusing on subject and object pronouns.

Direct students to page 215 in their Student Books and read the instructions. Point out that the passage is an excerpt from a radio broadcast. Ask students to consider whether this format will have an impact on the "voice" in the passage, especially on tone and pronoun usage.

Lesson 9 | Grammar

Find It: Pronouns

Circle the subject and object pronouns in the following passage. Underline the singular and plural possessive nouns. Write the pronouns and possessives on the appropriate lines below.

This is Jack Olsen, the voice of KOKA Radio.
Yesterday: Sunday, April 14, 1935.

The day dawned clear and dry across the southern Great Plains. Families went to church. Some planned to enjoy picnics, while others were bound for visits to friends and family. Everyone looked forward to the pleasant afternoon hours ahead.

Then, suddenly, in midafternoon, the air turned cooler. Birds began fluttering nervously and all at once, the wind picked up. Suddenly, a rolling black cloud of dust darkened the northern horizon. Everyone hurried home. We were trying desperately to beat the overwhelming "black blizzard" before it struck. Within minutes, the sky overhead was dark. Streetlights flickered in the gloom, and drivers turned on their headlights. Soon, the swirling dust storm blotted everything out.

"Black blizzards" are nothing new to us; we residents of the southwestern plains have experienced these terrible dust storms for several years now. We know their destruction. But the wall of flying soil that struck us yesterday was awesome. Its size and intensity had never been seen before.

In this morning's newspaper, one reporter observed, "An uncorked jug placed on a sidewalk for two hours was half filled with dust. Lady Godiva could have ridden through the streets, and even the horse wouldn't have seen her." One neighbor said, "All we could do about it was just sit in our dusty chairs, gaze at each other through the fog that filled the room, and watch that fog settle slowly and silently, covering everything—including ourselves—in a thick, brownish gray blanket."

We are getting the same reports from all over the Great Plains. Our region is becoming known as the Dust Bowl. The people we know—our families and friends—are experiencing tragedy the likes of which we have never seen. We have heard stories of attics collapsing under the weight of tons of dust. Farmers' tractors have been buried beneath six-foot drifts of dirt. Travelers are stranded in their cars, the roads disappearing under the dirt.

Subject pronouns: we, it Object pronouns: it, us, her

Possessive nouns: Its, morning's, farmers'

Unit 10 215

Read the passage, stopping after each paragraph to check student responses. Give students time to sort the pronouns, and then quickly review.

Note: While the lessons are written for a teacher read aloud, it is important that your students read as much and as often as they can. Assign readings that meet the needs of your students, based on your observations or data. This is a good opportunity to stretch students, but if they become frustrated, return to the read-aloud method.

This is Jack Olsen, the voice of KOKA Radio.
Yesterday: Sunday, April 14, 1935.

The day dawned clear and dry across the southern Great Plains. Families went to church. Some planned to enjoy picnics, while others were bound for visits to friends and family. Everyone looked forward to the pleasant afternoon hours ahead.

Then, suddenly, in midafternoon, the air turned cooler. Birds began fluttering nervously and all at once, the wind picked up. Suddenly, a rolling black cloud of dust darkened the northern horizon. Everyone hurried home. We were trying desperately to beat the overwhelming "black blizzard" before it struck. Within minutes, the sky overhead was dark. Streetlights flickered in the gloom, and drivers turned on their headlights. Soon, the swirling dust storm blotted everything out.

"Black blizzards" are nothing new to us; we residents of the southwestern plains have experienced these terrible dust storms for several years now. We know their destruction. But the wall of flying soil that struck us yesterday was awesome. Its size and intensity had never been seen before.

In this morning's newspaper, one reporter observed, "An uncorked jug placed on a sidewalk for two hours was half filled with dust. Lady Godiva could have ridden through the streets, and even the horse wouldn't have seen her." One neighbor said, "All we could do about it was just sit in our dusty chairs, gaze at each other through the fog that filled the room, and watch that fog settle slowly and silently, covering everything—including ourselves—in a thick, brownish gray blanket."

We are getting the same reports from all over the Great Plains. Our region is becoming known as the Dust Bowl. The people we know—our families and friends—are experiencing tragedy the likes of which we have never seen. We have heard stories of attics collapsing under the weight of tons of dust. Farmers' tractors have been buried beneath six-foot drifts of dirt. Travelers are stranded in their cars, the roads disappearing under the dirt.

Is this story told from the first-person, second-person, or third-person point of view? (first person) What is the effect of using first person in this passage? (The speaker is just like the listeners; he's one of them going through an experience they have in common.) Remember the effectiveness of using first person if one of your goals for writing is to form a close bond with your readers.

Reading

Objectives

- Read a text to develop fluency.
- Demonstrate comprehension by answering specific questions about a text.

Reading for Fluency

Direct students to pages 216 and 217 in their Student Books.

The following passage is decodable text. You have learned almost all the letters, sounds, and sight words. The purpose of the passage is to improve your fluency.

Have students read the passage independently or with partners.

Reading for Fluency

Read the passage with prosody. Chunk the words into phrases and create an image in your head as you read.

The Storm

The man on TV said the storm should hit just before dawn. That is between five and six a.m. There are storm warnings out. He said the winds will gust from 80–90 mph. Wind that hard can do a lot of harm. It can blow off a roof and move cars around. We may get five or six inches of water, as well. I need to be following the storm on the Web site with the tracking pictures.

This scares me a little. Why now? Mom and Dad are out of town on a trip to Rome. While they are away, Gram and Gramp are staying with my little sis and me. Gram and Gramp live out west, so they do not know about the kind of storms we get here. They get storms with wind, sand, and dust, but not the kind with lots of water. Gramp can do some tasks. He just mowed the lawn. The clumps of grass are smooth. Gram makes our meals and cleans. But, there is a lot of hard work to do before the storm hits. I know some of the things we need to do. But I wish I had a list of everything. I would like to check the things off, one by one. I need to be smart about what I need to do here. I can look out for our home while Mom and Dad are away, but I need to start now.

The bedrooms all have glass panes. So, it is not safe to ride out the storm there. We will plan on camping in the basement. I hate to think about time in the basement. It is damp, dark, and dank. And it stinks. But there is no glass. That is good. There is a bathroom down there. I will move the camping cots and sleeping bags down. We have an old stove in the basement, so I will bring in logs from the shed. We can use the stove to heat our food. We will need pans. Gram can get spoons, forks, plates, bowls, and glasses. We need a clock without a plug to tell time. I will put the stuff in boxes to take to the basement.

Reading for Fluency (*cont.*)

The Storm (*cont.*)

Mom has a storm kit in the shed. It has water to get us through two days. We may need more. There are flashlights. I need to check them for life. I may need to stop by the store for another box and more water, as well. Mom cans things. So, there are jars of corn and beans on the racks in the basement. And, right below there are jars of pork and fish. Sis needs to get the dog's dishes and food for her dog. I think we are good with food.

We each need a change of tops and shorts.

We can play a game in the light of our flashlights to pass the time. Or, I may read. It seems like it takes years for a storm to pass.

Here in town the wind may harm the roofs, the trees, bushes, and the plants. But, the people who live in the country have to think of their animals. Also, a storm can wash away the sand on the beaches. What do the fish, sharks, and whales do? How do they take care of the chimps and other animals at the zoo?

It is time to go pick up my little sis at school and go to the store. I think I will take her little dog, Spot, with me. Spot hates the sound of the wind. She whines and whines. But she feels safe when my sis has her in her arms.

The wind is up. Look at the flag in the air. It blows out; then it is limp. The trees are twisting and bending. That hawk glides in the wind. The temp is down. It is starting to get cool.

We are back home. Gramp can help take the small things off the deck so the wind will not blow them away. We have a tarp that hides the pool. But, we will not use it because the wind would just blow it away. We will take the grill inside off the porch. I will put the broom and dustpan and the wheeled cart inside. We may need them to clean up outside after the storm. I will get the planks from the shed. They fit over the panes to keep the glass whole. We should shut off the gas.

I look outside. Now, it is as dark as ink. The wind is howling. There are thumps on the roof. I think branches just broke out of the tree that hangs over the roof. The lamps are blinking. There is a green glow in the sky. I hope we have everything we need. Soon the town will blow the warning. Grab everything; it is time to go to the basement. The house is dark. The storm is here.

Ask students the following comprehension questions.

- There are at least three problems in the story. What are they? (Possible responses: The storm is approaching, Mom and Dad are gone, the author has only partial knowledge of the preparation needed, there are many things to do, Gram and Gramp can help with only some things.)
- Based on the author's description, what category do you think the hurricane might end up being? (Category 1 or 2)
- Based on the author's description, where do you think Gram and Gramp live? (Arizona, New Mexico, Texas)
- Did you notice anything the speaker forgot in his or her planning? (Answers will vary.)
- What should Mom and Dad have done differently before they left on their trip? (prepare a list of things to do in case of a storm)
- The speaker says he or she is scared. Why do you think the speaker feels that way, and what other emotions do you think he or she feels? (Answers will vary: The speaker is scared because of the intensity of the storm and the responsibility that falls on him or her to prepare for the hurricane. Other emotions: frustrated, nervous.)

Unit 10 Lesson 10

Lesson Opener

Before the lesson, choose one of the following activities to write on the board or post on the *LANGUAGE! Live* Class Wall online.

- *Write four meaningful sentences with the vocabulary words from this unit. Each sentence will contain two vocabulary words* (property, ordinary, definite, scale, threaten, surrounding, sustain, intense).
- *Describe the devastation that can be caused by a hurricane.*
- *If you received a late warning that a hurricane was coming at our school, who would you help escape and why?*

Vocabulary

Objectives

- Clarify the meaning of key passage vocabulary.
- Demonstrate an understanding of passage vocabulary by using words in sentences.

Review

Direct students to page 172 in their Student Books. Remind them of the review procedure. Have partners review the Key Passage Vocabulary.

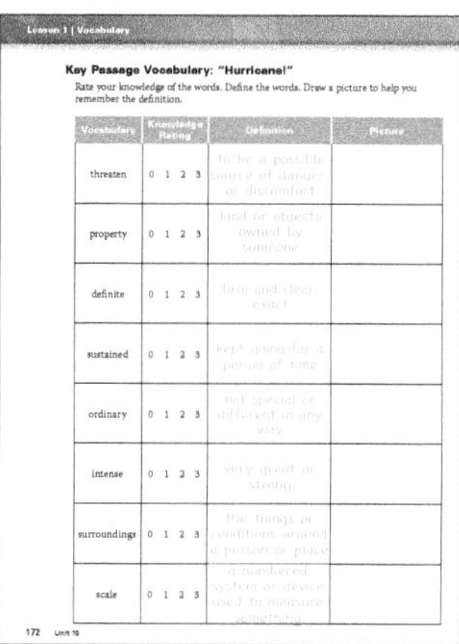
Lesson 1 | Vocabulary

Key Passage Vocabulary: "Hurricane!"

Rate your knowledge of the words. Define the words. Draw a picture to help you remember the definition.

Vocabulary	Knowledge Rating	Definition	Picture
threaten	0 1 2 3	to be a possible source of danger or discomfort	
property	0 1 2 3	land or objects owned by someone	
definite	0 1 2 3	firm and clear; exact	
sustained	0 1 2 3	kept going for a period of time	
ordinary	0 1 2 3	not special or different in any way	
intense	0 1 2 3	very great or strong	
surroundings	0 1 2 3	the things or conditions around a person or place	
scale	0 1 2 3	a numbered system or device used to measure something	

172 Unit 10

Review Procedure

- Student A reads the word.
- Student B tells the meaning.
- Students swap roles for each word.

Have students revisit their rating of the words. If they cannot change all ratings to a 3, pull them aside to discuss the vocabulary words they do not know.

Cloze Activity

Now we will read a paragraph. You will determine which vocabulary words are missing and write them on the lines. Direct students to page 218 in their Student Books. Remind them of the cloze procedure.

Cloze Procedure

- Teacher reads the text aloud, pausing at the blanks for students to write.
- Students fill in the blanks with words from the word bank.
- Teacher rereads the text as students chorally tell the correct word for each blank.
- Students correct errors.

Lesson 10 | Vocabulary

Using New Vocabulary

Fill in the blanks with the appropriate vocabulary words. If you need assistance, use the word bank at the bottom of the page.

Hurricane Katrina started out as an __ordinary__ storm forming over the Bahamas. It crossed Florida and became more __intense__ as it strengthened in the Gulf of Mexico. With __sustained__ winds as high as 175 miles per hour, it ranked as a Category 5 on the Saffir-Simpson Hurricane __Scale__. As it __threatened__ New Orleans and its __surroundings__, it weakened to a Category 3. Because the __definite__ path of the hurricane could not be predicted, many people were caught off guard. The storm surge caused severe damage to __property__ and 1,833 confirmed deaths. A significant number of those deaths occurred in New Orleans, where the levee system was not powerful enough to withstand the sustained rains.

Word Bank

definite	ordinary	scale	threatened
intense	property	surroundings	sustained

218 Unit 10

Reading

Objectives

- Discuss and answer questions to demonstrate an understanding of an author's or narrator's point of view in a text.
- Discuss and answer questions to demonstrate an understanding of the passages' main idea and key details.

Big Idea and Point of View

Direct students to page 171 in their Student Books.

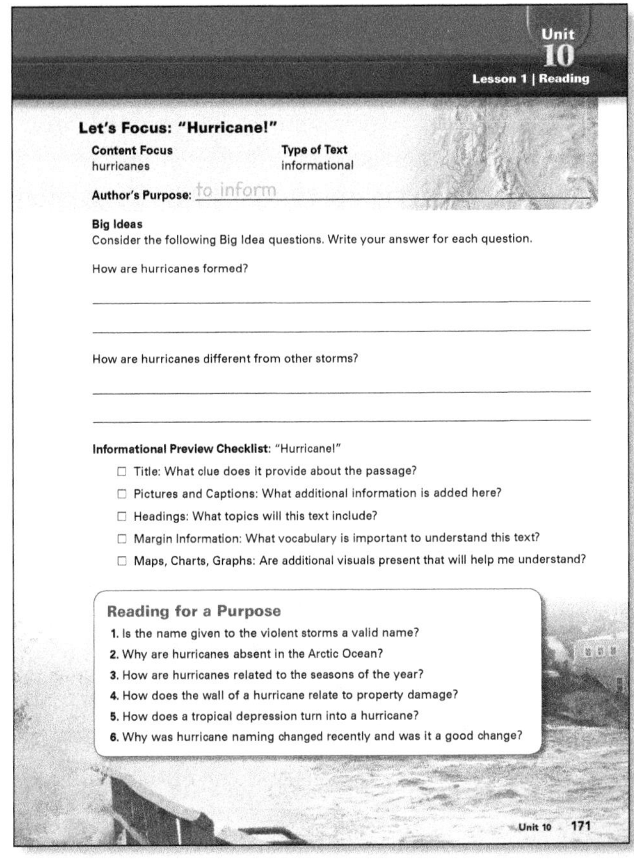
Unit 10
Lesson 1 | Reading

Let's Focus: "Hurricane!"

Content Focus
hurricanes

Type of Text
informational

Author's Purpose: to inform

Big Ideas
Consider the following Big Idea questions. Write your answer for each question.

How are hurricanes formed?

How are hurricanes different from other storms?

Informational Preview Checklist: "Hurricane!"

- ☐ Title: What clue does it provide about the passage?
- ☐ Pictures and Captions: What additional information is added here?
- ☐ Headings: What topics will this text include?
- ☐ Margin Information: What vocabulary is important to understand this text?
- ☐ Maps, Charts, Graphs: Are additional visuals present that will help me understand?

Reading for a Purpose

1. Is the name given to the violent storms a valid name?
2. Why are hurricanes absent in the Arctic Ocean?
3. How are hurricanes related to the seasons of the year?
4. How does the wall of a hurricane relate to property damage?
5. How does a tropical depression turn into a hurricane?
6. Why was hurricane naming changed recently and was it a good change?

Unit 10 171

Before we began reading "Hurricane!" we answered two Big Idea questions. Take a minute to look over your answers. Now that we have read the passage thoroughly and learned about other types of storms, how have your earlier ideas changed? What information can you add to your answers?

Discuss the questions and answers with the class. Scientists continue to study storms, trying to better understand why they form and better predict their destructive paths. Some scientists are experimenting with methods to control the weather, like cloud seeding. How do you feel about scientific efforts to control the weather? Do you think that's a good idea or a bad idea? What do you think some consequences may be if scientists are able to impact storms or exert some control over the weather? (Possible pros: protecting people from destructive storms, preventing floods or droughts, preventing extreme blizzards. Possible cons: We don't know the consequences of altering the natural patterns of weather; doing so may trigger more severe weather in nature's attempt to create balance on a larger scale.)

I want you to think for a minute how personal experience might impact how you feel about weather and how you might write about it. How do you think your answers would differ if you were a victim of a powerful storm? Do you think that would change how you look at storms and weather in general? How effective do you think an account of a catastrophic hurricane would be if it were told from the perspective of a storm victim—that is, in first person? Give students time to discuss the effects of using different points of view to describe a storm and the overall impact each voice would have on a piece of writing.

Writing

Objectives

- Discuss the value of specific details in creating imagery.
- Discuss the value of using strong verbs in writing.

Masterpiece Matchup

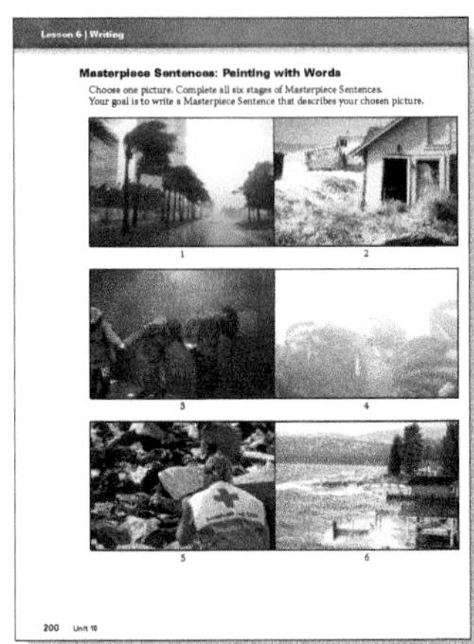

Lesson 6 | Writing

Masterpiece Sentences: Painting with Words

Choose one picture. Complete all six stages of Masterpiece Sentences.
Your goal is to write a Masterpiece Sentence that describes your chosen picture.

1 2

3 4

5 6

200 Unit 10

Direct students to the pictures that prompted their Masterpiece Sentences on page 200 in their Student Books. Call on students to read their Masterpiece Sentences and ask the class to decide which picture each sentence describes. Have students create a list containing each student's name and the number of the picture he or she described. After every sentence has been read, ask students to share their responses and see if they all agree.

Discuss the value of specific details to create an image in the reader's mind. If one picture was described in multiple sentences, ask students to compare the imagery in the sentences. Specifically examine the strength of the verbs in all of the sentences.

Alternative:

Display the pictures, or post the numbers 1–6, and have students write their sentences on sentence strips. Post all of the sentences, keeping the "authors" anonymous. Read each sentence aloud to the class and have them match the sentence to a picture as described above. As the sentence is read and matched to a picture, post the sentence underneath the picture or the corresponding number. Then compare sentences that describe the same picture as outlined above.

Discuss the power of word choice, word order (syntax), and the power of a strong verb as you discuss the effectiveness of each sentence in capturing the target image. If time permits, ask students to discuss their reasons for choosing the pictures they chose.

Reading

Objective for Content Mastery

- Demonstrate an understanding of how to interpret text by evaluating, analyzing, and connecting.

Responding to Prompts: *evaluate, analyze, connect*

Follow the procedure outlined below for the Reading Content Mastery questions and prompts.

Content Mastery Procedure

- Teacher reminds students to follow along with their pencils and listen.
- Teacher reads the question.
- Teacher reads each answer choice.
- Students choose the correct answer.
- Teacher repeats the question as students check their answers.

Have students turn to page 219 in their Student Books.

Let's look at the example first. Read the example aloud to students.

Listen: Connect each kind of storm with its wind speeds. To answer this prompt, I need to _____.

A form a critical opinion of each kind of storm

B break down or draw conclusions about the information

C tie ideas together about each kind of storm

D support my answer by using a direct quote about storms

Fill in the bubble for the correct response. Which bubble did you fill in? You should have filled in C, the bubble for "tie ideas together about each kind of storm." That is how you would respond to a question that asks you to connect one thing to something else.

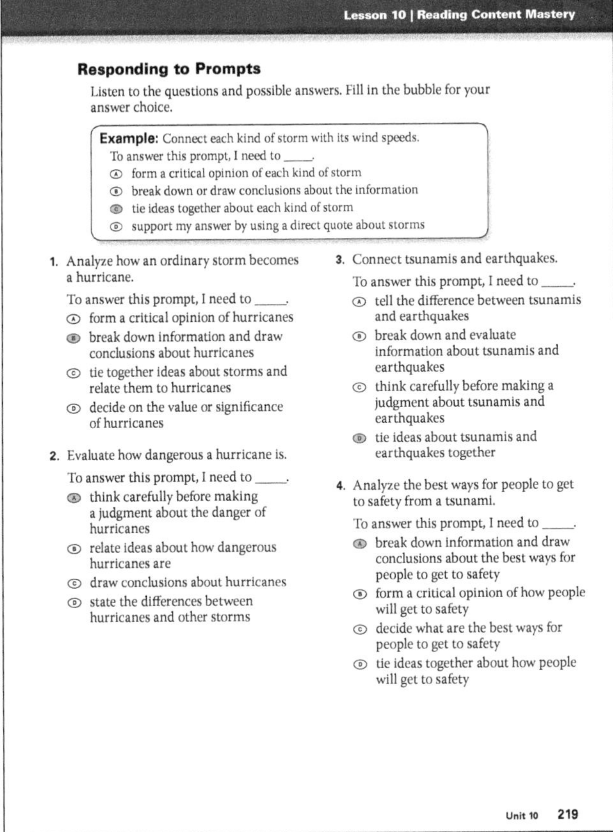

Lesson 10 | Reading Content Mastery

Responding to Prompts

Listen to the questions and possible answers. Fill in the bubble for your answer choice.

Example: Connect each kind of storm with its wind speeds.
To answer this prompt, I need to ____.
A form a critical opinion of each kind of storm
B break down or draw conclusions about the information
C tie ideas together about each kind of storm
D support my answer by using a direct quote about storms

1. Analyze how an ordinary storm becomes a hurricane.
To answer this prompt, I need to ____.
A form a critical opinion of hurricanes
B break down information and draw conclusions about hurricanes
C tie together ideas about storms and relate them to hurricanes
D decide on the value or significance of hurricanes

2. Evaluate how dangerous a hurricane is.
To answer this prompt, I need to ____.
A think carefully before making a judgment about the danger of hurricanes
B relate ideas about how dangerous hurricanes are
C draw conclusions about hurricanes
D state the differences between hurricanes and other storms

3. Connect tsunamis and earthquakes.
To answer this prompt, I need to ____.
A tell the difference between tsunamis and earthquakes
B break down and evaluate information about tsunamis and earthquakes
C think carefully before making a judgment about tsunamis and earthquakes
D tie ideas about tsunamis and earthquakes together

4. Analyze the best ways for people to get to safety from a tsunami.
To answer this prompt, I need to ____.
A break down information and draw conclusions about the best ways for people to get to safety
B form a critical opinion of how people will get to safety
C decide what are the best ways for people to get to safety
D tie ideas together about how people will get to safety

Unit 10 219

Follow along as I read aloud the questions and prompts. Fill in the bubble for your answer choice.

Use the following recommendations to reinforce or reteach according to student performance.

If...	Then...
Students miss 1 question	Review the question in a small group or individual setting, offering answer explanations.
Students miss 2 or more questions	Reteach the elements taught in Lesson 3 in a small group or individual setting. Unmarked copies of the student page can be reprinted from the online Teacher Resources.

Grammar

Objectives for Content Mastery

- Demonstrate an understanding of the function of direct objects in sentences.
- Demonstrate an understanding of the function of predicate modifiers in sentences.
- Demonstrate an understanding of the function of action verbs and linking verbs in sentences.

Direct Objects

Follow the procedure outlined below for each of the Grammar Content Mastery questions and prompts.

Content Mastery Procedure

- Teacher reminds students to follow along with their pencils and listen.
- Teacher reads the question.
- Teacher reads each answer choice.
- Students choose the correct answer.
- Teacher repeats the question as students check their answers.

Have students turn to page 220 in their Student Books.

Let's look at the example first. Read the example aloud to students.

Listen: Choose the sentence in which the word *reader* is a direct object. Fill in the bubble for your answer.

A Bart is the reader today.

B Our teacher told the reader to speak slowly.

C The reader turned the page.

D The teacher sat in a chair beside the reader.

Which bubble did you fill in? You should have filled in the bubble for B, "Our teacher told the reader to speak slowly." Remember, a direct object follows an action verb, in this sentence *told*. A direct object also answers the question, What? or Whom?

Follow along as I read aloud the sentences and possible answers. Fill in the bubble for your answer choice.

Lesson 10 | Grammar Content Mastery

Direct Objects

Listen to the questions and possible answers. Fill in the bubble for your answer choice.

Example: Choose the sentence in which the word *reader* is a direct object.
- Ⓐ Bart is the reader today.
- Ⓑ Our teacher told the reader to speak slowly.
- Ⓒ The reader turned the page.
- Ⓓ The teacher sat in a chair beside the reader.

1. Choose the sentence in which the word *ball* is a direct object.
   - Ⓐ The pitcher threw the ball.
   - Ⓑ The ball bounced on the ground.
   - Ⓒ That muddy blob is the ball.
   - Ⓓ The batter swung above the ball.
2. Choose the sentence in which the word *bowl* is a direct object.
   - Ⓐ The bowl is heaped with potatoes.
   - Ⓑ The only dish on the table is the blue bowl.
   - Ⓒ The potatoes are in the blue bowl.
   - Ⓓ Please pass the bowl of potatoes.
3. Choose the sentence in which the word *pen* is a direct object.
   - Ⓐ The pen writes in red ink
   - Ⓑ Mom bought the silver pen.
   - Ⓒ I like to write with this pen.
   - Ⓓ That silver thing is my pen.
4. Choose the sentence in which the word *storm* is a direct object.
   - Ⓐ The hail and wind were a bigger storm than we expected.
   - Ⓑ The weatherman predicted the storm.
   - Ⓒ The storm knocked out the electric power.
   - Ⓓ The air was cold after the storm.
5. Choose the sentence in which the word *tsunami* is a direct object.
   - Ⓐ The tsunami wiped out a whole village.
   - Ⓑ That huge wave was the tsunami.
   - Ⓒ The beach houses were swept away by the tsunami.
   - Ⓓ The earthquake caused a tsunami.

220 Unit 10

Use the following recommendations to reinforce or reteach according to student performance.

If...	Then...
Students miss 2 questions	Review the questions in a small group or individual setting, offering answer explanations.
Students miss 3 or more questions	Reteach the elements taught in Lesson 9 in a small group or individual setting. Unmarked copies of the student page can be reprinted from the online Teacher Resources.

Action Verb vs. Linking Verb

Have students turn to page 221 in their Student Books.

Let's look at the example first. Read the example aloud to students.

Listen: Choose the correct linking verb for this sentence: "He ______ very hungry." Fill in the bubble for your answer.

A are

B were

C felt

D was

Which bubble did you fill in? You should have filled in the bubble for D, "was," "He was very hungry." In this sentence *was* is the correct form of the linking verb. Remember, when a form of the verb *be* works as a linking verb, it connects the subject with a word that describes or renames the subject. When a form of the verb *be* is paired with another verb, it works as a helping verb. Then, the two verbs work together as an action verb.

Lesson 10 | Grammar Content Mastery

Action Verbs and Linking Verbs

Listen to the sentences and possible answers. Fill in the bubble for your answer choice.

Example: Choose the correct linking verb for this sentence:
He _____ very hungry.
Ⓐ are
Ⓑ were
Ⓒ felt
Ⓓ was

1. Choose the correct linking verb for this sentence: I _____ glad to help you.
Ⓐ am
Ⓑ are
Ⓒ is
Ⓓ were

2. Choose the correct action verb for this sentence: Drake _____ my name.
Ⓐ is
Ⓑ called
Ⓒ call
Ⓓ was

3. Choose the correct linking verb for this sentence: She _____ outside during recess.
Ⓐ played
Ⓑ were
Ⓒ was
Ⓓ went

4. Choose the correct action verb for this sentence: We _____ on the beach.
Ⓐ ran
Ⓑ is
Ⓒ runned
Ⓓ was

5. Choose the correct action verb for this sentence: The birds _____ in the tree.
Ⓐ was
Ⓑ were
Ⓒ sit
Ⓓ is

Unit 10 221

Follow along as I read aloud the sentences and possible answers. Fill in the bubble for your answer choice.

Use the following recommendations to reinforce or reteach according to student performance.

If...	Then...
Students miss 2 questions	Review the questions in a small group or individual setting, offering answer explanations.
Students miss 3 or more questions	Reteach the elements taught in Lesson 2 in a small group or individual setting. Unmarked copies of the student page can be reprinted from the online Teacher Resources.

Unit 11

Unit Plan

Primary Text:
"Twisters"

Text type: informational

Lesson 1	Lesson 2
Reading • Determine the topic of the text. • Determine the author's purpose. • Discuss the topic of the text. • Preview the text. **Vocabulary** • Determine the meaning of key passage vocabulary. **Reading** • Review text features. • Read an informational text. • Demonstrate an understanding of the text by asking and answering questions and referring to key details in the text.	**Vocabulary** • Use discussion and context to determine the meanings of the multiple-meaning words *contact* and *base*. • Demonstrate an understanding of the words by using them in written sentences. **Grammar** • Demonstrate an understanding of forming plurals using inflectional endings. • Demonstrate an understanding of using plural nouns and verbs with various inflectional endings in sentences. **Reading** • Discuss the purposes of informational and literary text types. • Discuss the features of informational and literary texts. • Compare and contrast informational and literary text types. • Analyze two types of text for specific words used to compare and to contrast.

Lesson 6	Lesson 7
Writing • Know spelling-sound correspondences for words with /oo/ as in *book*; words with /ā/ spelled *ai* and *ay*; words with the blends *sw* and *tw*; and words with /ō/ spelled *oa* and *ow*. **Vocabulary** • Use context to determine the meaning of words in text. • Consult reference materials to clarify the precise meaning of words. • Demonstrate an understanding of synonym word analogies. • Write synonym and antonym word analogies. **Writing** • Write sentences using concrete words and phrases and sensory details to convey information precisely. **Reading** • Compare and contrast informational and literary text types. • Analyze two types of text for specific words used to compare and to contrast.	**Reading** • Read with purpose and understanding. • Identify and explain explicit details from text. • Take notes on a text.

Lesson 3	Lesson 4	Lesson 5
Reading • Read words to develop fluency. Vocabulary • Review key passage vocabulary. • Demonstrate an understanding of common idioms. • Use a range of strategies (consult reference materials; use understanding of figurative language—including similes, metaphors, and idioms; use understanding of similes, antonyms, related words) to clarify the meaning of words. Reading • Use critical thinking skills to analyze a text. • Ask and answer questions and prompts using extended thinking skills to demonstrate an understanding of a text.	Reading • Read sentences to develop fluency. Grammar • Listen to oral sentences and write them accurately. • Demonstrate an understanding of the function of subject and object pronouns in sentences. Reading • Read sentence phrases with fluency to support comprehension. • Read an informational text. • Use critical thinking skills to respond to specific questions about a text.	Vocabulary • Review key passage vocabulary. Reading • Write questions or prompts about text to deepen comprehension. • Use critical thinking skills to respond orally to specific questions about a text. Writing • Use critical and extended thinking skills to write responses to prompts about a text. • Support written answers with evidence from a text.

Lesson 8	Lesson 9	Lesson 10
Writing • Gather relevant information from notes about a text. • Write a clear two-sentence introduction. Take notes on two texts about different topics. • Write a compare and contrast report.	Reading • Read words to develop fluency. Vocabulary • Use a range of strategies (consult reference materials; use understanding of figurative language—including similes, metaphors, and idioms; use understanding of similes, antonyms, related words) to clarify the meaning of words. Grammar • Demonstrate an understanding of the relationship of past, present, and future tense verbs. Writing • Demonstrate an understanding conventional patterns used in sentence structures. • Edit a text for basic conventions. • Edit a text using the Six Traits rubric.	Vocabulary • Clarify the meaning of key passage vocabulary. • Demonstrate an understanding of passage vocabulary by using them in sentences. Reading • Discuss and answer questions to demonstrate an understanding of main idea and key details in a text. • Discuss and answer questions to demonstrate an understanding of point of view in a text. Writing • Demonstrate an understanding of sentence structure by using key elements of sentences to create oral sentences.

Unit 11

Lesson 1

Lesson Opener

Before the lesson, choose one of the following activities to write on the board or post on the *LANGUAGE! Live* Class Wall online.

- *Write sentences with the following words:* mothers', dogs', students'*.*
- *Write three sentences about a hurricane that damaged homes. In the first sentence, the hurricane hasn't come yet. In the second sentence, the hurricane is there now. In the third sentence, the hurricane is already over.*
- *Explain what you would do if a hurricane flooded your neighborhood and the water was 10 feet above the ground.*

Reading

Objectives

- Determine the topic of the text.
- Determine the author's purpose.
- Discuss the topic of the text.
- Preview the text.

Unit Introduction

Direct students to page 223 in their Student Books.

Discuss the content focus of the unit.

Content Focus
tornadoes

What do you think this passage is about? (Answers will vary based on prior knowledge of tornadoes.)

Type of Text
informational

This text is expository, or informational. It will give us information, or facts. What will the information be about? (tornadoes)

Author's Purpose

The author's purpose is the reason that he or she wrote the text. Authors write for different purposes. Why do authors write? (to entertain, to persuade, and to inform or teach) Knowing an author's purpose can help a reader understand a text better. This text was written to inform others about how twisters form and why they are dangerous. Was "Twisters" written to inform or entertain? (inform) Is the author going to teach you something or entertain you? (teach) Have students write the answer on the page in their student books.

Unit 11
Lesson 1 | Reading

Let's Focus: "Twisters"

Content Focus
tornadoes

Type of Text
informational

Author's Purpose: to inform

Big Ideas
Consider the following Big Idea questions. Write your answer for each question.

Why do tornadoes cause fear in people?

How are tornadoes different from other storms?

Informational Preview Checklist: "Twisters"

- ☐ Title: What clue does it provide about the passage?
- ☐ Pictures and Captions: What additional information is added here?
- ☐ Headings: What topics will this text include?
- ☐ Margin Information: What vocabulary is important to understand this text?
- ☐ Maps, Charts, Graphs: Are additional visuals present that will help me understand?

Reading for a Purpose

1. How can a small tornado be more devastating than a large tornado?
2. How is the Fujita Scale similar to the Richter Scale and hurricane intensity chart? How is it different?
3. Why were tornado death rates elevated in 2011?
4. Do all tornadoes result in death?
5. Where did the deadliest tornado after 1950 occur?
6. What tornado milestones have occurred and when did they occur?
7. What do young children need to know about tornadoes?

Unit 11 223

Background Information

Twisters. What do you know about twisters? Have students share knowledge. Do you know another word that means the same as *twister?* (tornado) Twisters, also called tornadoes, are violent rotating columns of air. Stimulate discussion of background knowledge about tornadoes. Use these discussion starters as appropriate. As a child, I first learned about tornadoes watching *The Wizard of Oz*. Have you seen *The Wizard of Oz*? Where was Dorothy from? (Kansas) Are tornadoes common in Kansas? (yes) Compared with other states, Kansas ranks number three for frequency of tornadoes. What do you remember about the tornado in *The Wizard of Oz*? Do you remember what happens to Dorothy's house? When a tornado touches the ground, it can lift trees out of the ground.

Tornadoes and hurricanes are both weather-related natural disasters. Natural disasters like hurricanes and tornadoes cause fascination as well as fear in most people. We will learn how tornadoes are different from other storms and why people fear them.

What will we learn about? (twisters) What will we learn about them? (how they are different from other storms) We will learn how tornadoes are different from other storms and why they are dangerous.

Play the Unit 11 Text Training video found in the Teacher Resources online.

Before we read the passage about tornadoes, we will watch a short video to help build background knowledge. I want you to combine what you just heard with what you are about to watch on this video. Listen for two things you did not know about tornadoes. You will share this new information with a partner after the video. Play the Unit 11 Text Training video. Have partners discuss what they learned from the video.

Direct students to page 223 in their Student Books. Read the following Big Idea questions aloud:

Big Ideas

Why do tornadoes cause fear in people?

How are tornadoes different from other storms?

As a class, consider the two Big Idea questions. After discussing each question, have students write an answer. We'll come back to these questions after we finish learning about tornadoes. You will have much more to add to your answers. You can edit your answers as you gain information.

Preview

Good readers preview the features of a text independently and automatically. In order to strengthen this reading habit, you will preview text independently and then debrief with a partner.

Direct students to pages 225–227 in their Student Books to preview the text. Remind them of the Informational Preview Checklist on page 223. Give students permission to refer to the checklist during the preview if they need a reminder of text features.

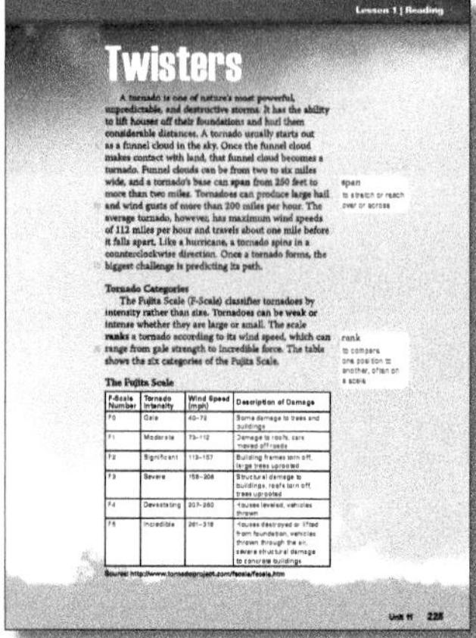

Note: Create a small teacher-led group for students who displayed dependence or confusion with the previewing process in the preceding unit. New students and truant students should also join this group until they reach independence.

Have individuals preview the text. After sufficient time, have partners use the checklist to evaluate each other's previewing skills. Gauge individual success as you circulate around the room. Determine which students need extra practice with the skills, and provide them with alternative practice sources.

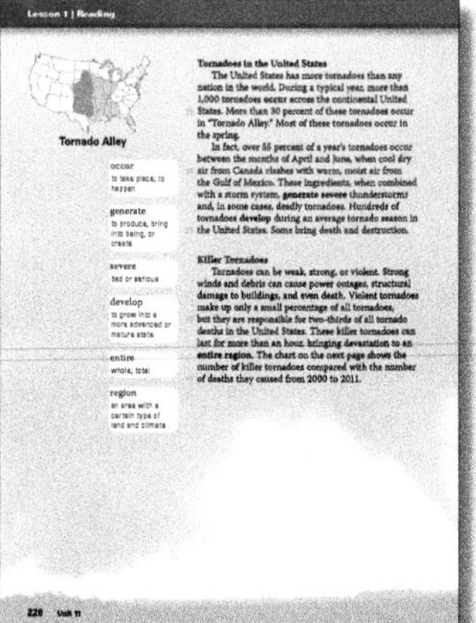

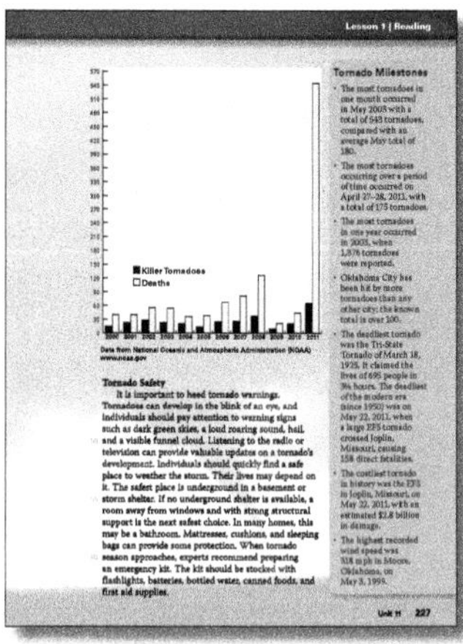

Vocabulary

Objective

- Determine the meaning of key passage vocabulary.

Rate Your Knowledge

Vocabulary Rating Scale poster

Direct students to page 224 in their Student Books. Display the Rating Scale poster or write the information on a board.

You will rate your word knowledge. The purpose of this activity is to recognize how familiar you are with this unit's Key Passage Vocabulary.

Review the Vocabulary Rating Scale with students.

Vocabulary Rating Scale

0—I have never heard the word before.

1—I have heard the word, but I'm not sure how to use it.

2—I am familiar with the word, but I'm not sure if I know the correct meaning.

3—I know the meaning of the word and can use it correctly in a sentence.

Lesson 1 | Vocabulary

Key Passage Vocabulary: "Twisters"

Rate your knowledge of the words. Define the words. Draw a picture to help you remember the definition.

Vocabulary	Knowledge Rating	Definition	Picture
span	0 1 2 3	to stretch or reach over or across	
rank	0 1 2 3	to compare one position with another, often on a scale	
occur	0 1 2 3	to take place; to happen	
generate	0 1 2 3	to produce, bring into being, or create	
severe	0 1 2 3	bad or serious	
develop	0 1 2 3	to grow into a more advanced or mature state	
entire	0 1 2 3	whole; total	
region	0 1 2 3	an area with a certain type of land and climate	

224 Unit 11

Read the list of words. Have students repeat each word. Provide time for students to rate their knowledge of each word.

Have partners discuss the words they rated as 3s and tell each other the meanings.

Preteach Vocabulary

You've rated your knowledge and talked about what you think the words mean. Now, let's discuss the words.

Preteach Procedure

This activity is intended to take only a short amount of time, so make it an oral exercise if your students aren't capable of writing quickly.

- Introduce each word as indicated on the word card.
- Read the definition and example sentences.
- Ask questions to clarify and deepen understanding.
- If time permits, allow students to share.

* Do not provide instruction time to write definitions or draw pictures, but explain that students should complete both as time permits during the unit.

Note: Research has proven that vocabulary is best learned when students represent their knowledge of words in linguistic and/or nonlinguistic ways. Thus, drawing a picture will help students remember the words. This strategy is especially effective for English language learners.

span

Let's read the first word together. *Span.*

Definition: *Span* means "to stretch or reach over or across." To stretch or reach over or across is to what? (span)

Example 1: The Golden Gate Bridge *spans* San Francisco Bay.

Example 2: The albatross's wings *span* 11 feet, 11 inches. Can you imagine having arms that long?

Example 3: The Watermelon Festival *spans* the entire month of June.

Question 1: Does a roof *span* a house? (yes)

Question 2: Does baseball season *span* the months of November through February? (no)

Pair Share: Tell your partner how many years your public education has *spanned.* Use the word *span* in your sentence.

rank

Let's read the next word together. *Rank.*

Definition: *Rank* means "to compare one position with another, often on a scale." To compare one position with another, often on a scale, is to what? (rank)

Example 1: I *rank* cleaning toilets at the very bottom of my list of favorite things to do.

Example 2: The girls' volleyball team was *ranked* first going into the state tournament.

Example 3: The artists were *ranked* best to worst after the art show.

Question 1: I can *rank* the meals in the cafeteria from best to worst? Yes or no? (yes)

Question 2: Are people in the military *ranked*? (yes)

Pair Share: With your neighbor, *rank* these words from hottest to coldest: *warm, cool, cold, scorching, freezing.*

occur

Let's read the next word together. *Occur.*

Definition: *Occur* means "to take place or happen." To take place or happen is to what? (occur)

Example 1: If a thunderstorm with lightning *occurs,* it is wise to go indoors.

Example 2: A leap year *occurs* every four years.

Example 3: A full moon *occurs* once every 28 days.

Question 1: Is learning *occurring* right now? Yes or no? (yes)

Question 2: Do rainbows *occur* at night? Yes or no? (no)

Pair Share: Turn to your partner and relate three important events that have *occurred* during your lifetime.

generate

Let's read the next word together. *Generate.*

Definition: *Generate* means "to produce, bring into being, or create." To produce, bring into being, or create is to what? (generate)

Example 1: Water from Niagara Falls is used to *generate* hydroelectric power.

Example 2: We have pep rallies to *generate* school spirit before games.

Example 3: We often *generate* questions about the text we are reading.

Question 1: What does an automobile factory *generate*? (cars)

Question 2: Does a fire *generate* heat? Yes or no? (yes)

Pair Share: With your partner, *generate* two sentences using the word *generate.*

severe

Let's read the next word together. *Severe.*

Definition: *Severe* means "bad or serious." If something is bad or serious, it is what? (severe)

Example 1: The accident caused *severe* damage to the car, but the occupants were all safe.

Example 2: When I saw the doctor's *severe* expression, I knew the news was not good.

Example 3: The man was *severely* injured when he fell off the ladder.

Question 1: When you think of baby bunnies, do you think of *severe*? (no)

Question 2: Can hurricanes and tsunamis cause *severe* damage? (yes)

Pair Share: Turn and give your partner a *severe* look—one that means you're serious.

develop

Let's read the next word together. *Develop.*

Definition: *Develop* means "to grow into a more advanced or mature state." To grow into a more advanced or mature state is to what? (develop)

Example 1: In their first two years of life, babies *develop* into toddlers.

Example 2: With daily practice, the boy who loved football *developed* into a top NFL quarterback.

Example 3: If you practice using Masterpiece Sentences, you will *develop* into a proficient writer.

Question 1: Can dogs *develop* into wolves? Yes or no? (no)

Question 2: Can you *develop* into a great reader? Yes or no? (yes)

Pair Share: Turn to your partner and discuss what caterpillars and tadpoles *develop* into.

entire

Let's read the next word together. *Entire.*

Definition: *Entire* means "whole or total." What word means whole or total? (entire)

Example 1: Once, I ate an *entire* watermelon! I was full for hours.

Example 2: Because my sister and I can't eat an *entire* pizza, we share it.

Example 3: The *entire* city, not just part of the city, uses water and electricity.

Question 1: Do you usually eat an *entire* chicken all by yourself? Yes or no? (no)

Question 2: Could you read an *entire* 800-page book in two days? Yes or no? (no)

Pair Share: Turn to your partner and finish this statement: I could go an *entire* _____ without using a phone.

region

Let's read the last word together. *Region.*

Definition: *Region* means "an area with a certain type of land and climate." An area with a certain type of land and climate is a what? (region)

Example 1: Maine is in the northeast *region* of the United States.

Example 2: Polar bears don't live in hot, dry *regions.*

Example 3: The Death Valley *region* in California is actually below sea level.

Question 1: Is *region* a verb? Yes or no? (no)

Question 2: Do palm trees grow in the northern *regions* of the United States? Yes or no? (no)

Pair Share: With your partner, cite examples of what the winter weather is like in the *region* where you live.

Reading

Objectives

- Review text features.
- Read an informational text.
- Demonstrate an understanding of the text by asking and answering questions and referring to key details in the text.

"Twisters"

Direct students to pages 225–227 in their Student Books.

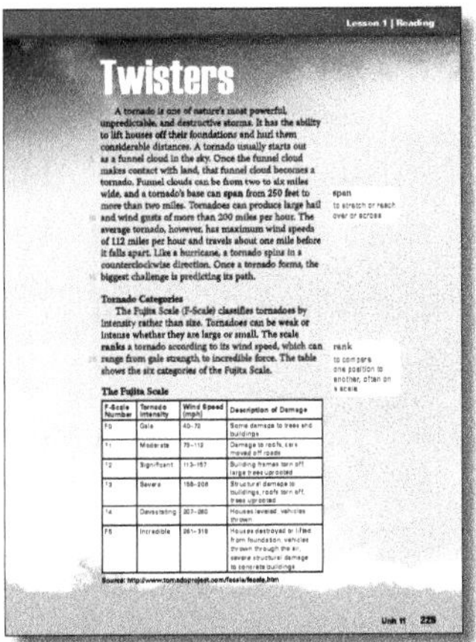

Words to Know

In addition to the vocabulary words, here are some words students might have trouble with:

ability the power or knowledge to do something; skill

classify to put in groups according to things that are similar

category a type of something based on similar characteristics

clash to come together with force

debris scattered pieces left after something has been destroyed

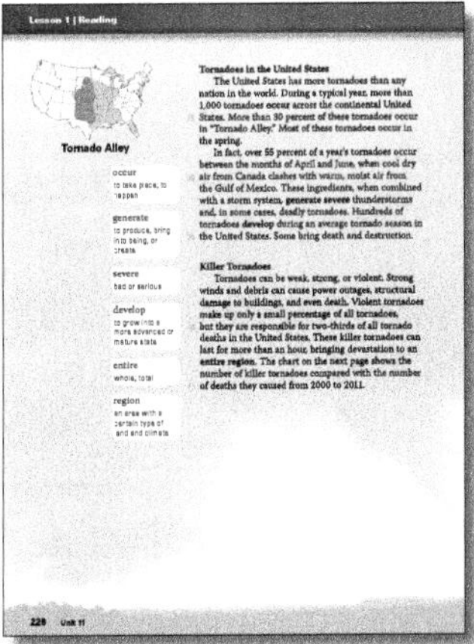

You and your partner have already previewed the text. Now let's discuss some key points before we read.

- Text features give us information about a text before we read it. Text features can sometimes help us identify the topic, which is the subject of the passage. What is the topic of this passage? (tornadoes)
- Which features gave you information about the text? Have students refer to the checklist in their Student Book, if necessary. Guide them to identify the following.
  - Headings: Tornado Categories, The Fujita Scale, Tornadoes in the United States, Killer Tornadoes, Tornado Safety
  - Margin Information: Tornado Milestones
    What are milestones? In this context, they are highlights or factoids.
  - Maps, Charts, Graphs: This text includes a chart, a map, and a graph. Point to the chart. Students should point to the chart on page 227. What information appears on this chart? (data about tornado F-Scale, intensity, wind speed, and damage) Find the map. What information appears on the map? (the location of Tornado Alley) What do you think *Tornado Alley* means? Accept reasonable responses. Is our state included in Tornado Alley? Help students find your state, if necessary.
    Find the graph. What information appears on the *x*-axis of the graph? (year) What information appears on the *y*-axis of the graph? (numbers in increments of 30) What color is used to represent killer

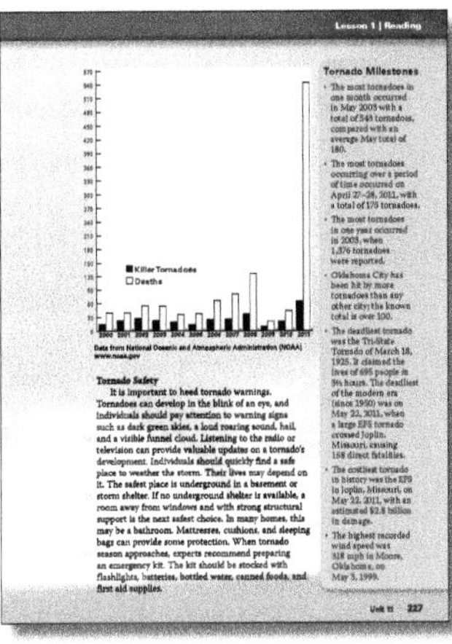

tornadoes? (black) What color is used to represent deaths? (gray) Can you tell from this graph if our state has had killer tornadoes? (no)

Direct students to page 223 in their Student Books. Have students follow along as you read the prompts aloud.

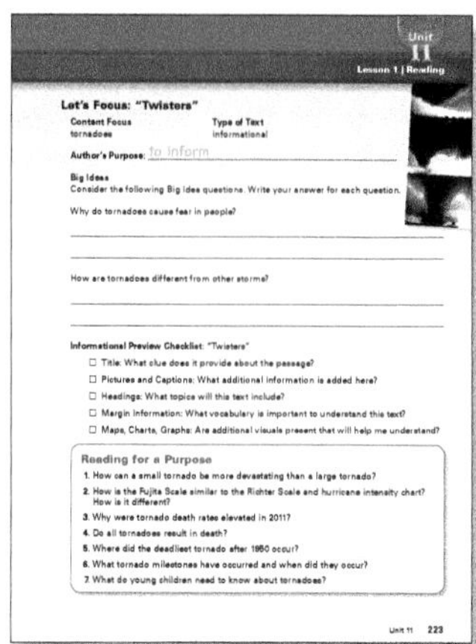

Reading for a Purpose

1. How can a small tornado be more devastating than a large tornado?
2. How is the Fujita Scale similar to the Richter Scale and hurricane intensity chart? How is it different?
3. Why were tornado death rates elevated in 2011?
4. Do all tornadoes result in death?
5. Where did the deadliest tornado after 1950 occur?
6. What tornado milestones have occurred and when did they occur?
7. What do young children need to know about tornadoes?

You will be better equipped to respond to these prompts after reading the passage. For now, let the prompts provide a focus for your reading. Be on the lookout for facts and concepts you could use to respond to them. While reading, you also should think about our two Big Idea questions: Why do tornadoes cause fear in people? and How are tornadoes different from other storms?

Now it's time to read. Let's review. Where are your eyes while I read? (on text) Where is your pencil? (following along, word for word) Eyes on text, pencil on words. Let's begin.

Guiding Students Toward Independent Reading

While the lessons are written for a teacher read aloud, it is important that your students read as much and as often as they can. Assign readings that meet the needs of your students, based on your observations or data. This is a good opportunity to stretch students, but if they become frustrated, return to the read-aloud method.

Options for reading text:

- Teacher read aloud
- Teacher-led or student-led choral read
- Independent read of small sections with frequent comprehension checks
- Paired read or independent read

Read the passage aloud.

Twisters

A tornado is one of nature's most powerful, unpredictable, and destructive storms. It has the ability to lift houses off their foundations and hurl them considerable distances. A tornado usually starts out as a funnel cloud in the sky. Once the funnel cloud makes contact with land, that funnel cloud becomes a tornado. Funnel clouds can be from two to six miles wide, and a tornado's base can span from 250 feet to more than two miles. Tornadoes can produce large hail and wind gusts of more than 200 miles per hour. The average tornado, however, has maximum wind speeds of 112 miles per hour and travels about one mile before it falls apart. Like a hurricane, a tornado spins in a counterclockwise direction. Once a tornado forms, the biggest challenge is predicting its path.

Timer

For confirmation of engagement, take 30 seconds to have students share one thing they learned with their partner. If needed, provide this example for students: While reading, I was thinking that the tornado in *The Wizard of Oz* seems like the tornadoes described here. Your turn. Share your thoughts and one thing you learned with your partner. Partners, you should listen carefully and ask questions to check understanding.

Tornado Categories

The Fujita Scale (F-Scale) classifies tornadoes by intensity rather than size. Tornadoes can be weak or intense whether they are large or small. The scale ranks a tornado according to its wind speed, which can range from gale strength to incredible force. The table shows the six categories of the Fujita Scale.

The Fujita Scale

F-Scale Number	Tornado Intensity	Wind Speed (mph)	Description of Damage
F0	Gale	40–72	Some damage to trees and buildings
F1	Moderate	73–112	Damage to roofs, cars moved off roads
F2	Significant	113–157	Building frames torn off, large trees uprooted
F3	Severe	158–206	Structural damage to buildings, roofs torn off, trees uprooted
F4	Devastating	207–260	Houses leveled, vehicles thrown
F5	Incredible	261–318	Houses destroyed or lifted from foundation, vehicles thrown through the air, severe structural damage to concrete buildings

Source: http://www.tornadoproject.com/fscale/fscale.htm

For confirmation of engagement, take 30 seconds to have students share one thing they learned with their partner. While reading, I was thinking that the tornado in *The Wizard of Oz* would be considered an F5 because the house was lifted off its foundation. Your turn. Switch roles. Share your thoughts and one thing you learned with your partner. Partners, you should listen carefully and ask questions to check understanding.

Tornadoes in the United States

The United States has more tornadoes than any nation in the world. During a typical year, more than 1,000 tornadoes occur across the continental United States. More than 30 percent of these tornadoes occur in "Tornado Alley." Most of these tornadoes occur in the spring.

In fact, over 55 percent of a year's tornadoes occur between the months of April and June, when cool dry air from Canada clashes with warm, moist air from the Gulf of Mexico. These ingredients, when combined with a storm system, generate severe thunderstorms and, in some cases, deadly tornadoes. Hundreds of tornadoes develop during an average tornado season in the United States. Some bring death and destruction.

For confirmation of engagement, take 30 seconds to have students share one thing they learned with their partner. Provide this example for students: While reading, I was thinking that Kansas is in Tornado Alley. Your turn. Switch roles. Share your thoughts and one thing you learned with your partner. Try to use one of the bold vocabulary words. Partners, you should listen carefully and ask questions to check understanding.

Killer Tornadoes

Tornadoes can be weak, strong, or violent. Strong winds and debris can cause power outages, structural damage to buildings, and even death. Violent tornadoes make up only a small percentage of all tornadoes, but they are responsible for two-thirds of all tornado deaths in the United States. These killer tornadoes can last for more than an hour, bringing devastation to an entire region. The chart on the next page shows the number of killer tornadoes compared with the number of deaths they caused from 2000 to 2011.

For confirmation of engagement, take 30 seconds to have students share one thing they learned with their partner. While reading, I was thinking that people should take tornado drills very seriously! Your turn. Switch roles. Share your thoughts and one thing you learned with your partner. Partners, you should listen carefully and ask questions to check understanding.

Tornado Safety

It is important to heed tornado warnings. Tornadoes can develop in the blink of an eye, and individuals should pay attention to warning signs such as dark green skies, a loud roaring sound, hail, and a visible funnel cloud. Listening to the radio or television can provide valuable updates on a tornado's development. Individuals should quickly find a safe place to weather the storm. Their lives may depend on it. The safest place is underground in a basement or storm shelter. If no underground shelter is available, a room away from windows and with strong structural support is the next safest choice. In many homes, this may be a bathroom. Mattresses, cushions, and sleeping bags can provide some protection. When tornado season approaches, experts recommend preparing an emergency kit. The kit should be stocked with flashlights, batteries, bottled water, canned foods, and first aid supplies.

For confirmation of engagement, take 30 seconds to have students share one thing they learned with their partner. While reading, I was wondering what *heed* means. From the context, I think it means pay attention to. I wonder if I'm correct. Your turn. Switch roles. Share your thoughts and one thing you learned with your partner. Partners, you should listen carefully and ask questions to check understanding.

Tornado Milestones

- The most tornadoes in one month occurred in May 2003 with a total of 543 tornadoes, compared with an average May total of 180.
- The most tornadoes occurring over a period of time occurred on April 27–28, 2011, with a total of 175 tornadoes.
- The most tornadoes in one year occurred in 2003, when 1,376 tornadoes were reported.
- Oklahoma City has been hit by more tornadoes than any other city; the known total is over 100.
- The deadliest tornado was the Tri-State Tornado of March 18, 1925. It claimed the lives of 695 people in 3½ hours. The deadliest of the modern era (since 1950) was on May 22, 2011, when a large EF5 tornado crossed Joplin, Missouri, causing 158 direct fatalities.
- The costliest tornado in history was the EF5 in Joplin, Missouri, on May 22, 2011, with an estimated $2.8 billion in damage.
- The highest recorded wind speed was 318 mph in Moore, Oklahoma, on May 3, 1999.

For confirmation of engagement, take 30 seconds to have students share one thing they learned with their partner. Now that you have read "Twisters," tell me something you shared with your partner during the reading. Call on students to share answers.

Unit 11

Lesson 2

Lesson Opener

Before the lesson, choose one of the following activities to write on the board or post on the *LANGUAGE! Live* Class Wall online.

- *How are tornadoes categorized and what is the strength of each category?*
- *Write a sentence with an action verb about what happens during a tornado. Then write a sentence with a linking verb that describes a tornado.*
- *Write a sentence about you and your best friend. Write a similar sentence using a subject pronoun. Then, write a third sentence using an object pronoun.*

Vocabulary

Objectives

- Use discussion and context to determine the meanings of the multiple-meaning words *contact* and *base*.
- Demonstrate an understanding of the words by using them in written sentences.

Multiple-Meaning Words: *contact, base*

Direct students to page 228 in their Student Books.

In this unit, we are talking about tornadoes—how they form and the damage they do when they contact the ground.

Contact is a word that has more than one meaning. For example, the word *contact* can be a noun, an adjective, or a verb.

So, how do we know which definition of the word is being used? It all depends on how it is used in a sentence. We look for clues around the word to help us.

Lead students in a discussion of the various meanings of the word *contact.* Have them write the meanings and sentences on the Multiple-Meaning Map in their Student Books.

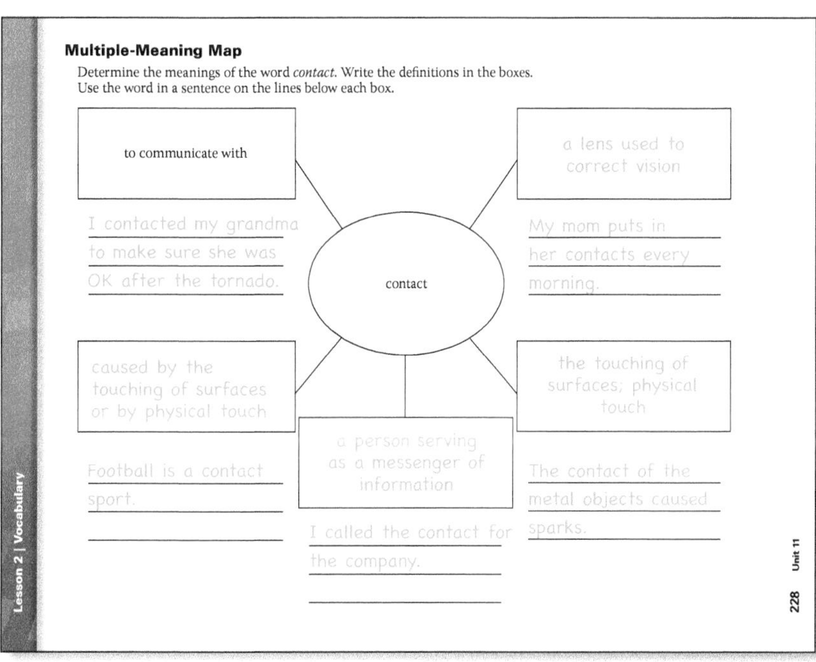

Multiple-Meaning Map
Determine the meanings of the word *contact.* Write the definitions in the boxes. Use the word in a sentence on the lines below each box.
contact
to communicate with
I contacted my grandma to make sure she was OK after the tornado.
a lens used to correct vision
My mom puts in her contacts every morning.
caused by the touching of surfaces or by physical touch
Football is a contact sport.
a person serving as a messenger of information
I called the contact for the company.
the touching of surfaces; physical touch
The contact of the metal objects caused sparks.
Lesson 2 | Vocabulary
228
Unit 11

Model

Have you ever made contact with someone? We often use *contact* as a verb meaning "to communicate." Listen to this sentence: I contacted my grandma to make sure she was okay after the tornado. Write the definition *to communicate with* on the board and have students find it on their map. Have students think of a good sentence for this usage and write it below the definition.

Guided Practice

I love to play sports. But I typically don't play sports that are physical in nature, like football and hockey. There is too much contact. Football and hockey are examples of contact sports. What is the definition of *contact* in this sentence? (caused by the touching of surfaces or physical touch) Write the definition on the board and have students write it on their map. Have students think of a good sentence for this usage and write it below the definition.

Independent Practice

Continue the process until the maps are complete. Review the sentences and correct as needed.

Note: Base the number of modeled and guided examples on student ability and progress. Challenge them with independent practice when appropriate.

Additional Definitions of *contact*

Noun

- communication

Verb

- to join

Direct students to page 229 in their Student Books. Repeat the process with the word *base.*

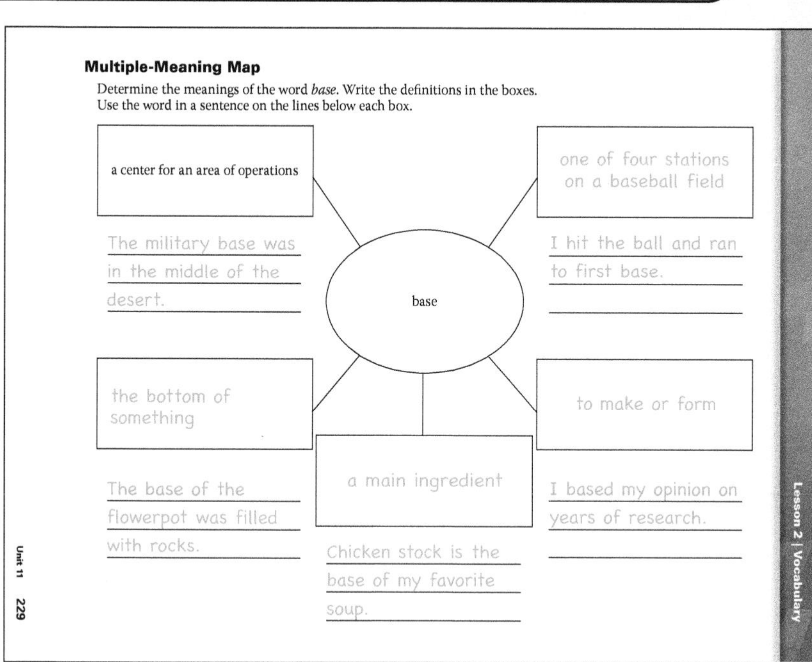
Multiple-Meaning Map

Determine the meanings of the word *base*. Write the definitions in the boxes. Use the word in a sentence on the lines below each box.

base

a center for an area of operations

The military base was in the middle of the desert.

one of four stations on a baseball field

I hit the ball and ran to first base.

the bottom of something

The base of the flowerpot was filled with rocks.

a main ingredient

Chicken stock is the base of my favorite soup.

to make or form

I based my opinion on years of research.

Unit 11 229

Lesson 2 | Vocabulary

Additional Definitions of *base*

Noun

- the lower part of the wall or column
- a number that is raised to a power
- the fundamental part of something
- the starting place or goal in a game
- a point to be considered
- compound with a pH greater than 7

Idiom

- *touch base:* make contact
- *cover all the bases:* anticipate all possibilities
- *off base:* mistaken; wrong

Grammar

Objectives

- Demonstrate an understanding of forming plurals using inflectional endings.
- Demonstrate an understanding of using plural nouns and verbs with various inflectional endings in sentences.

Inflectional Ending *-es*

We have learned how suffixes, or word endings, can impact meaning. We have also learned that good readers pay attention to all aspects of a word, looking for meaning clues. Write the following words on the board:

pitch

wish

buzz

If necessary, explain the sound the *-tch* trigraph makes. These words have multiple meanings and functions, so we need context to determine what any one of them means.

Nouns

Let's see whether any of them can function as a noun.

- What is a pitch? (the throwing of a ball, the sound of the human voice, slope, the presentation of an idea or action—sales pitch)
- What is a wish? (a longing, a desire, a hope)
- What is a buzz? (a sound)
- What is a tax? (money paid by people for public services)
- What is a pass? (the moving of a ball to another person, a try, written permission, a road through a mountain)

All five words can function as a noun, and most nouns can be either singular or plural.

Can we make these nouns plural so they mean more than one? (yes) What is one way to make a noun mean more than one? (add an *-s*) We can add an *-s* to some nouns to make them plural. But these words are different. Their final sounds make it difficult to simply add an *-s*. Model trying to pronounce the word *pitchs*. Instead of adding an *-s*, we have to add the letters *-es*. Add *-es* to each word on the board and then have students repeat the words.

Verbs

These words can also function as verbs, and we know that verbs take different forms and use different endings. When the subject of a sentence is a singular noun or a singular third-person pronoun such as *he, she,* or *it*, we have to add something to most regular verbs. Listen to these sentences: Sam pitches very well. He pitches the first inning in every game. Who pitches? (Sam, he)

Have volunteers use *wishes* as a verb in a sentence. Have students determine the subject. Repeat the process for the words *buzzes, passes,* and *taxes.*

What are ending letters and sounds that signal the need for *-es*? (words that end with the *s, x, z, sh, ch* sounds)

Direct students to page 230 in their Student Books and read the instruction aloud.

Lesson 2 | Grammar

Inflectional Ending *-es*

Add *-es* to the underlined word. Then use the new word in a sentence as the designated part of speech. Underline the word in the sentence. Answers will vary.

Base Word	Add -es	Part of Speech	Sentence
Example: catch	catches	verb	She catches the ball when I throw it.
Example: dish	dishes	noun	The dishes have a simple pattern on them.
1. fizz	fizzes	verb	The soda fizzes when it is poured over ice.
2. ax	axes	noun	He sells axes and hammers in his hardware store.
3. miss	misses	verb	Sara misses her friends.
4. flash	flashes	verb	Lightning flashes across the sky.
5. beach	beaches	noun	Beaches are favorite vacation spots.
6. wash	washes	verb	Ted washes the dishes.
7. fish	fishes	verb	Stan fishes in the lake.
8. box	boxes	noun	The boxes are empty.
9. reach	reaches	verb	She reaches for the salt.
10. class	classes	noun	Mrs. Smith teaches two reading classes.

230 Unit 11

Model

Model the process using the two examples.

Guided Practice

Guide students to complete the first sentence.

Independent Practice

Have students complete the remaining sentences independently. Review the answers as a class.

Note: Base the number of modeled and guided examples on student ability and progress. Challenge them with independent practice when appropriate.

Challenge students to make the nouns on the page possessive and use them in a sentence for the class.

Example Sentences with Possessive Nouns

The axes' handles are brown.

The beaches' visitors have a great time.

The boxes' lids are missing.

All the classes' books are missing.

Inflectional Ending Review

Let's review all of the inflectional endings we have learned. Write the following inflectional endings on the board:

-ing, -s, -ed, -'s, -s', -es, -es'

Write the following words on the board:

jump, pass, cat, class

Have volunteers create new words by adding endings to the verbs *jump* and *pass* and endings to the nouns *cat* and *class.*

> **Example Inflectional Endings**
>
> **Verbs:** past tense, present tense, present progressive (jumped, jumps, jumping; passed, passes, passing)
>
> **Nouns:** possessive, plural, plural possessive (cat's, cats, cats'; class's, classes, classes')

Provide other examples for extra practice, if needed.

Give students an example of a proper noun ending in *-s* (Wes) and explain how to form the possessive by adding an *-'s.*

Direct students to page 231 in their Student Books and read the inflectional endings in the box at the top of the page. Read the instructions for the activity.

Model

Then read the example sentence, omitting the target words.

A form of the word *prepare* goes in the first blank. I could say "I prepare" and use the present tense, but in that case, I wouldn't be adding an ending. I could also say "I am preparing," but there is no helping verb provided. To follow the instructions and add an ending, I will need to make the verb past tense: *prepared*. I will write *prepared* on the line. I now have "I prepared a great dish from . . . cookbook." The base word is *mother*. What part of speech is *mother*? It's a naming word, or a noun. My choices are to make it a plural or to make it possessive. I don't think it makes sense as a plural since I'm talking about my mother. Remember, the use of *I* signals first person. I'm thinking I need to make *mother* possessive. Because *mother* is singular, I will add *-'s*. Now, I will read the sentence again to make sure my choices

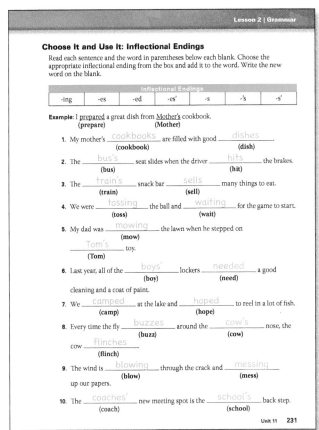

Lesson 2 | Grammar

Choose It and Use It: Inflectional Endings

Read each sentence and the word in parentheses below each blank. Choose the appropriate inflectional ending from the box and add it to the word. Write the new word on the blank.

Inflectional Endings						
-ing	-es	-ed	-es'	-s	-'s	-s'

Example: I prepared (prepare) a great dish from Mother's (Mother) cookbook.

1. My mother's cookbooks (cookbook) are filled with good dishes (dish).
2. The bus's (bus) seat slides when the driver hits (hit) the brakes.
3. The train's (train) snack bar sells (sell) many things to eat.
4. We were tossing (toss) the ball and waiting (wait) for the game to start.
5. My dad was mowing (mow) the lawn when he stepped on Tom's (Tom) toy.
6. Last year, all of the boys' (boy) lockers needed (need) a good cleaning and a coat of paint.
7. We camped (camp) at the lake and hoped (hope) to reel in a lot of fish.
8. Every time the fly buzzes (buzz) around the cow's (cow) nose, the cow flinches (flinch).
9. The wind is blowing (blow) through the crack and messing (mess) up our papers.
10. The coaches' (coach) new meeting spot is the school's (school) back step.

Unit 11 231

make sense in the sentence: "I prepared a great dish from mother's cookbook." I have added an ending to each word and they make sense in the sentence.

Guided Practice

Guide students to complete the first sentence.

Independent Practice

Read the next sentence and have students complete it independently. Review the answer immediately. If students struggle, continue to have them complete the sentence after you read it aloud, reviewing the answers to each sentence before students move to the next sentence. If students display mastery, then have them complete the remaining sentences independently. Review the answers as a class.

Note: Base the number of modeled and guided examples on student ability and progress. Challenge them with independent practice when appropriate.

Reading

Objectives

- Discuss the purposes of informational and literary text types.
- Discuss the features of informational and literary texts.
- Compare and contrast informational and literary text types.

Types of Text

We've been spending a lot of time identifying and analyzing text features. Many of these features provide strong clues to the content of a text and often present information in a clear and understandable format. Direct students to page 232 in their Student Books.

Let's talk about each type of text we've read. Let's start with expository, or informational, text. What is the purpose of an informational text? (to inform, to describe, to persuade, to teach) Have students write these purposes on the Types of Text chart. Then repeat the discussion with literary text. What is the purpose of literary text? (to express feelings, to tell a story, to entertain, to persuade) Have students add these purposes to the chart.

Next, have students brainstorm text features and examples of each type of text and use their ideas to complete the charts.

Direct students to page 233 in their Student Books. Draw a blank Venn diagram on the board. Informational and literary texts have many similarities and differences. Let's compare and contrast the two types of writing in a Venn diagram. This is a great tool to use when we want to organize our thoughts about similarities and differences. It makes it easier to "see" the differences and similarities. Have partners use their Types of Text charts to complete the Venn diagram. Review the answers as a class.

Types of Text

Fill in the chart below regarding purpose and form. Answers will vary.

Type of Text	Author's Purpose
expository/informational	to inform, to describe, to persuade, to teach
Text Features	**Examples**
charts graphs maps tables bold font pictures captions subheadings title	textbooks magazines encyclopedias Web sites newspapers letters nonfiction books diaries journals poetry

Type of Text	Author's Purpose
literary	to express feelings, to tell a story, to entertain, to persuade
Text Features	**Examples**
title chapter titles quotation marks illustrations bold words	fiction books picture books novels some magazines anthologies some Web sites poetry short stories letters diaries journals blogs

Text Features: Informational Text vs. Literary Text

Fill in the diagram to show how informational texts and literary texts are similar and different. Answers will vary.

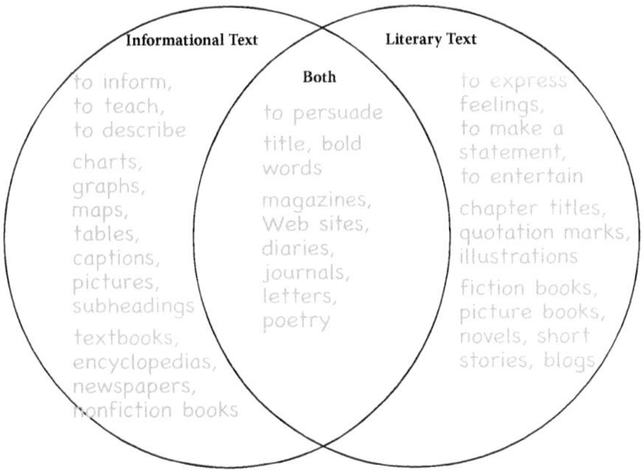

Informational Text

to inform, to teach, to describe

charts, graphs, maps, tables, captions, pictures, subheadings

textbooks, encyclopedias, newspapers, nonfiction books

Both

to persuade

title, bold words

magazines, Web sites, diaries, journals, letters, poetry

Literary Text

to express feelings, to make a statement, to entertain

chapter titles, quotation marks, illustrations

fiction books, picture books, novels, short stories, blogs

Unit 11 Lesson 3

Lesson Opener

Before the lesson, choose one of the following activities to write on the board or post on the *LANGUAGE! Live* Class Wall online.

- *Write three sentences with the word* base, *using a different meaning in each sentence.*
- *If a tornado ripped through your neighborhood and destroyed your home, what item in your bedroom would you spend the most time looking for in the debris? Why?*
- *Write a sentence about a tornado using a predicate modifier.*

Reading

Objective

- Read words to develop fluency.

Word Fluency: First Read

Timer

Follow the Fluency Procedure outlined below. If it is necessary, begin the fluency drill with a choral read of the words as you provide a rhythm (snap your fingers, tap your foot, tap your pencil). Direct students to page 234 in their Student Books and complete the process.

Word Fluency: First Read

Read the words fluently.

	Correct	Errors
1st Try		
2nd Try		

cooked	hook	goals	bowling	brains	sweet	slows	failed	twisted	moons	10
goals	bowling	brains	sweet	slows	failed	twisted	moons	swinging	stays	20
brains	sweet	slows	failed	twisted	moons	swinging	stays	coaches	tweeted	30
slows	failed	twisted	moons	swinging	stays	coaches	tweeted	swayed	loaned	40
twisted	moons	swinging	stays	coaches	tweeted	swayed	loaned	brooms	growing	50
swinging	stays	coaches	tweeted	swayed	loaned	brooms	growing	may	snails	60
coaches	tweeted	swayed	loaned	brooms	growing	may	snails	hook	cooked	70
swayed	loaned	brooms	growing	may	snails	hook	cooked	bowling	goals	80
brooms	growing	may	snails	hook	cooked	bowling	goals	sweet	brains	90
may	snails	hook	cooked	bowling	goals	sweet	brains	failed	slows	100

Lesson 3 | Reading

234 Unit 11

Fluency Procedure

- Partners switch books, so the recorder is marking errors in the reader's book.
- A timer is set for one minute.
- Readers and recorders move left to right, tracking each word with a pencil.
- As readers read the words aloud, recorders mark errors with a small x above the misread word.
- Recorders place a star to the right of the last word read when time ends.
- If the reader is able to read all words in the allotted time, the reader needs to start over at the beginning. The recorder must indicate this feat by placing two stars to the right of the last word read.
- When both students have read, partners switch books.
- Students calculate total words read, then subtract errors and record.
- Students record information on the progress chart in back of the Student Book.

Vocabulary

Objectives

- Review key passage vocabulary.
- Demonstrate an understanding of common idioms.
- Use a range of strategies (consult reference materials; use understanding of figurative language—including similes, metaphors, and idioms; use understanding of synonyms, antonyms, related words) to clarify the meaning of words.

Review

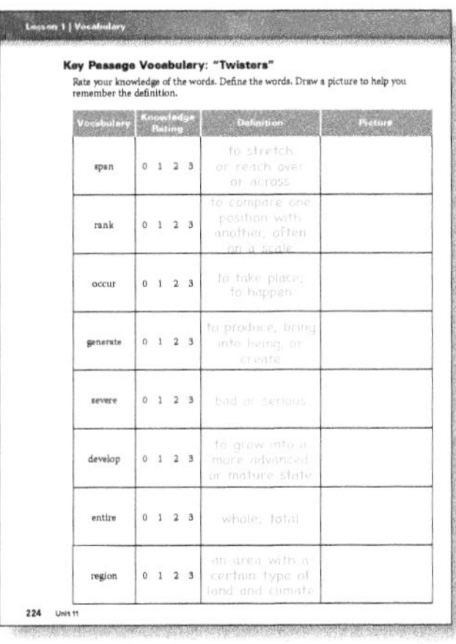

Direct students to page 224 in their Student Books.

Review the vocabulary words from the passage "Twisters." Have students answer in complete sentences.

- Can a tornado destroy an *entire* town? (Yes, a tornado can destroy an entire town.) A word meaning "whole or total" is what? (Entire means whole or total.)
- Do all thunderstorms *develop* into tornadoes? (No, not all thunderstorms develop into tornadoes.) To grow into a more mature state is to what? (To develop is to grow into a more mature state.)
- Is there *severe* wind in a tornado? (Yes, there is severe wind in a tornado.) If something is bad or serious, it is what? (If something is bad or serious, it is severe.)
- Do tornadoes happen more often in certain *regions* of the United States? (Yes, tornadoes happen more often in the Midwest region.) An area with a certain type of land and climate is a what? (A region is an area of land with a certain climate.)
- Are there specific actions you should take when a tornado *occurs*? (Yes, when a tornado occurs, you should go to the lowest point in the house without windows.) To take place or happen is to what? (To occur is to take place or happen.)
- Are tornadoes *ranked* on a numerical scale? (Yes, tornadoes are ranked on a numerical scale called the F-Scale.) To compare one position with another, often on a scale is to what? (To compare one position with another is to rank.)
- Can a tornado's base *span* 500 miles? (No, a tornado's base can span 250 miles.) To stretch or reach over or across is to what? (To stretch or reach over or across is to span.)
- Are tornadoes *generated* when warm, moist air meets cool, dry air? (Yes, tornadoes are generated when the two types of air clash.) To produce or bring into being is to what? (To produce or bring into being is to generate.)

Vocabulary Concept: Idioms

Figurative language activates our imagination by casting something in a new light or making a surprising comparison. Figurative language doesn't mean exactly what it says. It often uses exaggeration or irony for effect.

In this unit, we will study a form of figurative language called idioms. Idioms are common sayings that are used in a certain region or by a certain group of people. Take the idiom *raining cats and dogs,* for example. Most people know this idiom today, but it originated at a particular time in history. In the 1500s, in England, people lived in houses with thatched roofs and dirt floors. Thatch is straw that is layered to keep out water. The cats and other small animals slept overhead in the thatch at night. When it rained, the animals would fall to the floor. And that is the origin of the idiom *it's raining cats and dogs.* What do you think this idiom means now? (raining heavily)

Direct students to page 235 in their Student Books. Read the instructions.

Model

Complete the first item as a model.

Independent Practice

Have partners complete the activity. When all pairs are finished, discuss each idiom and its meaning.

Note: Base the number of modeled and guided examples on student ability and progress. Challenge them with independent practice when appropriate.

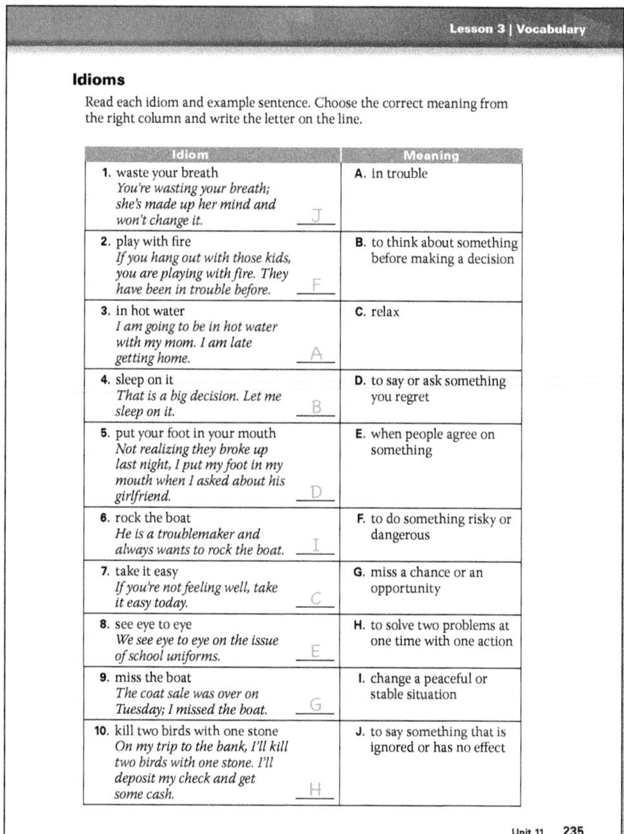

Lesson 3 | Vocabulary

Idioms

Read each idiom and example sentence. Choose the correct meaning from the right column and write the letter on the line.

Idiom	Meaning
1. waste your breath *You're wasting your breath; she's made up her mind and won't change it.* J	A. in trouble
2. play with fire *If you hang out with those kids, you are playing with fire. They have been in trouble before.* F	B. to think about something before making a decision
3. in hot water *I am going to be in hot water with my mom. I am late getting home.* A	C. relax
4. sleep on it *That is a big decision. Let me sleep on it.* B	D. to say or ask something you regret
5. put your foot in your mouth *Not realizing they broke up last night, I put my foot in my mouth when I asked about his girlfriend.* D	E. when people agree on something
6. rock the boat *He is a troublemaker and always wants to rock the boat.* I	F. to do something risky or dangerous
7. take it easy *If you're not feeling well, take it easy today.* C	G. miss a chance or an opportunity
8. see eye to eye *We see eye to eye on the issue of school uniforms.* E	H. to solve two problems at one time with one action
9. miss the boat *The coat sale was over on Tuesday; I missed the boat.* G	I. change a peaceful or stable situation
10. kill two birds with one stone *On my trip to the bank, I'll kill two birds with one stone. I'll deposit my check and get some cash.* H	J. to say something that is ignored or has no effect

Unit 11 235

Vocabulary Expansion

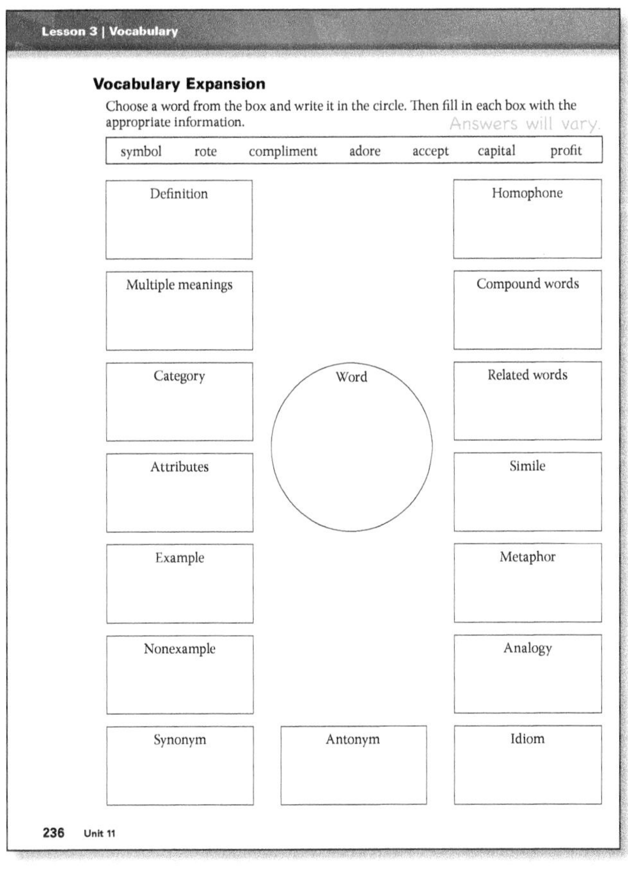

Direct students to page 236 in their Student Books. Review the definition of each concept in the Vocabulary Expansion chart.

- **Definition:** the meaning of the word
- **Multiple meanings:** other meanings and uses of the word
- **Category:** the broad group in which a word fits
- **Attributes:** specific characteristics of the word
- **Example:** something that models or patterns the word
- **Nonexample:** something that does not model or pattern the word
- **Synonym:** a word with a similar meaning
- **Antonym:** a word with the opposite meaning
- **Homophone:** a word that sounds the same but has a different meaning
- **Compound word:** two words combined to make one word
- **Related words:** words with the same root word and related meanings
- **Simile:** figurative language comparing two dissimilar things using like or as
- **Metaphor:** figurative language comparing two dissimilar things by saying one thing is another thing
- **Analogy:** a comparison of two pairs of words that share the same relationship
- **Idiom:** figurative language used in a certain region or by a certain group of people

In this unit and the last one, we've been discussing weather-related natural disasters. Write the word *weather* on the board. Let's take a closer look at this word, and see if we can use these Vocabulary Expansion concepts to create a deeper understanding of the word. Guide students as you discuss each concept and brainstorm possible answers. Write correct answers on the board.

Example Vocabulary Expansion of *weather*

Definition: the conditions in the atmosphere related to temperature and precipitation

Multiple meanings: *v.*: to go through something safely; *adj.* (weathered): affected or worn down by the elements

Category: conditions

Attributes: temperature, precipitation

Example: mild, sunny, windy, rainy, snow

Nonexample: indoor atmosphere

Synonym: climate

Antonym: N/A

Homophone: whether

Compound words: weathervane, weatherman, weathermen

Related words: N/A

Simile: as unpredictable as the weather

Metaphor: N/A

Analogy: weather : climate :: job : work

Idiom: weather the storm; under the weather

Dictionary or online access

Give each student a dictionary or provide Internet access. Read the instructions on page 236, then have students choose a word and use a dictionary (online or print) to complete the process. Explain the use of N/A for concepts that don't apply to the word. Have partners share their word expansions.

Reading

Objectives

- Use critical thinking skills to analyze a text.
- Ask and answer questions and prompts using extended thinking skills to demonstrate an understanding of a text.

Critical Understandings

Good readers demonstrate what they learned from a text when they answer questions and prompts. In this unit, we will work with more challenging prompts that require you to demonstrate critical thinking. Often, these higher level prompts ask you to find evidence in the text. Evidence can be a single word, a phrase, a sentence, or a group of sentences.

Proficient readers do more than recall and understand. Proficient readers are strategic thinkers who make connections between ideas in texts, are curious about new learning, and are able to reevaluate their opinions based on what they read. At the strategic thinking level, you are asked to show deeper knowledge about the subject matter discussed in a text.

At the extended thinking level of comprehension, you activate all of these ways of knowing. You recall information, you understand what the information means, you think strategically about new information, and you take time for extended, higher order thinking.

Direction Words: Extended Thinking poster

Direct students to the chart on page 16 or refer to the Extended Thinking poster if you have it displayed.

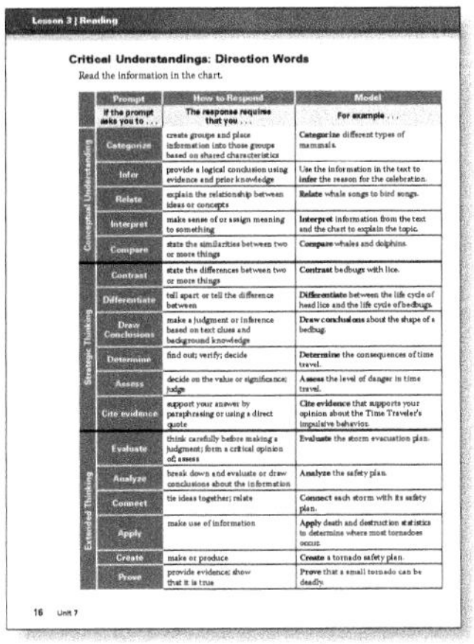

Lesson 3 | Reading

Critical Understandings: Direction Words

Read the information in the chart.

	Prompt	How to Respond	Model
	If the prompt asks you to . . .	The response requires that you . . .	For example . . .
Conceptual Understanding	Categorize	create groups and place information into those groups based on shared characteristics	**Categorize** different types of mammals.
	Infer	provide a logical conclusion using evidence and prior knowledge	Use the information in the text to **infer** the reason for the celebration.
	Relate	explain the relationship between ideas or concepts	**Relate** whale songs to bird songs.
	Interpret	make sense of or assign meaning to something	**Interpret** information from the text and the chart to explain the topic.
	Compare	state the similarities between two or more things	**Compare** whales and dolphins.
Strategic Thinking	Contrast	state the differences between two or more things	**Contrast** bedbugs with lice.
	Differentiate	tell apart or tell the difference between	**Differentiate** between the life cycle of head lice and the life cycle of bedbugs.
	Draw Conclusions	make a judgment or inference based on text clues and background knowledge	**Draw conclusions** about the shape of a bedbug.
	Determine	find out; verify; decide	**Determine** the consequences of time travel.
	Assess	decide on the value or significance; judge	**Assess** the level of danger in time travel.
	Cite evidence	support your answer by paraphrasing or using a direct quote	**Cite evidence** that supports your opinion about the Time Traveler's impulsive behavior.
Extended Thinking	Evaluate	think carefully before making a judgment; form a critical opinion of; assess	**Evaluate** the storm evacuation plan.
	Analyze	break down and evaluate or draw conclusions about the information	**Analyze** the safety plan.
	Connect	tie ideas together; relate	**Connect** each storm with its safety plan.
	Apply	make use of information	**Apply** death and destruction statistics to determine where most tornadoes occur.
	Create	make or produce	**Create** a tornado safety plan.
	Prove	provide evidence; show that it is true	**Prove** that a small tornado can be deadly.

16 Unit 7

In the last unit, you learned how to respond to prompts at the extended thinking level that contain the words *evaluate, analyze,* and *connect.* Today we will learn to respond to three more prompts at the extended thinking level that include the words *apply, create,* and *prove.*

Apply

If a prompt asks you to *apply,* it is asking you to make use of information. For example, if I asked you to apply death and destruction statistics to determine where most tornadoes occur, you would use that information and draw a new conclusion. How will you respond if a prompt asks you to apply? (make use of information)

Create

If the prompt asks you to *create,* the response requires you to make or produce something. Read the example with me. (Create a tornado safety plan.) When you create something, you use what you learned from the text *and* what you already know to make or produce something new.

Prove

If the prompt asks you to *prove,* you are being asked to provide evidence to show that something is true. Read the example with me. (Prove that a small tornado can be deadly.) When you prove something, you cite evidence from the text that makes it difficult to disagree with, or challenge, the given idea.

At each level, it is critical that you understand what the prompt is asking and how to respond. We will become automatic with these prompts and learn exactly how to respond at a mastery level.

Look at the How to Respond column in the chart for Conceptual Understanding, Strategic Thinking, and Extended Thinking. Each of these prompts requires you to construct a higher level response that uses information from the given sources and from your own prior knowledge. Proficient readers can identify "gaps" in the text—places where information is not given and must be found in another source. At the extended thinking level, you may find it necessary to confirm your answer with an outside source such as another book or an Internet search.

Direct students to pages 237–239 in their Student Books. Let's preview some prompts that require extended thinking using a short piece of text. I'll read the prompt, and you repeat the direction word in bold.

1. **Create** a model of the structure of the Earth. Label each of the four layers. (create)
2. **Apply** the theory of plate tectonics to earthquakes. (apply)
3. **Prove** that a 6.0 earthquake is 100 times as strong as a 4.0 earthquake. (prove)
4. **Prove** that scientists can predict where earthquakes occur but not when. (prove)
5. **Create** a survival plan for the next earthquake. (create)

With eyes on text, let's read this short text about a natural disaster that is not related to weather. Use your pencil eraser to follow along. Let's begin. Read the text aloud.

Note: While the lessons are written for a teacher read aloud, it is important that your students read as much and as often as they can. Assign readings that meet the needs of your students, based on your observations or data. This is a good opportunity to stretch students, but if they become frustrated, return to the read-aloud method.

Earthquakes

Destruction is not always caused by extreme weather. Sometimes, life and property are threatened by other natural disasters.

The ground is usually peaceful, but forces deep within the Earth can suddenly destroy that peacefulness. Seismologists, scientists who study earthquakes, are still learning about these dangerous events. To begin learning about earthquakes, it is necessary to understand the internal structure of our Earth. There is the thin outer crust, which is stiff and can break. There is a middle layer, the mantle, which is much hotter and not quite solid. The center of the Earth is called the core. It is made up of a liquid-like outer core and a solid inner core. When a vibration travels from deep within the Earth to its surface, an earthquake occurs.

Beneath the soil, rock, and water on the surface of our planet, the Earth is constantly changing. The top layer of the Earth is made of giant sheets of rock, like the pieces of a puzzle. The pieces of rock, called plates, make up the continents and ocean floors. Where the edges of the plates come together, there are often cracks and gaps called faults. Underneath the plates, the Earth is very hot. It is so hot that rock melts into a liquid called magma. The plates float on top of this liquid magma. The magma is always moving, and it drags the plates with it.

Seismologists believe that their theory of plate tectonics explains why earthquakes happen. The plates usually move very slowly. Sometimes, large pieces of the plates get caught. The plates keep trying to move, but other large blocks of rock hold them back. The pressure and energy build up. Then, suddenly, the plates give way, releasing the built-up pressure and energy. The plates jerk forward, and the ground shakes. Far above, on the surface, people feel an earthquake.

The damage and loss of life sustained during an earthquake result from falling structures and flying glass and objects. In certain areas, an earthquake can trigger mudslides. Wet earth slides down mountain slopes and can bury habitations below. An earthquake at sea can cause a tsunami, a series of damaging waves that ripple outward from the earthquake epicenter and flood coastal cities.

Scientists measure the strength of earthquakes on an instrument called a seismograph. Each earthquake is given a number from the Richter Scale depending on its strength. For each number on the Richter Scale, an earthquake is 10 times as strong as for the previous number. A 6.0 earthquake is 10 times as strong as a 5.0 earthquake. The largest earthquake ever recorded measured 9.5 on the Richter Scale.

Seismologists use instruments that allow them to see patterns along certain faults. These patterns indicate how likely it is that a major earthquake will happen along those faults, but it is impossible to say when. The next major earthquake could occur today, tomorrow, or 50 years from now.

Let's check our comprehension of this passage by responding to prompts that require extended thinking. For some of the prompts, you will need to consider learning outside of the text to support your answer.

Remember, each prompt is really a question—and we already know how to answer questions. If you struggle to remember how to respond to the prompt, it can be helpful to turn the prompt into a question so you know exactly how to answer it. We will practice responding to prompts that require extended thinking using evidence from text. Try asking yourself a question so that you know exactly how to respond.

Model

Read the first prompt aloud.

1. Create a model of the structure of the Earth. Label each of the four layers.

It is important to fully understand a prompt before constructing a response. Turn to your neighbor and restate the prompt as a question to demonstrate your understanding of it. **Provide partner time; confirm understanding.** The question would be, What are the layers of the structure of the Earth? To respond, we need to create or draw a model and then label the layers. Turn to your partner and discuss how to label the layers on the drawing. **While students are brainstorming, draw this graphic on the board without answers. If the students are having difficulty, help them label the parts using the text to guide them.**

Structure of the Earth

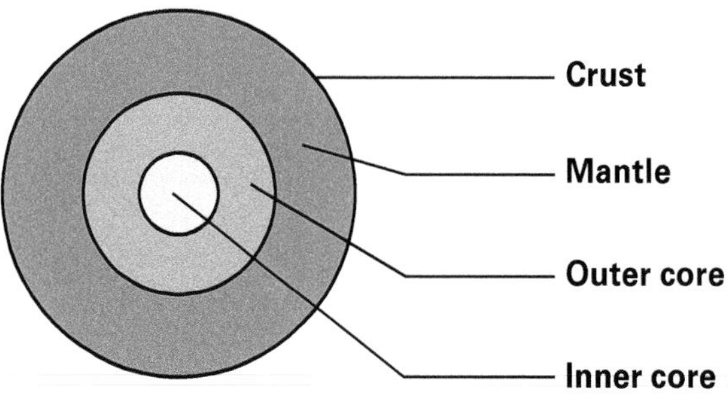

Lesson 3 | Reading

Critical Understandings

Review the extended thinking prompts on the Critical Understandings chart or on the poster. Read the prompts following the passage to establish a purpose for reading. Then read the passage and respond to the prompts.

Earthquakes

Destruction is not always caused by extreme weather. Sometimes, life and property are threatened by other natural disasters.

The ground is usually peaceful, but forces deep within the Earth can suddenly destroy that peacefulness. Seismologists, scientists who study earthquakes, are still learning about these dangerous events. To begin learning about earthquakes, it is necessary to understand the internal structure of our Earth. There is the thin outer crust, which is stiff and can break. There is a middle layer, the mantle, which is much hotter and not quite solid. The center of the Earth is called the core. It is made up of a liquid-like outer core and a solid inner core. When a vibration travels from deep within the Earth to its surface, an earthquake occurs.

Beneath the soil, rock, and water on the surface of our planet, the Earth is constantly changing. The top layer of the Earth is made of giant sheets of rock, like the pieces of a puzzle. The pieces of rock, called plates, make up the continents and ocean floors. Where the edges of the plates come together, there are often cracks and gaps called faults. Underneath the plates, the Earth is very hot. It is so hot that rock melts into a liquid called magma. The plates float on top of this liquid magma. The magma is always moving, and it drags the plates with it.

Seismologists believe that their theory of plate tectonics explains why earthquakes happen. The plates usually move very slowly. Sometimes, large pieces of the plates get caught. The plates keep trying to move, but other large blocks of rock hold them back. The pressure and energy build up. Then, suddenly, the plates give way, releasing the built-up pressure and energy. The plates jerk forward, and the ground shakes. Far above, on the surface, people feel an earthquake.

The damage and loss of life sustained during an earthquake result from falling structures and flying glass and objects. In certain areas, an earthquake can trigger mudslides. Wet earth slides down mountain slopes and can bury habitations below. An earthquake at sea can cause a tsunami, a series of damaging waves that ripple outward from the earthquake epicenter and flood coastal cities.

Scientists measure the strength of earthquakes on an instrument called a seismograph. Each earthquake is given a number from the Richter Scale depending on its strength. For each number on the Richter Scale, an earthquake is 10 times as strong as for the previous number. A 6.0 earthquake is 10 times as strong as a 5.0 earthquake. The largest earthquake ever recorded measured 9.5 on the Richter Scale.

Seismologists use instruments that allow them to see patterns along certain faults. These patterns indicate how likely it is that a major earthquake will happen along those faults, but it is impossible to say when. The next major earthquake could occur today, tomorrow, or 50 years from now.

Unit 11 237

Lesson 3 | Reading

Critical Understandings (*cont.*)

1. **Create** a model of the structure of the Earth. Label each of the four layers.

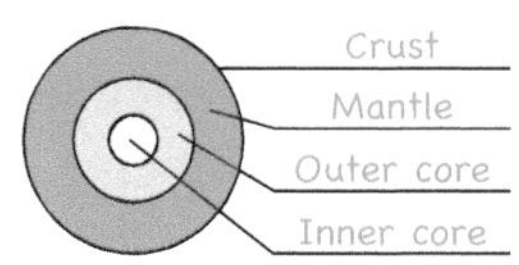

Answers will vary.

2. **Apply** the theory of plate tectonics to earthquakes.

Plate tectonics is the theory that the Earth's crust is made up of plates that are constantly moving. Occasionally, the plates get stuck. When they break apart or become unstuck, the force can cause an earthquake.

3. **Prove** that a 6.0 earthquake is 100 times as strong as a 4.0 earthquake.

Because an earthquake is 10 times as strong as the previous number, a 6.0 earthquake is 10 times as strong as a 5.0 earthquake and 100 times as strong as a 4.0 earthquake because 10 times 10 equals 100.

238 Unit 11

Guided Practice

Read the next prompt aloud.

2. Apply the theory of plate tectonics to earthquakes.

We can change this prompt into two separate questions and then decide how to respond. The first question would be, What is the theory of plate tectonics? The second question would be, How does that theory relate to earthquakes?

Have partners restate the prompt and answer the question. While students are working, write this sentence starter on the board:

Plate tectonics is the theory that ______.

Lesson 3 | Reading

Critical Understandings (*cont.*) Answers will vary.

4. **Prove** that scientists can predict where earthquakes occur but not when.
"Seismologists use instruments that allow them to see patterns along certain faults. These patterns indicate how likely it is that a major earthquake will happen along those faults, but it is impossible to say when." This quote from the text confirms that scientists are able to determine that earthquakes occur along those fault lines, but they cannot predict when they will occur.

5. **Create** a survival plan for the next earthquake.
During an earthquake, move away from buildings, trees, or other structures. Stay away from windows and other glass and metal objects. Find a stable place to hide. After the earthquake, stay clear of the bases of mountains and the coastlines.

Unit 11 239

Independent Practice

Have partners complete the remaining prompts. Review their answers as a class to ensure students understand what each prompt is asking.

Note: Base the number of modeled and guided examples on student ability and progress. Challenge them with independent practice when appropriate.

Provide these alternative questions and sentence starters for those who need additional help.

3. How can you confirm that a 6.0 earthquake is 100 times as strong as a 4.0 earthquake?

Because an earthquake is 10 times as strong as the previous number, ______________________________.

4. Can scientists predict where earthquakes occur? Can scientists predict when earthquakes happen? Explain your answer.

"Seismologists use instruments that allow them to see patterns along certain faults. These patterns indicate ______________________________."
This quote from the text confirms that ______________________________.

5. What should you do to survive the next earthquake? Write a survival plan.

During an earthquake, ______________________________.

Unit 11

Lesson 4

Lesson Opener

Before the lesson, choose one of the following activities to write on the board or post on the *LANGUAGE! Live* Class Wall online.

- *Write sentences using the following idioms. (Remember, it may be easier to write two sentences for each idiom to frame its meaning.)* waste your breath; rock the boat
- *Write a sentence about your favorite food. Use the word* entire *or* rank *in your sentence.*
- *Create your tornado-prepared avatar and post an explanation of its clothing.*

Reading

Objective

- Read sentences to develop fluency.

Sentence Fluency

Timer

Follow the Fluency Procedure outlined below. If it is necessary, begin the fluency drill with a choral read of all sentences. Direct students to page 240 in their Student Books and complete the process.

Fluency Procedure

- Partners switch books, so the recorder is marking errors in the reader's book.
- A timer is set for one minute.
- Readers and recorders move left to right, tracking each word with a pencil.
- As readers read the words aloud, recorders mark errors with a small x above the misread word.
- Recorders place a star to the right of the last word read when time ends.
- If the reader is able to read all words in the allotted time, the reader needs to start over at the beginning. The recorder must indicate this feat by placing two stars to the right of the last word read.
- When both students have read, partners switch books.
- Students calculate total words read, then subtract errors and record.
- Students record information on the progress chart in back of the Student Book.

Lesson 4 | Reading

Sentence Fluency

Read each sentence fluently.

	1st Try	2nd Try
Correct		
Errors		

1. She asked Mother for a pet goat. 7
2. Shawn went camping with them. 12
3. Who went with you to the pig roast? 20
4. They never found the song I wanted to play. 29
5. We went to the house with her. 36
6. What did you learn about the world on your Swiss train trip? 48
7. In the cookbook, I found a great roast beef dish. 58
8. I also thought you had the right answer. 66
9. Her mother's point was, if you study you get good grades. 77
10. Do you want to look at that house in the woods again before you spend cash on it? 95
11. Keep an eye out for any change in the way you look. 107
12. The football coach stood outside waiting for his team. 116
13. If you live in snow country, you can blow and scoop snow for a good part of the year. 135

240 Unit 11

Grammar

Objectives

- Listen to oral sentences and write them accurately.
- Demonstrate an understanding of the function of subject and object pronouns in sentences.

Pronouns

You have just read sentences for speed and accuracy. Now we will look closely at those sentences to reinforce what we have learned about pronouns.

Direct students to Part A on page 241 in their Student Books. Read the instructions and remind students of the procedure for sentence dictation.

Dictation Procedure

- Teacher reads the sentence.
- Students repeat the sentence.
- Students write the sentence.
- Teacher reads the sentence a second time as students check their work.

Dictate the following sentences:

1. She asked Mother for a pet goat.
2. Shawn went camping with them.
3. Who went with you to the pig roast?
4. They never found the song I wanted to play.
5. We went to the house with her.

Have students circle the subject and object pronouns and sort them in the chart. Review the answers as a class.

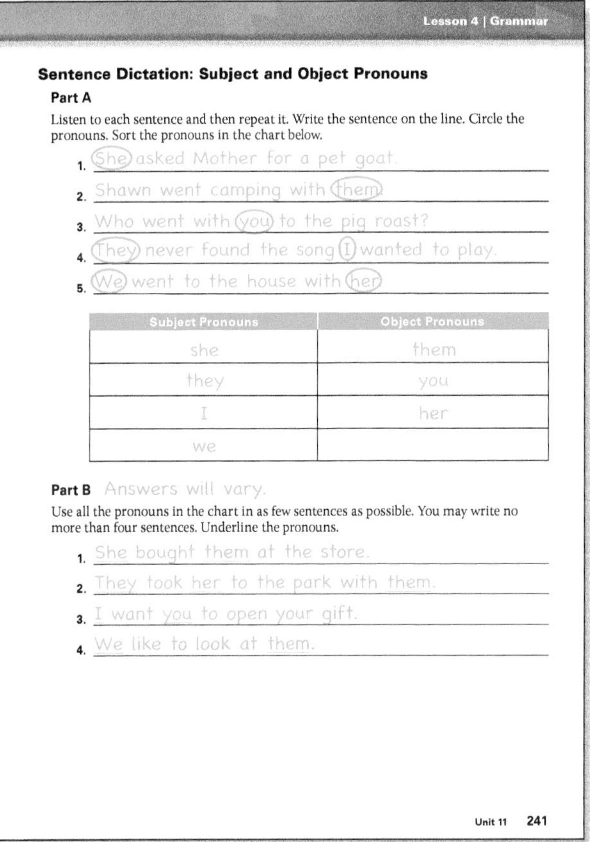
Lesson 4 | Grammar

Sentence Dictation: Subject and Object Pronouns

Part A

Listen to each sentence and then repeat it. Write the sentence on the line. Circle the pronouns. Sort the pronouns in the chart below.

1. She asked Mother for a pet goat.
2. Shawn went camping with them.
3. Who went with you to the pig roast?
4. They never found the song I wanted to play.
5. We went to the house with her.

Subject Pronouns	Object Pronouns
she	them
they	you
I	her
we	

Part B Answers will vary.

Use all the pronouns in the chart in as few sentences as possible. You may write no more than four sentences. Underline the pronouns.

1. She bought them at the store.
2. They took her to the park with them.
3. I want you to open your gift.
4. We like to look at them.

Unit 11 241

Note: In sentence 3, *you* is used as an object of the preposition and is placed accordingly in the chart. Point out that *you* can be used as either a subject pronoun or an object pronoun, and that students should take their time deciding how it is being used in any given sentence.

Direct students to Part B. Read the instructions aloud. Have students write sentences using all of the pronouns. Encourage them to use more than one pronoun in each sentence but to make sure the meaning is not clouded by the use of too many pronouns. Have students share their sentences with their partners, and then have volunteers share their sentences with the class.

Reading

Objectives

- Read sentence phrases with fluency to support comprehension.
- Read an informational text.
- Use critical thinking skills to respond to specific questions about a text.

Phrase It

Reading in phrases is an important step in becoming a proficient reader. Slowly read the following phrases, pausing in between so students can create a mental picture:

The cloud . . . turned black . . . and began to move . . . like a spinning top.

The cloud is the subject, and *turned black and began to move like a spinning top* is the predicate.

For Phrase It, we scoop phrases using our pencil. When we scoop a phrase, we form an image in our heads. The next phrase we read may add to or change the image. This process is what we call comprehension. The picture of the cloud changes as soon as we read the first part of the predicate—*turned black*. It changes again when we read the second part of the predicate—*and began to move*. It changes yet again when we read the third part of the predicate—*like a spinning top*. Our original image of a fluffy white cloud has gradually turned into an image of a dangerous tornado, and the feeling of the sentence has changed too. The addition of each *phrase*—not the addition of each *word*—changes our mental image. That's why we read in chunks.

Direct students to page 242 in their Student Books.

Model

Complete the first item as a model.

Guided Practice

Guide students to complete the next two.

Independent Practice

Read the remaining sentences and have students scoop the phrases. Review the answers as a class.

Note: Base the number of modeled and guided examples on student ability and progress. Challenge them with independent practice when appropriate.

There are various ways the sentences can be broken into phrases. Accept logical answers.

Lesson 4 | Reading

Phrase It

Read each phrase and scoop it with a pencil. As you read the phrase, form an image in your mind. Read the sentence with prosody.

1. While at the pool I jump off the high dive and swim to the wall.
2. My father and mother looked like a dream twisting and swaying around the room.
3. The twin boys played on the swings at the park.
4. Kay and Clay sailed into the little bay.
5. There were a few black tweed coats left at the sale.
6. The twins floated near the bank of the brook.
7. She came inside and shook the rain off her cloak.
8. I bent down to take a bite of the sweet pie, but the swift hawk swooped in and swiped it.
9. Which day can she do your nails and eyebrows?

242 Unit 11

Critical Understandings

Direction Words: Extended Thinking poster

We will continue responding to prompts at the extended thinking level. You will respond to prompts that include verbs such as *apply*, *create*, and *prove*. What level prompt are we studying in this unit? (extended thinking) These strategies will help you throughout school.

Direct students to pages 243–245 in their Student Books.

Let's preview some prompts that require extended thinking about another frightening power of nature. I'll read each prompt, and you repeat the key word in bold.

1. **Apply** what you learned about earthquakes to tsunamis. (apply)
2. **Prove** that not every earthquake near the ocean causes a tsunami. (prove)
3. **Prove** that tsunamis occur near volcanoes. (prove)
4. Use a highlighter to **create** a Ring of Fire on the diagram below. (create)
5. **Apply** your knowledge of volcanoes, earthquakes, and tsunamis to determine the best place to build a home. (apply)

Have students follow along as you read the text aloud.

Note: While the lessons are written for a teacher read aloud, it is important that your students read as much and as often as they can. Assign readings that meet the needs of your students, based on your observations or data. This is a good opportunity to stretch students, but if they become frustrated, return to the read-aloud method.

Frightening Powers of Nature

Earthquakes, volcanoes, and tsunamis are grim reminders of the power of nature. Earthquakes and volcanoes cause death and destruction. When they happen underwater, they can also cause deadly events known as tsunamis.

Earthquakes are a result of the movement of the Earth's crust. Volcanic eruptions are caused by the same thing. Volcanoes erupt all over the world. The danger and destruction of the eruptions vary based on how close to the volcano people live. The lava from a volcano can travel more than 30 miles. Some eruptions aren't even heard. But sometimes whole cities are buried under the lava and ashes. Parícutin is a volcano in Mexico. It began erupting in the 1940s and continued for nine years. In its path of destruction lay the city of Michoacán, which was completely buried in lava and ash. Mount Vesuvius is a volcano in Italy. Nearly two thousand years ago, an eruption of Vesuvius buried the city of Pompeii. Vesuvius has erupted many times since then and is still active today. For the three million people living near this dangerous volcano, the fear is constant.

The word *tsunami* is a Japanese word that means "harbor wave." It originated with Japanese fishermen who would return to port to find their towns destroyed by unusually large ocean waves that they hadn't even noticed while out at sea. Tsunamis can be devastating when they occur. Fortunately, they are very rare. There are usually six major tsunamis every one hundred years worldwide.

Earthquakes on the ocean floor cause most tsunamis. Underwater volcanic explosions also cause tsunamis. Not every earthquake or volcanic eruption in or near the ocean causes a tsunami. It depends on the strength of the earthquake and the kind of movement that occurs in the Earth's crust. An earthquake has to measure at least 6.75 on the Richter Scale to result in a tsunami.

Low-lying coastlines in areas where earthquakes are common have the greatest risk of tsunamis. The Ring of Fire is a line of volcanoes stretching around the entire Pacific Ocean. Where there are volcanoes, frequent earthquakes occur with the movement of the Earth's crust. Although we can't predict the exact time or location of an earthquake, we can estimate when an area is overdue for one.

Let's check our comprehension of this passage by responding to some prompts that require extended thinking.

Remember, each prompt is a question in disguise. If you struggle to remember how to respond to a prompt, try turning it into a question. Then use extended thinking and evidence from the text to answer it.

Model

Read the first prompt aloud.

1. **Apply** what you learned about earthquakes to tsunamis.

We can change this prompt into a question to determine how best to respond. The question would be, How do earthquakes cause tsunamis?

Work with your partner to answer the question. While students are working, write the sentence starter on the board. Work with students to formulate and record their answer.

Earthquakes can cause a tsunami when ______.

Guided Practice

Read the next prompt aloud.

2. **Prove** that not every earthquake near the ocean causes a tsunami.

We can change this prompt into a question and then decide how to respond. The question would be, Why doesn't every earthquake near the ocean cause a tsunami?

Work with your partner to answer the question. Explain your answer.

While students are working, write this sentence frame on the board. Work with students to formulate an answer and have them record it.

Only earthquakes near the ocean ______.

Critical Understandings

Read the prompts following the passage to establish a purpose for reading. Then read the passage and respond to the prompts.

Frightening Powers of Nature

Earthquakes, volcanoes, and tsunamis are grim reminders of the power of nature. Earthquakes and volcanoes cause death and destruction. When they happen underwater, they can also cause deadly events known as tsunamis.

Earthquakes are a result of the movement of the Earth's crust. Volcanic eruptions are caused by the same thing. Volcanoes erupt all over the world. The danger and destruction of the eruptions vary based on how close to the volcano people live. The lava from a volcano can travel more than 30 miles. Some eruptions aren't even heard. But sometimes whole cities are buried under the lava and ashes. Parícutin is a volcano in Mexico. It began erupting in the 1940s and continued for nine years. In its path of destruction lay the city of Michoacán, which was completely buried in lava and ash. Mount Vesuvius is a volcano in Italy. Nearly two thousand years ago, an eruption of Vesuvius buried the city of Pompeii. Vesuvius has erupted many times since then and is still active today. For the three million people living near this dangerous volcano, the fear is constant.

The word *tsunami* is a Japanese word that means "harbor wave." It originated with Japanese fishermen who would return to port to find their towns destroyed by unusually large ocean waves that they hadn't even noticed while out at sea. Tsunamis can be devastating when they occur. Fortunately, they are very rare. There are usually six major tsunamis every one hundred years worldwide.

Earthquakes on the ocean floor cause most tsunamis. Underwater volcanic explosions also cause tsunamis. Not every earthquake or volcanic eruption in or near the ocean causes a tsunami. It depends on the strength of the earthquake and the kind of movement that occurs in the Earth's crust. An earthquake has to measure at least 6.75 on the Richter Scale to result in a tsunami.

Low-lying coastlines in areas where earthquakes are common have the greatest risk of tsunamis. The Ring of Fire is a line of volcanoes stretching around the entire Pacific Ocean. Where there are volcanoes, frequent earthquakes occur with the movement of the Earth's crust. Although we can't predict the exact time or location of an earthquake, we can estimate when an area is overdue for one.

Critical Understandings (*cont.*)

1. **Apply** what you learned about earthquakes to tsunamis.
   Earthquakes can cause a tsunami when they occur on the ocean floor and measure greater than 6.75 on the Richter Scale, due to the vibration of the Earth's crust.

2. **Prove** that not every earthquake near the ocean causes a tsunami.
   Only earthquakes near the ocean that are greater than 6.75 on the Richter Scale cause a tsunami.

3. **Prove** that tsunamis occur near volcanoes.
   The text says, "low-lying coastlines in areas where earthquakes are common have the greatest risk of tsunamis. The Ring of Fire is a line of volcanoes stretching around the entire Pacific Ocean." This means that volcanic areas like the Ring of Fire are at risk for a tsunami.

Independent Practice

Have partners complete the remaining prompts. Review their answers as a class to ensure students understand what each prompt is asking.

Note: Base the number of modeled and guided examples on student ability and progress. Challenge them with independent practice when appropriate.

Lesson 4 | Reading

Critical Understandings (*cont.*)

4. Use a highlighter to **create** a Ring of Fire on the diagram below.

Kurile trench
Japan trench
Aleutian trench
Mt. Garibaldi
Mt. St. Helens
Izu-Ogasawara trench
Ryukyu trench
PACIFIC OCEAN
Puerto Rico trench
Philippine trench
Mt. Pinatubo
Mt. Mayon
Mariana trench
Middle America trench
Challenger Deep
Equator
Bougainville trench
Java (Sunda) trench
Tonga trench
Peru-Chile trench
Kermadec trench
South Sandwich trench

5. **Apply** your knowledge of volcanoes, earthquakes, and tsunamis to determine the best place to build a home.

When building a home, I would not choose to put it within 30 miles of a volcano to avoid its being destroyed by lava. I would also not build a home near a low-lying coastline, especially near the Ring of Fire near Asia. This would put my home at great risk from a tsunami. I would carefully look at the fault lines that run in the area I am looking to build in to ensure I am far away from a major fault line.

Unit 11 245

Provide these alternative questions and sentence starters for those who need additional help.

3. Do tsunamis occur near volcanoes? Explain your answer.

   The text says, "________________________________."
   This means that ________________________________.

4. Where is the Ring of Fire? Draw it on the map.

5. Where is a safe place to build a home?

   When building a home, I would ________________________________.

Lesson 5

Lesson Opener

Before the lesson, choose one of the following activities to write on the board or post on the *LANGUAGE! Live* Class Wall online.

- *Write sentences using words with the* -es *inflectional ending.*
- *Write a simile about a tornado.*
- *Pretend you are a super hero. What super power would you need to help you fight tornadoes?*

Vocabulary

Objective

- Review key passage vocabulary.

Recontextualize Passage Vocabulary

Direct students to page 224 in their Student Books.

Lesson 1 | Vocabulary

Key Passage Vocabulary: "Twisters"

Rate your knowledge of the words. Define the words. Draw a picture to help you remember the definition.

Vocabulary	Knowledge Rating	Definition	Picture
span	0 1 2 3	to stretch or reach over or across	
rank	0 1 2 3	to compare one position with another, often on a scale	
occur	0 1 2 3	to take place; to happen	
generate	0 1 2 3	to produce, bring into being, or create	
severe	0 1 2 3	bad or serious	
develop	0 1 2 3	to grow into a more advanced or mature state	
entire	0 1 2 3	whole; total	
region	0 1 2 3	an area with a certain type of land and climate	

224 Unit 11

Review the Key Passage Vocabulary from "Twisters."

- A word meaning "whole" or "total" is what? (entire) If I eat a piece of cake, did I eat the *entire* thing or part of it? (part of it) Another word for *whole* is what? (entire)
- To produce, bring into being, or create is to what? (generate) If I ask you to make a list of people you want to invite to a party, what am I asking you to do? (generate a list)
- If something is bad or serious, it is what? (severe) Being grounded for a year for missing a curfew would be considered a seriously bad punishment. What would it be? (severe)
- An area with a certain type of land and climate is a what? (region) The Southwest is an area of the United States that has warm weather and little rainfall. What is the Southwest? (a region)
- To take place or happen is to what? (occur) Does bullying *occur* in schools? (yes) You can help prevent it from happening. With your help, bullying might not what? (occur)
- To compare one position with another, often on a scale, is to what? (rank) *Rank* the days of the week in order from best to worst. Which day *ranks* the highest on your list? (Answers will vary.) What did you do when you compared the days of the week with each other? (ranked them)
- To stretch or reach over or across is to what? (span) Make a bridge with your arms that *spans* your desk. When your arms reach across the desk, what do they do? (span)
- To grow into a more advanced or mature state is to what? (develop) I know someone who had bronchitis that *developed* into pneumonia over time. It was scary. When small problems aren't addressed and taken care of, they often turn into bigger problems. What do they do? (develop)

Reading

Objectives

- Write questions or prompts about text to deepen comprehension.
- Use critical thinking skills to respond orally to specific questions about a text.

Guided Reading of "Twisters": Ask and Answer Questions

I already pointed out that skilled readers preview the text for text features such as headings and graphics. Proficient readers also reread text slowly and carefully to gain understanding. They monitor their thinking while reading to be sure that each sentence and paragraph make sense. Good readers look for answers to Big Idea questions. In this unit, we are answering these questions: Why do tornadoes cause fear in people? and How are tornadoes different from other storms?

Good readers also ask themselves and others questions about their reading. Challenging questions require readers to combine text and information in charts or maps with what they already know. Proficient readers understand that asking questions improves their own comprehension.

This time, when we read "Twisters," we will ask questions about the text. Doing this will help us understand what is important. We will also answer the questions that we ask, which should help clear up any confusion we had during our first read.

Direct students to page 225 in their Student Books or have them tear out the extra copy of "Twisters" from the back of their book.

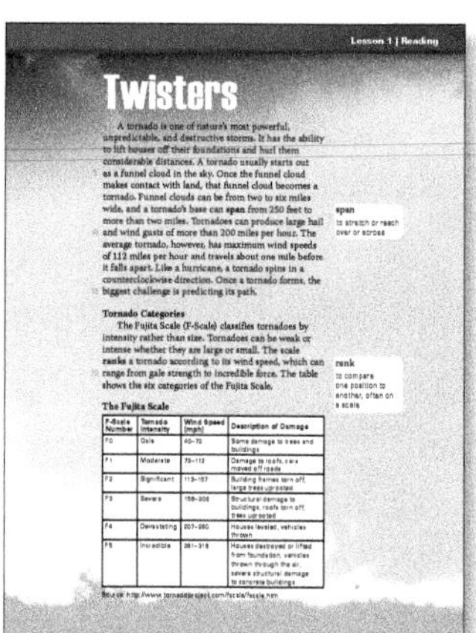

Lesson 1 | Reading

Twisters

A tornado is one of nature's most powerful, unpredictable, and destructive storms. It has the ability to lift houses off their foundations and hurl them considerable distances. A tornado usually starts out as a funnel cloud in the sky. Once the funnel cloud makes contact with land, that funnel cloud becomes a tornado. Funnel clouds can be from two to six miles wide, and a tornado's base can **span** from 250 feet to more than two miles. Tornadoes can produce large hail and wind gusts of more than 200 miles per hour. The average tornado, however, has maximum wind speeds of 112 miles per hour and travels about one mile before it falls apart. Like a hurricane, a tornado spins in a counterclockwise direction. Once a tornado forms, the biggest challenge is predicting its path.

span
to stretch or reach over or across

Tornado Categories

The Fujita Scale (F-Scale) classifies tornadoes by intensity rather than size. Tornadoes can be weak or intense whether they are large or small. The scale **ranks** a tornado according to its wind speed, which can range from gale strength to incredible force. The table shows the six categories of the Fujita Scale.

rank
to compare one position to another, often on a scale

The Fujita Scale

F-Scale Number	Tornado Intensity	Wind Speed (mph)	Description of Damage
F0	Gale	40–72	Some damage to trees and buildings
F1	Moderate	73–112	Damage to roofs, cars moved off roads
F2	Significant	113–157	Building frames torn off, large trees uprooted
F3	Severe	158–206	Structural damage to buildings, roofs torn off, trees uprooted
F4	Devastating	207–260	Houses leveled, vehicles thrown
F5	Incredible	261–318	Houses destroyed or lifted from foundation, vehicles thrown through the air, severe structural damage to concrete buildings

Source: http://www.tornadoproject.com/fscale/fscale.htm

Unit 11 225

> **Note:** To minimize flipping back and forth between the pages, a copy of each text has been included in the back of the Student Books. Encourage students to tear this out and use it when working on activities that require the use of the text.

Let's do what good readers do and reread "Twisters" with our minds on asking and answering questions.

Remember to track the text while your pencil points to the words. While reading, be aware of questions that come to your mind and questions that you could ask others.

Note: While the lessons are written for a teacher read aloud, it is important that your students read as much and as often as they can. Assign readings that meet the needs of your students, based on your observations or data. This is a good opportunity to stretch students, but if they become frustrated, return to the read-aloud method.

Eyes ready? Pencil ready? Let's begin.

Read the first paragraph.

Twisters

A tornado is one of nature's most powerful, unpredictable, and destructive storms. It has the ability to lift houses off their foundations and hurl them considerable distances. A tornado usually starts out as a funnel cloud in the sky. Once the funnel cloud makes contact with land, that funnel cloud becomes a tornado. Funnel clouds can be from two to six miles wide, and a tornado's base can span from 250 feet to more than two miles. Tornadoes can produce large hail and wind gusts of more than 200 miles per hour. The average tornado, however, has maximum wind speeds of 112 miles per hour and travels about one mile before it falls apart. Like a hurricane, a tornado spins in a counterclockwise direction. Once a tornado forms, the biggest challenge is predicting its path.

Direct students to page 246 in their Student Books. Think about the text. What questions to you still have? What should your peers have learned about tornadoes from this section?

- Choose one question word or prompt we have learned. Consider starting your question with *What*.
- If you want to challenge yourself to write a prompt, try using *Draw conclusions*.
- Write the question or prompt on the page. Be prepared to answer your question or prompt orally. Remember, questions require a question mark. Prompts require a period.

Lesson 5 | Reading

Ask and Answer Questions Answers will vary.

Reread "Twisters." After each section, write a question or prompt for your partner to answer using question or direction words that you have learned so far. Try not to use the same word twice. Be prepared to answer your questions orally. Use the Critical Understandings chart on page 16 or the poster to help you with the prompts.

Introduction *What?* *Draw conclusions*

1. ______

Tornado Categories *How?* *Apply*

2. ______

The Fujita Scale (table) *Compare* *Contrast*

3. ______

Tornadoes in the United States *Where?* *Create*

4. ______

Killer Tornadoes *When?* *Prove*

5. ______

Tornado Safety *Why?* *Assess*

6. ______

246 Unit 11

Direct students back to the passage. Now we will read the next section. Eyes ready? Pencil ready? Let's begin.

Read the next paragraph, Tornado Categories.

Tornado Categories

The Fujita Scale (F-Scale) classifies tornadoes by intensity rather than size. Tornadoes can be weak or intense whether they are large or small. The scale **ranks** a tornado according to its wind speed, which can range from gale strength to incredible force. The table shows the six categories of the Fujita Scale.

Direct students to page 246 in their Student Books.

- Choose a different direction or question word. Try using *How* or *Apply*.
- Write the question or prompt on the page. Be prepared to provide answers orally.

Direct students back to the passage. Now we will read the next section. Eyes ready? Pencil ready? Let's begin.

Read the table, The Fujita Scale.

The Fujita Scale

F-Scale Number	Tornado Intensity	Wind Speed (mph)	Description of Damage
F0	Gale	40–72	Some damage to trees and buildings
F1	Moderate	73–112	Damage to roofs, cars moved off roads
F2	Significant	113–157	Building frames torn off, large trees uprooted
F3	Severe	158–206	Structural damage to buildings, roofs torn off, trees uprooted
F4	Devastating	207–260	Houses leveled, vehicles thrown
F5	Incredible	261–318	Houses destroyed or lifted from foundation, vehicles thrown through the air, severe structural damage to concrete buildings

Source: http://www.tornadoproject.com/fscale/fscale.htm

Direct students to page 246 in their Student Books.

- Choose a different direction or question word. Try using *Compare* or *Contrast*.
- Write the question or prompt on the page. Be prepared to provide answers orally.

Direct students back to the passage. Now we will read the next section. Eyes ready? Pencil ready? Let's begin.

Read the next two paragraphs, Tornadoes in the United States.

Tornadoes in the United States

The United States has more tornadoes than any nation in the world. During a typical year, more than 1,000 tornadoes occur across the continental United States. More than 30 percent of these tornadoes occur in "Tornado Alley." Most of these tornadoes occur in the spring.

In fact, over 55 percent of a year's tornadoes occur between the months of April and June, when cool dry air from Canada clashes with warm, moist air from the Gulf of Mexico. These ingredients, when combined with a storm system, generate severe thunderstorms and, in some cases, deadly tornadoes. Hundreds of tornadoes develop during an average tornado season in the United States. Some bring death and destruction.

Direct students to page 246 in their Student Books.

- Choose a different direction or question word. Try using *Where* or *Create*.
- Write the question or prompt on the page. Be prepared to provide answers orally.

Direct students back to the passage. Now we will read the next section. Eyes ready? Pencil ready? Let's begin.

Read the next paragraph, Killer Tornadoes.

Killer Tornadoes

Tornadoes can be weak, strong, or violent. Strong winds and debris can cause power outages, structural damage to buildings, and even death. Violent tornadoes make up only a small percentage of all tornadoes, but they are responsible for two-thirds of all tornado deaths in the United States. These killer tornadoes can last for more than an hour, bringing devastation to an entire region. The chart on the next page shows the number of killer tornadoes compared with the number of deaths they caused from 2000 to 2011.

Direct students to page 246 in their Student Books.

- Choose a different direction or question word. Try using *When* or *Prove*.
- Write the question or prompt on the page. Be prepared to provide answers orally.

Direct students back to the passage. Now we will read the next section. Eyes ready? Pencil ready? Let's begin.

Read the last paragraph, Tornado Safety.

Tornado Safety

It is important to heed tornado warnings. Tornadoes can develop in the blink of an eye, and individuals should pay attention to warning signs such as dark green skies, a loud roaring sound, hail, and a visible funnel cloud. Listening to the radio or television can provide valuable updates on a tornado's development. Individuals should quickly find a safe place to weather the storm. Their lives may depend on it. The safest place is underground in a basement or storm shelter. If no underground shelter is available, a room away from windows and with strong structural support is the next safest choice. In many homes, this may be a bathroom. Mattresses, cushions, and sleeping bags can provide some protection. When tornado season approaches, experts recommend preparing an emergency kit. The kit should be stocked with flashlights, batteries, bottled water, canned foods, and first aid supplies.

Direct students to page 246 in their Student Books.

- Choose a different direction or question word. Try using *Why* or *Assess*.
- Write the question or prompt on the page. Be prepared to provide answers orally.

Share Questions or Prompts

Have partners read their questions or prompts to each other and answer them orally, correcting each other if needed. Each pair shares with another pair, then those four share with four others if time permits. Have volunteers share their questions or prompts and responses with the class.

Writing

Objectives

- Use critical and extended thinking skills to write responses to prompts about a text.
- Support written answers with evidence from a text.

Answer It: Direction Words

Direct students to pages 247–250 in their Student Books. Now, we will respond to prompts about "Twisters" for more practice. Some of the prompts may be similar to the prompts you already responded to.

Direction Words: Extended Thinking poster

- Read each prompt. Identify and underline the direction word.
- Use the Critical Understandings chart on page 16 or the Extended Thinking poster to review the information required by each kind of prompt.
- Use text headings or other text features to locate the information you need to respond.
- Reread the section to retrieve exact information to use as text evidence. Use the direction word to formulate a response.
- Don't forget to cite line numbers from the passage to show where you found your evidence.

Lesson 5 | Writing

Answer It: Direction Words

Underline the direction word in each prompt. Then respond to each prompt using a complete sentence. Provide line numbers for the text evidence.

1. Prove that a small tornado can be more devastating than a large tornado.

   A small tornado with incredible wind speed could be more damaging than a large tornado with gale winds because tornadoes are classified by intensity rather than size.

   Text Evidence: lines 16–18

2. Apply your knowledge of the Fujita Scale, intensity chart, and Richter Scale to determine their similarities and differences.

   The Fujita Scale, intensity chart, and Richter Scale are all scales that rate the strength of disasters caused by nature. The chart ranges from 1–5, with 5 being the most severe. The Fujita Scale measures damage from tornadoes at six levels. The intensity chart measures damage from hurricanes. The Richter Scale measures severity of earthquakes and ranges from 1–10, with 10 being the most severe.

   Text Evidence: chart and prior reading

Unit 11 247

Lesson 5 | Writing

Answer It: Direction Words (*cont.*)

3. Apply information from the margin and graph in "Twisters" to determine why the death rate was elevated in 2011.

   According to the margin and graph, 2011 had 175 tornadoes, 70 of them being killer tornadoes. This, along with the deadliest tornado in the modern era, combined to create an elevated tornado death rate.

   Text Evidence: margin and graph on page 229

4. Prove that many tornadoes do not result in death.

   This quote proves that many tornadoes do not result in death: "Violent tornadoes make up only a small percentage of all tornadoes, but they are responsible for two-thirds of all tornado deaths in the United States."

   Text Evidence: lines 38–41

5. Prove that the deadliest tornado since 1950 occurred in Joplin, Missouri.

   The text says, "The deadliest [tornado] of the modern era (since 1950), was on May 22, 2011, when a large EF5 tornado crossed Joplin, Missouri, causing 158 direct fatalities."

   Text Evidence: margin on page 229

248 Unit 11

Model

Read the first prompt aloud.

1. Prove that a small tornado can be more devastating than a large tornado.

What is the direction word? (prove) How do we respond to a prompt that asks us to *prove*? (We have to provide evidence to show that it is true.)

I can change this prompt into a question to determine how best to respond. To complete the first column, I would ask myself, "How can a small tornado be more devastating than a large tornado?" Next, I need to look back in the text to find evidence that a small tornado can be more devastating than a large tornado. Work with your partner to find information to use as proof.

Provide this sentence starter if needed.

A small tornado with _____ could be more damaging than a large tornado _____.

Guided Practice

Read the next prompt aloud.

2. Apply your knowledge of the Fujita Scale, intensity chart, and Richter Scale to determine their similarities and differences.

What is the direction word in this prompt? (apply) How do we respond to a prompt that begins with *apply*? (Make use of information.) I can also change that prompt into a question to determine how best to respond. What question could I ask? (How are the Fujita Scale, intensity chart, and Richter Scale similar? How are they different?)

Have volunteers model the sentence starter. Write the sentence starters on the board. Provide work time before sharing the answer. (Answers will vary.)

The Fujita Scale, intensity chart, and Richter ____________________.
The Fujita Scale and intensity chart range from ____________________.
The intensity chart measures ____________________.
The Richter Scale measures ____________________.

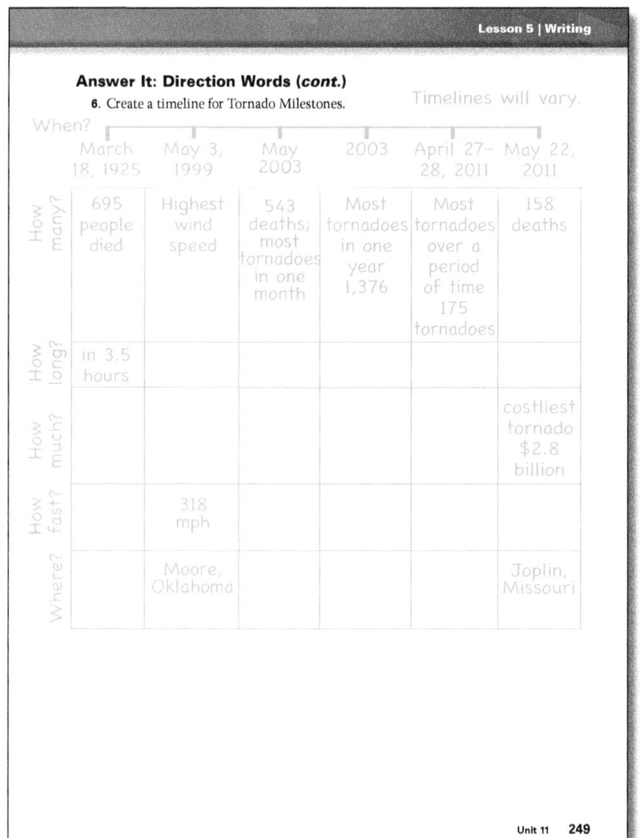

Lesson 5 | Writing

Answer It: Direction Words (*cont.*)

6. Create a timeline for Tornado Milestones.

Timelines will vary.

When?	March 18, 1925	May 3, 1999	May 2003	2003	April 27–28, 2011	May 22, 2011
How many?	695 people died	Highest wind speed	543 deaths; most tornadoes in one month	Most tornadoes in one year 1,376	Most tornadoes over a period of time 175 tornadoes	158 deaths
How long?	in 3.5 hours					
How much?						costliest tornado $2.8 billion
How fast?		318 mph				
Where?		Moore, Oklahoma				Joplin, Missouri

Unit 11 249

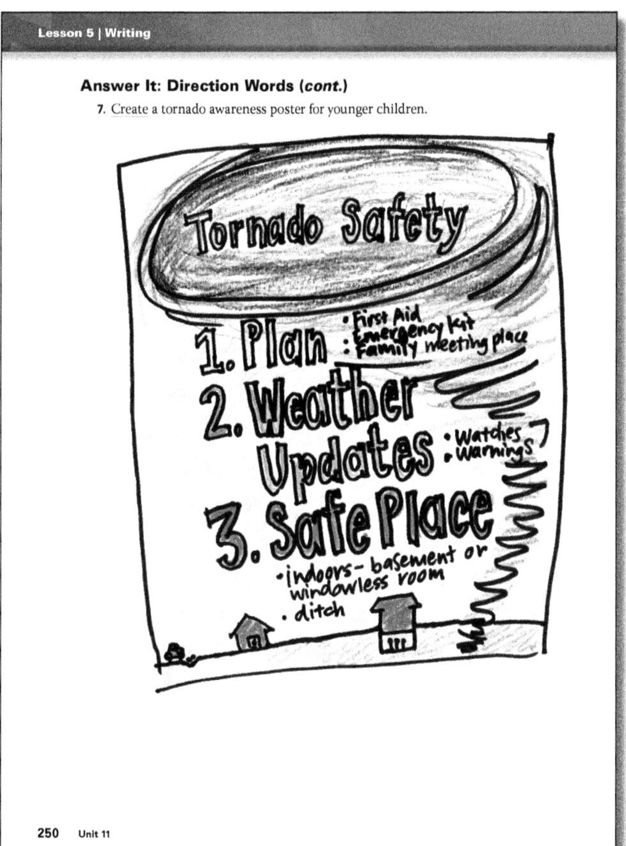

Lesson 5 | Writing

Answer It: Direction Words (*cont.*)

7. Create a tornado awareness poster for younger children.

250 Unit 11

Independent Practice

Have students answer the remaining questions independently. Create a small group for students who need more assistance, using question 3 as additional guided practice.

Note: Base the number of modeled and guided examples on student ability and progress. Challenge them with independent practice when appropriate.

Provide these alternative questions and sentence starters for those who need additional help.

3. Why were tornado death rates elevated in 2011? Cite evidence to support your answer.

   According to the margin and graph, 2011 ______________________________.

4. Do all tornadoes result in death?

   This quote proves that many tornadoes do not result in death: ____________."

5. Where did the deadliest tornado since 1950 occur? Cite evidence to support your answer.

   The text says, "____."

6. When did important dates and facts occur with regard to tornadoes? Create a chart showing Tornado Milestones.

When?						
How many?						
How long?						
How much?						
How fast?						
Where?						

7. What do young children need to know about tornadoes? Make a poster that teaches young children about the dangers of tornadoes.

Unit 11

Lesson 6

Lesson Opener

Before the lesson, choose one of the following activities to write on the board or post on the *LANGUAGE! Live* Class Wall online.

- *Turn to your Key Passage Vocabulary chart. Complete your drawings and add information to definitions as needed.*
- *Write three sentences about a tornado that lifted a home and dragged it for 100 feet. In the first sentence, the tornado hasn't come yet. In the second sentence, the tornado is there now. In the third sentence, the tornado is already over.*
- *If a tornado warning was issued and you had to go to an underground cellar for several hours, what would you take to the cellar? Why?*

Writing

Objectives

- Know spelling-sound correspondences for words with /o͝o/ as in *book*.
- Know spelling-sound correspondences for words with /ā/ spelled *ai* and *ay*.
- Know spelling-sound correspondences for words with the blends *sw* and *tw*.
- Know spelling-sound correspondences for words with /ō/ spelled *oa* and *ow*.

Spelling Words

Use this spelling activity to practice or assess the unit's spelling patterns students have learned online.

Direct students to Part A on page 251 in their Student Books. Read the instructions and remind students of the procedure for spelling. Use the spelling reminders to help struggling students.

1. brain; You must have a big brain.
2. soap; Wash your hands with soap.
3. clay; I made a vase out of clay.
4. sweet; These cookies are sweet.
5. crook; The crook robbed a store.
6. trains; The trains are loaded with cargo.
7. foam; The box was filled with foam peanuts.
8. twine; Tie the sticks up with twine.
9. paid; He paid for my lunch.
10. good; You are such a good friend.

Lesson 6 | Writing

Spelling

Part A

Write the words your teacher dictates.

1. brain
2. soap
3. clay
4. sweet
5. crook
6. trains
7. foam
8. twine
9. paid
10. good

Part B

Write the sentence your teacher dictates. Check for sentence signals—correct capitalization and end punctuation.

1. The twin goats like to play by the brook in the woods.
2. The boat sways as we load it with bowls of sweets.

Unit 11 251

Direct students to Part B on page 251 in their Student Books. Read the instructions and remind students of the procedure for sentence dictation.

The twin goats like to play by the brook in the woods.

The boat sways as we load it with bowls of sweets.

Spelling Words Procedure

- Teacher reads the word.
- Students repeat the word.
- Teacher reads the sentence.
- Students write the word.
- Teacher reads the word a second time as students check their work.

Sentence Dictation Procedure

- Teacher reads the sentence.
- Students repeat the sentence.
- Students write the sentence.
- Teacher reads the sentence a second time as students check their work.

Spelling Reminders

/o͝o/ as in *book*
In English, the phoneme /o͝o/ occurs only in the middle of words, such as in the word *book*. There are no words in English that begin or end with this vowel sound. We usually, but not always, use two *o*s to spell /o͝o/.

/ā/ Spelled *ai* and *ay*
Vowel teams often like certain places or spots in words. The long *a* phoneme is spelled *ai* in the middle of words, as in *pain*, and it's spelled *ay* when it's the last sound in a word or syllable, as in *play*.

Blends *sw* and *tw*
The initial blends *sw-* and *tw-* appear at the beginning of words or syllables. When you spell words with these blends, make sure you spell both sounds: /s/ /w/ and /t/ /w/.

/ō/ Spelled *oa* and *ow*
You know that long vowels often have several spellings. If the long *o* vowel is in the middle of a word, before a consonant, we can spell it *oa* as in *boat*, *soak*, and *road*. Long *o* can also be spelled *ow*, as in *show* and *grow*. The *ow* spelling is usually seen at the end of a word or before *n*.

Vocabulary

Objectives

- Use context to determine the meaning of words in text.
- Consult reference materials to clarify the precise meaning of words.
- Demonstrate an understanding of synonym word analogies.
- Write synonym and antonym word analogies.

Define It

Direct students to page 252 in their Student Books.

Lesson 6 | Vocabulary

Define It

Determine the category and attributes of each word. Then write the definition.

Word		Category		Attributes
nation	=	part of the world	+	area of land; one government; citizens with commonalities

Definition: A nation is an area of land in the world containing people with common characteristics who are united under one government.

Word		Category		Attributes
debris	=	trash	+	small pieces; after a disaster

Definition: Debris is small pieces of trash after a disaster.

Word		Category		Attributes
warning	=	signal	+	danger is coming; helpful

Definition: A warning is a helpful signal to alert people of possible danger.

Word		Category		Attributes

Definition:

252 Unit 11

To define words, we need to understand the words' categories and attributes. Categories are the broad groups. Attributes are things like size, shape, color, texture, and function.

Model

Direct students to the third paragraph of "Twisters" and have them find the word *nation.* We may not know what a *nation* is, but we can look at the context around the word to determine its category and attributes. The words following the word *nation* are "in the world." So, I can say that the category for *nation* is *a part of the world.*

Now I will read the entire paragraph to see if I can come up with some attributes of a *nation.* The text refers to the United States on multiple occasions. Based on the text, we know that the United States is a nation. What do we know about the United States that can help us understand the attributes of a nation? The United States is an area of land, it has a government, and it has citizens, or people, with common characteristics (who usually speak the same language).

These are all attributes of a *nation.* I didn't need to know the meaning. I just had to read closely and use my prior knowledge to figure out the meaning. Now that I have identified the term's category and attributes, I can write a definition. Write the definition on the board and read it aloud.

> *A nation is an area of land in the world containing people with common characteristics who are united under one government.*

Have students write the definition in their Student Books.

Guided and Independent Practice

Repeat the process for the second word, allowing students to provide the category, attributes, and definition. Then have partners complete the activity.

Dictionaries

Explain that they may choose and define any vocabulary word from the passage to complete the last item. Have partners verify their definitions in a dictionary and make corrections as needed.

> **Note:** Base the number of modeled and guided examples on student ability and progress. Challenge them with independent practice when appropriate.

Analogies

An analogy is a logic problem based on two pairs of words that have the same relationship.

Write the following antonym analogy on the board:

pretty : *ugly* :: *messy* : *neat.*

Write the following synonym analogy on the board:

pretty : *handsome* :: *tidy* : *neat.*

There are various types of analogies. In the last unit, we studied synonym analogies, which compare two sets of words that have similar meanings. An example would be: *pretty is to handsome as tidy is to neat.*

An antonym analogy is a comparison of two sets of words that have opposite meanings. An example would be: *pretty is to ugly as messy is to neat.*

A logic problem based on two pairs of words that share the same relationship is called what? (an analogy)

Words with similar meanings are called what? (synonyms)

A logic problem made up of two pairs of synonyms is called what? (a synonym analogy)

Words that have opposite meanings are called what? (antonyms)

A logic problem made up of two pairs of antonyms is called what? (an antonym analogy)

Direct students to Part A on page 253 in their Student Books. Read the instructions.

Model

Read the first analogy aloud. *Quick* is to *fast* as *small* is to *little.* I know that *quick* and *fast* are synonyms. I also know that *small* and *little* are synonyms. Together, the two sets form a synonym analogy. The colons between the words tell us that they are related. The double colons between the pairs of words tell us that the words in each pair are related in the same way.

Read the second analogy aloud. *Awake* is to *asleep* as *big* is to *little.* I know that *awake* and *asleep* are antonyms. I also know that *big* and *little* are antonyms. Together, these word pairs form an antonym analogy.

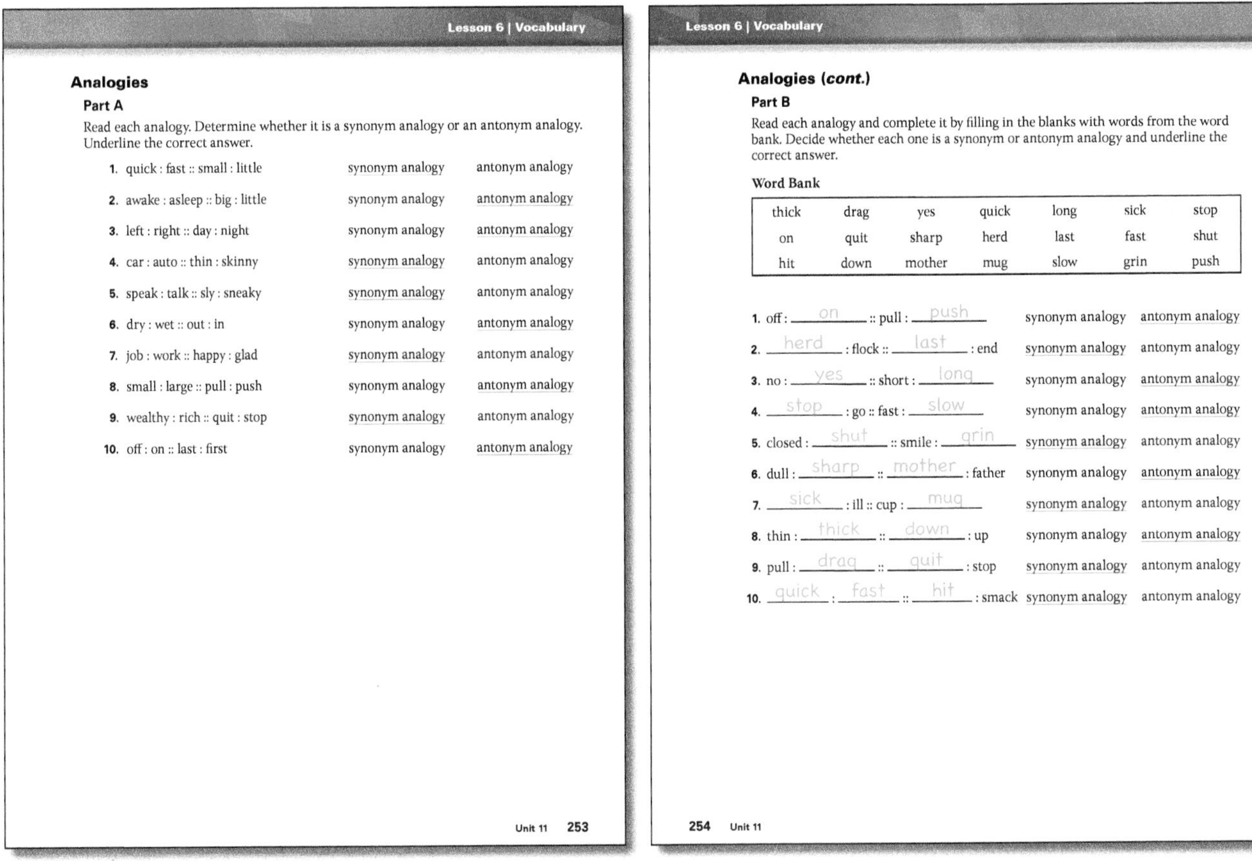
Lesson 6 | Vocabulary

Analogies

Part A

Read each analogy. Determine whether it is a synonym analogy or an antonym analogy. Underline the correct answer.

1.	quick : fast :: small : little	synonym analogy	antonym analogy
2.	awake : asleep :: big : little	synonym analogy	antonym analogy
3.	left : right :: day : night	synonym analogy	antonym analogy
4.	car : auto :: thin : skinny	synonym analogy	antonym analogy
5.	speak : talk :: sly : sneaky	synonym analogy	antonym analogy
6.	dry : wet :: out : in	synonym analogy	antonym analogy
7.	job : work :: happy : glad	synonym analogy	antonym analogy
8.	small : large :: pull : push	synonym analogy	antonym analogy
9.	wealthy : rich :: quit : stop	synonym analogy	antonym analogy
10.	off : on :: last : first	synonym analogy	antonym analogy

Unit 11 253

Lesson 6 | Vocabulary

Analogies (*cont.*)

Part B

Read each analogy and complete it by filling in the blanks with words from the word bank. Decide whether each one is a synonym or antonym analogy and underline the correct answer.

Word Bank

thick	drag	yes	quick	long	sick	stop
on	quit	sharp	herd	last	fast	shut
hit	down	mother	mug	slow	grin	push

1.	off : on :: pull : push	synonym analogy	antonym analogy
2.	herd : flock :: last : end	synonym analogy	antonym analogy
3.	no : yes :: short : long	synonym analogy	antonym analogy
4.	stop : go :: fast : slow	synonym analogy	antonym analogy
5.	closed : shut :: smile : grin	synonym analogy	antonym analogy
6.	dull : sharp :: mother : father	synonym analogy	antonym analogy
7.	sick : ill :: cup : mug	synonym analogy	antonym analogy
8.	thin : thick :: down : up	synonym analogy	antonym analogy
9.	pull : drag :: quit : stop	synonym analogy	antonym analogy
10.	quick : fast :: hit : smack	synonym analogy	antonym analogy

254 Unit 11

Guided Practice

Guide students to complete the next two analogies.

Independent Practice

Read the remaining analogies and have students determine whether each one is a synonym analogy or an antonym analogy and underline the correct choice. Review the answers as a class.

Direct students to Part B on page 254. Read the instructions. Have partners complete the analogies using the words in the box and then determine whether each analogy is a synonym or antonym analogy. Guide the process as needed and review the answers as a class.

Note: Base the number of modeled and guided examples on student ability and progress. Challenge them with independent practice when appropriate.

Writing

Objective

- Write sentences using concrete words and phrases and sensory details to convey information precisely.

Provide students with index cards for sentence manipulation if needed.

Masterpiece Sentences poster

Masterpiece Sentences

Direct students to page 255 in their Student Books. Discuss the picture and brainstorm words that students might use in preparing their canvas or when painting their subject and predicate. Create a word list on the board for students to refer to.

Review the stages of Masterpiece Sentences. Vividly describe the picture. Work through each stage of Masterpiece Sentences, writing your ideas next to the painter questions. Write your final sentence on the line at the bottom of the page.

Have students write their Masterpiece Sentence. Keep students moving through the stages by having them share their sentences in various stages. Students can use the frames in their Student Books or manipulative cards to build their sentences.

Have volunteers share their sentences.

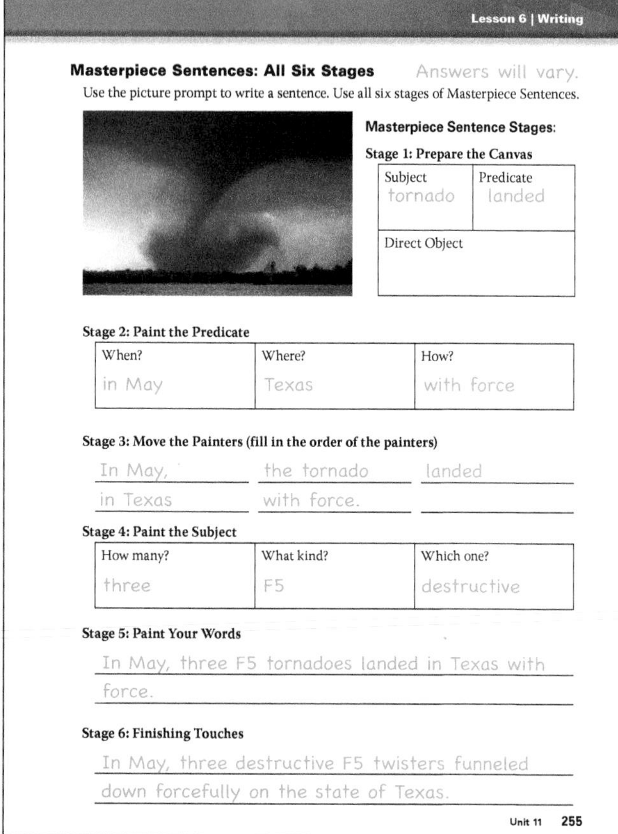
Lesson 6 | Writing

Masterpiece Sentences: All Six Stages Answers will vary.

Use the picture prompt to write a sentence. Use all six stages of Masterpiece Sentences.

Masterpiece Sentence Stages:

Stage 1: Prepare the Canvas

Subject	Predicate
tornado	landed
Direct Object	

Stage 2: Paint the Predicate

When?	Where?	How?
in May	Texas	with force

Stage 3: Move the Painters (fill in the order of the painters)

In May, | the tornado | landed
in Texas | with force.

Stage 4: Paint the Subject

How many?	What kind?	Which one?
three	F5	destructive

Stage 5: Paint Your Words

In May, three F5 tornadoes landed in Texas with force.

Stage 6: Finishing Touches

In May, three destructive F5 twisters funneled down forcefully on the state of Texas.

Unit 11 255

Reading

Objectives

- Compare and contrast informational and literary text types.
- Analyze two types of text for specific words used to compare and to contrast.

Compare and Contrast Paragraphs

In previous units, we have learned how to respond to prompts that ask us to compare and prompts that ask us to contrast. Remember, if you are asked to compare, you will state the similarities between two or more things. If you are asked to contrast, you will state the differences between two or more things. What do we look for when we compare? (similarities) What do we look for when we contrast? (differences) We're going to continue working on contrasting ideas as well as comparing them.

There are certain words that signal comparisons and certain words that signal contrasts. Direct students to pages 256 and 257 in their Student Books. Read the instructions and the lists of words for comparing and for contrasting.

> **Note:** While the lessons are written for a teacher read aloud, it is important that your students read as much and as often as they can. Assign readings that meet the needs of your students, based on your observations or data. This is a good opportunity to stretch students, but if they become frustrated, return to the read-aloud method.

Listen as I read the comparison paragraph and think about these two questions: What things are being compared? How are they alike? Read the compare paragraph.

Compare Paragraph

The Internet and print materials are alike in some ways. First, both the Internet and print media can be used to find information on everyday topics. People who want a telephone number for a business can look for it on the Internet. They can use a phone book, which is print material too. If you want the schedule for the movies for Saturday night, you can look up the times in the newspaper and on the Internet. What if you are looking for directions to get someplace? You can buy a map to see how to get there. You can also find a map on the Internet. Second, both the Internet and print media can be used to do research for school. For example, students can read magazines, newspapers, or even books on the Internet, just as they can in print. Students can find encyclopedias and dictionaries online too. If they want information about a person or a place or need to know the meaning of a word, people can choose between using a computer or looking up the information in a book.

What two things are being compared in this paragraph? (The Internet and print materials are being compared.) What are two things that the Internet and print materials have in common? (They are used to find information on everyday topics. They can be used to do research.)

Lesson 6 | Reading

Analyze Compare and Contrast Paragraphs

Read the compare and contrast paragraphs. Circle the words that signal similarities in the compare paragraph and the words that signal differences in the contrast paragraph. Then underline transition words that help the writer move from one similarity or difference to the next.

Words Used to Compare		Words Used to Contrast	
alike	similar	different	more . . . than
and	both	but	on the other hand
also	too	however	in contrast
just as	in common	unlike	vary

Compare Paragraph

The Internet and print materials are alike in some ways. First, both the Internet and print media can be used to find information on everyday topics. People who want a telephone number for a business can look for it on the Internet. They can use a phone book, which is print material too. If you want the schedule for the movies for Saturday night, you can look up the times in the newspaper and on the Internet. What if you are looking for directions to get someplace? You can buy a map to see how to get there. You can also find a map on the Internet. Second, both the Internet and print media can be used to do research for school. For example, students can read magazines, newspapers, or even books on the Internet, just as they can in print. Students can find encyclopedias and dictionaries online, too. If they want information about a person or a place or need to know the meaning of a word, people can choose between using a computer or looking up the information in a book.

256 Unit 11

Lesson 6 | Reading

Analyze Compare and Contrast Paragraphs (*cont.*)

Contrast Paragraph

The Internet and print materials also have many differences. First, people often can find more information on the Internet than they can in print media. For example, in a phone book, you can find some basic information about a place to order pizza, but on the Internet, you can find a lot more information. The Internet provides the telephone number of the restaurant, as well as the address and the hours it is open. You may also be able to read the pizza menu and look at a map to see how to get to the restaurant. Second, students can often find information they need for school faster on the Internet. It can take them a long time to find information for a report by looking through books. In contrast, they can usually find a lot of information quickly on the Internet. Although students still have to read the information, they can search for it much faster. That's because the Internet provides information from so many different sources.

Unit 11 257

Now, as I read the paragraph again, circle the words that signal comparisons are being made. We'll examine the paragraph one sentence at a time. Read the paragraph aloud, guiding students to circle the words as they appear in individual sentences. Read all of the comparing words chorally.

Now, as I read the contrasting paragraph, think about these questions: What things are being contrasted? How are they different? Read the paragraph aloud.

Contrast Paragraph

The Internet and print materials also have many differences. First, people can often find more information on the Internet than they can in print media. For example, in a phone book, you can find some basic information about a place to order pizza, but on the Internet, you can find a lot more information. The Internet provides the telephone number of the restaurant, as well as the address and the hours it is open. You may also be able to read the pizza menu and look at a map to see how to get to the restaurant. Second, students can often find information they need for school faster on the Internet. It can take them a long time to find information for a report by looking through books. In contrast, they can usually find a lot of information quickly on the Internet. Although students still have to read the information, they can search for it much faster. That's because the Internet provides information from so many different sources.

What two things are being contrasted in this paragraph? (The Internet and print materials are being contrasted.) As we reread the paragraph, circle the words that signal contrasting ideas. We will work our way through the paragraph, one sentence at a time. Be prepared to tell me how they differ. Read the paragraph aloud, guiding students to circle the contrasting words. Read all of the contrasting words chorally. How do the Internet and print materials differ? Tell me two ways. (The Internet offers more information and is faster than using print materials.)

Now I want you to look back at these two paragraphs and consider how the writer moved from one idea to the next. In both paragraphs, the writer used number transition words, *first* and *second*. In the compare paragraph, find the word *first* and underline it. It actually begins the second sentence. You will find *second* in line 6. Read both sentences aloud.

Direct students to the words *first* and *second* in the contrast paragraph and again read both sentences aloud. Instruct students to underline the words.

Unit 11

Lesson 7

Lesson Opener

Before the lesson, choose one of the following activities to write on the board or post on the *LANGUAGE! Live* Class Wall online.

- *Write sentences using the following idioms. (Remember, it may be easier to write two sentences for each idiom to frame its meaning.)* in hot water; take it easy
- *Use the word* debris *in a sentence about a tornado.*
- *Write a metaphor to describe your belongings after a tornado destroyed your home.*

Reading

Objectives

- Read with purpose and understanding.
- Identify and explain explicit details from text.
- Take notes on a text.

Guided Highlighting of "Twisters"

Let's do what skilled readers do and reread "Twisters" looking for the most important information and clarifying any misunderstandings.

Green, yellow, and pink highlighters or colored pencils

Have students get out a colored pencil or highlighter.

Direct students to pages 258–260 in their Student Books. We will review the text features of nonfiction or expository text. Please use your writing utensil to mark your answer according to my instructions.

- Draw a rectangle around the title, "Twisters."
- Circle each heading.

Listen and mark each highlighted vocabulary word as I read it aloud. I'm going to pause after every word to give you time to process whether you know the word and its meaning. We will review your ratings from Lesson 1 after we finish.

- span—*Span* means "to stretch or reach over or across." Say *span*. (span) Funnel clouds *span* two to six miles.
- ranks—*Ranks* means "to compare one position with others on a scale." Say *ranks*. (ranks) Each tornado will *rank* differently according to wind speed.

Lesson 7 | Reading

Guided Highlighting

Read the text.

Twisters

A tornado is one of nature's most powerful, unpredictable, and destructive storms. It has the ability to lift houses off their foundations and hurl them considerable distances. A tornado usually starts out as a funnel cloud in the sky. Once the funnel cloud makes contact with land, that funnel cloud becomes a tornado. Funnel clouds can be from two to six miles wide, and a tornado's base can **span** from 250 feet to more than two miles. Tornadoes can produce large hail and wind gusts of more than 200 miles per hour. The average tornado, however, has maximum wind speeds of 112 miles per hour and travels about one mile before it falls apart. Like a hurricane, a tornado spins in a counterclockwise direction. Once a tornado forms, the biggest challenge is predicting its path.

Tornado Categories

The Fujita Scale (F-Scale) classifies tornadoes by intensity rather than size. Tornadoes can be weak or intense whether they are large or small. The scale **ranks** a tornado on its wind speed, which can range from gale strength to incredible force. The table shows the six categories of the Fujita Scale.

The Fujita Scale

F-Scale Number	Tornado Intensity	Wind Speed (mph)	Description of Damage
F0	Gale	40–72	Some damage to trees and buildings
F1	Moderate	73–112	Damage to roofs, cars moved off roads
F2	Significant	113–157	Building frames torn off, large trees uprooted
F3	Severe	158–206	Structural damage to buildings, roofs torn off, trees uprooted
F4	Devastating	207–260	Houses leveled, vehicles thrown
F5	Incredible	261–318	Houses destroyed or lifted from foundation, vehicles thrown through the air, severe structural damage to concrete buildings

Source: http://www.tornadoproject.com/fscale/fscale.htm

258 Unit 11

- occur—*Occur* means "to happen." Say *occur.* (occur) Tornadoes typically *occur* in the spring.
- generate—*Generate* means "to produce or bring into being." Say *generate.* (generate) A tornado can *generate* a lot of debris.
- severe—*Severe* means "bad or serious." Say *severe.* (severe) *Severe* storms cause power outages.
- develop—*Develop* means "to grow into a more advanced or mature state." Say *develop.* (develop) Tornadoes *develop* quickly in the spring.
- entire—*Entire* means "whole or total." Say *entire.* (entire) Our *entire* school prepped for the tornado drill.
- region—A *region* is "an area with a certain type of land and climate." Say *region.* (region) The Great Plains *region* experiences frequent tornadoes.

Talk with your partner about any vocabulary word that is still confusing for you to read or understand. Share your ratings from Lesson 1. Were you honest about your word knowledge? Now is the time to do something about it!

Give students time to discuss their understanding of the vocabulary words with a partner.

It's time to reread the text the way proficient readers do. You will read the text "Twisters" one section at a time. Please be sure to draw a question mark over any confusing words, phrases, or sentences. I will provide specific instructions on how to mark the text that will help with your comprehension and writing.

Note: If you feel your students are capable, instruct them to highlight the main idea of each paragraph or section in green, and the supporting details in yellow. Then make all additional marks in another color.

Lesson 7 | Reading

Guided Highlighting (*cont.*)

Tornadoes in the United States

The United States has more tornadoes than any nation in the world. During a typical year, more than 1,000 tornadoes **occur** across the continental United States. More than 30 percent of these tornadoes occur in "Tornado Alley." Most of these tornadoes occur in the spring.

In fact, over 55 percent of a year's tornadoes occur between the months of April and June, when cool dry air from Canada clashes with warm, moist air from the Gulf of Mexico. These ingredients, when combined with a storm system, **generate severe** thunderstorms and, in some cases, deadly tornadoes. Hundreds of tornadoes **develop** during an average tornado season in the United States. Some bring death and destruction.

Killer Tornadoes

Tornadoes can be weak, strong, or violent. Strong winds and debris can cause power outages, structural damage to buildings, and even death. Violent tornadoes make up only a small percentage of all tornadoes, but they are responsible for two-thirds of all tornado deaths in the United States. These killer tornadoes can last for more than an hour, bringing devastation to an **entire region**. The chart on the next page shows the number of killer tornadoes compared with the number of deaths they caused from 2000 to 2011.

Unit 11 259

Lesson 7 | Reading

Guided Highlighting (*cont.*)

Tornado Safety

It is important to heed tornado warnings. Tornadoes can develop in the blink of an eye, and individuals should pay attention to warning signs such as dark green skies, a loud roaring sound, hail, and a visible funnel cloud. Listening to the radio or television can provide valuable updates on a tornado's development. Individuals should quickly find a safe place to weather the storm. Their lives may depend on it. The safest place is underground in a basement or storm shelter. If no underground shelter is available, a room away from windows and with strong structural support is the next safest choice. In many homes, this may be a bathroom. Mattresses, cushions, and sleeping bags can provide some protection. When tornado season approaches, experts recommend preparing an emergency kit. The kit should be stocked with flashlights, batteries, bottled water, canned foods, and first aid supplies.

Tornado Milestones

- The most tornadoes in one month occurred in May 2003 with a total of 543 tornadoes, compared with an average May total of 180.
- The most tornadoes occurring over a period of time occurred on April 27–28, 2011, with a total of 175 tornadoes.
- The most tornadoes in one year occurred in 2003, when 1,376 tornadoes were reported.
- Oklahoma City has been hit by more tornadoes than any other city; the known total is over 100.
- The deadliest tornado was the Tri-State Tornado of March 18, 1925. It claimed the lives of 695 people in 3½ hours. The deadliest of the modern era (since 1950) was on May 22, 2011, when a large EF5 tornado crossed Joplin, Missouri, causing 158 direct fatalities.
- The costliest tornado in history was the EF5 in Joplin, Missouri, on May 22, 2011, with an estimated $2.8 billion in damage.
- The highest recorded wind speed was 318 mph in Moore, Oklahoma, on May 3, 1999.

260 Unit 11

With eyes on text, listen to each section as it is read to you. Use your pencil eraser to follow along.

Note: While the lessons are written for a teacher read aloud, it is important that your students read as much and as often as they can. Assign readings that meet the needs of your students, based on your observations or data. This is a good opportunity to stretch students, but if they become frustrated, return to the read-aloud method.

Let's read the first paragraph, lines 1–11. Read the paragraph.

Twisters

A tornado is one of nature's most powerful, unpredictable, and destructive storms. It has the ability to lift houses off their foundations and hurl them considerable distances. A tornado usually starts out as a funnel cloud in the sky. Once the funnel cloud makes contact with land, that funnel cloud becomes a tornado. Funnel clouds can be from two to six miles wide, and a tornado's base can span from 250 feet to more than two miles. Tornadoes can produce large hail and wind gusts of more than 200 miles per hour. The average tornado, however, has maximum wind speeds of 112 miles per hour and travels about one mile before it falls apart. Like a hurricane, a tornado spins in a counterclockwise direction. Once a tornado forms, the biggest challenge is predicting its path.

- Circle the check mark or question mark for this paragraph. Draw a question mark over any confusing words or phrases.
- On lines 1 and 2, mark three adjectives that describe tornadoes. (powerful, unpredictable, destructive)
- Go to line 3. Mark the synonym for *throw*. (hurl)
- Mark what a tornado can do to a house. (lift houses off their foundation and hurl them)
- Mark how a tornado starts. (a funnel cloud)
- Mark what changes a funnel cloud to a tornado. (contact with land)
- Mark the size of a funnel cloud. (two to six miles wide)
- Mark the two things produced by a tornado. (large hail; wind gusts)
- Mark the maximum wind speeds of an average tornado. (112 mph)
- Mark how a tornado is "like a hurricane." (spins in a counterclockwise direction)
- Mark the challenge of tornadoes. (predicting its path)

Let's read the next section, Tornado Categories, along with the table, The Fujita Scale. Read the paragraph and table.

Tornado Categories

The Fujita Scale (F-Scale) classifies tornadoes by intensity rather than size. Tornadoes can be weak or intense whether they are large or small. The scale **ranks** a tornado according to its wind speed, which can range from gale strength to incredible force. The table shows the six categories of the Fujita Scale.

The Fujita Scale

F-Scale Number	Tornado Intensity	Wind Speed (mph)	Description of Damage
F0	Gale	40–72	Some damage to trees and buildings
F1	Moderate	73–112	Damage to roofs, cars moved off roads
F2	Significant	113–157	Building frames torn off, large trees uprooted
F3	Severe	158–206	Structural damage to buildings, roofs torn off, trees uprooted
F4	Devastating	207–260	Houses leveled, vehicles thrown
F5	Incredible	261–318	Houses destroyed or lifted from foundation, vehicles thrown through the air, severe structural damage to concrete buildings

Source: http://www.tornadoproject.com/fscale/fscale.htm

- Circle the check mark or question mark for the paragraph and table. Draw a question mark over any confusing words or phrases.
- Go to line 12. Mark the abbreviation for Fujita Scale. (F-Scale)
- Mark how the Fujita Scale classifies tornadoes. (intensity)
- Go to line 13. Mark the antonym pair that describes the intensity of tornadoes. (weak, intense)

- Go to line 14. Mark the indicator that determines a tornado's F-Scale number. (wind speed)
- Mark the lowest level of wind speed and the highest level of wind speed. (gale; incredible force)
- Go to the table, The Fujita Scale. Number four categories of information. (1. F-Scale Number; 2. Tornado Intensity; 3. Wind Speed; 4. Description of Damage)
- Mark the destruction of buildings at each level.

Let's read the next section, Tornadoes in the United States. Read the paragraphs.

Tornadoes in the United States

The United States has more tornadoes than any nation in the world. During a typical year, more than 1,000 tornadoes occur across the continental United States. More than 30 percent of these tornadoes occur in "Tornado Alley." Most of these tornadoes occur in the spring.

In fact, over 55 percent of a year's tornadoes occur between the months of April and June, when cool dry air from Canada clashes with warm, moist air from the Gulf of Mexico. These ingredients, when combined with a storm system, generate severe thunderstorms and, in some cases, deadly tornadoes. Hundreds of tornadoes develop during an average tornado season in the United States. Some bring death and destruction.

- Circle the check mark or question mark for each paragraph. Draw a question mark over any confusing words or phrases.
- Mark the nation what has the most tornadoes. (United States)
- In the first paragraph, underline the phrase that answers *when* tornadoes occur. (in the spring)
- Go to line 19. Put a box around the prepositional phrase that answers *where* more than 30 percent of tornadoes occur. (Tornado Alley)
- In the second paragraph, circle the phrase that answers *how many* tornadoes occur between April and June. (over 55 percent)
- Mark what happens from April to June that make tornadoes possible. (cool dry air from Canada clashes with warm, moist air from the Gulf of Mexico)
- Mark what two things can happen when the clash of air combines with a storm system. (severe thunderstorms; deadly tornadoes)
- Mark the number of tornadoes in the United States during one season. (Hundreds)
- Mark the two things tornadoes can bring. (death; destruction)

Let's read the next section, Killer Tornadoes. Read the paragraph.

Killer Tornadoes

Tornadoes can be weak, strong, or violent. Strong winds and debris can cause power outages, structural damage to buildings, and even death. Violent tornadoes make up only a small percentage of all tornadoes, but they are responsible for two-thirds of all tornado deaths in the United States. These killer tornadoes can last for more than an hour, bringing devastation to an entire region. The chart on the next page shows the number of killer tornadoes compared with the number of deaths they caused from 2000 to 2011.

- Circle the check mark or question mark for this paragraph. Draw a question mark over any confusing words or phrases.
- Go to line 27. Mark the effects of a tornado. (power outages, structural damage to buildings, death)
- Mark the two things that cause the effects. (strong wind; debris)
- Go to line 30. Mark the adjective that describes *tornadoes.* (killer)
- On the same line, circle the phrase "these killer tornadoes." Now go to line 28 and circle what the phrase is referring to. (violent tornadoes) Draw a line connecting the two.

Let's read the next section, Tornado Safety. Read the paragraph.

Tornado Safety

It is important to heed tornado warnings. Tornadoes can develop in the blink of an eye, and individuals should pay attention to warning signs such as dark green skies, a loud roaring sound, hail, and a visible funnel cloud. Listening to the radio or television can provide valuable updates on a tornado's development. Individuals should quickly find a safe place to weather the storm. Their lives may depend on it. The safest place is underground in a basement or storm shelter. If no underground shelter is available, a room away from windows and with strong structural support is the next safest choice. In many homes, this may be a bathroom. Mattresses, cushions, and sleeping bags can provide some protection. When tornado season approaches, experts recommend preparing an emergency kit. The kit should be stocked with flashlights, batteries, bottled water, canned foods, and first aid supplies.

- Circle the check mark or question mark for this paragraph. Draw a question mark over any confusing words or phrases.
- Go to line 34. Mark the antonym for *ignore.* (heed)
- Go to lines 34 and 35. Mark the idiom that means "extremely quickly." (in the blink of an eye)
- Number the warning signs that a tornado is coming. (1. dark green skies; 2. loud roaring sound; 3. hail; 4. visible funnel cloud)

- Mark the two ways to stay updated on tornado happenings. (listening to the radio or television)
- Go to line 39. Mark the idiom that means "to experience something and survive it." (weather the storm)
- Mark the safest place to be during a tornado. (underground in a basement or storm shelter)
- Mark where you should go if an underground shelter isn't available. (room away from windows)
- Mark what experts recommend you have during tornado season. (emergency kit)
- Mark the five things that should in an emergency kit. (flashlights, batteries, bottled water, canned foods, first aid supplies)

Let's read Tornado Milestones. Read the section.

Tornado Milestones

- The most tornadoes in one month occurred in May 2003 with a total of 543 tornadoes, compared with an average May total of 180.
- The most tornadoes occurring over a period of time occurred on April 27–28, 2011, with a total of 175 tornadoes.
- The most tornadoes in one year occurred in 2003, when 1,376 tornadoes were reported.
- Oklahoma City has been hit by more tornadoes than any other city; the known total is over 100.
- The deadliest tornado was the Tri-State Tornado of March 18, 1925. It claimed the lives of 695 people in 3½ hours. The deadliest of the modern era (since 1950) was on May 22, 2011, when a large EF5 tornado crossed Joplin, Missouri, causing 158 direct fatalities.
- The costliest tornado in history was the EF5 in Joplin, Missouri, on May 22, 2011, with an estimated $2.8 billion in damage.
- The highest recorded wind speed was 318 mph in Moore, Oklahoma, on May 3, 1999.

- Circle the check mark or question mark for this section. Draw a question mark over any confusing words or phrases.
- Mark how many tornadoes occurred in May 2003. (543)
- Mark how many tornadoes were reported in 2003. (1,376)
- Mark the city that has been hit with the most tornadoes. (Oklahoma City)
- Mark the fastest recorded wind speed in a tornado. (318 mph)

Have partners compare text markings and correct any errors.

Unit 11

Lesson 8

Lesson Opener

Before the lesson, choose one of the following activities to write on the board or post on the *LANGUAGE! Live* Class Wall online.

- *Complete the analogies:* look : see :: _____ : _____; pass : fail :: _____ : _____.
- *Use the word* warning *in a sentence about a tornado.*
- *Write a compound sentence comparing hurricanes and tornadoes.*

Writing

Objectives

- Gather relevant information from notes about a text.
- Write a clear two-sentence introduction.
- Take notes on two texts about different topics.
- Write a compare and contrast report.

Prepare to Write

Colored pencils

Before taking notes on "Twisters," let's consider our writing assignment. Direct students to pages 261 and 262 in their Student Books and read the prompt aloud. Discuss the topic and writing expectations, then have students identify the topic, directions, and purpose for writing. Have them write their responses in their Student Books.

Lesson 8 | Writing

Prepare to Write

Part A. Study the Prompt Answers will vary.

Read the prompt. Identify the topic, directions, and purpose for writing.

Write a multi-paragraph essay that analyzes the similarities and differences between tornadoes and hurricanes. Use information from "Hurricane!" and "Twisters" to make comparisons and contrasts.

Topic: tornadoes and hurricanes

Directions: write a multi-paragraph compare/contrast essay

Purpose for writing: tell the similarities and differences between hurricanes and tornadoes; use evidence to support comparisons and contrasts

Part B. Write an Introductory Paragraph: Topic Sentence + Elaboration

Write an opening paragraph that begins with a topic sentence. Add sentences that frame the similarities and differences to be analyzed.

Hurricanes and tornadoes are both powerful storms. These storms have several common attributes. They also have some distinct differences. In unique ways, hurricanes and tornadoes illustrate nature's powerful and destructive forces.

Unit 11 261

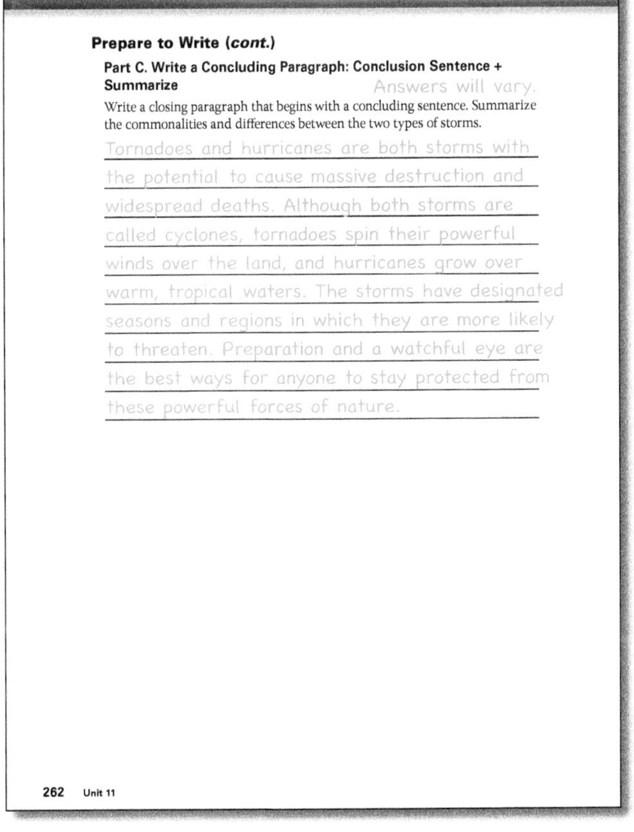
Lesson 8 | Writing

Prepare to Write (*cont.*)

Part C. Write a Concluding Paragraph: Conclusion Sentence + Summarize Answers will vary.

Write a closing paragraph that begins with a concluding sentence. Summarize the commonalities and differences between the two types of storms.

Tornadoes and hurricanes are both storms with the potential to cause massive destruction and widespread deaths. Although both storms are called cyclones, tornadoes spin their powerful winds over the land, and hurricanes grow over warm, tropical waters. The storms have designated seasons and regions in which they are more likely to threaten. Preparation and a watchful eye are the best ways for anyone to stay protected from these powerful forces of nature.

262 Unit 11

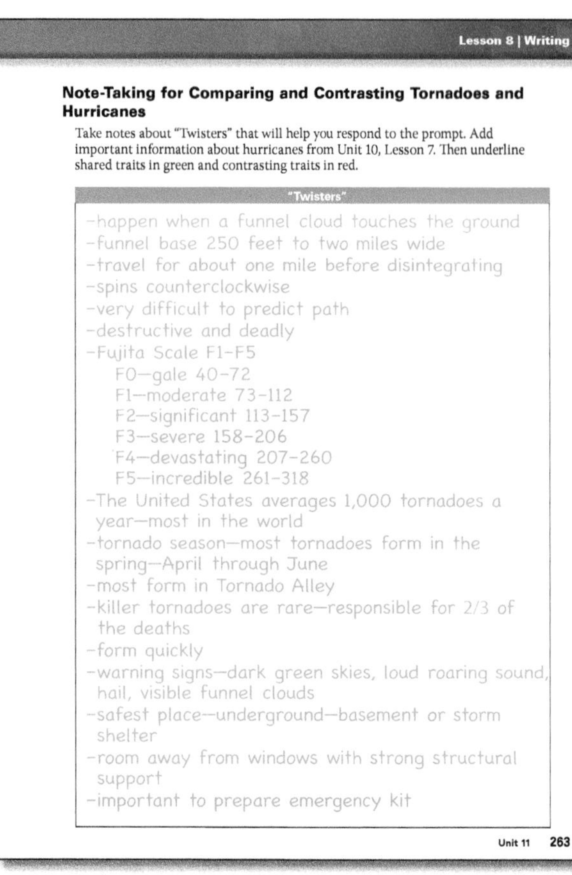

Lesson 8 | Writing

Note-Taking for Comparing and Contrasting Tornadoes and Hurricanes

Take notes about "Twisters" that will help you respond to the prompt. Add important information about hurricanes from Unit 10, Lesson 7. Then underline shared traits in green and contrasting traits in red.

"Twisters"

-happen when a funnel cloud touches the ground
-funnel base 250 feet to two miles wide
-travel for about one mile before disintegrating
-spins counterclockwise
-very difficult to predict path
-destructive and deadly
-Fujita Scale F1–F5
F0—gale 40–72
F1—moderate 73–112
F2—significant 113–157
F3—severe 158–206
F4—devastating 207–260
F5—incredible 261–318
-The United States averages 1,000 tornadoes a year—most in the world
-tornado season—most tornadoes form in the spring—April through June
-most form in Tornado Alley
-killer tornadoes are rare—responsible for 2/3 of the deaths
-form quickly
-warning signs—dark green skies, loud roaring sound, hail, visible funnel clouds
-safest place—underground—basement or storm shelter
-room away from windows with strong structural support
-important to prepare emergency kit

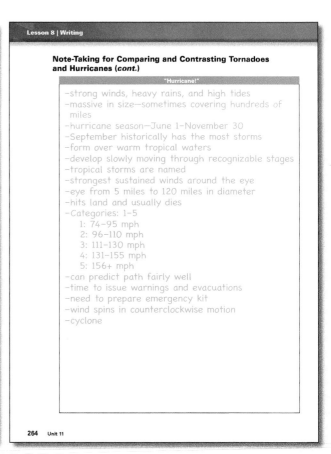

Unit 11 263

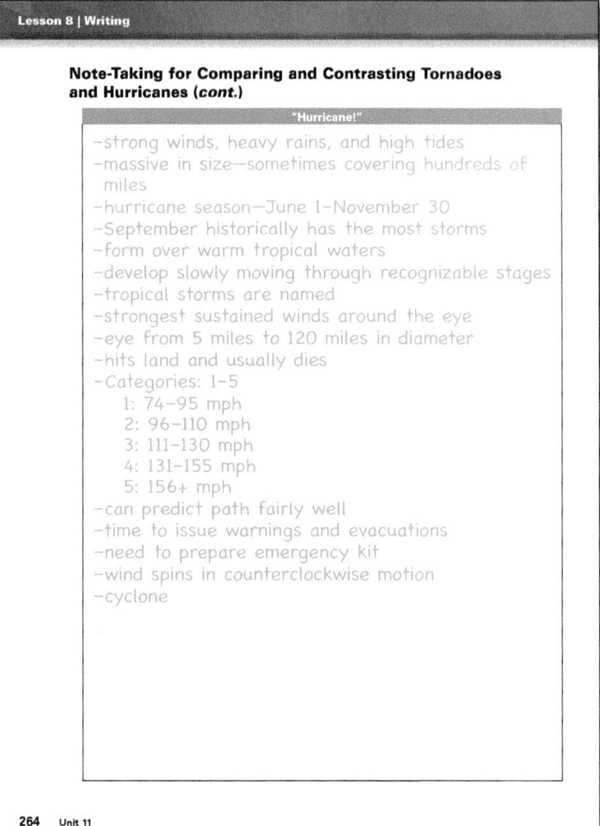

Lesson 8 | Writing

Note-Taking for Comparing and Contrasting Tornadoes and Hurricanes (*cont.*)

"Hurricane!"

-strong winds, heavy rains, and high tides
-massive in size—sometimes covering hundreds of miles
-hurricane season—June 1–November 30
-September historically has the most storms
-form over warm tropical waters
-develop slowly moving through recognizable stages
-tropical storms are named
-strongest sustained winds around the eye
-eye from 5 miles to 120 miles in diameter
-hits land and usually dies
-Categories: 1–5
1: 74–95 mph
2: 96–110 mph
3: 111–130 mph
4: 131–155 mph
5: 156+ mph
-can predict path fairly well
-time to issue warnings and evacuations
-need to prepare emergency kit
-wind spins in counterclockwise motion
-cyclone

264 Unit 11

Direct students to pages 263 and 264 in their Student Books. You will look at your Guided Highlighting of "Twisters" and take notes. You are looking for information that will help you compare and contrast hurricanes and tornadoes. Anything you think you might be able to use, you need to record. When you finish, you will return to your Guided Highlighting of "Hurricane!" and do the same.

We will be looking for information about how the storms form, what they are, and what kind of damage they cause. And because they are both classified using a scale, we will want information about that as well. Remember, since we are comparing and contrasting, we want to take notes on things that make them similar as well as things that make them different.

Have partners use their Guided Highlighting of "Hurricanes" from Unit 10, pages 203–205, and "Twisters" from this unit, pages 258–260, to complete the notes.

Note: If necessary, use answers above to guide the note-taking process.

Have students underline the common traits in one color and the contrasting traits in another color.

Write a Two-Sentence Introduction

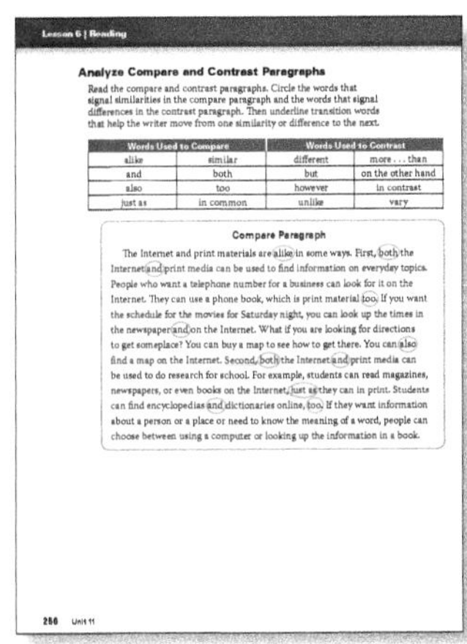

Lesson 6 | Reading

Analyze Compare and Contrast Paragraphs

Read the compare and contrast paragraphs. Circle the words that signal similarities in the compare paragraph and the words that signal differences in the contrast paragraph. Then underline transition words that help the writer move from one similarity or difference to the next.

Words Used to Compare		Words Used to Contrast	
alike	similar	different	more . . . than
and	both	but	on the other hand
also	too	however	in contrast
just as	in common	unlike	vary

Compare Paragraph

The Internet and print materials are alike in some ways. First, both the Internet and print media can be used to find information on everyday topics. People who want a telephone number for a business can look for it on the Internet. They can use a phone book, which is print material too. If you want the schedule for the movies for Saturday night, you can look up the times in the newspaper and on the Internet. What if you are looking for directions to get someplace? You can buy a map to see how to get there. You can also find a map on the Internet. Second, both the Internet and print media can be used to do research for school. For example, students can read magazines, newspapers, or even books on the Internet, just as they can in print. Students can find encyclopedias and dictionaries online, too. If they want information about a person or a place or need to know the meaning of a word, people can choose between using a computer or looking up the information in a book.

256 Unit 11

Remember that we discussed words used to signal comparisons and contrasts between two things. Direct students to page 256 in their Student Books to review the compare and contrast words and the topic sentences in each paragraph. Display the word chart or write it on the board for students to refer to as they begin to write. Keep these words in mind as you work on your topic sentences.

Direct students to Prepare to Write on pages 261 and 262 in their Student Books. We need to write an introduction that will set up the purpose for our writing and our main idea. Discuss ideas for an introductory sentence with your partner, and work together to write your own sentences. Consider quantifying the points of comparison and contrast as you write your opening paragraph.

Write Compare and Contrast Report

Notebook paper

Steps for Paragraph Writing poster

Before we write the conclusion, let's consider what will go in the "middle" or body of our paper. In that section, we will need to expand on the commonalities and the differences between hurricanes and tornadoes. We've already made a general reference to those elements in our introductory paragraph. Now, let's consider how we might summarize or restate our main idea to create a powerful conclusion. Brainstorm ways to restate the topic sentence and main points. Have students write their concluding paragraph.

Have partners discuss the big ideas for comparing the two storms. After a few minutes, have volunteers share their ideas.

Have partners discuss the differences between the two storms. After a few minutes, have volunteers share their answers.

Draw a Venn diagram on the board and write student ideas into the overlapping area for commonalities and the outer sides for unique attributes. Have students consider these main points and write their concluding paragraph.

With the time remaining, have students write the two paragraphs that compare and contrast the storms. Circulate and monitor student progress, answering questions and providing ideas when students seem to be struggling. Use the example report, if needed, to guide students as they write.

> **Note:** Because this is the first assigned multi-paragraph report, students may struggle pulling ideas together in a cohesive manner. Have struggling students use the House Blueprint for Writing with stars, dashes, and bullets from the back of their books to help with organization. Explain that the walls are now topic sentences for each body paragraph, the dashes are the supporting details, and the bullets are the elaborations.

Example Compare and Contrast Report

Hurricanes and tornadoes are both powerful storms. These storms have several common attributes. They also have some distinct differences. In unique ways, hurricanes and tornadoes illustrate nature's powerful and destructive forces.

Strong swirling winds are at the core of both storms. Spinning counterclockwise, they strengthen into threatening cyclones. Their strong winds cause death and destruction. Systems for categorizing the strength of each storm are based on wind strength. Tornadoes are more likely to occur in certain geographic regions of the United States and at certain times of the year. Like tornadoes, hurricanes have specific times and places in which they are more likely to form. Both storms pose a common threat of disruption and destruction. Because of this potential, people living in the path of tornadoes and hurricanes are urged to make emergency kits and safety plans.

Different parts of the country are threatened by each type of cyclone. Tornadoes form over land, while hurricanes require warm, tropical waters for development. Tornadoes can form in the blink of an eye, but hurricanes develop slowly and move through predictable stages of development. April and May are the prime months for tornado activity and put residents of Tornado Alley on alert. June 1st through November 30th is hurricane season and all of the residents along the southeastern coast of the United States make preparations.

Tornado strength is measured according to wind speeds and ranked on the Fujita Scale. The weakest rating for a tornado is F0, which signifies gale force winds gusting from 40 to 72 miles per hour. Tornado strength is measured by wind gusts, but hurricane strength is rated by its sustained winds. A minimal hurricane, or Category 1 hurricane, has sustained winds that range from 74 to 95 miles per hour. The strongest hurricane category, Category 5, has sustained winds of over 156 miles per hour. These winds last for hours and cause devastating flooding. The strongest tornado, an F5, has wind gusts over 261 miles per hour. Although these winds may not last very long, they leave death and total destruction in their wake. The most frightening aspect of a powerful tornado is its unpredictability. Because scientists have not been able to predict the occurrence of these storms, people have very little time to prepare and find a safe place to wait out the storm.

Tornadoes and hurricanes are both storms with the potential to cause massive destruction. Although both storms are called cyclones, tornadoes spin their powerful winds over the land, and hurricanes grow over warm, tropical waters. The storms have seasons and regions in which they are more likely to threaten. Preparation and a watchful eye are the best ways for anyone to stay protected from these powerful forces of nature.

Lesson 9

Lesson Opener

Before the lesson, choose one of the following activities to write on the board or post on the *LANGUAGE! Live* Class Wall online.

- *Write sentences with the words* vanish *and* vanishes. *Use each word as a noun and as a verb.*
- *Would you rather live in a region where hurricanes are possible or a region where tornadoes are possible? Explain your answer.*
- *Write a sentence about tornadoes with the following sentence structure: where + subject + which one + predicate.*

Reading

Objective

- Read words to develop fluency.

Word Fluency: Second Read

Timer

Follow the Fluency Procedure outlined below. If it is necessary, begin the fluency drill with a choral read of the words as you provide a rhythm (snap your fingers, tap your foot, tap your pencil). Direct students to page 265 in their Student Books and complete the process.

Word Fluency: Second Read

Read the words fluently.

	Correct	Errors
1st Try		
2nd Try		

cooked	hook	goals	bowling	brains	sweet	slows	failed	twisted	moons	10
goals	bowling	brains	sweet	slows	failed	twisted	moons	swinging	stays	20
brains	sweet	slows	failed	twisted	moons	swinging	stays	coaches	tweeted	30
slows	failed	twisted	moons	swinging	stays	coaches	tweeted	swayed	loaned	40
twisted	moons	swinging	stays	coaches	tweeted	swayed	loaned	brooms	growing	50
swinging	stays	coaches	tweeted	swayed	loaned	brooms	growing	may	snails	60
coaches	tweeted	swayed	loaned	brooms	growing	may	snails	hook	cooked	70
swayed	loaned	brooms	growing	may	snails	hook	cooked	bowling	goals	80
brooms	growing	may	snails	hook	cooked	bowling	goals	sweet	brains	90
may	snails	hook	cooked	bowling	goals	sweet	brains	failed	slows	100

Unit 11 265

Lesson 9 | Reading

Fluency Procedure

- Partners switch books, so the recorder is marking errors in the reader's book.
- A timer is set for one minute.
- Readers and recorders move left to right, tracking each word with a pencil.
- As readers read the words aloud, recorders mark errors with a small x above the misread word.
- Recorders place a star to the right of the last word read when time ends.
- If the reader is able to read all words in the allotted time, the reader needs to start over at the beginning. The recorder must indicate this feat by placing two stars to the right of the last word read.
- When both students have read, partners switch books.
- Students calculate total words read, then subtract errors and record.
- Students record information on the progress chart in back of the Student Book.

Vocabulary

Objective

- Use a range of strategies (consult reference materials; use understanding of figurative language—including similes, metaphors, and idioms; use understanding of synonyms, antonyms, related words) to clarify the meaning of words.

Vocabulary Expansion

Direct students to page 266 in their Student Books. Review the definition of each concept in the Vocabulary Expansion chart.

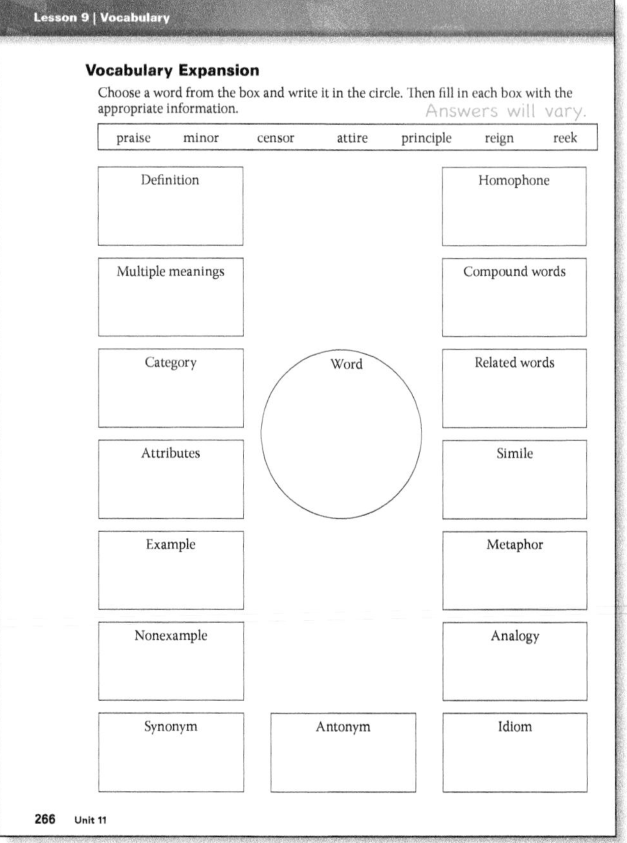

- **Definition:** the meaning of the word
- **Multiple meanings:** other meanings and uses of the word
- **Category:** the broad group in which a word fits
- **Attributes:** specific characteristics of the word
- **Example:** something that models or patterns the word
- **Nonexample:** something that does not model or pattern the word
- **Synonym:** a word with a similar meaning
- **Antonym:** a word with the opposite meaning
- **Homophone:** a word that sounds the same but has a different meaning
- **Compound word:** two words combined to make one word
- **Related words:** words with the same root word and related meanings
- **Simile:** figurative language comparing two dissimilar things using like or as
- **Metaphor:** figurative language comparing two dissimilar things by saying one thing is another thing
- **Analogy:** a comparison of two pairs of words that share the same relationship
- **Idiom:** figurative language used in a certain region or by a certain group of people

In this unit, we have been discussing how tornadoes form and the damage they cause. If people are warned about tornadoes, lives can be saved. Write the word *warn* on the board. Let's take a closer look at this word, and see if we can use the Vocabulary Expansion concepts to create a deeper understanding of this word. Guide students as you discuss each of the concepts and brainstorm possible answers. Write correct answers on the board.

Example Vocabulary Expansion of *warn*

Definition: to give notice of danger or evil

Multiple meanings: *v.:* to call to one's attention

Category: action

Attributes: notice, danger is coming, sounds, words, body language

Example: "Stop," "Be careful," tornado siren, flashing light, signs

Nonexample: invitation

Synonym: advise, alert, caution

Antonym: N/A

Homophone: worn

Compound words: N/A

Related words: warned, warning, forewarn

Simile: She interrupted me like a weather warning.

Metaphor: N/A

Analogy: warn : advise :: hop : jump

Idiom: Forewarned is forearmed.

Dictionaries or online access

Give each student a dictionary or provide Internet access. Read the instructions, then have students choose a word and use a dictionary (online or print) to complete the process. Have partners share their word expansions.

Grammar

Objective

- Demonstrate an understanding of the relationship of past, present, and future tense verbs.

Tense Timeline: Past, Present, Future

Create verb index cards.

Tense Timeline poster

Create index cards with verbs in a variety of tenses. Distribute index cards to students. Create a physical tense timeline, possibly across the front of the room, designating places for past, present, and future tense. Have students place themselves along the timeline according to the verb on the index card. Once they have "sorted" themselves, call on students in each segment of the timeline to read their verbs. Ask other students to determine the accuracy of each placement.

Verbs for Index Cards

generates	generated	is generating	will generate
seasons	seasoned	will season	
develops	developed	was developing	
threatens	threatened	will threaten	
sustains	is sustaining	was sustaining	
occurs	will occur		
related	will relate		
defines			
intrigues			
vanishes			
was scaling			

Note: The verbs listed for use are vocabulary words, but not necessarily decodable. If you think students will struggle, change the verbs to decodable verbs that they've already learned in class.

If time permits, ask students to use their verb in a sentence.

Activity variation: Give students multiple cards and have them place the cards along the timeline.

Writing

Objectives

- Demonstrate an understanding of conventional patterns used in sentence structures.
- Edit a text for basic conventions.
- Edit a text using the Six Traits rubric.

Sentence Structure

We have worked on a variety of sentence structures and patterns. Write the following words in a list on the board:

subject

predicate

direct object

predicate adjective

predicate nominative

conjunction

Write example sentences on the board to review the components. Have students identify the components as you point to them.

The fish is blue.
(*fish*: subject; *is*: predicate; *blue*: predicate adjective)

Maria reads a book.
(*Maria*: subject; *reads*: predicate; *book*: direct object)

Stan and Sam are my brothers.
(*Stan, Sam*: subject; *and*: conjunction; *brothers*: predicate nominative)

Direct students to page 267 in their Student Books and read the instructions aloud.

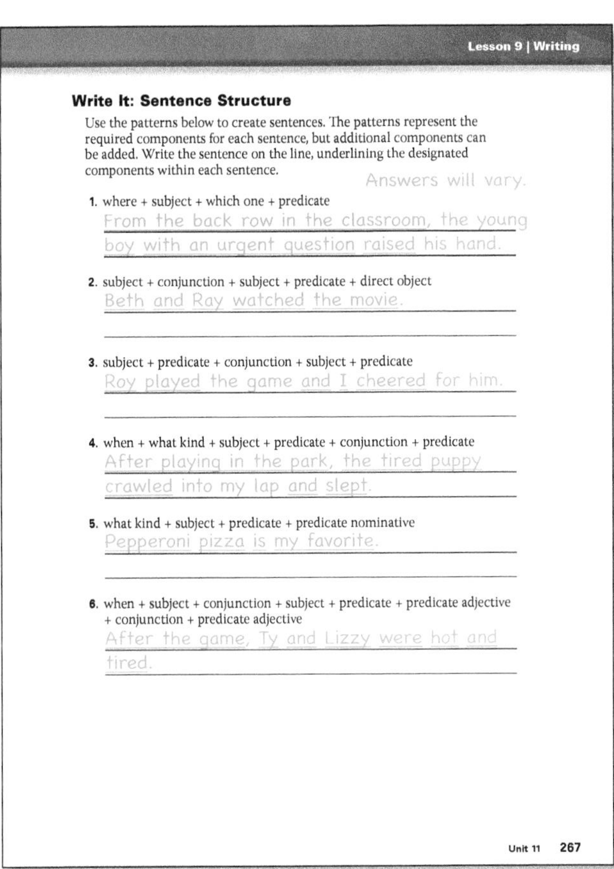
Lesson 9 | Writing

Write It: Sentence Structure

Use the patterns below to create sentences. The patterns represent the required components for each sentence, but additional components can be added. Write the sentence on the line, underlining the designated components within each sentence.

Answers will vary.

1. where + subject + which one + predicate
From the back row in the classroom, the young boy with an urgent question raised his hand.
2. subject + conjunction + subject + predicate + direct object
Beth and Ray watched the movie.
3. subject + predicate + conjunction + subject + predicate
Roy played the game and I cheered for him.
4. when + what kind + subject + predicate + conjunction + predicate
After playing in the park, the tired puppy crawled into my lap and slept.
5. what kind + subject + predicate + predicate nominative
Pepperoni pizza is my favorite.
6. when + subject + conjunction + subject + predicate + predicate adjective + conjunction + predicate adjective
After the game, Ty and Lizzy were hot and tired.

Unit 11 267

Model

Read the first pattern. There are a couple of different ways to follow the pattern and create a sentence. We can start by looking at the heart of the sentence, the subject and predicate, and create a kernel sentence. We need to look at all of the components before we commit to a kernel sentence, though, because what follows the verb will influence our verb choice.

For this first sentence, let's start with our kernel sentence, or simple subject and simple predicate. Have students generate several kernel sentences and choose one to write on the board.

Now, we have to answer two questions about this sentence: *where* and *which one*. Where did it happen? We need to add some details to our predicate, or the verb in the sentence. Encourage a variety of responses and choose one to write on the board. We need to add some details about our subject. Which one did it? Encourage a variety of responses and choose one to write on the board. Let's read our sentence and make sure it makes sense. Read the sentence.

The last thing we need to do is underline all of the components that appear in the pattern. Underline each component. Now it's your turn. Write your own sentence that follows this pattern. Have volunteers share their completed sentences.

Another way to accomplish the task is to work through the pattern in order. Read the next pattern aloud. We know we need a compound subject and that we have to choose a verb that will take a direct object. Keeping that in mind, let's think of some different subject nouns we could use to create a compound subject. Encourage a variety of responses and choose one to write on the board.

Now, we have to choose a verb. We have to be able to answer the direct object question: *What did they do it to?* Encourage a variety of responses for the verb and choose one to write on the board. Then ask students to answer the question and provide a direct object. Choose one and write it on the board. Now, let's read our sentence to make sure it makes sense and then underline all of the required components.

Guided and Independent Practice

Read the remaining patterns and have students work independently to write the sentences. Have volunteers share their answers.

Note: Base the number of modeled and guided examples on student ability and progress. Challenge them with independent practice when appropriate.

Writer's Checklist

Direct students to page 268 in their Student Books. Have students work independently, using the Writer's Checklist to make final revisions to their compare and contrast essay.

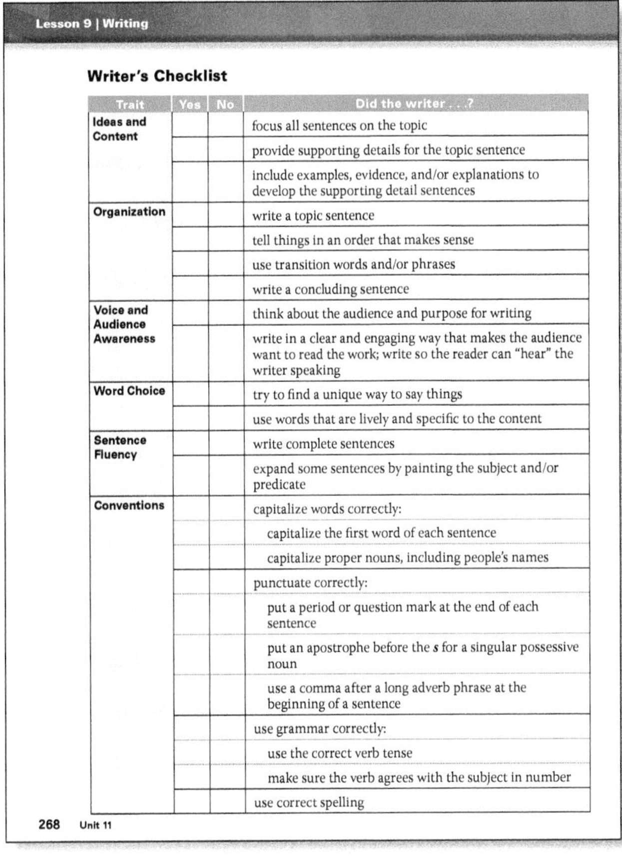

Lesson 9 | Writing

Writer's Checklist

Trait	Yes	No	Did the writer . . .?
Ideas and Content			focus all sentences on the topic
			provide supporting details for the topic sentence
			include examples, evidence, and/or explanations to develop the supporting detail sentences
Organization			write a topic sentence
			tell things in an order that makes sense
			use transition words and/or phrases
			write a concluding sentence
Voice and Audience Awareness			think about the audience and purpose for writing
			write in a clear and engaging way that makes the audience want to read the work; write so the reader can "hear" the writer speaking
Word Choice			try to find a unique way to say things
			use words that are lively and specific to the content
Sentence Fluency			write complete sentences
			expand some sentences by painting the subject and/or predicate
Conventions			capitalize words correctly:
			capitalize the first word of each sentence
			capitalize proper nouns, including people's names
			punctuate correctly:
			put a period or question mark at the end of each sentence
			put an apostrophe before the *s* for a singular possessive noun
			use a comma after a long adverb phrase at the beginning of a sentence
			use grammar correctly:
			use the correct verb tense
			make sure the verb agrees with the subject in number
			use correct spelling

268 Unit 11

Six Traits of Writing

Direct students to page 269 in their Student Books. Have students work with their partners to apply all six traits on the rubric to their writing.

Look over your rough draft and see if you want to make any more edits to your compare and contrast essay. Then work with your partner to make sure you have applied all six traits to your writing.

Six Traits Rubric: Compare and Contrast Report

Trait	Criteria 4	3	2	1	Value	Comments
Ideas and Content	Clear focus on the topic. Body paragraphs begin with transition topic sentences that are fully supported with elaborations. No irrelevant information.	Mostly focuses on the topic. Body paragraphs begin with transition topic sentences that are adequately supported with elaborations. Limited irrelevant information.	Unclear focus on the topic. May have too few or minimally developed body paragraphs. Too repetitious or too much irrelevant information.	Does not address prompt and/or lacks focus on the topic. Ideas undeveloped or are unrelated to the topic.	____	
Organization	Introductory paragraph clearly states the topic and the plan. Ideas are logically organized. Transition topic sentences link paragraphs. Contains a concluding paragraph.	Introductory paragraph states the topic and the plan. Ideas are mostly logically sequenced. Transition topic sentences may not clearly link body paragraphs, or some paragraphs may lack transition. Contains a concluding paragraph.	Introductory paragraph absent or does not state topic and/or plan. Body paragraphs not developed logically and/or fully. Transition topic sentences may be missing. Report is list-like or hard to follow. Conclusion missing or unrelated to topic.	No evident structure. Lack of organization seriously interferes with meaning.	____	
Voice and Audience Awareness	Strong sense of person and purpose behind the words. Brings topic to life.	Some sense of person and purpose behind the words.	Little sense of person or purpose behind the words.	No sense of person or purpose behind the words.	____	
Word Choice	Words are specific, accurate, and vivid. Word choice enhances meaning and reader's enjoyment.	Words are correctly used but may be somewhat general and unspecific.	Word choice limited. Words may be used inaccurately or repetitively.	Extremely limited range of words. Restricted vocabulary impedes message.	____	
Sentence Fluency	Writes complete sentences and varies sentence patterns and beginnings.	Writes complete sentences with some expansion.	Writes mostly simple and/or awkwardly constructed sentences. May include some run-ons and fragments.	Numerous run-ons and/or sentence fragments interfere with meaning.	____	
Conventions	*Capitalization & Punctuation* 0–1 error. Indents paragraphs.	*Capitalization & Punctuation* 2 errors. Indents paragraphs.	*Capitalization & Punctuation* 3 errors. May not indent paragraphs.	*Capitalization & Punctuation* 4+ errors. May not indent paragraphs.	____	
	Grammar/Usage 0–1 error	*Grammar/Usage* 2 errors	*Grammar/Usage* 3 errors	*Grammar/Usage* 4+ errors	____	
	Spelling 0–1 error	*Spelling* 2 errors	*Spelling* 3 errors	*Spelling* 4+ errors	____	

Unit 11 269

Lesson 9 | Writing

Lesson 10

Lesson Opener

Before the lesson, choose one of the following activities to write on the board or post on the *LANGUAGE! Live* Class Wall online.

- *Write four meaningful sentences with the vocabulary words from this unit. Each sentence will contain two vocabulary words* (span, rank, occur, generate, severe, develop, entire, region).
- *Write a technical (step-by-step) paragraph about the steps you would take if you heard a tornado siren.*
- *Write a sentence about tornadoes and hurricanes with the following sentence structure: when + subject + conjunction + subject + predicate + predicate adjective + conjunction + predicate adjective.*

Vocabulary

Objectives

- Clarify the meaning of key passage vocabulary.
- Demonstrate an understanding of passage vocabulary by using them in sentences.

Review

Direct students to page 224 in their Student Books. Remind them of the review procedure. Have partners review the Key Passage Vocabulary.

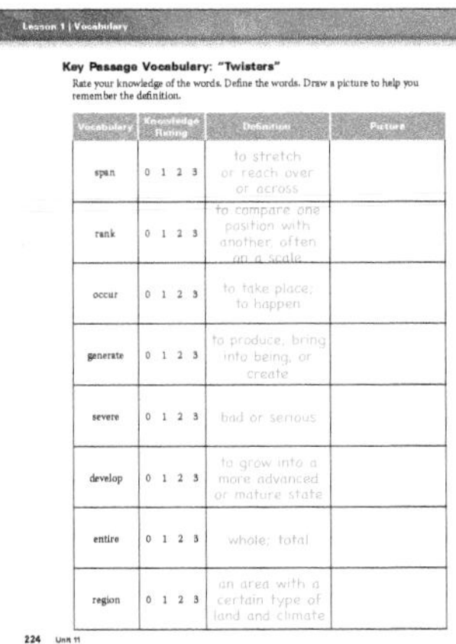
Lesson 1 | Vocabulary

Key Passage Vocabulary: "Twisters"

Rate your knowledge of the words. Define the words. Draw a picture to help you remember the definition.

Vocabulary	Knowledge Rating	Definition	Picture
span	0 1 2 3	to stretch or reach over or across	
rank	0 1 2 3	to compare one position with another, often on a scale	
occur	0 1 2 3	to take place; to happen	
generate	0 1 2 3	to produce, bring into being, or create	
severe	0 1 2 3	bad or serious	
develop	0 1 2 3	to grow into a more advanced or mature state	
entire	0 1 2 3	whole; total	
region	0 1 2 3	an area with a certain type of land and climate	

224 Unit 11

Review Procedure

- Student A reads the word.
- Student B tells the meaning.
- Students swap roles for each word.

Have students revisit their rating of the words. If they cannot change all ratings to a 3, pull them aside to discuss the vocabulary words they do not know.

Cloze Activity

Now we will read a paragraph. You will determine which vocabulary words are missing and write them on the lines. Direct students to page 270 in their Student Books. Remind them of the cloze procedure.

Cloze Procedure

- Teacher reads the text aloud, pausing at the blanks for students to write.
- Students fill in the blanks with words from the word bank.
- Teacher rereads the text as students chorally tell the correct word for each blank.
- Students correct errors.

Lesson 10 | Vocabulary

Using New Vocabulary

Fill in the blanks with the appropriate vocabulary words. If you need assistance, use the word bank at the bottom of the page.

The tornado in Joplin, Missouri, was one of the most __severe__ in U.S. history. It __occurred__ on Sunday, May 22, 2011. As a part of a tornado outbreak, deadly tornadoes __developed__ over the Midwest __region__ for several days. The base of the Joplin tornado __spanned__ a width of more than one mile. On the Enhanced Fujita Scale, the tornado __ranked__ as an EF5 tornado and __generated__ winds that peaked between 225 to 250 mph. It wiped out __entire__ neighborhoods in the town. It killed 158 people and about 1,000 were injured. It was the deadliest tornado in the United States since 1947.

Word Bank

severe	generated	ranked	entire
developed	spanned	region	occurred

270 Unit 11

Reading

Objectives

- Discuss and answer questions to demonstrate an understanding of main idea and key details in a text.
- Discuss and answer questions to demonstrate an understanding of point of view in a text.

Big Idea and Point of View

Direct students to page 223 in their Student Books.

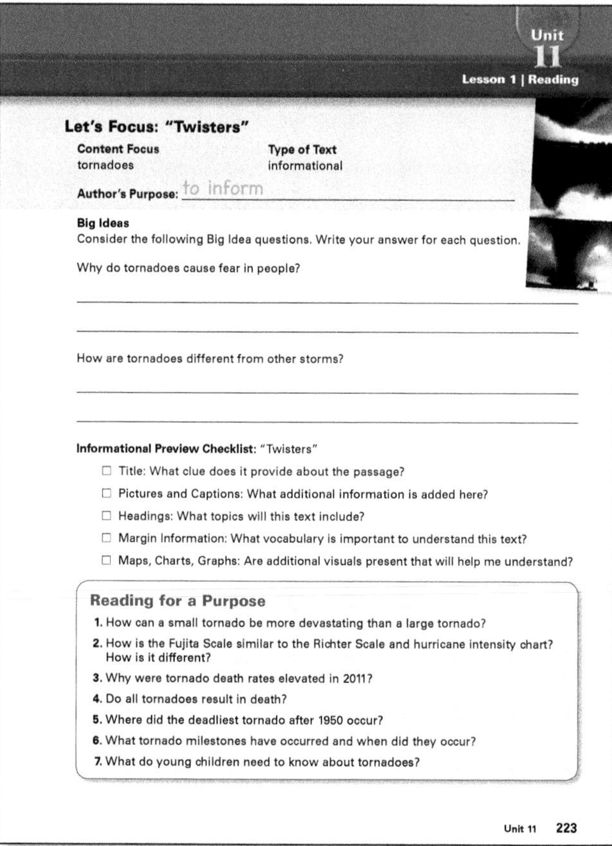
Unit 11

Lesson 1 | Reading

Let's Focus: "Twisters"

Content Focus
tornadoes

Type of Text
informational

Author's Purpose: to inform

Big Ideas

Consider the following Big Idea questions. Write your answer for each question.

Why do tornadoes cause fear in people?

How are tornadoes different from other storms?

Informational Preview Checklist: "Twisters"

- ☐ Title: What clue does it provide about the passage?
- ☐ Pictures and Captions: What additional information is added here?
- ☐ Headings: What topics will this text include?
- ☐ Margin Information: What vocabulary is important to understand this text?
- ☐ Maps, Charts, Graphs: Are additional visuals present that will help me understand?

Reading for a Purpose

1. How can a small tornado be more devastating than a large tornado?
2. How is the Fujita Scale similar to the Richter Scale and hurricane intensity chart? How is it different?
3. Why were tornado death rates elevated in 2011?
4. Do all tornadoes result in death?
5. Where did the deadliest tornado after 1950 occur?
6. What tornado milestones have occurred and when did they occur?
7. What do young children need to know about tornadoes?

Unit 11 223

Before we began reading "Twisters," we answered two Big Idea questions. Take a minute to look over your answers. Now that we have read the passage thoroughly and learned more about tornadoes, how have your earlier ideas changed? What information can you add to your answers?

Discuss the questions and answers with the class.

In the last unit, we talked about the pros and cons of trying to control violent storms. Do you think the impact we have on the environment inadvertently affects the weather? Do you think the consequences of continued air pollution or deforestation include a negative impact on our planet's weather? Give students time to discuss their thoughts. Whatever their position, encourage students to support it with examples or evidence.

We have spent time talking about point of view. What are the three perspectives from which you can write? (first person, second person, third person) As a writer, what are some reasons to choose one point of view over another? Think about why a writer would choose to write from the first-person perspective. Call on several students to share their thoughts. (Possible responses: personalization for drama, personal feelings, "eyewitness" perspective, to make the character come alive)

Ask similar questions about the second- and third-person points of view. Encourage students to consider whether any single point of view communicates more credibility or authority than the others.

If time permits, have students identify what point of view "Twisters" is written in. Have students use their knowledge of point of view to determine how the author views tornadoes.

Writing

Objective

- Demonstrate an understanding of sentence structure by using key elements of sentences to create oral sentences.

Sentence Structure

Create a set of sentence element index cards for each group.

Make sets of index cards using the sentence elements below, one per card. Each set should contain duplicates.

Markers for use on game board

Direct partners or groups to page 271 in their Student Books. Only one game board will be used per group. Distribute a set of cards to each pair or team, along with a game board marker for each student.

To play, students should take turns drawing a card. When a player successfully uses the element shown on the card in a complete sentence, he or she may advance one space.

The game can be played in small groups or as a whole class divided into two teams.

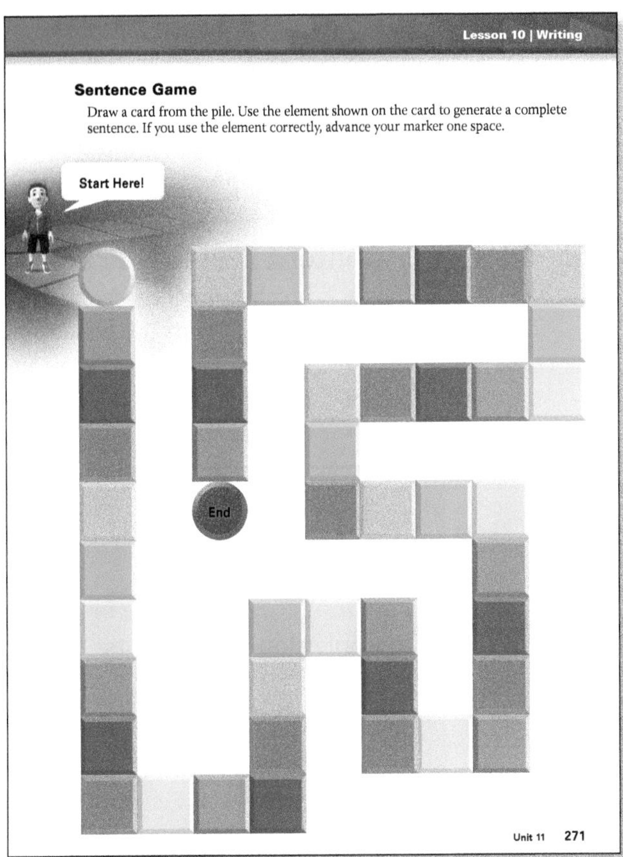

Lesson 10 | Writing
Sentence Game
Draw a card from the pile. Use the element shown on the card to generate a complete sentence. If you use the element correctly, advance your marker one space.
Start Here!
End
Unit 11 271

Sentence Elements for Index Cards

predicate adjective	predicate nominative
direct object	compound subject
compound predicate	compound sentence (and)
compound sentence (but)	compound sentence (or)
question/answer	future tense
present tense	present progressive
past tense	past progressive

Reading

Objectives for Content Mastery

- Demonstrate an understanding of how to analyze text.
- Demonstrate an understanding of comparison and contrast in text.
- Demonstrate an understanding of how to analyze informational text features to find information.

Responding to Prompts: *apply, create, prove*

Follow the procedure outlined below for each of the Reading Content Mastery questions and prompts.

Content Mastery Procedure

- Teacher reminds students to follow along with their pencils and listen.
- Teacher reads the question.
- Teacher reads each answer choice.
- Students choose the correct answer.
- Teacher repeats the question as students check their answers.

Have students turn to page 272 in their Student Books.

Let's look at the example first. Read the example aloud to students.

Listen: Apply what you know about your neighborhood to write a story about it. To answer this prompt, I need to ______.

A make or produce

B make use of information

C provide evidence; show that it is true

D tie ideas together; relate

Fill in the bubble for the correct response. Which bubble did you fill in? You should have filled in B, the bubble for "make use of information." That is how you would respond to a question that asks you to apply.

Follow along as I read the questions and prompts aloud. Fill in the bubble for your answer choice.

Lesson 10 | Reading Content Mastery

Responding to Prompts

Listen to the prompts and possible answers. Fill in the bubble for your answer choice.

Example: Apply what you know about your neighborhood to write a story about it.

To answer this prompt, I need to ____.
- Ⓐ make or produce
- ● make use of information
- Ⓒ provide evidence; show that it is true
- Ⓓ tie ideas together; relate

1. Create a map of the school.

   To answer this prompt, I need to ____.
   - Ⓐ provide evidence of a map
   - Ⓑ make use of information about the school
   - Ⓒ break down and evaluate or draw conclusions about the map
   - ● make or produce a map

2. Prove that hurricanes blow around a central eye.

   To answer this prompt, I need to ____.
   - Ⓐ explain the relationship between hurricanes and the eye
   - Ⓑ make use of information about hurricanes
   - Ⓒ make or produce a graph of a hurricane
   - ● provide evidence about how hurricanes work

3. Apply the skills you have learned to diagram this sentence.

   To answer this prompt, I need to ____.
   - Ⓐ make or produce a diagram
   - Ⓑ provide evidence of a sentence diagram
   - ● make use of information to diagram a sentence
   - Ⓓ tie ideas about diagrams together

4. Create a play showing what to do if a tornado is expected.

   To answer this prompt, I need to ____.
   - ● make or produce a play
   - Ⓑ provide evidence about an expected tornado
   - Ⓒ make use of information about tornadoes
   - Ⓓ break down and evaluate or draw conclusions about tornadoes

5. Prove that a cellar is the safest place to be if a tornado hits.

   To answer this prompt, I need to ____.
   - Ⓐ make use of information about cellars
   - ● show why a cellar is the safest place
   - Ⓒ make or produce a map of a cellar
   - Ⓓ explain the relationship between cellars and tornadoes

272 Unit 11

Use the following recommendations to reinforce or reteach according to student performance.

If...	Then...
Students miss 2 questions	Review the questions in a small group or individual setting, offering answer explanations.
Students miss 3 or more questions	Reteach the elements taught in Lessons 3 and 4 in a small group or individual setting. Unmarked copies of the student page can be reprinted from the online Teacher Resources.

Compare and Contrast

Have students turn to page 273 in their Student Books.

Lesson 10 | Reading Content Mastery

Compare and Contrast

Listen to the questions and possible answers. Fill in the bubble for your answer choice.

Example: Which sentence compares two things?
- Ⓐ Scientists can estimate the path a hurricane will take, but not the path of a tornado.
- Ⓑ Most tornadoes happen in the United States.
- Ⓒ Tornadoes and hurricanes are similar because they both spin counterclockwise.
- Ⓓ With hurricanes, there is time to issue warnings.

1. Which sentence contrasts two things?
   - Ⓐ Hurricanes develop slowly, through specific stages.
   - Ⓑ A tornado is a powerful storm, just as a hurricane is.
   - Ⓒ It's important to prepare an emergency kit for hurricanes.
   - Ⓓ Tornado bases are less than two miles wide; however, hurricanes can be miles across.
2. Which sentence compares two things?
   - Ⓐ Tornado winds start at 40 mph, but hurricanes start at 74 mph.
   - Ⓑ Tornadoes can cause serious damage and loss of life, and hurricanes can, too.
   - Ⓒ Killer tornadoes are rare, but cause most of the deaths.
   - Ⓓ Tropical storms are given names.
3. Which sentence contrasts two things?
   - Ⓐ Tornadoes occur in the spring, while hurricanes occur in the summer and fall.
   - Ⓑ Both hurricanes and tornadoes occur during specific seasons of the year.
   - Ⓒ Most tornadoes are formed in Tornado Alley.
   - Ⓓ Hurricanes cause heavy rains and high tides.
4. Which sentence compares two things?
   - Ⓐ The United States has one thousand tornadoes every year.
   - Ⓑ Hurricanes start out at sea, but tornadoes almost always form over land.
   - Ⓒ Both hurricanes and tornadoes are measured by the speed of the wind.
   - Ⓓ Hurricanes start as tropical storms over warm water.
5. Which sentence contrasts two things?
   - Ⓐ People need to be prepared for both hurricanes and tornadoes.
   - Ⓑ Unlike tornadoes, which are sudden, we know when a hurricane is going to hit.
   - Ⓒ Tornadoes only travel a mile on the ground before disappearing.
   - Ⓓ Hurricanes usually die when they hit land.

Unit 11 273

Let's look at the example first. Read the example aloud to students.

Listen: Which sentence compares two things?

Fill in the bubble for your answer.

A Scientists can estimate the path a hurricane will take, but not the path of a tornado.

B Most tornadoes happen in the United States.

C Tornadoes and hurricanes are similar because they both spin counterclockwise.

D With hurricanes, there is time to issue warnings.

Which bubble did you fill in? You should have filled in C. To compare, we use words like *both, and,* and *similar.* "Tornadoes *and* hurricanes are *similar* because they *both* spin counterclockwise." When we contrast, we use words like *but, however,* and *different.*

Follow along as I read aloud the definitions and possible answers. Fill in the bubble for your answer choice.

Use the following recommendations to reinforce or reteach according to student performance.

If...	Then...
Students miss 2 questions	Review the questions in a small group or individual setting, offering answer explanations.
Students miss 3 or more questions	Reteach the elements taught in Lesson 6 in a small group or individual setting. Unmarked copies of the student page can be reprinted from the online Teacher Resources.

Analyzing Text Features (Charts and Graphs)

Have students turn to page 274 in their Student Books.

Let's look at the example first. Read the example aloud to students.

Listen: Look at the chart. What is the title of the chart?

Fill in the bubble for your answer.

A When?

B Facts about Tornadoes

C How many?

D Where?

Which bubble did you fill in? You should have filled in B, the bubble for "Facts about Tornadoes." The title is usually above the chart.

Follow along as I read the definitions and possible answers aloud. Fill in the bubble for your answer choice.

Use the following recommendations to reinforce or reteach according to student performance.

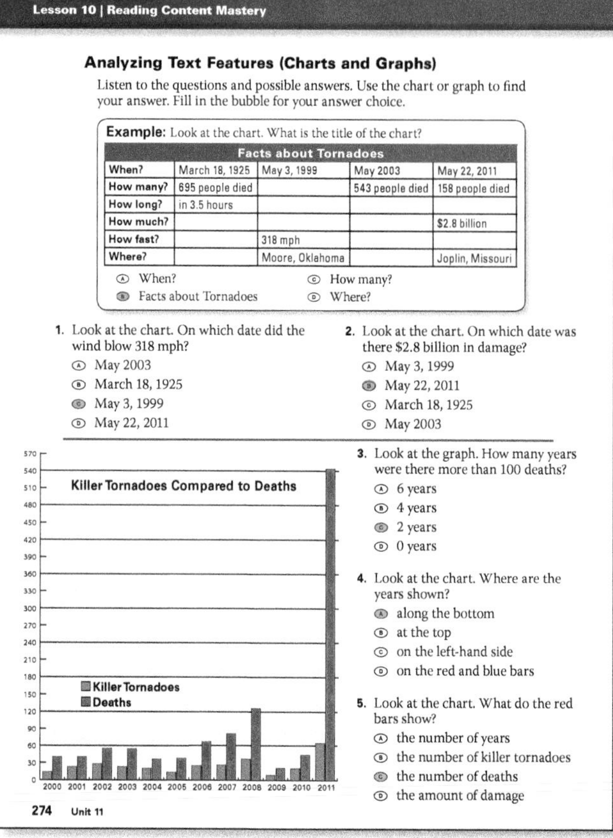

Lesson 10 | Reading Content Mastery

Analyzing Text Features (Charts and Graphs)

Listen to the questions and possible answers. Use the chart or graph to find your answer. Fill in the bubble for your answer choice.

Example: Look at the chart. What is the title of the chart?

Facts about Tornadoes				
When?	March 18, 1925	May 3, 1999	May 2003	May 22, 2011
How many?	695 people died		543 people died	158 people died
How long?	in 3.5 hours			
How much?				$2.8 billion
How fast?		318 mph		
Where?		Moore, Oklahoma		Joplin, Missouri

Ⓐ When? Ⓑ Facts about Tornadoes Ⓒ How many? Ⓓ Where?

1. Look at the chart. On which date did the wind blow 318 mph?
   Ⓐ May 2003
   Ⓑ March 18, 1925
   Ⓒ May 3, 1999
   Ⓓ May 22, 2011

2. Look at the chart. On which date was there $2.8 billion in damage?
   Ⓐ May 3, 1999
   Ⓑ May 22, 2011
   Ⓒ March 18, 1925
   Ⓓ May 2003

3. Look at the graph. How many years were there more than 100 deaths?
   Ⓐ 6 years
   Ⓑ 4 years
   Ⓒ 2 years
   Ⓓ 0 years

4. Look at the chart. Where are the years shown?
   Ⓐ along the bottom
   Ⓑ at the top
   Ⓒ on the left-hand side
   Ⓓ on the red and blue bars

5. Look at the chart. What do the red bars show?
   Ⓐ the number of years
   Ⓑ the number of killer tornadoes
   Ⓒ the number of deaths
   Ⓓ the amount of damage

274 Unit 11

If...	Then...
Students miss 2 questions	Review the questions in a small group or individual setting, offering answer explanations.
Students miss 3 or more questions	Reteach the elements taught in Lessons 5 and 6 in a small group or individual setting. Unmarked copies of the student page can be reprinted from the online Teacher Resources.

Vocabulary

Objectives for Content Mastery

- Demonstrate an understanding of the meanings of common idioms.
- Demonstrate an understanding of synonym and antonym word analogies.

Idioms

Follow the procedure outlined below for each of the Vocabulary Content Mastery questions and prompts.

Content Mastery Procedure

- Teacher reminds students to follow along with their pencils and listen.
- Teacher reads the question.
- Teacher reads each answer choice.
- Students choose the correct answer.
- Teacher repeats the question as students check their answers.

Have students turn to page 275 in their Student Books.

Let's look at the example first. Read the example aloud to students.

Listen: Which idiom most likely means "everyone has the same problem to solve." Fill in the bubble for your answer.

A on pins and needles

B all in the same boat

C backseat driver

D pull the plug

Which bubble did you fill in? You should have filled in the bubble for B because "all in the same boat" means "everyone has the same problem to solve."

Follow along as I read aloud each idiom. Fill in the bubble for your answer choice.

Lesson 10 | Vocabulary Content Mastery

Idioms

Listen to the questions and possible answers. Fill in the bubble for your answer choice.

Example: Which idiom most likely means "everyone has the same problem to solve"?
- Ⓐ on pins and needles
- Ⓑ all in the same boat
- Ⓒ backseat driver
- Ⓓ pull the plug

1. Which idiom most likely means "getting a bad start"?
   - Ⓐ great minds think alike
   - Ⓑ a dime a dozen
   - Ⓒ cross your fingers
   - Ⓓ off on the wrong foot
2. Which idiom most likely means "a very small part of something big"?
   - Ⓐ a drop in the bucket
   - Ⓑ all bark and no bite
   - Ⓒ ride off into the sunset
   - Ⓓ out on a limb
3. Which idiom most likely means "to do whatever you have to, to get the job done"?
   - Ⓐ once in a blue moon
   - Ⓑ go the extra mile
   - Ⓒ chip on your shoulder
   - Ⓓ don't count your chickens before they hatch
4. Which idiom most likely means "even bad times will lead to better days"?
   - Ⓐ everything but the kitchen sink
   - Ⓑ hit the nail on the head
   - Ⓒ every cloud has a silver lining
   - Ⓓ you are what you eat
5. Which idiom most likely means "study for a test"?
   - Ⓐ hit the books
   - Ⓑ hold your horses
   - Ⓒ keep your chin up
   - Ⓓ run out of steam

Unit 11 275

Use the following recommendations to reinforce or reteach according to student performance.

If...	Then...
Students miss 2 questions	Review the questions in a small group or individual setting, offering answer explanations.
Students miss 3 or more questions	Reteach the elements taught in Lesson 3 in a small group or individual setting. Unmarked copies of the student page can be reprinted from the online Teacher Resources.

Analogies

Have students turn to page 276 in their Student Books.

Let's look at the example first. **Read the example aloud to students.**

Listen: Which pair of words make the best synonym analogy for *three : triangle*? Fill in the bubble for your answer.

A kitchen : cooking

B jog : run

C four : square

D wet : dry

Which bubble did you fill in? You should have filled in the bubble for C. *Three* is to *triangle* as *four* is to *square*. *Three* is the number of sides on a *triangle*. *Four* is the number of sides on a *square*.

Follow along as I read aloud each question and the word pairs. Fill in the bubble for your answer choice.

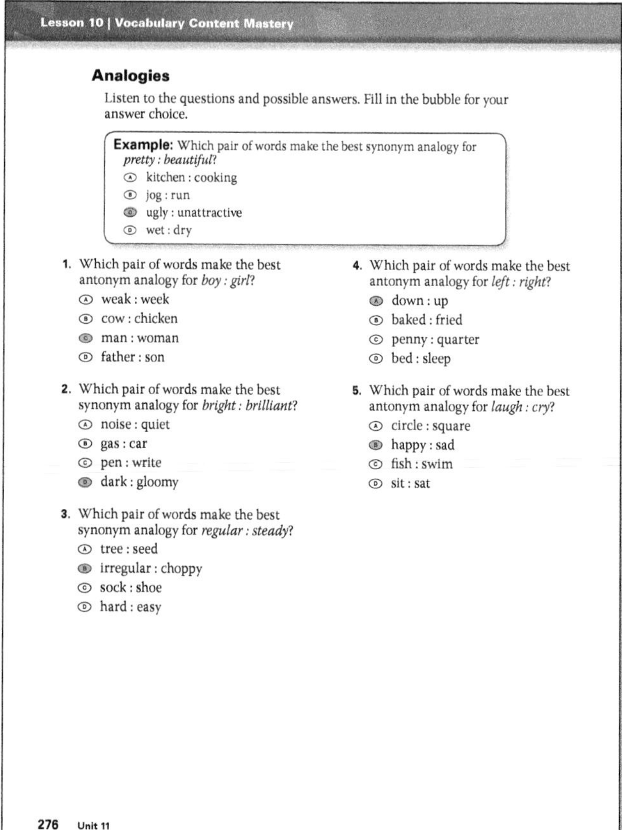

Lesson 10 | Vocabulary Content Mastery

Analogies

Listen to the questions and possible answers. Fill in the bubble for your answer choice.

Example: Which pair of words make the best synonym analogy for *pretty : beautiful*?

- Ⓐ kitchen : cooking
- Ⓑ jog : run
- Ⓒ ugly : unattractive (filled)
- Ⓓ wet : dry

1. Which pair of words make the best antonym analogy for *boy : girl*?
   - Ⓐ weak : week
   - Ⓑ cow : chicken
   - Ⓒ man : woman (filled)
   - Ⓓ father : son

2. Which pair of words make the best synonym analogy for *bright : brilliant*?
   - Ⓐ noise : quiet
   - Ⓑ gas : car
   - Ⓒ pen : write
   - Ⓓ dark : gloomy (filled)

3. Which pair of words make the best synonym analogy for *regular : steady*?
   - Ⓐ tree : seed
   - Ⓑ irregular : choppy (filled)
   - Ⓒ sock : shoe
   - Ⓓ hard : easy

4. Which pair of words make the best antonym analogy for *left : right*?
   - Ⓐ down : up (filled)
   - Ⓑ baked : fried
   - Ⓒ penny : quarter
   - Ⓓ bed : sleep

5. Which pair of words make the best antonym analogy for *laugh : cry*?
   - Ⓐ circle : square
   - Ⓑ happy : sad (filled)
   - Ⓒ fish : swim
   - Ⓓ sit : sat

276 Unit 11

Use the following recommendations to reinforce or reteach according to student performance.

If...	Then...
Students miss 2 questions	Review the questions in a small group or individual setting, offering answer explanations.
Students miss 3 or more questions	Reteach the elements taught in Lesson 3 in a small group or individual setting. Unmarked copies of the student page can be reprinted from the online Teacher Resources.

Grammar

Objectives for Content Mastery

- Demonstrate an understanding of how subject and object pronouns are used in sentences.
- Demonstrate an understanding of the order of past, present, and future verb tenses.

All Tenses

Follow the procedure outlined below for each of the Grammar Content Mastery questions and prompts.

Content Mastery Procedure

- Teacher reminds students to follow along with their pencils and listen.
- Teacher reads the question.
- Teacher reads each answer choice.
- Students choose the correct answer.
- Teacher repeats the question as students check their answers.

Have students turn to page 277 in their Student Books.

Let's look at the example first. Read the example aloud to students.

Listen: On a verb tense timeline, what is the order of these verbs, from past to future? Fill in the bubble for your answer.

A predicted, are predicting, will predict

B predict, predicted, will predict

C will predict, predicted, are predicting

D will predict, predict, predicted

Which bubble did you fill in? You should have filled in the bubble for A. *Predicted* is past tense, *are predicting* is present tense, and *will predict* is future tense.

Follow along as I read aloud the questions and possible answers. Fill in the bubble for your answer choice.

Lesson 10 | Grammar Content Mastery

All Tenses

Listen to the questions and possible answers. Fill in the bubble for your answer choice.

Example: On a verb tense timeline, what is the order of these verbs, from past to future?
- Ⓐ predicted, are predicting, will predict
- Ⓑ predict, predicted, will predict
- Ⓒ will predict, predicted, are predicting
- Ⓓ will predict, predict, predicted

1. On a verb tense timeline, what is the order of these verbs, from past to future?
   - Ⓐ will bury, bury, buried
   - Ⓑ bury, buried, will bury
   - Ⓒ will bury, buried, is burying
   - Ⓓ buried, is burying, will bury
2. On a verb tense timeline, what is the order of these verbs, from past to future?
   - Ⓐ will call, called, is calling
   - Ⓑ call, called, will call
   - Ⓒ called, is calling, will call
   - Ⓓ will call, call, called
3. On a verb tense timeline, what is the order of these verbs, from past to future?
   - Ⓐ erupts, erupted, will erupt
   - Ⓑ erupted, is erupting, will erupt
   - Ⓒ will erupt, erupted, is erupting
   - Ⓓ will erupt, erupts, erupted
4. On a verb tense timeline, what is the order of these verbs, from past to future?
   - Ⓐ released, is releasing, will release
   - Ⓑ release, released, will release
   - Ⓒ will release, released, is releasing
   - Ⓓ will release, release, released
5. On a verb tense timeline, what is the order of these verbs, from past to future?
   - Ⓐ will develop, develop, developed
   - Ⓑ develop, developed, will develop
   - Ⓒ will develop, developed, is developing
   - Ⓓ developed, is developing, will develop

Unit 11 277

Use the following recommendations to reinforce or reteach according to student performance.

If...	Then...
Students miss 2 questions	Review the questions in a small group or individual setting, offering answer explanations.
Students miss 3 or more questions	Reteach the elements taught in Lessons 2 and 9 in a small group or individual setting. Unmarked copies of the student page can be reprinted from the online Teacher Resources.

Subject and Object Pronouns

Have students turn to page 278 in their Student Books.

Let's look at the example first. Read the example aloud to students.

Listen: In which of the following sentences is a subject pronoun underlined? Fill in the bubble for your answer.

A We bought him new shoes.

B They ate the whole pizza.

C Dad gave the box to Fred.

D I hit it out of the park.

Which bubble did you fill in? You should have filled in the bubble for B, "They ate the whole pizza." *They* is a subject pronoun. *They* answers the question, Who ate it?

Follow along as I read aloud the questions and possible answers. Fill in the bubble for your answer choice.

Lesson 10 | Grammar Content Mastery

Subject and Object Pronouns

Listen to the questions and possible answers. Fill in the bubble for your answer choice.

Example: In which of the following sentences is a subject pronoun underlined?

- Ⓐ We bought him new shoes.
- Ⓑ They ate the whole pizza.
- Ⓒ Dad gave the box to Fred.
- Ⓓ I hit it out of the park.

1. In which of the following sentences is an object pronoun underlined?
   - Ⓐ We waited there all night.
   - Ⓑ I asked him to bring me a hammer.
   - Ⓒ You look good in red.
   - Ⓓ She cut out a paper pattern.
2. In which of the following sentences is a subject pronoun underlined?
   - Ⓐ I told him to wait for us.
   - Ⓑ Give them to the man.
   - Ⓒ She is eating dinner.
   - Ⓓ Ice on the roads is dangerous.
3. In which of the following sentences is a subject pronoun underlined?
   - Ⓐ He wore muddy shoes.
   - Ⓑ You should try it.
   - Ⓒ The dog made them late.
   - Ⓓ Kites are hard to fly.
4. In which of the following sentences is an object pronoun underlined?
   - Ⓐ I'm going to stop here.
   - Ⓑ I am ready for bed.
   - Ⓒ Some friends are coming over to study.
   - Ⓓ Jock bought me a new puppy.
5. In which of the following sentences is an object pronoun underlined?
   - Ⓐ The teacher took it away.
   - Ⓑ Where are all the tools?
   - Ⓒ Some of them play on a different team.
   - Ⓓ Their house is at the end of the block.

278 Unit 11

Use the following recommendations to reinforce or reteach according to student performance.

If...	Then...
Students miss 2 questions	Review the questions in a small group or individual setting, offering answer explanations.
Students miss 3 or more questions	Reteach the elements taught in Lesson 4 in a small group or individual setting. Unmarked copies of the student page can be reprinted from the online Teacher Resources.

Unit 12 Unit Plan

Primary Text:
"The Gorgon's Head"

Text type: literary

Secondary Text:
"Mythological Women"

Text type: informational

Lesson 1	Lesson 2
Reading • Determine the topic of the text. • Determine the author's purpose. • Discuss the topic of the text. • Preview the text. Vocabulary • Determine the meaning of key passage vocabulary. Reading • Review text features. • Read a myth. • Demonstrate an understanding of the text by asking and answering questions and referring to key details in the text.	Vocabulary • Use discussion and context to determine the meanings of the multiple-meaning words *eye* and *blind*. • Demonstrate an understanding of words by using them in written sentences. Grammar • Demonstrate an understanding of forming and using comparative and superlative endings. • Demonstrate an understanding of irregular comparative and superlative adjectives. • Demonstrate an understanding of the Royal Order of Adjectives. • Use the Royal Order of Adjectives to order adjectives in phrases.

Lesson 6	Lesson 7
Writing • Know spelling-sound correspondences for words with /oo/ as in *book*. • Know spelling-sound correspondences for words with soft *c* and *g*. Vocabulary • Use context to determine the meaning of words in text. • Consult reference materials to clarify the precise meaning of words. • Demonstrate an understanding of word analogies by completing written analogies. • Identify various types of word analogies. Writing • Accurately write orally dictated sentences. • Write sentences using a variety of adjectives to add interest. Reading • Read an informational text. • Demonstrate an understanding of character traits. • Analyze a text to identify stated and inferred character traits.	Vocabulary • Review key passage vocabulary. Reading • Read with purpose and understanding. • Identify and explain explicit details from text. • Take notes on a text. • Identify idioms in text.

Lesson 3	Lesson 4	Lesson 5
Reading • Read words to develop fluency. **Vocabulary** • Review key passage vocabulary. • Demonstrate an understanding of basic proverbs and their meanings. • Use context to determine the meaning of words in text. • Consult reference materials to clarify the meaning of words. • Demonstrate an understanding of synonyms and word analogies. **Reading** • Use critical thinking skills to analyze a text. • Ask and answer questions and prompts using conceptual understanding, strategic thinking, and extended thinking skills to demonstrate an understanding of a text.	**Reading** • Read sentences to develop fluency. **Grammar** • Demonstrate an understanding of the modals *could*, *would*, and *should*. • Listen to oral sentences and write them accurately. • Use modals in written sentences. **Reading** • Read sentence phrases with fluency to support comprehension. • Read an informational text. • Use critical thinking skills to respond to specific questions about a text.	**Reading** • Write questions or prompts about text to deepen comprehension. • Use critical thinking skills to respond orally to specific questions about a text. **Writing** • Use critical and extended thinking skills to write responses to prompts about a text. • Support written answers with evidence from text.

Lesson 8	Lesson 9	Lesson 10
Reading • Identify characters, setting, and basic plot elements in a narrative. **Writing** • Determine a setting, characters, problem, and solution for an original myth. • Write a rough draft of a myth.	**Reading** • Read words to develop fluency. **Vocabulary** • Use a range of strategies (consult reference materials; use understanding of figurative language—including similes, metaphors, and idioms; use understanding of similes, antonyms, related words) to clarify the meaning of words. **Grammar** • Demonstrate an understanding of the conditional tense in sentences. • Write sentences using the conditional tense. **Reading** • Read a text to develop fluency. • Demonstrate comprehension by answering specific questions about a text. **Writing** • Edit a narrative for content, details, word choice, and basic conventions.	**Vocabulary** • Clarify the meaning of key passage vocabulary. • Demonstrate an understanding of passage vocabulary by using words in sentences. **Reading** • Discuss and answer questions to demonstrate an understanding of the main idea of the myth. • Demonstrate an understanding of point of view. • Retell a story from a different point of view. **Writing** • Tell a story using descriptive details. • Speak clearly at an understandable pace.

Lesson 1

Lesson Opener

Before the lesson, choose one of the following activities to write on the board or post on the *LANGUAGE! Live* Class Wall online.

- *Use each pronoun pair in a sentence:* she–him; he–them; they–her.
- *Write a sentence using a plural possessive noun.*
- *Write a sentence about your avatar using a verb with the inflectional ending* -es.

Reading

Objectives

- Determine the topic of the text.
- Determine the author's purpose.
- Discuss the topic of the text.
- Preview the text.

Unit Introduction

Direct students to page 279 in their Student Books.

Discuss the content focus of the unit.

Content Focus
mythology

What do you think of when you hear the term *mythology*? (Answers will vary based on prior knowledge of mythology.)

Type of Text
literary

This text is literary. Myths are ancient, or very old, stories filled with adventure. The characters face many challenges and the stories usually involve supernatural creatures. Often the title of a fictional piece does not provide the same clues for content as the title of an expository piece. In Unit 11, we read "Twisters!" and it was a little easier to predict the content. Have you ever heard of a Gorgon? Knowing that myths typically contain supernatural creatures, do you think a Gorgon might be a supernatural creature? The title makes me wonder what's so special about its head.

Unit 12
Lesson 1 | Reading

Let's Focus: "The Gorgon's Head"

Content Focus	Type of Text
mythology	literary

Author's Purpose: to entertain; to explain the unknown

Big Ideas
Consider the following Big Idea questions. Write your answer for each question.

Why did people create myths?

______

How are myths relevant to modern times?

______

Narrative Preview Checklist: "The Gorgon's Head"

- ☐ Title: What clue does it provide about the passage?
- ☐ Pictures: What additional information is added here?
- ☐ Margin Information: What vocabulary is important to understand this text?

Reading for a Purpose

1. Why did Perseus accept the king's request to bring him Medusa's head?
2. Why do Hermes and Athena help Perseus, and was it a good decision?
3. What do we know about Perseus based on his dealings with the Three Gray Women?
4. Why does Perseus think Hermes has magical powers?
5. What is the value of the gifts Perseus received from the Nymphs? Could he have succeeded without them?
6. How did Perseus feel when he faced Medusa?
7. How else could the story have ended?

Unit 12 279

Author's Purpose

The author's purpose is the reason that he or she wrote the text. We learned in previous units that the purpose of expository text is to inform. What is the purpose of fictional text? (to entertain) The purpose of fictional text is primarily to entertain. In addition to providing entertainment, many myths provide an explanation for things ancient people didn't understand. In Unit 2, we read about constellations and we learned the myth of Gemini, which explained why the stars were in the sky. Knowing that the passage we are about to read is a myth, why do you think the author wrote the story? (Answers will vary.)

Have students write the answer on the page in their Student Books.

Background Information

Many ancient cultures have created stories that answer questions about their world. Why do we have different seasons or predictable changes in our weather each year? (Answers will vary based on knowledge of science and weather.) It has to do with Earth's rotation, the tilt of the axis, and our orbital path around the sun. Because ancient people did not understand these things, they made up a story to help explain the changes in weather associated with spring, summer, fall, and winter. Myths from ancient civilizations represent their ideas about religion, history, and the world.

"The Gorgon's Head" is a Greek myth. Greek mythology is a series of elaborate stories about gods, goddesses, and monsters and their interactions with humans. These stories also sought to explain the natural world. References from Greek mythology can be found in pop culture, literature, music, and in great works of art. What kind of story are we going to read? (a myth)

Note: The complete unabridged text of *The Gorgon's Head* can be found in the ebook *Myths That Every Child Should Know* which is available as a free download at http://www.gutenberg.org/ebooks/16537.

Play the Unit 12 Text Training video found in the Teacher Resources online.

Before we read "The Gorgon's Head," we will watch a short video to help build background knowledge. Listen for two things you did not know about mythological characters. You will share your new knowledge with your partner after the video. Play the Unit 12 Text Training video. Have partners discuss what they learned.

Direct students to page 279 in their Student Books. Read the following Big Idea questions aloud:

Big Ideas

Why did people create myths?

How are myths relevant to modern times?

As a class, consider the two Big Idea questions. After discussing each question, have students write an answer in their Student Books. We'll come back to these questions after we finish reading the myth. You can edit your answers as you gain information.

Preview

Good readers preview text features automatically, every time they begin to read. To develop this reading habit, you will preview today's text on your own, and then discuss what you noticed with a partner.

Note: Create a small teacher-led group for students who displayed dependence or confusion with the previewing process in the preceding unit. New students and truant students should also join this group until they reach independence.

Before we preview this text, let's review the differences between informational text and literary text. What are some of the typical features found in informational text? (headings, charts, graphs, pictures with captions) In Unit 9, we read "The Time Machine," a literary text selection. Did we find the same text features in literary text that we found in informational text? (no)

Direct students to page 281 in their Student Books to preview the text. Remind them of the Narrative Preview Checklist on page 279. Have individuals preview the text and predict what it will be about. After sufficient time, have partners use the Narrative Preview Checklist to evaluate each other's previewing skills. Gauge individual success as you circulate around the room.

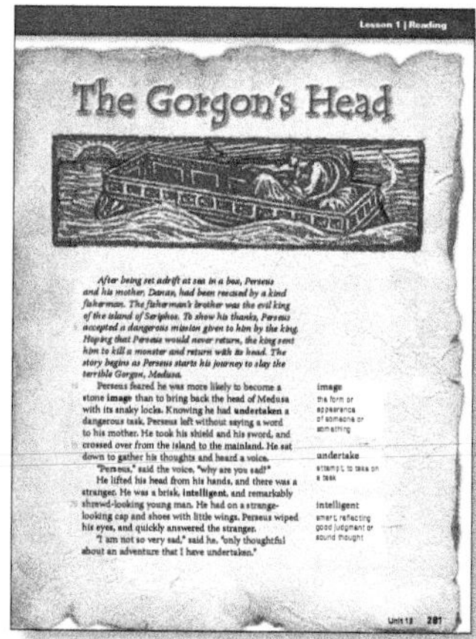

Vocabulary

Objective

- Determine the meaning of key passage vocabulary.

Rate Your Knowledge

Direct students to page 280 in their Student Books.

You will rate your word knowledge. The purpose of this activity is to recognize how familiar you are with this unit's Key Passage Vocabulary.

Vocabulary Rating Scale poster

Review the Vocabulary Rating Scale with students.

Vocabulary Rating Scale

0—I have never heard the word before.

1—I have heard the word, but I'm not sure how to use it.

2—I am familiar with the word, but I'm not sure if I know the correct meaning.

3—I know the meaning of the word and can use it correctly in a sentence.

Lesson 1 | Vocabulary

Key Passage Vocabulary: "The Gorgon's Head"

Rate your knowledge of the words. Define the words. Draw a picture to help you remember the definition.

Vocabulary	Knowledge Rating	Definition	Picture
image	0 1 2 3	the form or appearance of someone or something	
undertake	0 1 2 3	attempt; to take on a task	
intelligent	0 1 2 3	smart; reflecting good judgment or sound thought	
proceed	0 1 2 3	to begin and carry on an action or movement	
recover	0 1 2 3	to get back something lost; regain	
invisible	0 1 2 3	impossible to see; not visible	
perceive	0 1 2 3	to become aware of through sight or observation	
enormous	0 1 2 3	very great in size or amount	

280 Unit 12

Read the list of words. Have students repeat each word. Provide time for students to rate their knowledge of each word.

Have partners discuss the words they rated as 3s and tell each other the meanings.

Preteach Vocabulary

You've rated your knowledge and talked about what you think the words mean. Now, let's discuss the words.

Preteach Procedure

This activity is intended to take only a short amount of time, so make it an oral exercise if your students aren't capable of writing quickly.

- Introduce each word as indicated on the word card.
- Read the definition and example sentences.
- Ask questions to clarify and deepen understanding.
- If time permits, allow students to share.

* Do not provide instruction time to write definitions or draw pictures, but explain that students should complete both as time permits during the unit.

Note: Research has proven that vocabulary is best learned when students represent their knowledge of words in linguistic and/or nonlinguistic ways. Thus, drawing a picture will help students remember the words. This strategy is especially effective for English language learners.

image

Let's read the first word together. *Image.*

Definition: *Image* means "the form or appearance of someone or something." The form or appearance of someone or something is what? (image)

Example 1: The *image* of a dog is on the bag of dog food.

Example 2: When you look into water, you can sometimes see your *image.*

Example 3: The mirrors in a fun house can distort a person's *image.*

Question 1: An *image* can be someone's face. Yes or no? (yes)

Question 2: Can *images* be in your mind? Yes or no? (yes)

Pair Share: What is your favorite *image* to see when you enter the school?

undertake

Let's read the next word together. *Undertake.*

Definition: *Undertake* means "to attempt or take on a task." If you were to attempt a task you would what? (undertake it)

Example 1: I will *undertake* the project of monitoring our school's recycling program.

Example 2: Before you *undertake* the job of class president, make sure you understand all of the responsibilities.

Example 3: The work you are *undertaking* in this class may be difficult, but it is very important and rewarding.

Question 1: Can you *undertake* a simple task? (yes)

Question 2: If you *undertake* a job, are you attempting to do it? (yes)

Pair Share: Tell your partner a task around the school you would like to *undertake.*

intelligent

Let's read the next word together. *Intelligent.*

Definition: *Intelligent* means "smart, reflecting good judgment or sound thought." If you are smart, or reflect good judgment or sound thought, what are you? (intelligent)

Example 1: The *intelligent* young man made a wise decision regarding his education.

Example 2: Although he was very excitable, the puppy was very *intelligent* and easily understood the trainer's commands.

Example 3: If you study, you will be able to answer the teacher's questions *intelligently.*

Question 1: Are scientists *intelligent*? (yes)

Question 2: Do most teachers think dropping out of school is an *intelligent* decision? (no)

Pair Share: With your partner, discuss which animals you think are *intelligent* and why.

proceed

Let's read the next word together. *Proceed.*

Definition: *Proceed* means "to begin and carry on an action or movement." What is another word for "beginning an action"? (proceed)

Example 1: The football player *proceeded* to stretch and warm up for the championship game.

Example 2: The group of dancers will *proceed* with practice even though the director is late.

Example 3: In spite of interruptions by students, I *proceed* with the daily lessons.

Question 1: If the baseball game *proceeded* after the rain delay, did they continue playing the game? (yes)

Question 2: Would members of the track team *proceed* with practice if they had been cut from the team? (no)

Pair Share: Complete this sentence and share it with your partner: In spite of the cold weather, the _____ *proceeded* with _____.

recover

Let's read the next word together. *Recover.*

Definition: *Recover* means "to get back something lost or regain." If you get back something that was lost you what? (recover it)

Example 1: Police often *recover* stolen property when they catch thieves.

Example 2: I was so thankful when I *recovered* my lost watch.

Example 3: Searching through the old house, they *recovered* many valuable family heirlooms.

Question 1: If you found something that was lost, did you *recover* it? (yes)

Question 2: Can you *recover* something that was not lost or taken? (no)

Pair Share: Tell your partner about something you lost and then *recovered.*

invisible

Let's read the next word together. *Invisible.*

Definition: *Invisible* means "impossible to see or not visible." If you can't see something, what is it? (invisible)

Example 1: A cloudy night makes the stars *invisible.*

Example 2: I saw a movie in which the superhero can make himself *invisible.*

Example 3: Some bugs are *invisible* unless you use a high-power microscope.

Question 1: If something is *invisible,* can you see it? (no)

Question 2: Could you run into an *invisible* force field? (yes)

Pair Share: Tell your partner about a time you wished you were *invisible.*

perceive

Let's read the next word together. *Perceive.*

Definition: *Perceive* means "to become aware of something through sight or observation." If you become aware of something, what do you do? (perceive it)

Example 1: By noticing their stern tone of voice and harsh facial expressions, I can *perceive* when my parents are upset.

Example 2: As the fog cleared, she was able to *perceive* the city's skyline.

Example 3: After close examination of the building, the engineer *perceived* the extent of the damage caused by the earthquake.

Question 1: Is it easy to *perceive* the difference between a crocodile and an alligator? (no)

Question 2: If you *perceive* the outline of a building does that mean that you see it? (yes)

Pair Share: Discuss with your partner what you would hope to *perceive* upon opening a treasure chest.

enormous

Let's read the last word together. *Enormous.*

Definition: *Enormous* means "very great in size or amount." If something is great in size, what is it? (enormous)

Example 1: The *enormous* fire covered hundreds of square miles and caused vast destruction.

Example 2: The elephant is *enormous* compared with an ant.

Example 3: A tsunami is an *enormous* wave that can cause tremendous damage.

Question 1: Would a bug the size of a rabbit be called *enormous*? (yes)

Question 2: Would a cracker be considered an *enormous* feast? (no)

Pair Share: Work with your partner to finish the sentence: The snake was so *enormous* that ____.

Reading

Objectives

- Review text features.
- Read a myth.
- Demonstrate an understanding of the text by asking and answering questions and referring to key details in the text.

"The Gorgon's Head"

Direct students to page 281 in their Student Books.

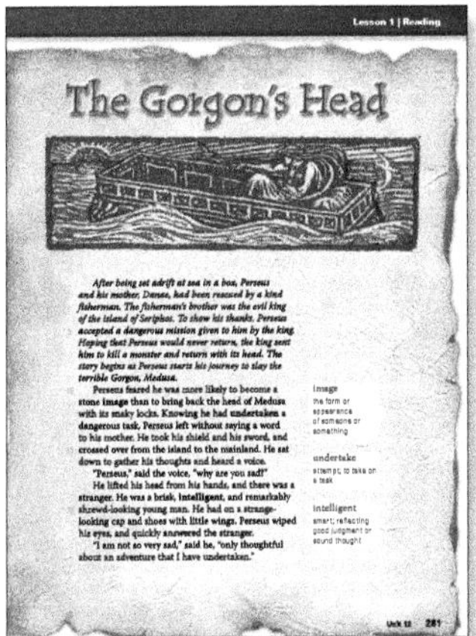
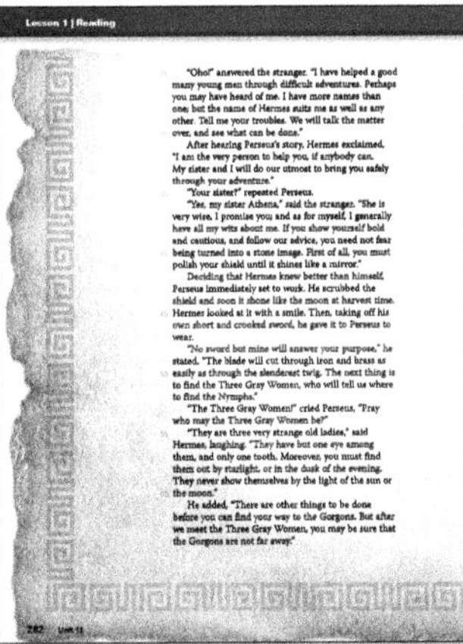
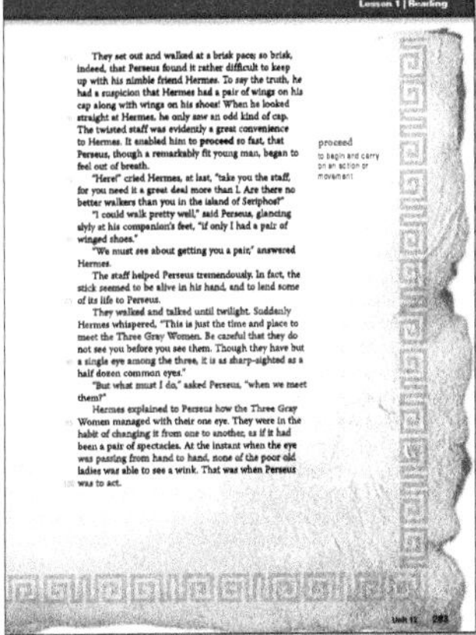
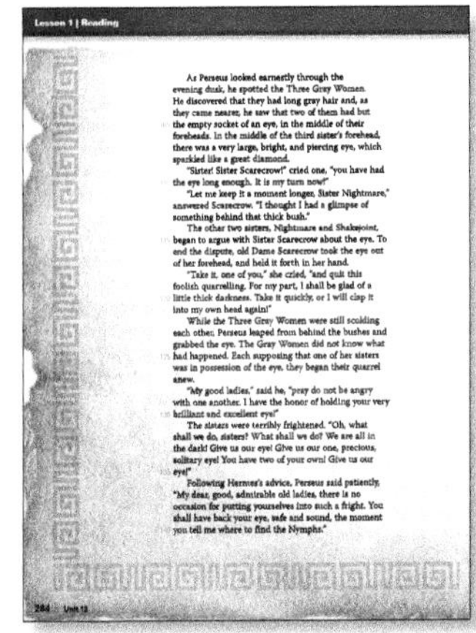
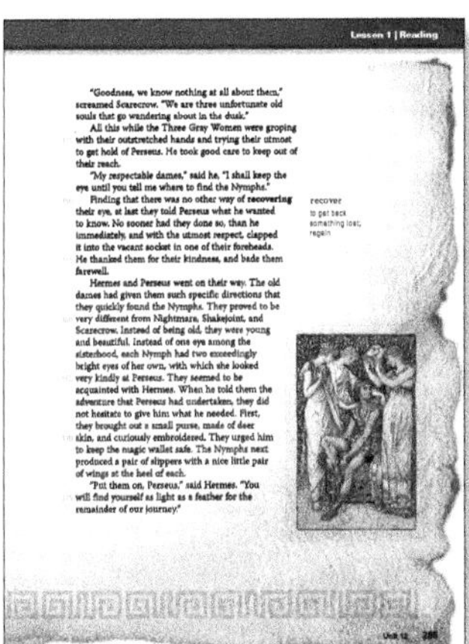
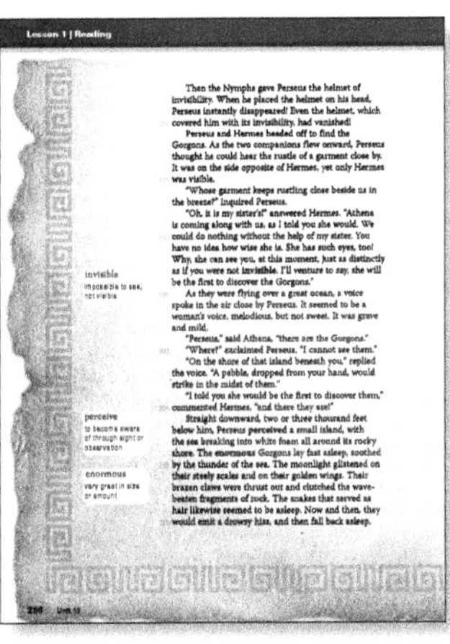
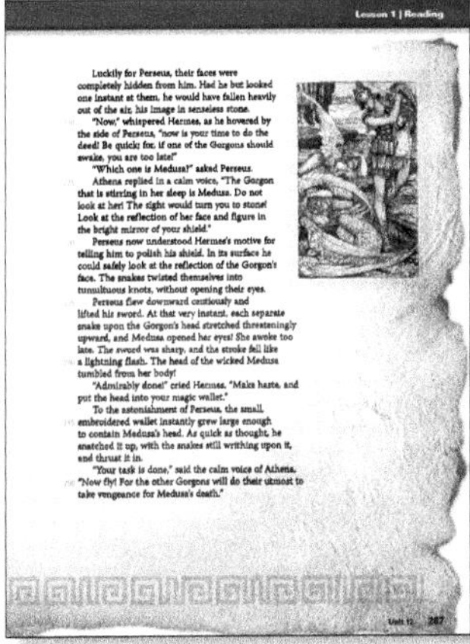

Words to Know

In addition to the vocabulary words, here are some words students might have trouble with:

adrift without power to move or anchor to remain
locks hair
gather bring together
shrewd clever
utmost of the greatest or highest degree
wits reason; sense; intellect
harvest the season for gathering agricultural crops
nimble quick and light in motion; agile
suspicion the act of thinking something is wrong without proof or evidence; doubt
dozen twelve
dusk the beginning of the darkness of night
socket an opening that holds something
glimpse a quick look
respect a high or special regard
fragments a broken off piece of a larger thing
emit to send out or give off
deed task; job
tumultuous tending to cause upheaval or unrest; not calm
haste rapidity of motion
vengeance punishment inflicted in retaliation for injury or offense
loath unwilling to do something; reluctant
pity a sympathetic sorrow for someone who is suffering

Direct students to page 279 in their Student Books. Have students follow along while you read the prompts aloud.

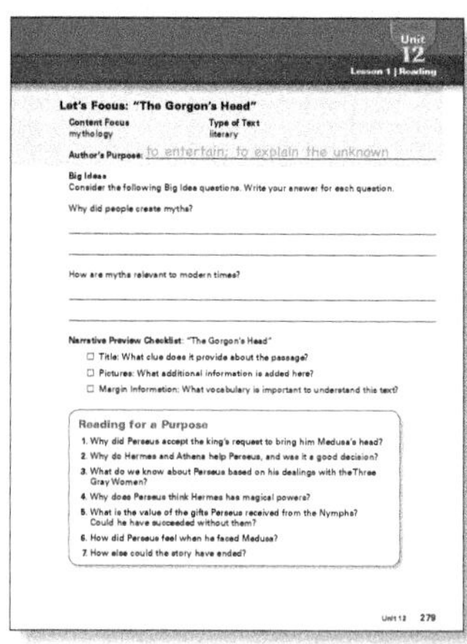

Unit 12
Lesson 1 | Reading

Let's Focus: "The Gorgon's Head"

Content Focus
mythology

Type of Text
literary

Author's Purpose: to entertain; to explain the unknown

Big Ideas
Consider the following Big Idea questions. Write your answer for each question.

Why did people create myths?

How are myths relevant to modern times?

Narrative Preview Checklist: "The Gorgon's Head"

- ☐ Title: What clue does it provide about the passage?
- ☐ Pictures: What additional information is added here?
- ☐ Margin Information: What vocabulary is important to understand this text?

Reading for a Purpose

1. Why did Perseus accept the king's request to bring him Medusa's head?
2. Why do Hermes and Athena help Perseus, and was it a good decision?
3. What do we know about Perseus based on his dealings with theThree Gray Women?
4. Why does Perseus think Hermes has magical powers?
5. What is the value of the gifts Perseus received from the Nymphs? Could he have succeeded without them?
6. How did Perseus feel when he faced Medusa?
7. How else could the story have ended?

Unit 12 279

Reading for a Purpose

1. Why did Perseus accept the king's request to bring him Medusa's head?
2. Why do Hermes and Athena help Perseus, and was it a good decision?
3. What do we know about Perseus based on his dealings with the Three Gray Women?
4. Why does Perseus think Hermes has magical powers?
5. What is the value of the gifts Perseus received from the Nymphs? Could he have succeeded without them?
6. How did Perseus feel when he faced Medusa?
7. How else could the story have ended?

You will become equipped to answer these questions by reading the passage. For now, let the prompts guide your reading. Be on the lookout for information you could use to respond to them. While reading, you also should think about our two Big Idea questions: Why did people create myths? and How are myths relevant to modern times?

Direct students to page 281 in their Student Books. Now it's time to read. Where are your eyes while I read? (on text) Where is your pencil? (following along, word for word) Eyes on text, pencil on words. Follow along with your pencil eraser as I read the text. Read the passage aloud.

Guiding Students Toward Independent Reading

While the lessons are written for a teacher read aloud, it is important that your students read as much and as often as they can. Assign readings that meet the needs of your students, based on your observations or data. This is a good opportunity to stretch students, but if they become frustrated, return to the read-aloud method.

Options for reading text:

- Teacher read aloud
- Teacher-led or student-led choral read
- Independent read of small sections with frequent comprehension checks
- Paired read or independent read

The Gorgon's Head

After being set adrift at sea in a box, Perseus and his mother, Danae, had been rescued by a kind fisherman. The fisherman's brother was the evil king of the island of Seriphos. To show his thanks, Perseus accepted a dangerous mission given to him by the king. Hoping that Perseus would never return, the king sent him to kill a monster and return with its head. The story begins as Perseus starts his journey to slay the terrible Gorgon, Medusa.

Timer

For confirmation of engagement, take 30 seconds to have students share one thing they learned about the characters and the setting with their partner.

Share some of the following details if necessary: Perseus and his mother, Danae, have already faced danger; they are living on an island ruled by the king; the king doesn't want Perseus around; a Gorgon is a monster.

Follow along with your pencil erasers as I continue reading the text. Read the entire text without interruption.

Perseus feared he was more likely to become a stone image than to bring back the head of Medusa with its snaky locks. Knowing he had undertaken a dangerous task, Perseus left without saying a word to his mother. He took his shield and his sword, and crossed over from the island to the mainland. He sat down to gather his thoughts and heard a voice.

"Perseus," said the voice, "why are you sad?"

He lifted his head from his hands, and there was a stranger. He was a brisk, intelligent, and remarkably shrewd-looking young man. He had on a strange-looking cap and shoes with little wings. Perseus wiped his eyes, and quickly answered the stranger.

"I am not so very sad," said he, "only thoughtful about an adventure that I have undertaken."

"Oho!" answered the stranger. "I have helped a good many young men through difficult adventures. Perhaps you may have heard of me. I have more names than one; but the name of Hermes suits me as well as any other. Tell me your troubles. We will talk the matter over, and see what can be done."

After hearing Perseus's story, Hermes exclaimed, "I am the very person to help you, if anybody can. My sister and I will do our utmost to bring you safely through your adventure."

"Your sister?" repeated Perseus.

"Yes, my sister Athena," said the stranger. "She is very wise, I promise you; and as for myself, I generally have all my wits about me. If you show yourself bold and cautious, and follow our advice, you need not fear being turned into a stone image. First of all, you must polish your shield until it shines like a mirror."

Deciding that Hermes knew better than himself, Perseus immediately set to work. He scrubbed the shield and soon it shone like the moon at harvest time. Hermes looked at it with a smile. Then, taking off his own short and crooked sword, he gave it to Perseus to wear.

"No sword but mine will answer your purpose," he stated. "The blade will cut through iron and brass as easily as through the slenderest twig. The next thing is to find the Three Gray Women, who will tell us where to find the Nymphs."

"The Three Gray Women!" cried Perseus, "Pray who may the Three Gray Women be?"

"They are three very strange old ladies," said Hermes, laughing. "They have but one eye among them, and only one tooth. Moreover, you must find them out by starlight, or in the dusk of the evening. They never show themselves by the light of the sun or the moon."

He added, "There are other things to be done before you can find your way to the Gorgons. But after we meet the Three Gray Women, you may be sure that the Gorgons are not far away."

They set out and walked at a brisk pace; so brisk, indeed, that Perseus found it rather difficult to keep up with his nimble friend Hermes. To say the truth, he had a suspicion that Hermes had a pair of wings on his cap along with wings on his shoes! When he looked straight at Hermes, he only saw an odd kind of cap. The twisted staff was evidently a great convenience to Hermes. It enabled him to proceed so fast, that Perseus, though a remarkably fit young man, began to feel out of breath.

"Here!" cried Hermes, at last, "take you the staff, for you need it a great deal more than I. Are there no better walkers than you in the island of Seriphos?"

"I could walk pretty well," said Perseus, glancing slyly at his companion's feet, "if only I had a pair of winged shoes."

"We must see about getting you a pair," answered Hermes.

The staff helped Perseus tremendously. In fact, the stick seemed to be alive in his hand, and to lend some of its life to Perseus.

They walked and talked until twilight. Suddenly Hermes whispered, "This is just the time and place to meet the Three Gray Women. Be careful that they do not see you before you see them. Though they have but a single eye among the three, it is as sharp-sighted as a half dozen common eyes."

"But what must I do," asked Perseus, "when we meet them?"

Hermes explained to Perseus how the Three Gray Women managed with their one eye. They were in the habit of changing it from one to another, as if it had been a pair of spectacles. At the instant when the eye was passing from hand to hand, none of the poor old ladies was able to see a wink. That was when Perseus was to act.

As Perseus looked earnestly through the evening dusk, he spotted the Three Gray Women. He discovered that they had long gray hair and, as they came nearer, he saw that two of them had but the empty socket of an eye, in the middle of their foreheads. In the middle of the third sister's forehead, there was a very large, bright, and piercing eye, which sparkled like a great diamond.

"Sister! Sister Scarecrow!" cried one, "you have had the eye long enough. It is my turn now!"

"Let me keep it a moment longer, Sister Nightmare," answered Scarecrow. "I thought I had a glimpse of something behind that thick bush."

The other two sisters, Nightmare and Shakejoint, began to argue with Sister Scarecrow about the eye. To end the dispute, old Dame Scarecrow took the eye out of her forehead, and held it forth in her hand.

"Take it, one of you," she cried, "and quit this foolish quarrelling. For my part, I shall be glad of a little thick darkness. Take it quickly, or I will clap it into my own head again!"

While the Three Gray Women were still scolding each other, Perseus leaped from behind the bushes and grabbed the eye. The Gray Women did not know what had happened. Each supposing that one of her sisters was in possession of the eye, they began their quarrel anew.

"My good ladies," said he, "pray do not be angry with one another. I have the honor of holding your very brilliant and excellent eye!"

The sisters were terribly frightened. "Oh, what shall we do, sisters? What shall we do? We are all in the dark! Give us our eye! Give us our one, precious, solitary eye! You have two of your own! Give us our eye!"

Following Hermes's advice, Perseus said patiently, "My dear, good, admirable old ladies, there is no occasion for putting yourselves into such a fright. You shall have back your eye, safe and sound, the moment you tell me where to find the Nymphs."

"Goodness, we know nothing at all about them," screamed Scarecrow. "We are three unfortunate old souls that go wandering about in the dusk."

All this while the Three Gray Women were groping with their outstretched hands and trying their utmost to get hold of Perseus. He took good care to keep out of their reach.

"My respectable dames," said he, "I shall keep the eye until you tell me where to find the Nymphs."

Finding that there was no other way of recovering their eye, at last they told Perseus what he wanted to know. No sooner had they done so, than he immediately, and with the utmost respect, clapped it into the vacant socket in one of their foreheads. He thanked them for their kindness, and bade them farewell.

Hermes and Perseus went on their way. The old dames had given them such specific directions that they quickly found the Nymphs. They proved to be very different from Nightmare, Shakejoint, and Scarecrow. Instead of being old, they were young and beautiful. Instead of one eye among the sisterhood, each Nymph had two exceedingly bright eyes of her own, with which she looked very kindly at Perseus. They seemed to be acquainted with Hermes. When he told them the adventure that Perseus had undertaken, they did not hesitate to give him what he needed. First, they brought out a small purse, made of deer skin, and curiously embroidered. They urged him to keep the magic wallet safe. The Nymphs next produced a pair of slippers with a nice little pair of wings at the heel of each.

"Put them on, Perseus," said Hermes. "You will find yourself as light as a feather for the remainder of our journey."

Then the Nymphs gave Perseus the helmet of invisibility. When he placed the helmet on his head, Perseus instantly disappeared! Even the helmet, which covered him with its invisibility, had vanished!

Perseus and Hermes headed off to find the Gorgons. As the two companions flew onward, Perseus thought he could hear the rustle of a garment close by. It was on the side opposite of Hermes, yet only Hermes was visible.

"Whose garment keeps rustling close beside us in the breeze?" inquired Perseus.

"Oh, it is my sister's!" answered Hermes. "Athena is coming along with us, as I told you she would. We could do nothing without the help of my sister. You have no idea how wise she is. She has such eyes, too! Why, she can see you, at this moment, just as distinctly as if you were not invisible. I'll venture to say, she will be the first to discover the Gorgons."

As they were flying over a great ocean, a voice spoke in the air close by Perseus. It seemed to be a woman's voice, melodious, but not sweet. It was grave and mild.

"Perseus," said Athena, "there are the Gorgons."

"Where?" exclaimed Perseus. "I cannot see them."

"On the shore of that island beneath you," replied the voice. "A pebble, dropped from your hand, would strike in the midst of them."

"I told you she would be the first to discover them," commented Hermes, "and there they are!"

Straight downward, two or three thousand feet below him, Perseus perceived a small island, with the sea breaking into white foam all around its rocky shore. The enormous Gorgons lay fast asleep, soothed by the thunder of the sea. The moonlight glistened on their steely scales and on their golden wings. Their brazen claws were thrust out and clutched the wave-beaten fragments of rock. The snakes that served as hair likewise seemed to be asleep. Now and then, they would emit a drowsy hiss, and then fall back asleep.

Luckily for Perseus, their faces were completely hidden from him. Had he but looked one instant at them, he would have fallen heavily out of the air, his image in senseless stone.

"Now," whispered Hermes, as he hovered by the side of Perseus, "now is your time to do the deed! Be quick; for, if one of the Gorgons should awake, you are too late!"

"Which one is Medusa?" asked Perseus.

Athena replied in a calm voice, "The Gorgon that is stirring in her sleep is Medusa. Do not look at her! The sight would turn you to stone! Look at the reflection of her face and figure in the bright mirror of your shield."

Perseus now understood Hermes's motive for telling him to polish his shield. In its surface he could safely look at the reflection of the Gorgon's face. The snakes twisted themselves into tumultuous knots, without opening their eyes.

Perseus flew downward cautiously and lifted his sword. At that very instant, each separate snake upon the Gorgon's head stretched threateningly upward, and Medusa opened her eyes! She awoke too late. The sword was sharp, and the stroke fell like a lightning flash. The head of the wicked Medusa tumbled from her body!

"Admirably done!" cried Hermes. "Make haste, and put the head into your magic wallet."

To the astonishment of Perseus, the small, embroidered wallet instantly grew large enough to contain Medusa's head. As quick as thought, he snatched it up, with the snakes still writhing upon it, and thrust it in.

"Your task is done," said the calm voice of Athena. "Now fly! For the other Gorgons will do their utmost to take vengeance for Medusa's death."

Perseus flew directly to the island of Seriphos to carry Medusa's head to King Polydectes.

Not finding his mother at home, Perseus went straight to the palace and was immediately taken to the king. Polydectes was by no means happy to see him. He had felt certain, in his own evil mind, that Perseus would be killed by the Gorgons.

The king asked, "Have you performed your promise? Have you brought me the head of Medusa with the snaky locks?"

"Yes," answered Perseus with a casual tone. "I have brought you the Gorgon's head, snaky locks and all!"

"Indeed! Pray let me see it," cried King Polydectes. "It must be a very curious spectacle, if all that travelers tell about it be true!"

Perseus persuaded the king to invite all of his subjects to see the terrible head of Medusa.

"Show us the head! Show us the head of Medusa with the snaky locks!" shouted the people.

A feeling of sorrow and pity came over the youthful Perseus. "O King Polydectes," cried he, "and ye many people, I am loath to show you the Gorgon's head!"

"Show me the Gorgon's head, or I will cut off your own!" proclaimed the king.

Perseus sighed and cried out in a voice like a trumpet, "Behold it then!"

Instantly the king and all of his subjects were turned into stone. Perseus thrust the head back into the wallet, and went to tell his dear mother that she need no longer be afraid of the wicked King Polydectes.

For confirmation of engagement, take 30 seconds to have students share an example of the supernatural powers or characters in this story. While reading, I was struck by the supernatural powers of the Three Gray Women. Your turn, share your thoughts about this mythological adventure with your partner.

Have students share their answers.

Lesson 2

Lesson Opener

Before the lesson, choose one of the following activities to write on the board or post on the *LANGUAGE! Live* Class Wall online.

- *Name three of the main characters and three different settings found in "The Gorgon's Head."*
- *Write sentences with the following possessive nouns:* Gorgon's, Medusa's, Perseus's.
- *Write a sentence with a possessive noun and a verb phrase with the inflectional ending* -ing.

Vocabulary

Objectives

- Use discussion and context to determine the meanings of the multiple-meaning words *eye* and *blind.*
- Demonstrate an understanding of words by using them in written sentences.

Multiple-Meaning Words: *eye, blind*

Direct students to page 289 in their Student Books.

In this unit, we are learning about mythological characters and their adventures. Many of these characters are strange, and they possess supernatural abilities. The Three Gray Women had a very special eye. *Eye* is a word that has more than one meaning. The word *eye* can be a noun or a verb.

So how do we know which definition of the word is being used? It all depends on how it is used in a sentence, or in context. We look for clues around the word to help us.

Lead students in a discussion of the various meanings of the word *eye.* Have them write the meanings and sentences on the map.

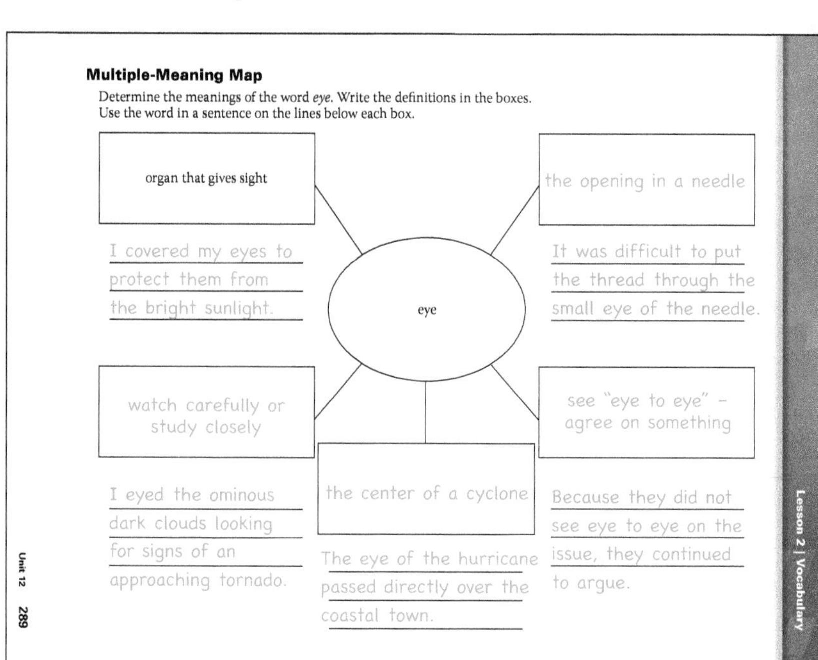

Multiple-Meaning Map

Determine the meanings of the word *eye.* Write the definitions in the boxes. Use the word in a sentence on the lines below each box.

eye

organ that gives sight

I covered my eyes to protect them from the bright sunlight.

the opening in a needle

It was difficult to put the thread through the small eye of the needle.

watch carefully or study closely

I eyed the ominous dark clouds looking for signs of an approaching tornado.

the center of a cyclone

The eye of the hurricane passed directly over the coastal town.

see "eye to eye" – agree on something

Because they did not see eye to eye on the issue, they continued to argue.

Unit 12 289

Lesson 2 | Vocabulary

Model

Have you ever rubbed your eyes because they were irritated? We often use the word *eye* as a noun referring to the organ that allows us to see. Listen to this sentence: I covered my eyes to protect them from the bright sunlight. Write the definition *the organ that gives sight* on the board and have students find it on the Multiple-Meaning Map in their Student Books. Have students think of a good sentence for this usage and write it below that definition.

Guided and Independent Practice

Each spring, I enjoy watching the birds in my backyard build their nests. I eye them closely as they fly back and forth with small bits of grass and straw. After eyeing them for a while, I notice the progress they have made on their nests. What is the definition of *eye* used in these sentences? (watch carefully or study closely) Write the definition on the board and have students write it on their map. Have students think of a good sentence for this usage and write it below the definition.

Continue the process until the maps are complete. Review the sentences and correct as needed.

Note: Base the number of modeled and guided examples on student ability and progress. Challenge them with independent practice when appropriate.

Additional Definitions of *eye*

Noun

- the center of a cyclone

Verb

- to look at; observe
- contemplate; consider

Idiom

- *an eye for an eye:* if someone does something wrong, they should have the same thing done to them
- *catch someone's eye:* to attract
- *have an eye for:* to be good at noticing a particular thing
- *keep an eye on:* watch

Direct students to page 290 in their Student Books. Repeat the process with the word *blind.*

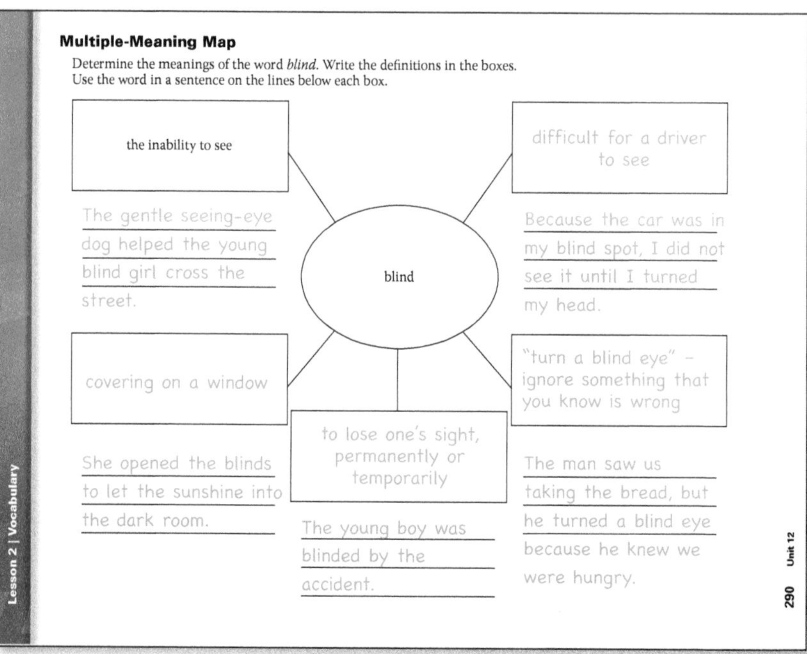
Multiple-Meaning Map

Determine the meanings of the word *blind.* Write the definitions in the boxes. Use the word in a sentence on the lines below each box.

blind

the inability to see

The gentle seeing-eye dog helped the young blind girl cross the street.

difficult for a driver to see

Because the car was in my blind spot, I did not see it until I turned my head.

covering on a window

She opened the blinds to let the sunshine into the dark room.

to lose one's sight, permanently or temporarily

The young boy was blinded by the accident.

"turn a blind eye" – ignore something that you know is wrong

The man saw us taking the bread, but he turned a blind eye because he knew we were hungry.

Lesson 2 | Vocabulary

290 Unit 12

Additional Definitions of *blind*

Noun

- camouflage for hunters
- people who have lost their sight

Idiom

- *the blind leading the blind:* someone is trying to show someone how to do something that they do not know how to do themselves

Grammar

Objectives

- Demonstrate an understanding of forming and using comparative and superlative endings.
- Demonstrate an understanding of irregular comparative and superlative adjectives.
- Demonstrate an understanding of the Royal Order of Adjectives.
- Use the Royal Order of Adjectives to order adjectives in phrases.

Adjectives: Comparative and Superlative

Collect like items of differing sizes for comparison, for example, three blocks or three books.

Let's review adjectives. When we want to compare two or more things, we can add inflectional suffixes to adjectives to convey the comparison. What can we add to adjectives to compare things? (inflectional suffixes) Yes, the two inflectional suffixes that we will use are *-er* and *-est*. What are the inflectional suffixes we can use? (-er and -est)

We use *-er* when we compare two things, and we can use *-est* when we compare more than two things. Think about the adjective *small*. Write ***small*** on the board and hold up the largest of your items. I can use *small* as an adjective to describe (item). The small (item) is in my hand. If I want to compare it with another (item), I could say: The (item 2) is smaller than (item 1). Write ***smaller*** on the board. But if I want to compare three (items), I could say: The (item 3) is the smallest of all the (items). Write ***smallest*** on the board.

Have partners compare items in the classroom using the comparatives and superlatives of *pretty, big, nice,* and *wide*. Have volunteers share their sentences.

Unfortunately, some adjectives do not follow this pattern. Some adjectives, like some verbs, are irregular. *Bad* is an example of an irregular adjective. If I want to compare two foods I don't like, I have to change the word completely. I do not add *-er* to the base word! Write *bad, worse, worst* on the board.

I think peas are *bad*. They are *worse* than spinach. In fact, I think they are the *worst* vegetable of all. Have partners tell each other about their three least favorite movies using *bad, worse,* and *worst*. Have volunteers share their sentences.

Repeat the process with *good* using different foods, like pudding, cupcakes, and ice cream. Have partners tell each other about their three favorite movies using *good, better,* and *best*.

Note: Point out the use of *the* in front of *worst* and *best*.

Direct students to page 291 in their Student Books and read the instructions aloud.

Model

Model the activity by completing the two example sentences.

Guided and Independent Practice

Read the remaining sentences aloud, giving students time to write their responses. Review the answers as a class.

Note: Base the number of modeled and guided examples on student ability and progress. Challenge them with independent practice when appropriate.

Lesson 2 | Grammar

Adjectives: Comparative and Superlative

Use the adjective provided for each sentence and rewrite it as a comparative or superlative adjective.

Examples:

Out of all of the boys on my basketball team, Mark is the tallest one. (tall)

Her eyes are greener than her sister's. (green)

1. I am so glad this story is shorter than the last one because I don't have very much time to devote to it. (short)
2. People were wrapped in their coats and gloves as they braced for the coldest day of the year. (cold)
3. The steak knife is sharper than the butter knife, so it is a better choice for slicing the meat. (sharp)
4. Melissa was the quickest one on the team, and her accurate responses helped them win the contest. (quick)
5. The path around the lake is longer and more peaceful than the path that cuts behind the school. (long)
6. When it comes to watching scary movies, you are much braver than I am. (brave)
7. Tonight's dinner was better than last night's. (good)
8. With an average rainfall of over 39 feet, Mt. Wai'ale'ale on the island of Kaua'i is the wettest spot on the planet. (wet)
9. The tortoise may be slower than the hare, but his steady pace helped him finish first. (slow)
10. We listened to the news about the storm all night, and the latest forecast shows it is beginning to weaken. (late)

Unit 12 291

Adjective Order (Royal Order of Adjectives)

Print the Royal Order of Adjectives poster from the Teacher Resources online and display where students can easily see it.

When we expand our subjects by answering the subject painter questions, we typically generate adjectives or adjectival phrases. The next step in the process is putting these descriptors or painters into the sentence. We choose the best order by moving the painters around and deciding which way sounds the best. This process helps you figure out the proper order for adjectives.

Today, we will learn the formal rule for the order of adjectives in a sentence. **Direct students to Part A on page 292 in their Student Books.**

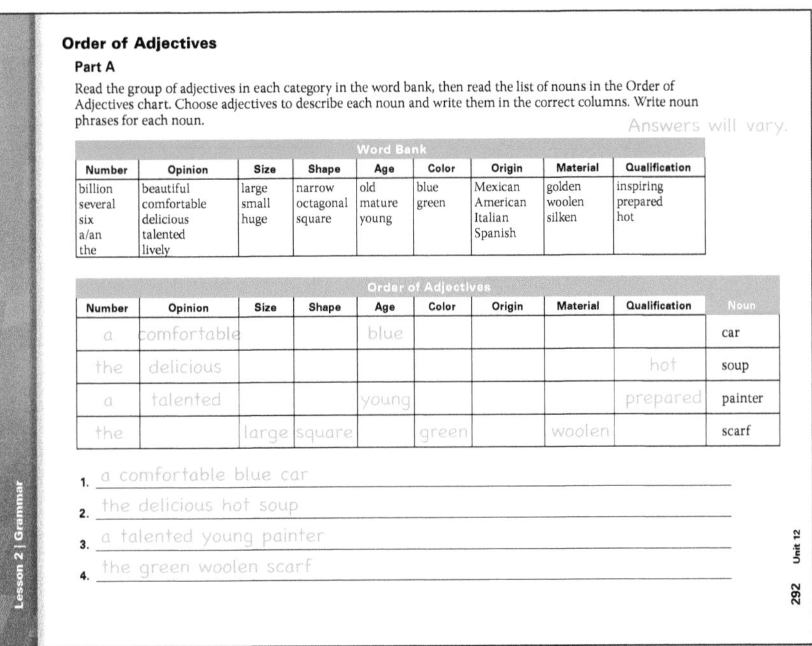

Order of Adjectives

Part A

Read the group of adjectives in each category in the word bank, then read the list of nouns in the Order of Adjectives chart. Choose adjectives to describe each noun and write them in the correct columns. Write noun phrases for each noun.

Answers will vary.

Word Bank

Number	Opinion	Size	Shape	Age	Color	Origin	Material	Qualification
billion	beautiful	large	narrow	old	blue	Mexican	golden	inspiring
several	comfortable	small	octagonal	mature	green	American	woolen	prepared
six	delicious	huge	square	young		Italian	silken	hot
a/an	talented					Spanish		
the	lively							

Order of Adjectives

Number	Opinion	Size	Shape	Age	Color	Origin	Material	Qualification	Noun
a	comfortable			blue					car
the	delicious							hot	soup
a	talented			young				prepared	painter
the		large	square		green		woolen		scarf

1. a comfortable blue car
2. the delicious hot soup
3. a talented young painter
4. the green woolen scarf

Lesson 2 | Grammar

292 Unit 12

The word bank on the top of this page shows the correct order of adjectives when you want to use more than one descriptor for a noun.

- If you have a number word, it will always go first. What is the first number word listed in the word bank? **(billion)**
- Next you have opinion words. The first word in the word bank is *beautiful.* That is considered an opinion word because people have very different ideas about what they consider beautiful. There's no way to prove that something is or isn't beautiful. What is another word that would fit the opinion category? **(Answers will vary, but may include words like fun, lovely, fabulous, awful, terrible, easy, difficult.)**

Continue reviewing the word bank and ensure that students understand the type of words that fit each category.

Have students chorally read all of the words in the word bank.

Model and Guided Practice

Read the instructions aloud and model the activity using the first noun in the Order of Adjectives chart, *car.* Think about a car and consider words from the word bank that could describe a car. First of all, could we use number word? Yes, the noun is singular, so what number words would be appropriate? **(a or the)** Yes, write your choice in the first box under Number. Let's consider the opinion words that are listed and could any of them be used to describe a car? **(beautiful or comfortable)** That's right. We probably wouldn't describe a car as *delicious, talented,* or *lively.* Write your choice in the first box under Opinion. You would never have a descriptor from every category when describing a noun. Choose one more descriptor for the car and write it in the appropriate box. I chose *blue*, so my phrase would read: a comfortable blue car. Have volunteers share their phrases aloud.

Independent Practice

Have students complete the chart and write their phrases. Have students share their phrases with their partners.

> **Note:** Base the number of modeled and guided examples on student ability and progress. Challenge them with independent practice when appropriate.

Direct students to Part B on page 293 in their Student Books and read the instructions aloud. Model the activity describing yourself using *teacher* as the noun. Generate a descriptor for each category except Material.

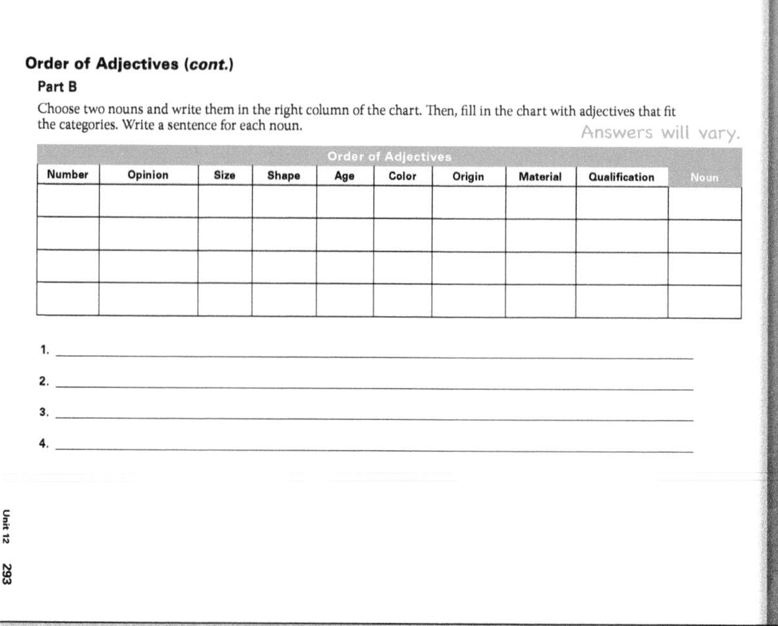

Order of Adjectives (*cont.*)

Part B

Choose two nouns and write them in the right column of the chart. Then, fill in the chart with adjectives that fit the categories. Write a sentence for each noun.

Answers will vary.

Order of Adjectives									
Number	Opinion	Size	Shape	Age	Color	Origin	Material	Qualification	Noun

1. ______
2. ______
3. ______
4. ______

Unit 12 293

Lesson 2 | Grammar

Example

a funny short round old white Russian skilled teacher

Have partners complete the chart. Challenge them to generate descriptors in every category. Have students write two sentences for each noun using different adjectives in each. Model with your example on the board.

Example

A short old white teacher walked into the room.

A funny round Russian teacher taught the lesson.

Unit 12 Lesson 3

Lesson Opener

Before the lesson, choose one of the following activities to write on the board or post on the *LANGUAGE! Live* Class Wall online.

- *Write three sentences with the word* eye, *using a different meaning in each sentence.*
- *Write two sentences using the base word* fast. *Use the comparative in the first sentence and the superlative in the second sentence.*
- *Complete the analogy:* Medusa : Gorgon :: Perseus : _____.

Reading

Objective

- Read words to develop fluency.

Word Fluency: First Read

Timer

Follow the Fluency Procedure outlined below. If it is necessary, begin the fluency drill with a choral read of the words as you provide a rhythm (snap your fingers, tap your foot, tap your pencil). Direct students to page 294 in their Student Books and complete the process.

Lesson 3 | Reading

Word Fluency: First Read

Read the words fluently.

	Correct	Errors
1st Try		
2nd Try		

maybe	brace	chopping	gems	straining	germs	moonbeams	pavement	rainbow	cookbooks	10
chopping	gems	straining	germs	moonbeams	pavement	rainbow	cookbooks	chatted	sprained	20
straining	germs	moonbeams	pavement	rainbow	cookbooks	chatted	sprained	basement	railroad	30
moonbeams	pavement	rainbow	cookbooks	chatted	sprained	basement	railroad	planned	spruce	40
rainbow	cookbooks	chatted	sprained	basement	railroad	planned	spruce	spraying	shredding	50
chatted	sprained	basement	railroad	planned	spruce	spraying	shredding	strayed	center	60
basement	railroad	planned	spruce	spraying	shredding	strayed	center	brace	maybe	70
planned	spruce	spraying	shredding	strayed	center	brace	maybe	gems	chopping	80
spraying	shredding	strayed	center	brace	maybe	gems	chopping	germs	straining	90
strayed	center	moonbeams	maybe	gems	chopping	germs	straining	pavement	brace	100

294 Unit 12

Fluency Procedure

- Partners switch books, so the recorder is marking errors in the reader's book.
- A timer is set for one minute.
- Readers and recorders move left to right, tracking each word with a pencil.
- As readers read the words aloud, recorders mark errors with a small x above the misread word.
- Recorders place a star to the right of the last word read when time ends.
- If the reader is able to read all words in the allotted time, the reader needs to start over at the beginning. The recorder must indicate this feat by placing two stars to the right of the last word read.
- When both students have read, partners switch books.
- Students calculate total words read, then subtract errors and record.
- Students record information on the progress chart in back of the Student Book.

Vocabulary

Objectives

- Review key passage vocabulary.
- Demonstrate an understanding of basic proverbs and their meanings.
- Use a range of strategies (consult reference materials; use understanding of figurative language—including similes, metaphors, and idioms; use understanding of synonyms, antonyms, related words) to clarify the meaning of words.

Review

Direct students to page 280 in their Student Books.

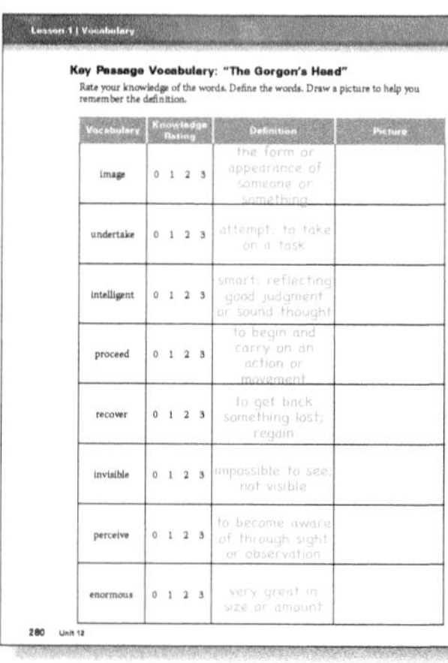

Lesson 1 | Vocabulary

Key Passage Vocabulary: "The Gorgon's Head"

Rate your knowledge of the words. Define the words. Draw a picture to help you remember the definition.

Vocabulary	Knowledge Rating	Definition	Picture
image	0 1 2 3	the form or appearance of someone or something	
undertake	0 1 2 3	attempt; to take on a task	
intelligent	0 1 2 3	smart; reflecting good judgment or sound thought	
proceed	0 1 2 3	to begin and carry on an action or movement	
recover	0 1 2 3	to get back something lost; regain	
invisible	0 1 2 3	impossible to see; not visible	
perceive	0 1 2 3	to become aware of through sight or observation	
enormous	0 1 2 3	very great in size or amount	

280 Unit 12

Review the vocabulary words from the passage "The Gorgon's Head." Have students answer in complete sentences.

- Did Hermes and his sister Athena prove to be *intelligent* allies for Perseus? (Yes, Hermes and Athena proved to be intelligent allies for Perseus.) To be smart, reflect good judgment or sound thought is to be what? (To be smart, reflect good judgment or sound thought is to be intelligent.)
- Did Perseus wear a helmet that made him *invisible*? (Yes, Perseus wore a helmet that made him invisible.) To not be visible or seen is to be what? (To not be visible or seen is to be invisible.)
- When Perseus first received the wallet from the Nymphs, was it *enormous*? (No, the wallet was not enormous when Perseus received it from the Nymphs.) To be very great in size or amount is to be what? (To be very great in size or amount is to be enormous.)
- Would looking at Medusa's face turn someone into a stone *image*? (Yes, looking at Medusa's face would turn someone into a stone image.) A word meaning the form or appearance of someone or something is what? (A word meaning the form or appearance of someone or something is *image*.)
- Did the Three Gray Women *recover* their eye from Perseus? (Yes, the Three Gray Women recovered their eye from Perseus.) To regain or get back something lost is to what? (To regain or get back something lost is to recover.)
- Did Hermes's crooked staff help him *proceed* quickly on the journey? (Yes, Hermes's crooked staff help him proceed quickly on the journey.) To begin and carry on an action or movement is to what? (To begin and carry on an action or movement is to proceed.)
- Did Perseus *perceive* the image of Medusa when he looked in his shield? (Yes, Perseus perceived Medusa when he looked in his shield.) What is it to become aware of through sight or observation? (To perceive is to become aware of through sight or observation.)
- Did Perseus *undertake* a dangerous mission to repay the king's kindness? (Yes, Perseus did undertake a dangerous mission to repay the king's kindness.) To attempt or to take on a task is to what? (To attempt or take on a task is to undertake.)

Vocabulary Concept: Proverbs

We have been working with idioms as well as other forms of figurative language. We use figurative language to create vivid images and to place emphasis on events or characters. It is not meant to be taken literally. We use phrases such as *blind as a bat* or *stubborn as a mule* to make a point. Today we're going to explore a new type of figurative language—proverbs. It's very possible that you've heard proverbs being used, but you may not have completely understood their meaning. They would be very difficult to understand if you thought you were supposed to take them literally. A proverb is a phrase or a saying that gives advice in an unusual way.

Understanding proverbs requires extended thinking skills! You first have to figure out the literal meaning of the expression and then consider how that applies to people or a certain situation. Only by extending your thinking can you appreciate the wisdom in a proverb.

Use the proverbs in a multisentence example and have students figure out the meaning. Offer the explanation if it is needed.

- *The early bird gets the worm.* Beth, I know you want to go to the big sale tomorrow. You should make sure you get there well before the store opens because the early bird gets the worm!
  Explanation: Think about birds looking for food in the ground. Earthworms often come out of the ground in the morning when it is cool. The bird who gets there first will likely be the one that gets to eat the worm.
- *Birds of a feather flock together.* I looked out the window and saw three of the meanest boys in school throwing dirt at each other. It doesn't surprise me because birds of a feather flock together.
  Explanation: Think about looking at the wires strung between utility poles and often there are birds sitting together. Usually they are all the same kind of bird. *Birds of a feather* means "birds that are the same kind." What do birds of a feather do, according to this proverb? (flock together)
- *Don't put all of your eggs in one basket.* I know you really like to play football and you are really good at it, but be sure to try other things and pay attention to your studies. You don't want to put all of your eggs in one basket.
  Explanation: Think about how fragile eggs are and how easy it is to break one accidentally. So, if all of your eggs were in one basket and you dropped the basket, what would happen to all of the eggs? (All of the eggs would break.) If you put everything into one option and it goes badly, you have lost everything. The proverb is recommending you keep several choices open. If one goes badly, you still have other options you can choose.

Direct students to page 295 in their Student Books and read the instructions aloud.

Model

The first proverb is *all that glitters is not gold*. What does that mean? (If something looks good, it doesn't mean that it is good.) Let's look at the events and see if we can find an example of when you might give this advice. Read aloud the events and explain why C is the best answer.

Guided Practice

Guide students in finding the event that matches the second proverb.

Independent Practice

Have partners complete the activity. Review the answers as a class.

Note: Base the number of modeled and guided examples on student ability and progress. Challenge them with independent practice when appropriate.

Lesson 3 | Vocabulary

Proverbs

Read each proverb and its meaning. Then find an event that proves the wisdom of the proverb. Write the letter on the line of the appropriate proverb.

Proverb	Meaning
1. All that glitters is not gold. *Meaning: If something looks good, it doesn't mean that it is good.* C	A. Bill wanted to improve his bowling game, so he played every day.
2. When in Rome, do as the Romans do. *Meaning: When in a new situation or place, follow the customs and practices of that place.* B	B. Sara went to a new place for take-out and was not sure of how things worked, so she watched another customer before she ordered.
3. A picture is worth a thousand words. *Meaning: Pictures capture some emotions and ideas more effectively than written or spoken explanations.* E	C. The car looked great, but it turned out to be a very bad buy.
4. Actions speak louder than words. *Meaning: It means more to carry through on what you say than to just say it.* G	D. The old man walking into the bank looked like a beggar. He turned out to be a millionaire!
5. Practice makes perfect. *Meaning: To become really good at something, you have to practice.* A	E. Sam could not describe the destruction caused by the storm. He ended up using his camera to show his friends what was left of the town.
6. Beauty is in the eye of the beholder. *Meaning: People have different ideas about what is beautiful.* F	F. You may not think my purple hair is attractive, but I love it!
7. You can't judge a book by its cover. *Meaning: Things sometimes look different than they really are, so you need to look more closely before you decide.* D	G. When I started volunteering at the shelter, my son finally followed my advice and found someplace to volunteer too.

Unit 12 295

Vocabulary Expansion

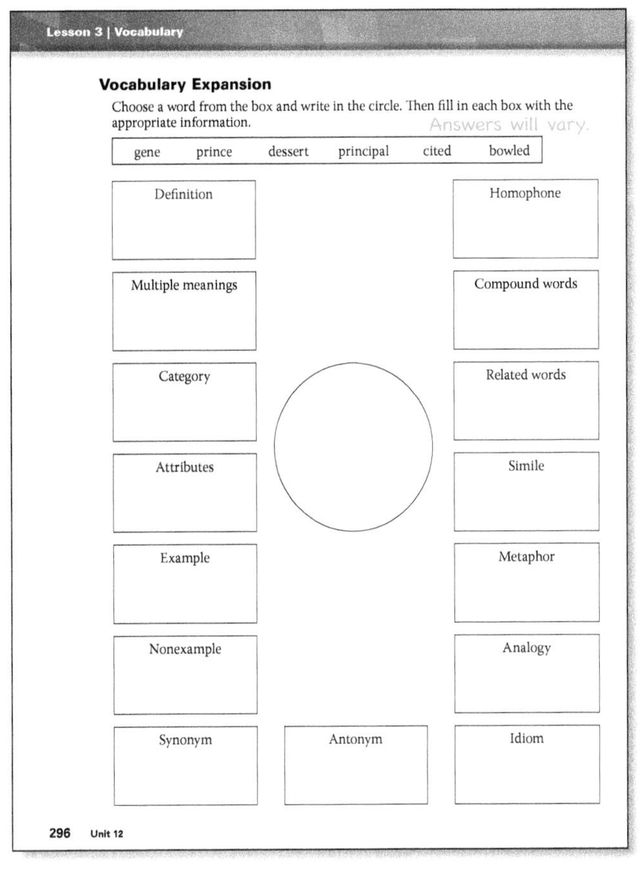

Direct students to page 296 in their Student Books. Review the definition of each concept in the Vocabulary Expansion chart.

- **Definition:** the meaning of the word
- **Multiple meanings:** other meanings and uses of the word
- **Category:** the broad group to which a word belongs
- **Attributes:** specific characteristics of the word
- **Example:** something that models or patterns the word
- **Nonexample:** something that does not model or pattern the word
- **Synonym:** a word with a similar meaning
- **Antonym:** a word with the opposite meaning
- **Homophone:** a word that sounds the same but is spelled differently and has a different meaning
- **Compound word:** two words combined to make one word
- **Related words:** words with the same root and related meanings
- **Simile:** figurative language comparing two dissimilar things using *like* or *as*
- **Metaphor:** figurative language comparing two dissimilar things by saying one thing is another thing
- **Analogy:** a comparison of two pairs of words that share the same relationship
- **Idiom:** figurative language used in a certain region or by a certain group of people

In this unit we read a tale from Greek mythology. Write the word *tale* on the board. Let's take a closer look at this word and see if we can use these concepts to create a deeper understanding of the word.

Example Expansion of *tale*

Definition: a story about imaginary events; an exciting or dramatic story

Multiple meanings: n: a falsehood; n: count, or tally

Category: stories

Attributes: exciting, mysterious, unbelievable, funny, adventurous

Example: fable, Cinderella, Tortoise and the Hare, myth

Nonexample: news broadcast

Synonym: story, narrative

Antonym: N/A

Homophone: tail

Compound words: telltale, folktale, fairytale

Related words: tales

Simile: Your life is like a fairytale.

Metaphor: The fairytale creature walked in the room and had us all wondering what he did to his hair.

Analogy: tale : read :: movie : watch

Idiom: old wives' tale

Dictionaries or online access

Give each student a dictionary or provide Internet access. Read the instructions, then have students choose a word and use a dictionary (online or print) to complete the process. Explain the use of N/A for concepts that don't apply to the word. Have partners share their word expansions.

Explain that they will use the dictionary again during this unit to help them master the skill.

Reading

Objectives

- Use critical thinking skills to analyze a text.
- Ask and answer questions and prompts using conceptual understanding, strategic thinking, and extended thinking skills to demonstrate an understanding of a text.

Critical Understandings

All Direction Words posters

Direct students to page 16 in their Student Books or refer to the Direction Words posters if you have them displayed.

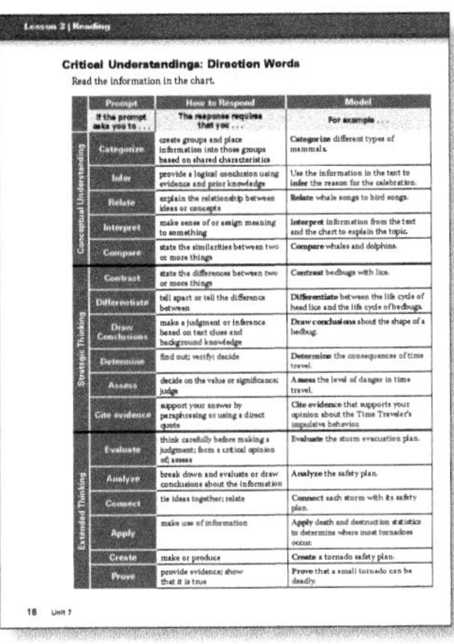

Lesson 2 | Reading

Critical Understandings: Direction Words

Read the information in the chart.

	Prompt	How to Respond	Model
	If the prompt asks you to . . .	The response requires that you . . .	For example . . .
Conceptual Understanding	Categorize	create groups and place information into those groups based on shared characteristics	**Categorize** different types of mammals.
	Infer	provide a logical conclusion using evidence and prior knowledge	Use the information in the text to **infer** the reason for the celebration.
	Relate	explain the relationship between ideas or concepts	**Relate** whale songs to bird songs.
	Interpret	make sense of or assign meaning to something	**Interpret** information from the text and the chart to explain the topic.
	Compare	state the similarities between two or more things	**Compare** whales and dolphins.
Strategic Thinking	Contrast	state the differences between two or more things	**Contrast** bedbugs with lice.
	Differentiate	tell apart or tell the difference between	**Differentiate** between the life cycle of head lice and the life cycle of bedbugs.
	Draw Conclusions	make a judgment or inference based on text clues and background knowledge	**Draw conclusions** about the shape of a bedbug.
	Determine	find out; verify; decide	**Determine** the consequences of time travel.
	Assess	decide on the value or significance; judge	**Assess** the level of danger in time travel.
	Cite evidence	support your answer by paraphrasing or using a direct quote	**Cite evidence** that supports your opinion about the Time Traveler's impulsive behavior.
Extended Thinking	Evaluate	think carefully before making a judgment; form a critical opinion of; assess	**Evaluate** the storm evacuation plan.
	Analyze	break down and evaluate or draw conclusions about the information	**Analyze** the safety plan.
	Connect	tie ideas together; relate	**Connect** each storm with its safety plan.
	Apply	make use of information	**Apply** death and destruction statistics to determine where most tornadoes occur.
	Create	make or produce	**Create** a tornado safety plan.
	Prove	provide evidence; show that it is true	**Prove** that a small tornado can be deadly.

16 Unit 7

Good readers can answer questions at a variety of difficulty levels and in a variety of forms. Often you are asked to respond to a statement or a prompt instead of a question. Your comprehension of a text is often evaluated by your ability to respond accurately to these different types of prompts or questions. We have worked with prompts that require you to use different levels of thought: conceptual understanding, strategic thinking, and extended thinking. In this lesson we will review the prompts for all levels of thinking.

Conceptual Understanding

Looking at the chart on page 16 or at the posters, what prompts require you to think conceptually? (categorize, infer, relate, interpret, compare)

> **Note:** If you are referring to the Conceptual Understanding poster, there are several other prompts listed. (describe, show, explain, summarize)

Have students identify what is required in the response for each prompt at this level.

Strategic Thinking

The next level of prompt calls for readers to think strategically. What are the different prompts for Strategic Thinking? (contrast, differentiate, draw conclusions, determine, assess, cite evidence) Answers to complex questions require you to apply lower level and higher level thinking skills. They require a solid understanding of the information and the ability to draw conclusions that often take you beyond the text.

Have students identify what is required in the response for each prompt at this level.

Extended Thinking

The most complex prompts require you to extend your thinking. What are the different prompts for Extended Thinking? (evaluate, analyze, connect, apply, create, prove) Have students identify what is required in the response for each prompt at this level.

We have responded to prompts at these differing levels throughout this program. We know that at each level, it is critical to understand exactly what the prompt is asking.

Direct students to pages 297 and 298 in their Student Books. Let's preview the prompts for the short piece of text we will read. I'll read the prompt, and you repeat the direction word in bold.

1. **Infer** what happened when Odysseus's men jumped out of the Trojan Horse. (infer)
2. **Contrast** the mythological characters Odin and Odysseus. (contrast)
3. **Assess** the importance of magical powers for a mythological hero. (assess)
4. **Prove** that different cultures created their own myths. (prove)
5. **Create** a mythological hero that would be able to help you in school. (create)

Lesson 3 | Reading

Critical Understandings

Review the prompts on the Critical Understandings chart or on the Direction Words posters. Read the prompts at the bottom of the page to establish a purpose for reading. Then read the passage and respond to the prompts. Identify each prompt according to the level of thinking required to respond.

Heroes from Mythology

The myths created by people from different ancient cultures revolved around heroic characters. These heroes faced special challenges and encounters with supernatural characters. Mythological heroes possessed a variety of unique traits that enabled them to overcome great obstacles.

First of all, most legendary heroes have some kind of superhuman power. The heroes of ancient Greek legends were usually related to the gods. This meant they would be very strong, extremely clever, and very lucky. Hercules, for example, was only a baby when he strangled two snakes that had been sent to kill him.

Also, some heroes used magic. Odin was a very important Norse god. He had an invincible spear called Gungnir. He also had two ravens. They would perch on his shoulder and fly off to spy on his enemies. His son, Thor, had a hammer called Mjolnir ("the destroyer"). The hammer returned like a boomerang whenever he threw it. Thor also had a magic belt. This belt doubled his strength.

Odysseus was a hero who did not have any magic powers. He captured the city of Troy by hiding his army inside a huge wooden horse. The Trojans thought it was a gift from the Greeks, but they got an unpleasant surprise when Odysseus's men jumped out!

In addition, many heroes from myths and legends have a fatal flaw. Few heroes are totally invincible. Most have one weakness that can destroy them. In the case of Achilles, the great Greek warrior of the Trojan War, it was his heel. When Achilles was a baby, his mother dipped him in the magic river Styx. This made his whole body invulnerable—except for his heel where she held him. He finally died when a poisoned arrow struck him on the heel.

Answers will vary.

1. **Infer** what happened when Odysseus's men jumped out of the Trojan Horse.
Odysseus's men attacked the men of Troy, and the element of surprise helped them win.

Level of thinking: conceptual understanding

Unit 12 297

Have partners identify the level of each prompt and change the prompt to a question.

Example Questions

1. Conceptual understanding: What do you think happened when Odysseus's men jumped out of the Trojan Horse?
2. Strategic thinking: How are Odin and Odysseus different?
3. Extended thinking: Were magical powers important for mythological heroes? Why or why not?
4. Extended thinking: What evidence from the text is proof that different cultures created their own myths?
5. Extended thinking: What traits would a mythological hero need to help you in school?

Now that you know what information you are looking for, we will read the text. With eyes on text, listen while I read this short text on mythological heroes. Use your pencil eraser to follow along. Let's begin. Read the text aloud.

Note: While the lessons are written for a teacher read aloud, it is important that your students read as much and as often as they can. Assign readings that meet the needs of your students, based on your observations or data. This is a good opportunity to stretch students, but if they become frustrated, return to the read-aloud method.

Heroes from Mythology

The myths created by people from different ancient cultures revolved around heroic characters. These heroes faced special challenges and encounters with supernatural characters. Mythological heroes possessed a variety of unique traits that enabled them to overcome great obstacles.

First of all, most legendary heroes have some kind of superhuman power. The heroes of ancient Greek legends were usually related to the gods. This meant they would be very strong, extremely clever, and very lucky. Hercules, for example, was only a baby when he strangled two snakes that had been sent to kill him.

Also, some heroes used magic. Odin was a very important Norse god. He had an invincible spear called Gungnir. He also had two ravens. They would perch on his shoulder and fly off to spy on his enemies. His son, Thor, had a hammer called Mjolnir ("the destroyer"). The hammer returned like a boomerang whenever he threw it. Thor also had a magic belt. This belt doubled his strength.

Odysseus was a hero who did not have any magic powers. He captured the city of Troy by hiding his army inside a huge wooden horse. The Trojans thought it was a gift from the Greeks, but they got an unpleasant surprise when Odysseus's men jumped out!

In addition, many heroes from myths and legends have a fatal flaw. Few heroes are totally invincible. Most have one weakness that can destroy them. In the case of Achilles, the great Greek warrior of the Trojan War, it was his heel. When Achilles was a baby, his mother dipped him in the magic river Styx. This made his whole body invulnerable—except for his heel where she held him. He finally died when a poisoned arrow struck him on the heel.

Let's check our comprehension of this passage by responding to the prompts that require different levels of thinking. For some prompts, you will need to consider learning outside of the text to support your answer.

Model

Read the first prompt aloud.

1. **Infer** what happened when Odysseus's men jumped out of the Trojan Horse.

We can change this prompt into a question to determine how best to respond. Have partners share their questions. The question would be, What do you think happened when Odysseus's men jumped out of the Trojan Horse?

To respond, we need to check back in the text and see if we can find any clues. Look at the fourth paragraph. The text tells us "Odysseus captured the city of Troy" and that the men of Troy were in for "an unpleasant surprise." These clues confirm that Odysseus and his men fought the Trojans and won the battle because of the element of surprise. So, the answer would be: Odysseus's men attacked the men of Troy, and the element of surprise helped them win.

Guided Practice

Read the next prompt aloud.

2. **Contrast** the mythological characters Odin and Odysseus.

Have partners share their questions. The question would be, How are Odin and Odysseus different? Remember when you see the word *contrast*, focus on the differences not the similarities. Think about origin, magic, and status when looking for the differences between these two characters. Write the words *origin, magic, status* on the board.

What is their origin or where were they from? Did they have magical powers? What was their status, meaning were they gods, creatures, or mortal men? Have partners answer the question. While students are working, write the following answer on the board:

> *Odin was a god from Norse mythology, while Odysseus was a man from Greek mythology. Odin had magical powers, but Odysseus had to rely on his wits.*

Compare student responses.

Independent Practice

Have partners complete the remaining prompts. Review the answers as a class to ensure students understand what each prompt is asking.

Note: Base the number of modeled and guided examples on student ability and progress. Challenge them with independent practice when appropriate.

Lesson 3 | Reading

Critical Understandings (*cont.*) Answers will vary.

2. **Contrast** the mythological characters Odin and Odysseus.
Odin was a god from Norse mythology, while Odysseus was a man from Greek mythology. Odin had magical powers, but Odysseus had to rely on his wits.
Level of thinking: strategic thinking

3. **Assess** the importance of magical powers for a mythological hero.
Magical powers were not important for all mythological heroes. Some heroes found ways to face and overcome their challenges without magic. Odysseus was clever and brave; benefited from the magical powers of others. However, Odin relied on a magical spear and ravens, and Thor relied on a magical hammer.
Level of thinking: strategic thinking

4. **Prove** that different cultures created their own myths.
Line 1 of the text says "myths created by people from different ancient cultures." The text also makes reference to Odin, a god from Norse mythology, and Odysseus, a hero from Greek mythology. This proves that myths were created across cultures.
Level of thinking: extended thinking

5. **Create** a mythological hero that would be able to help you in school.
Possible Answer: Scninia is a Greek heroine who is the daughter of Athena and Hercules. She is very wise and strong. Her ball of wisdom allows her to explain concepts to me in a way I will understand. Her strength keeps me safe from bullies. Her fatal flaw is that she is so open-minded, there is actually a gap in her skull.
Level of thinking: extended thinking

298 Unit 12

Provide these alternative questions and sentence starters for those who need additional help.

3. Were magical powers important for mythological heroes? Why or why not?

   Magical powers ____________________ important for all mythological heroes.
   Some heroes, ____.
   Characters like ____.

4. What evidence from the text is proof that different cultures created their own myths?

   Line ______ of the text says "________________________________."
   This proves ____.

5. What traits would a mythological hero need to help you in school?

Unit 12 Lesson 4

Lesson Opener

Before the lesson, choose one of the following activities to write on the board or post on the *LANGUAGE! Live* Class Wall online.

- *What do you think the following proverb means?* People who live in glass houses should not throw stones.
- *Write one sentence about Medusa and her snakes. Then write a second sentence replacing the nouns with pronouns. Example: Medusa fed her snakes. She fed them.*
- *Complete these analogies:* piece : whole :: ____ : ____; occur : happen :: ____ : ____.

Reading

Objective

- Read sentences to develop fluency.

Sentence Fluency

Timer

Follow the Fluency Procedure outlined below. If it is necessary, begin the fluency drill with a choral read of all sentences. Direct students to page 299 in their Student Books and complete the process.

Fluency Procedure

- Partners switch books, so the recorder is marking errors in the reader's book.
- A timer is set for one minute.
- Readers and recorders move left to right, tracking each word with a pencil.
- As readers read the words aloud, recorders mark errors with a small x above the misread word.
- Recorders place a star to the right of the last word read when time ends.
- If the reader is able to read all words in the allotted time, the reader needs to start over at the beginning. The recorder must indicate this feat by placing two stars to the right of the last word read.
- When both students have read, partners switch books.
- Students calculate total words read, then subtract errors and record.
- Students record information on the progress chart in back of the Student Book.

Lesson 4 | Reading

Sentence Fluency

Read each sentence fluently.

	Correct	Errors
1st Try		
2nd Try		

	Sentence	Words
1.	The rain could make the streets slick, so you should drive slowly.	12
2.	If you exceed the speed limit, you could get a ticket.	23
3.	You would not strain your back when you lift if you would just use your legs.	39
4.	She sprained her hand when she took a turn on the zip line.	52
5.	The students had a chance to ride in the open railroad cars on the class trip.	68
6.	Her mother's ring contains large, bright red gems.	76
7.	If I had time, I would spray the flowers with a fine mist.	89
8.	Tom is finishing his homework and his chores, so he will be allowed to go on the class trip.	108
9.	Moonbeams filled the basement with pale yellow light, and I used the light to follow her up the stairs.	127
10.	She is shredding the papers with a strange device.	136
11.	The crowd cheered as the gifted dancer stepped into the spotlight at the center of the stage.	153
12.	If you don't clean your hands well, the germs could make you sick.	166
13.	Beth and Susan planned the dinner after looking at their cookbooks.	177

Unit 12 299

Grammar

Objectives

- Demonstrate an understanding of the modals *could, would,* and *should.*
- Listen to oral sentences and write them accurately.
- Use modals in written sentences.

Modals: *could, would, should*

We've been working with helping verbs and learning how they enhance the meaning of the base or main verb. Helping verbs are sometimes used as a way to express time or tense. We've learned how to place events in the past, present, and future. One thing we haven't talked about is expressing the possibility that something "might" happen.

Write the following sentence on the board and read it aloud.

> *I will clean my room.*

Look at the sentence on the board. What is the verb? (will clean) What tense is *will clean*? (future tense) This sentence is about something I plan to do in the future. However, there *might* be something that keeps me from doing it.

Write the following sentences on the board and read them aloud.

> *I know I should clean my room. I would clean it today, if I could open the door.*

The words *should, would,* and *could* are being used. Notice that nothing is happening in the sentences. The first sentence with *should* is simply advice. I know that my room needs to be cleaned, so I should do it. The next word, *would,* shows that I have a desire to clean it. The remainder of the sentence uses the word *could*—which means something is possible. In this instance, it is being used to say that if it was possible to open the door, I would clean my room.

Write the following explanations on the board.

> *could = possibility*
>
> *would = desire*
>
> *should = advice*

The differences are not huge, but they are there. When we speak, listen, and read, we need to pay attention to these more subtle differences in meaning. Little clues sometimes make a big difference in the outcome of an event. As readers, we can anticipate where an author is going with greater certainty when we pay attention to all of the clues.

Model

Begin students with this starter: If I take a trip to the beach, _____. Then have them complete the sentence using *could, would,* or *should.*

Example Sentences

I could swim in the ocean.

I should pack plenty of sunscreen.

I would enjoy the sand and the sun.

Begin students with this starter: If I get a puppy, _____. Then have them complete the sentence using *could, would,* or *should.*

Example Sentences

I could take it on walks.

I should feed it twice a day.

I would love it so much.

Guided and Independent Practice

Direct students to page 300 in their Student Books. Read the instructions aloud and remind students of the procedure for sentence dictation, but explain that this time it will be different because you will only be telling them part of the sentence, and they will be completing the sentence on their own.

Dictation Procedure

- Teacher reads the sentence starter.
- Students repeat the sentence starter.
- Students write the sentence starter and complete the sentence.
- Teacher reads the sentence starter a second time as students check their work.

Lesson 4 | Grammar

Sentence Dictation: Conditional Tense Answers will vary.

Listen to each sentence starter and repeat it. Write the sentence starter on the line, then complete the sentence using *could, would,* or *should.*

1. If you do not clean your hands well, the germs could make you sick.
2. If I had time, I would spray the flowers with a fine mist.
3. If you want to get an A on your test, you should study the night before.
4. If I could travel to another place, I would go to Tahiti.
5. If you want to get there on time, you should leave by 9:00.
6. If you eat too much candy, you could get a stomachache.
7. If you want to get a cat, you should go to the animal shelter.
8. If he opens the door quickly, you could get knocked over.
9. If you work hard in school, you could get a scholarship.
10. If I were old enough to drive, I would get a fast car.

300 Unit 12

Dictate the following sentence starters, and have students complete the sentences using *should, could,* or *would.*

1. If you do not clean your hands well, _____.
2. If I had time, _____.
3. If you want to get an A on your test, _____.
4. If I could travel to another place, _____.
5. If you want to get there on time, _____.
6. If you eat too much candy, _____.
7. If you want to get a cat, _____.
8. If he opens the door quickly, _____.
9. If you work hard in school, _____.
10. If I were old enough to drive, _____.

Have volunteers share their answers.

Reading

Objectives

- Read sentence phrases with fluency to support comprehension.
- Read an informational text.
- Use critical thinking skills to respond to specific questions about a text.

Phrase It

Reading in phrases is an important step in becoming a proficient reader. We must practice this skill often, until it becomes a habit.

Read the following phrases, pausing in between for students to create a mental picture.

> At that very instant . . . each separate snake . . . upon the Gorgon's head . . . stretched threateningly upward . . . and Medusa . . . opened her eyes!

At that very instant answers the *when* question and we often start sentences, especially masterpiece sentences, with a *when* or *where* phrase. *Each separate snake upon the Gorgon's head* is the subject, and *stretched threateningly upward* is the predicate. We have a compound sentence, so we read on to find *and Medusa* is the second subject and *opened her eyes* is the second predicate. Reading in phrases is especially helpful when the sentences are long and complex.

For Phrase It, we scoop phrases using our pencil. When we scoop a phrase, we form an image in our heads. The next phrase we read may add or change the image. Reading for meaning, or comprehension, requires this level of attention to how images should be growing or changing in our minds. We learned more about what happened "at that very instant" as we read the sentence. The image of the snakes changed from a normal reptile to Medusa's hair as we continued reading. Meaning and significance is added to the snakes by the way they move, and their movement sets up more danger when we learn that Medusa wakes up. We get a real sense of danger as we continue reading the sentence and that helps to build drama in a story.

Direct students to page 301 in their Student Books.

Model

Complete the first sentence as a model.

Guided Practice

Guide students to complete the next two sentences and share options for responses.

Independent Practice

Have students read the remaining sentences and scoop the phrases. Review the answers as a class.

Note: Base the number of modeled and guided examples on student ability and progress. Challenge them with independent practice when appropriate.

There are various ways the sentences can be broken into phrases. Accept logical answers.

Phrase It

Read each phrase and scoop it with a pencil. As you read the phrase, form an image in your mind. Read the sentence with prosody.

1. When I run on the track, I think about winning first place in a race.
2. The storm passed, and I strained my eyes to see the pale rainbow.
3. Mark and Sam are spraying the garden to keep the bugs from eating the new plants.
4. Will you stop at the store on your way home and pick up a loaf of bread?
5. After the team stretched, they practiced the new plays for the upcoming big game.
6. The dance was a huge success, and it helped the club raise funds for their important project.
7. We sprinted in the damp grass and when we turned to look back at our tracks, we slipped.
8. Will you tell me when you plan to take the exam for this class?
9. The towering spruce trees swayed back and forth in the morning breeze.
10. Do you like to ride horses on the trails at the beach?

Critical Understandings

All Direction Words posters

We have worked with prompts that require you to use different levels of thinking: conceptual thinking, strategic thinking, and extended thinking. In this lesson we will review the prompts for all levels of thinking. What levels of prompts are we reviewing in this unit? (conceptual, strategic, extended) These strategies will help you throughout school. What are some of the things you have to do to show different levels of comprehension? (recall, understand, think strategically, and extend thinking) Would these strategies work in other classes? (yes)

Direct students to pages 302–304 in their Student Books.

Let's preview some prompts that require conceptual understanding, strategic thinking, and extended thinking about myths from different cultures. I'll read each prompt, and you repeat the key word in bold. Ready? Let's begin.

1. **Categorize** the gods and heroes according to their cultural origins. (categorize)
2. **Draw conclusions** about why people turned to myths for answers. (draw conclusions)
3. **Cite evidence** that supports your opinion of Hercules. (cite evidence)
4. **Evaluate** Thor's title of "god of thunder." (evaluate)
5. **Connect** Odin to the idea of sacrifice. (connect)

Lesson 4 | Reading

Critical Understandings

Read the prompts below the passage to establish a purpose for rereading. Then read the passage and respond to the prompts. Identify each prompt according to the level of thinking required to respond.

Myths from Ancient Cultures

The people of Norway, the people of Greece, and the people of Rome had something in common. They all created myths to help them understand the world around them.

Odin and Thor are two heroes from Norse mythology. Odin was the Norse god of war and wisdom. He rode upon an eight-footed horse, Sleipnir. Odin had only one eye. He loved learning so much that he traded one of his eyes for a drink from the well of wisdom. This drink gave him knowledge. Thor, Odin's son, was the Norse god of thunder. He was large and powerful. He had a red beard and eyes of lightning. Despite his threatening appearance, he was very popular. He protected both the gods and humans from the forces of evil. Thor got into frequent fights with giants. One of them was Skrymir, a huge frost giant. The giant was so big that Thor slept in the thumb of his empty glove—thinking he was inside a house.

In Greek mythology, 12 gods ruled the universe and they lived on Mount Olympus. Zeus was the supreme god of the Olympians and he had several sons, one of which was Perseus. The ancient Greeks admired cunning and trickery. Many of their gods and heroes possessed a gift for deceptions. Hercules was famous for the 12 tasks, or labors, set for him by King Eurystheus of Tiryns. These tasks included killing monsters, cleaning a stable by diverting a river, and taming a herd of man-eating horses. He proved his amazing strength many times. Once, he even held up the sky in place of the giant named Atlas. Jason was another Greek hero who set out to capture the Golden Fleece, the hide from a magical ram. With the help of a witch and many other heroes, he was finally able to take the fleece and claim his rightful place as king.

302 Unit 12

Have partners identify the level of each prompt and change the prompt to a question.

Example Questions

1. Conceptual understanding: What culture does each god and hero come from?
2. Strategic thinking: Why did people turn to myths for answers?
3. Strategic thinking: What is your opinion of Hercules, and what textual evidence supports this opinion?
4. Extended thinking: Why was Thor called the "god of thunder"? Was this a good name for him?
5. Extended thinking: How is Odin connected to the idea of sacrifice?

With eyes on text, listen while I read this short text on myths from different cultures. Use your pencil eraser to follow along. Let's begin. Read the text aloud.

Note: While the lessons are written for a teacher read aloud, it is important that your students read as much and as often as they can. Assign readings that meet the needs of your students, based on your observations or data. This is a good opportunity to stretch students, but if they become frustrated, return to the read-aloud method.

Myths from Ancient Cultures

The people of Norway, the people of Greece, and the people of Rome had something in common. They all created myths to help them understand the world around them.

Odin and Thor are two heroes from Norse mythology. Odin was the Norse god of war and wisdom. He rode upon an eight-footed horse, Sleipnir. Odin had only one eye. He loved learning so much that he traded one of his eyes for a drink from the well of wisdom. This drink gave him knowledge. Thor, Odin's son, was the Norse god of thunder. He was large and powerful. He had a red beard and eyes of lightning. Despite his threatening appearance, he was very popular. He protected both the gods and humans from the forces of evil. Thor got into frequent fights with giants. One of them was Skrymir, a huge frost giant. The giant was so big that Thor slept in the thumb of his empty glove—thinking he was inside a house.

In Greek mythology, 12 gods ruled the universe and they lived on Mount Olympus. Zeus was the supreme god of the Olympians and he had several sons, one of which was Perseus. The ancient Greeks admired cunning and trickery. Many of their gods and heroes possessed a gift for deceptions. Hercules was famous for the 12 tasks, or labors, set for him by King Eurystheus of Tiryns. These tasks included killing monsters, cleaning a stable by diverting a river, and taming a herd of man-eating horses. He proved his amazing strength many times. Once, he even held up the sky in place of the giant named Atlas. Jason was another Greek hero who set out to capture the Golden Fleece, the hide from a magical ram. With the help of a witch and many other heroes, he was finally able to take the fleece and claim his rightful place as king.

The Romans also told about their gods in myths. Many of their gods were based on gods from Greek mythology, but the Romans gave them different names. Saturn was one of their gods, the god of time. Saturn had three sons: Jupiter, Neptune, and Pluto. Jupiter ruled the air and was the king of the gods. He was the strongest god. Juno was Jupiter's wife, and the goddess of husbands and wives. Neptune ruled the seas. He gave the waves the white caps and made the waters still. He held the fate of ships in his hands, so a trip could be safe or unsafe. His brother, Pluto, ruled over the dead. His kingdom was a dark and gloomy land. Pluto ruled over all who entered his kingdom. Once the dead entered Pluto's underworld, they could never leave.

People in all three cultures created stories about their gods and the challenges faced by heroic characters. These stories helped them make sense of their world. The stories were thrilling as well as entertaining and offered the common person a sense of hope in overcoming life's many challenges.

Let's check our comprehension of this passage by responding to some prompts that require different levels of thinking.

Model

Read the first prompt aloud.

1. **Categorize** the gods and heroes according to their cultural origins.

Have partners share their questions. The question would be, What culture does each god and hero come from? I can look through the text to find this answer fairly quickly. Work with your partner to answer the question in sentence format. Consider creating a chart to help you sort.

While students are working, draw this chart on the board. Ask the students to name the characters that fit into each category.

Norse Mythology	*Roman Mythology*	*Greek Mythology*

Critical Understandings (*cont.*)

The Romans also told about their gods in myths. Many of their gods were based on gods from Greek mythology, but the Romans gave them different names. Saturn was one of their gods, the god of time. Saturn had three sons: Jupiter, Neptune, and Pluto. Jupiter ruled the air and was the king of the gods. He was the strongest god. Juno was Jupiter's wife, and the goddess of husbands and wives. Neptune ruled the seas. He gave the waves the white caps and made the waters still. He held the fate of ships in his hands, so a trip could be safe or unsafe. His brother, Pluto, ruled over the dead. His kingdom was a dark and gloomy land. Pluto ruled over all who entered his kingdom. Once the dead entered Pluto's underworld, they could never leave.

People in all three cultures created stories about their gods and the challenges faced by heroic characters. These stories helped them make sense of their world. The stories were thrilling as well as entertaining and offered the common person a sense of hope in overcoming life's many challenges.

1. **Categorize** the gods and heroes according to their cultural origins.

Norse Mythology	Roman Mythology	Greek Mythology
Odin Thor Skrymir	Saturn Jupiter Neptune Pluto Juno	Zeus Perseus Hercules King Eurystheus Atlas Jason

Level of thinking: conceptual understanding

Critical Understandings (*cont.*)

2. **Draw conclusions** about why people turned to myths for answers.

People from different cultures turned to myths because they wanted to make sense of their world. People from ancient cultures didn't have access to books and the Internet to explain things. Myths helped them feel more secure in a world they didn't understand.

Level of thinking: strategic thinking

Answers will vary.

3. **Cite evidence** that supports your opinion of Hercules.

I think Hercules was very brave and honorable. The text tells of him "killing monsters, cleaning a stable by diverting a river, and taming a herd of man-eating horses." "He even held up the sky" for Atlas, the giant. He showed his honor by completing the tasks set for him.

Level of thinking: strategic thinking

4. **Evaluate** Thor's title of "god of thunder."

Thor was called the god of thunder because he was very powerful, like thunder. He had eyes of lightning and was threatening—both of which are connected to thunder. Thunder is the sound of lightning, and thunder is heard as a threat of an impending storm.

Level of thinking: extended thinking

5. **Connect** Odin to the idea of sacrifice.

To sacrifice means to give up something that you need. Odin sacrificed his vision to be able to learn more. I would say Odin made a huge sacrifice for something he desperately wanted.

Level of thinking: extended thinking

Guided Practice

Read the second prompt aloud.

2. **Draw conclusions** about why people turned to myths for answers.

Have partners share their questions. The question would be, Why did people turn to myths for answers? Have partners answer the question.

While students are working, write the following sentence frame on the board. Work with students to formulate an answer and have them record it.

People from different cultures turned to myths because _____.

Help students understand that the first part of the answer is found in the text. The second part of the answer offers a conclusion not found in the text but is based on information in the text.

Independent Practice

Have partners complete the remaining prompts. Review the answers as a class to ensure students understand what each prompt is asking.

Note: Base the number of modeled and guided examples on student ability and progress. Challenge them with independent practice when appropriate.

Provide these alternative questions and sentence starters for those who need additional help.

3. What is your opinion of Hercules, and what textual evidence supports this opinion?

   I think Hercules ____.
   The text ____.

4. Why was Thor called the "god of thunder"? Was this a good name for him?

   Thor was called the god of thunder because ______________________.
   Thunder ____.

5. How is Odin connected to the idea of sacrifice?

   To sacrifice means ____.
   Odin sacrificed ____.

Unit 12

Lesson 5

Lesson Opener

Before the lesson, choose one of the following activities to write on the board or post on the *LANGUAGE! Live* Class Wall online.

- *Review Key Passage Vocabulary; add to definitions and complete pictures.*
- *Use the word* recover *in a sentence.*
- *If you had a choice, would you rather learn scientific or mythological explanations about the natural world? Explain your answer.*

Vocabulary

Objective

- Review key passage vocabulary.

Recontextualize Passage Vocabulary

Direct students to page 280 in their Student Books.

Lesson 1 | Vocabulary

Key Passage Vocabulary: "The Gorgon's Head"

Rate your knowledge of the words. Define the words. Draw a picture to help you remember the definition.

Vocabulary	Knowledge Rating	Definition	Picture
image	0 1 2 3	the form or appearance of someone or something	
undertake	0 1 2 3	attempt; to take on a task	
intelligent	0 1 2 3	smart; reflecting good judgment or sound thought	
proceed	0 1 2 3	to begin and carry on an action or movement	
recover	0 1 2 3	to get back something lost; regain	
invisible	0 1 2 3	impossible to see; not visible	
perceive	0 1 2 3	to become aware of through sight or observation	
enormous	0 1 2 3	very great in size or amount	

280 Unit 12

Review the vocabulary words from "The Gorgon's Head."

- A word meaning "to move forward with an action or movement" is what? (proceed) If I begin my homework, did I *proceed* with my work? (yes) What do you do when you begin to do something? (proceed)
- If something is huge or very big, what is it? (enormous) If I cut a thin slice of cake, would it be small or *enormous*? (small) Another word for *huge* is what? (enormous)
- A word meaning "very smart" is what? (intelligent) Would studying for an upcoming exam be an *intelligent* or dumb choice? (intelligent)
  If you are smart, you are what? (intelligent)
- What is another word for "becoming aware of something through sight or observation"? (perceive) If you *perceive* that someone is becoming annoyed with your behavior, are you aware of how you are making someone feel? (yes) To become aware of something is what? (perceive)
- If something can be seen, it is called visible. If something cannot be seen, what is it? (invisible) Ink that doesn't show up on the paper is what kind of ink? (invisible) What word is the opposite of *visible*? (invisible)
- A word meaning "to get something back or regain" is what? (recover) If you lost your wallet and found it, did you *recover* it? (yes) If you get something back, what do you do? (recover it)
- What is another word for "the form or appearance of someone or something"? (image) If you see yourself in the mirror, is that your *image*? (yes) When you see someone's appearance, you see what? (an image)
- If you attempt or take on a task, what did you do? (undertake) When you put off starting on your science project, are you *undertaking* the project? (no) What is another word for "attempting a task"? (undertake)

Reading

Objectives

- Write questions or prompts about text to deepen comprehension.
- Use critical thinking skills to respond orally to specific questions about a text.

Guided Reading of "The Gorgon's Head": Ask and Answer Questions

You know that skilled readers preview the text for text features such as headings, bolded or italicized text, and illustrations. Proficient readers also reread text slowly and carefully to gain a better understanding of the text. They monitor their thinking while reading to be sure that each sentence and paragraph makes sense. Good readers continue to think about the Big Idea questions as they read and look for information that would help them formulate their answers. What are our two Big Idea questions for this text selection? Remember you can turn back to page 279 in your Student Books to find the questions. (Why did people create myths? How are myths relevant to modern times?)

Good readers also ask questions. They ask themselves and others questions about their reading. These questions help them clarify their understanding and extend their thinking about the text. Challenging questions force readers to combine information found in the text with what they already know about the subject. Proficient readers understand that this level of questioning helps them improve their own comprehension. After listening to the questions of others, they ask themselves new questions. This time when we read "The Gorgon's Head," we will ask questions about the text. We will also answer the questions we ask and this should clear up any confusion we have about the text.

Direct students to page 281 in their Student Books or have them tear out the extra copy of "The Gorgon's Head" from the back of their book.

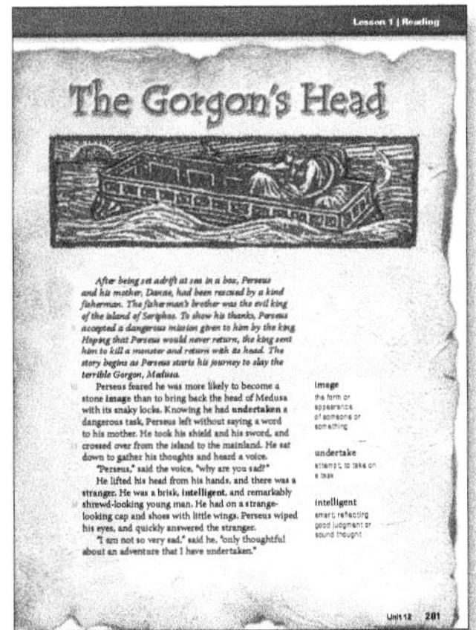

Note: To minimize flipping back and forth between the pages, a copy of each text has been included in the back of the Student Books. Encourage students to tear this out and use it when working on activities that require the use of the text.

Let's do what good readers do and reread "The Gorgon's Head" thinking about asking and answering questions that will further our comprehension.

Remember to track the text while your pencil points to the words. While reading, be aware of questions that come to your mind and questions that you could ask others. Eyes ready? Pencils ready? Let's begin.

Note: While the lessons are written for a teacher read aloud, it is important that your students read as much and as often as they can. Assign readings that meet the needs of your students, based on your observations or data. This is a good opportunity to stretch students, but if they become frustrated, return to the read-aloud method.

Read the first paragraph.

The Gorgon's Head

After being set adrift at sea in a box, Perseus and his mother, Danae, had been rescued by a kind fisherman. The fisherman's brother was the evil king of the island of Seriphos. To show his thanks, Perseus accepted a dangerous mission given to him by the king. Hoping that Perseus would never return, the king sent him to kill a monster and return with its head. The story begins as Perseus starts his journey to slay the terrible Gorgon, Medusa.

Direct students to page 305 in their Student Books.

Think about the text. What questions do you have? What should your peers have learned about Perseus and his mission in this section?

- Choose one question word or prompt we have learned. Consider starting your question with *Where*.
- For a more challenging question, consider a prompt that uses *Infer*.
- Write the question or prompt on the page in your Student Books. Be prepared to answer your question or prompt orally. What end mark is required for a question? (question mark) What end mark is required for a prompt? (period)

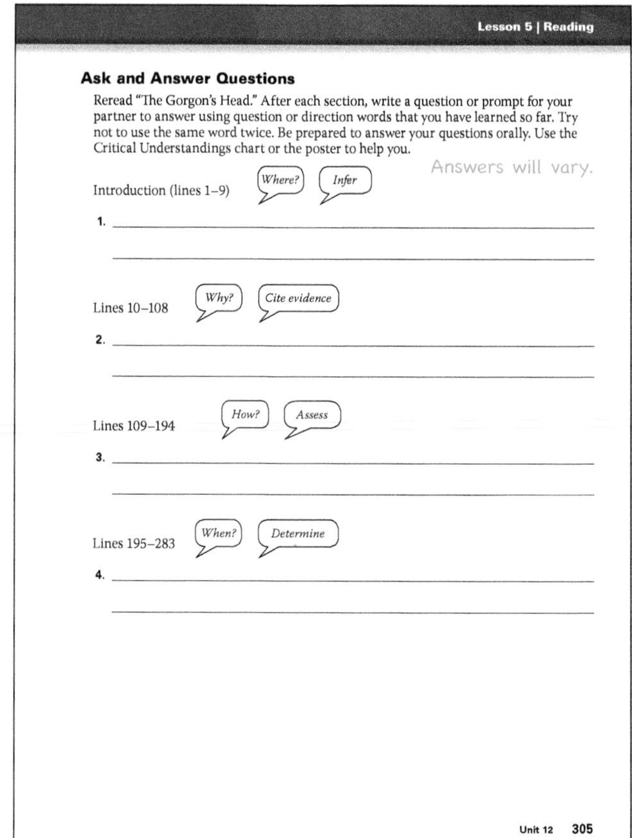
Lesson 5 | Reading

Ask and Answer Questions

Reread "The Gorgon's Head." After each section, write a question or prompt for your partner to answer using question or direction words that you have learned so far. Try not to use the same word twice. Be prepared to answer your questions orally. Use the Critical Understandings chart or the poster to help you.

Answers will vary.

Introduction (lines 1–9) *Where?* *Infer*

1. ______

Lines 10–108 *Why?* *Cite evidence*

2. ______

Lines 109–194 *How?* *Assess*

3. ______

Lines 195–283 *When?* *Determine*

4. ______

Unit 12 305

Direct students back to the passage. Now we will read the next section. Eyes ready? Pencils ready? Let's begin.

Perseus feared he was more likely to become a stone image than to bring back the head of Medusa with its snaky locks. Knowing he had undertaken a dangerous task, Perseus left without saying a word to his mother. He took his shield and his sword, and crossed over from the island to the mainland. He sat down to gather his thoughts and heard a voice.

"Perseus," said the voice, "why are you sad?"

He lifted his head from his hands, and there was a stranger. He was a brisk, intelligent, and remarkably shrewd-looking young man. He had on a strange-looking cap and shoes with little wings. Perseus wiped his eyes, and quickly answered the stranger.

"I am not so very sad," said he, "only thoughtful about an adventure that I have undertaken."

"Oho!" answered the stranger. "I have helped a good many young men through difficult adventures. Perhaps you may have heard of me. I have more names than one; but the name of Hermes suits me as well as any other. Tell me your troubles. We will talk the matter over, and see what can be done."

After hearing Perseus's story, Hermes exclaimed, "I am the very person to help you, if anybody can. My sister and I will do our utmost to bring you safely through your adventure."

"Your sister?" repeated Perseus.

"Yes, my sister Athena," said the stranger. "She is very wise, I promise you; and as for myself, I generally have all my wits about me. If you show yourself bold and cautious, and follow our advice, you need not fear being turned into a stone image. First of all, you must polish your shield until it shines like a mirror."

Deciding that Hermes knew better than himself, Perseus immediately set to work. He scrubbed the shield and soon it shone like the moon at harvest time. Hermes looked at it with a smile. Then, taking off his own short and crooked sword, he gave it to Perseus to wear.

"No sword but mine will answer your purpose," he stated. "The blade will cut through iron and brass as easily as through the slenderest twig. The next thing is to find the Three Gray Women, who will tell us where to find the Nymphs."

"The Three Gray Women!" cried Perseus, "Pray who may the Three Gray Women be?

"They are three very strange old ladies," said Hermes, laughing. "They have but one eye among them, and only one tooth. Moreover, you must find them out by starlight, or in the dusk of the evening. They never show themselves by the light of the sun or the moon."

He added, "There are other things to be done before you can find your way to the Gorgons. But after we meet the Three Gray Women, you may be sure that the Gorgons are not far away."

They set out and walked at a brisk pace; so brisk, indeed, that Perseus found it rather difficult to keep up with his nimble friend Hermes. To say the truth, he had a suspicion that Hermes had a pair of wings on his cap along with wings on his shoes! When he looked straight at Hermes, he only saw an odd kind of cap. The twisted staff was evidently a great convenience to Hermes. It enabled him to proceed so fast, that Perseus, though a remarkably fit young man, began to feel out of breath.

"Here!" cried Hermes, at last, "take you the staff, for you need it a great deal more than I. Are there no better walkers than you in the island of Seriphos?"

"I could walk pretty well," said Perseus, glancing slyly at his companion's feet, "if only I had a pair of winged shoes."

"We must see about getting you a pair," answered Hermes.

The staff helped Perseus tremendously. In fact, the stick seemed to be alive in his hand, and to lend some of its life to Perseus.

They walked and talked until twilight. Suddenly Hermes whispered, "This is just the time and place to meet the Three Gray Women. Be careful that they do not see you before you see them. Though they have but a single eye among the three, it is as sharp-sighted as a half dozen common eyes."

"But what must I do," asked Perseus, "when we meet them?"

Hermes explained to Perseus how the Three Gray Women managed with their one eye. They were in the habit of changing it from one to another, as if it had been a pair of spectacles. At the instant when the eye was passing from hand to hand, none of the poor old ladies was able to see a wink. That was when Perseus was to act.

As Perseus looked earnestly through the evening dusk, he spotted the Three Gray Women. He discovered that they had long gray hair and, as they came nearer, he saw that two of them had but the empty socket of an eye, in the middle of their foreheads. In the middle of the third sister's forehead, there was a very large, bright, and piercing eye, which sparkled like a great diamond.

Direct students to page 305 in their Student Books.

- Choose a different direction or question word. Try using *Why* or *Cite evidence.*
- Write the question or prompt on the page. Be prepared to provide answers orally.

Direct students to back to the passage. Now we will read the next section. Eyes and pencils ready? Let's begin.

"Sister! Sister Scarecrow!" cried one, "you have had the eye long enough. It is my turn now!"

"Let me keep it a moment longer, Sister Nightmare," answered Scarecrow. "I thought I had a glimpse of something behind that thick bush."

The other two sisters, Nightmare and Shakejoint, began to argue with Sister Scarecrow about the eye. To end the dispute, old Dame Scarecrow took the eye out of her forehead, and held it forth in her hand.

"Take it, one of you," she cried, "and quit this foolish quarrelling. For my part, I shall be glad of a little thick darkness. Take it quickly, or I will clap it into my own head again!"

While the Three Gray Women were still scolding each other, Perseus leaped from behind the bushes and grabbed the eye. The Gray Women did not know what had happened. Each supposing that one of her sisters was in possession of the eye, they began their quarrel anew.

"My good ladies," said he, "pray do not be angry with one another. I have the honor of holding your very brilliant and excellent eye!"

The sisters were terribly frightened. "Oh, what shall we do, sisters? What shall we do? We are all in the dark! Give us our eye! Give us our one, precious, solitary eye! You have two of your own! Give us our eye!"

Following Hermes's advice, Perseus said patiently, "My dear, good, admirable old ladies, there is no occasion for putting yourselves into such a fright. You shall have back your eye, safe and sound, the moment you tell me where to find the Nymphs."

"Goodness, we know nothing at all about them," screamed Scarecrow. "We are three unfortunate old souls that go wandering about in the dusk."

All this while the Three Gray Women were groping with their outstretched hands and trying their utmost to get hold of Perseus. He took good care to keep out of their reach.

"My respectable dames," said he, "I shall keep the eye until you tell me where to find the Nymphs."

Finding that there was no other way of recovering their eye, at last they told Perseus what he wanted to know. No sooner had they done so, than he immediately, and with the utmost respect, clapped it into the vacant socket in one of their foreheads. He thanked them for their kindness, and bade them farewell.

Hermes and Perseus went on their way. The old dames had given them such specific directions that they quickly found the Nymphs. They proved to be very different from Nightmare, Shakejoint, and Scarecrow. Instead of being old, they were young and beautiful. Instead of one eye among the sisterhood, each Nymph had two exceedingly bright eyes of her own, with which she looked very kindly at Perseus. They seemed to be acquainted with Hermes. When he told them the adventure that Perseus had undertaken, they did not hesitate to give him what he needed. First, they brought out a small purse, made of deer skin, and curiously embroidered. They urged him to keep the magic wallet safe. The Nymphs next produced a pair of slippers with a nice little pair of wings at the heel of each.

"Put them on, Perseus," said Hermes. "You will find yourself as light as a feather for the remainder of our journey."

Then the Nymphs gave Perseus the helmet of invisibility. When he placed the helmet on his head, Perseus instantly disappeared! Even the helmet, which covered him with its invisibility, had vanished!

Perseus and Hermes headed off to find the Gorgons. As the two companions flew onward, Perseus thought he could hear the rustle of a garment close by. It was on the side opposite of Hermes, yet only Hermes was visible.

"Whose garment keeps rustling close beside us in the breeze?" inquired Perseus.

"Oh, it is my sister's!" answered Hermes. "Athena is coming along with us, as I told you she would. We could do nothing without the help of my sister. You have no idea how wise she is. She has such eyes, too! Why, she can see you, at this moment, just as distinctly as if you were not invisible. I'll venture to say, she will be the first to discover the Gorgons."

Direct students to page 305 in their Student Books.

- Choose a different direction or question word. Try using *How* or *Assess*.
- Write the question or prompt on the page. Be prepared to provide answers orally.

Direct students back to the passage. Now we will read the next section. Eyes and pencils ready? Let's begin.

As they were flying over a great ocean, a voice spoke in the air close by Perseus. It seemed to be a woman's voice, melodious, but not sweet. It was grave and mild.

"Perseus," said Athena, "there are the Gorgons."

"Where?" exclaimed Perseus. "I cannot see them."

"On the shore of that island beneath you," replied the voice. "A pebble, dropped from your hand, would strike in the midst of them."

"I told you she would be the first to discover them," commented Hermes, "and there they are!"

Straight downward, two or three thousand feet below him, Perseus perceived a small island, with the sea breaking into white foam all around its rocky shore. The enormous Gorgons lay fast asleep, soothed by the thunder of the sea. The moonlight glistened on their steely scales and on their golden wings. Their brazen claws were thrust out and clutched the wave-beaten fragments of rock. The snakes that served as hair likewise seemed to be asleep. Now and then, they would emit a drowsy hiss, and then fall back asleep.

Luckily for Perseus, their faces were completely hidden from him. Had he but looked one instant at them, he would have fallen heavily out of the air, his image in senseless stone.

"Now," whispered Hermes, as he hovered by the side of Perseus, "now is your time to do the deed! Be quick; for, if one of the Gorgons should awake, you are too late!"

"Which one is Medusa?" asked Perseus.

Athena replied in a calm voice, "The Gorgon that is stirring in her sleep is Medusa. Do not look at her! The sight would turn you to stone! Look at the reflection of her face and figure in the bright mirror of your shield."

Perseus now understood Hermes's motive for telling him to polish his shield. In its surface he could safely look at the reflection of the Gorgon's face. The snakes twisted themselves into tumultuous knots, without opening their eyes.

Perseus flew downward cautiously and lifted his sword. At that very instant, each separate snake upon the Gorgon's head stretched threateningly upward, and Medusa opened her eyes! She awoke too late. The sword was sharp, and the stroke fell like a lightning flash. The head of the wicked Medusa tumbled from her body!

"Admirably done!" cried Hermes. "Make haste, and put the head into your magic wallet."

To the astonishment of Perseus, the small, embroidered wallet instantly grew large enough to contain Medusa's head. As quick as thought, he snatched it up, with the snakes still writhing upon it, and thrust it in.

"Your task is done," said the calm voice of Athena. "Now fly! For the other Gorgons will do their utmost to take vengeance for Medusa's death."

Perseus flew directly to the island of Seriphos to carry Medusa's head to King Polydectes.

Not finding his mother at home, Perseus went straight to the palace and was immediately taken to the king. Polydectes was by no means happy to see him. He had felt certain, in his own evil mind, that Perseus would be killed by the Gorgons.

The king asked, "Have you performed your promise? Have you brought me the head of Medusa with the snaky locks?"

"Yes," answered Perseus with a casual tone. "I have brought you the Gorgon's head, snaky locks and all!"

"Indeed! Pray let me see it," cried King Polydectes. "It must be a very curious spectacle, if all that travelers tell about it be true!"

Perseus persuaded the king to invite all of his subjects to see the terrible head of Medusa.

"Show us the head! Show us the head of Medusa with the snaky locks!" shouted the people.

A feeling of sorrow and pity came over the youthful Perseus. "O King Polydectes," cried he, "and ye many people, I am loath to show you the Gorgon's head!"

"Show me the Gorgon's head, or I will cut off your own!" proclaimed the king.

Perseus sighed and cried out in a voice like a trumpet, "Behold it then!"

Instantly the king and all of his subjects were turned into stone. Perseus thrust the head back into the wallet, and went to tell his dear mother that she need no longer be afraid of the wicked King Polydectes.

Direct students to page 305 in their Student Books.

- Choose a different direction or question word. Try using *When* or *Determine*.
- Write the question or prompt on the page. Be prepared to provide answers orally.

Share Questions or Prompts

Have partners read their questions or prompts to each other and answer them orally, correcting each other if needed. Each pair shares with another pair, then those four share with four others if time permits. Have volunteers share their questions or prompts and responses with the class.

Writing

Objectives

- Use critical and extended thinking skills to write responses to prompts about a text.
- Support written answers with evidence from text.

Answer It: Direction Words

Direct students to the questions on pages 306–308 in their Student Books.

Now, we will respond to prompts about "The Gorgon's Head" for more practice. Some of the prompts may be similar to the prompts you already responded to, which should make them easier to answer.

- Read each prompt. Identify and underline the direction word(s).
- Use the Critical Understandings chart on page 16 or the Direction Words posters to review the type of information required by each kind of prompt.
- Locate the information you need to answer the question.
- Reread the section to retrieve exact information to use as text evidence. Use the direction word to formulate a response.

All Direction Words posters

Lesson 5 | Writing

Answer It: Direction Words

Underline the direction word in each prompt. Then respond to each prompt using a complete sentence. Provide line numbers for the text evidence.

1. Determine the reason Perseus accepts the king's request to bring him Medusa's head.

   Perseus accepts the king's request to show his thanks for being able to live and grow up on the island.

   Text Evidence: Lines 4–5

2. Analyze Hermes and Athena's decision to help Perseus.

   Hermes and Athena helped Perseus because they liked helping young men who were bold and willing to follow their advice. The decision was good because Perseus was successful and the reward for Perseus was greater than he imagined.

   Text Evidence: Lines 35–40

3. Assess Perseus's character based on his dealings with the Gray Sisters.

   Perseus is an honorable and intelligent hero when dealing with the Gray Sisters. He listens to Hermes's advice and watches them carefully as they grope for their eye. He speaks to them respectfully, yet he is not deceived by their denial of knowledge. To prove he is a man of his word, he returns the eye once the sisters tell him where to find the Nymphs.

   Text Evidence: Lines 123–156

306 Unit 12

Model

Read the first prompt aloud.

1. Determine the reason Perseus accepts the king's request to bring him Medusa's head.

What is the direction word? (determine) How do we respond to a prompt that asks us to determine? (find out; verify; or decide) If I change this to a question, it would be "Why does Perseus accept the king's request to bring him Medusa's head?" Let's use part of the prompt as our sentence starter. Call on a student to help you write the sentence starter. Write the sentence starter on the board.

Perseus accepts the king's request _____.

Have students write the answer in their Student Books.

Next, we need to go into the text to find out why he accepted the king's request. Take a look at the introductory paragraph. What does the text tells us? (to show his thanks) Why would he feel the need to show thanks? (They have been living on the island since their rescue from a box set adrift on the sea.) Write the answer on the board and read it aloud.

Perseus accepts the king's request to show his thanks for being able to live and grow up on the island.

Guided Practice

Read the next prompt aloud.

2. Analyze Hermes and Athena's decision to help Perseus.

What is the direction word in this prompt? (analyze) How do we respond to a prompt that asks us to analyze? (evaluate and draw conclusions about the information) If I change this to a question, it would be, Why do Hermes and Athena help Perseus, and was it a good decision? Work with your partner to use part of the prompt as a sentence starter. Have a volunteer provide the sentence starter and write it on the board:

Hermes and Athena helped Perseus because _____.

The decision was _____ because _____.

Now work with your partner to find the answer in the text. If students need help finding the answer, direct them to lines 35–40. After giving students time to formulate their responses, call on a student to help you finish the answer. Write the answer on the board and read it aloud.

Hermes and Athena helped Perseus because they liked helping young men who were bold and willing to follow their advice. The decision was good because Perseus was successful and the reward for Perseus was greater than he imagined.

Lesson 5 | Writing

Answer It: Direction Words (*cont.*) Answers will vary.

4. Evaluate Perseus's conclusion that Hermes possessed magical powers. Cite evidence to support your position.

Perseus believes that Hermes has magical powers because although young and physically fit, Perseus couldn't keep up with Hermes and this made him suspicious. Hermes confirms that his shoes are magical when he responds to Perseus saying, "We must see about getting you a pair." When Hermes gave him his staff, Perseus noticed that "the stick seemed to be alive in his hands and to lend some of its life to Perseus."

Text Evidence: Lines 65–85

5. Evaluate the value of the gifts Perseus received from the Nymphs and decide if he could have succeeded without them. Provide reasons as well as cite evidence to support your position.

The gifts Perseus received from the Nymphs were critical to his success in killing Medusa. The winged sandals allowed him to travel swiftly: "the two companions flew onward, . . . they were flying over a great ocean." They also allowed him to get close to Medusa. "Perseus flew downward cautiously and lifted his sword." They also helped him to escape. Being invisible was critical for approaching the Gorgons and Medusa. The wallet expanded magically allowing him to place the head in it. "To the astonishment of Perseus, the small, embroidered wallet instantly grew large enough to contain Medusa's head."

Text Evidence: Lines 169–180, 235–248

Unit 12 307

Lesson 5 | Writing

Answer It: Direction Words (*cont.*)

6. Imagine what Perseus was feeling when he faced Medusa in battle and describe the emotions, citing evidence from the text where possible.

Perseus must have felt many different things when he faced Medusa. Appreciative of the advice from Hermes, he must have been relieved to understand the role the shield played in his success, which made him more confident. Athena's wise and soothing voice should have helped him act with courage. It must have been a terrible surprise when he saw Medusa open her eyes. He felt relief when his sharp sword cut her head off so quickly.

Text Evidence: Lines 225, 230–233, 236–240

7. Create an alternate ending to "The Gorgon's Head" in which Perseus and his mother still gain their freedom from the king.

Upon returning to the island, Perseus goes to find his mother. He leaves the magic wallet holding Medusa's head with the guards. He warns them not to look inside. The guards cannot resist and they look. They are immediately turned to stone. The king sends guards to find Perseus. The guards bring back the bag and pull out the head. Everyone in the room turns to stone. When Perseus returns with his mother, he finds the palace eerily quiet. He warns his mother to cover her eyes, and he uses his shield to guide him. He finds the stone king and his guards and returns Medusa's head to the wallet. The people of the island beg Perseus to remain as their king.

308 Unit 12

Independent Practice

Have students find and use text evidence to answer the remaining prompts independently.

Note: Base the number of modeled and guided examples on student ability and progress. Challenge students with independent practice when appropriate.

Provide these alternative questions and sentence starters for those who need additional help.

3. What do we know about Perseus based on his dealings with the Three Gray Women?

   Perseus is ______________________________ when dealing with the Gray Sisters. He____.

4. Why does Perseus think Hermes has magical powers? How do you know?

   Perseus believes that Hermes has magical powers because _________________.

5. What is the value of the gifts Perseus received from the Nymphs? Could he have succeeded without them? What proof is in the text?

   The gifts Perseus received from the Nymphs were ________________________.

6. How did Perseus feel when he faced Medusa?

   Perseus must have felt ____.

7. How else could the story have ended?

   Upon returning to the island, ____.

Unit 12 Lesson 6

Lesson Opener

Before the lesson, choose one of the following activities to write on the board or post on the *LANGUAGE! Live* Class Wall online.

- *Write sentences using the following verb phrases:* could walk, should study, would attend.
- *Use the word* perceive *in a sentence.*
- *Write a mythological explanation for night. In other words, if you didn't know about the earth's rotation, how would you explain the change from light to darkness about every 12 hours?*

Writing

Objectives

- Know spelling-sound correspondences for words ending in *-se* or *-ve*.
- Know spelling-sound correspondences for words with soft *c* and *g*.
- Know the spelling-sound correspondences for words with three letter blends.

Spelling Words

Use this spelling activity to practice or assess the unit's spelling patterns students have learned online.

Direct students to Part A on page 309 in their Student Books. Read the instructions and remind students of the procedure for spelling. Use the spelling reminders to help struggling students.

1. shrimp; I ate some fried shrimp.
2. horse; The horse ran through the field.
3. place; I won first place in the contest.
4. thrilling; That movie was thrilling.
5. germs; Wash the germs off your hands.
6. splash; My dog likes to splash in puddles.
7. lease; Her lease is up next month.
8. ice; I put a lot of ice in my glass.
9. wheeze; My allergies make me wheeze.
10. huge; I ate a huge plate of spaghetti.

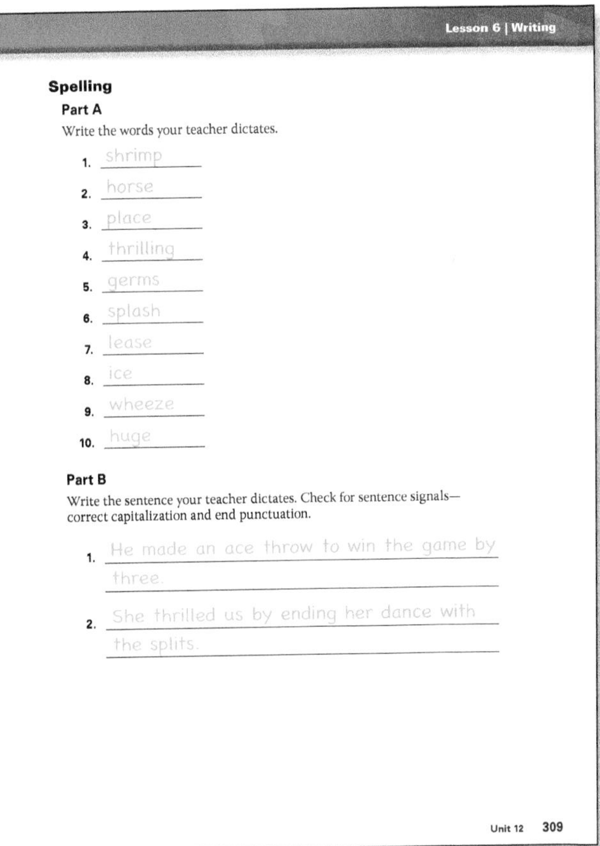

Lesson 6 | Writing

Spelling

Part A

Write the words your teacher dictates.

1. shrimp
2. horse
3. place
4. thrilling
5. germs
6. splash
7. lease
8. ice
9. wheeze
10. huge

Part B

Write the sentence your teacher dictates. Check for sentence signals—correct capitalization and end punctuation.

1. He made an ace throw to win the game by three.
2. She thrilled us by ending her dance with the splits.

Unit 12 309

Direct students to Part B on page 309 in their Student Books. Read the instructions and remind students of the procedure for sentence dictation.

He made an ace throw to win the game by three.

She thrilled us by ending her dance with the splits.

Spelling Words Procedure

- Teacher reads the word.
- Students repeat the word.
- Teacher reads the sentence.
- Students write the word.
- Teacher reads the word a second time as students check their work.

Sentence Dictation Procedure

- Teacher reads the sentence.
- Students repeat the sentence.
- Students write the sentence.
- Teacher reads the sentence a second time as students check their work.

Spelling Reminders

Words ending in *-se* or *-ve*

Some words have a vowel team or *r*-controlled vowel followed by a consonant and silent *-e*. In these words, the *-e* does not change the sound of the first vowel, as in a VC*e* word. So that is why it is "truly just silent." Many of these words end with the letter *-s* or letter *-v* before the silent *-e*, such as *please* and *horse*.

Words with Soft *c* and *g*

The way you pronounce *c* and *g* can depend on their placement in words. If *c* or *g* is followed by *e, i,* or *y*, the pronunciation may be "soft." That means that the letters make the soft sounds /s/ and /j/ instead of the hard sounds /k/ and /g/.

Vocabulary

Objectives

- Use context to determine the meaning of words in text.
- Consult reference materials to clarify the precise meaning of words.
- Demonstrate an understanding of word analogies by completing written analogies.
- Identify various types of word analogies.

Define It

Direct students to page 310 in their Student Books.

We have learned that to define words, we need to understand the words' categories and attributes. Categories are the broad groups to which words belong. Attributes are descriptors such as size, shape, color, texture, and function.

Lesson 6 | Vocabulary

Define It

Determine the category and attributes of each word. Then write the definition.

Word		Category		Attributes
mission	=	job or task	+	often requires travel

Definition: A mission is a job or task that often requires travel.

Word		Category		Attributes
brisk	=	pace or speed	+	difficult to keep up with; fast

Definition: Brisk is a pace that is fast and difficult to keep up with.

Word		Category		Attributes
whisper	=	sound	+	barely able to hear; usually a human voice

Definition: A whisper is a sound usually made by a human voice that is barely able to be heard.

Word		Category		Attributes

Definition:

310 Unit 12

Model

Direct students to the third sentence in "The Gorgon's Head" and have them find the word *mission*.

We may not know what a *mission* is, but we can look at the context around the word to determine its category and attributes. The text says that the king sent him to kill a monster and return with its head. Killing a monster was his specific job or task. That is the category.

Now let's read the rest of the surrounding text and see if we can generate attributes or descriptors for a mission. Killing a monster sounds like a dangerous task. However, when the word *mission* is used in the text, it is described as dangerous. So, I don't think all missions are dangerous, otherwise they wouldn't have needed the adjective. Let's keep looking. Because the king hoped he would "never return," we know that means he had to leave. So a mission must require travel. That is an attribute. I didn't have to know anything about mission; I just had to read closely. Now that I have my category and attributes, I can write a definition: *A mission is a job or task that often requires travel.*

Guided and Independent Practice

Dictionaries

Repeat the process for the second word, allowing students to provide the category, attributes, and definition for you. Then, have partners complete the activity. Explain that they may choose and define any unknown word from the passage for the last item. Have partners use a dictionary to verify their definitions and make corrections as needed.

Note: Base the number of modeled and guided examples on student ability and progress. Challenge them with independent practice when appropriate.

Vocabulary Concept: Analogies

We have been working on different types of analogies in the past two units. We learned that analogies are logic problems based on two pairs of words that have the same relationship. What is an analogy? (a logic problem based on two pairs of words that have the same relationship)

Antonym and Synonym Analogies

We explored antonym analogies and synonym analogies. Words that are antonyms have what kind of meanings? (opposite meanings) Words that are synonyms have what kind of meanings? (similar meanings) Write the following analogies on the board:

dark : light :: hot : cold

blanket : quilt :: slacks : pants

Look at the two analogies on the board. Read the first analogy. What kind of analogy is this? (an antonym analogy) Correct, because both sets of words are antonyms. They have opposite meanings. Read the second analogy. What kind of analogy is this? (a synonym analogy) Yes, both pairs of words have similar meanings.

Part-to-Whole Analogies

Words can be related in different ways. Another way words are related is that they can give us more information about an object. It can name a part of an object or tell how something is used. Write the word *desk* on the board.

Look at my desk. One part of my desk is its legs. Write the word *book* on the board. One part of a book is its cover. So I could create an analogy that describes parts of things. Complete the analogy so it reads: leg : desk :: cover : book.

This is a part-to-whole analogy. It's important to note the word order in an analogy. It would not be correct to say *desk* is to *leg* as *cover* is to *book*. Each word pair has to mirror the same word order or relationship. I could say *leg* is to *desk* as *cover* is to *book* because now both pairs start with the part and end with the whole. Think about computers and video game systems. Work with your partner to create a part-to-whole analogy. After sufficient time, have volunteers share their analogies.

Function Analogies

We can also create relationships between words by talking about their function or use. Write the word *pens* on the board. What do we use pens for? (to write) Write *pens : write* on the board. Correct, so we have the first part of an analogy based on the purpose or function of something.

Write *feet* on the board. What do we use our feet for? (to walk) Add *:: feet : walk* to complete the analogy on the board. Now we can say *pens* are to *write* as *feet* are to *walk*.

Direct students to Part A on page 311 in their Student Books and read the instructions aloud.

Model

Listen as I read the first analogy. *Finger* is to *hand* as *leaf* is to *tree.* I have to ask myself what is the relationship of *finger* to *hand* and *leaf* to *tree*? Hands have fingers and trees have leaves. I realize this is a part-to-whole analogy. Write the following sentence on the board:

> *A finger is part of a hand, and a leaf is part of a tree.*

Have students write the explanation in their Student Books.

Guided and Independent Practice

Read the remaining analogies and guide students in developing their explanations.

Lesson 6 | Vocabulary

Analogies

Part A

Read each analogy and determine the relationship between the pairs of words. Write a sentence that explains the relationship.

1. finger : hand :: leaf : tree
   A finger is part of a hand, and a leaf is part of a tree.
2. glasses : see :: cane : walk
   Glasses help you see, and a cane helps you walk.
3. spend : save :: give : get
   The opposite of spend is to save, and the opposite of give is to get.
4. great : good :: strange : odd
   If something is great it is good, and if something is strange it is odd.
5. moan : whale :: chirp : bird
   Whales communicate through moans, and birds communicate through chirps.

Unit 12 311

Note: Base the number of modeled and guided examples on student ability and progress. Challenge them with independent practice when appropriate.

Direct students to Part B on page 312 in their Student Books and read the instructions aloud. Have students choral read the words in the word bank.

Lesson 6 | Vocabulary

Analogies (*cont.*)

Part B

Use the word bank to complete the analogies.

Word Bank

movie	bus	necklace	soft	dog
transport	easy	axe	book	feet

1. gloves : hands :: socks: feet
2. now : later :: easy : hard
3. rap: music :: horror : movie
4. ring : finger :: necklace : neck
5. kitten : cat :: puppy : dog
6. music : listen :: book : read
7. rock : hard :: velvet : soft
8. hammer : strike :: axe : cut
9. shield : protect :: car : transport
10. boat : river :: bus : pavement

312 Unit 12

Model

Listen as I read the first part of the analogy: *gloves* are to *hands*. I know gloves are something you wear on your hands, so this could be a function analogy. The next word is *socks*, so I am going to look for a word that tells what you do with socks. I think *feet* is my best choice because you wear socks on your feet. I'll put *feet* in the blank. The analogy is: Gloves are to hands as socks are to feet. I need to check my analogy by explaining the relationship. Gloves are worn on hands, and socks are worn on feet. That makes sense, and my word order is consistent.

Guided Practice

Guide students in completion of the second analogy, asking students to help you determine the missing word and dictate an explanation sentence.

Independent Practice

Have students complete the remaining analogies independently. Review the answers as a class.

Note: Base the number of modeled and guided examples on student ability and progress. Challenge them with independent practice when appropriate.

Writing

Objective

- Write sentences using a variety of adjectives to add interest.

Masterpiece Sentences poster

Masterpiece Sentences

Direct students to page 313 in their Student Books. Today, you will work on Step 4: Paint the Subject using a variety of adjectives. You will need to pay special attention to the order of your chosen adjectives. After answering the painter questions, write your final sentences on the lines. Have students share their final sentences with the class.

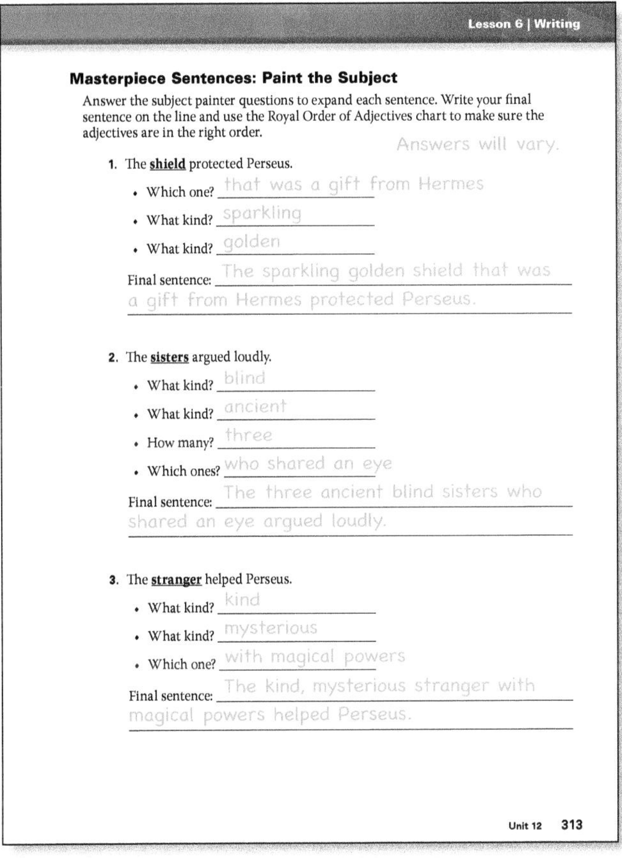

Lesson 6 | Writing

Masterpiece Sentences: Paint the Subject

Answer the subject painter questions to expand each sentence. Write your final sentence on the line and use the Royal Order of Adjectives chart to make sure the adjectives are in the right order.

Answers will vary.

1. The **shield** protected Perseus.
   - Which one? that was a gift from Hermes
   - What kind? sparkling
   - What kind? golden

   Final sentence: The sparkling golden shield that was a gift from Hermes protected Perseus.

2. The **sisters** argued loudly.
   - What kind? blind
   - What kind? ancient
   - How many? three
   - Which ones? who shared an eye

   Final sentence: The three ancient blind sisters who shared an eye argued loudly.

3. The **stranger** helped Perseus.
   - What kind? kind
   - What kind? mysterious
   - Which one? with magical powers

   Final sentence: The kind, mysterious stranger with magical powers helped Perseus.

Unit 12 313

Reading

Objective

- Read an informational text.

Introduction of Secondary Text: "Mythological Women"

Direct students to pages 314 and 315 in their Student Books or have them tear out the extra copy of "Mythological Women" from the back of their book.

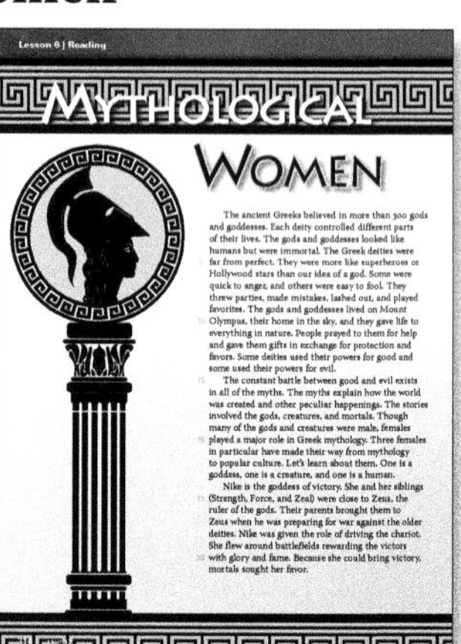

Lesson 6 | Reading

MYTHOLOGICAL WOMEN

The ancient Greeks believed in more than 300 gods and goddesses. Each deity controlled different parts of their lives. The gods and goddesses looked like humans but were immortal. The Greek deities were far from perfect. They were more like superheroes or Hollywood stars than our idea of a god. Some were quick to anger, and others were easy to fool. They threw parties, made mistakes, lashed out, and played favorites. The gods and goddesses lived on Mount Olympus, their home in the sky, and they gave life to everything in nature. People prayed to them for help and gave them gifts in exchange for protection and favors. Some deities used their powers for good and some used their powers for evil.

The constant battle between good and evil exists in all of the myths. The myths explain how the world was created and other peculiar happenings. The stories involved the gods, creatures, and mortals. Though many of the gods and creatures were male, females played a major role in Greek mythology. Three females in particular have made their way from mythology to popular culture. Let's learn about them. One is a goddess, one is a creature, and one is a human.

Nike is the goddess of victory. She and her siblings (Strength, Force, and Zeal) were close to Zeus, the ruler of the gods. Their parents brought them to Zeus when he was preparing for war against the older deities. Nike was given the role of driving the chariot. She flew around battlefields rewarding the victors with glory and fame. Because she could bring victory, mortals sought her favor.

Note: To minimize flipping back and forth between the pages, a copy of each text has been included in the back of the Student Books. Encourage students to tear this out and use it when working on activities that require the use of the text.

To gain a better understanding of Greek mythology and deepen your knowledge of mythological characters, we have a second text selection for this unit. With the exception of Athena, all of the characters you have met through the text readings have been male. This text explores the role of women in Greek mythology. You will read about three different kinds of mythological characters: goddesses, creatures, and humans.

To ensure engagement, let's get ready to read. You know what that means. It means eyes and pencils on text. It also means to constantly question your understanding of the text as it is being read. Remember, proficient readers monitor their comprehension through this type of questioning. Ready? Let's begin.

Read the text aloud.

Note: While the lessons are written for a teacher read aloud, it is important that your students read as much and as often as they can. Assign readings that meet the needs of your students, based on your observations or data. This is a good opportunity to stretch students, but if they become frustrated, return to the read-aloud method.

Mythological Women

The ancient Greeks believed in more than 300 gods and goddesses. Each deity controlled different parts of their lives. The gods and goddesses looked like humans but were immortal. The Greek deities were far from perfect. They were more like superheroes or Hollywood stars than our idea of a god. Some were quick to anger, and others were easy to fool. They threw parties, made mistakes, lashed out, and played favorites. The gods and goddesses lived on Mount Olympus, their home in the sky, and they gave life to everything in nature. People prayed to them for help and gave them gifts in exchange for protection and favors. Some deities used their powers for good and some used their powers for evil.

The constant battle between good and evil exists in all of the myths. The myths explain how the world was created and other peculiar happenings. The stories involved the gods, creatures, and mortals. Though many of the gods and creatures were male, females played a major role in Greek mythology. Three females in particular have made their way from mythology to popular culture. Let's learn about them. One is a goddess, one is a creature, and one is a human.

Nike is the goddess of victory. She and her siblings (Strength, Force, and Zeal) were close to Zeus, the ruler of the gods. Their parents brought them to Zeus when he was preparing for war against the older deities. Nike was given the role of driving the chariot. She flew around battlefields rewarding the victors with glory and fame. Because she could bring victory, mortals sought her favor.

Medusa was once very beautiful and lived far in the north where the sun didn't visit. Being very curious, she wanted to see the sun. She asked the goddess Athena for permission to visit the south, but Athena refused. Medusa got angry and accused Athena of being jealous of her beauty. Athena was angered and punished Medusa by turning her hair into snakes. She made Medusa so ugly that whoever looked at her eyes would turn to stone. As punishment for her vanity, Medusa would live a life of solitude. Nobody would find her beautiful again for as long as she lived.

Pandora, the first mortal woman, was created by the gods and was given many gifts. She was beautiful, charming, cunning, deceitful, skillful, and very curious. She was made to punish Prometheus, a Titan who liked humans. Prometheus had stolen fire from the gods and given it to man against the wishes of the gods. Zeus decided to punish Prometheus and man, with the creation of Pandora, whom he offered to Prometheus's brother as a gift.

Zeus gave Pandora a box, which she was forbidden to open. Pandora always wondered what was in the box, and finally, her curiosity overcame her. She opened the box, and from it flew hate, anger, sickness, poverty, and every bad thing in the world. Luckily, before she was able to slam the lid down, the final thing escaped—hope. If hope had been left in the box, people would have struggled against all of these bad things without hope for something better. As Zeus had intended, Pandora's opening of the box brought great despair to Prometheus. To watch people suffer was just as bad as suffering himself.

Ancient Greeks believed the gods and goddesses held the world in their hands and that they controlled all of nature and the people on Earth. Their punishments were cruel and ruthless, but the morals of the stories have survived the test of time.

Have partners discuss the text.

Lesson 7

Lesson Opener

Before the lesson, choose one of the following activities to write on the board or post on the *LANGUAGE! Live* Class Wall online.

- *Write three sentences in conditional tense about Pandora, Nike, and Medusa.*
- *Write a sentence describing Pandora using at least three adjectives. Remember the royal order.*
- *If you could have a "super power," what would it be and why?*

Reading

Objectives

- Read with purpose and understanding.
- Identify and explain explicit details from text.
- Take notes on a text.
- Identify idioms in text.
- Identify characters, setting, and basic plot elements in a narrative.

Guided Highlighting of "The Gorgon's Head"

Today we're going to reread "The Gorgon's Head." We will pay close attention to how the author develops the plot or story. We will note how the characters are introduced and how they contribute to the story.

Good writers use characters to help develop their plot or story line. They use dialogue and descriptors to make the characters believable. Good readers pay attention to the details shared by authors because these details provide clues about how the story will develop.

As we read today, we will mark places in the text that illustrate the story elements. This will include setting, characters, and events that contribute to the development of the plot.

Direct students to the Story Elements chart on page 163 in their Student Books. Review the story elements.

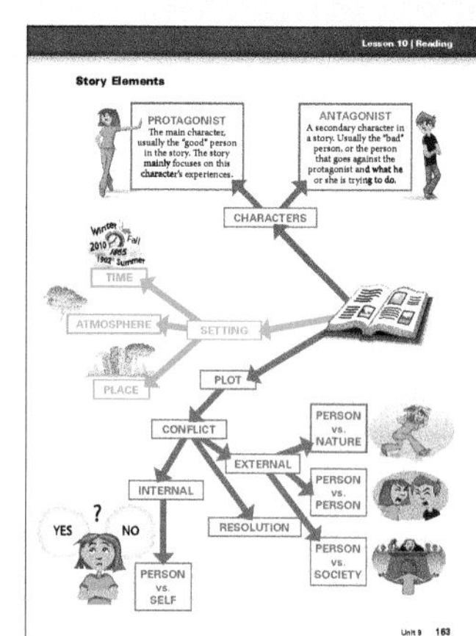

The major elements of this chart are setting, characters, and plot. Under the plot, notice we have a conflict and a resolution. Every story needs a problem, something that prompts the characters into action in an attempt to solve the problem. In some stories the characters never really solve their problem, but in "The Gorgon's Head," Perseus succeeds in accomplishing a very dangerous mission.

Highlighters or colored pencils

Direct students to page 316 in their Student books. Have students get out a colored pencil or highlighter. Listen and mark each bold vocabulary word as I read it aloud. I will pause after every word to give you time to process whether you know the word and its meaning. We will review your ratings from Lesson 1 after we finish.

- image—*Image* means "the form or appearance of someone or something." Say *image.* (image) Perseus saw Medusa's *image* reflected in his shield.
- intelligent—If someone is *intelligent,* he is smart or he reflects good judgment or sound thought. Say *intelligent.* (intelligent) Perseus made the *intelligent* decision to follow Hermes's advice.
- undertake—*Undertake* means "to attempt or take on a task." Say *undertake.* (undertake) If Perseus had not made the decision to *undertake* the mission, he and his mom would have likely been treated poorly by the king for many more years.
- recover—*Recover* means "to get back something lost or to regain." Say *recover.* (recover) The Three Gray Women were able to *recover* their stolen eye.
- invisible—*Invisible* means "impossible to see or not visible." Say *invisible.* (invisible) The *invisible* Athena flew beside Perseus without being noticed.
- enormous—If something is *enormous* it is very great in size or amount. Say *enormous.* (enormous) The Gorgons were *enormous,* though they appeared to be small from the sky above.
- perceive—*Perceive* means "to become aware of through sight or observation." Say *perceive.* (perceive) Though she was invisible, Perseus was able to *perceive* Athena's presence because of a sound.
- proceed—*Proceed* means "to begin and carry on an action or movement." Say *proceed.* (proceed) With Hermes's help, Perseus agreed to *proceed* with the dangerous mission, though he was clearly scared.

Talk with your partners about any vocabulary word that is still confusing for you to read or understand. Share your ratings from Lesson 1. Were you honest about your word knowledge? Now is the time to do something about it!

It's time to reread the text the way proficient readers do. You will read the text "The Gorgon's Head" one section at a time. After each section, you will monitor your understanding by circling the check mark or the question mark. I will provide specific instructions on how to mark the text that will help you with your comprehension and writing.

Note: Because this is the final unit and students should have mastered the concepts in guided highlighting, line numbers have been omitted intentionally. If you feel your students cannot handle the task of highlighting important information without line numbers, please provide them for students.

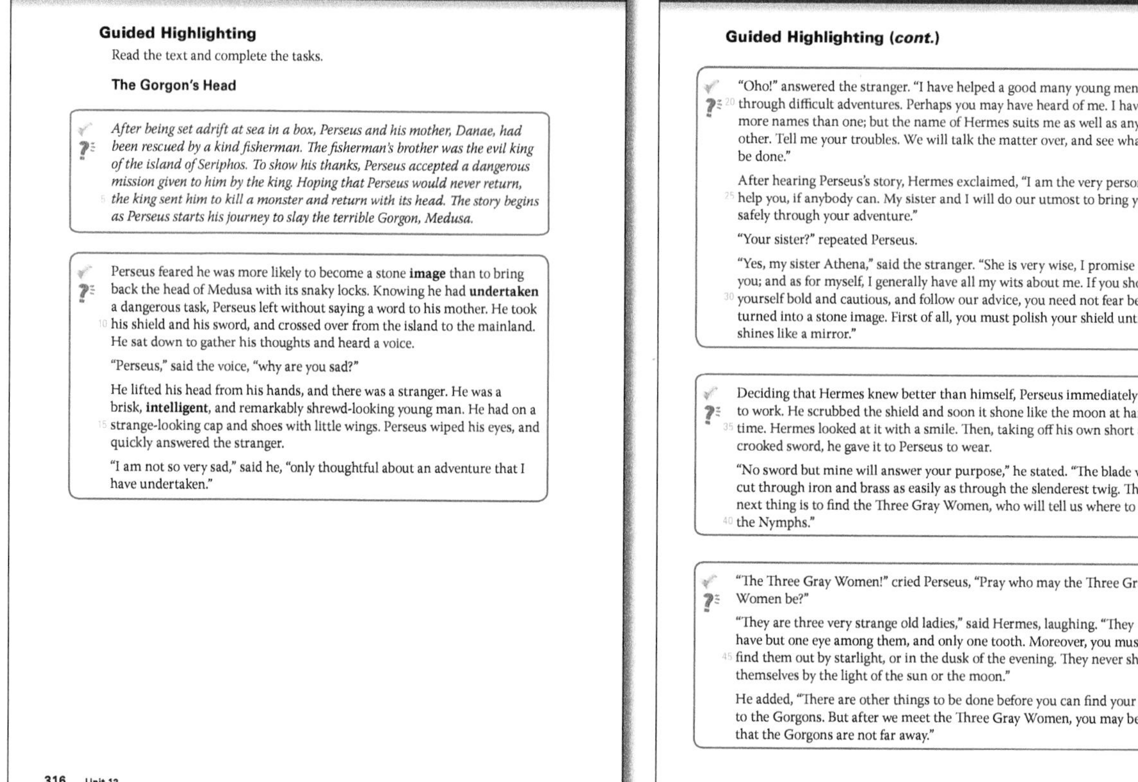
Lesson 7 | Reading

Guided Highlighting

Read the text and complete the tasks.

The Gorgon's Head

After being set adrift at sea in a box, Perseus and his mother, Danae, had been rescued by a kind fisherman. The fisherman's brother was the evil king of the island of Seriphos. To show his thanks, Perseus accepted a dangerous mission given to him by the king. Hoping that Perseus would never return, the king sent him to kill a monster and return with its head. The story begins as Perseus starts his journey to slay the terrible Gorgon, Medusa.

Perseus feared he was more likely to become a stone **image** than to bring back the head of Medusa with its snaky locks. Knowing he had **undertaken** a dangerous task, Perseus left without saying a word to his mother. He took his shield and his sword, and crossed over from the island to the mainland. He sat down to gather his thoughts and heard a voice.

"Perseus," said the voice, "why are you sad?"

He lifted his head from his hands, and there was a stranger. He was a brisk, **intelligent**, and remarkably shrewd-looking young man. He had on a strange-looking cap and shoes with little wings. Perseus wiped his eyes, and quickly answered the stranger.

"I am not so very sad," said he, "only thoughtful about an adventure that I have undertaken."

316 Unit 12

Lesson 7 | Reading

Guided Highlighting (*cont.*)

"Oho!" answered the stranger. "I have helped a good many young men through difficult adventures. Perhaps you may have heard of me. I have more names than one; but the name of Hermes suits me as well as any other. Tell me your troubles. We will talk the matter over, and see what can be done."

After hearing Perseus's story, Hermes exclaimed, "I am the very person to help you, if anybody can. My sister and I will do our utmost to bring you safely through your adventure."

"Your sister?" repeated Perseus.

"Yes, my sister Athena," said the stranger. "She is very wise, I promise you; and as for myself, I generally have all my wits about me. If you show yourself bold and cautious, and follow our advice, you need not fear being turned into a stone image. First of all, you must polish your shield until it shines like a mirror."

Deciding that Hermes knew better than himself, Perseus immediately set to work. He scrubbed the shield and soon it shone like the moon at harvest time. Hermes looked at it with a smile. Then, taking off his own short and crooked sword, he gave it to Perseus to wear.

"No sword but mine will answer your purpose," he stated. "The blade will cut through iron and brass as easily as through the slenderest twig. The next thing is to find the Three Gray Women, who will tell us where to find the Nymphs."

"The Three Gray Women!" cried Perseus, "Pray who may the Three Gray Women be?"

"They are three very strange old ladies," said Hermes, laughing. "They have but one eye among them, and only one tooth. Moreover, you must find them out by starlight, or in the dusk of the evening. They never show themselves by the light of the sun or the moon."

He added, "There are other things to be done before you can find your way to the Gorgons. But after we meet the Three Gray Women, you may be sure that the Gorgons are not far away."

Unit 12 317

With eyes on text, listen to each section as it is read to you. Use your pencil eraser to follow along. Let's read the introductory paragraph, lines 1–6. Read the paragraph.

Note: While the lessons are written for a teacher read aloud, it is important that your students read as much and as often as they can. Assign readings that meet the needs of your students, based on your observations or data. This is a good opportunity to stretch students, but if they become frustrated, return to the read-aloud method.

The Gorgon's Head

After being set adrift at sea in a box, Perseus and his mother, Danae, had been rescued by a kind fisherman. The fisherman's brother was the evil king of the island of Seriphos. To show his thanks, Perseus accepted a dangerous mission given to him by the king. Hoping that Perseus would never return, the king sent him to kill a monster and return with its head. The story begins as Perseus starts his journey to slay the terrible Gorgon, Medusa.

- Circle the check mark or question mark for this section. Draw a question mark over words or phrases that confuse you.
- Mark the characters referenced in this paragraph. (Perseus, Danae, kind fisherman, king)

- Mark the setting. (Seriphos)
- Mark Perseus's mission. (slay the terrible Gorgon)

Let's read the next section. Read the section.

Perseus feared he was more likely to become a stone image than to bring back the head of Medusa with its snaky locks. Knowing he had undertaken a dangerous task, Perseus left without saying a word to his mother. He took his shield and his sword, and crossed over from the island to the mainland. He sat down to gather his thoughts and heard a voice.

"Perseus," said the voice, "why are you sad?"

He lifted his head from his hands, and there was a stranger. He was a brisk, intelligent, and remarkably shrewd-looking young man. He had on a strange-looking cap and shoes with little wings. Perseus wiped his eyes, and quickly answered the stranger.

"I am not so very sad," said he, "only thoughtful about an adventure that I have undertaken."

- Circle the check mark or question mark for this section. Draw a question mark over words or phrases that confuse you.
- Mark why Perseus did not tell his mother good-bye. (knowing he had undertaken a dangerous task)
- Mark how you know Perseus was sad, despite his response. (wiped his eyes)

Let's read the next section. Read the section.

"Oho!" answered the stranger. "I have helped a good many young men through difficult adventures. Perhaps you may have heard of me. I have more names than one; but the name of Hermes suits me as well as any other. Tell me your troubles. We will talk the matter over, and see what can be done."

After hearing Perseus's story, Hermes exclaimed, "I am the very person to help you, if anybody can. My sister and I will do our utmost to bring you safely through your adventure."

"Your sister?" repeated Perseus.

"Yes, my sister Athena," said the stranger. "She is very wise, I promise you; and as for myself, I generally have all my wits about me. If you show yourself bold and cautious, and follow our advice, you need not fear being turned into a stone image. First of all, you must polish your shield until it shines like a mirror."

- Circle the check mark or question mark for this section. Draw a question mark over words or phrases that confuse you.
- Mark the names of the new characters. (Hermes, Athena)

- Mark character traits of Athena. (She is very wise)
- Mark character traits of Hermes. (I generally have all my wits about me)
- Mark what is required of Perseus to keep himself from becoming stone. (show yourself bold and cautious, follow our advice)
- Mark his first task. (polish your shield)
- Mark the simile that describes how the polished shield should look. (like a mirror)

Let's read the next section. Read the section.

Deciding that Hermes knew better than himself, Perseus immediately set to work. He scrubbed the shield and soon it shone like the moon at harvest time. Hermes looked at it with a smile. Then, taking off his own short and crooked sword, he gave it to Perseus to wear.

"No sword but mine will answer your purpose," he stated. "The blade will cut through iron and brass as easily as through the slenderest twig. The next thing is to find the Three Gray Women, who will tell us where to find the Nymphs."

- Circle the check mark or question mark for this section. Draw a question mark over words or phrases that confuse you.
- Mark the simile that describes the brightness of the shield. (shone like the moon at harvest time)
- Mark how you know Hermes is pleased with Perseus's work. (Hermes looked at it with a smile)
- Mark how you know his sword is sharp. (cut through iron and brass as easily as through the slenderest twig)
- Mark the next thing they must do. (find the Three Gray Women)
- Mark what they hope to learn from the Three Gray Women. (where to find the Nymphs)

Let's read the next section. Read the section.

"The Three Gray Women!" cried Perseus, "Pray who may the Three Gray Women be?"

"They are three very strange old ladies," said Hermes, laughing. "They have but one eye among them, and only one tooth. Moreover, you must find them out by starlight, or in the dusk of the evening. They never show themselves by the light of the sun or the moon."

He added, "There are other things to be done before you can find your way to the Gorgons. But after we meet the Three Gray Women, you may be sure that the Gorgons are not far away."

- Circle the check mark or question mark for this section. Draw a question mark over words or phrases that confuse you.
- Mark what is unusual about the Three Gray Women. (have but one eye, one tooth, never show themselves by the light of the sun or the moon)
- Mark why Perseus can't go straight to the Gorgons. (There are other things to be done)

Let's read the next section. Read the section.

They set out and walked at a brisk pace; so brisk, indeed, that Perseus found it rather difficult to keep up with his nimble friend Hermes. To say the truth, he had a suspicion that Hermes had a pair of wings on his cap along with wings on his shoes! When he looked straight at Hermes, he only saw an odd kind of cap. The twisted staff was evidently a great convenience to Hermes. It enabled him to proceed so fast, that Perseus, though a remarkably fit young man, began to feel out of breath.

"Here!" cried Hermes, at last, "take you the staff, for you need it a great deal more than I. Are there no better walkers than you in the island of Seriphos?"

"I could walk pretty well," said Perseus, glancing slyly at his companion's feet, "if only I had a pair of winged shoes."

"We must see about getting you a pair," answered Hermes.

The staff helped Perseus tremendously. In fact, the stick seemed to be alive in his hand, and to lend some of its life to Perseus.

- Circle the check mark or question mark for this section. Draw a question mark over words or phrases that confuse you.
- Mark the evidence that proves they were moving too fast for Perseus. (difficult to keep up; out of breath)
- Mark the attributes of Hermes that enabled him to move so quickly. (pair of winged shoes, wings on the side of his head, staff)
- Mark the description of Perseus. (remarkably fit; young)
- Mark the way Perseus looked at Hermes's feet. (slyly)
- Mark words that describe the power of the staff. (alive in his hand, and to lend some of its life)

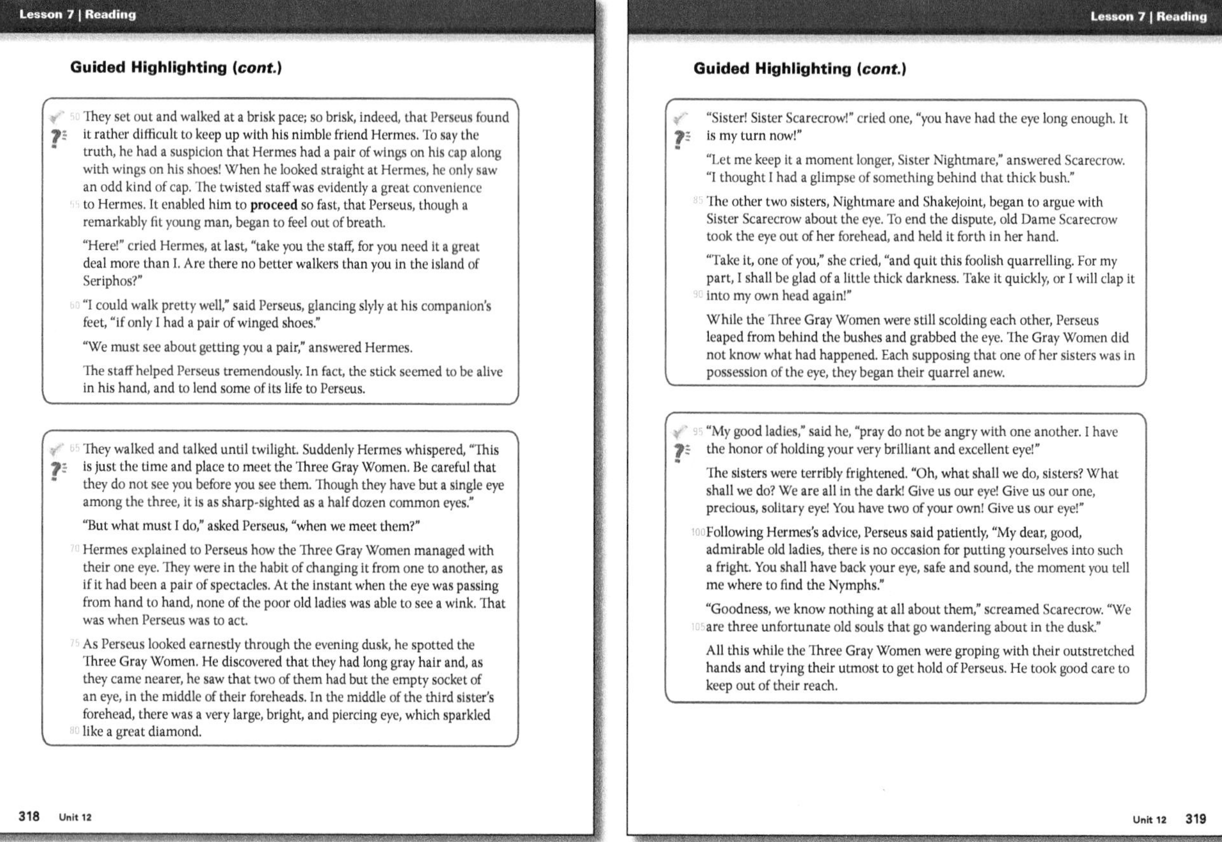

Lesson 7 | Reading

Guided Highlighting (*cont.*)

They set out and walked at a brisk pace; so brisk, indeed, that Perseus found it rather difficult to keep up with his nimble friend Hermes. To say the truth, he had a suspicion that Hermes had a pair of wings on his cap along with wings on his shoes! When he looked straight at Hermes, he only saw an odd kind of cap. The twisted staff was evidently a great convenience to Hermes. It enabled him to **proceed** so fast, that Perseus, though a remarkably fit young man, began to feel out of breath.

"Here!" cried Hermes, at last, "take you the staff, for you need it a great deal more than I. Are there no better walkers than you in the island of Seriphos?"

"I could walk pretty well," said Perseus, glancing slyly at his companion's feet, "if only I had a pair of winged shoes."

"We must see about getting you a pair," answered Hermes.

The staff helped Perseus tremendously. In fact, the stick seemed to be alive in his hand, and to lend some of its life to Perseus.

They walked and talked until twilight. Suddenly Hermes whispered, "This is just the time and place to meet the Three Gray Women. Be careful that they do not see you before you see them. Though they have but a single eye among the three, it is as sharp-sighted as a half dozen common eyes."

"But what must I do," asked Perseus, "when we meet them?"

Hermes explained to Perseus how the Three Gray Women managed with their one eye. They were in the habit of changing it from one to another, as if it had been a pair of spectacles. At the instant when the eye was passing from hand to hand, none of the poor old ladies was able to see a wink. That was when Perseus was to act.

As Perseus looked earnestly through the evening dusk, he spotted the Three Gray Women. He discovered that they had long gray hair and, as they came nearer, he saw that two of them had but the empty socket of an eye, in the middle of their foreheads. In the middle of the third sister's forehead, there was a very large, bright, and piercing eye, which sparkled like a great diamond.

318 Unit 12

Lesson 7 | Reading

Guided Highlighting (*cont.*)

"Sister! Sister Scarecrow!" cried one, "you have had the eye long enough. It is my turn now!"

"Let me keep it a moment longer, Sister Nightmare," answered Scarecrow. "I thought I had a glimpse of something behind that thick bush."

The other two sisters, Nightmare and Shakejoint, began to argue with Sister Scarecrow about the eye. To end the dispute, old Dame Scarecrow took the eye out of her forehead, and held it forth in her hand.

"Take it, one of you," she cried, "and quit this foolish quarrelling. For my part, I shall be glad of a little thick darkness. Take it quickly, or I will clap it into my own head again!"

While the Three Gray Women were still scolding each other, Perseus leaped from behind the bushes and grabbed the eye. The Gray Women did not know what had happened. Each supposing that one of her sisters was in possession of the eye, they began their quarrel anew.

"My good ladies," said he, "pray do not be angry with one another. I have the honor of holding your very brilliant and excellent eye!"

The sisters were terribly frightened. "Oh, what shall we do, sisters? What shall we do? We are all in the dark! Give us our eye! Give us our one, precious, solitary eye! You have two of your own! Give us our eye!"

Following Hermes's advice, Perseus said patiently, "My dear, good, admirable old ladies, there is no occasion for putting yourselves into such a fright. You shall have back your eye, safe and sound, the moment you tell me where to find the Nymphs."

"Goodness, we know nothing at all about them," screamed Scarecrow. "We are three unfortunate old souls that go wandering about in the dusk."

All this while the Three Gray Women were groping with their outstretched hands and trying their utmost to get hold of Perseus. He took good care to keep out of their reach.

Unit 12 319

Let's read the next section. Read the section.

They walked and talked until twilight. Suddenly Hermes whispered, "This is just the time and place to meet the Three Gray Women. Be careful that they do not see you before you see them. Though they have but a single eye among the three, it is as sharp-sighted as a half dozen common eyes."

"But what must I do," asked Perseus, "when we meet them?"

Hermes explained to Perseus how the Three Gray Women managed with their one eye. They were in the habit of changing it from one to another, as if it had been a pair of spectacles. At the instant when the eye was passing from hand to hand, none of the poor old ladies was able to see a wink. That was when Perseus was to act.

As Perseus looked earnestly through the evening dusk, he spotted the Three Gray Women. He discovered that they had long gray hair and, as they came nearer, he saw that two of them had but the empty socket of an eye, in the middle of their foreheads. In the middle of the third sister's forehead, there was a very large, bright, and piercing eye, which sparkled like a great diamond.

- Circle the check mark or question mark for this section. Draw a question mark over words or phrases that confuse you.

- Mark the word that indicates Hermes didn't want to be noticed. (whispered)
- Mark what the women do with the eye. (changing it from one to another)
- Mark the proof that they can see very well with their eye. (as sharp sighted as half a dozen common eyes)
- Mark the line that tells when Perseus should grab the eye. (At the instant when the eye was passing from hand to hand, none of the poor old ladies was able to see a wink.)
- Mark what Perseus spotted through the dusk of the evening. (the Three Gray Women)

Let's read the next section. Read the section.

"Sister! Sister Scarecrow!" cried one, "you have had the eye long enough. It is my turn now!"

"Let me keep it a moment longer, Sister Nightmare," answered Scarecrow. "I thought I had a glimpse of something behind that thick bush."

The other two sisters, Nightmare and Shakejoint, began to argue with Sister Scarecrow about the eye. To end the dispute, old Dame Scarecrow took the eye out of her forehead, and held it forth in her hand.

"Take it, one of you," she cried, "and quit this foolish quarrelling. For my part, I shall be glad of a little thick darkness. Take it quickly, or I will clap it into my own head again!"

While the Three Gray Women were still scolding each other, Perseus leaped from behind the bushes and grabbed the eye. The Gray Women did not know what had happened. Each supposing that one of her sisters was in possession of the eye, they began their quarrel anew.

- Circle the check mark or question mark for this section. Draw a question mark over words or phrases that confuse you.
- Mark the evidence that Scarecrow may have known Perseus was near. (I thought I had a glimpse of something behind that thick bush.)
- Mark the evidence that proves Scarecrow was right about something hiding in the bushes. (Perseus leaped from behind the bushes)
- Mark the four words that mean fight or fighting that explain what the sisters often do. (argue, quarrelling, scolding, quarrel)
- Mark the names of the sisters. (Scarecrow, Nightmare, Shakejoint)
- Mark what the sisters did, unaware that Perseus had their eye. (began their quarrel anew)

Let's read the next section. **Read the section.**

"My good ladies," said he, "pray do not be angry with one another. I have the honor of holding your very brilliant and excellent eye!"

The sisters were terribly frightened. "Oh, what shall we do, sisters? What shall we do? We are all in the dark! Give us our eye! Give us our one, precious, solitary eye! You have two of your own! Give us our eye!"

Following Hermes's advice, Perseus said patiently, "My dear, good, admirable old ladies, there is no occasion for putting yourselves into such a fright. You shall have back your eye, safe and sound, the moment you tell me where to find the Nymphs."

"Goodness, we know nothing at all about them," screamed Scarecrow. "We are three unfortunate old souls that go wandering about in the dusk."

All this while the Three Gray Women were groping with their outstretched hands and trying their utmost to get hold of Perseus. He took good care to keep out of their reach.

- Circle the check mark or question mark for this section. Draw a question mark over words or phrases that confuse you.
- Mark the pronouns in line 95. Above them, write who they are referring to. (he, I; Perseus)
- Mark an assumption that the sisters made. (You have two of your own!)
- Mark evidence that Perseus is attempting to flatter the ladies. (honor, dear, good, admirable)
- Mark what Perseus wants in exchange for the eye. (where to find the Nymphs)
- Mark how Perseus describes the eye. (very brilliant and excellent eye)
- Mark the lie that the sisters told. (we know nothing at all about them)
- Mark how Scarecrow describes herself and her sisters. (three unfortunate old souls that go wandering about in the dusk)

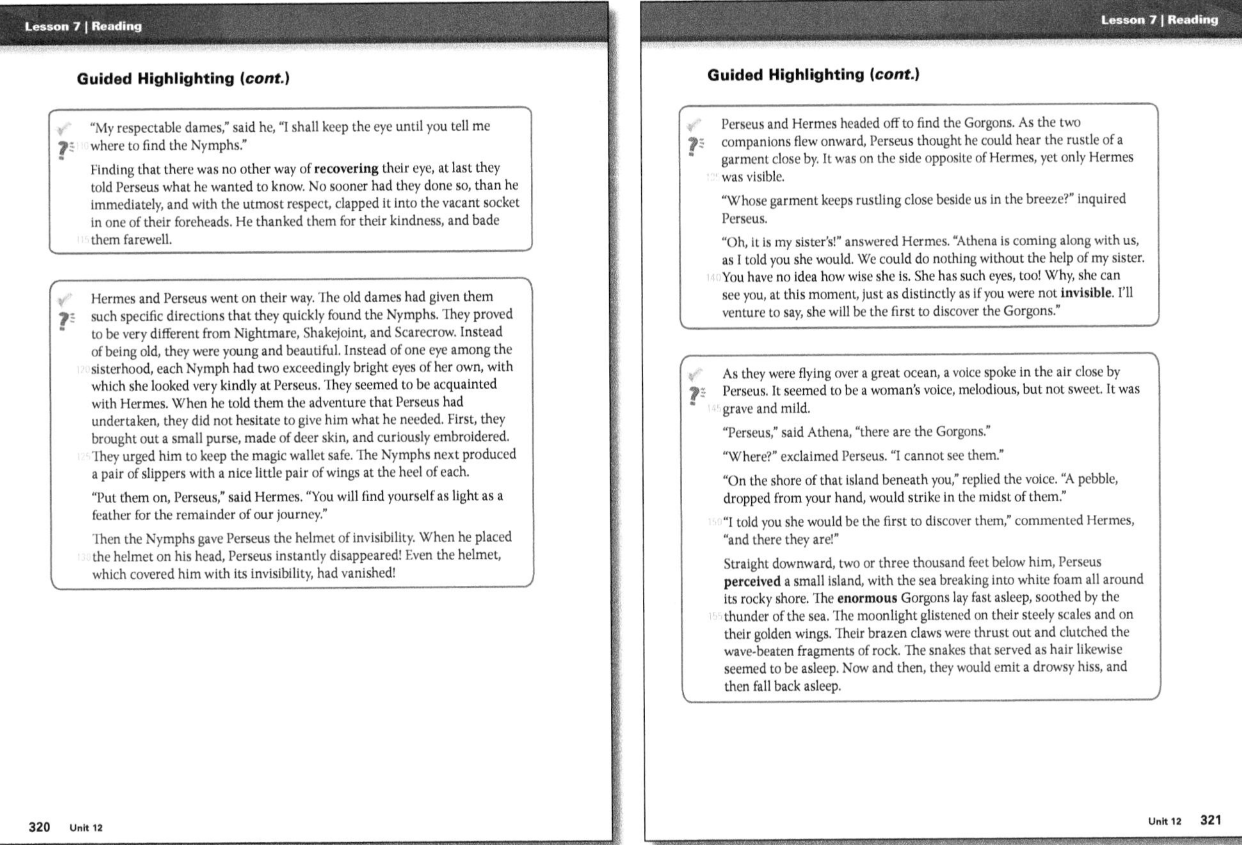
Lesson 7 | Reading

Guided Highlighting (*cont.*)

"My respectable dames," said he, "I shall keep the eye until you tell me where to find the Nymphs."

Finding that there was no other way of **recovering** their eye, at last they told Perseus what he wanted to know. No sooner had they done so, than he immediately, and with the utmost respect, clapped it into the vacant socket in one of their foreheads. He thanked them for their kindness, and bade them farewell.

Hermes and Perseus went on their way. The old dames had given them such specific directions that they quickly found the Nymphs. They proved to be very different from Nightmare, Shakejoint, and Scarecrow. Instead of being old, they were young and beautiful. Instead of one eye among the sisterhood, each Nymph had two exceedingly bright eyes of her own, with which she looked very kindly at Perseus. They seemed to be acquainted with Hermes. When he told them the adventure that Perseus had undertaken, they did not hesitate to give him what he needed. First, they brought out a small purse, made of deer skin, and curiously embroidered. They urged him to keep the magic wallet safe. The Nymphs next produced a pair of slippers with a nice little pair of wings at the heel of each.

"Put them on, Perseus," said Hermes. "You will find yourself as light as a feather for the remainder of our journey."

Then the Nymphs gave Perseus the helmet of invisibility. When he placed the helmet on his head, Perseus instantly disappeared! Even the helmet, which covered him with its invisibility, had vanished!

320 Unit 12

Lesson 7 | Reading

Guided Highlighting (*cont.*)

Perseus and Hermes headed off to find the Gorgons. As the two companions flew onward, Perseus thought he could hear the rustle of a garment close by. It was on the side opposite of Hermes, yet only Hermes was visible.

"Whose garment keeps rustling close beside us in the breeze?" inquired Perseus.

"Oh, it is my sister's!" answered Hermes. "Athena is coming along with us, as I told you she would. We could do nothing without the help of my sister. You have no idea how wise she is. She has such eyes, too! Why, she can see you, at this moment, just as distinctly as if you were not **invisible**. I'll venture to say, she will be the first to discover the Gorgons."

As they were flying over a great ocean, a voice spoke in the air close by Perseus. It seemed to be a woman's voice, melodious, but not sweet. It was grave and mild.

"Perseus," said Athena, "there are the Gorgons."

"Where?" exclaimed Perseus. "I cannot see them."

"On the shore of that island beneath you," replied the voice. "A pebble, dropped from your hand, would strike in the midst of them."

"I told you she would be the first to discover them," commented Hermes, "and there they are!"

Straight downward, two or three thousand feet below him, Perseus **perceived** a small island, with the sea breaking into white foam all around its rocky shore. The **enormous** Gorgons lay fast asleep, soothed by the thunder of the sea. The moonlight glistened on their steely scales and on their golden wings. Their brazen claws were thrust out and clutched the wave-beaten fragments of rock. The snakes that served as hair likewise seemed to be asleep. Now and then, they would emit a drowsy hiss, and then fall back asleep.

Unit 12 321

Let's read the next section. Read the section.

"My respectable dames," said he, "I shall keep the eye until you tell me where to find the Nymphs."

Finding that there was no other way of recovering their eye, at last they told Perseus what he wanted to know. No sooner had they done so, than he immediately, and with the utmost respect, clapped it into the vacant socket in one of their foreheads. He thanked them for their kindness, and bade them farewell.

- Circle the check mark or question mark for this section. Draw a question mark over words or phrases that confuse you.
- Go to line 113. Mark the pronoun and write the noun that it is replacing above it. (it; the eye)
- Mark the synonym for *empty*. (vacant)
- Mark the phrase that means the same as "said good-bye." (bade them farewell)
- Mark how Perseus showed he was a man of his word. (with the utmost respect, thanked them for their kindness)

Let's read the next section. Read the section.

Hermes and Perseus went on their way. The old dames had given them such specific directions that they quickly found the Nymphs. They proved to be very different from Nightmare, Shakejoint, and Scarecrow. Instead of being old, they were young and beautiful. Instead of one eye among the sisterhood, each Nymph had two exceedingly bright eyes of her own, with which she looked very kindly at Perseus. They seemed to be acquainted with Hermes. When he told them the adventure that Perseus had undertaken, they did not hesitate to give him what he needed. First, they brought out a small purse, made of deer skin, and curiously embroidered. They urged him to keep the magic wallet safe. The Nymphs next produced a pair of slippers with a nice little pair of wings at the heel of each.

"Put them on, Perseus," said Hermes. "You will find yourself as light as a feather for the remainder of our journey."

Then the Nymphs gave Perseus the helmet of invisibility. When he placed the helmet on his head, Perseus instantly disappeared! Even the helmet, which covered him with its invisibility, had vanished!

- Circle the check mark or question mark for this section. Draw a question mark over words or phrases that confuse you.
- Mark who Hermes and Perseus found. (the Nymphs)
- Mark the details that create the image of the three Nymphs. (young and beautiful, two exceedingly bright eyes, looked very kindly at Perseus)
- Mark the evidence that they knew Hermes. (They seemed to be acquainted with Hermes.)
- Mark the evidence that they were eager to help Perseus complete his mission. (they did not hesitate to give him what he needed)
- Mark the three items Perseus received from the Nymphs. (small purse, pair of slippers with a nice little pair of wings at the heel of each, helmet of invisibility)
- Mark the synonyms in lines 130 and 131. (disappeared; vanished)

Let's read the next section. Read the section.

Perseus and Hermes headed off to find the Gorgons. As the two companions flew onward, Perseus thought he could hear the rustle of a garment close by. It was on the side opposite of Hermes, yet only Hermes was visible.

"Whose garment keeps rustling close beside us in the breeze?" inquired Perseus.

"Oh, it is my sister's!" answered Hermes. "Athena is coming along with us, as I told you she would. We could do nothing without the help of my sister. You have no idea how wise she is. She has such eyes, too! Why, she can see you, at this moment, just as distinctly as if you were not invisible. I'll venture to say, she will be the first to discover the Gorgons."

- Circle the check mark or question mark for this section. Draw a question mark over words or phrases that confuse you.
- Mark how Perseus knew someone was flying next to him besides Hermes. (thought he could hear the rustle of a garment close by his side)
- Mark the proof in line 134 and 135 that Athena is invisible. (yet only Hermes was visible)
- Mark how Hermes describes his sister. (how wise she is, has such eyes)
- Mark why Athena will be the first to discover the Gorgons. (she can see you, at this moment, just as distinctly as if you were not invisible)

Let's read the next section. Read the section.

As they were flying over a great ocean, a voice spoke in the air close by Perseus. It seemed to be a woman's voice, melodious, but not sweet. It was grave and mild.

"Perseus," said Athena, "there are the Gorgons."

"Where?" exclaimed Perseus. "I cannot see them."

"On the shore of that island beneath you," replied the voice. "A pebble, dropped from your hand, would strike in the midst of them."

"I told you she would be the first to discover them," commented Hermes, "and there they are!"

Straight downward, two or three thousand feet below him, Perseus perceived a small island, with the sea breaking into white foam all around its rocky shore. The enormous Gorgons lay fast asleep, soothed by the thunder of the sea. The moonlight glistened on their steely scales and on their golden wings. Their brazen claws were thrust out and clutched the wave-beaten fragments of rock. The snakes that served as hair likewise seemed to be asleep. Now and then, they would emit a drowsy hiss, and then fall back asleep.

- Circle the check mark or question mark for this section. Draw a question mark over words or phrases that confuse you.
- Mark the words that describe Athena's voice. (melodious; not sweet; grave and mild)
- Mark the proof that Athena has superior vision. (I cannot see them.)
- Mark where they found the Gorgons. (a small island, sea breaking into white foam around its rocky shore)
- Mark the words and phrases that paint an image of the Gorgons. (steely scales, golden wings, brazen claws, snakes instead of hair, emit a drowsy hiss)

Let's read the next section. Read the section.

Luckily for Perseus, their faces were completely hidden from him. Had he but looked one instant at them, he would have fallen heavily out of the air, his image in senseless stone.

"Now," whispered Hermes, as he hovered by the side of Perseus, "now is your time to do the deed! Be quick; for, if one of the Gorgons should awake, you are too late!"

"Which one is Medusa?" asked Perseus.

Athena replied in a calm voice, "The Gorgon that is stirring in her sleep is Medusa. Do not look at her! The sight would turn you to stone! Look at the reflection of her face and figure in the bright mirror of your shield."

Perseus now understood Hermes's motive for telling him to polish his shield. In its surface he could safely look at the reflection of the Gorgon's face. The snakes twisted themselves into tumultuous knots, without opening their eyes.

- Circle the check mark or question mark for this section. Draw a question mark over words or phrases that confuse you.
- Mark the part of the Gorgons that Perseus could not look at. (faces)
- Mark what would have happened to Perseus had he looked at one of the Gorgon's faces. (fallen heavily out of the air, an image in senseless stone)
- Go to line 170. Mark the synonym for reason. (motive)
- Mark how Perseus used his shield. (in its surface he could safely look at the reflection of the Gorgon's face)
- Mark how the snakes are described. (twisted themselves into tumultuous knots, without opening their eyes)

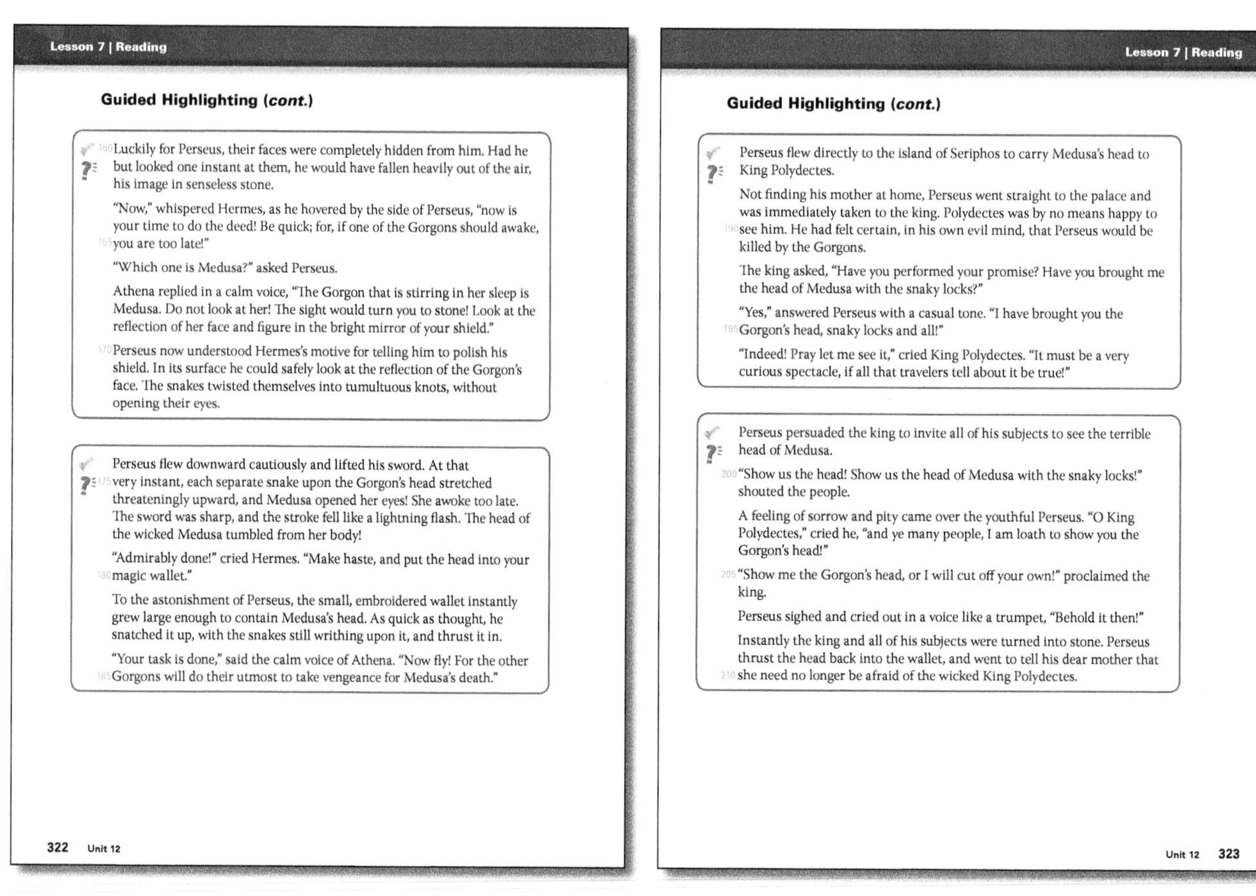

Lesson 7 | Reading

Guided Highlighting (*cont.*)

Luckily for Perseus, their faces were completely hidden from him. Had he but looked one instant at them, he would have fallen heavily out of the air, his image in senseless stone.

"Now," whispered Hermes, as he hovered by the side of Perseus, "now is your time to do the deed! Be quick; for, if one of the Gorgons should awake, you are too late!"

"Which one is Medusa?" asked Perseus.

Athena replied in a calm voice, "The Gorgon that is stirring in her sleep is Medusa. Do not look at her! The sight would turn you to stone! Look at the reflection of her face and figure in the bright mirror of your shield."

Perseus now understood Hermes's motive for telling him to polish his shield. In its surface he could safely look at the reflection of the Gorgon's face. The snakes twisted themselves into tumultuous knots, without opening their eyes.

Perseus flew downward cautiously and lifted his sword. At that very instant, each separate snake upon the Gorgon's head stretched threateningly upward, and Medusa opened her eyes! She awoke too late. The sword was sharp, and the stroke fell like a lightning flash. The head of the wicked Medusa tumbled from her body!

"Admirably done!" cried Hermes. "Make haste, and put the head into your magic wallet."

To the astonishment of Perseus, the small, embroidered wallet instantly grew large enough to contain Medusa's head. As quick as thought, he snatched it up, with the snakes still writhing upon it, and thrust it in.

"Your task is done," said the calm voice of Athena. "Now fly! For the other Gorgons will do their utmost to take vengeance for Medusa's death."

322 Unit 12

Lesson 7 | Reading

Guided Highlighting (*cont.*)

Perseus flew directly to the island of Seriphos to carry Medusa's head to King Polydectes.

Not finding his mother at home, Perseus went straight to the palace and was immediately taken to the king. Polydectes was by no means happy to see him. He had felt certain, in his own evil mind, that Perseus would be killed by the Gorgons.

The king asked, "Have you performed your promise? Have you brought me the head of Medusa with the snaky locks?"

"Yes," answered Perseus with a casual tone. "I have brought you the Gorgon's head, snaky locks and all!"

"Indeed! Pray let me see it," cried King Polydectes. "It must be a very curious spectacle, if all that travelers tell about it be true!"

Perseus persuaded the king to invite all of his subjects to see the terrible head of Medusa.

"Show us the head! Show us the head of Medusa with the snaky locks!" shouted the people.

A feeling of sorrow and pity came over the youthful Perseus. "O King Polydectes," cried he, "and ye many people, I am loath to show you the Gorgon's head!"

"Show me the Gorgon's head, or I will cut off your own!" proclaimed the king.

Perseus sighed and cried out in a voice like a trumpet, "Behold it then!"

Instantly the king and all of his subjects were turned into stone. Perseus thrust the head back into the wallet, and went to tell his dear mother that she need no longer be afraid of the wicked King Polydectes.

Unit 12 323

Let's read the next section. Read the section.

Perseus flew downward cautiously and lifted his sword. At that very instant, each separate snake upon the Gorgon's head stretched threateningly upward, and Medusa opened her eyes! She awoke too late. The sword was sharp, and the stroke fell like a lightning flash. The head of the wicked Medusa tumbled from her body!

"Admirably done!" cried Hermes. "Make haste, and put the head into your magic wallet."

To the astonishment of Perseus, the small, embroidered wallet instantly grew large enough to contain Medusa's head. As quick as thought, he snatched it up, with the snakes still writhing upon it, and thrust it in.

"Your task is done," said the calm voice of Athena. "Now fly! For the other Gorgons will do their utmost to take vengeance for Medusa's death."

- Circle the check mark or question mark for this section. Draw a question mark over words or phrases that confuse you.
- Mark what happened as Perseus lifted his sword. (each separate snake upon the Gorgon's head stretched threateningly upward, and Medusa opened her eyes!)
- Mark the simile that describes the quickness of the sword. (fell like a lightning flash)

- Mark how you know that Perseus is surprised by the size of the wallet. (to the astonishment of Perseus)
- Mark the simile that describes how quickly Perseus picks up Medusa's head. (as quick as thought)
- Mark why Perseus was still in danger. (the other Gorgons will do their utmost to take vengeance for Medusa's death.)

Let's read the next section. Read the section.

Perseus flew directly to the island of Seriphos to carry Medusa's head to King Polydectes.

Not finding his mother at home, Perseus went straight to the palace and was immediately taken to the king. Polydectes was by no means happy to see him. He had felt certain, in his own evil mind, that Perseus would be killed by the Gorgons.

The king asked, "Have you performed your promise? Have you brought me the head of Medusa with the snaky locks?"

"Yes," answered Perseus with a casual tone. "I have brought you the Gorgon's head, snaky locks and all!"

"Indeed! Pray let me see it," cried King Polydectes. "It must be a very curious spectacle, if all that travelers tell about it be true!"

- Circle the check mark or question mark for this section. Draw a question mark over words or phrases that confuse you.
- Mark where Perseus goes. (to the island of Seriphos)
- Mark the true purpose the king sent Perseus on the mission. (Perseus would be killed)
- Mark how you know the king is not an honorable man. (by no means happy to see him; felt certain, in his own evil mind, that Perseus would be killed by the Gorgons)
- Mark the descriptors for the Gorgon's head. (snaky locks and all, a very curious spectacle)

Let's read the last section. Read the section.

> Perseus persuaded the king to invite all of his subjects to see the terrible head of Medusa.
>
> "Show us the head! Show us the head of Medusa with the snaky locks!" shouted the people.
>
> A feeling of sorrow and pity came over the youthful Perseus. "O King Polydectes," cried he, "and ye many people, I am loath to show you the Gorgon's head!"
>
> "Show me the Gorgon's head, or I will cut off your own!" proclaimed the king.
>
> Perseus sighed and cried out in a voice like a trumpet, "Behold it then!"
>
> Instantly the king and all of his subjects were turned into stone. Perseus thrust the head back into the wallet, and went to tell his dear mother that she need no longer be afraid of the wicked King Polydectes.

- Circle the check mark or question mark for this section. Draw a question mark over words or phrases that confuse you.
- Mark the evidence that Perseus knows what will happen and feels bad about it. (A feeling of sorrow and pity; I am loath to show you the Gorgon's head)
- Mark why Perseus's mother need no longer be afraid. (the king and all of his subjects were turned into stone)

Have partners compare text markings and correct any errors.

Plot Analysis

Direct students to page 324 in their Student Books and read the instructions aloud. Have students use their Guided Highlighting to fill in the plot map. Assist students as needed.

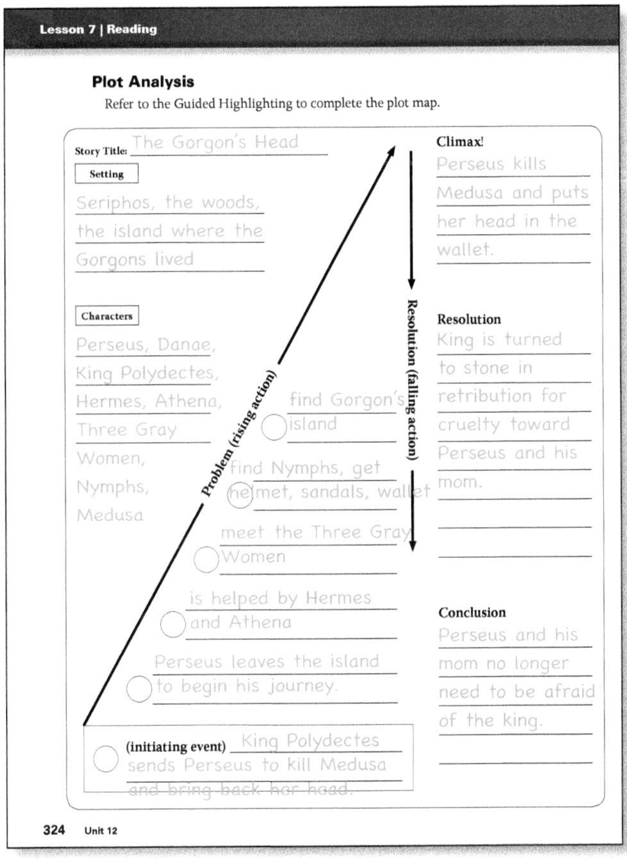

Lesson 7 | Reading
Plot Analysis
Refer to the Guided Highlighting to complete the plot map.
Story Title: The Gorgon's Head
Setting
Seriphos, the woods, the island where the Gorgons lived
Characters
Perseus, Danae, King Polydectes, Hermes, Athena, Three Gray Women, Nymphs, Medusa
Problem (rising action)
(initiating event) King Polydectes sends Perseus to kill Medusa and bring back her head.
Perseus leaves the island to begin his journey.
is helped by Hermes and Athena
meet the Three Gray Women
find Nymphs, get helmet, sandals, wallet
find Gorgon's island
Climax!
Perseus kills Medusa and puts her head in the wallet.
Resolution (falling action)
Resolution
King is turned to stone in retribution for cruelty toward Perseus and his mom.
Conclusion
Perseus and his mom no longer need to be afraid of the king.
324 Unit 12

Unit 12

Lesson 8

Lesson Opener

Before the lesson, choose one of the following activities to write on the board or post on the *LANGUAGE! Live* Class Wall online.

- *Use the word* brisk *in a sentence.*
- *If you were a god or goddess, what part of nature would you want to control?*
- *Complete the analogies.*

  thorns : roses :: bark : _____

  car : window :: tiger : _____

Writing

Objectives

- Determine a setting, characters, problem, and solution for an original myth.
- Write a rough draft of a myth.

Prepare to Write

Direct students to Part A on page 325 in their Student Books. Read the instructions and guide students through the steps to identify the topic, directions, and purpose for the writing prompt.

Map It

Direct students to Part B on page 326 in their Student Books. Explain that the plot map will provide support for students who may struggle with ideas for writing.

The plot map is your story organizer. Before you start writing your story, you need to decide on these critical elements. We analyzed "The Gorgon's Head" and found all of these elements for that story. The author made the story more vivid by including descriptions of the settings and characters. The author also started with a problem for the main character. What was Perseus's problem? (He had to kill a dangerous monster and bring back her head.) Perseus received unexpected help with his problem. As it turns out, he probably would never have returned to the island of Seriphos without that help.

Everyone's story will start in the same place, Seriphos, so everyone can put that as one of the settings in their story.

Who is the main character? (Perseus) Yes, so put his name as one of the characters.

You must decide on a problem before you think about other settings and characters. What problems could Perseus, and possibly his mother, Danae, face? Do you think they will stay on the island of Seriphos or try to get back home? If they choose to leave the island, how will they travel? Could something bad happen to them along the way? Take a few minutes and talk to your partner about some ideas for the problem in your story.

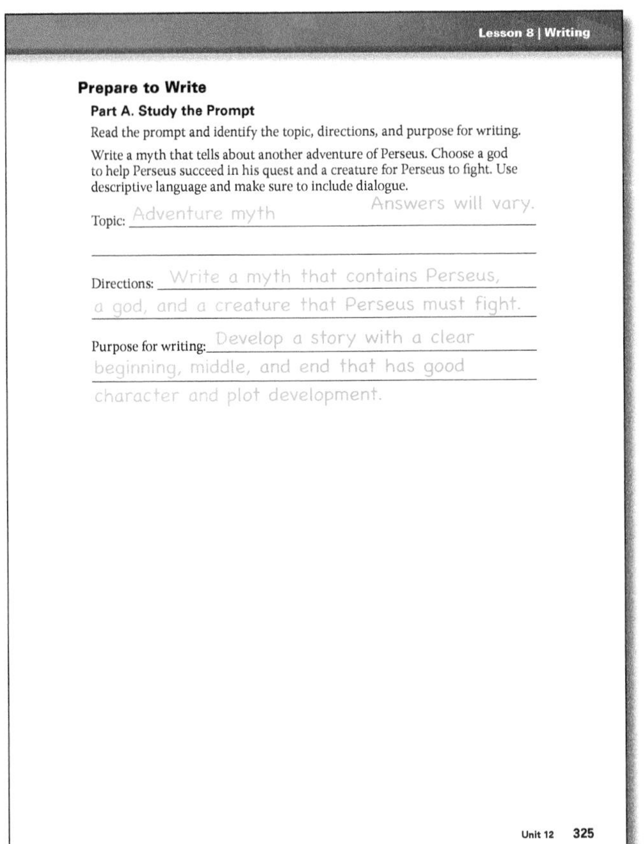
Lesson 8 | Writing

Prepare to Write

Part A. Study the Prompt

Read the prompt and identify the topic, directions, and purpose for writing.

Write a myth that tells about another adventure of Perseus. Choose a god to help Perseus succeed in his quest and a creature for Perseus to fight. Use descriptive language and make sure to include dialogue.

Topic: Adventure myth   Answers will vary.

Directions: Write a myth that contains Perseus, a god, and a creature that Perseus must fight.

Purpose for writing: Develop a story with a clear beginning, middle, and end that has good character and plot development.

Unit 12 325

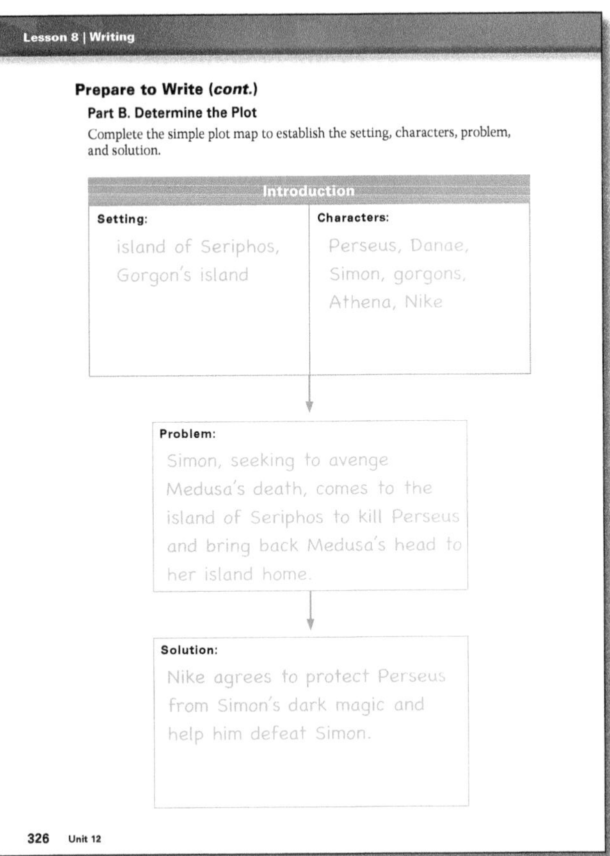
Lesson 8 | Writing

Prepare to Write (*cont.*)

Part B. Determine the Plot

Complete the simple plot map to establish the setting, characters, problem, and solution.

Introduction	
Setting: island of Seriphos, Gorgon's island	**Characters:** Perseus, Danae, Simon, gorgons, Athena, Nike

Problem: Simon, seeking to avenge Medusa's death, comes to the island of Seriphos to kill Perseus and bring back Medusa's head to her island home.

Solution: Nike agrees to protect Perseus from Simon's dark magic and help him defeat Simon.

326 Unit 12

After students have been given time to discuss their ideas, have them write the problem for their story in their Student Books. Have volunteers share their ideas.

Example Problem

On the way home, Perseus encounters a monster loyal to the Gorgons who wants to avenge Medusa's death. He kidnaps Perseus's mother and will exchange her only for Perseus's life.

How will Perseus solve his problem? Will he meet another god or creature that will offer him help? Think about the Greek gods we read about when we worked on responding to prompts. Have students brainstorm gods, characters, and creatures from Greek mythology and write them on the board. (Possible responses: Hermes, Athena, Pandora, Nike, Strength, Force, Zeal, Hercules, Zeus, Atlas, Jason, Odysseus, Prometheus.) If students have any background knowledge, allow them to share other deities or characters from other Greek myths.

Have students discuss possible solutions with their partners. As they discuss, write your example solution on the board. After students have been given time to discuss their ideas, have them write their solution on the map. Have volunteers share their ideas.

Example Solution

Perseus is befriended by Nike, the goddess of victory and learns about the creature's weakness. He pours saltwater over the creature and that turns him back into a man. He had been cursed by one of the gods for his friendship with Prometheus.

In creating my problem and solution, I figured out who some of my characters would be and also more details about my setting. You should have as well. Fill in these details as I fill in mine. **Give students a few minutes to add their characters and setting.**

Example Settings

ocean, woods

Example Characters

creature – Neron; Nike, Prometheus, Danae

Story Starters

Now that you have identified your problem and decided on how the problem will be resolved, you are ready to start filling in the details. Direct students to Part C on page 327 in their Student Books. Read the ideas for ways to start a story. As you read each one, write an example from your myth to provide another illustration of each strategy. Ask students to brainstorm other examples as you discuss each story starter.

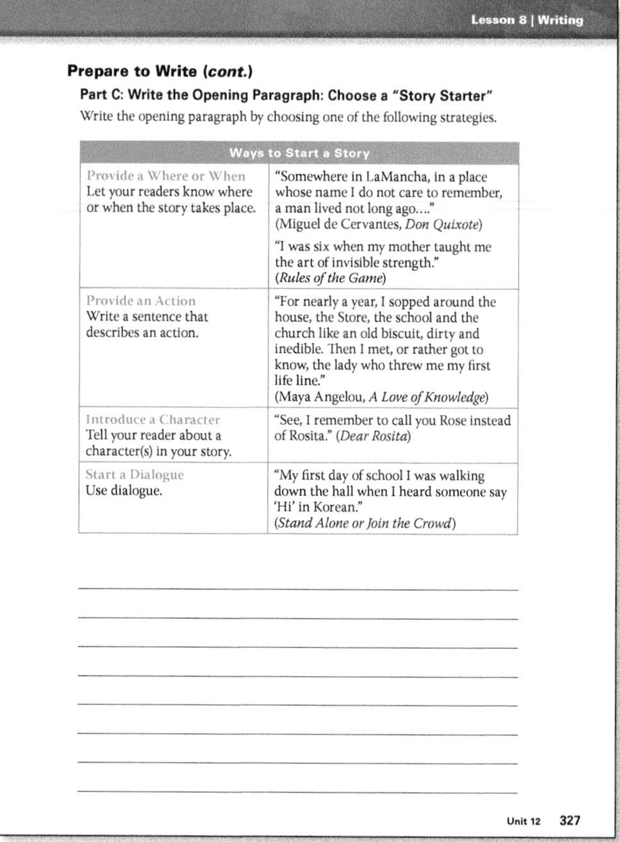

Lesson 8 | Writing

Prepare to Write (*cont.*)

Part C: Write the Opening Paragraph: Choose a "Story Starter"

Write the opening paragraph by choosing one of the following strategies.

Ways to Start a Story	
Provide a Where or When Let your readers know where or when the story takes place.	"Somewhere in LaMancha, in a place whose name I do not care to remember, a man lived not long ago...." (Miguel de Cervantes, *Don Quixote*) "I was six when my mother taught me the art of invisible strength." (*Rules of the Game*)
Provide an Action Write a sentence that describes an action.	"For nearly a year, I sopped around the house, the Store, the school and the church like an old biscuit, dirty and inedible. Then I met, or rather got to know, the lady who threw me my first life line." (Maya Angelou, *A Love of Knowledge*)
Introduce a Character Tell your reader about a character(s) in your story.	"See, I remember to call you Rose instead of Rosita." (*Dear Rosita*)
Start a Dialogue Use dialogue.	"My first day of school I was walking down the hall when I heard someone say 'Hi' in Korean." (*Stand Alone or Join the Crowd*)

Unit 12 327

Example Story Starters

Provide a Where or When
The woods were lit with an eerie light, as Perseus and his mother walked along the narrow path.

Provide an Action
Perseus's heart leapt with fear when the huge shadow appeared on their path.

Introduce a Character
The enormous creature stood in front of Perseus and his mother, looking menacingly at the two of them.

Start a Dialogue
As Perseus slowly sat up, rubbing the knot on his head, he heard a soft voice. "Don't fear for your mother's life, Perseus. I have been watching you and know you are worthy of my help."

Have partners discuss possible beginnings. Getting started is often the hardest part of writing a story. Once you've decided how to you will begin, write your opening lines on a blank sheet of paper. After students have had time to decide on their beginning, have volunteers share their story starters.

Develop the Plot

Notebook Paper

Steps for Paragraph Writing poster

You have made some important decisions about your story, and you should be ready to write your rough draft. Remember this is just your rough draft so develop your characters and your story, knowing you will have an opportunity to refine your wording and check for mechanics like spelling and punctuation later. Remember to skip lines on your notebook paper, so you will be able to edit your writing more easily.

Give students time to work on their stories. If students seem to struggle with getting started, encourage them to use your ideas on the board.

Write the Closing Paragraph

Direct students to Part D on page 328 in their Student Books. Read the ideas for ways to end a story. As you read each one, write an example from your myth to provide another illustration of the strategy.

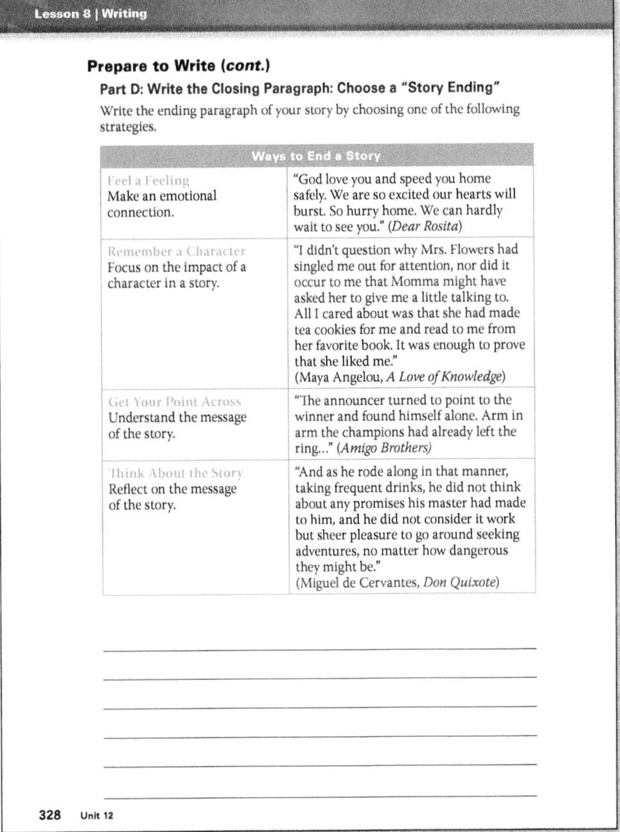

Lesson 8 | Writing

Prepare to Write (*cont.*)

Part D: Write the Closing Paragraph: Choose a "Story Ending"

Write the ending paragraph of your story by choosing one of the following strategies.

Ways to End a Story	
Feel a Feeling Make an emotional connection.	"God love you and speed you home safely. We are so excited our hearts will burst. So hurry home. We can hardly wait to see you." (*Dear Rosita*)
Remember a Character Focus on the impact of a character in a story.	"I didn't question why Mrs. Flowers had singled me out for attention, nor did it occur to me that Momma might have asked her to give me a little talking to. All I cared about was that she had made tea cookies for me and read to me from her favorite book. It was enough to prove that she liked me." (Maya Angelou, *A Love of Knowledge*)
Get Your Point Across Understand the message of the story.	"The announcer turned to point to the winner and found himself alone. Arm in arm the champions had already left the ring..." (*Amigo Brothers*)
Think About the Story Reflect on the message of the story.	"And as he rode along in that manner, taking frequent drinks, he did not think about any promises his master had made to him, and he did not consider it work but sheer pleasure to go around seeking adventures, no matter how dangerous they might be." (Miguel de Cervantes, *Don Quixote*)

328 Unit 12

Example Story Endings

Feel a Feeling

Relief washed over Perseus as he held his mother in his arms. He couldn't help but wonder what other challenges would face them as they continued their journey home.

Remember a Character

As the three of them continued on the journey home, Perseus thought of Nike and her encouraging voice when he had been overcome by fear. Looking around with a little smile on his face, he hoped she was still watching over them.

Get Your Point Across

True to his character, Perseus invited Neron to join them on their journey home. He had learned the value of friendship and hoped to be a friend to others in need.

Think About the Story

Perseus knew how kind and fickle the gods could be. He walked slowly down the path with his mother and new companion. He had the strange feeling that if they were to encounter more danger along their journey, he would also encounter a new ally to help him in his battle.

Decide how you will end your story. Once you have written it, read it aloud to your partner. Work together to see if you can strengthen your endings.

Example Myth

Simon sat on the beach at the feet of the terrifying Gorgons and wept. He had been a frequent visitor to their rocky beach and never had to worry about being harmed by them. Simon had known Medusa when she was still beautiful and had fallen in love with her. Simon still loved her even though Athena had turned her into a hideous creature. Armed with powerful dark magic, he stepped into his small boat. He promised the Gorgons that he would avenge her death. He had learned that Perseus had succeeded due largely to the help of Hermes and Athena. He had waited a long time to find a way to punish Athena for what she had done to his beloved Medusa and now he hoped he could get his revenge by killing Perseus. Athena had obviously thought Perseus was worthy of her help and now Simon would make him pay. He knew he had to travel a great distance in his small boat and thought he would put the time to good use to plot his attack.

Example Myth (*cont.*)

On the island of Seriphos, Perseus was proving to be a very wise ruler. The decent people of the island had not come to see the spectacle at the palace and had been spared from Medusa's deadly glare. They were grateful to Perseus for ridding them of their evil king and the wicked members of the court. Knowing that Perseus was brave and fair, they had persuaded Perseus to stay on the island as their ruler. Perseus refused to be called king, but agreed to rule over the island and its people. Perseus began to ask his mother many questions about his father and how they came to be adrift at sea. Danae's answers were very vague and unsatisfying. Eager for news of the world, he spent a great deal of time talking with sailors who brought their goods to trade with the people of the island.

One day, a small boat landed on the shores of Seriphos and a dark, brooding man stepped ashore. People wondered what he was doing on their island as he had no goods to trade or sell. Instead, he said he had interesting news about Perseus's father and wondered if they could tell him how to find Perseus. Eager to hear news of his father, Perseus sent word to invite the stranger to have dinner with them that evening.

As soon as the messenger left the palace with the invitation, Perseus heard a familiar voice. "Perseus, beware of this stranger," the wise and gentle voice of Athena sounded in his ear. Startled, Perseus spun around and found her standing there. Her elegant pale blue gown matched her intense eyes. A calm, but concerned, gaze met his stare.

"This stranger has come with an unspoken agenda," warned Athena. "I know him. He's hoping to catch you with your guard down. Do not be tempted to follow him in search of your father." Athena told Perseus about Simon and his love for Medusa. "He is protected by dark magic, so you need someone more accustomed to battle than I am."

"But you helped me successfully kill the most horrible monster I had ever seen. Who could be more knowledgeable than you in such matters?" asked Perseus in disbelief.

"Nike, the goddess of victory, will see you through this fight," proclaimed Athena. "And she has arrived just in the nick of time." Suddenly the room filled with a bright flash and Perseus beheld the most beautiful warrior he had ever seen. Dressed in armor that sparkled like silver, she moved across the room as light as air and as quick as thought.

"Perseus, we have but a few hours to prepare you for the most dangerous fight of your life. Simon, the mysterious stranger, has powerful magic to help him in his attempt to avenge Medusa's death. His voice is like a siren song and you will find his words irresistible. Against all reason, you will believe his news and be ready to follow him anywhere," explained Nike in words that came tumbling out as if in a race against time.

Example Myth (*cont.*)

"What can I possibly do to protect myself from his bewitching voice?" asked Perseus urgently.

"Put these small pieces of cloth in your ears. They will not stop you from hearing, but they will protect you from the spell he casts with his words," advised Nike as she handed over the small balls of pale gauze. "You must act as if you are under his spell and then strike quickly. As with Medusa, it will take a special blade to cut through his protective shield. Take my sword and keep it hidden under your clothing."

"How will I ever get close enough to use it before he does me harm?" asked Perseus, afraid to admit his doubts about the plan.

"Ah," said Nike as she handed him a golden tunic, "this will protect you from his blade. You must let him draw you near and you must lean forward as if to whisper in his ear. There will be but a split-second that you can catch him unaware and successfully penetrate his defenses. Serve your best wine and be patient. Simon loves to hear his own voice, so it's easy to get him to elaborate on a tale."

Simon entered the palace ready to make good on his promise to the Gorgons. He believed that Perseus was completely unaware of his true identity and that the evening would bring him the head of his beloved Medusa. Perseus graciously welcomed Simon into his palace and urged him to quickly share his news of Perseus's father. As Danae sat spellbound by Simon's words, Perseus acted as if he too was under the storyteller's powers. After dinner, Perseus decided to tell Simon about his battle with Medusa. He watched Simon become more agitated and impatient. He told him of Medusa's horrendous power to turn people to stone, knowing that this would only upset Simon. When he mentioned the fact that Athena had helped him succeed in his quest, Simon almost came unglued. Perseus leaned forward and whispered to Simon, "Do you want to see her grotesque face?"

Simon screamed as if in pain, "She was beautiful, so beautiful..." but he didn't finish his sentence because Perseus drove Nike's sword into his chest. Simon fell with a look of disbelief on his face.

Athena and Nike instantly appeared and in unison said, "Simon, you should have known that we would continue to protect the brave and good warriors of Greece. The dark magic of the Gorgons could never match ours." Echoing in his head, these were the last words Simon heard.

"Once again, I am in your debt," said Perseus as he bowed low to both women. He sent Simon's body out to sea in the small boat. Nike and Athena used their skills to push the boat back to the rocky beach of the Gorgons' island. The Gorgons began to shriek and cry out against the gods and became even more determined to seek their revenge.

Unit 12 Lesson 9

Lesson Opener

Before the lesson, choose one of the following activities to write on the board or post on the *LANGUAGE! Live* Class Wall online.

- *Write two sentences that contain a simile and a metaphor describing characters from your myth.*
- *Share the first and last sentence of your myth.*
- *Write a sentence to compare your avatar to your true self. Use the conjunction* but.

Reading

Objective

- Read words to develop fluency.

Word Fluency: Second Read

Timer

Follow the Fluency Procedure outlined below. If it is necessary, begin the fluency drill with a choral read of the words as you provide a rhythm (snap your fingers, tap your foot, tap your pencil).

Direct students to page 329 in their Student Books and complete the process.

Word Fluency: Second Read

Read the words fluently.

	Correct	Errors
1st Try		
2nd Try		

maybe	brace	chopping	gems	straining	germs	moonbeams	pavement	rainbow	cookbooks	10
chopping	gems	straining	germs	moonbeams	pavement	rainbow	cookbooks	chatted	sprained	20
straining	germs	moonbeams	pavement	rainbow	cookbooks	chatted	sprained	basement	railroad	30
moonbeams	pavement	rainbow	cookbooks	chatted	sprained	basement	railroad	planned	spruce	40
rainbow	cookbooks	chatted	sprained	basement	railroad	planned	spruce	spraying	shredding	50
chatted	sprained	basement	railroad	planned	spruce	spraying	shredding	strayed	center	60
basement	railroad	planned	spruce	spraying	shredding	strayed	center	brace	maybe	70
planned	spruce	spraying	shredding	strayed	center	brace	maybe	gems	chopping	80
spraying	shredding	strayed	center	brace	maybe	gems	chopping	germs	straining	90
strayed	center	moonbeams	maybe	gems	chopping	germs	straining	pavement	brace	100

Unit 12 329

Lesson 9 | Reading

Fluency Procedure

- Partners switch books, so the recorder is marking errors in the reader's book.
- A timer is set for one minute.
- Readers and recorders move left to right, tracking each word with a pencil.
- As readers read the words aloud, recorders mark errors with a small x above the misread word.
- Recorders place a star to the right of the last word read when time ends.
- If the reader is able to read all words in the allotted time, the reader needs to start over at the beginning. The recorder must indicate this feat by placing two stars to the right of the last word read.
- When both students have read, partners switch books.
- Students calculate total words read, then subtract errors and record.
- Students record information on the progress chart in back of the Student Book.

Vocabulary

Objective

- Use a range of strategies (consult reference materials; use understanding of figurative language—including similes, metaphors, and idioms; use understanding of synonyms, antonyms, related words) to clarify the meaning of words.

Vocabulary Expansion

Direct students to page 330 in their Student Books. Review the definition of each concept in the Vocabulary Expansion chart.

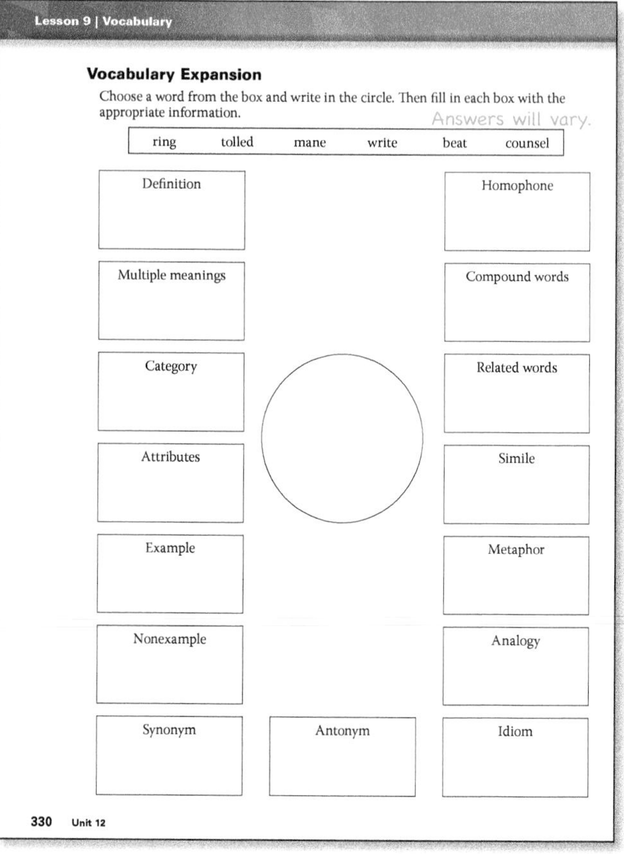
Lesson 9 | Vocabulary

Vocabulary Expansion

Choose a word from the box and write in the circle. Then fill in each box with the appropriate information. Answers will vary.

ring	tolled	mane	write	beat	counsel

Definition
Multiple meanings
Category
Attributes
Example
Nonexample
Synonym
Antonym
Homophone
Compound words
Related words
Simile
Metaphor
Analogy
Idiom

330 Unit 12

- **Definition:** the meaning of the word
- **Multiple meanings:** other meanings and uses of the word
- **Category:** the broad group to which a word belongs
- **Attributes:** specific characteristics of the word
- **Example:** something that models or patterns the word
- **Nonexample:** something that does not model or pattern the word
- **Synonym:** a word with a similar meaning
- **Antonym:** a word with the opposite meaning
- **Homophone:** a word that sounds the same but is spelled differently and has a different meaning
- **Compound word:** two words combined to make one word
- **Related words:** words with the same root and related meanings
- **Simile:** figurative language comparing two dissimilar things using *like* or *as*
- **Metaphor:** figurative language comparing two dissimilar things by saying one thing is another thing
- **Analogy:** a comparison of two pairs of words that share the same relationship
- **Idiom:** figurative language used in a certain region or by a certain group of people

In this unit we have been reading about heroes in ancient tales. Another kind of hero from English folklore is a knight. Write the word *knight* on the board. Arthur and his Knights of the Round Table dedicated their lives to rescuing innocent people who were in danger. Let's take a close look at this word, and see if we can use the concepts in the Vocabulary Expansion chart to create a deeper understanding of this word.

Example Expansion of *knight*

Definition: a warrior of ancient times who fought on horseback, served a king, and swore to behave in a noble and honorable way

Multiple meanings: military rank; a chess piece; rank of English nobility; a member of an order or society

Category: person/rank of distinction

Attributes: brave, honorable, dedicated, proficient horse rider, armed to defend, usually wears armor

Example: Sir Lancelot, Knight of the Round Table

Nonexample: a villain

Synonym: advocate, champion, supporter, defender

Antonym: enemy, foe, rival

Homophone: night

Compound word: N/A

Related words: knighthood; knightly, knighted

Simile: You are as noble as a knight from King Arthur's Round Table.

Metaphor: He is my defender, my knight.

Analogy: knight : horse :: pilot : jet

Idiom: knight in shining armor; a white knight

Dictionaries or online access

Give each student a dictionary or provide Internet access. Read the instructions, then have students choose a word and use a dictionary (online or print) to complete the process. Explain the use of N/A for concepts that don't apply to the word. Have partners share their word expansions.

Grammar

Objectives

- Demonstrate an understanding of the conditional tense in sentences.
- Write sentences using the conditional tense.

Sentence Structure and Conditional Tense

Let's review what we have learned about modals and conditional tense. Write the words *could, should,* and *would* on the board. Ask students to tell you the implications of using each modal. (Answers need to include: *could* implies possibility, *would* implies intent, *should* implies advice or a directive.)

Unlike any other helping verbs we've worked with, these words don't change based on the point of view—first, second, or third person. They are not changed in any way to fit into the sentence. If you think about the verb *be*, you will realize how this simplifies the use of these modals. Write *be* on the board along with the pronouns *I, you, he, we, they.*

Help me use the verb *be* with these pronouns, keeping it in the present tense. I (am), you (are), he (is), we (are), they (are). Nice job. You know that these would change again if we wanted to talk about something that has already happened, or the past tense.

While we've worked with these words and examined how they impact meaning, we really haven't focused on the structure of sentences written with words. We will start with the basic sentence structure that contains an *if* clause. By starting with the word *if*, the writer immediately lets you know that a *then* is coming. With the conditional tense, you start with the situation or condition and then you end with a specified action. Tell me if this is a complete thought or sentence: If you want to win the race. (no) It doesn't sound finished does it? I need to finish the thought. Right now, I have a question still unanswered in my head: What do I have to do if I want to win the race? Listen and tell me if I now have a complete sentence: If you want to win the race, you should become familiar with the track. (yes) It is a complete thought. I now know what I need to do, at least according to this person, if I want to win the race. What is this person recommending I do? (become more familiar with the track) Yes, so we need two parts, or elements, to a sentence written in the conditional tense.

Direct students to Part A on page 331 in their Student Books and read the instructions. Let's take a look at these sentences. The *if* phrase contains a subject noun and a verb, but it cannot stand alone. The word *if* is a signal that this group of words is dependent on other words to make it complete.

Lesson 9 | Grammar

Sentence Structure and Conditional Tense

Part A

Read the following the sentences and underline the *if* statement once and the remainder of the sentence twice. Circle the comma.

1. If you had made your bed, you could go to the park.
2. If you wanted to have some extra money, you should have cut the grass yesterday.
3. If you practiced free throws every day, you would score more points during the game.

Part B

Turn each one of the following sentences into a conditional sentence.

Example: We cannot go to the park because you did not finish your chores.
If you had finished your chores, we could go to the park.

1. Our class will not win the contest because we didn't read enough books.
If our class had read more books, we would have won the contest.
2. Too many students were talking, so we did not finish the lesson in class.
If students had not been talking so much, we could have finished the lesson in class.
3. You must not have wanted to make the team because you were not at tryouts.
If you wanted to make the team, you should have been at tryouts.
4. Not many people were at the party, so they will not have it next year.
If more people had come to the party, they would have it again next year.
5. People were making too much noise in the hall because they were not aware of the testing.
If the people had been aware of the testing, they would not have made so much noise.

Unit 12 331

Model

Follow along as I read the first sentence. Read the first sentence.

What is the *if* part of the sentence? (if you had made your bed) Right, underline that part of the sentence once. Is it a complete thought? (no) It leaves me with the question: what could/would/should happen if I made my bed? How is the question answered? (you could go to the park) Yes, I could go to the park if I had made my bed. Is *you could go to the park* a complete thought? Yes, it is. Even though I don't know what would make it possible, it can stand alone. Underline that part of the sentence twice.

The last thing I want to point out in this type of sentence is the need for a comma. Find the comma in the sentence and circle it. You need a comma to separate the *if* statement from the rest of the sentence. Remember, a comma signals us to pause, and when reading it helps us separate chunks of meaning within a longer sentence. Complete the process with the remaining sentences.

Direct students to Part B. Now, we will use information to practice writing this type of sentence. Listen to this sentence: We cannot go the park because you did not finish your chores.

What were you supposed to do, but didn't? (finish my chores) Right, and what would have happened had you finished your chores? (we could go to the park) Yes, we can use the information in this sentence to write a sentence that states the condition or is in the conditional tense. The *if* statement tells what you were supposed to do: If you had finished your chores. Then we place a comma and tell what could/would/should have happened. In this sentence, what would have been the outcome? (we could go to the park)

Guided Practice

Complete the first two sentences with students, asking questions to guide students in constructing the new sentences.

Independent Practice

Have students work with their partner to complete the remaining sentences. When students have completed the sentences, check responses as a class to ensure understanding.

Note: Base the number of modeled and guided examples on student ability and progress. Challenge them with independent practice when appropriate.

Reading

Objectives

- Read a text to develop fluency.
- Demonstrate comprehension by answering specific questions about a text.

Reading for Fluency

Direct students to pages 332 and 333 in their Student Books.

The following text is decodable. You have learned almost all the letters, sounds, and sight words that appear in it. Reading this text will help you improve your fluency.

Have students read the text.

Reading for Fluency

Read the passage with prosody. Chunk the words into phrases and create an image in your head as you read.

A Trip to Crete

The plane landed. Beth grinned as the wheels skidded on the path. "Here at last. We're in Greece!" she said to herself. Her little sister, Genna, was sitting next to her. A bell dinged and belts clicked as other people grabbed their bags. "Don't leave your book," Beth's mom prompted from a seat in the next row. "Genna, your book is still in the seat. Grab it now and let's go."

It felt as if they were standing in a warm, damp tent as they waited for a cab. They grabbed their sunglasses to keep from squinting in the strong sun. They took a van to their beach home. The kids' chatter filled the van. Dan was nine and could not be still. At sixteen, Beth was the oldest and used to his chatter. Genna was thirteen, and Dan drove her nuts. Mrs. Wells was starting to make a book on Crete and needed to visit the site of a dig. The team had dug up parts of a very old ship. The trip would be a mix of work and play for all of them.

From their porch they looked out at the Sea of Crete. Waves of teal were rimmed by clean white sand. As quick as a wink, the three kids ran out to swim and play in the waves. A soft breeze and the fresh water kept them cool as they played on the shore. No one had stopped to put on sunscreen or grab a hat, so by the end of the day they were all red as beets.

"Mom, did you pack any soothing cream for our sunburns?" asked Genna. Their skin was hurting. They ate fresh seafood for dinner. Later, they played a card game. The kids were so worn out, they went to bed as soon as the game ended.

They woke to sunshine. "Mom, can we come with you to the dig site this morning?" asked Beth.

"Yes, but I need to leave soon. Please eat fast, so we can get on the road," said Mrs. Wells. She shook her head as the other kids came dragging down the steps. They all put on sunscreen and grabbed their hats. "Dan, where are your boots?" asked Mom. "It will be hard to hike in your flip-flops!"

"I forgot to pack them," Dan said. The frown on his face showed he wasn't kidding. His mom had asked him to use a list for packing, but he did not take the time. Now, he wished he had checked his bag one last time.

Reading for Fluency (*cont.*)

"Well, I bet you will not forget them the next time you pack!" Genna yelled. Dan shot her a mean look, but he did not say a thing. He hated to say that she was right.

At the dig, all of the kids felt the sting of their sunburn. They looked for shade and were glad they had their hats. The workers at the dig were glad to see them. They were very glad about the boat and what it would add to the ancient history of Crete. When they took a break, Beth chatted with one of the men on the team. He asked her if she had ever read any Greek myths. "Yes, my class just read some myths," said Beth.

"Did you know that Crete is said to be the place where Zeus was born?" asked the man. "Other gods and goddesses were said to be born close to here!" he added.

"Spending time here makes the myths feel so much more real," she said and he nodded his head.

"Will you go to see Athens on this trip?" he asked her. She shook her head no.

"My mom needs to spend all of her time here on Crete. She hopes to add new facts to her book after spending time at the dig." Beth said.

They sat on big rocks to eat their lunch. After a long day at the site, they rode back to the beach home with the windows rolled down. The breeze felt good on their hot, sunburned faces. Dan rubbed his feet and frowned. How he wished he had packed his boots!

The rest of the trip was a blur of sun, water, and sand. Mrs. Wells spent time at the dig site each day. She had many things to do. The kids went to the beach. They ate dinner on the back porch every day. Dan, Genna and Beth would show her the shells they had found on the beach. They wanted to know about the boat and their mom's book.

As they packed their bags Dan said, "Time does fly when you have fun! I wish we could stay longer." They all nodded yes and said they were sad to leave. No one said a thing as they drove away from the site. They all slept on the plane ride home, dreaming of their next trip.

After reading, ask students the following comprehension questions.

- Why did the Wells travel to Crete? (Mrs. Wells was doing research for her book on the history of Crete.)
- What problems did they have while on their trip? (They forgot to put on sunscreen and got sunburned. Dan forgot his tennis shoes, so he had to hike in his flip-flops.)
- How could they have avoided these problems? (They should have put on sunscreen especially because it was their first day. Dan should have made a list of things to pack.)
- Have you ever had a similar experience as the kids in this story? (Answers will vary.)
- Do you think the vacation sounded like fun? (Answers will vary.)
- What had the archeologists at the site found that was so special? (They had found an ancient ship.)
- Is there a connection between the island of Crete and Greek mythology? (Yes, Crete is said to be the birthplace of Zeus.)

Writing

Objectives

- Edit a narrative for content, details, word choice, and basic conventions.

Writer's Checklist

Reread your rough draft and make changes that strengthen your story. Use the Writer's Checklist on page 334 in your Student Book to help you. Decide if you need to add more details about your characters. Make sure you have written meaningful dialogue that advances the story.

Give students time to work independently, reading over their rough draft and using the checklist to make edits.

Lesson 9 | Writing

Writer's Checklist

Trait	Yes	No	Did the writer . . .?
Ideas and Content			focus all sentences on the topic
			provide supporting details for the topic sentence
			include examples, evidence, and/or explanations to develop the supporting detail sentences
Organization			write a topic sentence
			tell things in an order that makes sense
			use transition words and/or phrases
			write a concluding sentence
Voice and Audience Awareness			think about the audience and purpose for writing
			write in a clear and engaging way that makes the audience want to read the work; write so the reader can "hear" the writer speaking
Word Choice			try to find a unique way to say things
			use words that are lively and specific to the content
Sentence Fluency			write complete sentences
			expand some sentences by painting the subject and/or predicate
Conventions			capitalize words correctly:
			capitalize the first word of each sentence
			capitalize proper nouns, including people's names
			punctuate correctly:
			put a period or question mark at the end of each sentence
			put an apostrophe before the *s* for a singular possessive noun
			use a comma after a long adverb phrase at the beginning of a sentence
			use grammar correctly:
			use the correct verb tense
			make sure the verb agrees with the subject in number
			use correct spelling

334 Unit 12

Six Traits of Writing

Now that you have rewritten your rough draft, think about how to evaluate your writing. Focus on Word Choice and Mechanics. Give yourself a score based on those two elements of the Six Traits rubric.

Give students time to score their writing.

Have students use the Six Traits chart on page 335 in their Student Books.

Six Traits of Writing

	Ideas and Development	Organization	Voice and Audience Awareness	Word Choice	Sentence Fluency	Language Conventions
5	The paper is very clear and well focused. Supporting details make the paper very easy and interesting to understand.	Ideas are very clearly organized. All parts of the essay (introduction, body, and conclusion) work together to support the thesis.	The writer's voice is distinctive and shows an interest in the topic. The writer knows who his or her audience is.	Words are used correctly and are very well chosen. They create pictures in the reader's mind.	Sentences have an easy flow and rhythm. Transitions are very smooth.	There are no grammar errors. There are few or no errors in spelling, capitalization, or punctuation.
4	The paper is clear and well focused. Supporting details make the paper easy to understand.	Ideas are clearly organized. The paper includes all parts of an essay (introduction, body, and conclusion).	The writer's voice is natural and shows an interest in the topic. The writer knows who his or her audience is.	Words are used correctly. Some words may be a bit general.	Sentences are formed correctly and are varied in structure. Transitions are clear.	There are no major grammar errors. There are few errors in spelling, capitalization, or punctuation.
3	The paper has a clear thesis. The ideas are somewhat developed, but there are only a few details.	Ideas are fairly well organized. The paper includes all parts of an essay (introduction, body, and conclusion).	The writer's voice is natural, but the writer is not fully engaged in the topic. At times the writer's viewpoint may be vague.	Most words are used correctly. A few words are too general. Some words are repeated.	Sentences are formed correctly, although they may be similar in structure. Most transitions are clear.	There are a few grammar errors. There are a few errors in spelling, capitalization, or punctuation.
2	The thesis of the paper is unclear. The paper is poorly developed.	Ideas are not clearly organized. The paper may be missing an introduction or a conclusion.	The writer seems somewhat uninterested in the topic and unaware of his or her audience.	Some words are used incorrectly, some are too general, or some words are repeated often.	The sentences do not flow well. They are short and choppy, or long and confusing.	There are many grammar or spelling errors. There are quite a few errors in capitalization and punctuation.
1	The paper is missing a thesis. The paper is very confusing or poorly developed.	The paper has no organization. There is no introduction or conclusion.	The writer is uninterested in the topic and unaware of his or her audience.	Many words are used incorrectly, many words are general, or many words are repeated.	The sentences are not correctly structured and they do not flow well.	There are many spelling and grammar errors. There are many errors in capitalization and punctuation.

Unit 12 335

Lesson 9 | Writing

Unit 12 Lesson 10

Lesson Opener

Before the lesson, choose one of the following activities to write on the board or post on the *LANGUAGE! Live* Class Wall online.

- *Write four meaningful sentences with the vocabulary words from this unit. Each sentence will contain two vocabulary words (*image, proceed, perceive, invisible, intelligent, undertake, recover, enormous*).*
- *Write three sentences about your favorite mythological character we have learned about in this unit.*
- *Mythology is a part of our everyday world. Where have you heard the names of mythological characters in your daily life?*

Vocabulary

Objectives

- Clarify the meaning of key passage vocabulary.
- Demonstrate an understanding of passage vocabulary by using words in sentences.

Review

Direct students to page 280 in their Student Books. Remind them of the review procedure. Have partners review the Key Passage Vocabulary.

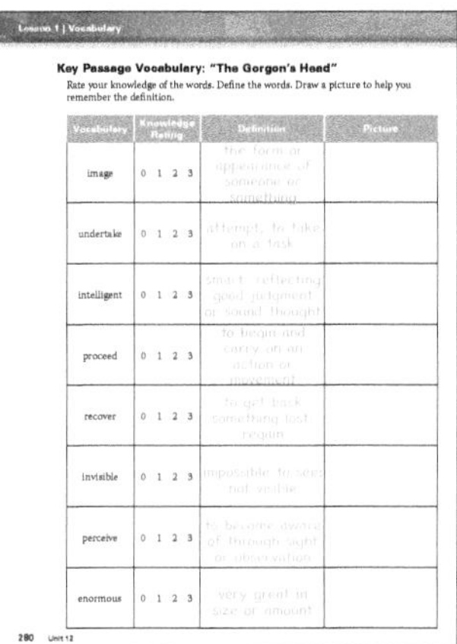

Lesson 1 | Vocabulary

Key Passage Vocabulary: "The Gorgon's Head"

Rate your knowledge of the words. Define the words. Draw a picture to help you remember the definition.

Vocabulary	Knowledge Rating	Definition	Picture
image	0 1 2 3	the form or appearance of someone or something	
undertake	0 1 2 3	attempt; to take on a task	
intelligent	0 1 2 3	smart; reflecting good judgment or sound thought	
proceed	0 1 2 3	to begin and carry on an action or movement	
recover	0 1 2 3	to get back something lost; regain	
invisible	0 1 2 3	impossible to see; not visible	
perceive	0 1 2 3	to become aware of through sight or observation	
enormous	0 1 2 3	very great in size or amount	

280 Unit 12

Review Procedure

- Student A reads the word.
- Student B tells the meaning.
- Students swap roles for each word.

Have students revisit their rating of the words. If they cannot change all ratings to a 3, pull them aside to discuss the vocabulary words they do not know.

Cloze Activity

Now we will read a paragraph. You will determine which vocabulary words are missing and write them on the lines.

Direct students to page 336 in their Student Books. Remind them of the cloze procedure.

Cloze Procedure

- Teacher reads the text aloud, pausing at the blanks for students to write.
- Students fill in the blanks with words from the word bank.
- Teacher rereads the text as students chorally tell the correct word for each blank.
- Students correct errors.

Lesson 10 | Vocabulary

Using New Vocabulary

Fill in the blanks with the appropriate vocabulary words. If you need assistance, use the word bank at the bottom of the page.

Comic book heroes are very similar to mythological characters. Superheroes like Superman (who can fly), The Invisible Woman (who can make herself ___invisible___), and Spiderman (who can catch people in his webs) keep the world safe. These characters have superhuman powers that set them apart from the rest of the world. However, they live a double life. In their "non super" form, they may be out for a walk or shopping at the grocery store when they ___perceive___ that someone is in danger. Once the hero has donned his mask, he can ___proceed___ to help the victim. These heroes often ___undertake___ dangerous missions to save lives, prevent crime, and ___recover___ stolen property. These strong and ___intelligent___ heroes overpower and outwit the villains they fight. The people know them only as heroes and display their ___images___ all over town, hoping one day they will come to know the man or woman behind the mask. This ___enormous___ responsibility can be overwhelming, but it is well worth it when a life is saved.

Word Bank

enormous	perceive	proceed	images
undertake	recover	intelligent	invisible

336 Unit 12

Reading

Objectives

- Discuss and answer questions to demonstrate an understanding of the main idea of the myth.
- Demonstrate an understanding of point of view.
- Retell a story from a different point of view.

Big Idea and Point of View

Direct students to page 279 in their Student Books.

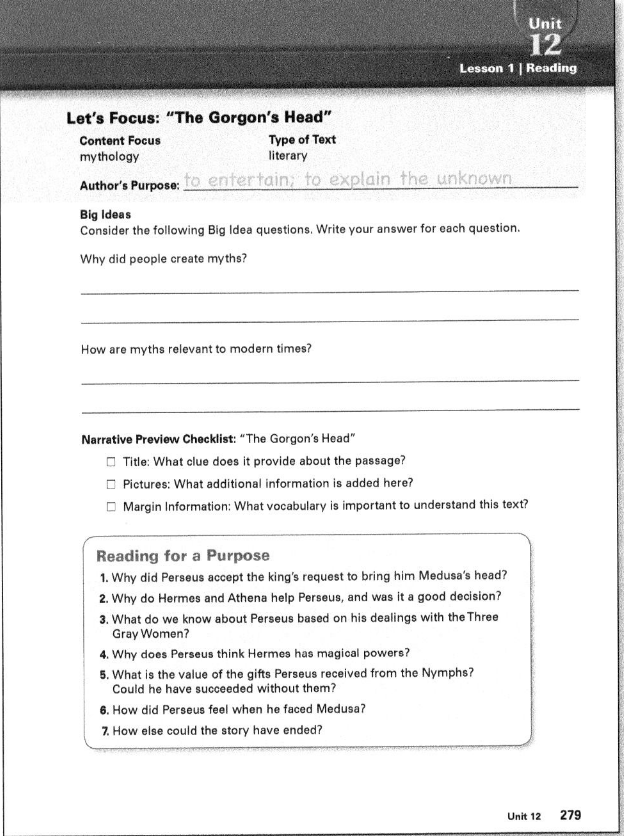
Unit 12
Lesson 1 | Reading

Let's Focus: "The Gorgon's Head"

Content Focus: mythology
Type of Text: literary

Author's Purpose: to entertain; to explain the unknown

Big Ideas
Consider the following Big Idea questions. Write your answer for each question.

Why did people create myths?

How are myths relevant to modern times?

Narrative Preview Checklist: "The Gorgon's Head"

- ☐ Title: What clue does it provide about the passage?
- ☐ Pictures: What additional information is added here?
- ☐ Margin Information: What vocabulary is important to understand this text?

Reading for a Purpose

1. Why did Perseus accept the king's request to bring him Medusa's head?
2. Why do Hermes and Athena help Perseus, and was it a good decision?
3. What do we know about Perseus based on his dealings with the Three Gray Women?
4. Why does Perseus think Hermes has magical powers?
5. What is the value of the gifts Perseus received from the Nymphs? Could he have succeeded without them?
6. How did Perseus feel when he faced Medusa?
7. How else could the story have ended?

Unit 12 279

Before we began reading "The Gorgon's Head," we answered two Big Idea questions. Take a minute to look over your answers. Now that we have read the story and learned more about mythological characters and different cultures' myths, how have your earlier ideas changed? What information can you add to your answers?

Discuss the questions and answers with the class.

"The Gorgon's Head" is a Greek myth. We learned that Greek mythology is a series of elaborate stories about gods, goddesses, and creatures and their interactions with humans. These stories sought to explain the natural world and why things happen. Often they were written to teach the reader a lesson. In ancient Greece, people relied on the stories to teach difficult life lessons. The mythological tales helped people know right from wrong and how to behave.

Think back on the myths that we read about. What was the lesson learned from Pandora? (Be careful what you wish for; don't give in to your urges; don't be greedy) What was the lesson learned from Medusa? (Don't be vain; be humble) What was the lesson learned from King Polydectes? (Be kind or it may come back to bite you; listen to the warnings of others; good prevails over evil)

The lessons taught in stories are referred to as *themes*. Themes are universal and repeated throughout literature. As you read other stories, pay close attention to the way they address themes such as good vs. evil, greed, and pride. References from Greek mythology can be found in pop culture, literature, music, and art. The lessons the ancient authors wanted to teach are a daily part of our lives.

In many of the previous units, we have discussed point of view. As a review, tell your partner the three perspectives from which you can write. (first person, second person, third person)

What was the point of view of "The Gorgon's Head?" (third person) Consider how differently the story may have been if it had been told from Perseus's point of view, or even Medusa's.

Point of view is a powerful tool for a writer. Choose a character from "The Gorgon's Head" and think about a scene from the story and how it might have sounded had it been told from that character's point of view. For example, how differently would the scene with the Three Gray Women have been if Shakejoint had told the story? She wouldn't have known how the information they gave Perseus impacted the story. Because the story was being told from the third person, the reader knew everything that was going on as it happened.

Work with your partner to retell one of the scenes from a different character's point of view. Be prepared to share. If time permits, have students identify the scenes and the character's point of view for their retell.

Writing

Objectives

- Tell a story using descriptive details.
- Use technology to produce and publish writing.

Creating a Myth

Have students use their myths to create illustrated books. This can be done on the computer. When the books are complete, create a library in your classroom and have students read each other's myths.

Vocabulary

Objectives for Content Mastery

- Demonstrate an understanding of word meanings by relating them to their other words.
- Demonstrate an understanding of word analogies.

Part-to-Whole and Function Analogies

Follow the procedure outlined below for the Vocabulary Content Mastery questions and prompts.

Content Mastery Procedure

- Teacher reminds students to follow along with their pencils and listen.
- Teacher reads the question.
- Teacher reads each answer choice.
- Students choose the correct answer.
- Teacher repeats the question as students check their answers.

Have students turn to page 337 in their Student Books.

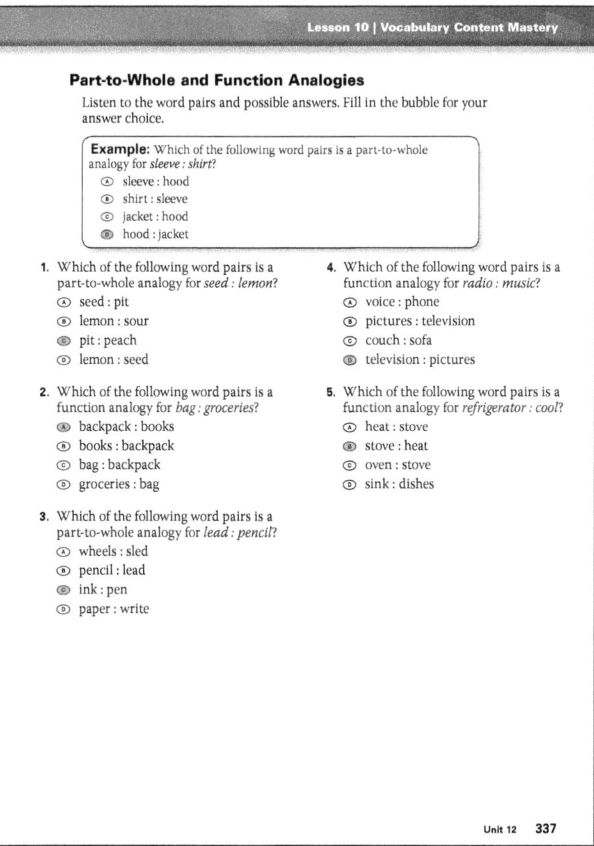

Lesson 10 | Vocabulary Content Mastery

Part-to-Whole and Function Analogies

Listen to the word pairs and possible answers. Fill in the bubble for your answer choice.

Example: Which of the following word pairs is a part-to-whole analogy for *sleeve : shirt?*
- Ⓐ sleeve : hood
- Ⓑ shirt : sleeve
- Ⓒ jacket : hood
- Ⓓ hood : jacket

1. Which of the following word pairs is a part-to-whole analogy for *seed : lemon?*
   - Ⓐ seed : pit
   - Ⓑ lemon : sour
   - Ⓒ pit : peach
   - Ⓓ lemon : seed
2. Which of the following word pairs is a function analogy for *bag : groceries?*
   - Ⓐ backpack : books
   - Ⓑ books : backpack
   - Ⓒ bag : backpack
   - Ⓓ groceries : bag
3. Which of the following word pairs is a part-to-whole analogy for *lead : pencil?*
   - Ⓐ wheels : sled
   - Ⓑ pencil : lead
   - Ⓒ ink : pen
   - Ⓓ paper : write
4. Which of the following word pairs is a function analogy for *radio : music?*
   - Ⓐ voice : phone
   - Ⓑ pictures : television
   - Ⓒ couch : sofa
   - Ⓓ television : pictures
5. Which of the following word pairs is a function analogy for *refrigerator : cool?*
   - Ⓐ heat : stove
   - Ⓑ stove : heat
   - Ⓒ oven : stove
   - Ⓓ sink : dishes

Unit 12 337

Let's look at the example first. Read the example aloud to students.

Listen: Which of the following word pairs is a part-to-whole analogy for *sleeve : shirt?*

A sleeve : hood

B shirt : sleeve

C jacket : hood

D hood : jacket

Fill in the bubble for the correct response. Which bubble did you fill in? You should have filled in D, the bubble for "hood : jacket." *Sleeve : shirt :: hood : jacket.* A *sleeve* is part of a *shirt*; a *hood* is part of a *jacket*. Notice that the order of the words is important. A *jacket* is not part of a *hood*.

Follow along as I read aloud the questions and prompts. Fill in the bubble for your answer choice.

Use the following recommendations to reinforce or reteach according to student performance.

If...	Then...
Students miss 2 questions	Review the questions in a small group or individual setting, offering answer explanations.
Students miss 3 or more questions	Reteach the elements taught in Lesson 6 in a small group or individual setting. Unmarked copies of the student page can be reprinted from the online Teacher Resources.

Grammar

Objectives for Content Mastery

- Demonstrate an understanding of how comparatives and superlatives convey meaning.
- Demonstrate an understanding of the use of modals (*could, would, should*) to convey various conditions.

Comparatives and Superlatives

Follow the procedure outlined below for each of the Grammar Content Mastery questions and prompts.

Content Mastery Procedure

- Teacher reminds students to follow along with their pencils and listen.
- Teacher reads the question.
- Teacher reads each answer choice.
- Students choose the correct answer.
- Teacher repeats the question as students check their answers.

Have students turn to page 338 in their Student Books.

Let's look at the example first. Read the example aloud to students.

Listen: Follow along as I read the sentence aloud. Choose the correct adjective to fill in the blank: *A meter is ______ than a yard.* Fill in the bubble for your answer.

A longer

B long

C longest

D most long

Which bubble did you fill in? You should have filled in the bubble for A, "longer." Remember, when you compare two things, use the comparative form that usually ends in *-er.* When you compare three or more things, use the superlative form that usually ends in *-est.*

Lesson 10 | Grammar Content Mastery

Comparatives and Superlatives

Listen to the sentences and possible answers. Fill in the bubble for your answer choice.

Example: Choose the correct adjective to fill in the blank:
A meter is ____ than a yard.
Ⓐ longer
Ⓑ long
Ⓒ longest
Ⓓ most long

1. Choose the correct adjective to fill in the blank:
This glass is ____ than that one.
Ⓐ largest
Ⓑ larger
Ⓒ large
Ⓓ most large

2. Choose the correct adjective to fill in the blank:
Canada is ____ than Mexico.
Ⓐ big
Ⓑ biggest
Ⓒ bigger
Ⓓ most big

3. Choose the correct adjective to fill in the blank:
Of all the animals in the zoo, the monkey is the ____ climber.
Ⓐ best
Ⓑ better
Ⓒ good
Ⓓ most good

4. Choose the correct adjective to fill in the blank:
The green car is the ____ one in the whole parking lot.
Ⓐ most bright
Ⓑ brighter
Ⓒ bright
Ⓓ brightest

5. Choose the correct adjective to fill in the blank:
Henry and Vicki had on dark shirts, but Marco's was the ____ one.
Ⓐ darkier
Ⓑ darkest
Ⓒ dark
Ⓓ most darkest

338 Unit 12

Follow along as I read aloud the sentences and possible answers. Fill in the bubble for your answer choice.

Use the following recommendations to reinforce or reteach according to student performance.

If...	Then...
Students miss 2 questions	Review the questions in a small group or individual setting, offering answer explanations.
Students miss 3 or more questions	Reteach the elements taught in Lesson 2 in a small group or individual setting. Unmarked copies of the student page can be reprinted from the online Teacher Resources.

Modals: *could, would, should*

Have students turn to page 339 in their Student Books.

Let's look at the example first. Read the example aloud to students.

Listen: Choose the correct word to complete the sentence: *If Peter wants to learn his spelling words, he ______ practice every day.*

A should

B would

C could

D none of the above

Which bubble did you fill in? You should have filled in the bubble for A, "If Peter wants to learn his spelling words, he *should* practice every day."

Follow along as I read aloud the sentences and possible answers. Fill in the bubble for your answer choice.

Lesson 10 | Grammar Content Mastery

Modals: *could, would, should*

Listen to the sentences and possible answers. Fill in the bubble for your answer choice.

Example: Choose the correct word to complete the sentence:
If Peter wants to learn his spelling words, he _____ practice every day.
- Ⓐ should
- Ⓑ would
- Ⓒ could
- Ⓓ none of the above

1. Choose the correct word to complete the sentence:
   If Perseus wants to succeed with his quest, he _____ follow the advice Hermes gives him.
   - Ⓐ would
   - Ⓑ should
   - Ⓒ could
   - Ⓓ none of the above
2. Choose the correct word to complete the sentence:
   Dana _____ keep his room in order, but he didn't care enough to do it.
   - Ⓐ would
   - Ⓑ should
   - Ⓒ could
   - Ⓓ none of the above
3. Choose the correct word to complete the sentence:
   If I'm correct, the gates to the water park _____ open at noon.
   - Ⓐ could
   - Ⓑ would
   - Ⓒ should
   - Ⓓ none of the above
4. Choose the correct word to complete the sentence:
   Perseus _____ have kept the head of Medusa hidden if the king had not insisted he show it.
   - Ⓐ would
   - Ⓑ should
   - Ⓒ could
   - Ⓓ none of the above
5. Choose the correct word to complete the sentence:
   I _____ mow the lawn, but it's raining.
   - Ⓐ could
   - Ⓑ should
   - Ⓒ would
   - Ⓓ none of the above

Unit 12 339

Use the following recommendations to reinforce or reteach according to student performance.

If...	Then...
Students miss 2 questions	Review the questions in a small group or individual setting, offering answer explanations.
Students miss 3 or more questions	Reteach the elements taught in Lessons 2 and 4 in a small group or individual setting. Unmarked copies of the student page can be reprinted from the online Teacher Resources.

Additional Resources

Posters

Reading

Posters can also be printed from the Teacher Resources online.

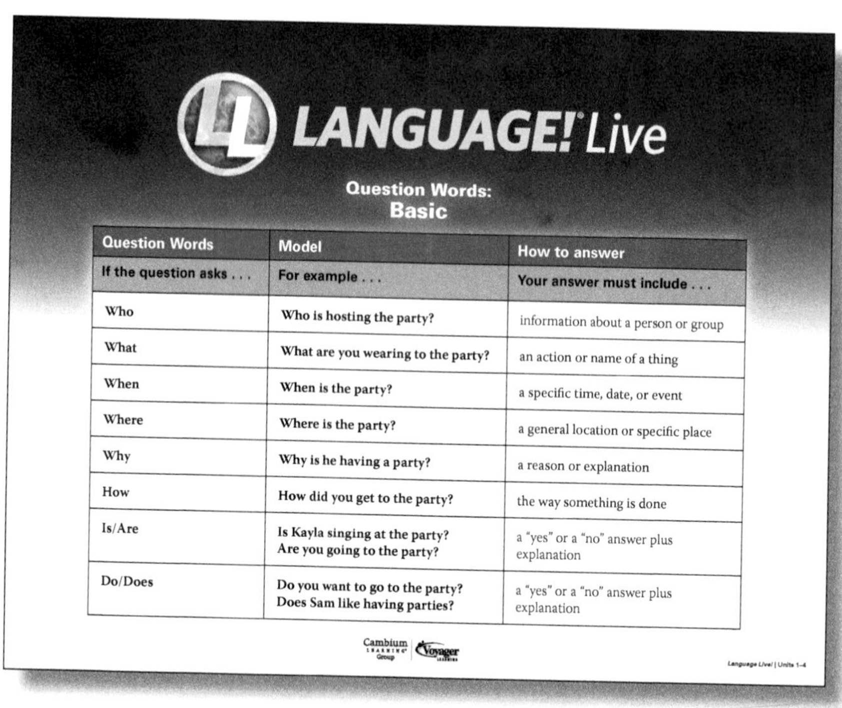

LANGUAGE! Live

Question Words: Basic

Question Words	Model	How to answer
If the question asks . . .	**For example . . .**	**Your answer must include . . .**
Who	Who is hosting the party?	information about a person or group
What	What are you wearing to the party?	an action or name of a thing
When	When is the party?	a specific time, date, or event
Where	Where is the party?	a general location or specific place
Why	Why is he having a party?	a reason or explanation
How	How did you get to the party?	the way something is done
Is/Are	Is Kayla singing at the party? Are you going to the party?	a "yes" or a "no" answer plus explanation
Do/Does	Do you want to go to the party? Does Sam like having parties?	a "yes" or a "no" answer plus explanation

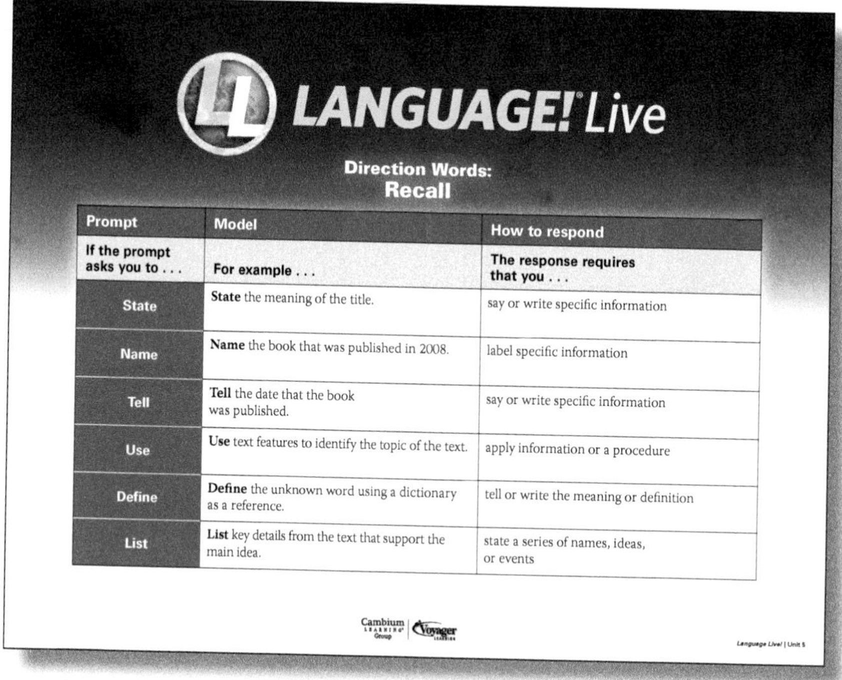

LANGUAGE! Live

Direction Words: Recall

Prompt	Model	How to respond
If the prompt asks you to . . .	**For example . . .**	**The response requires that you . . .**
State	**State** the meaning of the title.	say or write specific information
Name	**Name** the book that was published in 2008.	label specific information
Tell	**Tell** the date that the book was published.	say or write specific information
Use	**Use** text features to identify the topic of the text.	apply information or a procedure
Define	**Define** the unknown word using a dictionary as a reference.	tell or write the meaning or definition
List	**List** key details from the text that support the main idea.	state a series of names, ideas, or events

Reading

Posters can also be printed from the Teacher Resources online.

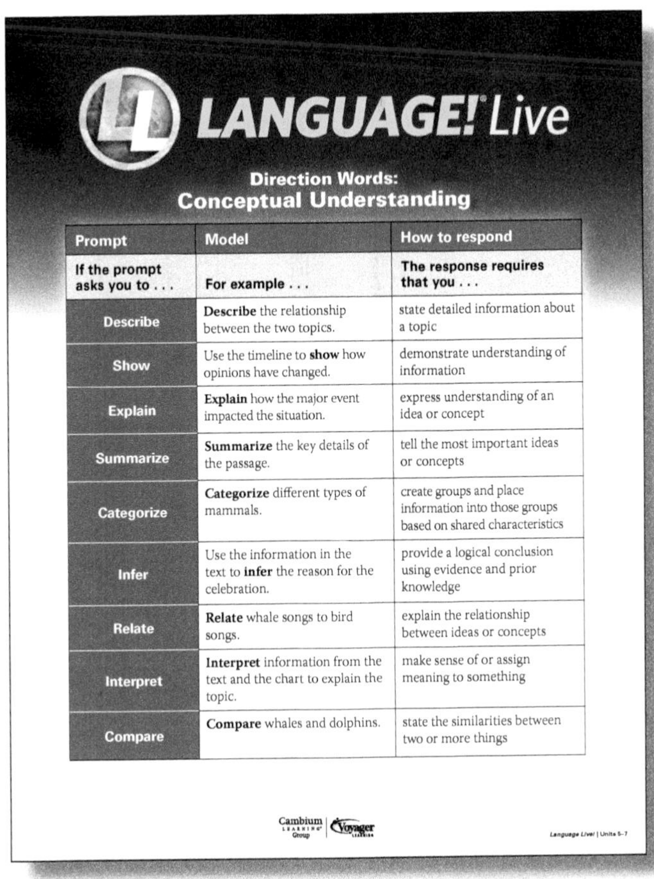

LANGUAGE! Live

Direction Words: Conceptual Understanding

Prompt	Model	How to respond
If the prompt asks you to . . .	**For example . . .**	**The response requires that you . . .**
Describe	**Describe** the relationship between the two topics.	state detailed information about a topic
Show	Use the timeline to **show** how opinions have changed.	demonstrate understanding of information
Explain	**Explain** how the major event impacted the situation.	express understanding of an idea or concept
Summarize	**Summarize** the key details of the passage.	tell the most important ideas or concepts
Categorize	**Categorize** different types of mammals.	create groups and place information into those groups based on shared characteristics
Infer	Use the information in the text to **infer** the reason for the celebration.	provide a logical conclusion using evidence and prior knowledge
Relate	**Relate** whale songs to bird songs.	explain the relationship between ideas or concepts
Interpret	**Interpret** information from the text and the chart to explain the topic.	make sense of or assign meaning to something
Compare	**Compare** whales and dolphins.	state the similarities between two or more things

Cambium Learning Group | Voyager Learning

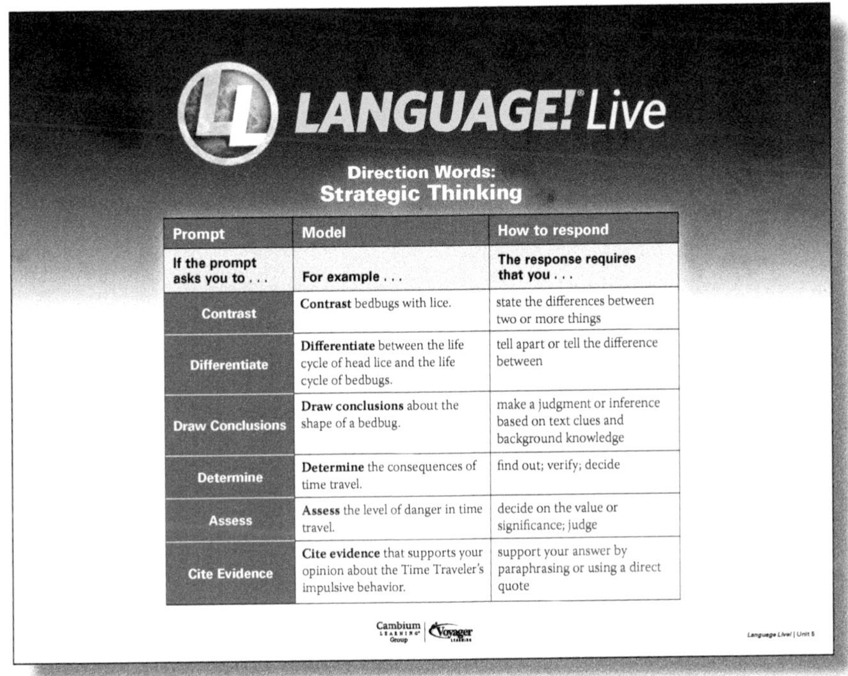

LANGUAGE! Live

Direction Words: Strategic Thinking

Prompt	Model	How to respond
If the prompt asks you to . . .	**For example . . .**	**The response requires that you . . .**
Contrast	**Contrast** bedbugs with lice.	state the differences between two or more things
Differentiate	**Differentiate** between the life cycle of head lice and the life cycle of bedbugs.	tell apart or tell the difference between
Draw Conclusions	**Draw conclusions** about the shape of a bedbug.	make a judgment or inference based on text clues and background knowledge
Determine	**Determine** the consequences of time travel.	find out; verify; decide
Assess	**Assess** the level of danger in time travel.	decide on the value or significance; judge
Cite Evidence	**Cite evidence** that supports your opinion about the Time Traveler's impulsive behavior.	support your answer by paraphrasing or using a direct quote

Cambium Learning Group | Voyager Learning

Posters

Reading

Posters can also be printed from the Teacher Resources online.

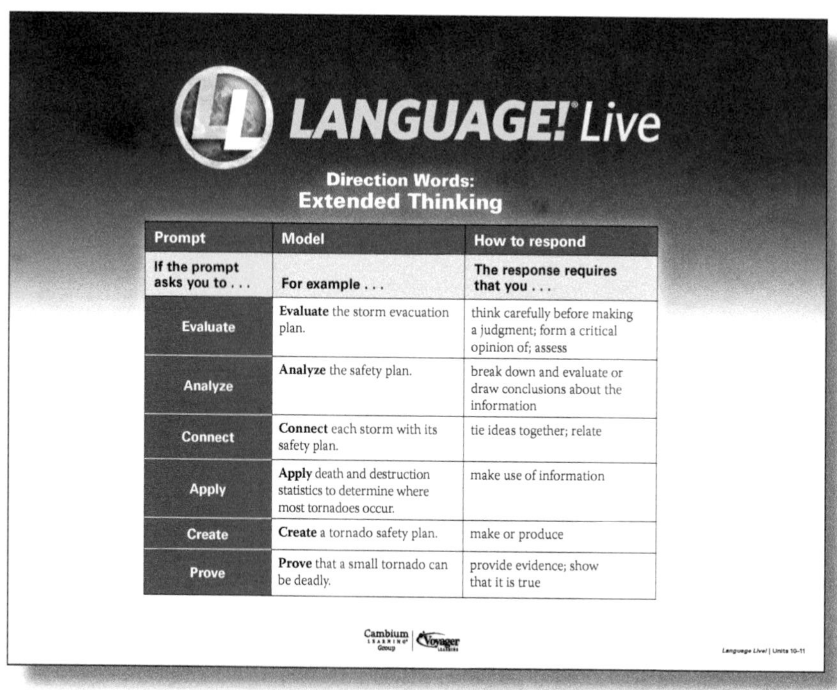

Prompt	Model	How to respond
If the prompt asks you to . . .	For example . . .	The response requires that you . . .
Evaluate	**Evaluate** the storm evacuation plan.	think carefully before making a judgment; form a critical opinion of; assess
Analyze	**Analyze** the safety plan.	break down and evaluate or draw conclusions about the information
Connect	**Connect** each storm with its safety plan.	tie ideas together; relate
Apply	**Apply** death and destruction statistics to determine where most tornadoes occur.	make use of information
Create	**Create** a tornado safety plan.	make or produce
Prove	**Prove** that a small tornado can be deadly.	provide evidence; show that it is true

Vocabulary

Posters can also be printed from the Teacher Resources online.

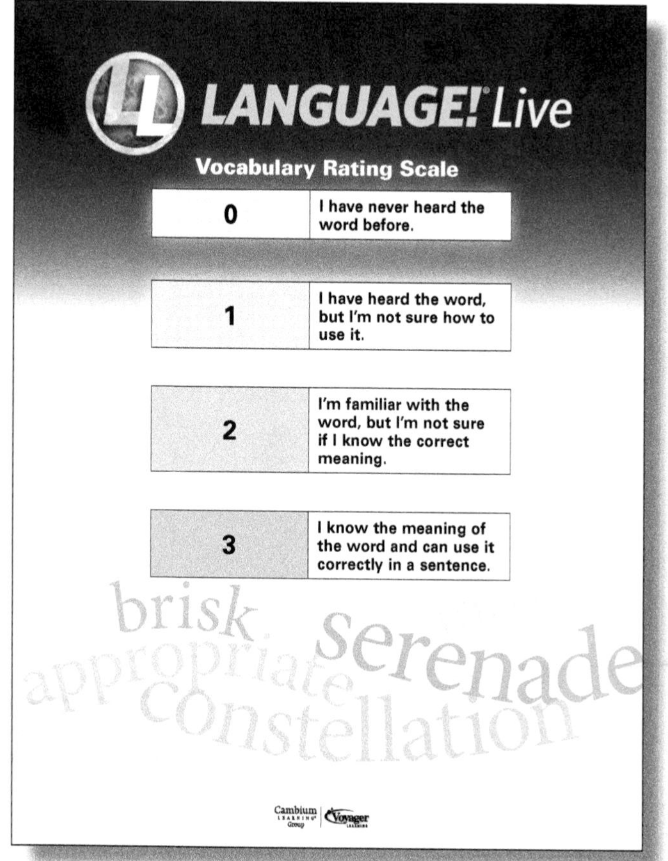

0	I have never heard the word before.
1	I have heard the word, but I'm not sure how to use it.
2	I'm familiar with the word, but I'm not sure if I know the correct meaning.
3	I know the meaning of the word and can use it correctly in a sentence.

Grammar

Posters can also be printed from the Teacher Resources online.

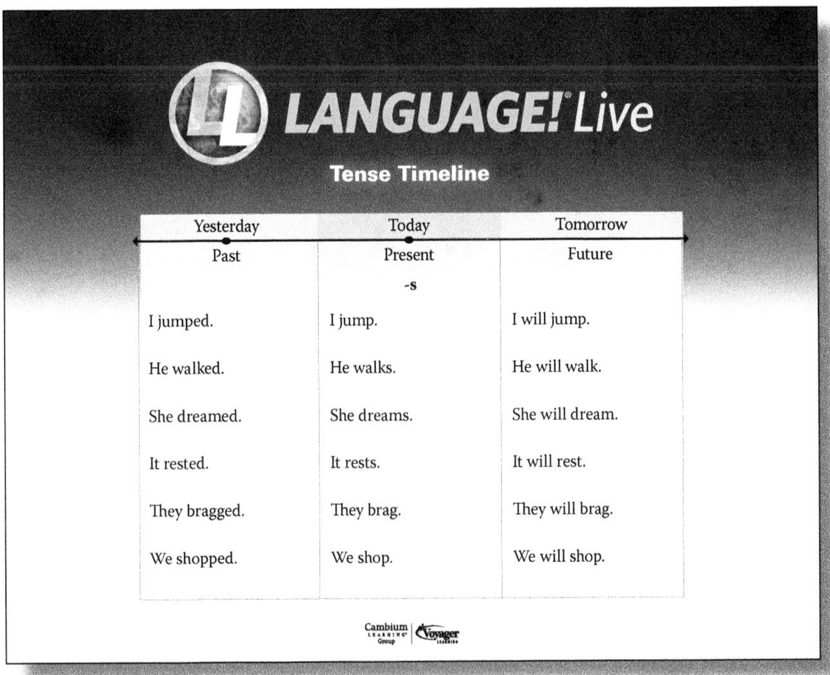

LANGUAGE! Live
Tense Timeline
Yesterday
Today
Tomorrow
Past
Present
Future
-s
I jumped.
I jump.
I will jump.
He walked.
He walks.
He will walk.
She dreamed.
She dreams.
She will dream.
It rested.
It rests.
It will rest.
They bragged.
They brag.
They will brag.
We shopped.
We shop.
We will shop.
Cambium Learning Group
Voyager Learning

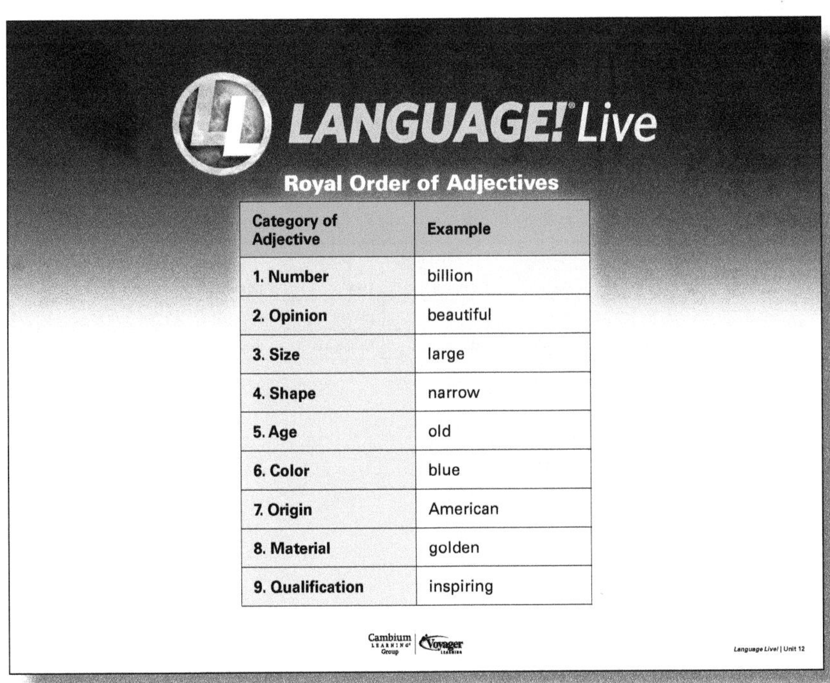

LANGUAGE! Live
Royal Order of Adjectives
Category of Adjective
Example
1. Number
billion
2. Opinion
beautiful
3. Size
large
4. Shape
narrow
5. Age
old
6. Color
blue
7. Origin
American
8. Material
golden
9. Qualification
inspiring
Cambium Learning Group
Voyager Learning

Posters

Grammar

Posters can also be printed from the Teacher Resources online.

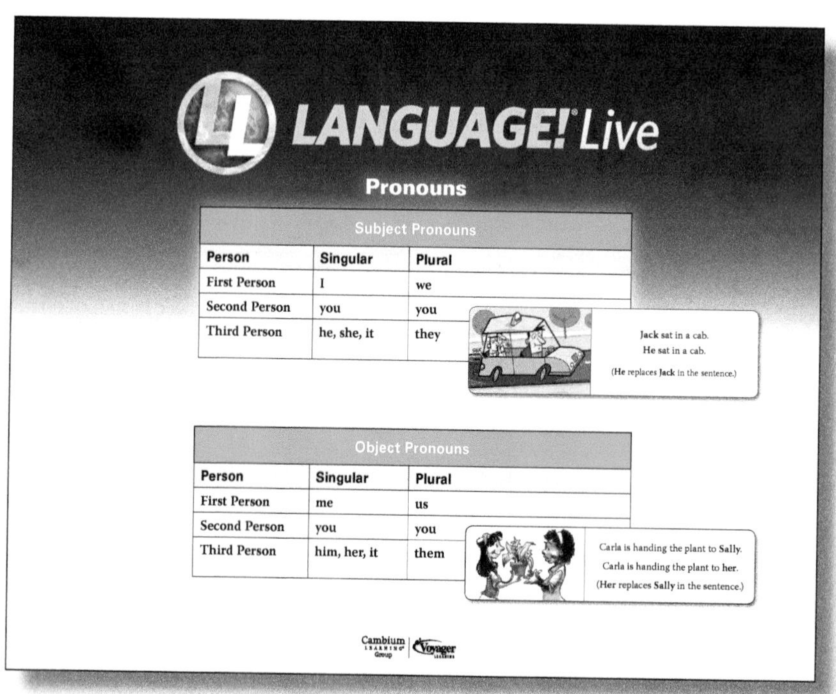

Subject Pronouns		
Person	**Singular**	**Plural**
First Person	I	we
Second Person	you	you
Third Person	he, she, it	they

Object Pronouns		
Person	**Singular**	**Plural**
First Person	me	us
Second Person	you	you
Third Person	him, her, it	them

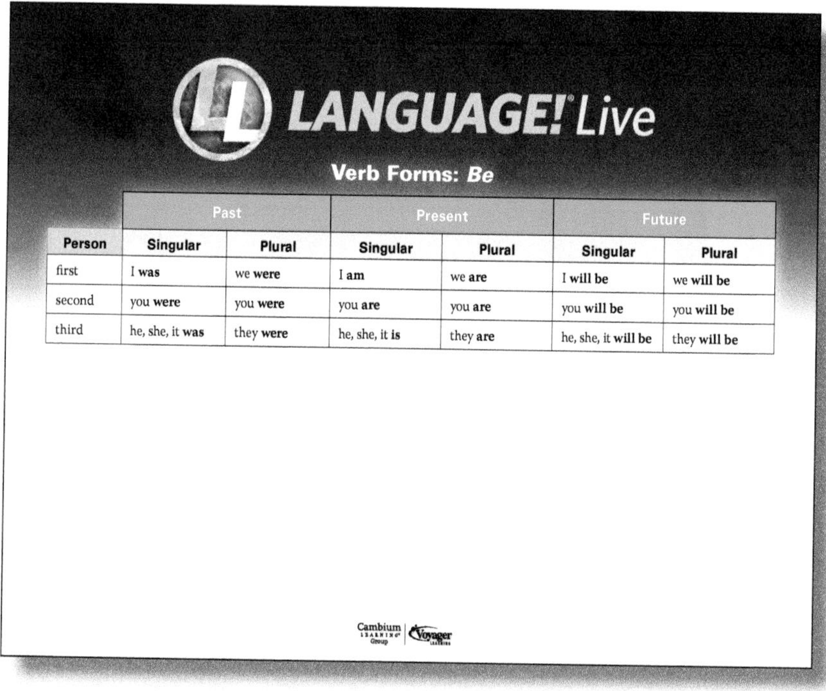

	Past		Present		Future	
Person	**Singular**	**Plural**	**Singular**	**Plural**	**Singular**	**Plural**
first	I **was**	we **were**	I **am**	we **are**	I **will be**	we **will be**
second	you **were**	you **were**	you **are**	you **are**	you **will be**	you **will be**
third	he, she, it **was**	they **were**	he, she, it **is**	they **are**	he, she, it **will be**	they **will be**

Writing

Posters can also be printed from the Teacher Resources online.

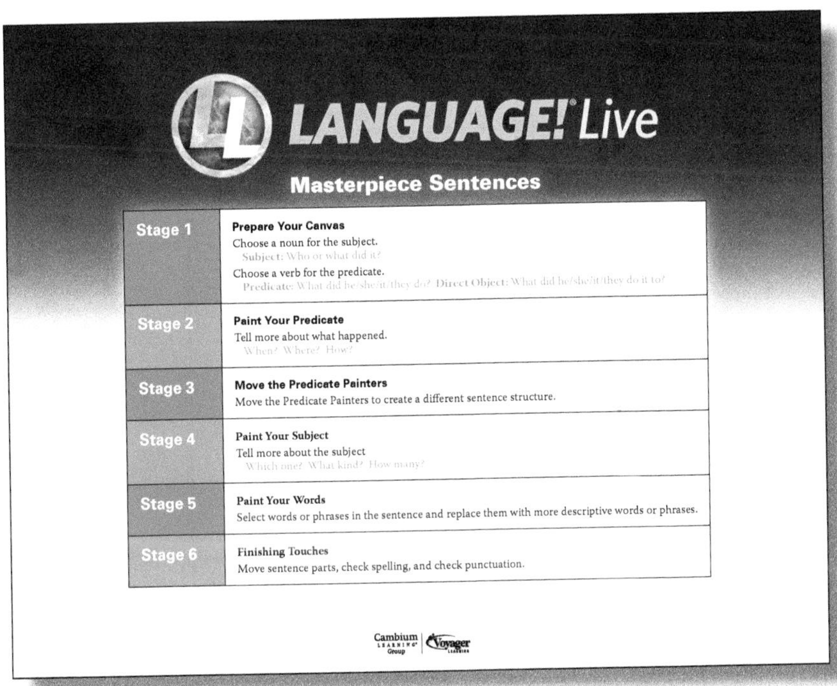

ultiple-Meaning Map

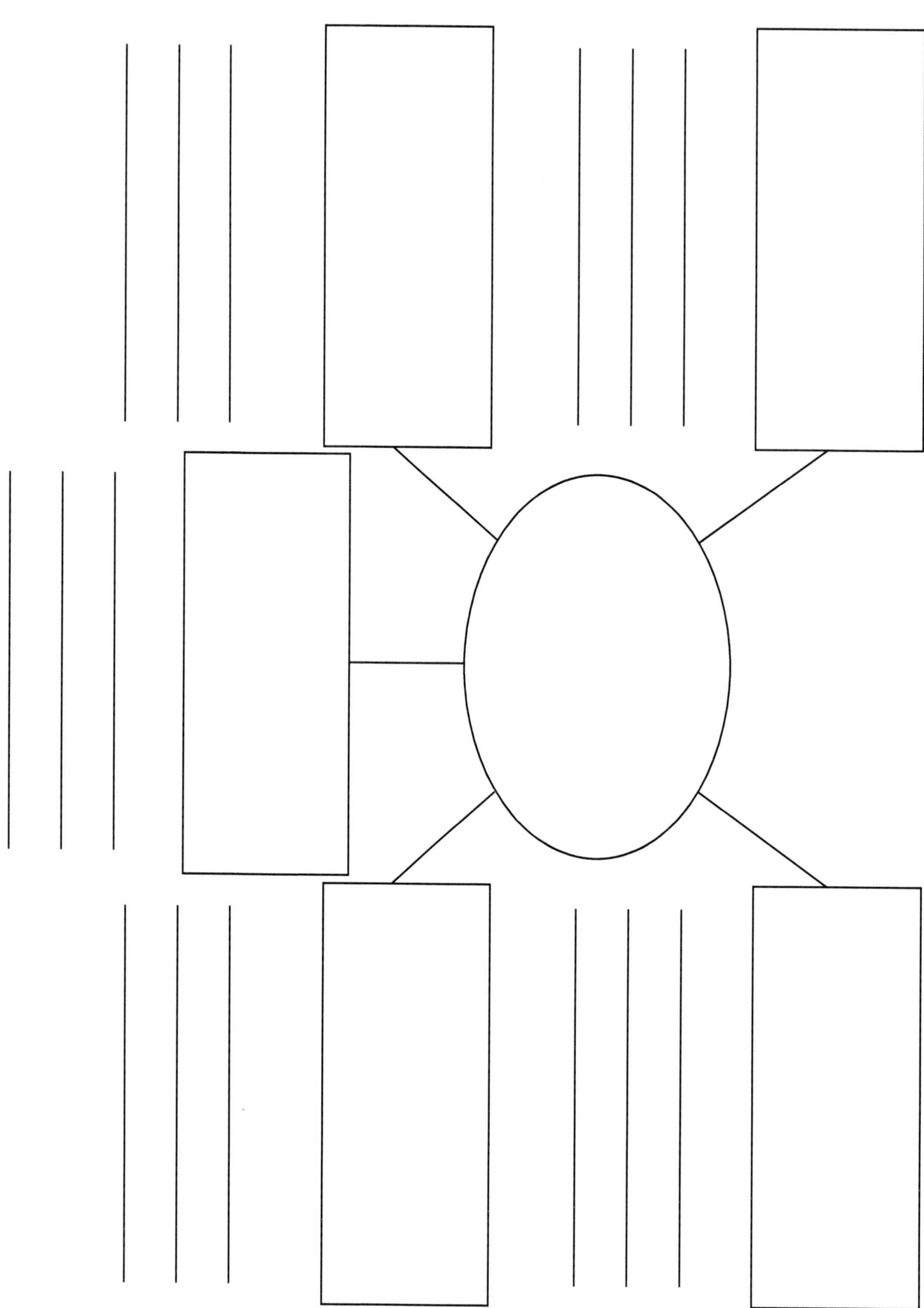

Define It

Word		Category		Attributes
	=		+	

Definition: ____

____

Word		Category		Attributes
	=		+	

Definition: ____

____

Word		Category		Attributes
	=		+	

Definition: ____

____

Word		Category		Attributes
	=		+	

Definition: ____

____

Four-Square

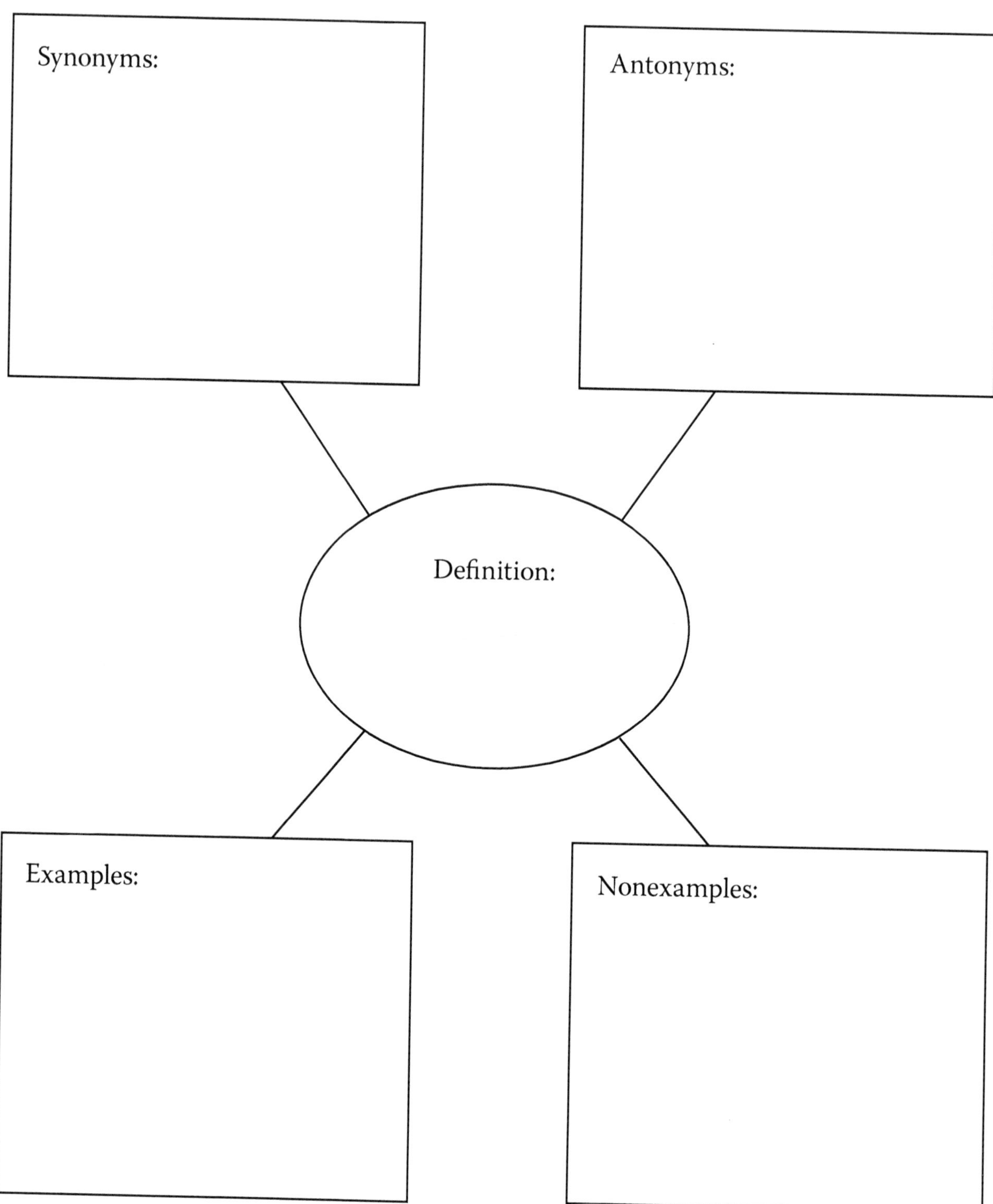

Making Connections

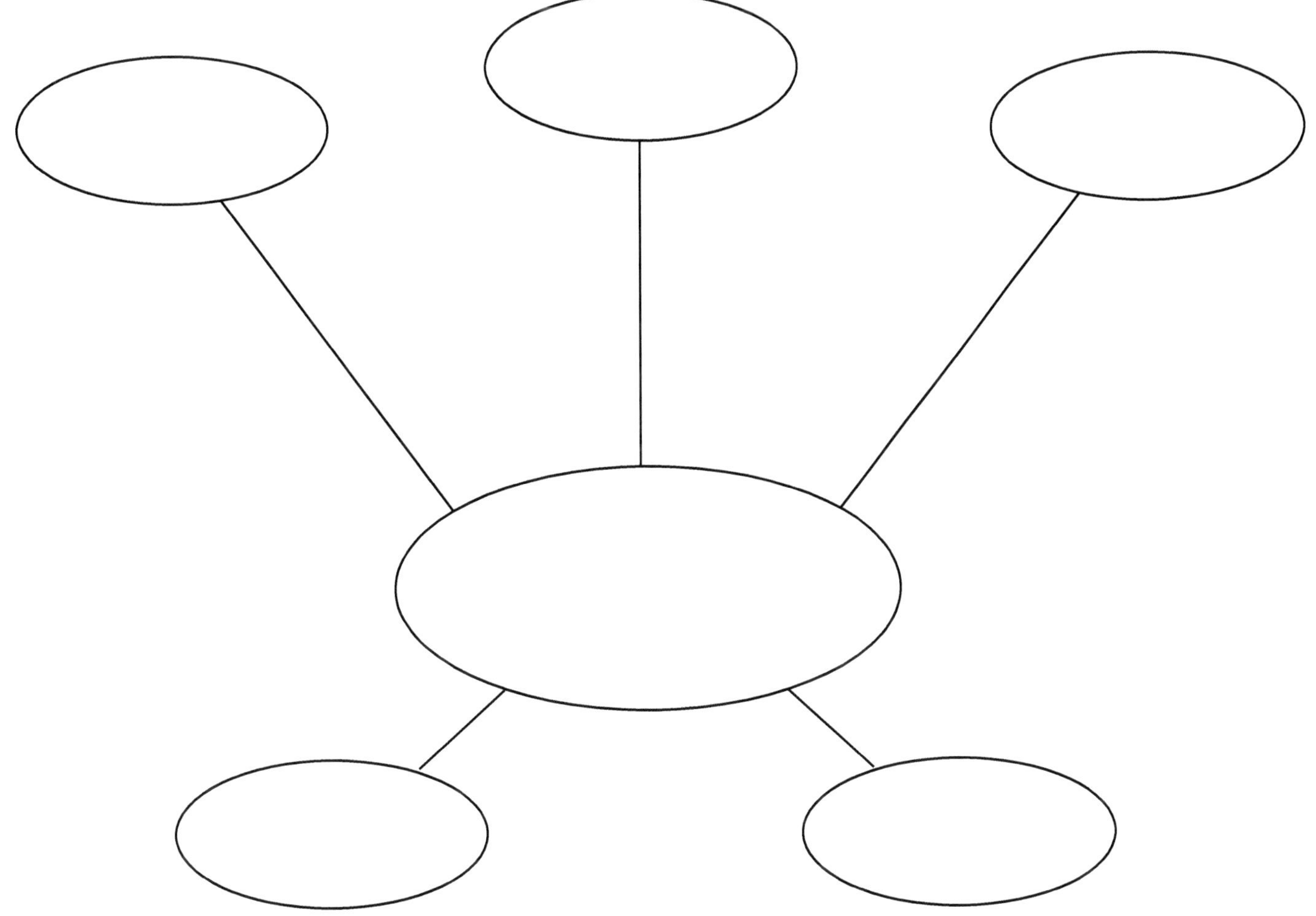

Blueprint for Writing

Vocabulary

The following words are passage vocabulary, context vocabulary, and multiple-meaning words used in Text Training.

ancient
appropriate
attempt
average
bacteria
ballad
band
banjo
base
basic
bat
battle
brilliant
bug
chemicals
coarse
colony
combine
connect
consequence
constellation
contact
contain
coordinate
create
creature
dance
danger
debris
definite
demand
desert
destroy
develop
device
devoted
dig
digest
dinosaur
display
element
eliminate
emerge
entire
exclude
expert
express
fine
fragile
generate
god
graphic
guideline
horror
hurricane
ignorance
indecency
infection
intense
interest
interfere
intestines
intrigue
jazz
legend
lice
log
mammal
mean
message
migrate
modern
moment
mortal
mosquito
multiply
musician
nation
negligence
network
occur
ordinary
oxygen
pattern
pause
permit
pesticide
philosopher
plant
plantation
poet
pollution
port
precise
property
protagonist
pulley
rank
recipe
region
regulate
relate
scale
scalp
scholar
scientist
season
serenade
severe
shield
simple
slight
smog
social
sonar
span
specific
spoil
spread
square
star
steady
substance
support
surface
surroundings
sustained
termite
test
theme
threaten
tint
tropical depression
tropical storm
vanish
variety
version
victim
vision
warning
waste
wonder

Sight Words

The following sight words are introduced by Unit and cumulatively reviewed online in Word Training and reinforced in Text Training.

Unit 1	Unit 2	Unit 3	Unit 4	Unit 5	Unit 6
I	are	be	over	most	about
a	you	he	them	find	their
on	for	or	there	more	that
have	his	not	all	put	been
one	into	what	long	should	each
by	with	said	want	out	many
live	has	do	her	here	only
in	from	when	she	see	then
my	just	we	so	time	very
is	but	your	no	make	they
it				made	
as				these	
at				would	
had				could	
and				like	
to				this	
give				than	
was				how	
				some	

Unit 7	Unit 8	Unit 9	Unit 10	Unit 11	Unit 12
those	after	sound	animals	house	won
which	words	little	why	point	flew
does	who	work	different	mother	paper
look	water	place	move	answer	hair
were	two	years	kind	father	night
people	other	good	picture	study	today
where	day	great	again	learn	city
know	way	through	change	world	light
more	may	before	air	high	head
come	first	right	away	found	story
		old	every	never	group
		any	between	eyes	example
		following	below	thought	always
		show	country	don't	both
		also	school	few	together
		around			
		another			
		large			
		even			
		because			

Word Training Unit Skills

The following phonemes, graphemes, and skills are introduced by Unit and cumulatively reviewed online in Word Training and reinforced in Text Training.

Unit 1	Unit 2	Unit 3
1. m, l, s, t, ă 2. p, f, c, n 3. b, r, j 4. ĭ, v, k	5. g, w, d 6. h; -ck; plural -s 7. ŭ, -ll 8. y, z, x	9. verb marker -ing 10. ŏ, blend st 11. blends sm, sn, qu 12. blends sp, sl, sk
Unit 4	**Unit 5**	**Unit 6**
13. ĕ; ll, ss, ff, zz ("floss" rule) 14. past tense -ed 15. digraphs, floss rule, inflection review 16. digraphs, floss rule, inflection review	17. short vowels in closed syllables 18. /ō/, /ā/; Vce pattern 19. /ū/, /yū/; digraph sh	20. /ē/; vowel team ee 21. bl, cl blends; ea for /ē/ 22. fl, gl, pl blends; /ī/; y spells /ī/ 23. digraph ch
Unit 7	**Unit 8**	**Unit 9**
24. -ing, -ang, -ung 25. ar 26. unvoiced /th/ and digraph th 27. oy	28. -all word family; voiced th 29. br, cr; ow for /ou/ 30. dr, fr; digraph review 31. gr, pr, tr	32. er 33. /ū/ spelled oo; contrast with /yū/ 34. past-tense -ed has three sounds, /d/, /t/, /ed/ 35. or, /ō/ spelled ow
Unit 10	**Unit 11**	**Unit 12**
36. wh, contrast with /w/; plural -es 37. aw 38. ink, ank, onk, unk 39. blends nt, nd, mp; other blends	40. oo as in "book" 41. ai, ay, blends sw, tw 42. oa, ow; ow and ou as /ou/	43. words with silent -e that are not VCe 44. soft c and g 45. blends with three consonants 46. y as ē; oi vowel team

Research and Evidence of Effectiveness

Alliance for Excellent Education (2010). *Issue brief – There's a crisis in America's high schools.* Alliance for Excellent Education: Washington, DC. Retrievable from: http://www.all4ed.org/about_the_crisis

Archer, A. L., Gleason, M. M., & Vachon, V. (2003). Decoding and fluency: Foundation skills for older struggling readers. *Learning Disability Quarterly, 26*(2), 89-101.

August, D., & Shanahan, T. (Eds.) (2006) Developing Literacy in Second-Language Learners: Report of the National Literacy Panel on Language-Minority Children and Youth. Mahwah, NJ: Lawrence Erlbaum.

Balfanz, R., & Herzog, L. (2006). *Keeping middle grades students on track to graduation. Part A: Early identification.* Paper presented at the Annual Meeting of the American Educational Research Association, San Francisco, CA.

Bhattacharya, A., & Ehri, L. (2004). Graphosyllabic analysis helps adolescent struggling readers read and spell words. *Journal of Learning Disabilities, 37*(4), 331-348.

Biancarosa, C., & Snow, C. E. (2006). Reading next—A vision for action and research in middle and high school literacy:A report to Carnegie Corporation of New York (2nd ed.). Washington, DC: Alliance for Excellent Education.

Boardman, A. G., Roberts, G., Vaughn, S., Wexler, J., Murray, C. S., & Kosanovich, M. (2008). *Effective instruction for adolescent struggling readers: A practice brief.* Portsmouth, NH: RMC Research Corporation, Center on Instruction. Available from: http://www.centeroninstruction.org/files/Adol%20Struggling%20Readers%20Practice%20Brief.pdf

Byrd, M. (2001). Technology helps increase reading scores. *Media & Methods, 37*(3), 12-15.

Calhoon, M. B. (2005). Effects of a peer-mediated phonological skill and reading comprehension program on reading skill acquisition of middle school students with reading disabilities. *Journal of Learning Disabilities*, 38(5), 424–433.

Calhoon, M.B., & Petscher Y. (2013). Individual and group sensitivity to remedial reading program design: Examining reading gains across three middle school reading projects. *Reading and Writing, 26*(4), 565-592.

Calhoon, M.B., Sandow, A., & Hunter, C.V. (2010) Reorganizing the instructional reading components: Could there be a better way to design remedial reading programs to maximize middle school students with reading disabilities' response to treatment? *Annals of Dyslexia, 60*, 57–85.

Carnegie Council on Advancing Adolescent Literacy. (2010). Time to act: An agenda for advancing adolescent literacy for college and career success. New York, NY: Carnegie Corporation of New York.

Cheung, A. C., & Slavin, R. E. (2011). *The effectiveness of education technology for enhancing reading achievement: A meta-analysis.* Best Evidence Encyclopedia, John Hopkins University School of Education's Center for Data-Driven Reform in Education and the Institute of Education Sciences, U.S. Department of Education. Retrievable from: www.bestevidence.org

Curtis, M. (2004). Adolescents who struggle with word identification: Research and practice. In T. Jetton & J. Dole (Eds.), *Adolescent literacy research and practice* (pp. 119-134). New York: Guilford.

Curtis, M., & Longo, A.M. (1999) *When adolescents can't read: Methods and materials that work.* Cambridge, MA: Brookline Books.

Denson, K. (2008). *Passport Reading Journeys effectiveness with ninth grade students identified for reading improvement instruction in an urban high school.* Dallas, TX: Voyager Expanded Learning, Inc.. Retrievable from: http://www.voyagerlearning.com

Deshler, D. D., Palincsar, A. S., Biancarosa, G., & Nair, M. (2007). *Informed choices for struggling adolescent readers: A researched-based guide to instructional programs and practices.* Newark, DE: International Reading Association.

Ehri, L. (2004). Teaching phonemic awareness and phonics: An explanation of the National Reading Panel meta-analysis. In P. McCardle. and L. Chhabra, (Eds.), *The Voice of Evidence in Reading Research* (pp. 153-186). Baltimore, MD: Brookes Publishing Company.

Fletcher, J. M., Lyon, G. R., Barnes, M., Stuebing, K. K., Francis, D. J., Olson, R. K., ... & Shaywitz, B. A. (2002). Classification of learning disabilities: An evidenced-based evaluation. In R. Bradley, L. Danielson, & D. P. Hallahan (Eds.). *Identification of learning disabilities: Research to practice* (pp. 185-250). Mahwah, NJ: Erlbaum.

Fletcher, J. M., Lyon, G. R., Fuchs, L. S., & Barnes, M. A. (2007). *Learning disabilities: From identification to intervention.* New York, NY: Guilford.

Foorman, B. R., Francis, D. J., Fletcher, J. M., Schatschneider, C., & Mehta, P. (1998). The role of instruction in learning to read: Preventing reading failure in at-risk children. *Journal of Educational Psychology, 90*(1), 37-55.

Foorman, B. R., & Torgesen, J. K. (2001). Critical elements of classroom and small group instruction promote reading success in all children. *Learning Disabilities Research & Practice 16(4)*, 203-212.

Guskey, T. R. (1997). *Implementing mastery learning.* Belmont, CA: Wadsworth Publishing.

Hall, T. E., Hughes, C. A., & Filbert, M. (2000). Computer assisted instruction in reading for students with learning disabilities: A research synthesis. *Education and Treatment of Children, 23*(3), 173-193.

Hook, P. E., Macaruso, P., & Jones, S. (2001). Efficacy of fast forward training on facilitating acquisition of reading skills by children with reading difficulties—a longitudinal study. *Annals of Dyslexia, 51*, 75-96.

Kamil, M. L., Borman, G. D., Dole, J., Kral, C. C., Salinger, T., & Torgesen, J. (2008). *Improving adolescent literacy: Effective classroom and intervention practices: A Practice Guide* (NCEE #2008-4027). Washington, DC: National Center for Education Evaluation and Regional Assistance, Institute of Education Sciences, U.S. Department of Education.

Kluger, A., & Adler, S. (1993). Person-versus computer-mediated feedback. *Computers in Human Behavior, 9*(1), 1-16.

Kulik, J. A. (1994). Meta-analytic studies of findings on computer-based instruction. In E. L. Baker and H. F. O'Neil, Jr. (Eds.). *Technology assessment in education and training.* Hillsdale, NJ: Lawrence Erlbaum.

Lee, C.D., & Spratley, A. (2010). *Reading in the disciplines: The challenges of adolescent literacy.* New York, NY: Carnegie Corporation of New York. Available from: http://carnegie.org/fileadmin/Media/Publications/PDF/tta_Lee.pdf

Lovett, M.W., Lacerenza, L., De Palma, M., & Frijters, J.C. (2012) Evaluating the efficacy of remediation for struggling readers in high school. *Journal of Learning Disabilities*, 45(2), 151-169

Lyon, G. R. (1995). Toward a definition of dyslexia. *Annals of Dyslexia*, 45, 3-27.

MacArthur, C. A., Ferretti, R. P., Okolo, C. M., & Cavalier, A. R. (2001). Technology applications for students with literacy problems: A critical review. *The Elementary School Journal, 101*, 273-301.

Moats, L. C. (2010). *Speech to print: Language essentials for teachers.* Baltimore: Paul Brookes.

Morris, R. D., Lovett, M.W., Wolf, M., Sevcik, R.A., Steinbach, K.A., Frijters, J.C. & Shapiro, M.B. (2012) Multiple-component remediation for developmental reading disabilities: IQ, socioeconomic status, and race as factors in remedial outcome. *Journal of Learning Disabilities*, 45(2), 99-127.

Nagy, W.E., & Anderson, R.C. (1984). How many words are there in printed English? *Reading Research Quarterly, 19*, 304-330.

National Association of State Boards of Education (2005). *Reading at risk: How states can respond to the crisis in adolescent literacy.* Alexandria, VA: Author. Available from http://www.centeroninstruction.org/files/Reading_At_Risk_Full_Report.pdf

National Center for Education Statistics (2009). *The nation's report card: Reading 2009* (NCES 2010–458). Washington, DC: Institute of Education Sciences, U.S. Department of Education.

National Institute for Literacy (2007). *What content area teachers should know about adolescent literacy.* Jessup, MD: EdPubs. Retrievable from: http://lincs.ed.gov/publications/pdf/adolescent_literacy07.pdf

National Joint Committee on Learning Disabilities (2008). *Adolescent Literacy and Older Students with Learning Disabilities* [Technical Report]. Retrieved from: www.asha.org/policy

National Longitudinal Transition Study II. (2003). *National Center for Special Education Research at the Institute of Education Sciences.* Washington, DC: U.S. Department of Education.

National Reading Panel (2000). *Teaching children to read: An evidence-based assessment of the scientific research literature on reading and its implications for reading instruction.* National Institute of Child Health and Human Development, Washington, D.C.

Niemiec, C. P., & Ryan, R. M. (2009). Autonomy, competence, and relatedness in the classroom: Applying self-determination theory to educational practice. *Theory and Research in Education 7*(2), 133-144.

Reed, D. K., & Vaughn, S. (2010). Reading interventions for older students. In T. A. Glover & S. Vaughn (Eds.), *Response to intervention: Empowering all students to learn, a critical account of the science and practice* (pp. 143-186). New York, NY: Guilford Press.

Scammacca, N., Roberts, G., Vaughn, S., Edmonds, M., Wexler, J., Reutebuch, C. K., & Torgesen, J. (2007). *Reading interventions for adolescent struggling readers: A meta-analysis with implications for practice.* Portsmouth, NH: RMC Research Corporation, Center on Instruction.

Scarborough, HS and Brady, SA 2002. Toward a common terminology for talking about speech and reading: A glossary of the "phon" words and some related terms. *Journal of Literacy Research, 34*(3), 299–334

Schacter, J. (1999). *The impact of educational technology on student achievement: What the most current research has to say.* Milken Exchange on Educational Technology, Santa Monica, CA. Retrievable from: http://www.eric.ed.gov/PDFS/ED430537.pdf

Schatschneider, C., Buck, J., Torgesen, J., Wagner, R., Hassler, L., Hecht, S., & Powell-Smith, K. (2004). A Multivariate Study of Individual Differences in Performance on the Reading Portion of the Florida Comprehensive Assessment Test:A Preliminary Report. Technical report #5 , Florida Center for Reading Research

Shankweiler, D., Lundquist, E., Katz, L., Stuebing, K. K., Fletcher, J. M., Brady, S., ...Shaywitz, B. A. (1999). Comprehension and decoding: Patterns of association in children with reading difficulties. *Scientific Studies of Reading,* 3, 69-94.

Slavin, R. E., Cheung, A., Groff, C., & Lake, C. (2008). Effective reading programs for middle and high schools: A best-evidence synthesis. *Reading Research Quarterly, 43*(3), 290-322.

Snow, C. E., & Biancarosa, G. (2003). *Adolescent literacy and the achievement gap: What do we know and where do we go from here?* New York: Carnegie Corporation of New York.

Soe, K., Koki, S., & Chang, J. M. (2000). *Effect of computer-assisted instruction (CAI) on reading achievement: A meta-analysis.* Pacific Resources for Education and Learning: Honolulu, HI. Retrievable from: http://www.prel.org/products/products/effect-cai.htm

Tillman, P. S. (2010). *Computer-assisted instruction (CAI) and reading acquisition: A synthesis of the literature.* Retrievable from: http://teach.valdosta.edu/are/TillmanPLRFinal.pdf

Torgesen, J.K. (2004). Avoiding the devastating downward spiral: The evidence that early intervention prevents reading failure. *American Educator, 28,* 6-19.

Torgesen, A.W., Alexander, R. K., Wagner, C. A., Rashotte, K., Conway, T., & Rose, E. (2001). Intensive remedial instruction for children with severe reading disabilities: Immediate and long-term outcomes from two instructional approaches. *Journal of Learning Disabilities, 34,* 33-58.

Torgesen, J. K., Wagner, R. K., Rashotte, C. A., Herron, J., & Lindamood, P. (2010). Computer-assisted instruction to prevent early reading difficulties in students at risk for dyslexia: Outcomes from two instructional approaches. *Annals of Dyslexia, 60*(1), 40-56, doi:10.1007/s11881-009-0032-y

Tsesmeli, S. N., & Seymour, P. H. K. (2009). The effects of training of morphological structure on spelling derived words by dyslexic adolescents. *British Journal of Psychology, 100,* 565-592.

Vadasy, P. F., Sanders, E. A., & Tudor, S. (2007). Effectiveness of paraeducator supplemented individual instruction: Beyond basic decoding skill. *Journal of Learning Disabilities, 40*(6), 508-524.

Vaughn, S., Gersten, R., & Chard, D. J. (2000). The underlying message in LD intervention research: Findings from research syntheses. *Exceptional Children, 67*(1), 99-114.

Vellutino, F. R., Tunmer, W. E., Jaccard, J. J., & Chen, R. (2007). Components of reading ability: Multivariate evidence for a convergent skills model of reading development. *Scientific Studies of Reading, 11*(1), 3-32.

Index

A

B

C

D

Index

Index

Index